RECORDS OF EARLY ENGLISH DRAMA

Records of Early English Drama

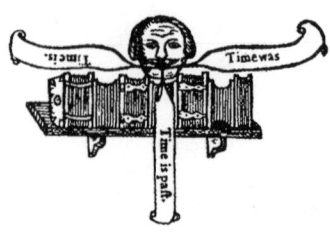

OXFORD

EDITED BY JOHN R. ELLIOTT, JR, and ALAN H. NELSON (University)
ALEXANDRA F. JOHNSTON and DIANA WYATT (City)

1
The Records

THE BRITISH LIBRARY

and

UNIVERSITY OF TORONTO PRESS

© University of Toronto Press Incorporated 2004
Toronto Buffalo
Printed in Canada

First published in North America in 2004 by University of Toronto Press Incorporated
ISBN 0-8020-3905-7
and in the European Union in 2004 by
The British Library
96 Euston Road
London NW1 2DB

British Library Cataloguing in Publication Data
A catalogue record for this title is available from The British Library

ISBN 0-7123-4856-5

Printed on acid-free paper

National Library of Canada Cataloguing in Publication

Oxford / edited by John R. Elliott ... [et al.].

(Records of early English drama)
Includes bibliographical references and index.
Contents: 1. The records – 2. Editorial apparatus.
ISBN 0-8020-3905-7

1. Performing arts – England – Oxford – History – Sources.
2. Theater – England – Oxford – History – Sources. 3. Oxford
(England) – History – Sources. I. Elliott, John R. II. Series.

PN2596.O93O93 2004   790.2'09425'74   C2004-900153-1

1003911700T

The research and typesetting costs of
Records of Early English Drama
have been underwritten by the
National Endowment for the Humanities and the
Social Sciences and Humanities Research Council of Canada

Contents

Records of Early English Drama

The aim of Records of Early English Drama (REED) is to find, transcribe, and publish external evidence of dramatic, ceremonial, and minstrel activity in Great Britain before 1642. The executive editor would be grateful for comments on and corrections to the present volume and for having any relevant additional material drawn to her attention at REED, 150 Charles St West, Toronto, Ontario, Canada M5S 1K9 or s.maclean@utoronto.ca. Detailed information about the REED series can be found on the internet at http://www.chass.utoronto.ca/~reed/reed.html.

Acknowledgments

More than any previous publication in the Records of Early English Drama series, this collection of records from Oxford is the result of a cooperative effort by many scholars over many years.

It is with great pleasure mixed with great sadness that three of the present editors record their admiration and affection for the fourth (or rather the first), John R. Elliott, Jr, of the Department of English at Syracuse University. Professor Elliott was a member of the REED team almost from its inception. As prospective editors were invited to declare an interest in a particular city, county, or institution, he secured the editorship of the records of Oxford University and colleges. In the late 1970s and early 1980s REED researchers fanned out across England, he to Oxford (usually with digs in Manchester College) over several summers and for one full academic year. Although publication of his research was delayed to facilitate coordination with research on Oxford city and parishes, editing was finally well advanced, with e-mail messages flying back and forth between Toronto and Syracuse, when in February 2002 Professor Elliott was felled by a disabling stroke. Despite this blow, which concluded his active participation in the project, his name remains at the head of the list of editors, as he had essentially completed the identification and transcription of records in his domain, compiled endnotes, drafted his part of the Introduction, and begun work on the Appendixes. We his fellow editors, including Alan H. Nelson who took over his part of the project, along with the entire REED staff, dedicate our labours to Professor Elliott with best wishes for further recovery. We also express our appreciation to Mark Elliott, who has helped us maintain our ties to his father and supported the work of the project at every turn.

On the civic side the present editors are in the debt of Marianne Briscoe, who initiated REED research into the records of Oxford city and its parishes. We gratefully acknowledge her pioneering efforts, especially among the antiquarian records in the Bodleian Library that preserve references from parish documents now lost. When we came to take over the task we were able to build on a solid foundation.

All REED collections depend heavily on the expertise and dedication of librarians and archivists, and the institutions they serve. With respect to Oxford academia our acknowledgments are vexed by the passage of time and events beyond our control. We nevertheless confidently thank All Souls College, Norma Aubertin-Potter, Archivist and Librarian; Balliol College, John Jones, Vice-Master and Archivist; Brasenose College, the late Robin Peedell, Librarian, and

Elizabeth Boardman, Archivist; Christ Church, June Wells, former Assistant Archivist, Judith Curthoys, Archivist, John Wing and John Mason, former Librarians, and Janet McMullin, Librarian; Corpus Christi College, the late Trevor Aston, Fellow Librarian and Archivist, Joanna Snelling, Librarian-in-Charge, and Julian Reid, Archivist; Exeter College, Juliet Chadwick, Archivist; Jesus College, Rosemary Dunhill, Archivist; Lincoln College, John Newman and Andrew Mussell, Archivists; Magdalen College, Brenda Parry-Jones, former Archivist, Janie Cottis, former Archivist, Robin Darwall-Smith, Archivist, and Christine Ferdinand, Fellow Librarian; Merton College, Julian Reid and Robin Darwall-Smith, Archivists; New College, the late G.V. Bennett, Archivist, and Caroline Dalton, Archivist; Oriel College, Marjory Szurko, Librarian; Pembroke College, Ellena Pike, Librarian-Archivist; The Queen's College, Michael Riordan, Assistant Archivist, and Amanda Saville, Librarian; St John's College, the late Angela Williams, Librarian, Ruth Ogden, Library Administrator, Catherine Hilliard, Librarian, and Michael Riordan, Archivist; Trinity College, Clare Hopkins, Archivist; University College, Robin Darwall-Smith, Archivist; Wardham College; Worcester College; Oxford University Archives, the late Trevor Aston, Keeper 1969–85, Ruth Vyse, then Assistant Archivist, and Simon Bailey, Keeper (currently); and finally the Bodleian Library and its ever-helpful staff. We know that Professor Elliott would have wished to thank institutions and persons unknown to the rest of us.

With respect to Oxford city and parishes we wish to thank the staff of the Oxfordshire Record Office both in their basement lair in County Hall in New Road, and later in their fine new quarters on the Cowley Road: Carl Boardman, County Archivist, Senior Archivists Liz Finn and Mark Priddey, Archivists Jenny Childs, Robin Darwall-Smith, Karen Garvey, Chris Gilliam, Jeanette Grisold, Ruth Imeson, Giles Morris, Eleanor Roberts, and Madeleine Simms, and their several assistants. Oxford records held by the city were brought to us for consultation at both the Record Office and the Centre for Oxfordshire Studies at Oxford Central Library. We are grateful to Malcolm Graham, the Head of the Centre, and his staff for making these documents available.

Outside Oxford we wish to thank Archivo General de Simancas, Spain; the Beinecke Library of Yale University; the British Library; the Centre for Kentish Studies, Maidstone; the Cheshire and Chester Archives, Jonathan Peplar, County Archivist; the Durham University Library, Alan Piper, Archives & Special Collections; the Folger Shakespeare Library, Laetitia Yeandle and Heather Woolfe, Curators of Manuscripts; the Hampshire Record Office; Lord Salisbury, Hatfield House, Robin Harcourt-Williams, Librarian and Archivist; the Houghton Library and the Harvard Theatre Collection of Harvard University; the Huntington Library, Mary Robertson, Chief Curator of Manuscripts; the Inner Temple Library, Adrian Blunt, Deputy Librarian; the Magdalene College Library, Cambridge, Aude Fitzsimmons, Assistant Librarian; the Public Record Office (now The National Archives), both in Chancery Lane and at Kew; the Staffordshire Record Office, Michael Dorrington, Principal Archivist; the Surrey History Centre, Michael Page, Archivist; and the Venetian State Archives.

We are grateful to the following for formal permission to publish excerpts from manuscripts in their possession: The Principal and Fellows of Brasenose College, Oxford; Christ Church, by kind permission of the Governing Body of Christ Church, Oxford; Corpus Christi College, by permission of The President and Fellows of Corpus Christi College, Oxford; The Rector and Fellows of Exeter College, Oxford; The President and Fellows of Magdalen College, Oxford; The Warden and Fellows of New College, Oxford; The Provost and Fellows of Oriel College, Oxford; The Master, Fellows, and Scholars of Pembroke College, Oxford; The Master and Fellows of University College, Oxford; the Keeper of the Archives, University of Oxford; the Syndics of Cambridge University Library; the Masters of the Bench of the Inner Temple; the Oxford City Council's Archives; and the Oxfordshire Record Office.

Work on this project could not have been brought to a successful conclusion without the support of the editorial team in Toronto – a remarkable and talented group of scholars and technicians, each of whom brings his or her special talents to the task with patience and good humour. The team has been directed and coordinated from the beginning by Sally-Beth MacLean, whose determination that this work would be completed has sustained all our efforts and whose scholarly rigour has made this collective work of scholarship as good as it has become. Generations of REED staff have made their contributions to these pages. First to be thanked are the bibliographers, Ian Lancashire, Theodore DeWelles, Miriam Skey, and John Lehr, assisted most recently by Lindsey Bell, Tanya Hagen, and Milton Kooistra, who sought out fugitive references and who as a team remained with the editors on their journey through to the final check for accuracy of citation. Next come the English paleographers, Heather Phillips, Edward English, Arleane Ralph, and William Cooke (who rejoined the project to prepare the English Glossary); also their colleagues the Latin paleographers Abigail Ann Young (who also prepared the Latin Glossary) and Patrick Gregory (who also prepared the translations from Latin). Translations from other languages were provided by Josiah Blackmore, Dario Brancato, and William Edwards. Early technical support was provided by Donna Ballman and William Rowcliffe, assisted by Barbara Sella. The last few years of production have prospered under the watchful eye of Arleane Ralph, who expertly kept all the strands separate yet parallel as the several parts of the volumes took shape. Initial fact-checking for Appendix 6 and for the University Index fell to Agnes Ormsby and for the Index to Julia Pope. John Lehr took responsibility for Patrons and Travelling Companies: other contributors are separately acknow-ledged in the headnote to that section. Subhash Shanbhag prepared the maps. Carolyn Black copy-edited each section of the final text, tactfully coordinating the work of three editors and several co-workers. Marion Filipiuk compiled the complex Index. Gord Oxley typeset the collection with a keen sense of how his technical work was assisting the rest of us as we worked on the final parts of the back matter.

We have been greatly assisted by scholars outside the REED Toronto office. A major contribu-tion was made by Kirstie Jackson in completing transcriptions and document descriptions in Oxford record repositories, especially college archives. Other on-site checks were undertaken in the early days by Annette Jacob and more recently by Penny Tucker and Jessica Freeman in London, and by Jenny Sisk at Yale and Betty Falsey at Harvard. Many colleagues in many disciplines have provided expert knowledge in fields ranging from academic drama and naut-ical terminology to visitation records. These include James Alsop, Jane Cowling, Charles B. Faulhaber, Carl Hammer, David Klausner, James McConica, John McKinnell, Dana R. Sutton, and Robert Tittler. John Finnis not only alerted us to a document hitherto unnoticed by historians of Oxford academic drama (Laurence Humphrey's Ash Wednesday sermon of 1582) but provided advice on the law. David Palliser read an early version of the Introduction and provided sound direction for improvement.

Alan Nelson wishes especially to thank Nicole Asaro for help with fact-checking and Annette Fern (of the Harvard Theatre Collection), Paul Hammer, and Steven W. May for advice; and to acknowledge three funding sources from within the University of California at Berkeley: the Academic Senate Committee on Research; a Humanities Research Fellowship; and a Graduate Research Assistantship.

Alexandra Johnston wishes especially to thank Caroline Barron and John Barron for their personal friendship and hospitality; and the latter, as master of St Peter's College, Oxford, for arranging for the Canadian scholars who worked on these records to live in the college during many research visits.

The research and publication costs of these volumes have been provided in Canada by the Social Sciences and Humanities Research Council of Canada, Father Edward Jackman and the Jackman Foundation of Toronto, and Patricia McCain; in the United States by the National Endowment for the Humanities and the Andrew W. Mellon Foundation of New York; in the United Kingdom by the British Academy, the Marc Fitch Fund, The Warden and Fellows of All Souls College, The President and Fellows of Corpus Christi College, The Warden and Fellows of Merton College, The President and Fellows of St John's College, and the English Faculty of Oxford University. Alexandra Johnston and Alan Nelson are also pleased to recall the late Stanley J. Kahrl and the Ohio State University, joint-shepherds of NEH funding in the earliest years of REED.

Finally, more than with any previous publication in the Records of Early English Drama series, the editors are aware that individuals or institutions who contributed one way or another to the collection may have been overlooked. To any such, they extend an apology – but beg for understanding.

RECORDS OF EARLY ENGLISH DRAMA

Symbols

ASC	All Souls College		MC	Magdalen College
BC	Balliol College		MCR	Merton College Records
BL	British Library		MtC	Merton College
BNC	Brasenose College		NC	New College
Bodl.	Bodleian Library		OC	Oriel College
CCC	Corpus Christi College		OCA	Oxford City Archives
CCCA	Corpus Christi College Archives		ORO	Oxfordshire Record Office
ChCh	Christ Church		OUA	Oxford University Archives
Crd	Cardinal College		PRO	Public Record Office
EC	Exeter College		QC	The Queen's College
GC	Gloucester College		SJC	St John's College
JC	Jesus College		TC	Trinity College
LC	Lincoln College		UC	University College

A	Antiquarian Compilation
AC	Antiquarian Collection
DNB	*Dictionary of National Biography*
OED	*The Oxford English Dictionary*, compact ed, 2 vols (New York, 1971)
OUF	Oxford University Financial
OUM	Oxford University Miscellaneous
OUS	Oxford University Statutes
REED	Records of Early English Drama
STC	A.W. Pollard and G.R. Redgrave (comps), *Short-Title Catalogue ... 1475–1640*
VCH	*Victoria History of the Counties of England*
Wing	D.G. Wing (comp), *Short-Title Catalogue ... 1641–1700*

*	(after folio, membrane, page, or sheet number) see endnote
⟨...⟩	lost or illegible letters in the original
[ ]	cancellation in the original
(blank)	a blank in the original where writing would be expected
° °	matter in the original added in another hand
⌈ ⌉	text written above the line
⌊ ⌋	text written below the line
^	caret mark in the original
...	ellipsis of original matter
|	change of folio, membrane, page, or sheet in continuous text
®	right-hand marginale
†	marginale too long for the left-hand margin

The Records

1284–5
Archbishop Pecham's Register
Lambeth Palace Library: MS Archbishop Pecham's Register
f 223   *(November)*

…   5

℞ ¶ Godestowe   ¶ Frater Iohannes permissione diuina Cantuariensis ecclesie Minister
humilis tocius Anglie primas dilectis in Christo filiabus . . Abbatisse
℞ de celebracione   et Conuentui de Godestowe salutem, gratiam & benediccionem…. vt
diuini officij   uidelicet ecclesiasticum officium in quo habetis sponsum alloqui &
eius suscipere spiramina temporibus debitis cum omni reuerencia   10
celebretis quo tempore nulli sane a choro se liceat absentare/ nisi Sit
obediencialiter in necessarijs non in forinsecis colloquijs occupata.
Ipsum autem officium precise & integre precipimus Decantari. precise
inquam ut tam in missis chori quam beate virginis excludentur per
annum totum superuacue nouitates nec nouum aliquid inibi Decantetur/   15
nisi de consilio Magistri & Abbatisse pariter ac cantricis/ sed nouis
omnibus vetera preponantur. Integre eciam officium celebretur reiecta
penitus mutilacione officij Monastici/ quam inuenerunt nuper
presidentes Capituli Monachorum Abundonie celebrati. Puerilia
autem sollempnia que in festo solent fieri innocentium post uesperas   20
sancti Iohannis tantum inchoari permittimus et in crastino in ipsa
die Innocentium totaliter terminentur. Pro regimine insuper Conuentus
maturiores ac prudenciores teneatur Abbatissa uocare pro negocijs
domus intrinsecis & extrinsecis salubriter disponendis. Quod si aliqua
secundo vocata/ uenire contempserit? in Sequenti prandio ei pitancia   25
subtrahatur. Quod si tercio non ueniens aurem obstruxerit imperanti/
panis ei & aqua in proximo prandio tantum modo concedantur. Idem
dicimus in omnibus illis quecunque quandocunque inobedientes proprie
inheserint uoluntati….

20, 22/ innocentium, Innocentium: *2 minims for* iu *in* MS

1292

Chancellor's Register   OUA: NEP/Supra/A
f 55v   *(University College statutes)*

…

20.

¶ Item viua*n*t o*mne*s honeste vt cl*er*ici p*r*out decet *s*anc*t*os no*n* pu∧⌐g⌐na*n*tes   5
no*n* scurrilia v*e*l t*ur*pia loqu*ent*es n*o*n ca*n*tilenas s*eu* fabulas de amasijs v*e*l
luxurosis aut ad libidine*m* sona*n*tib*us* narra*n*tes canta*n*tes a*u*t libe*n*t*er*
audientes non irridentes v*e*l a*liqu*e*m* ad ira*m* moue*n*tes no*n* clama*n*tes ut
studentes a studio v*e*l quiete impedia*n*t*ur*…

10

1297–8

University Response to Town Complaints of a Riot   OUA: SEP/Y/12a
mb [3]*

…

En dreit du conflict qe fu fet Lundi en la gra*n*t Rue pur ceo qe de par ceus   15
La Vile fut le fet de tote la Co*m*mune od seyns & od corns & a co*m*mune
criee presenz les baillifs armez e de la p*ar*tie des Clers ni aueyt for qe singulers
p*er*sones sanz auctorite & sanz chif, & sanz co*m*mune criee aa La Vniu*er*site
ordine qe les clers puissent leur damages qe il receuient, en p*er*sones ou en
biens demaunder de La co*m*munete deua*n*t le Chauncelyr en forme de dreit   20
& les lays qe pleyndre se vodereynt des Clers, ausi deua*n*t le Chauncelyr len
lor fra dreit, issi qe cete syute ne de vne part*e* ne de autre, ne seit fete for qe
enfourme de simple trespas, sanz peril de vie e de membre….

…

25

c **1300**

Chancellor's Register   OUA: NEP/Supra/A
f 63*   *(Decree against observance of local festivals)*

…

De modo interdicendi festa nac*i*onum   30
Avctoritate domini cancellarij & Magistrorum regencium cum vnanimi
conse*n*su non regencium decretum est & statutum quod nullum festum
nat*i*onis cui*us*que cum solempnitate & conuocat*i*one consueta Magistro*rum* &
scolarium seu aliorum notorum in quacumq*ue* eccl*es*i*a* amodo celebretur. nisi

®°Festa   quatenus aliqui festum alicuius sancti sue proprie dyocesis cum deuoc*i*one in   35
diocesiu*m*°   suis parochiis vbi deg*un*t volu*er*int celebrare alterius tamen parochie u*e*l sue
Magistros scolares seu alios quoscumq*ue* notos non vocando. sicut nec fit

Collation with OUA: NEP/Supra/B *(B)* ff 87–8v and OUA: NEP/Supra/C *(C)* ff 99–
100v: 5m 20.] 21 *C*   6 s*eu*] siue ⌐°uel°⌐ *B;* siue *C*   7 luxurosis] luxuriosis *BC*
7 narra*n*tes] *corrected from* narrantibus *B*

7/ luxurosis: *for* luxuriosis; *single minim for second* u   15/ Lundi: *24 February 1297/8*

®°Ludi *in*
publi*cis* plateis
prohibe*antur*°

in festis sancte kat*er*ine sancti Nicholai & similium. ⁅Hoc etiam decretum
auctoritate eiusdem Cancellarij sub pena maioris exco*mm*unicat*i*onis precipimus
obseruari vt nequis correas cum laruis seu strepitu aliquo? in ecclesijs u*e*l plateis
ducat u*e*l sertatus uel coronatus corona ex folijs arborum u*e*l florum u*e*l aliunde
compo*s*ita alicubi incedat sub pena excommunicatonis quam exnu*n*c ferimus   5
et incarcerat*i*onis diutine prohibemus.

…

1305–6

AC   ***A Report on the Inquest into the Death of Gilbert Foxlee***   10
Bodl.: MS. Twyne 4
pp 32–3*

…

®Edward I

®Thom*as*
Lisewys.

®Ci*ss*or*um* Oxoni*æ*
tripudi*um*
et *vide* litter*as*
Reg*is* Hen*ri*ci 6ⁱ
contra circuitus
in vigilijs *Sancti*
Ioh*annis* Baptist*æ*
et Apost*olorum*
Petri et Pauli.
Aaa p. 38 .1.
anno 1444. ·

®Draperia

Contigit die do*mi*nica *proxima* post festu*m* Assumptionis Beat*æ* Mari*æ* virg*inis*
an*n*o regni regis Edw*ardi* 34 . qu*od* Gilb*er*tus de Foxlee clericus obijt in   15
Hospitio suo ubi ipse manebat in *parochia Sancti* Petri Oriental*is* Oxoni*æ*
circa hora*m* nonam, Et die lun*æ proximo* sequent*i* visus fuit p*er* Thom*am*
Lisewys coron*atorem* dom*i*ni Regis vill*æ* Oxoni*æ* et h*a*buit vna*m* plaga*m* in
tibia sua sinistra iuxta genu suum latitudinis 4 pellicu*m* circumquaqu*e* et
*pro*funditatis vnius pellicis et dim*idij*. Inquisitio capta fuit inde cora*m* ₍dicto₎   20
Coronatore p*er* sacramentu*m* &c: omnia pene Iuratorum no*mi*na illic desunt .
deinde sequit*ur*. Qui dicunt sup*er* sacramentu*m* suum qu*od* die Iouis in vigilia
natiuitatis *Sancti* Ioh*annis* Baptist*æ proxima præ*cedenti Cissores Oxoni*æ*
et alij de villa q*ui* fuerant cum eis vigilabant in Shoppis suis p*er* totam
noctem cantantes et facientes solatia sua cum Cytharis viellis et alijs diu*er*sis   25
instrumentis prout moris e*st* et consuetudo ibi*dem* et alibi facere *propter*
solennitatem illius festi. Et post media*m* noctem cum intellexisse*nt* neminem
vagantem ibi in stratis, exierunt de Shoppis suis et alij q*ui* erant cum eis
et ducebant coreas suas in alto vico contra draperiam; et ut sic ludebant
sup*er*uenit *præ*dictus Gilb*er*tus de Foxle cu*m* quoda*m* gladio nudo et extracto   30
in manu sua et mouebat statim contentionem vers*ù*s eos volens o*mn*imodo
penetrasse coream illa*m*: videntes autem quida*m* illor*um* | q*ui* h*a*buerunt
notitiam p*er*son*æ* venerunt ad eum et voluerunt eu*m* abduxisse ab eis et
rogabant eu*m* ne malefaceret cuiquam at idem Gilb*er*tus *propter* hoc noluit
[p]₍o₎mittere sed statim prosilijt ab eis et venit retro insultu*m* faciendo in   35
quenda*m* Will*el*mu*m* de Cleydon et voluit cum gladio suo amputasse manu*m*
sua*m* ut iuit in corea illa nisi se citius retraxisset; et statim currebant ad eum
Henricus de Beumont Coruiser Thom*as* de Bloxham Will*el*mus de Leye
seruiens Ioh*ann*is de Leye, et *præ*dictus Will*el*mus de Cleydon, et *præ*dictus

---

5/ excommunicatonis: *for* excommunicat*i*onis;
   abbreviation mark missing
14/ die do*mi*nica … virg*inis*: *21 August 1306*

22–3/ die Iouis … *præ*cedenti: *23 June 1306*
25/ cantantes: *first* ant *corrected over other letters*
38/ Beumont: *n corrected over another letter*

Henricus cu*m* quodam gladio vulnerauit ipsu*m* in brachio suo dextro, et
pr*æ*dictus Thomas vulnerauit ipsu*m* cu*m* quoda*m* misericorde in dorso:
pr*æ*dictus vero Will*elmus* de Cleydon vulnerauit ipsu*m* in capite, ita q*u*od
cecidit. et statim postea Will*elmus* de Leye cum quadam hach*a* q*ue* vocat*ur*
sparth vulnerauit ipsu*m* in tibia sua sinistra et fecit ei pr*æ*dicta*m* plag*am*   5
iuxta genu vnde obijt die d*omi*nico supradicto sed vixit *per* 8 hebdom*ades*
et 2 dies et dim*idium* et h*a*buit om*n*ia iura sua ecclesiastica.
...

1340   10

A   ***The Queen's College Statutes***   QC Arch
    p 18   *(Chapter 20)*
    ...

...Conueniantq*ue* simul ad prandiu*m* et c*æ*nam, quantu*m* comodè poterint,
horà vocationis ad eadem. Fiat aute*m* vocatio per Clarionem in loco   15
competente, ab vno seruiente qui ad illud fuerit deputatus, vbi ab omnibus
et singulis audiri poterit aptius....
    ...

    pp 26–7   *(Chapter 31)*   20
    ...

§   Et quoniam non congruit pauperibus præcipue de eleemosyna viuentibus
    dare panem filioru*m* hominu*m* canibus ad manducandu*m*: v*æ*que sit eis
    imprecatu*m* qui in auibus c*æ*li ludunt, nullus scholariu*m* dict*æ* Aul*æ*, in eàdem
    vel locis coniunctis, leporariu*m* teneat, cane*m* venaticum, vel aliu*m* priuatum,   25
    accipitrem, vel auem reclamatoriam, aut aliam habeat qualemcunque. Et
    quonia*m* solet frequentia instrumentorum musicoru*m* leuitatem et insolentiam
    qua*m* pluries prouocare, occasionémq*ue* adferre distractionis a studio et
    profectu; huiusmodi instrumentorum vsum infra suu*m* mansum, nisi
    temporibus co*m*munis solatij, scholares pr*æ*dicti omnino sibi nouerint   30
    interdictu*m*, omnimodu*m*q*ue* taxilloru*m* ludu*m* et scaccorum, omne*m*que
    alium ludum dantem occasione*m* perditionis monet*æ*, et pecuni*æ* cuiuscunq*ue*
    in Aulâ cameris, seu eoru*m* manso, nisi fortè quis vel qui, causâ recreationis,
    extra Aulam, absq*ue* suâ vel socioru*m* distractione à studio vel diuino officio,
    honestè et pacificè iocari voluerint aliquando; in quo caueatur præcipuè ludus   35
    taxilloru*m*, et huiusmodi ex quibus solet insurgere dissentionis materia, et
    frequenter contingere ludenti penuria; et ad declinatione*m* ludoru*m* talium,
    ad modu*m* scholariu*m*, capellani, pauperes, clerici, omnésq*ue* ministri seu
    habitantes dictam Aula*m*, nouerint se astringi sub | pæna a præposito infligenda.

15/ eadem: d *corrected over* n   24/ qui ... ludunt: *Bar 3.17*
15/ Clarionem: *underlined*   34/ Aula*m*: a *corrected over* u
23/ dare ... manducandu*m*: *cp Mt 15.26*   39/ sub ... infligenda: *underlined*

Præpositus verò, et locum eius tenens, ad omnia præmissa compescenda,
nisi quatenus necessitas exigit, vel honestas permittit, vinculo iuramenti
nouerint se astrictos.

…

5

1360–1
Exeter College Rectors' Accounts   EC Arch: A.1
single mb*   *(10 July–17 October 1361)*   *(Internal and external expenses)*
…
…Item. *reddit compotum* de viij. d. *solutis pro* expens*is* parochianor*um* de West   10
Wyttenham in die decollac*i*onis *sancti* Ioh*ann*is Baptist*e quando* lud*us* erat…

…

1378
Continuatio Eulogii   BL: Cotton MS Galba E.VII   15
f 194 col 2–f 194v col 1

…

Eode*m a*nno miles q*ui*da*m* de familia Reg*is* ve*n*it de wodstoke ad oxoniam
Scolares q*ui*dam nocte vene*r*unt & staba*n*t cora*m* hospicio suo facie*n*tes de eo
q*ue*ndam cantum ritmicem anglico continente*m* certa verba co*n*tra honorem   20
Reg*is* Et mise*r*unt sag*i*ttas ad fenestram hospicij ¶Miles mane surge*n*s conquest*us*
est Regi/ Stati*m* cancellari*us* & su*us* vicecancel*larius* vocati su*n*t londoni*am* &
statuu*n*tur cora*m* cancellario Reg*n*i & consilio Reg*is* Et q*ue*rebatur a cancellario
vniuersi*tatis* quare non puniuit derisores Reg*is* ¶*Resp*ondebat cancella*rius* | q*ui*a
timuit irregularitate*m* Cui cancella*rius* reg*n*i Tu probare vis q*uod* oxoni*a* non   25
potest regi per clericum Rex non potest conte*m*pni oxoni*am* sic*ut n*ec alibi/ Et
si vos de oxoni*a* no*n* potestis corrigere & castigare reg*is* contemptores propter
irregularitate*m* vt dic*it* cancella*rius* Sequitur q*uod* oxoni*a* non potest regi per
cleric*os* Sed oporte*t* regem subtrahere priuilegia Tu deberes maxime priuilegia
vniuersi*tatis* defendere & propter officium tuu*m* & *etiam* propter Iurame*n*tum   30
tuu*m* & contra ipsa priuile*gi*a tu loqueris. Nos te deponim*us* ab officio tuo/
*Resp*ondebat vniu*er*si*tatis* Cancella*rius* Officiu*m* meu*m* h*ab*eo a papa & a rege
¶Q*uod* a rege h*ab*eo Rex potest auferre Sed non illud q*uod* a papa h*ab*eo Cui
cancella*rius* angl*ie* & nos priuam*us* te p*ar*te regia & tu*n*c videas si poteris
gaud*ere* p*ar*te pape/ te ad dictum officium inhabilita*n*tes ¶Rex potest ab oxoni*a*   35
ammouere vniu*er*sitatem & te ¶vicecancella*rius* monach*us* adiudicat*us* fuit
carcerib*us* q*ui*a ad mandatu*m* pape incarcerauerat vt superi*us* dictu*m* est
Ioh*ann*em wicclif q*ui* postea ad rogatu*m* amicor*um* liberat*us* est. Cancellari*us*
deposit*us* pallia*n*s deposic*i*onem sua*m* resignauit spo*n*te in conuocac*i*one vt
dix*i*t no*n* coact*us*…   40

…

10–11/ West Wyttenham: *Long Wittenham, Berkshire (now Oxfordshire), a college estate*

1386–7
Merton College Supervisors of Founders' Kin Accounts   MCR: 4109
single mb dorse   *(1 August–1 August)* *(Necessary commons expenses)*
...
...Item p*ro* gaudijs q*uando* omne*s* socij a*u*le tr*ansiu*erunt ad mayyng*e* ij s....   5

1389–90
Gaol Delivery Roll   PRO: JUST 3/180
mbs 2c–d*   *(18 February)*

10

Gaol delivery held at Oxford Castle before John Hulle and other JPs for Oxfordshire
...

Oxon*ie*   ¶ Will*elmu*s Gymel et Petrus Ardach capti p*ro* eo q*uo*d ind*i*ct*a*ti fuerunt coram
Robert*o* Cherlton et soc*ijs* suis Iustic*iarijs* d*omi*ni Regis ad pac*em* in Com*itatu*
pred*icto* conseruand*am* assign*atis* de eo q*uo*d ipsi sim*u*l cum alijs ignotis   15
felon*ibus* eis armat*is* alligat*is* modo guerrino arraiat*is* apud Oxon*iam* die Iouis
et die ven*er*is in quarta septim*ana* quadragesime anno regni d*omi*ni Regis nunc
angli*e* duodecimo ordinauerunt int*er* eos c*er*tos capitaneos & gubernatores
insurgendo cont*ra* | *(blank)* Wallicos quoscu*m*que in villa Oxon*ie* existent*es*
sagittando in diu*er*sis vicis et venellis ante se clamando Ware Ware Ware   20
sle sle sle the Walsh dogges and here helpes and ho so loketh out of his
hous he shal be ded & quosdam occiderunt v*t* inferius et quosdam graui*ter*
vuln*er*auerunt et quosdam Wallicos genuflexebant abiurare villam fecerunt
ducentes eos ad portas d*i*ct*e* ville et sup*er* eas fec*er*unt eos mingere & osculare
portam & sic osculando tundebant capita ad portam ita q*uo*d quandoq*ue*   25
sanguis de naso int*er*dum lacrime exibant ab oc*u*lis eor*u*ndem et quandam
aulam in Oxon*ia* vocat*am* Depehalle felon*ice* fregerunt & ib*idem* vnu*m* libru*m*
vnu*m* pennar*ium* cu*m* cornu unu*m* par braccar*um* Will*elm*i Whetehull et
vnu*m* gladiu*m* et libros Ioh*ann*is Hoby ad valenc*iam* triginta & octo solid*orum*
felon*ice* furati fuerunt et asportauerunt & q*uo*d ˄⌜dicto⌝ die ven*er*is noctanter   30
cameram Thome ffrenssh in d*i*cta aula situat*am* felon*ice* fregerunt et duos
gladios vnam p*ar*mam duos arcus cum viginti et sex sagittis vnu*m* iak de
fustian vnam togam rubeam duo p*ar*ia manic*arum* albar*um* vnu*m* par
linthiaminu*m* vnam armilausam dupplicatam quinq*ue* p*ar*ia caligar*um* et
duas vlnas de caneuas vnu*m* par linee tele et alia bona et catalla ipsius Thome   35
ffrench p*re*cij sexaginta solid*orum* felon*ice* furati fuerunt et asportauerunt et
alias cam*er*as diu*er*sor*um* scolarium in aula pred*i*cta manenc*ium* pred*ic*to die
ven*er*is felon*ice* fregerunt et bona et catalla ibidem inuenta vide*l*icet libros
pannos lineos et laneos felon*ice* furati fuer*unt* & d*i*cto die ven*er*is noctant*er*

16–18/ die Iouis ... duodecimo: *1–2 April 1389*
19/ *(blank)*: *blank at top of membrane; missing text likely* pacem domini Regis et quiesiuerunt *as in*
parallel passage on mb 3

introitum nuncupat*um* Neuylesentre in Oxon*ia* felon*ice* freg*er*unt et bona et
catalla videl*icet* hostia fenestras ac libros gramaticales ac pannos lineos et laneos
Will*elm*i Dannay principal*is* eiusdem introitus Ioh*ann*is Halkyn scolaris ib*ide*m
et alior*um* scolariu*m* ib*ide*m morancium ad valenc*iam* sexaginta solidor*um*
felon*ice* furati fuerunt et asportauerunt; et eodem die ven*er*is noctant*er* aulam 5
vocat*am* sent Agase halle in Oxon*ia* felon*ice* fregerunt et bona et catalla ib*ide*m
inuenta videl*icet* pannos lineos et laneos libros gramaticales simul diolecticales
gladios arcus citheras Will*elm*i Getton Ioh*ann*is Mulle Ioh*ann*is Gloue et
alior*um* scolariu*m* ib*ide*m existencium ad valenciam quatuor librar*um* felon*ice*
furati fuerunt & q*u*od die sab*at*i in d*ic*ta quarta septi*m*ana quadragesime anno 10
supra*dic*to pre*dic*ti Will*elm*us Gymel & Petrus sim*u*l cum alijs felon*ibus* ignotis
aulam vocat*am* Pyrihalle in Oxon*ia* felon*ice* freg*er*unt et bona principalis
eiusdem aule mathei alco et Ric*ard*i Olyuere videl*icet* duos gladios clocos
dupplic*atos* diu*er*sorum colorum vnum baselard*um* vnam securim ac arcus et
sagittas ad valenc*iam* quatuor librar*um* felon*ice* furati fuerunt et alias aulas et 15
introitus ib*ide*m eodem die intrauerunt videl*icet* Mildredhalle Hamptonhalle
Bastaplesentre & diu*er*sa bona diuersorum scolarium in d*ic*ta aula manencium
ad valenc*iam* quinquaginta solidor*um* felon*ice* furati fu*er*unt Et q*u*od in d*ic*ta
surexione occis*i* fuerunt p*er* d*ic*tos felon*es* videl*icet* Edwardus Nuton Galf*ri*dus
Hanlane de Wall*ia* Thomas Repton et Ioh*ann*es Bowman Et q*u*od d*ic*to die 20
Iouis p*re*d*ic*ti felones et diu*er*si ignoti exportar*unt* ostia tabulas et petras de
d*ic*tis aulis spoliat*is* in altum vicum iuxta ecclesiam beate Marie & acceperunt
lignu*m* truncos & hostia laicor*um* inuitis illis et clauserunt se a cherltonesyn
vsq*ue* ad Penchurclane & ibi de nocte p*er*manserunt? ven*iunt* coram Iustic*iarijs*
hic p*er* vice*m* ducti et allucati qualit*er* se velint de felonijs p*re*d*ic*tis acquietare? 25
dic*unt* q*u*od ipsi in nullo sunt inde culpabiles Et de hoc pon*unt* se de bono et
malo sup*er* p*at*riam? Ideo fiat inde Iur*at*a. Iuratores ven*iunt* qui ad hoc electi
triati et iurati dic*unt* sup*er* sacr*a*mentu*m* suum q*u*od pre*dic*ti Will*elm*u*s* Gymel
& Petrus non sunt culpabiles de felon*ijs* p*re*d*ic*tis nec ea occ*asi*one vnqu*am*
se retraxerunt 30

Quieti Ideo consid*eratum* est q*u*od pre*dic*ti Will*elm*us Gymel & Petrus eant inde
Quieti &c

…

mb 3d* 35

…& eodem die ven*er*is noctant*er* aulam vocat*am* Seynteagace halle in
Oxon*ia* felon*ice* fregerunt & bona & catalla ib*ide*m inuenta videl*icet*
pannos lineos et laneos libros gramaticales sim*u*l diolec*ticales* gladios
arcus citheras Willelmi Gitton Ioh*ann*is Mulle Ioh*ann*is Gloue & alior*um* 40

8/ Gloue: *3 minims in* MS   37/ eodem die ven*er*is: *2 April 1389*
10–11/ die sab*at*i … supra*dic*to: *3 April 1389*

scolari*um* ibi*de*m existenc*ium* ad valenc*iam* quatuor librar*um* felon*ice* furati fuerunt...

mb 5d*

...& eodem die ven*eris* noctant*er* aulam vocat*am* Seynt agace halle in Oxon*ia* felon*ice* fregit & bona & catalla ibi*de*m inuenta vide*licet* pannos lineos et laneos libros gramaticales Sim*ul* diolectic*ales* gladios arcus citheras Willelmi Gitton Ioh*annis* Mulle Ioh*annis* Gloue & alior*um* scolariu*m* ibi*de*m existenc*ium* ad valenc*iam* quatuor librar*um* felon*ice* furatus fuit...   10

1395
AC   *Expenses for a Degree Feast at Canterbury College*
Pantin: *Canterbury College*, vol 3
p 56   15
...
Item dat*um* fistulatoribus xx s.
...

c 1396   20
Letter Recommending a Father Remove His Son from Oxford
BL: MS Royal 17.B.xlvii
f 44v*
...

          Alia forma consimilis.   25
Amice confidentissime licet alias vobis consulerim vt capientes exemplum de pro*uerbijs* antiquitus promulgatis. Quod noua testa capit inueterata sapit/ Debuistis ve*str*um filium ad Oxon*ie* scolas transmittere sic qu*od* ibidem potuisset tam *scientia* qu*am* morib*us* informari. Concipiens attamen p*er* relac*iones* qu*am* plurimu*m* qu*od* non proficiet in doctrina sed mores   30
detestabiles derelinquit su*m*mus d*omi*n*us* collaudet*ur* et tam in scriptura qu*am* in ludo lire commendabilit*er* est imbutus vobis consulo puro corde quatinus eundem ad s*er*uiend*um* in Curia d*omi*ni Regis vel Ducis lancastr*ie* volu*eritis* sagaciter ordinare.
...   35

c 1398
New College Statutes   NC Arch: 9429
ff 14–14v
...   40
®.xviij.   De mora non facienda in aula post prandium & cenam.

6/ eodem die veneris: *2 April 1389*   27/ inueterata: *corrected from* necueterata (?)

Item quia post refeccionem corporum *per* ciborum & potuum sumpcionem
homines ad scurrilitates turpiloquia & quod peius est detracciones & iurgia
necnon alia mala q*u*am plura & *per*iculosa *per*petranda efficiuntur co*mmun*it*er*
*pro*mpciores minusq*ue* tunc q*u*am ieiuno stomaco excessus h*uiu*sm*odi*
ponderantes animos plerumq*ue* ad lites contumelias & excessus alios   5
commouent simplicium *per*sonarum. Statuimus ordinamus & volumus vt
singulis diebus post prandium & cenam *per*soluta prius altissimo *pro* susceptis
graciar*um* accione/ deinde sine temporis interuallo potu caritatis bibere
volentibus ministrato & post potaciones in aula hora ignitegij seniores singuli
cuiuscumq*ue* status aut gradus fuerint ad studia sua vel loca | alia se transferant 10
nec iuniores alios ibidem moram facere vlterius *per*mittant nisi in festis
principalibus & festis maioribus duplicibus & nisi quando consilia domus
disputaciones aut alia negocia ardua Collegium tangencia i*m*mediate post in
aula debeant *per*tractari aut nisi quando ob dei reu*er*enciam ac sue matris vel
alterius sancti cuiuscumq*ue* tempo*re* yemali ignis in aula socijs ministrat*ur*   15
tunc scolarib*us* & socijs post temp*us* prandij aut cene liceat gracia recreac*i*onis
in aula in cantilenis & alijs solacijs honestis moram facere condecentem &
poemata regnor*um* cronicas & mundi huius mirabilia ac cetera que statum
clericalem condecorant seriosius *per*tractare.
...   20

f 16   *(Chapter 24)* *(Students and fellows not to leave the University without*
permission)
...

...Et q*u*od dum absentes fuerint in patria sicut decet clericos induantur &   25
honeste moribus conu*er*sentur. Nec *pro* tunc aut dum in vniuersitate *pre*sentes
fuerint ijdem scolares & socij vel alij in ip*so* Collegio manentes quicumq*ue*
tabernas spectacula vel alia loca inhonesta exerceant aut frequentent set a
comitiuis suspectis penitus se abstineant ne q*u*od absit ex co*mmun*ione
inhonesta vel suspecta aut alias ex eorum insolencijs quibuscumq*ue* dicto   30
Collegio n*ost*ro scolaribus vel socijs ciusdem scandalum dampnum vel
preiudicium eueniat aut quomodolibet generetur....

f 24*   *(Chapter 42)* *(Manner of saying mass, matins, and the other hours in*
the college chapel)   35

...In alijs vero festis infrascriptis videlicet sanctorum stephani Iohannis ap*osto*li
Innocencium sancti Thome martiris & in feria secunda tercia & quarta
ebdomade Pasche & Pentecostes Inuencionis & Exaltacionis sancte Crucis
Translacionis sancti Thome sanctorum Andree & Thome ap*osto*lorum/ Mathie/ 40

16/ scolarib*us* ... temp*us*: *corrected over illegible erasure*
32/ quomodolibet: modo *corrected over illegible erasure*

Marci/ Apostolorum Philippi & Iacobi & sancti Iacobi ap*osto*li/ Bartholomei/
Mathei Michaelis luce/ Simonis & Iude/ Martini/ Nicholai/ Translacionis
sancti Swithuni Katerine & Magdalene minores & inferiores *per*sone socij
ip*s*ius Collegij habitis relacione & consideracione debitis ad festa & *per*sonas
huiusmodi sec*un*d*u*m maioritatem minoritatem seu dignitatem dictorum   5
festorum officia modo debito exequantur. Que omnia et singula premissis
singulis diebus huiusmodi *per* dicti Collegij Scolares & socios predictos modo
& forma *pre*dictis volumus & precipimus exequi fieri & adimpleri excepto
festo sanctorum Innocencium supradicto in quo festo permittimus q*uo*d pueri
vesp*er*as matutinas & alia diuina officia legendo & cantando dicere & exequi   10
valeant sec*un*d*u*m vsum & consuetudinem eccl*es*ie Sarum...

...

ff 34v–5*

...   15

lxiij. De Saltibus luctacionibus & alijs ludis inordinatis in Capella vel aula
non fiendis.
Item quia in intermedio capitali siue transu*er*sali muro Capelle n*os*tri
Collegij Supradicti quidam murus lapideus int*er* ip*s*am Capellam &
aulam ip*s*ius Collegij mediare noscitur ac etiam Sep*ar*are ymago sanctissime   20
ac indiuidue trinitatis patibulum sancte Crucis cum ymagine crucifixi
beatissime Marie virginis sanctor*um*que plurium alior*um* ymagines sculpture
fenestre vitree ac picture varie nonnullaq*ue* alia op*er*a sumptuosa ad dei
laudem gloriam & honorem ip*s*iusq*ue* matris *pre*dicte subtiliter fabricata
varijsq*ue* coloribus *per*ornata ex p*ar*te dicte Capelle deuotissime situant*ur*   25
ac multifarie collocantur que quidem crux & ymagines sculpture fenestre
vitree picture ac alia op*er*a supradicta ex impericia inaduertencia & insolencia
diuersorum socior*um* | & scolarium aliarum eciam *per*sonarum *per* diuersos
iactus lapidum pilarum vel aliarum rerum ad parietem memoratum in
p*ar*te aule *pre*dicte vel *per* saltus luctaciones alios ve incautos & inordinatos   30
ludos in aula vel in Capella ipsa forsan fiendos defacili & casualiter &
verisimiliter ledi poterint deturpari ammoueri frangi cancellari seu alias
damnificari dictus quoq*ue* murus in p*ar*te vel in toto deterior fieri vel
eciam debilitari. Nos vero ymaginum sculpturarum fenestrarum & op*er*um
*pre*dictorum indempnitati *pro*spicere cupientes iactus lapidum & pilarum   35
necnon rerum quarumlibet aliarum ad parietem memoratum saltus
insup*er* luctaciones aliosq*ue* incautos & inordinatos ludos quoscumq*ue* in
Capella vel aula predicta vllo vmq*uam* temp*or*e fieri districtius *pro*hibemus
per que vel eorum aliquod ymaginibus sculpturis fenestris vitreis picturis
vel alijs sumptuosis op*er*ibus supradictis seu *pre*fato parieti capitali in sui   40

Collation with NC Arch: 9431 *(N)* ff 14–14v, 23–3v, 33–3v: 10 officia] *N omits*

composicione vel fabrica in materia vel in forma dampnum inferri poterit
quomodolibet vel iactura. Item quia subtus aulam predictam que in modum
solarij desuper terram eleuata & edificata consistit plures diuerse camere
ordinantur in quibus scolares vel socij dicti nostri Collegij necnon sacerdotes
clerici & ministri & alij in Capella ipsius Collegij seruire debentes morari   5
iacere quiescere ac eciam studere debebunt qui per luctaciones coreas
tripudia saltus cantus clamores tumultus & strepitus inordinatos aquarum
ceruisie & liquorum aliorum effusiones ludosque tumultuosos in aula ipsa
forsan fiendos ab ipsorum studio dormicione tranquillitate requie ac quiete
defacili & verisimiliter poterunt impediri & alias in libris vestibus alijsque   10
rebus suis dampna grauia Sustinere. Nos vero ipsorum vtilitati pariter &
quieti prospicere cupientes omnes huiusmodi luctaciones/ coreas/ tripudia/
saltus/ cantus/ clamores/ tumultus & strepitus inordinatos aquarum
ceruisie aliorumque liquorum omnium effusiones ludos quoque tumultuosos
& alias insolencias quascumque in aula vel Capella predicta vllo vmquam   15
tempore fieri districtius prohibemus per que vel eorum aliquod prefati
studentes sacerdotes & alij in dictis cameris commorantes ab ipsorum
studio dormicione tranquillitate requie vel quiete quomodolibet poterunt
impediri seu alias in libris vestibus alijs ve rebus suis dampnum sustineant
vel grauamen seu per que aula ipsa in ipsius ornatu vel fabrica deorsum   20
vel superius infra vel extra in aliqua sui parte deturpetur lesionem ve seu
dampnum aliquod paciatur. Et si quis in premissis vel aliquo premissorum
culpabilis inuentus fuerit pro dampno per ipsum illato satisfaciat competenter.
Et nichilominus vt pena vnius sit metus multorum per subtraccionem
communarum suarum vel alias iuxta discrecionem & ordinacionem   25
Custodis vicecustodis decanorum & sex aliorum sociorum seniorum
dicti Collegij iuxta quantitatem excessus acriter puniatur sine fauore
quocumque.
...

                                                                                  30

1399–1400
Durham College Accounts   Durham University Library:
  Durham Cathedral Muniments, Oxford Ac. 1399–1400
single mb*   *(3 or 7 July–28 May)* *(Expenses at Oxford)*
...   35
Item episcopo elemosinarie   ij s.
...

8, 14/ ceruisie: cer *corrected over illegible erasure*
10–11/ alijsque rebus: *corrected over illegible erasure*
12/ cupientes: *corrected over illegible erasure*

1400–1
Merton College Supervisors of Founders' Kin Accounts   MCR: 4114
single mb*   *(1 August–1 August)* *(Necessary expenses noted)*
...
...It*em pro* maio ij d....   5
...

1401–2
Durham College Accounts   Durham University Library:
  Durham Cathedral Muniments, Oxford Ac. 1401–2   10
single mb   *(13 May–5 May)* *(Expenses at Oxford)*
...
Item Ep*iscop*o Elimosinarie   xx d.
...

                                                                              15

1410–11
Expenses for Inception at Canterbury College
Bodl.: MS. Tanner 165
f 147*   *(Necessary expenses and wages)*
...   20
...Item In soluc*ione fac*ta hist*ri*onib*us* vj s. viij d....

Merton College Supervisors of Founders' Kin Accounts   MCR: 4115
single mb*   *(1 August–1 August)* *(Necessary expenses noted)*
...   25
...Item p*ro* ceretecis dat*is* p*ro* tr*i*humpho metr*i*fica*n*di iiij d....
...

single mb dorse*
...   30
...Item p*ro* maiac*ione* vj d....
...

1414
AC   *Chamberlains' Accounts*   Bodl.: MS. Twyne 23   35
p 242*
...
...Item pro 7. petris plumbi pro repara*t*ione de le bullringe 7 s. 6 d....
...

1422–3
St Michael at the North Gate Churchwardens' Accounts
ORO: PAR 211/4/F1/1, item 5
single mb* *(6 January 1422/3–6 January 1423/4) (Receipts)*
...

...Item payd for Bowez of treez ij d....

...

1427–8
Chancellor's Register OUA: Hyp/A/1, Register Aaa
f 13 *(31 July) (Goods found in Thomas Cooper's study)*
...

...Item j antiqua cithara Item j lute fractum...

...

1431–2
Merton College Bursars' Accounts MCR: 3754
mb 1 *(23 March–27 July)*
...

...Item histrion' domini ducis glow⟨...⟩ vj d....

...

c 1440
All Souls College Inventory Bodl.: MS. D.D. All Souls c.268, no 210
mb 2 col 1* *(Contents of the vestry)*

...Item j chemisia j capicium & mitra pro episcopo Nicholai

1443
All Souls College Foundation Statutes ASC Arch
ff [25–5v] *(That fellows and scholars shall not leave the town without permission)*
...

...Et quod dum absentes fuerint in patria sicut decet clericos induantur & honeste moribus conuersentur. Nec protunc aut dum in vniuersitate presentes fuerint ijdem scolares aut socij vel alij in ipso collegio manentes capellani quicumque tabernas spectacula vel alia loca inhonesta exerceant aut frequen|tent Set a comituis suspectis se abstineant ne quod absit ex communione inhonesta vel suspecta aut alias ex eorum insolencijs quibuscumque dicto collegio

20/ glow⟨...⟩: *right edge of roll torn*

scolarib*us* vel socijs eiusdem scandalum vel dampn*um* aut preiudicium
eueniat aut quomodoli*bet* genere*tur*...

...

1443–4
St Peter in the East Churchwardens' Accounts   ORO: PAR 213/4/F1/1
single mb   *(Receipts)*

...

...Et. de. xiij. s. ij. d. de ceruisia eccl*es*ia/...

...

1444–5
AC *St Peter in the East Churchwardens' Accounts*
Bodl.: MS. Top.Oxon c.403
f 39   *(Receipts)*

...

...Et de XIIs. in ceruisia ecclesie ad festum Pentecost*es*...

...

1447–8
Chancellor's Register   OUA: Hyp/A/1, Register Aaa
f 63v col 2   *(20 July)* *(Valuation of the goods leased by Simon Berynton*
   at Coleshill Hall)

...

It*em* j horn*e*pipe pr*ecio* j d.

...

1456–7
Lincoln College Computus   LC Arch: Computus 1
f 3   *(21 September–21 December 1456)* *(Offerings of All Saints' Church)*

...

Item i*n* die s*an*c*t*i Nicholai   v d. ob.
reliqua *p*ars qu*o*d se exte*n*debit ad vj d. datos u*idelice*t ep*iscop*o ex precepto
M*agist*ri rectoris

...

f 14v   *(21 December 1455–21 December 1456)* *(Necessary expenses)*

Post *fes*t*um* s*an*c*t*i Michael*is* archang*e*li

...

17/ festum Pentecostes: *16 May 1445*   32/ Nicholai: N *corrected over another letter, possibly* P

5

10

15

20

25

30

35

40

Item Clerico ecclesie *sancti* Michal*is in* vigilia *sancti* Nicholai   vj d.

...

St Michael at the North Gate Churchwardens' Accounts
ORO: PAR 211/4/F1/1, item 25   5
single mb   *(6 January 1456/7–6 January 1457/8) (Receipts)*

...

Item receuyd att Wesontyde for ye ⟨.⟩hirch all   xj s. iij d.

...

10

1460–1
New College Bursars' Accounts   NC Arch: 7713
mb 5   *(External payments)*

...

...Et so*lutum* histrionib*us* do*mi*ni Regis *pro* Rewardo eis dato iij s. iiij d.... 15

...

1461–2
St Peter in the East Churchwardens' Accounts   ORO: PAR 213/4/F1/1
single mb*   *(Receipts)*   20

...

Et de iiij s. iij d. ob. recept*is* int*er* *p*arochianos in festo Pentecost*es* *pro*
c*er*uisia eccl*esie*...

...

25

1462
Chancellor's Register   OUA: Hyp/A/1, Register Aaa
f 200v   *(Valuation of the goods of W. Lydbery)*

...

...It*em* a lewt *pre*cio vj d.   30

...

1463
Chancellor's Register   OUA: Hyp/A/1, Register Aaa
f 210   *(Valuation of the goods of John Hosear)*   35

...

Item An harpe iiij d.

...

8/ Wesontyde: *5–11 June 1457*
22/ festo Pentecost*es*: *6 June 1462*

1463-4

St Michael at the North Gate Churchwardens' Accounts
ORO: PAR 211/4/F1/1, item 33
single mb   *(6 January 1463/4-6 January 1464/5)* *(Receipts)*

...

Item rec*eperunt* de m*u*lierib*us* apud Hocketyde   iiij s. vij d.

...

1464-5

St Peter le Bailey Churchwardens' Accounts   ORO: PAR 214/4/F1/3
single mb*   *(Receipts)*

...

Item Rec*eptos pro* ceruisia Ap*u*d Pentechost*am*   viij s.

...

1465-6

AC   *St Peter in the East Churchwardens' Accounts*
Bodl.: MS. Top.Oxon c.403
f 42*   *(Receipts)*

...

...Et de XIs. IId. receptis in ceruisia vendita erga Pentecost*em*...

...

St Peter le Bailey Churchwardens' Accounts   ORO: PAR 214/4/F1/4
single mb*   *(Receipts)*

...

Et cu*m* vij s. rec*eptis* ad fes*tum* Pentecoste p*ro* ceruisia
Et cu*m* iij s. iij d. rec*eptis* at hocke Tewn*es* day

...

1466

Chancellor's Register   OUA: Hyp/A/1, Register Aaa
f 236

...

Mr Rober*tus* passlew condux*it* in s*er*uu*m* suu*m* Iohann*em* harrys. harpemak*er*.
p*ro* toga v*el* precio vj s. viij d. & id*em* Iohann*es* iurat*us* e*st* ad priuilegior*um*
vniuersit*atis* obseruanciam &c

...

6/ Hocketyde: *8-9 April 1464*   27/ festum Pentecoste: *25 May 1466*
13/ Pentechost*am*: *23 April 1465*   28/ hocke Tewn*es* day: *14 April 1466*
21/ Pentecost*em*: *25 May 1466*

5

10

15

20

25

30

35

1466–7
St Peter le Bailey Churchwardens' Accounts ORO: PAR 214/4/F1/5
single mb* *(Receipts)*

...

Item Ad Festum Pentecoste pro ceruisia   vj s. ij d. 5

...

1467–8
All Souls College Bursars' Accounts Bodl.: MS. D.D. All Souls c.278
mb 4* *(2 November–2 November) (Rewards)*   10

...

Et de ij d. datis vni ludenti the hobyhors tempore natalis domini

...

mb 5* *(Various expenses)*   15

...

Et de xvj d. solutis diuersis ludentibus in aula tempore purificacionis

...

St Michael at the North Gate Churchwardens' Accounts   20
ORO: PAR 211/4/F1/1, item 38
single mb *(8 March 1467/8–8 March 1468/9) (Receipts)*

...

Item receperunt apud hoctyde   xv s. viij d.

...   25

St Peter le Bailey Churchwardens' Accounts ORO: PAR 214/4/F1/6
single mb *(Receipts)*

...

Item in d⌈i⌉e Pentechoste pro ceruisia   xx s. 30
Item in die *(blank)* ceruisia   xxiij d.
Item ad duae Vices receptos pro ceruisia v s. viij d. datos Ad pannuel

...

5/ Festum: *scribe habitually uses the form* fcm *with marks of abbreviation*
5/ Pentecoste: *17 May 1467*
24/ hoctyde: *25–6 April 1468*
30/ d⌈i⌉e Pentechoste: *5 June 1468*
32/ duae: *for* duas

1468–9

St Michael at the North Gate Churchwardens' Accounts
ORO: PAR 211/4/F1/1, item 39
single mb   *(8 March 1468/9–29 March 1470) (Receipts)*

...   5

Item Apud hoctyde   xv s.

...

St Peter le Bailey Churchwardens' Accounts   ORO: PAR 214/4/F1/7
single mb*   *(Receipts)*   10

...

Item pro ceruisia data per Iohannem Rogger   xvij d.
Item pro ceruisia data per Thomam Dalton   xx d.

...

Item festum Pentecoste pro ceruisia   xx s. 15

...

(Payments)
Item pro portacione cepularum cum leo & draco in ceruisio   ij d.

...   20

Item for lyuerye at Wytsuntyde   viij d.

...

1469

Chancellor's Register   OUA: Hyp/A/1, Register Aaa   25
f 270 col 2   *(Valuation of the goods of Reginald Stone)*

...

Item j harpe ij s.

...

                                                                          30

1469–70

Merton College Bursars' Accounts   MCR: 3785
single mb   *(28 July–24 November) (External expenses)*

...

...Item in regarda ex precepto domini custodis lusoribus apud holywell pro   35
ecclesia sancti petri in oriente xij d....

...

6/ hoctyde: *10–11 April 1469*
15/ festum: *scribe habitually uses the form* fcm *with marks of abbreviation*
15/ Pentecoste: *21 May 1469*
19/ cum leo & draco: *for* cum leone & dracone
21/ Wytsuntyde: *21–7 May 1469*

New College Bursars' Accounts   NC Arch: 7720
mb 4   *(Necessary external costs)*
…
…Et solut*um* histrionib*us* D*om*ini Regis p*ro* Rewardo *sibi* dat*o* ij s.…
…   5

St Michael at the North Gate Churchwardens' Accounts
ORO: PAR 211/4/F1/1, item 42
single mb*   *(20 March 1469/70–7 March 1470/1)*   *(Receipts)*
…   10
It*em* Aput hoctyde vnus torche pondr*ans*
xxx libr*arum* precij cuiuslib*et* libr*e*   iiij d. *summa*/ et in pecu*n*ia j d. ob.
…

1471–2   15
OUF   **Proctors' Accounts**   OUA: NW/5/3
single mb   *(29 April 1471–30 April 1472)*   *(Payments)*
…
It*em* tubicinibus regis pro regarda   iij s. iiij d.
…   20

St Michael at the North Gate Churchwardens' Accounts
ORO: PAR 211/4/F1/1, item 43
single mb*   *(25 December–25 December)*   *(Receipts)*
…   25
De recept*ione* in hockday   ij s. vj d.
De recept*ione* p*ro* ceruisia uendit*a* in Septimana Pentecoste   xiiij s.
…

St Peter le Bailey Churchwardens' Accounts   ORO: PAR 214/4/F1/8   30
single mb   *(Receipts)*
…
It*em* rec*eiued* for Ale at Wytsontyde   xvj s. ix d.
…

                                                                                            35
(Expenses)
It*em* sol*utum* est to the [pyper] ⌜luter⌝ at wyssontyde   ij s. vj d.
…

11/ hoctyde: *30 April–1 May 1470*   27/ Septimana Pentecoste: *17–23 May 1472*
26/ hockday: *7 April 1472*   33, 37/ Wytsontyde, wyssontyde: *17–23 May 1472*

1472-3
St Michael at the North Gate Churchwardens' Accounts
ORO: PAR 211/4/F1/1, item 46
single mb*   *(2 February 1472/3-2 February 1473/4) (Receipts)*
…   5

De recepcione pro seruisia vendida in septimana Penthacoste   xvij s. j d.
…
De recepcione pro seruisia vendida ex donacione Iohannis Roger   iiij s. vj d.
…

                                                                              10

1473-4
St Peter le Bailey Churchwardens' Accounts   ORO: PAR 214/4/F1/9
single mb   *(Receipts)*
…
Item receptis Ad ffestum Pentechoste pro ceruisia   xiiij s. 15
…

(Payments)
Item for the pyper at Wytson tyde   iij s. viij d.
…   20

1474-5
St Michael at the North Gate Churchwardens' Accounts
ORO: PAR 211/4/F1/1, item 49
single mb*   *(2 February 1474/5-2 February 1475/6) (Receipts)*   25
…
Item receperunt de claro pro seruisia vendida in
septimana penthacoste   xiij s. vj d.
Item receperunt de seruisia vendida ex dono Iohannis
Rogers in festo sancte Anne   ij s. v d. 30
…

St Peter in the East Churchwardens' Accounts   ORO: PAR 213/4/F1/1
single mb   *(8 December-8 December) (Receipts)*
…   35
Item illi receperunt ad hoktide   viij s. j d.

6/ septimana Penthacoste: *6-12 June 1473*   28/ septimana penthacoste: *14-20 May 1475*
15/ ffestum: *scribe habitually uses the form fcm with*   36/ illi: *predicti collectores; mentioned in the first*
  marks of abbreviation   *receipts item*
15/ Pentechoste: *29 May 1474*   36/ hoktide: *3-4 April 1475*
19/ Wytson tyde: *29 May-4 June 1474*

Item pro ceruisia vendida in septimana penthecostes   xiij s. vij d.

...

1475–6
St Michael at the North Gate Churchwardens' Accounts   5
ORO: PAR 211/4/F1/1, item 50
single mb   *(25 December–25 December) (Receipts)*

...

...Et de iiij s. v d. pro seruisia uendita ... Et cum xvj d. receptis in die
nuncupato hocday ... Et cum xv s. x d. ob. pro seruisia uendita ad festum   10
Pentecosten...

...

St Peter le Bailey Churchwardens' Accounts   ORO: PAR 214/4/F1/10
single mb*   *(Receipts)*   15

...

Item receptis pro ceruisia Ad festum Pentechos   xvij s.
Item receptis pro ceruisia data per Iohannem holywode   iij s. iiij d.
Item receptis pro ceruisia data per Petrum Schormolode   ij s. viij d.
Item receptis pro ceruisia data per Ricardum Rust   iij s. 20
Item receptis pro ceruisia data Iohanne Smyth   v s.
Item receptis pro ceruisia data Thoma Dalton   iij s. iij d.

...

1476–7   25
Lincoln College Computus   LC Arch: Computus 1
f 32v   *(21 September–21 December 1476) (Necessary expenses)*

...

Item clerico ecclesie Michaelis in vigilia sancti nicholai   vj d.

...   30

St Peter le Bailey Churchwardens' Accounts   ORO: PAR 214/4/F1/11
single mb   *(Receipts)*

...

Item in die Pentecoste pro ceruisia   xiij s. 35

...

1/ septimana penthecostes: *14–20 May 1475*
10/ hocday: *23 April 1476*
10–11/ festum Pentecosten: *2 June 1476*
17/ festum: *scribe habitually uses the form* fcm *with marks of abbreviation*
17/ Penthecos: *for* Pentecoste, *2 June 1476*
35/ die Pentecoste: *25 May 1477*

1477–8
St Michael at the North Gate Churchwardens' Accounts
ORO: PAR 211/4/F1/1, item 53
single mb   *(2 February 1477/8–2 February 1478/9) (Receipts)*

...   5

...Et cum xxj d. *(blank)* receptis in die nuncupato hockeday Et cum xv⟨..⟩ s. ob.
receptis in septimana Pentecosten ⌈In seruisia uendita⌉ ... Et cum vij s. viij d.
Receptis de pecunie collecta ⌈per feminas⌉ in hock monday Et cum ij s. iij d.
Receptis quam summam Iuuenes colligerunt de seruisia uendita post festum
pentecoste...   10

...

St Peter le Bailey Churchwardens' Accounts   ORO: PAR 214/4/F1/12
single mb   *(Receipts)*

...   15

Item pro ceruisia [d] Ad festum Pentechoste   xvj s. vj d.

...

1478–9
St Michael at the North Gate Churchwardens' Accounts   20
ORO: PAR 211/4/F1/1, item 54
single mb   *(25 December–25 December) (Receipts)*

...

...Item xxiij d. Received on hockeday
...Item of xix s. ix d. att Wytsontyd for Alle   25

...

1479–80
All Souls College Bursars' Accounts   Bodl.: MS. D.D. All Souls c.278
sheet 9*   *(2 November–2 November) (Various expenses)*   30

...

Et de xij d. solutis ludentibus pro ecclesia de evissam

...

6/ hockeday: *31 March 1478*
7/ septimana Pentecosten: *10–16 May 1478*
8/ pecunie: *for* pecunia
8/ hock monday: *30 March 1478*
16/ festum: *scribe habitually uses the form* fcm *with marks of abbreviation*
16/ Pentechoste: *10 May 1478*
24/ hockeday: *20 April 1479*
25/ Wytsontyd: *30 May–5 June 1479*

New College Bursars' Accounts   NC Arch: 7722
mb 7   *(Necessary external costs)*
…

…Et in vino dato *seruientibus* ville Oxonie in festo Circumcisionis vj d. Et
in vino dato histrionibus *domini* principis xij d. Et in Rewardo dato eisd*em*   5
vj s. viij d.…

St Michael at the North Gate Churchwardens' Accounts
ORO: PAR 211/4/F1/1, item 55
single mb   *(25 December–25 December) (Receipts)*   10
…

…It*em* of xij s. ix d. resseuyd Att Hoktide It*em* of xxv s. resseuyd At
Witsuntyde for Ale all cownted and Allowed…
…

15

St Peter le Bailey Churchwardens' Accounts   ORO: PAR 214/4/F1/13
single mb*   *(Receipts)*
…

Item rece*perunt* de Ioh*anne* Robyns ex seruisia dat*a*   ij s. viij d.
…   20
Item rece*perunt pro* ceruisia in fest*o* pentecost*e*   xj s. j d.
…

1480–1
St Peter in the East Churchwardens' Accounts   ORO: PAR 213/4/F1/1   25
single mb*   *(Receipts)*
…

It*em* in pecunia apud hoctyd   vj s. viij d.
It*em* in s*er*uicia vendid*a* in septimana pentecost*es*   xvj s. vj d.
…   30

1481–2
St Michael at the North Gate Churchwardens' Accounts
ORO: PAR 211/4/F1/1, item 59
single mb   *(25 December–25 December) (Receipts)*   35
…

Item *with* ix s. viij d. Rec*eyuyd* At Hockeday

12/ Hoktide: *10–11 April 1480*	28/ hoctyd: *30 April–1 May 1481*
13/ Witsuntyde: *21–7 May 1480*	29/ septimana pentecost*es*: *10–16 June 1481*
21/ ceruisia: c *written over another letter, probably* s	37/ Hockeday: *16 April 1482*
21/ fest*o* pentecost*e*: *21 May 1480*	

Item w*ith* xiij s. iiij d. Rec*eyuyd* At Whytsontydde for Ale

...

St Peter in the East Churchwardens' Accounts   ORO: PAR 213/4/F1/1
single mb*   *(Receipts)*   5

...

It*em* In pecunias apud hoctyd   viij s. vj d.
Item in s*er*uicia vendid*a* in septimana penticost*es*   ix s. ij d.

...
                                                                                                   10

1482–3
Magdalen College Liber Computi 1482–3   MC Arch
f 26v   *(Chapel costs)*

...Item v°° die dece*m*bris pro cerothecis ep*iscop*i in ffesto *sanct*i Nicholai   15
iiij d....

AC   **All Saints Churchwardens' Accounts**   Bodl.: MS. Wood D.2
p 328*   *(Rendered 29 January 1483/4) (Receipts)*

...
                                                                                                   20
® ye k*in*g game.   It*em* rec*eiv*ed at whitsontyde for ye kinge game 17 s. 3 d.

St Peter in the East Churchwardens' Accounts   ORO: PAR 213/4/F1/1
single mb*   *(Receipts)*

...
                                                                                                   25
It*em* In pecunijs apud hoctyd   ix s.
Item In s*er*uicia vendid*a* in septimana pentecost*es*   x s. iij d.

...

1483   30
Magdalen College Statutes   MC Arch: MS 277
f 20v   *(That fellows and students should not leave town without permission)*
...
...Et q*uo*d dum absentes fu*er*int in p*at*ria. sicut decet Cl*er*icos induant*ur* et
honeste moribus conu*er*sentur. Nec p*ro* tunc aut dum in vniu*er*sitate p*re*sentes   35

Collation with NC Arch: MS 276 *(A)* ff 22–3v, 41 and MC Arch: MS 278 *(B)* ff 25,
43–3v: 34 dum] *A omits*   35 presentes] *AB omit*

1/ Whytsontydde: *26 May–1 June 1482*   21/ whitsontyde: *18–24 May 1483*
7/ pecunias: *for* pecunijs *(?)*   26/ pecunijs: ij *written over* ia *(?)*
7/ hoctyd: *16–17 April 1482*   26/ hoctyd: *8–9 April 1483*
8/ septimana penticost*es*: *26 May–1 June 1482* 27/ septimana pentecost*es*: *18–24 May 1483*

fuerint Iidem scolares & socij vel alij in ipso Collegio manentes Capellani
seu Clerici quicunque tabernas spectacula vel alia loca inhonesta exerceant aut
frequentent sed a comitiuis suspectis penitus se abstineant Ne quod absit
ex communione inhonesta vel suspecta aut alias ex ipsorum insolencijs
quibuscumque dicto Collegio scolaribus vel socijs eiusdem scandalum 5
dampnum vel preiudicium eueniat aut quomodolibet generetur…

f 38v

De mora non facienda in Aula post prandium 10
Item quia post refeccionem Corporis per Ciborum & potuum sumpcionem
homines ad scruri_⌐li⌐tates & turpiloquia & quod peius est ad detractiones
& iurgia necnon alia mala quam plurima & periculosa perpetranda efficiuntur
communiter promciores minusque tunc quam ieiuno stomaco excessus
huiusmodi ponderantes animos plerumque ad lites contumelias & excessus 15
alios commouent simplicium personarum. Statuimus ordinamus & volumus
quod singulis diebus post prandium & cenam persoluta prius altissimo pro
susceptis graciarum accione deinde sine temporis intervallo potu caritatis libere
volentibus ministrato & post potaciones in Aula hora ignitegij seniores singuli
cuiuscumque status aut gradus fuerint ad studia sua vel loca alia se transferant 20
nec Iuniores alios ibidem moram facere vlterius permittant nisi quando Consilia
domus aut alia negocia ardua Collegium tangencia inmediate post in Aula
debeant pertractari Nisi eciam disputaciones aut Capitulorum biblie temporibus
refeccionum lectorum declaraciones per aliquem sociorum Theologum iuxta
discrecionem presidentis vicepresidentis vel senioris tunc presentis absque 25
premunicione deputandum quem quidem ex improuiso sic deputatum si
in dicta declaracione renuens vel multum negligens repertus fuerit penam
huiusmodi incurrere volumus que pro linguis suis abutentibus in ydiomate
materno ordinata existit quas quidem declaraciones vt singuli presentes dicte
lecture reddantur attenciores singulis diebus quibus presidenti & in eius 30
abscncia vicepresidenti videbitur expedire ⌐fieri⌐ volumus aut nisi quando ob
dei reuerenciam ac sue matris vel alterius sancti cuiuscumque ignis quem ex

Collation continued: 1 Iidem] Idem AB   1 in ipso] in [q] ipso A   3 suspectis]
suspectus A   3 se] AB omit   11 & potuum] potuumque B   12 scruri_⌐li⌐tates]
scurrilitates AB   16 simplicium] supplicium AB   17 & cenam persoluta] [persolut']
& cenam persoluta B   18 temporis] temporibus A; temporibus B   29 existit]
existat B   32 quem] A adds [dei reuerentiam] after quem

3/ comitiuis: corrected from comtiuis by interlinear
   addition of minim
3/ suspectis: i corrected by erasure from u
12/ scruri_⌐li⌐tates: for scurrilitates

23–31/ Nisi eciam … ⌐fieri⌐ volumus: enclosed in
   parentheses in another, likely later, hand
26/ premunicione: 7 minims in MS
27/ penam: e corrected over erasure

solis Carbonibus fieri volumus in Aula socijs ministrat*ur* tunc socijs &
scolaribus post tempus prandij aut Cene liceat gr*acia* recreacionis in
Cantulenis & alijs solacijs honestis moram fac*ere* condecentem & poemata
regnor*um* cronicas & mundi huius mirabilia ac cet*er*a que statum Clericalem
condecorant ⌊seriosius p*er*tractare⌋   5

1483–4
Magdalen College Liber Computi 1483–4   MC Arch
f 68   *(Chapel costs)*

…   10

x   …Et solut*um* p*ro* Ceroticis ep*iscop*i festo Sanc*t*i Nich*o*l*a*i & eius crucem ferent*is*
viij. d.…

f 68v*

                                                                                   15

…Et p*ro* pane consecrabili & h*o*minibus facientib*us* Tab*er*naculum *pro*phete
pro istoriis…

St Michael at the North Gate Churchwardens' Accounts
ORO: PAR 211/4/F1/1, item 62   20
single mb   *(2 February 1483/4–2 February 1484/5)* *(Receipts)*
…
…It*em* At hoktyde clere resseuyd vj s. j d.…
…

                                                                                   25

1484–5
Merton College Register   MCR: 1.2
f 17v
…

Iniu*n*ctio fact*a*   Eod*em* die Iniu*n*ctum e*st* ibid*em* Iunioribus Magist*r*is vt caueant de nimia   30
Iunio*ribus*   familiaritate. arrogantia et p*re*sumptione erga seniores Magist*r*os sub pena
Magistris   incumbenti. Iniunctum ₍ᵉˢᵗ₎ etiam ibid*em* eisd*em* Iunioribus Magist*r*is ne
                   de cet*er*o in Noctib*us* solemnib*us* faciant vel clamores. vel strepit*us*. in
                   detrimentu*m* dom*us*. aut socior*um* inquietationes. sub pe*n*a expulsio*n*is [⟨.⟩] a
Iniu*n*ctio fact*a*   commu*n*is. Et ibid*em* Iniu*n*ctum erat Magist*r*o hesington ne de cet*er*o vtat*ur*   35
Magist*r*o   instrum*entis* musicalib*us* infra q*u*adratu*m* n*ec* an*te* propositio*n*em tituli n*ec* post.
hesington   …

Collation continued: 1 Carbonibus] carnibonib*us* A   1 ministrat*ur*] ministretur *AB*

16–17/ Et … istoriis: *no sum given; part of list of*
   unrelated sacrist's expenses totalling 5s 9½d
16/ prophete: h *corrected from* p

23/ hoktyde: *26–7 April 1484*
30/ Eodem die: *17 January 1484/5*

f 18*

…

°Ignis
Magistrorum
Regentium°

® de igne
regentium

Eodem die celebratus est ignis regentium in aula. Magistro wodwarde
existente seniore regente. et hec consuetudo a multis annis in dissuetudinem
abijt. 5

…

f 18v*

…

ignis in die
capituli./.

Eodem die celebratus est in alta aula ignis post vltimum biberium quod ab 10
antiquis temporibus fieri consueuit illo die quo celebratur capitulum si ante
quadragesimam teneatur. & propter hanc causam dilata est propositio tituli
in crastinum diem

…

15

1485–6
Magdalen College Battells Book   MC Arch: CP 8/49
f 49   (10–16 December)

…

In die mercurij ad prandium cum socijs duo vrsarij domini Stanlay… 20

…

f 83 col 1   (22–8 July)

Item die sabati [vij] viz die sancte marie magdalene Ad prandium 25
…& cum socijs in alia tabula … 3es cantatores…

…

In die dominica ad prandium cum socijs duo iuuenes cantatores … Et ad
cenam cum socijs vnus cantator de Westbury…

… 30

Magdalen College Liber Computi 1485–6   MC Arch
f 100v*   (Other external expenses)

…

…Solutum xxvijo die decembris satrape maioris, pro pensione sua & 35
consuetudine antiqua ij s. ij d.…

3/ Eodem die: *17 January 1484/5*
3/ ignis regentium: *underlined*
10/ Eodem die: *18 January 1484/5*
20/ die mercurij: *14 December 1485*
25/ die sabati: *22 July 1486*
28/ die dominica: *23 July 1486*

f 103   *(25 December–25 March)   (Hall costs)*

…

…Solut*um* ⌜2° term*ino*⌝ *M*agistro Croff*tes* decano pro pictura ornam*en*t'
lus' tempore natal*is* d*om*i*n*i vt p*atet* p*er* billa*m* sua*m* iij s. v d.…

Merton College Register   MCR: 1.2
f 22*

…

parsons Elig*itur*
rex

°Rex°

*M*agis*te*r p*ar*sons Elig*itur* rex Collegij †®
decimo octauo die [eiusd*em*] Nouembris elect*us* est pro [⟨.⟩] rege fabaru*m*
in collegio *secundum* antiqua*m* *consue*tudine*m* *M*agis*te*r Ioh*an*n*es* p*ar*sons
et ho*c* q*uia* tu*nc* promot*us* erat ad Collegiu*m* Eton*en*se

…

f 23*

® de igne
capitulari

Eod*em* die celebrat*us* e*st* ignis in alta aula post cena*m*. q*ui* d*icitu*r ignis capituli

…

New College Hall Book   NC Arch: 5529
f [90v]   *(15–21 July)*

…

Marc*ur*ij v*enerunt* ad cen*am* c*um* so*cijs* … tres mimi d*om*i*n*i sta*n*ley…

…

1486–7
Magdalen College Liber Computi 1486–7   MC Arch
f 130v*   *(25 December–25 March)   (Itemized hall costs)*

…

Solut*um* vj° die Ianuarij citharist' & mimis te*m*pore lud*i* in
aula ex co*n*sensu decanor*um* & burs*ariorum* in regard*o*   viij d.

• Solut*um* pro quod*am* ornamento lusor*um* vocat*o* le capp
maynte*n*aunce vt p*er* billa*m* decani   ix d.

…

Merton College Register   MCR: 1.2
f 30v

*M*agis*te*r Byrde
elect*us* est In
rege*m*

…

Die prec*e*cente viz. nonodecimo [*com*put] *M*agis*te*r Birde [q*uia*] promot*us*

17–18m/ de igne capitulari: *underlined*   39/ prec*e*cente: *for* precedente
17/ Eod*em* die: *19 January 1485/6*   39/ nonodecimo: *19 November 1486*
23/ Marc*ur*ij: *19 July 1486*

®°Rex° est in regem non obstante tunc temporis Bacallario hanchyrch promoto et eodem anno procuratore existente Magistro Ardern

…

f 31v 5

…

Ignis Regencium Quintodecimo die eiusdem mensis erat ignis regencium In Alta Aula Magistro
®°Ignis Ardern procuratore tunc seniore regente
Regencium°

…

10

1487–8
Lincoln College Computus LC Arch: Computus 2
p 20 *(21 December 1486–21 December 1487) (Necessary expenses and other costs)*

…

15

Item solui Clerico ⌈festo⌉ sancti Nicholai   vj ⟨.⟩

…

Magdalen College Liber Computi 1487–8 MC Arch
f 145v *(Hall costs)*   20

…

Solutum pro vestimentis lusorum tempore natiuitatis domini
consilio vnius Decani ut patet per billam magistri Radcliff   ij s. ij d.

Merton College Register MCR: 1.2   25
f 34v

…

19o die eiusdem mensis electus est in regem Magister willelmus Nele.

…

30

f 35v

…

ignis regencium 30o die eiusdem erat ignis regencium in alta aula seniore regente Magistro
Roberto Ardern

…   35

7l eiusdem mensis: *February 1486/7*
28l eiusdem mensis: *November 1487*
33l eiusdem: *January 1487/8*

1488–9
Lincoln College Computus   LC Arch: Computus 1
f 89   *(21 December 1487–21 December 1488)* *(Necessary expenses)*
...
Item Clerico *sancti* Michaelis *in* vig*ilia sancti* Nicho*le*   vj d.   5
...

Magdalen College Liber Computi 1488–9   MC Arch
f 176v   *(Chapel costs)*

10

...Solut*um* Ioh*anni* Wynman pro scrip*tura* vni*us* libri de *ser*uic*io* Ep*iscop*i
pro die Innocenci*um*. v d....

Merton College Register   MCR: 1.2
f 39v   15

Molland elect*us*
est in reg*em*   ...
®°Rex°   19o die ei*us*d*em* m*agiste*r Symon Molland vno o*mnium* consensu socior*um*
                   elect*us* est in reg*em*.

Mens*is*
decembris   ...
                   18 die Mens*is* decebris viz. 8o die an*te* natale d*omin*i celebratu*m* est   20
Scrutin*ium*   scrutiniu*m*. [⟨.⟩] in q*u*o deposit*um* co*ntra* indiscretu*m* modu*m* quor*undam*
celebratum an*te*   m*agist*ror*um* erga bacca∧⌈la⌉rios in vig*ilia* *Sancti* Edmu*n*di impune a decanis
natale d*omi*ni   *per*miss*um* & alia deposita su*n*t s*ed* no*n* magni oneris & dissolutum est
                   scrutiniu*m*
                   ...   25

f 40
                   ...
®Ignis regenciu*m* 20o die ei*us*d*em* erat ignis regenciu*m* in alta aula seniore regente M*agist*ro
                   Thoma Kent.   30
                   ...

St Peter in the East Churchwardens' Accounts   ORO: PAR 213/4/F1/1
single mb   *(8 December–8 December)* *(Receipts)*
...   35
Item recep*er*unt de claro ap*u*d hoktide   xj s. j d.
...

5/ Nicho*le*: *for* Nicholai   23/ oneris: i *corrected over* o
17/ eiusdem: *November 1488*   29/ eiusdem: *February 1488/9*
20/ decebris: *for* decembris; *abbreviation mark missing*   36/ hoktide: *27–8 April 1489*

Item In septimana pentacostes receperunt de claro xiij s. j d.

...

Item de Incremento 1 quarterij seruisie Et pro players garmentes ix d.

...

5

1489–90
Merton College Bursars' Accounts MCR: 3808
mb 1 *(27 March–7 August) (External expenses)*

...

...pro in regardis quibusdem lusoribus ad mandatum custodis xij d.... 10

...

Merton College Register MCR: 1.2
f 43

...

15

® harper electus
est in regem

19o die eiusdem Magister Thomas harper ex vnanimi consensu sociorum
electus est in regem.

...

St Michael at the North Gate Churchwardens' Accounts 20
ORO: PAR 211/4/F1/1, item 67
single mb *(11 March 1489/90–10 March 1490/1) (Receipts)*

...

...Item At hoctyde v s. x d....

...

25

1490–1
Magdalen College Battells Book MC Arch: CP 8/50
f 30 *(26 March–1 April)*

30

In die dominico ad cena cum socijs vnus firmarius vocatus Phylyppe Harrys
Et alius venne cantans. In die mercurij idem cantator ad prandium cum socijs/
Et idem in die veneris ad prandium cum socijs...

f 47 *(25 June–1 July)* 35

...In die Iouis ... ad prandium cum socijs [vn] quidam cantor de abendonia...

...

1/ septimana pentacostes: *7–13 June 1489*   32/ die mercurij: *30 March 1491*
16/ eiusdem: *November 1489*   33/ die veneris: *1 April 1491*
24/ hoctyde: *19–20 April 1490*   37/ die Iouis: *30 June 1491*
31/ die dominico: *27 March 1491*

f 50   *(23–9 July)*

...In die veneris ad prandium in aula ... Nicholaus cantator...

f 52   *(6–12 August)*

In die dominico ... ad cena cum socijs vnus cantator londonensis...

...

f 55   *(27 August–2 September)*

...

In die dominico ad prandium cum socijs duo cantatores capelle domini episcopi hartfordensis

...

Magdalen College Liber Computi 1490–1   MC Arch
f 11   *(Hall costs)*

...

...Solutum pro Candelis consumptis tempore ludorum in Natali vj d....

Merton College Register   MCR: 1.2
f 47v

...

20º die eiusdem ex vnanimi consensu sociorum magister georgius weldysch
2ᵘˢ quattuor seniorum electus est in regem pro anno futuro

...

® °Rex°

weldysch
eligitur in
regem

St Michael at the North Gate Churchwardens' Accounts
ORO: PAR 211/4/F1/1, item 69
single mb   *(31 March 1491–29 March 1492) (Receipts)*

...

...Item at Hocday receyued viij s. vij d. ob. Item receyued at Witsontid x s.
iij d. ob....

...

3/ die veneris: *29 July 1491*
7/ die dominico: *7 August 1491*
12/ die dominico: *28 August 1491*
13/ hartfordensis: *for herefordensis*
24/ eiusdem: *November 1490*
32/ Hocday: *12 April 1491*
32/ Witsontid: *22–8 May 1491*

AC   *Order for Receiving the Mayor*   Bodl.: MS. Twyne 23
p 560*

...

    Here followeth vnder what forme any Mayre when he is come home
          from London shalbe receyued at ye Trinitie chappell   5
First ye Crier of ye Court must goe before all ye company.
After him ye Commons in their liueries as they be assigned to weare
After ye commons must goe ye Constables of ye Southwest and Northwestwards
After them ye Common Counsell
Then ye Constable of ye North East and south East wardes   10
Then such chamberlaynes as be in ye Bayliues liueries
After them all, ye Baylifs, ye yonger first and so orderly as followeth, and as
it was ordered in ye 6 yeare of ye raigne of king Henry ye 7th in ye time of
Richard Hewes beinge mayr of ye towne of oxford
And then shall come ye Mynstrels (or Mynster) and then ye Baylifs serieants,   15
ye towne clerke next after & ye Mayors Serieant with him; and then ye
Bayliues newe chosen bearinge in their hands 2 white longe rodds, that time
beinge Bayliffs ∧⸢of Oxford⸣ William Wotton, Dauid Dyer
After them ye Mayor and his 2 followers that time beinge Mayer Richard
Hewes.   20
Then ye Aldermen and such as followeth them or ought so doe

1491–2
St Michael at the North Gate Churchwardens' Accounts
ORO: PAR 211/4/F1/1, item 70   25
single mb   *(29 March 1492–28 March 1493)* (Receipts)

...

...Item at Hocday *receyued* xij s. Item at Witsontide x s. viij d....

...

                                                                                  30

1492–3
Lincoln College Computus   LC Arch: Computus 1
f 106v   *(21 December 1491–21 December 1492)* (Necessary internal expenses)

...

Item clerico parochiali in vigilia Sancti Nicholai   vj d.   35

...

15/ Mynster: *for* Mynstrel (?)
21/ ought so doe: *for* ought so to doe
28/ Hocday: *1 May 1492*
28/ Witsontide: *10–16 June 1492*

Merton College Register   MCR: 1.2
f 97v

...

® °Rex°
Rawlyns eligi*tur*
i*n* rege*m*

20o die me*nsis* eiusde*m* ex vnanimi *consensu* soci*orum* M*agister* Ricard*us*
Rawlyns 4t*us* de 4or senioribus elect*us* est in rege*m pro* anno futuro q*uia*   5
tunc te*m*poris erat promot*us*

...

New College Hall Book   NC Arch: 5529
f [166v]   *(8–14 June)*   10

...

D*omi*nica vener*unt* ... duo [my] mimi d*omi*ni pri*nci*pis ij fa*muli cum* eis ad
pra*n*d*ium cum* soc*ijs*...

...

15

1493–4
Merton College Register   MCR: 1.2
f 101

°Rex Regni
Fabarum°
® Molder elect*us*
i*n* rege*m*

...

19o die me*nsis* eiusde*m* elect*us* erat M*agiste*r Ioha*n*nes Molder in regem   20
regni fabar*um*

...

New College Hall Book   NC Arch: 5529
f [179]   *(7–13 December)*   25

...

Sa*bb*ato vene*runt* ... [ij mi*mus* no*n*] ij mimi no*n* Inuita*n*tes seip*s*os ad
pra*n*d*ium cum* soc*ijs*.

...

30

f [182]   *(11–17 January)*

...

Martis. ve*n*er*unt* duo mimi ad c*en*am cum soc*ijs*.

...

35

f [183v]   *(1–7 February)*

Sa*bb*ato vene*runt* ... ij mimi ad pra*n*d*ium cum* soc*ijs*...

...

4/ me*nsis* eiusde*m*: *November 1492*   27/ Sa*bb*ato: *7 December 1493*
12/ D*omi*nica: *9 June 1493*   33/ Martis: *14 January 1493/4*
20/ me*nsis* eiusde*m*: *November 1493*   38/ Sa*bb*ato: *1 February 1493/4*

Mercurij ve*nerunt* … .j. mimus ad p*randium cum socijs*…

…

1494–5
Merton College Register   MCR: 1.2
f 103v

…

Eode*m* die electus est in rege*m* regni fabar*um* ex vnanimi co*n*sensu singul*orum*
m*agiste*r Robert*us* dale t*un*c temp*or*is p*ro*curator vniu*er*sit*atis*

…

c 1495
Magdalen School Copy Book   BL: MS Arundel 249
f 15

…

All the yonge folk*es* almoste of this towne dyde rune yesterday to the castell
to se a bere batyde/ w*ith* fers dogg*es* within the wallys. It was greatly to be
wondred/ for he dyde defend hy[s]*m* selfe so/ w*ith* hys craftynes and his
wyllynes from the cruell doggys/ me thought he sett not a whitt be their
woodenes nor by their fersnes:
Heri tota pene Iuuent*us* huius oppidi ad ergastulum: vrsu*m* intra menia
atrocissimis canibus exagitatu*m*/ grat*i*a visendi confluxere/ Res sane no*n* p*ar*uo
stupore: digna. Na*m* ita sua solercia atq*ue* astutia sese a seuissimis liciscis
tutabatur/ ut eoru*m* rabiem atq*ue* ferocitatem: prorsus naucipe*n*dere mihi
visus est.

ff 52v–3*   *(A play of King Solomon)*

…

I remembre not þat eu*er* I sawe a play þat more delityd me þa*n* yesterdays.
and All be it chefe prayse be to the doer þerof. yete ar none of þe players to
be disapoyntede of þer praise. for eu*ery* ma*n*n plaid so his part*es* þat (except |
hym þat plaide kynge Salomo*n*n it is harde to say whom a ma*n*n may praise
be fore other./
Non memini vidisse me vnq*uam* ludicru*m* q*uo*d maiore me voluptate afficeret
q*uam* histernum. cui*us* & si laus p*re*cipua auctori debet*ur*? no*n* su*n*t tame*n*
actores sua laude fraudendi. Ita enim suas quisq*ue* partes agebat? ut (excepto
eo qui regem salomone*m* egerat) difficile sit dictu que*m* cui anteponas./

…

1/ Mercurij: *5 February 1493/4*
8/ Eodem die: *19 November 1494*
23/ liciscis: *underlined*

31–2/ (except … Salomonn: *closing parenthesis
missing*

f 85v*   *(Letter of Thomas More to John Holt)*

...

Thomas Morus Iohanni Holto Salutem.

℃   Misim*us* ad te que volebas om*n*ia *pr*eter eas *p*artes quas in comediam illa*m*
que de salamone est adiecimus illas ad te modo no*n* potui mittere. quippe que   5
apud me no*n* su*n*t dabo op*er*am ut ebdomada *pr*oxima recipias & quicq*uid*
aliud ex meis reb*us* volueris....

1495–6

Lincoln College Computus   LC Arch: Computus 1   10
f 123   *(21 December 1494–21 December 1495) (Necessary expenses)*

...

Ite*m* *in* festo *sanct*i nicholai clerico	vj d.
Ite*m* *in* vino to the byshop	ij d. ob.

...   15

Magdalen College Liber Computi 1495–6   MC Arch
f 41v   *(Chapel costs)*

...

Solut*um* henrico Mertyn pro Lino alyn & alijs empt*is* *pro* ludo   20
in die pasche vt *p*atet *per* billa*m*   xvij d. ob.

...

f 42v   *(Hall costs)*

...   25

x   Solut*um* *pro* pane & potu consu*m*pt*is* *in* t*em*poribus ludor*um*
in nati*uita*te *do*mi*n*i   xij d.

...

Merton College Register   MCR: 1.2   30
f 106v

...

M*agiste*r thomas beamavnt eligitur in regem
®°Rex°

Eodem die ex vnanimi consensu & assensu singulor*um* electus est in rege*m*
nostri regni fabar*um* m*agiste*r thomas Beamont

...   35

New College Hall Book   NC Arch: 5529
f [208v]*   *(6–12 February)*

...

Mart*is* vener*un*t ... ij° mimi ducis bedfordie ad *pr*an*dium* *cum* soc*ijs*...   40

...

33/ Eodem die: *19 November 1495*   40/ Martis: *9 February 1495/6*

St Peter in the East Churchwardens' Accounts   ORO: PAR 213/4/F1/1
single mb   *(8 December–8 December) (Receipts)*

…

Item in festo hoctyde	xxij s. ij d.
Item dicti procuratores receperunt in festo Pentecostes	xlix s. 5

…

Item receyvyd att christmas for playing garmentes   x⟨…⟩

c 1496–1502
St Peter in the East Churchwardens' Accounts   ORO: PAR 213/4/F1/1   10
single mb*   *(Receipts)*

…

Item in festo Hocktyde de claro Receperunt	xx s.
Item Receperunt in festo pentecoste	xlvj s. vij d.

…   15

1496–7
Magdalen College Liber Computi 1496–7   MC Arch
f 81v   *(Hall costs)*

…   20

Solutum pro carbonibus & candelis consumptis tempore ludorum   iij s. iiij d.

…

Merton College Register   MCR: 1.2
f 109   25

…

°Rex°
® Claxton eligitur
in regem

19mo die mensis eiusdem ex vnanimi assensu & consensu sociorum presentium
electus est in regem nostri fabarum scilicet regni magister Robertus Claxton.

…

30

1497–8
Merton College Register   MCR: 1.2
f 113

…

°Rex°
® walgrave eligitur
in regem

Eodem die magister Iohannes walgrave electus in regem vno suffragio omnium.   35

…

4/ festo hoctyde: *11–12 April 1496*
5/ festo Pentecostes: *22 May 1496*
7/ x⟨…⟩: *rest of the sum lost; large hole in* MS
27/ mensis eiusdem: *November 1496*
35/ Eodem die: *19 November 1497*

1498–9
Merton College Register   MCR: 1.2
f 117v

…

®˚Rex˚   xix⁰ die eiusdem mensis magister Edwardus Bernardus electus est In regem.   5
Edwardus   vno suffragio omnium
bernard eligitur
in regem   …

1499–1500
Merton College Register   MCR: 1.2   10
f 121

…

˚Rex˚   xix⁰ die mensis eiusdem Magister Thomas kynge Electus est in regem vno
®Thomas kyng est   suffragio omnium sociorum
electus in Regem   …   15

f 121v

…

Mensis februarij   iiij^to. die mensis eiusdem. hora decima ante meridiem conuocauit vicecustos
.6. seniores ad domum Custodis pro reformacione habenda de quadam   20
immoderata vigilia excessiue facta per Magistrum irlande in die purificacionis
beate marie ad noctem. cum clamoribus strepitibus & pulsacionibus ad hostia
sociorum & Capellanorum cum quodam canto inhonesto. vbi ostensum est
Quodam decretum. factum anno regni regis Ricardi tercij 2⁰ contra huiusmodi
indiscretas vigilias. In quo Iniunctum erat Iunioribus Magistris ne de cetero   25
in noctibus recreacionum faciant huiusmodi indiscretas vigilias clamores vel
strepitus in detrimentum domus. aut sociorum ve Capellanorum inquietacionem
quo minus ad diuina apti fuerint celebranda officia. sub pena expulcionis a
communis. super quo habita est ibidem communicacio inter seniores. an
huiusmodi immoderate vigilie erant simpliciter dampnate sub pena illa predicta.   30
vbi quidam affirmauerunt quod non. si facte [sun] essent autoritate alicuius
decani & non excessiue. omnes tamen [conuenerat] conuenerunt in isto quod
iste vigilie nuper facte per magistrum irlonde erant excessiue facte & sola sua
Iniunctio   autoritate seruate. propterea vnanimi consensu seniorum ad maiorem Cautelam
Irlonde   eius & exemplum aliorum iniunctum est sibi quod soluat vj d. pro communis   35
suis. decretum eciam est ibidem preterea quod nullus sociorum cuiuscumque
status aut gradus de cetero faciat vel obseruet huiusmodi vigilias clamores vel
strepitus ad inquietacionem sociorum vel Capellanorum sub pena expulcionis
a communis:/

…   40

5/ eiusdem mensis: *November 1498*   20/ .6.: *underlined*
13/ mensis eiusdem: *November 1499*   27/ ve: *for* vel

Chancellor's Register   OUA: Hyp/A/2, Register D (or D reversed)
f 39v   *(12 August)* *(Valuation of the goods of Thomas Fodergill of Broadgates Hall)*

...

Item j casement *pro* doulcemeryes ij d.   5

...

St Michael at the North Gate Churchwardens' Accounts
ORO: PAR 211/4/F1/2, item 77
single mb   *(5 March 1499/1500–12 March 1500/1)* *(Receipts)*   10

...

...Item Rec*euyd* at Whytsu*n*tyde xxiiij s....

...

St Peter le Bailey Churchwardens' Accounts   ORO: PAR 214/4/F1/14   15
single mb*   *(25 November–25 November)* *(Receipts)*

...

Item de collect*is* apud w*h*itsontide   xl s.
Item apud hoctide   ix s. vj d.
...   20

1500–1
Merton College Register   MCR: 1.2
f 126

...   25

®goodhugh
eligi*tur* rex.

19 die mensis eiusd*em* M*a*giste*r* Ioha*n*ne*s* goodhugh vn*a*nimi c*on*sensu
socior*um* elect*us* e*st* in regem q*uia* promotus ad magistr*um* c*on*tuberni*j* de
Wigh in Cancia

...

                                                                                 30

Chancellor's Register   OUA: Hyp/A/2, Register D (or D reversed)
f 93*   *(29 May)*

Proceedings of the court held before Thomas Bank, commissary
...   35

4*to* Kalend*arum* Iunij ve*n*it cora*m* nob*is* quida*m* Willi*mus* Iannys Citherari*us*
& ex*tr*ane*us* & c*on*quest*us* e*st* q*uod* duo Viri: *scilicet*. Pitt*es* & Hawkinse de
p*a*rochia sa*n*c*t*i Micha*elis* ad Porta boriale*m* sua*m* cithera*m* i*n*iuste retinere*n*t

---

12, 18/ Whytsu*n*tyde, w*h*itsontide: *7–13 June 1500*
19/ hoctide: *27–8 April 1500*
26/ mensis eiusd*em*: *November 1500*

27–8/ contubernij de Wigh in Cancia: *probably the College of Sts Gregory and Martin, Wye, Kent*
38/ Porta: *for* Portam; *abbreviation mark missing*

vendica*n*tes ab eo *seruicium* q*uod* nu*n*quam eis debuit n*ec* promisit & [ab] ad
h*oc* proband*um* indux*it* Ioha*n*nem Huskinse de p*ar*ochia Sa*n*cte Marie qui se
promisit & fideiusit q*uod* idem *pro*bare. *scilicet* q*uod* predict*us* Willi*m*o no*n*
promisit predic*tis* Pittes & Hawkinse [a⟨.⟩] [&] Aliquod *seruicium* sed promisit
*ser*uicium *sibi* Ioha*n*ni Huskinse & socij ei*us* Et i*deo* requisiuit me ta*m* predict*us*   5
Willimus q*uam* prefat*us* Ioha*n*nes vt registrare*tur* q*uod* Willimus sepedict*us*
*pro*mouit suam *causam* coram Commissario Vni*uersitatis* Ne iniuste ve∧⌈x⌉aret*ur*
per Villanos balliuos *vel* per maiorem ∧⌈ville⌉ Eo q*uod* ext*r*aneus esset promittens
fidem sua se *res*po*n*surum pariturum facturum & acceptu⟨…⟩ q*uod* iust*i*cia
exigeret si ad h*oc* esset co*n*uentus &c.   10
Willi*m*us Ia*n*nys Ioha*n*nes Huskinse Pitt*es* & Hawkinse

1501–2
Merton College Register   MCR: 1.2
f 131   15
…

°Doctor in
Theologia Rex°

® Saunde*rs* elect*us*
es*t* in rege*m*

decimonono die Eiusd*em* electus est M*agister* hugo Saunders in Sacra theologia
doctor. ex omni*um* socior*um* consensu electus est in Rege*m*. tu*m* q*uia* senior
q*ui* regiu*m* mun*us* prius no*n* subierat tu*m* q*uia* promotus ad vicariam Ecclesie
p*ar*ochialis de Mepham in Dioc*esi* Cantuar*ie*   20
…

f 131v
…

® de igne
regentiu*m*

®°Ignis°

xvij° die Eiusd*em* habitus est ignis regentiu*m* cu*m* iocundissimis i*n*terlud*is*   25
senior ex*iste*nte M*agist*ro Tho*m*a Skirsbreke
…

New College Hall Book   NC Arch: 5530
f [26v]   *(29 January–4 February)*   30
…

Mercurij venerunt … 2° mimi ad *pr*andi*um* cu*m* soc*ijs* … 2.° mimi ad
cena*m* cu*m* soc*ijs*
Iouis venerunt … vn*us* cithereda … ad *pr*andi*um* cu*m* soc*ijs*…

3/ fideiusit: *2 minims for* iu *in* MS
3/ probare: *for* probaret
3/ Willi*m*o: *for* Willimus
5/ socij: *for* socio *or* socijs
9/ fidem sua: *for* fide sua
17/ Eiusdem: *November 1501*

20/ Mepham in Dioc*esi* Cantuar*ie*: *Meopham, Kent*
25/ Eiusdem: *January 1501/2*
26/ senior: *for* seniore
32/ Mercurij: *2 February 1501/2*
34/ Iouis: *3 February 1501/2*

St Michael at the South Gate Churchwardens' Account
ORO: DD Par. Oxford St Aldate c. 33, item l
mb [1]   *(8 December–8 December) (Receipts)*

...

Item *ressayuyd* of hocketide money	viij s. x d. 5
Item *ressayuyd* of Whitsontide money	xxj s. [viij d.] iij d.

...

mb [2] col 1   *(Expenses)*

...   10

Item paid to A mynstrell at Whitsontid	ij s.

...

1502–3
Magdalen College Liber Computi 1502–3   MC Arch   15
f 126   *(External payments)*

...

– Solut*um* in expens*is* fact*is* *tempore* na*talis* d*omi*ni in biberijs	
p*ost* in*ter*ludia & alia	xiij s. iiij d.

...   20

Merton College Register   MCR: 1.2
f 137

...

°Rex°   Eodem die Idem magist*er* Wille*lm*us Ireland ex vna*n*imi consensu o*mn*ium   25
® Ireland elect*us*   socior*um* electus est in rege*m* nostru*m* p*ro* hoc anno primu*m* q*uia* ra*ci*one
est in regem   senior*itat*is hoc mu*n*eris sibi ⌐aduen*er*at¬ inde ecia*m* q*uia* promotus erat hoc
                         anno ad Rectoria*m* de Cuxham

...

                                                                                    30

1503–4
Lincoln College Computus   LC Arch: Computus 1
f 155*   *(21 December 1502–21 December 1503) (Necessary expenses)*

...

Item for a q*u*art of wy*n*e whe*n* sent nicholas clark*es* was at ye coleg	ij d. 35
Item at ye same tyme to ye parish clarke	vj d.

...

5/ hocketide: *4–5 April 1502*
6, 11/ Whitsontide, Whitsontid: *15–21 May 1502*
25/ Eodem die: *19 November 1502*
27/ muneris: *for* munus
28/ Cuxham: *Cuxham, Oxfordshire*

Merton College Register　MCR: 1.2
f 144v

…

Iohannes adams
eligitur in regem

°vicecustos. in
Regem°

Decimo Nono die eiusdem mensis. ex vnanimi consensu omnium magistrorum
qui tunc interfuerant qui paucissimi erant ex causa que supradicta est. magister　5
Iohannes ∧⌈adams⌉ vicecustos tunc senior racione noue constitutionis. (que
supra proximo folio precedenti ponitur) in Regem electus est

…

f 145v　　　　　　　　　　　　　　　　　　　　　　　　　　　　　　　10

…

Ignis regentium

Tricesimo die Eiusdem mensis Magister Ioannes Mattston tunc Senior Regens
conuiuauit Magistros & bachillarios cum igne regentium & alijs lauticijs
secundum antiquum morem

…　　　　　　　　　　　　　　　　　　　　　　　　　　　　　　　　　15

St Peter in the East Churchwardens' Accounts　ORO: PAR 213/4/F1/1
single mb　(8 December–8 December)　(Receipts)

…

Item in festo hocktyd de claro　　　　　　　　　　　　　　　xix s.　20
Item in festo pentecostes　　　　　　　　　　　　　　　xxxvj s. viij d.

…

1504

AC　**St Peter le Bailey Churchwardens' Accounts**　Bodl.: MS. Wood C.1　25
p 78*　(Receipts)

…

de pecunijs collectis apud Hocktyde 8 s. 4 d.

…

　　　　　　　　　　　　　　　　　　　　　　　　　　　　　　　　30

1504–5
Merton College Register　MCR: 1.2
f 151v*

…

.A.

Gydding eligitur
in regem

°Rex°

Decimo nono die Eiusdem mensis. magister Willelmus Gidding ex vnanimi　35
consensu omnium sociorum eligitur in Regem ffabarum/ tum quia Senior socius/
tum quia promotus ad Ecclesiam parochialem de Mepham. Cantuarie diocesi

…

4, 12/ eiusdem mensis, Eiusdem mensis: *November*
1503
5/ ex causa que supradicta est: *ie, plague in the college*
20/ festo hocktyd: *15–16 April 1504*

21/ festo pentecostes: *26 May 1504*
35/ Eiusdem mensis: *November 1504*
36/ Regem ffabarum: *underlined*
37/ de Mepham. Cantuarie diocesi: *Meopham, Kent*

St Peter in the East Churchwardens' Accounts ORO: PAR 213/4/F1/1
single mb *(8 December–8 December) (Receipts)*

...

Item in festo hoctyde declaro	xix s. iij d.
Item receperunt in ffesto Pentecostes declaro	xxx s. viij d. 5

...

1505–6
Lincoln College Computus LC Arch: Computus 2
p 19* *(21 September–21 December 1505) (Commons costs)* 10

...

for ye chaplain of owr ladys day & ffor sayntt nicholas clerkes †®

⟨..⟩mus	xij d. ob. qua.

...

15

p 27 *(21 December 1504–21 December 1505) (Necessary internal expenses)*

...

Item for wyn to sant nycholas Clarkes	ij d.
Item to ye parych clark ye saym nyght	vj d.

...

20

Merton College Register MCR: 1.2
f 158

...

® elegitur consaunt | decimo Nono die eiusdem mensis vnanimi concensu omnium Magistrorum et 25
in regem sub | sociorum & aliorum baccalariorum qui tunc interfuerant Magister Nicholaus
condicione | consaunt vicecustos eligitur in regem sub condicione. quod si magister skarysbryke
®°Rex° | erat inductus in beneficium [per] sicuti dicebatur a multis ille susciperet onus
| sin minus predictus vicecustos vnus tamen erat pronunciatus propter assistentes
| & modum antiquuum & condicio tantum inter socios erat cognita 30

...

f 158v

...

Ianuarius | Primo die istius mensis venerunt ad collegium nostrum satrapes ville vti 35
| consueti sunt ad cantandum vnum canticum ∧⌜in alta aula⌝ et ad
de satrapis ville | recipiendum a bursario ex humanitate & dono gratuito vnum nobile
quomodo | sed propter eorum ingratitudinem et quia dicunt se ex debito recipere
negatum erat | debere et non ex liberalitate nostra ideo cum verbis honestis & aliquali
eis nobile ex | humanitate eis ostensa negauimus ∧⌜eis⌝ pro isto tempore. dictas pecunias. 40
liberalitate |
antiquitus |
concessum |

4/ festo hoctyde: *31 March–1 April 1505*   25/ eiusdem mensis: *November 1505*
5/ ffesto Pentecostes: *11 May 1505*

et ita recesserunt ad collegium diue marie Magdalene vbi vt audiuimus consimile responsum acceperunt

...

Ignis Regencium   decimo quarto die istius mensis Magister Iohannes wayte tunc senior regens convivavit Magistros et baccalarios cum igne regentium & lauticijs secundum   5
antiquum morem

...

St Peter in the East Churchwardens' Accounts   ORO: PAR 213/4/F1/1
single mb   *(8 December–8 December) (Receipts)*   10
...

Item dicti procuratores receperunt in ffesto hoctyd declaro   xviij s. ij d.
Item dicti procuratores receperunt in ffesto pentecostes declaro   xliij s.
...

15

1506-7
Lincoln College Computus   LC Arch: Computus 2
p 30   *(21 December 1505–21 December 1506) (Necessary internal expenses)*
...
Item clerico sancti michaelis   vj d. 20
...

Magdalen College Battells Book   MC Arch: CP 8/51
f 63*   *(3–9 January)*
...   25
Die epiphanie ad prandium cum socijs in ferculo ... In 4º refectionibus
Citharista...
...

Magdalen College Liber Computi 1506–7   MC Arch   30
f 200*   *(11 November–11 November) (External payments)*
...
x   Solutum domino burges pro scriptura lusi beate marie magdalene   x d.
...
x   Solutum homini ducenti Cantica a magistro Edwardo martyn   35
ad mandatum vicepresidis   viij d.
...
x   Solutum Kendall pro diligentia sua in luso Sancte marie
Magdalene Mandato vicepresidis   xij d.
...   40

12/ ffesto hoctyd: *20–1 April 1506*   13/ ffesto pentecostes: *31 May 1506* f 201*

...

x   Solut*um* d*omino* burges *pro* notac*ione* diuersor*um* Canticor*um*
ad ma*n*datu*m* M*agistri* vice*presidis per* bill*am*   v s.

...   5

f 201v

...

–   Solut*um pro* expens*is* mimi *tempore* nat*alis* do*mini* hoc a*n*no   iiij s.

...   10

Episcopal Visitation of Magdalen College
Hampshire Record Office: 21M65/A1/18
f 47*   *(20 January)* *(Interrogatories for Bishop Richard Fox's visitation taken*
   before John Dowman, LLD, vicar general)   15

...

41. Item in*terrogetur* qualit*er* libri orname*n*ta Iocalia et alia bona d*icti* Collegij
su*n*t custodit*a*

...

45. Item in*terrogetur* an aliquis socius vel scolaris dict*i* Collegij mantellis aut   20
liripipijs extra precinctum Collegij vtitur

...

f 58v*   *(Reply of Mr John Burgess, MA)*

...   25

Ad xl articulu*m* dicit q*uod* sacrista negligens est accomodando libros socijs ad
eor*um* cubicula et *tempore* Nat*a*lis in In*ter*ludijs lusores vtu*n*tur capis/

...

f 69*   *(Reply of Sir John Burgess, BA)*   30

...

...dicit insup*er* q*uod* pollard de sc*ien*ci*a* istius Iur*a*ti exiuit Collegiu*m* in veste
laicali et more vnius ex*er*cent*is* interludia...

Merton College Register   MCR: 1.2   35
f 165

® Ioh*annes*
chambre elegit*ur*   ...
in rege*m*   Decimo nono die eiusd*em* m*ensis* ex *consensu* magistror*um* et socior*um*

38/ eiusd*em* m*ensis*: *November 1506*

electus est in regem Magister Iohannes chambre doctor in medicinis tunc
rome existens

...

f 165v   5

...

xj die istius mensis Magister wayte senior regens conuivauit omnes socios cum
igne regencium & alijs lauticijs secundum antiquum modum et consuetudinem

New College Hall Book   NC Arch: 5530   10
f [157]   *(2–8 January)*

...

[Lune] Eodem die mimus quidam ad cenam cum socijs...

...

                                                                                    15

St Peter le Bailey Churchwardens' Accounts   ORO: PAR 214/4/F1/15
single sheet   *(25 November–25 November)* *(Receipts)*

...

Item at hoctide   xiiij s. ⟨...⟩ d.
Item at Whitsontide   [iiij iiij d.] liij s. iiij d.   20

...

1507
Balliol College Statutes   BC Arch: Statutes 1
f [31]   *(Concerning serious prohibitions)*   25

...prohibemus etiam ne quis ullo loco aut tempore loca frequentet inhonesta/
aut suspecta negociationes aut commercia/ clericis interdicta exerceat assidua
crapula et ebrietate crebra se non ingurgitet iniurijs agendis aut conuicijs
obprobriosis ⌈ne⌉ quemquam exagitet aut vexet ludis inhonestis et prohibitis   30
aut vicium incitantibus aut doctrinam impedientibus et contentionem
prouocantibus non intersit/ histrionibus aut iaculatoribus se non immisceat
quibus sic a nobis prohibitis aut similibus alijs maioribus si deliquerit bis
admonitus a magistro aut eius vicem gerente cum suo decano tercio offendens
expellatur...   35

1–2/ electus ... existens: *underlined*
7/ istius mensis: *February 1506/7*
13/ Eodem die: *3 January 1506/7*
19/ hoctide: *12–13 April 1507*
19/ ⟨...⟩ d.: *hole in MS*
20/ Whitsontide: *23–9 May 1507*

1507–8
Lincoln College Computus LC Arch: Computus 2
p 23   *(21 December 1506–21 December 1507)* *(Necessary internal expenses)*

...

⟨...⟩ *pro* vino ep*iscop*o s*cilicet* s*an*cto nicholaye   v d.   5
⟨...⟩ clerico s*an*c*ti* Michael*is*   vj d.

...

Magdalen College Liber Computi 1507–8   MC Arch
f 216v   *(External expenses)*   10

+   Solut*um* *pro* biberio dat*o* ep*iscop*o vigilia S*an*c*ti* nichol*a*i in vino
⌈ij d. ob.⌉ in s*er*uisia ⌈ij d. ob.⌉ et in igne ⌈ij d. ob.⌉   vj d. ob.

...
                                                                                            15

Merton College Register   MCR: 1.2
f 175

...

®wayt co*n*uivauit
socios *pro*
offi*ci*o regali

decimo die me*n*sis Ianuarij m*agiste*r Io*hann*es waytt *pro* offi*ci*o regali co*n*uiuauit
om*ne*s soc*i*os cu*m* igne ∧⌈et⌉ [cu*m*] alijs lauticinijs sec*un*d*u*m more*m* antiquu*m* 20

®wyngar senior
rege*n*s co*n*uiuat
rege*n*t*es*

Conuiuauit m*agiste*r wyngar tu*n*c senior regens decimo quinto die mensis
predict*i* om*ne*s regentes

...
                                                                                            25

St Peter in the East Churchwardens' Accounts   ORO: PAR 213/4/F1/1
single mb   *(8 December–8 December)* *(Receipts)*

...

Item d*i*c*ti* procuratores receperu*n*t in ffesto hoctyde declar*o*   xvij s.
It*em* d*i*c*ti* procuratores receperu*n*t in ffesto pentecostes declar*o*   xl s. 30

...

1508–9
Lincoln College Computus   LC Arch: Computus 2
p 33*   *(21 December 1507–21 December 1508)* *(Necessary internal expenses)* 35

...

It*em* to sent nycholas clark*es*   vj d.
Item eode*m* nocte *pro* vino   v d.

...

13/ vj d. ob.: *for* vij d. ob.   30/ ffesto pentecostes: *11 June 1508*
29/ ffesto hoctyde: *1–2 May 1508*   37/ sent: t *corrected over* d

Item for cristinmes cowles the last yer. *scilicet* a quarter for
candilmes a quarter for sent nicholes & xvj for cristinmes   xij s.

...

Item for iij quarteres of cowles on for alhalo day an odre for
our dedicacion day the therd for sent nycholas   ij s.   5

...

Magdalen College Liber Computi 1508–9   MC Arch
f 231v   *(11 November–11 November)*   *(External payments)*

...   10

Solutum pro vino ⌈ij d. ob.⌉ dato Episcopo et Igne ⌈ij d.⌉
& Biberio ⌈ij d.⌉ in vigilia Sancti Nycholai   vj d. ob.

...

Solutum ffamulo Regis ducenti Vrsam ad Collegium ex
mandato vicepresidis   xij d. 15

...

Merton College Register   MCR: 1.2
f 191

...   20

°Rex°
® magister hyll
electus in regale
officium

Vicesimo primo die huius Mensis lecta littera in aula ex more antiquo omnes
socij ex vnanimi consensu eligerunt magistrum hyll regem pro anno futuro

...

f 194*   25

...

® Satrapes ville
® °ex debito nihil.
vide supra fol.
(blank) et infra
fol. 242.b et
fol. 256 ⟨.⟩°
® conuiuium Regis

primo die huius mensis venerunt ad collegium nostrum satrapes ville ad
cantandum coram socijs vnum canticum in alta aula vbi receperunt a
bursario in nomine collegii ex humanitate ad respondendum pro nobis in
domo conuocacionis eorum pro possessione nostra in villa vj s. viij d.   30
Magister hyll electus pro rege conviuauit omnes socios cum pluribus lauticinis
octauo die huius mensis

...

f 194v   35

...

°Ignis
Regentium°

decimo quinto die magister wyngar senior regens cum igne in nocte conviuauit
omnes socios secundum consuetudinem antiquam

...

21/ huius Mensis: *November 1508*
27m/ Satrapes: S *overwritten in darker ink by later hand*
27, 32/ huius mensis, huius mensis: *January 1508/9*

37–8m/ Ignis Regentium: *written over* ignis
regencium, *apparently in first hand*
37/ decimo quinto die: *15 January 1508/9*

ignis regentiu*m* decim*o* quinto die huius mensis erat ignis regentiu*m* m*a*gist*r*o wyngar
seniore regent*e*

...

f 195

...

°prandiu*m*
Capitulare° Vicesimo primo die hui*us* mens*is* fecit *secundus* burs*a*rius prandiu*m*
® prandiu*m* capitulare p*ro* dissoluc*ione* capituli et in aula magna in ead*em* nocte ignis
capitular*e* capitularis
® °ignis capitularis°

...

ff 196–6v

...

® °Ludi° Decimo nono die eiusdem me*n*sis senior bacularius vna cu*m* Iuniore
Inuitaru*n*t custode*m* vt nocte seque*n*te In alta collegij aula solacia pro suo
adue*n*tu dedicata dignaret*ur* aspicere quibus assenciens q*uando* tempus
recreacionis aduenisset illuc sese contulit cu*m* multis alijs venerabilibus
°Dapes° finitoq*ue* ludo ad domu*m* custodis Introducti om*n*es | collegij socij cu*m* alijs
no*n*nullis vicinaru*m* aularu*m* contubernialib*us* obsonium varijs *con*feccionib*us*
paratu*m* habuerunt. In cuius fine venie*n*tes om*n*es bacularij pallinodia
(vnusquisq*ue* In ordine suo) ca*n*taueru*n*t

...

St Peter in the East Churchwardens' Accounts   ORO: PAR 213/4/F1/1
single mb   *(8 December–8 December) (Receipts)*

...

Item receperu*n*t in ffes*t*o hoctyde declar*o*   xxv s. vj d.
Item receperu*n*t in ffes*t*o pentecostes   iij li. vij s. vij d.

...

1509–10
Lincoln College Computus   LC Arch: Computus 2
p 28   *(21 December 1508–21 December 1509) (Necessary internal expenses)*

...

Ite*m* to p*a*rych Clark   vj d.
Ite*m* for wyn to sant nicholas clark*es*   v d.

...

1, 7/ huius mensis, hui*us* mens*is*: *January 1508/9*   18/ finitoq*ue* ludo: *underlined*
14/ eiusdem me*n*sis: *February 1508/9*   27/ ffes*t*o hoctyde: *16–17 April 1509*
14/ senior ... Iuniore: *underlined*   28/ ffes*t*o pentecostes: *27 May 1509*

Magdalen College Liber Computi 1509–10   MC Arch
f 6   *(11 November–11 November)* *(External payments)*

...

So*lutum* Mimo temp*ore* na*talis* do*mi*ni mandat*o* vic*e*p*residis*   xij d.

...   5

f 6v

...

So*lutum* pane cibo & alijs dat*is* pu*er*is luden*tibus* in
die pasche man*dato* vic*e*p*residis*   xvij d. ob. 10

...

Merton College Register   MCR: 1.2
f 204

...   15

Ignis rege*n*cium   Vicesimo quarto ⌈die⌉ mensis Ianuarij Magister wyngar senior Regens
conuiuauit o*mne*s socios cu*m* igne & epulis in nocte *secundu*m *con*suetudi*n*em
Antiquam & hic finis illius on*er*is q*uia* vltim*us* ann*us* sue regencie in facul₍ₐ⌈ta⌉te
Arcium modo t*er*minabitur

...   20

AC   **St Mary the Virgin Churchwardens' Accounts**   Bodl.: MS. Wood D.3
p 267*   *(Receipts)*

...

Hoctyde   It*em* re*ceiv*ed atte Hoctyde of ye wifes gaderyng xv s. ij d.   25

...

St Peter in the East Churchwardens' Accounts   ORO: PAR 213/4/F1/1
single mb   *(8 December–8 December)* *(Receipts)*

...   30

Item rec*e*per*unt* in festo hoctyde declar*o*   ⟨...⟩
Item rec*e*per*unt* in ffes*to* pentecost*es*   ⟨...⟩

...

1510–11   35
Lincoln College Computus   LC Arch: Computus 2
p 34   *(21 December 1509–21 December 1510)* *(Necessary internal expenses)*

...

It*em* for wyen to saynt nycolas clark*es*   vj d.

10/ die pasche: *31 March 1510*   32/ ffes*to* pentecost*es*: *19 May 1510*
25, 31/ Hoctyde, festo hoctyde: *8–9 April 1510*

Item to ye clark   vj d.
…

Magdalen College Liber Computi 1510–11   MC Arch
f 19   *(External payments)*   5
…
Solutum cuidam mimo tempore natalis domini in regardo   viij d.
…

Merton College Register   MCR: 1.2   10
f 209
…
In die sancti vlstani conuiuauit magister wyngar Rex omnes socios cum
pluribus ferculis
…   15
Decimo die huius mensis magister huys procurator senior regens fecit ignem
regentium & conuiuauit eosdem
…

AC   **St Mary Magdalen Churchwardens' Accounts**   Bodl.: MS. Wood D.2   20
p 301*   *(Rendered 25 May) (Payments)*
…
Item for a minstreill on May day 4 d.
…

                                                                                    25
St Peter in the East Churchwardens' Accounts   ORO: PAR 213/4/F1/1
single mb*   *(8 December–8 December) (Receipts)*
…
Item receperunt in festo hoctyde declaro   xxiij s.
Item receperunt in festo pentecostes   liij s. iiij d.   30
…

1511–12
Magdalen College Liber Computi 1511–12   MC Arch
f 61*   *(Hall costs)*   35
…
Solutum pro biberijs datis socijs & scholaribus
post interludia   vj s. viij d. ij s. viij d.
…

16/ huius mensis: *February 1510/11*   30/ festo pentecostes: *8 June 1511*
29/ festo hoctyde: *28–9 April 1511*

Register of Congregation and Convocation   OUA: NEP/Supra/G
f 143*

…

® Wattson   Eodem die supradicto Edwardus Watson scolaris grammatice quatenus studium
® °vide in proxima   4or annorum cum praxi ad docendum sufficiente vt admittatur ad docendum   5
pagina°   in eadem facultate hec est concessa sic quod componat C carmina in laudem
vniversitatis et vnnam commodeam infra annum post gradum susceptum

…

f 143v*   10

…

Admissio ad   Eodem die admissus est ad informandum in grammatica dominus edwardus
informandum   Wattson
in grammatica

…

15

Merton College Register   MCR: 1.2
f 214

…

°Rex°   In vigilia sancti edmundi regis completis consuetudinibus antiquis & littera
® Electio regis   perlecta omnes socij ex vnanimi consensu eligerunt magistrum morvent   20
regem pro anno futuro

…

St Michael at the North Gate Churchwardens' Accounts
ORO: PAR 211/4/F1/2, item 90   25
single mb   (18 March 1511/12–17 March 1512/13) (Receipts)

…

Item recewyd Att hocketyde   xiij s.
Item recewyd of Whyttson Ale Clere   xlvj s. viiij d.

…   30

St Peter in the East Churchwardens' Accounts   ORO: PAR 213/4/F1/1
single mb   (8 December–8 December) (Receipts)

…

Item Receperunt in festo hoktyde declaro   xxj s. iiij d. 35
Item Receperunt In festo pentecostes   lvj s. viij d.

…

4/ Eodem die supradicto: 11 March 1511/12   28, 35/ hocketyde, festo hoktyde: 19–20 April 1512
5–6m/ °vide … pagina°: in Anthony Wood's hand   29/ Whyttson: Whitsuntide was 30 May–5 June 1512
12/ Eodem die: 18 March 1511/12   36/ festo pentecostes: 30 May 1512
28, 29/ Item: 2 minims in MS

c 1512–27
Magdalen School Exercise Book BL: MS Royal 12.B.xx
f 35

...

          Relictis ludis iocis atque salibus quibus hisce natalis christi   5
          diebus festis animos expleuiumus. nunc videtur mihi tempus
          ut vicissim feria agamus. nam si rebus iocularibus assidue
          dediti fuerimus diu erit antequam ad scientiam que summa
          cura summa opera summa que diligentia acquerenda que
          aspirandique   10
Me semeth it is tyme to leue owr pleys sportes and mery conseittes yat we
haue fullyd your myndes with this cristinnmes holidays & to fall in hand a
nother while with maters of sadnes for and if we giue your selfe styll [to] a
pease to maters of sport it wilbe long or we cum to connyng which must be
gotten with grett labour and diligence   15

...

f 39*

...

          Eunti hesterna die ad templum diue virginis marie quam   20
          plurime mulieres confluentes iter mihi intercludere ceperunt,
          adeo ut neque progredi neque regredi per eas mihi licebat.
          quas cum interrogassem quidnam sibi volebant. respondere
          moris esse pretermittere neminem eo die A quo quippiam
          non exigerent. Itaque velim nolim aliquid elargiri cogebat.   25
          neque mecum solo sed et multis cum alijs sic actum esse,
          postea cernebam. quippe preteribat nemo cui non aut iure
          aut iniuria aliquid extorquebant
As I went hesterday to sant mari [ser] church yer cam a grett meny of women
a bowte me and be gane to stope me of my gate. so yat cowde nother go   30
forwarde nother backwarde for them. and when I axid them what ye ment
thei answerd yat it was the gyys to let no man pase yat day. but yei wold haue
sumwhat of hym. & so wether I wold or no I was fayne to giue them sumwhat.
& I dyd se after ward yat I was not seruid soo onli. but many other men
wher so seruid as well as y. for ther was no man passid by them but the got   35
sumwhat of hym other by hocke or by crocke

...

f 44*

...

   40
          hic puer agit dominum heri inter suos equales suum singulis

10/ aspirandique: d *corrected from* q

mun*us* assignans aliu*m* structore*m* instituit: Aliu*m*
pince*r*nam. aliu*m* Ianitore*m*. aliu*m* q*ue* imp*er*ata fac*er*e
recusauit appr*e*hensu*m* m*ulti*s v*er*beris effecit. ac ne pauc*is*
absoluam quemadmodu*m* cyru*m* olim pueror*um* regem
egit. ita hic suor*um* equaliu*m* regem agere cepit: q*uam*quam   5
[*esse*] euentu haudquaq*uam* opinor simili. Cyrus cu*m*
nobilis claroq*ue* loco natus ad regia*m* magestate*m* revera
tande*m* aspirauit. hic v*er*o ignobilis obscuro q*ue* natus[*tus*]
loco nisi p*er* temp*us* flagisiquos mores corrigat in o*m*ni
reliqua vita verisimilit*er* ignobilem est acturus   10

this boye playd the lord yester day a mong his co*m*panyou*n*ce a poyntyng
eu*er*y man his office. oon he mayd his carver an other his butlere: an other
his porter. an other bi cause [col] he wold not do as he co*m*mandyd hym he
toke and [all] to bete hyme. and to make and ende at few word*es* lykewyse as
[Cys] Cyrus pleyd oons ye kyng of boyes so he be gane to play ye kyng of his   15
co*m*paniou*n*s hoo be it I trow in an vn lyke chaun*n*ce. for as for cyrus was a
noble man borne and at ye last he cam to ye riallthe of a kyng in veri dede.
but as for this is a knawe borne and be lykelyhode wyll playe the knawe all
ye remna*n*t of his lyffe except he mend his vnhappy man*er*s betyme

                                                                            20

ff 45v–6

...

ludere tessaris ocillis alueis . calculis . canere . saltare potare
queq*ue* ad a*nim*i oblectac*i*one*m* p*er*tinere putassis fac*er*e
uobis ia*m*diu p*er*missu*m* est . nu*n*c hic dies aliud viuendi   25
modu*m* affert . alios mores postulat. Vestru*m* *est* ig*itur* alias
res agere id est libros ⌈re⌉visere . studia litt*er*arum int*er*missa .
resarcere ad eaque animos vestros adiu*n*gere . na*m* si assidue
reb*us* iocularib*us* dediti fuerit*is*. ad erudic*i*one*m* quaru*m*
exoptat*is* nu*n*q*uam* aspirabit*is*. | 30

ye had your liberte now a grette whill to play at dise at card*es* at tabl*es* at
chest*es* to syng to daunce to drynke to reuell and to do suche thyng*es* as ys
thowght p*er*tynyd to ye pleasur of mynde now this day begyng*es* in another
mano*r* of lernyng . yt requirith other manor*es* it is yo*ur* parte therfor to go
a bowght other thyng[g]*es* y*a*t is to sa go se a nother whyll yo*ur* bok*es* &   35
renew yo*ur* studis y*a*t haue ben discontinuyd . and set yo*ur* mynd*es* to them
for & you begynne all to pla styll a pece ye shall neu*er* cu*m* to ye lernyng
y*a*t ye desire

...

9/ flagisiquos: *second* i *corrected from* s   33/ begyng*es*: *for* begynes
24/ putassis: *for* putasses

1512–13
Lincoln College Computus   LC Arch: Computus 3
f 28v*   *(21 December–21 December)*

…

Domus ⌈for ye play⌉   iij s. ij d.   5

Magdalen College Liber Computi 1512–13   MC Arch
f 33v   *(11 November–11 November)* *(External payments)*

…

Solutum petro pyper pro pypyng in interludio nocte sancti Iohannis   vj d. 10

…

f 34

…

+   Solutum Iohanni tabourner pro lusione in interludio octava epiphanie   vj d. 15

…

+   Solutum Roberto Ionson pro vna tunica pro interludijs   iiij s.

…

Merton College Register   MCR: 1.2   20
f 218v

…

huys electus est   In vigilia sancti Edmundi regis venerunt nuncij de partibus longinquis
Rex   afferentes secum litteras pro rege eligendo quibus perlectis ac alijs consuetudinibus
peractis ex unanimi consensu omnium electus est magister huys pro rege   25
anni sequentis

…

f 219

…   30

°Symons   decimo die huius mensis magister Symons procurator et senior regens
senior regens   conuiuauit in nocte omnes magistros per ignem splendide cum pluribus
procurator.°   epulis cum vino
® mensis Ianuarij
® °Ignis Regens.°   …

                                                            35

f 219v

…

conuiuium   vicesimo die huius mensis conuiuauit magister custos omnes magistros in
magistri custodis   domo sua in nocte & habuerunt ludum optimum in magna aula

17/ Ionson: *3 minims for first n in MS*   39/ habuerunt … aula: *underlined*
38/ huius mensis: *January 1512/13*

conuiuium
magistri huys

vicesimo quarto die huius mensis conviuauit magister huys rex anni presentis
omnes magistros in prandio & in nocte

...

Tailors' Wardens' Accounts   Bodl.: MS. Morrell 9   5
f 8*   (Payments)

...

Item for the synggers   xij d.

...

10

St Peter in the East Churchwardens' Accounts   ORO: PAR 213/4/F1/1
single mb   (8 December–8 December) (Receipts)

...

Item apud hoktide   xix s. viij d.
Item in festo Pentecostes   lij s. iiij d. 15

...

1513–14
Lincoln College Computus   LC Arch: Computus 3
f 46   (21 December 1512–21 December 1513) (Necessary internal expenses) 20

...

Item for wyen off saynt nycholas euyn   vj d.
Item to ye parysche Clark   vj d.

...

25

Merton College Register   MCR: 1.2
f 222

...

°rex°

®symons electus
est rex

In vigilia sancti edmondi regis venerunt nuncij de partibus remotis afferentes
secum litteras pro rege eligendo quibus lectis alijsque consuetudinibus peractis ex 30
vnanimi omnium concensu electus est magister Symons in regem anni sequentis

...

f 222v

...

35

mensis februarij

Ignis regencium

xxvjto die februarij magister Ricardus walcar tunc senior regens conuiuauit
Magistros et bacchilarios cum igne regencium et alijs lauticijs secundum
antiquum morem:

...

1/ huius mensis: *January 1512/13*   15/ festo Pentecostes: *13 May 1513*
14/ hoktide: *4–5 April 1513*

Tailors' Wardens' Accounts   Bodl.: MS. Morrell 9
f 9*   *(Payments)*

…

Item payd to ye synggers on sanct Iohn day   xij d.

…   5

1514–15
Merton College Register   MCR: 1.2
f 227v

…   10

Conuiuium | 29º die huius mensis Magister poxwell Rex conuiuauit omnes socios in prandio
poxwell Regis | cum caponibus & vino & in nocte cum igne & multis farculis honorifice

Conuiuium | Quarto die februarij Magister walkar senior Regens conuiuauit omnes socios
walar senior | cum multis farculis & vino.
regens

…   15

St Michael at the North Gate Churchwardens' Accounts
ORO: PAR 211/4/F1/2, item 94
single mb   *(15 March 1514/15–13 March 1515/16) (Receipts)*

…   20

Item receuyde at Hoctyde   viij s.
Item receuyde of Wytson Ayll Cleyr to the box   xl s. xl d.

…

1515–16   25
Merton College Register   MCR: 1.2
f 230v

…

Knyght electus | Decimo Nono eiusdem mensis Magister Willelmus Kny⟨.⟩ht ex vnanimi
est in Regem:/ | consensu omnium Sociorum electus est in Regem pro anno futuro:/.   30

…

St Michael at the North Gate Churchwardens' Accounts
ORO: PAR 211/4/F1/2, item 96
f [1]   *(13 March 1515/16–19 March 1516/17) (Receipts)*   35

…

Item receyved of the Hokmoney   ix s. iiij d.

11/ huius mensis: *January 1514/15*   22/ Wytson: *Whitsuntide was 27 May–2 June 1515*
14m/ walar: *for* walkar   29/ eiusdem mensis: *November 1515*
21/ Hoctyde: *16–17 April 1515*   37/ Hokmoney: *Hocktide was 31 March–1 April 1516*

Item receyved of the Whitson Ale   iiij Merkes

...

1516–17
Corpus Christi College Statutes   CCCA: A/4/1/1   5
ff 60–60v   *(22 June)*
...

De mora non trahenda in Aula post refectiones
Turpiloquia detractiones, iurgia Scurrilitates verbositas & cetera lingue vicia
raro vacuum comitantur ventrem at crebro inflatum & repletum. quocirca   10
vt obstemus principijs mandamus Statuentes, vt in nostro collegio singulis
diebus post prandium & cenam, persoluta prius altissimo pro acceptis
gratiarum accione & potu caritatis libere volentibus minstrato, ac etiam
post illas potaciones, (quas bibesia vocant) de more vniuersitatis pro tempore
consuetas, Seniores singuli cuiuscumque gradus aut status extiterint statim   15
sine vllo interuallo ad studia sua vel loca alia se conferant, nec Iuniores alios
ibidem moram facere vlterius permittant, nisi quando vel consilia domus
vel alia negotia ardua collegium tangentia immediate debeant pertractari,
vel lectiones disputaciones aut biblie exposiciones et declaraciones continuo
consequantur, quibus etiam absolutis & finitis statim decedant, vel quando   20
ob dei reuerentiam sue gloriose matris vel alterius sancte ad solacium omni
inhabitancium ibidem construatur ignis, tunc enim liceat socijs et scholaribus
nostri collegij post dictas refectiones et potaciones gratia recreacionis modeste
ut decet clericos in canticis et alijs solacijs honestis in aula moram facere &
poemata historias ac mundi mirabilia & cetera huius generis inter se conferre   25
legere & enarrare.

De cubiculorum disposicione.
Ab aula discedimus ad cubicula vt loca quietis et somni et post curas &
labores receptacula, Statuimus igitur vt vnusquisque nostri collegij in suo   30
cubiculo se honeste gerat et modeste tam cum suo cubiculario quam cum
alijs vicinis vtque nullum quouis tempore a somno quiete aut studio impediat
per immoderatos clamores risus cantica strepitus saltaciones musicorum
instrumentorum pulsaciones, Sed si aliquando ante ignem aut alibi animi
ₐ⌈laxandi⌉ causa cum alijs libeat conuersari producatur tempus cum moderato   35
silentio in hijs que ad virtutem et doctrinam attinent. neque in hijs fiant
serotine commessaciones aut potaciones sed temperate et salubres.
...

1/ Whitson: *Whitsuntide was 11–17 May 1516*

St Michael at the North Gate Churchwardens' Accounts
ORO: PAR 211/4/F1/2, item 97
pt 1, f [4]* *(Expenses)*
...

Item payd to ye mynstrell for Whyttsontyde   vj s. viij d.   5

pt 3, f [1]* *(Receipts)*
...

Item Resiuyd A octyde   xv s. iij d.
Item Resiuyd at wytsontyd for wytson all   xxx s. ij d. ob.   10
...

1517–18
Lincoln College Computus   LC Arch: Computus 3
f 64v *(21 December 1516–21 December 1517)* *(Necessary internal expenses)*   15
...

Item payd to saynt nycolas clarkes   vj d.
...

Item payd for wyne to saynt nycolas clarkis   v d.
...   20

Magdalen College Liber Computi 1517–18   MC Arch
f 123v* *(11 November–11 November)* *(External payments)*
...

+ Solutum vnj adducenti tunicam lusoriam a magistro burges   ij d.   25
...

f 126* *(Chapel costs)*
...

Solutum domino porett pro tinctura et factura tunice eius qui   30
ageret partem Christi et pro crinibus mulieribus   ij s. vj d.
...

Merton College Register   MCR: 1.2
f 239   35
...

® Pleyn electus   xixno die eiusdem mensis magister Iohannes [Knythe] poleyn electus est in
   est in Regem   Regem ex concenssu omnium Sociorum pro anno futuro:/
...

5/ mynstrell: *first* l *written over* y   9/ octyde: *20–1 April 1517*
5, 10/ Whyttsontyde, wytsontyd: *31 May–*   37/ eiusdem mensis: *November 1517*
   6 June 1517

f 239v

December
°Rex°

Iniunctio
Senioris
bacularij

Huius mensis decimo die Custos audita negligencia Senioris bacularij in providendo litteram cum Sigillo iuxta antiquam consuetudinem pro regis electione Iniunxit eidem vt ne denarium vnum exhibicionis williot accipiat neque 5 Senioris Locum et ordinem (donec de eius penitencia laudabili testimonium habeat) vendicet quoniam in vigilia Edmundi Regis eius exemplo et Incuria bacularij eodem tempore peregrinis vestibus laruati non accesserunt:/

...

10

St Peter in the East Churchwardens' Accounts   ORO: PAR 213/4/F1/1
single mb   *(8 December–8 December)* *(Receipts)*

...

| Item In festo pethecostes | iij li. vj s. viij d. |
| Item receperunt in festo hocktyde declaro | xxij s. 15 |

...

(Expenses)

Item payd to G⟨..⟩rgij Coke for hys hows at wytsontyd	iii s. viij d.
...	20
Item p⟨..⟩ to the mynstrels at wytsontyd	[ij s. iiij d.] xij d.

...

1518–19
Merton College Register   MCR: 1.2   25
f 241

...

® ffrenschyppe
Electus in regem:

In vigilia sancti Emundi regis electus est in regem pro hoc anno Magister ffrenschypp. duobus solum bachalarijs scilicet seniore & Iuniore circueuntibus ignem cum litteris & sigillo modo quo solitum est antea fieri ceremonijs seruatis 30

...

f 241v

...

Nota de
Satrapis ville
qua condicione
receperunt hoc
anno vnum
nobile

Primo die Ianuarij venerunt ad collegium nostrum ville satrapes vti sunt consueti 35 ad cantandum vnum canticum in alta aula et cantauerunt postea eisdem unum nobile datum ᴧ⌐est⌐ per bursarium presente vicecustode. vbi declaratum est eis. hoc munus scilicet regale non datum esse illis a collegio nostro ex debito

14/ festo pethecostes: *23 May 1518*   19, 21/ wytsontyd: *23–9 May 1518*
14/ pethecostes: *for* penthecostes   28–9m/ ffrenschyppe ... regem: *underlined*
15/ festo hocktyde: *12–13 April 1518*   28/ Emundi: *for* Edmundi

aliquo ∧⌜quia per 2. aut 3. annos nichil receperunt⌝ sed solum ex humanitate
et liberalitate nostra. vt Inuicem amici essemus vti consuetum est. Et placuit illis
sermo & recesserunt

St Michael at the North Gate Churchwardens' Accounts   5
ORO: PAR 211/4/F1/2, item 100
single mb   (17 March 1518/19–15 March 1519/20) (Receipts)
...

Item Reysevyd At hoctyde	xiij s. j d.
Item Reysevyd off Witson Ayle cleyr	vj s. viij d. 10

...

1519–20
Magdalen College Liber Computi 1519–20   MC Arch
f 141   (Chapel costs)   15
...

Solutum domino Magott pro 2obus paribus cyrothecarum
pro episcopo diui nicolai   iiij d.
...

20

f 141v

...

Solutum Roberto payntar pro cruce et corona & diligentia
sua circa ludum die pasche   viij d.
...   25

Merton College Register   MCR: 1.2
f 245
...

® Holdar electus   In vigilia sancti emundi regis electus est in Regem pro hoc anno futuro   30
In Regem.   Magister Holdar Octo bachalarijs prius ignem in aula circueuntibus cum
litteris & sigillo modo quo solitum est antea fieri ceremonijs seruatis:
...

f 248v   35

Ianuarius   Primo die Ianuarij ad collegium ville satrapes venerunt vnum canticum in aula
alta cantaturi quo finito eisdem vnum Nobile per Howper 2m bursarium
datum est. quo gratanter accepto gratias agentes Recesserunt
...   40

9/ hoctyde: 2–3 May 1519   30/ emundi: for edmundi
10/ Witson: Whitsuntide was 12–18 June 1519

St Peter in the East Churchwardens' Accounts   ORO: PAR 213/4/F1/1
single mb   *(8 December–8 December) (Receipts)*
…

It*em* at hoctyde	xxj s.
It*em* at wytsu*n*tyde	liij s. iiij d. 5

…

1520–1

Lincoln College Computus   LC Arch: Computus 3
f 85v   *(21 December 1519–21 December 1520) (Necessary internal expenses)*   10
…

It*em* for wyne on seynt nycolasse ny3the	vj d. ob.
It*em* to ye clerke ye same ny3the	vj d.

…

15

Magdalen College Liber Computi 1520–1   MC Arch
f 170v   *(External payments)*
…

[Solut*um* pro carbonib*us* consumpt*is* in vig*i*lia sanct*i* Nicolai in aula ⌜iiij d.⌝
et pro carbonib*us* consumpt*is* in diu*er*sis interludijs t*em*po*r*e natalis do*m*ini   20
xvj d. et pro candel*is* consumpt*is* in noctib*us* ⌜xj d.⌝]

…

St Peter in the East Churchwardens' Accounts   ORO: PAR 213/4/F1/1
single mb   *(8 December–8 December) (Receipts)*   25
…

It*em* receyuyd At hoctyde	xxiij s. viij d.
It*em* receyuyd At whytsontyde	lij s. ij d.

…

30

1521

A   ***Brasenose College Statutes***   BNC Arch: A.2.3
p 36   *(Chapter 23)*

…præterea uero statuentes q*u*od null*us* socior*um* aut scholari*um* siue   35
serui*en*tium aliqu*em* can*em* siue au*em* q*u*alemc*um*q*ue* seu aliud q*u*odc*um*q*ue*
a*n*imal infra dict*um* Collegi*um* uel extra ad damn*um* seu detrim*en*tu*m*
ei*us*dem siue ad nocum*en*tum, inquietatio*n*em aut p*er*turbatio*n*em alicuius
socior*um* uel scholari*um* ei*us*dem Collegij nutriat seu custodiat Nec etia*m*

4/ hoctyde: *16–17 April 1520*   27/ hoctyde: *8–9 April 1521*
5/ wytsuntyde: *27 May–2 June 1520*   28/ whytsontyde: *19–25 May 1521*

cantu, clamore, vociferatione, instrumento musico aut quouis genere tumultus
socium aut scholarem quemcumque dicti Collegij quominus studere aut dormire
ualeat quoquo modo impediat....

...

1521–2
Merton College Register   MCR: 1.2
f 256

...

® Cantilena per
Satrapas ville

Ianuarius

Primo die Ianuarij venerunt ad collegium satrape ville Oxonie qui postquam   10
ex more vnam cantilenam cantauerunt in aula communi receperunt ex sola
humanitate & non ex debito vj s. viij d.

...

1522–3   15
Lincoln College Computus   LC Arch: Computus 3
f 105   *(21 December 1521–21 December 1522)* *(Necessary internal
   payments and expenses)*

...

Item for wyne & ayll to sant nycholas clarkes   v d. 20
Item to ye paryshe clarke for hys Reward   vj d.

...

Merton College Register   MCR: 1.2
f 257   25

...

Primo die Ianuarij venerunt ad collegium iuxta consuetudinem Satrape ville
qui et vnam cantilenam in aula nostra cantauerunt deinde ex sola beneuolentia
et non ex debito vj s. viij d. a bursario receperunt

...   30

AC   ***St Mary the Virgin Churchwardens' Accounts***   Bodl.: MS. Wood D.3
p 268   *(Receipts)*

...

received of ye wifes gathering at Hocktyde 16 s. 8 d.   35

...

28/ cantilenam: i *corrected over* a
35/ Hocktyde: *13–14 April 1523*

St Michael at the North Gate Churchwardens' Accounts
ORO: PAR 211/4/F1/2, item 101
single mb   *(19 March 1522/3–17 March 1523/4)   (Receipts)*
…

Item Receuyde Att hoctyde & All chargys borne	x s. [vij d.] ij d. 5
Item þat We made att Wytsontyde clyre & All costys borne	xlvj s. viij d.

…

St Peter in the East Churchwardens' Accounts   ORO: PAR 213/4/F1/1
single mb   *(8 December–8 December) (Receipts)*   10
…

Item resauid at hoctyde	xxj s.
Item resauid at Whitsuntyde	iij li.

…

15

1523-4
Merton College Register   MCR: 1.2
f 258v
…

®Ianuar*ius*   1o die Ianuarij veneru*nt* ad collegiu*m* satrape ville qui iux*ta* antiqua*m*   20
consuetudi*nem* postqu*am* cantilenam in aula commu*n*i cecieru*nt* vj s. viij d.
[iux*ta*] ex sola benevole*n*tia et no*n* ex debit*o* recipientes gratant*er* abieru*nt*.

…

St Peter in the East Churchwardens' Accounts   ORO: PAR 213/4/F1/1   25
single mb   *(8 December–8 December) (Receipts)*
…

Item receyuyd at hoctyde	xviij s.
Item made of the ale at Whitsontyde	iij li. xvj d.

…   30

1524-5
Merton College Register   MCR: 1.2
f 261v
…   35

nobile   Primo die hui*us* me*n*sis accesseru*nt* ad collegiu*m* satrapes ville oxon*ie*
ad cantand*um* vnum cantic*um* i*n* aula iux*ta* antiqu*um* morem quo finito
eisd*em* ex mera ben*e*uolentia socior*um* datu*m* est vnu*m* nobile p*er* M*a*gist*r*um

---

5, 12/ hoctyde: *13–14 April 1523*	29/ Whitsontyde: *15–21 May 1524*
6, 13/ Wytsontyde, Whitsuntyde: *24–30 May 1523*	36/ hui*us* mensis: *January 1524/5*
28/ hoctyde: *4–5 April 1524*	38/ vnu*m* nobile: *underlined*

ball 2ᵐ burssarium quod grato animo acceperunt & gratias agentes recesserunt

…

New College Bursars' Accounts   NC Arch: 7477
mb 4   *(Hall costs)*

…

…Et solutum Senescallo in die Natiuitatis pro ludo iiij d.…

…

St Michael at the North Gate Churchwardens' Accounts
ORO: PAR 211/4/F1/2, item 104
single mb   *(16 March 1524/5–15 March 1525/6)* *(Receipts)*

…

Item haue receuyde att hoktyde & all schargys borne	x s. ob.
Item haue receuyde of þe Wytson All & All thyng payde	xl s. viij d.

…

1525–6
Lincoln College Computus   LC Arch: Computus 3
f 144   *(21 December 1524–21 December 1525)* *(Necessary internal payments and expenses)*

Item payde for wyne on saynt nicholas evyn	vj d.
Item to ye paryssh clerke for his reward	vj d.

…

Merton College Register   MCR: 1.2
f 266

…

® Electio regis

In vigilia sancti edmundi regis electus est in regem Iohannes Cloterboke ex vnanimi consensu sociorum pro anno futuro

…

® accessus
satrapum ad
aulam

Primo die Ianuarij accesserunt ad collegium satrapes ville oxonie ad cantandum vnum canticum in aula iuxta antiquam consuetudinem quo finito eisdem ex mera beniuolentia sociorum datum est vnum nobile quod grato animo acceperunt & gratias agentes recesserunt.

…

15/ hoktyde: *24–5 April 1525*
16/ Wytson: *Whitsuntide was 4–10 June 1525*
34/ oxonie: *3 minims in MS*

St Michael at the North Gate Churchwardens' Accounts
ORO: PAR 211/4/F1/2, item 105
single mb   *(15 March 1525/6–14 March 1526/7)*   *(Receipts)*

…

Item receyvyd at hocktyde all charges alowed   xij s.   5
Item receyvyd of the Wysson ale all charges payd   xxx s. iiij d.

…

1526–7
Lincoln College Computus   LC Arch: Computus 4   10
p 28   *(21 December 1525–21 December 1526)*   *(Necessary internal expenses)*

…

It*em* for wyne on say*n*t nycholas evy*n*   ⟨…⟩
Item to the clerke for a reward   vj d.

…   15

Merton College Register   MCR: 1.2
f 268v

…

In vigilia *sancti* edmu*n*di elect*us* erat in rege*m* mayst*er* ball.   20

…

St Michael at the North Gate Churchwardens' Accounts
ORO: PAR 211/4/F1/2, item 106
single mb   *(14 March 1526/7–13 March 1527/8)*   *(Receipts)*   25

…

Item Receuyd Att hoctyde All The Charges born   xvj s. ob.
Item Receuyd of The Wytson A⌈y⌉ll All Charges born   l s. viij d.

…
                                                                             30

St Peter in the East Churchwardens' Accounts   ORO: PAR 213/4/F1/1
single mb   *(8 December–8 December)*   *(Receipts)*

…

Item recevyd at hoketyde of the Wyvys   xx⟨..⟩
…   35
Item recevyd for whytson ale & all thyng payd for   iij li. ⟨…⟩

…

5/ hocktyde: *9–10 April 1526*   34/ xx⟨..⟩: *edge of MS torn*
6/ Wysson: *Whitsuntide was 20–6 May 1526*   36/ iij li. ⟨…⟩: *sum faded*
27, 34/ hoctyde, hoketyde: *29–30 April 1527*
28, 36/ Wytson, whytson: *Whitsuntide was*
    9–15 June 1527

1527–8
Lincoln College Computus LC Arch: Computus 4
p 75 *(21 December 1526–21 December 1527)* *(Necessary internal expenses)*
…

Item to ye clerke on saynt nycholas evyn	vj d. 5
Item for wyne & ale for ye bysshop & hys clerkes	vj d.

…

Merton College Register MCR: 1.2
f 270v 10
…

Elexio regis In vigilia sancti edmundi electus est in regem magister tresham
…

f 271 15

® Accessus
satrapum ad
aulam

Prima die Ianuarij accesserunt satrapes uille ad altam aulam ut consuetum est
et ibidem cantabant unam cantilenam quo facto ex beniuolentia datum erat
illis nobile quod grato animo acceperunt et sic statim reccesserunt.
… 20

AC ***St Mary the Virgin Churchwardens' Accounts*** Bodl.: MS. Wood D.3
p 270 *(Receipts)*
…

® Hocktyde Item ye wifes gathering at hocktyde de claro xvi s. iv d. 25
…

1528–9
Lincoln College Computus LC Arch: Computus 4
p 125 *(21 December 1527–21 December 1528)* *(Necessary internal expenses)* 30
…

⟨…⟩ the clarke on sanyte nycholas evyn	vj d.
⟨…⟩ wyne & ale for ye bysshope & hys clerkes	viij d.

…

35

Merton College Register MCR: 1.2
f 272v

Electio regis In vigilia sancti edmundi electus est magister blewet in regem
… 40

12/ magister tresham: *underlined*　　　32/ sanyte: *for* saynte
25/ hocktyde: *20–1 April 1528*

satrapes ville

In die circumcisionis domini venerunt satrapes ville et habuerunt vj s. viij d.
ut solebant a burssario

…

St Michael at the North Gate Churchwardens' Accounts

ORO: PAR 211/4/F1/2, item 108
single mb*   *(12 March 1528/9–12 March 1529/30)*   *(Receipts)*

…

Item receuyd Att Octyde declaro   xiiij s. iij d.
Item receuyd for the Witson Ale & all charges borne   xxx s.

…

1529–30
Cardinal College Expense Book   PRO: E/36/104
f 12v   *(1 November–1 November)*

…

Solutum in regardo Duobus histrionibus famulis Ducis
Northfolcie ad mandatum [D] Decani 15 Iulij   ij s. vj d.

…

f 14

…

Solutum pro battellis canonicorum 2ⁱ ordinis quando
parabant agere comediam superiore anno vt patet per
billam promi   vj s. xj d. ob. qua.

…

Lincoln College Computus   LC Arch: Computus 4
p 169   *(21 December 1528–21 December 1529)*   *(Necessary internal expenses)*

…

⟨…⟩m to the clerke on sent Nycholace even   vj d.
⟨.⟩tem for wyine & alle for sent nycholace & hys clerkes   vj d.

…

Magdalen College Liber Computi 1529–30   MC Arch
f 248   *(External payments)*

…

x   solutum merkame pro vino dato episcopo nicolai in biberio   xj d.

…

9/ Octyde: *5–6 April 1529*
10/ Witson: *Whitsuntide was 16–22 May 1529*

++   solutum pro gaudimonijs datis socijs & scolaribus tempore
     natalis post ludos peractos & pro alijs gaudimonijs prout
     patet per billam   [xxvij s. vij d. ob.]
+   solutum pro cerothecis datis episcopo nicolai   iiij d.
     ...   5

Merton College Register   MCR: 1.2
f 273

...

® Electio regis   In vigilia sancti emundi electus est magister Raynaldes rex   10
® satrapes ville In die circumcisionis domini venerunt satrapes ville & habuerunt vj s. viij d.
                a bursario ut solebant

...

St Michael at the North Gate Churchwardens' Accounts   15
ORO: PAR 211/4/F1/2, item 110
single mb*   (12 March 1529/30–12 March 1530/1)   (Receipts)

...

Item Receyued at Octide for the Ale   xvj s. x d.
Item receyued at whitson ale and all charges born   xxxvij s. 20

...

St Peter le Bailey Churchwardens' Accounts   ORO: PAR 214/4/F1/16
single sheet   (25 November–25 November)   (Receipts)

...   25

Item recevyd for hoctyd money   x s. ij d. ob.
Item recevyd for whytsonetyde ale   xlj s. ij d.

...

1530–1   30
Lincoln College Computus   LC Arch: Computus 4
p 205   (21 December 1529–21 December 1530)   (Necessary internal expenses)

...

⟨...⟩ to ye clarke off sant nycoleys nyhte   vj d.

...   35

⟨...⟩m for wyne ale & breyd off sant ⟨..⟩coleys nyhte   vj d.

...

10/ emundi: for edmundi
19/ Octide: 25–6 April 1530
20/ whitson: Whitsuntide was 5–11 June 1530
26/ hoctyd: 25–6 April 1530
27/ whytsonetyde: 5–11 June 1530

Magdalen College Liber Computi 1530–1   MC Arch
f 7v   *(External payments)*

…

Solut*um* Mimis d*om*ine principisshe   xx d.

…   5

f 8v

…

+   Solut*um* *pro* biberio dato sotijs et sco*lar*ib*us* post
interludia in te*m*pore natalis d*om*ini   [vj s. viij d.] 10

…

Merton College Register   MCR: 1.2
f 274

…   15

® Electio reg*is*   In vigilia *sancti* edmu*n*di m*a*g*iste*r [Henricus] ⌈°Ricardus°⌉ ewer elect*us* *est*
in rege*m*

…

St Michael at the North Gate Churchwardens' Accounts   20
ORO: PAR 211/4/F1/2, item 111
single mb*   *(12 March 1530/1–12 March 1531/2) (Receipts)*

…

It*em* reseuyd At hoctyde for the Ale   xvj s. x d.
It*em* reseuyd At Whitson Ale And All Charg*es* boren   xxx[x]j s. 25

St Peter in the East Churchwardens' Accounts   ORO: PAR 213/4/F1/1
single mb*   *(8 December–8 December) (Receipts)*

…

It*em* Resauyd Att hochtyde   xxviij s. ix d. 30
It*em* Resauyd Att wyttson hayll Clere   iij li. v s. iij d.

…

St Peter le Bailey Churchwardens' Accounts   ORO: PAR 214/4/F1/17
sheet [1]   *(25 November–25 November) (Receipts)*   35

…

It*em* rece*vy*d for hoctyd money   ix s. viij d.

4/ principisshe: *for* principisse
9/ sotijs: *for* socijs
16/ ewer: w *corrected over* u
24, 30, 37/ hoctyde, hochtyde, hoctyd: *17–18 April 1531*
25, 31/ Whitson, wyttson: *Whitsuntide was 28 May–3 June 1531*

Item rece*vyd* for whytson ale xxx s. vij d.

…

1531–2
Magdalen College Liber Computi 1531–2 MC Arch
f 21* *(External payments)* 5

…

So*lutum* lusori*bus* Reginæ mandato d*omi*ni p*re*sidis xij d.

…

billa So*lutum* p*ro* biberio dato soci*js* post ludu*m* baccalaureor*um*
in magna aula ut pa*tet* per billa*m* vj s. iij d. 10

…

Merton College Register MCR: 1.2
f 276 15

® Electio Reg*is* Vigialia Edmundi Regis congregatis soci*js* ad igne*m* in aula more *pr*isco delectus
& deputatus in Regem *pro* anno futuro est m*agiste*r Robertus Tailer Register
vni*uersitatis* principalis aule albane & in collegio vic*ecustos* vice*m* gerens post
Clutturbucchi discessu*m* & ad sacellatu*m* Wynsorie *per* custode*m* promotu*m*. 20

…

Chancellor's Court Register OUA: Hyp/A/4, Register EEE (or B reversed)
f 248*

… 25

Lyndesy con*tra* vij^mo die mensis Iunij m*agiste*r doctor Lyndesey sacre theologie professor
Knyght allegavit cora*m* d*omi*no substituto *pre*dicto q*uod* commodauit m*agist*ro Ioh*ann*i
°Dr lyndesy Knyght artiu*m* m*agist*ro quodda*m* par de ly clerycordes quod petijt ab eodem
obijt 2º martij restitui et noluit sed dicebat q*uod* dict*us* m*agiste*r doctor lyndesy dabat dictu*m*
1534 Al*um*ni par eidem con*s*intendo q*uod* ab eo receperat i*n* p*re*sentia dicti doct(.)ris negand*i* 30
Oxon*ienses* q*uod* dabat sed q*uod* commodauit du*m*taxat et petijt iustici*am* sibi fieri i*n* hac
f 672° *p*arte vna cu*m* expensis fact*is* et faciendis et tunc dict*us* m*agiste*r Ioh*ann*es
Knyght petijt termin*um* ad probandu*m* q*uod* dict*us* m*agiste*r doctor lyndesy
dabat ei dictu*m* par de ly clerycordes et d*omi*nus assignauit ei diem lune
proxim*um* hora prima et post m*er*idiem ex consensu dict*i* m*agist*ri doctoris et 35
monuit *p*artes ad interessendum

lyndesy con*tra* ix^no die mens*is* Iunij predicti ∧⌜hora predicta⌝ *pre*fatus m*agiste*r doctor
Knyght Lyndesey comp*ar*uit et petebat a d*omi*no commissario quatin*us* cogeret

1/ whytson: *Whitsuntide was 28 May–3 June 1531*   30/ consintendo: *in corrected from c; for* consentiendo
17/ Vigialia: *for* vigilia   35/ et¹: *possibly intended for cancellation*
28/ quod: *o corrected over* e

dictum magistrum Knyght ad restituendum dicta ly clerycordes & eorum
verum valorem in presentia dicti magistri Knyght nullam probacionem inducentis
quod dictus magister doctor dedit eidem prenominatum par de ly clericordes.
ad cuius videlicet magistri peticionem condemnauit prefatum magistrum
[Robertum] ⌜Iohannem⌝ Knyght ad restituendum dictum par de ly clericordes   5
[intra] infra octo dies in equo bono statu quo tempore tradicionis fuerunt &
ad satisfaciendum partibus viz. magistro Bawdwyn et Beest quorum consensu
prefatum ∧⌜par⌝ ly clericordes erant sequestratum in manus dicti magistri
doctoris lyndesey et in expensis per dominum commissarium taxandis. et ad
[eod] exonerandum dictum Magistrum doctorum aduersus partes predictas per   10
sufficientes fideiussores infra octo dies proximos sequentes prenominata sub pena
ut supra

St Michael at the North Gate Churchwardens' Accounts
ORO: PAR 211/4/F1/2, item 113   15
single mb *(12 March 1531/2–12 March 1532/3) (Receipts)*
…

Item Receyued At Hoctetyde for the Ale   xij s.
Item Receyued At Whysontyde for the Ale   xxxiij s.
…   20

St Peter le Bailey Churchwardens' Accounts ORO: PAR 214/4/F1/18
single mb *(25 November–25 November) (Receipts)*
…

Item recevyd for the hoctyd money   x s. 25
Item recevyd for the Wytsun hale   xxviij s. viij d.
…

1532–3
Lincoln College Computus LC Arch: Computus 4   30
p 240 *(21 December 1531–21 December 1532) (Necessary internal expenses)*
…

Item to ye clerke on saynt nycolace evyn   ⟨…⟩
Item for wyne and ayle ye same evyn   vj ⟨.⟩
                                                                                 35

Merton College Register MCR: 1.2
f 277v
…

Electio Regis   vigilia Edmundi Regis Congregatis socijs ad Ignem in aula more prisco

---

8/ erant: n *corrected over another letter; for* erat
10/ doctorum: *for* doctorem
18, 25/ Hoctetyde, hoctyd: *8–9 April 1532*

19/ Whysontyde: *19–25 May 1532*
26/ Wytsun: *Whitsuntide was 19–25 May 1532*

delect*us* & deputat*us* in rege*m* *pro* anno futuro est magis*ter* Iohannes David
...

St Michael at the North Gate Churchwardens' Accounts
ORO: PAR 211/4/F1/2, item 114   5
single mb   *(12 March 1532/3–12 March 1533/4)*   *(Receipts)*
...

It*em* Receyued At Hoctyde for the Ale	xij s.
It*em* Rec*eyued* At Whytsontyde for the Ale	xxxiiij s.

...   10

1533–4
GC **Letter of Richard Croke to Thomas Cromwell**   PRO: SP/1/82
f [2]   *(26 January)*
...   15

Syr the warde*n* off Cant*er*burye College ys a e*n*nymye to the king*es* cause, and
albeyt ou3t off tewen harpyth in his *ser*mon of *familiar* commu*n*ication ayenste
the same in lykewyse as doctor holyma*n* and Morema*n* doth thou off the
whiche ij ys lyke to haue the diuinite lecture here onles [*prouisio*n] remedy be
prouyded For doctor Mortym*er* late doctor off the chayre ys called vnto the   20
quenys *ser*uice I dou3t not but your Maist*er*shippe hathe seene the [play]
ent*er*lude [⟨.⟩] deuysed to haue bene playd in Glocestre college a place off
Monk*es* yff Mr Cart*er* had not stoppyd the same. The co*m*myssarye hathe the
said play aboue wit*h* hy*m*. And ye wol not bylyue how the monkes and chano*ns*
and al other ignorante *r*eligious *per*sons and sutche as be e*n*nymyes vnto the 25
king*es* cause reioyse at the stay off the wark*es* and college nor what they take
off the same Nor what truste they haue off the vndoynge off the same and
ho⟨.⟩ that *r*eligious me*n* shal ayene e*n*ioye ⌜there⌝ to the distruction off flat*er*ers
and fals hypocrites and traytors for so they cal vs that fauor the king*es* cause
...   30

Magdalen College Liber Computi 1533–4   MC Arch
f 44   *(External payments)*
...

billa +   Solut*um* Ricard*o* Alard *pro* duab*us* refectionib*us* post   35
          ludos socioru*m* & scho*l*ariu*m* vt *p*atet *per* duas billas
          in vnu*m* coiunctas   xij s. ij d.
...

8/ Hoctyde: *21–2 April 1533*
9/ Whytsontyde: *1–7 June 1533*
19/ onles: e *written over* y

37/ coiunctas: *for* coniunctas; *abbreviation mark*
    missing

Merton College Register   MCR: 1.2
f 279

...

Devynel eligitur
in regem

19 die novembris vz. in vigilia Edmundi regis electus est magister Henricus
devynell in regem quia promotus est ad rectoriam de Burporte in comitatu   5
Dorsetie

...

New College Bursars' Accounts   NC Arch: 7488
mb 7   *(Necessary external costs)*   10

...

...Solutum in regardo lusoribus regis ad mandatum Custodis iij s. iiij d....

mb 8

                                                                                  15

...Solutum in regardo dato Tympanistrijs ly Calysse ad mandatum vicecustodis
xij d....

...

Chancellor's Court Register   OUA: Hyp/A/4, Register EEE (or B reversed)   20
f 257v   *(A Christmas play at Broadgates Hall)*

...

Eodem die comparuit Robertus woodward mancipium domus aule latarum
portarum et allegauit se commodasse domino Ioanni Moore scolari dicte aule
xv s. ad emendum certa vestimenta ob ludos et pegmata tempore natalis christi   25
quos petijt a dicto domino Iohanne more ᴧ⌐cum expensis litis⌐ et ad probandum
commodationem induxit georgium wymbsley legum baccallaurium et Thomam
burgon scolares dicte aule qui tactis sacrosanctis euangelijs deposuerunt
prenominatum mancipium prefatam summam x[x] ⌐v s.⌐ eidem ᴧ⌐domino⌐
Iohanni ᴧ⌐commodasse⌐ more sub ea conditione quod eandem restitueret   30
⌐summam⌐ post [quam] collectionem sol[d]⌐itam⌐ fieri inter [eo] scolares dicte
domus ad contribuendum solutioni in presentia dicti domini Ioannis more
confitentis se recepisse prefatam summam a dicto mancipio sed dicit se soluisse
vijtem solidos prefato mancipio [et] quam summam vijtem solidorum prefatus
mancipium confessus est se recepisse et [dominus] ⌐Iudex⌐ [precepit dicto domino 35
Iohanni more] prelibatum dominum more in residuum puta in viijto solidos
ᴧ⌐vna cum expensis litis⌐ condemnauit et precepit eidem ut dictam summam
ᴧ⌐vna cum expensis litis⌐ prefato mancipio intra viijto dies proximos sequentes

5–6/ Burporte in comitatu Dorsetie: *probably*   23/ Eodem die: *4 December 1533*
  Bridport, Dorset   29, 35/ mancipium: *2 minims for* iu *in* MS
16/ ly Calysse: *Calais, France*

solu*e*ret sub pe*n*a Iuris et i*n*continen*ti* Iudex taxauit expe*n*s*as* i*n* x denar*ios*

…

AC **St Mary the Virgin Churchwardens' Accounts**   Bodl.: MS. Wood D.3
p 276   *(Receipts)*   5

…

It*em* at Hocktyde 31 s. 7 d. ob.

…

1534–5   10
Magdalen College Liber Computi 1534–5   MC Arch
f 77   *(External payments)*

…

– Solutu*m* mimo pro solatijs fact*is* sotijs te*mpo*re
  natiuitat*is* Do*m*ini   iiij s. iiij d. 15

…

– Solutu*m* pro mere*n*da fact*a* post comedia*m* acta*m*
  vt p*atet per* libru*m* alarde   ix s. iij d.

…

  Solutu*m* Ioculatorib*us* do*m*ini regis ma*n*dato d*omini* presidis   xx d. 20

New College Bursars' Accounts   NC Arch: 7489
mb 8   *(Necessary external costs)*

…so*lutum* in regardo dato lusorib*us* regiis ij s.…   25

…

St Michael at the North Gate Churchwardens' Accounts
ORO: PAR 211/4/F1/2, item 116
single mb   *(12 March 1534/5–12 March 1535/6)* *(Receipts)*   30

…

Item Receyued At hockctyde declaroe   xiij s.
Item Receyued At Whytsontyde declaroe   xx s. j d.

…
                                                                             35

(Payments)
Item p*a*yd to the Mynstrell At Whytsontyde   iij s. vij d.

…

7/ Hocktyde: *13–14 April 1534*   32/ hocketyde: *5–6 April 1535*
14/ sotijs: *for* socijs   33, 37/ Whytsontyde: *16–22 May 1535*

St Peter le Bailey Churchwardens' Accounts   ORO: PAR 214/4/F1/19
single mb   *(25 November–25 November) (Receipts)*

...

Item made At hoctyde	viij s.
Item made of Whytsun ale	xl s. 5

...

1535-6
Magdalen College Liber Computi 1535-6   MC Arch
f 67   *(External payments)*   10

...

Solutum Mimo pro solatijs factis sociis et scholasticis
tempore nativitatis domini   iiij s.

...

                                                                              15

St Aldate Churchwardens' Accounts   ORO: DD Par. Oxford St Aldate c.15/2
mb [2]   *(4 February 1535/6–4 February 1536/7) (Receipts)*

...

Item recevyd at whytsontyd	*(blank)*
Item recevyd at hoctyde	vij s. iij d. ob. 20

...

Item recevyd for ye may polle	ij s.

...

mb [3]   *(Expenses)*   25

...

Item to Ihon peese of hynxhye for caryge of ye maypoll	xij d.

...

St Michael at the North Gate Churchwardens' Accounts   30
ORO: PAR 211/4/F1/2, item 117
single mb*   *(12 March 1535/6–12 March 1536/7) (Receipts)*

...

Item Receyued At Hoctyde declaroe	viij s. x d.
Item Receyued at Whytsontyde declaro	xxiiij s. 35

...

4/ hoctyde: *5–6 April 1535*
5/ Whytsun: *Whitsuntide was 16–22 May 1535*
19, 35/ whytsontyd, Whytsontyde: *4–10 June 1536*
20, 34/ hoctyde, Hoctyde: *24–5 April 1536*
27/ hynxhye: *Hinksey, Oxfordshire*

St Peter le Bailey Churchwardens' Accounts ORO: PAR 214/4/F1/20
single mb *(25 November–25 November) (Receipts)*

...

Item Receyvid At Octyde   ix s. v d.
Item Receyvid At Whytsontide   xx s. 5

...

1536–7
Lincoln College Computus LC Arch: Computus 4
p 269 *(21 December 1535–21 December 1536) (Necessary internal expenses)* 10

...

⟨...⟩ to the clerke off sant nycolys nyght   vj d.
⟨...⟩ for wyne the same nyght   *(blank)*

...

15

New College Bursars' Accounts NC Arch: 7493
mb 5 *(Necessary external costs)*

...*so*l*utum* lusoribus regis *per* man*us* vic*e*custodis xx d....

...   20

1537–8
Magdalen College Liber Computi 1537–8 MC Arch
f 120v *(External payments)*

...   25

x Solut*um* duob*us* tympanist*is* pro laborib*us* in fest*is* natalitijs   iiij s. viij d.

...

f 122

...   30

Solut*um pro* bellarijs dat*is* socijs c*um* ageretur com*æ*dia   vj s. viij d.

...

Merton College Register MCR: 1.2
f 283 *(November)*   35

...

M*a*gist*er* Ramgryg elect*us* e*st* in regem

4/ Octyde: *24–5 April 1536*
5/ Whytsontide: *4–10 June 1536*
12/ nycolys: *s corrected over another letter, possibly* c

New College Bursars' Accounts   NC Arch: 7495
mb 4   *(Necessary external expenses)*

...

...In regardo dato histrionibus d*omini* Crumwelli vij s....

...   5

St Peter le Bailey Churchwardens' Accounts   ORO: PAR 214/4/F1/21
single mb*   *(25 November–25 November) (Receipts)*

...

Item receyued of the Ale at Octide   vij s. j d. q*u*a. 10

...

It*e*m receyued of the Ale at Whitsontide   xxxj s. viij d.

...

(Payments)   15
Item paid for mendyng of a gowne and kyrtell   v d.

...

1538–9
Magdalen College Liber Computi 1538–9   MC Arch   20
f 131v   *(Hall costs)*

...

Solutu*m* Hammond p*ro* labore trium dier*um* circa proscænium   xviij d.

...

                                                                                          25

f 136   *(External payments)*

...

x   Solutu*m* p*ro* bellariis datis sociis cu*m* ageretur comedia   viij s.

...

                                                                                          30

Merton College Register   MCR: 1.2
f 284v

...

20 die electus erat magister borow vicari*us* de Croden in regem
martonensem   35

...

10/ Octide: *29–30 May 1538*
12/ Whitsontide: *9–15 June 1538*
34/ 20 die: *20 November 1538*
34/ Croden: *probably Croydon, Surrey*

St Mary the Virgin Churchwardens' Accounts
Bodl.: MS. Rolls Oxon Box 1, #15
sheet 1*   *(Receipts)*

...

Item At hoktyde clere Aboue All charges   vij s. j d.   5

...

St Peter le Bailey Churchwardens' Accounts   ORO: PAR 214/4/F1/22
single mb   *(25 November–25 November) (Receipts)*

...   10

Item Receyved and made of the Ale at Octide   v s. iiij d.

...

Item Receyued and made of the Ale at Whitsontide   xxxj s.

...

                                                                                    15

(Payments)
Item paid to the Mynstrell at Whitsontide   vj s. viij d.

...

1539–40   20
Lincoln College Computus   LC Arch: Computus 5
f 14   *(21 December 1538–21 December 1539) (Necessary internal expenses)*

...

Item to ye clerk of sanct nicholas nyght   *(blank)*

                                                                                    25

Magdalen College Liber Computi 1539–40   MC Arch
f 150v   *(External payments)*

...

Solutum duobus cytharedis tempore Natiuitatis Christi   iiij s. viij d.
...   30
Solutum pro epulis datis sociis eo tempore quo agebatur
tragedia   viij s. iiij d.

...

– Solutum pro pane et potu datis semicommunnariis dum
curabant publicam exhibere comediam   xx d. 35

...

Merton College Register   MCR: 1.2
f 285v

...   40
Estwyke electus
est in regem   19 die nouembris electus est magister estwyke in vigilia Edmundi regis in regem

5, 11/ hoktyde, Octide: *14–15 April 1539*   13, 17/ Whitsontide: *25–31 May 1539*

f 286

...

®accessus
Satrapum ad
aulam

Primo die ianuarij accesserunt ad collegium satrapes ville oxonie ad cantandum
vnum canticum in aula quo finito eisdem ex mera beniuolentia sotiorum datum
est vnum nobile quod grato animo acceperunt & gratias agentes recesserunt   5

...

St Peter le Bailey Churchwardens' Accounts   ORO: PAR 214/4/F1/23
single mb   *(25 November–25 November) (Receipts)*

...   10

Item receyued and made of the ock Ale   v s. j d.

...

Item Receyued and made of the Ale at Whitsontyde
all costes and charges born   (blank)

...   15

1540–1
Magdalen College Liber Computi 1540–1   MC Arch
f 158   *(Hall costs)*

...   20

Solutum pro candelis consumptis in Aula tempore
actarum comediarum   v s.

f 162*   *(External payments)*

...   25

Solutum pro biberio dato sociis post actas comedias   xij s. iiij d.

...

Solutum Magistro harley pro conducto timpanista in
ferijs nataliciis   iiij s.

...   30

St Peter in the East Churchwardens' Accounts   ORO: PAR 213/4/F1/1
single mb   *(8 December–8 December) (Receipts)*

...

Item Recevyd and made at octyde   xvj s. ix d. 35
Item Recevyd and made of the Whytson alle   xliij s. xj d.

...

11/ ock: *Hocktide was 5–6 April 1540*
13/ Whitsontyde: *16–22 May 1540*
35/ octyde: *24–5 April 1541*
36/ Whytson: *Whitsuntide was 5–11 June 1541*

St Peter le Bailey Churchwardens' Accounts ORO: PAR 214/4/F1/24
single mb* *(25 November–25 November) (Receipts)*

...

Item Receyued and made of the ale at Whitsontyde
all cost*es* and charg*es* borne   liij s. iiij d. 5
Item Receyued and made of the Ale at Ocke tyde
all cost*es* and charg*es* borne   viij s. xj d.

...

(Payments)   10
It*em* for mendyng of the Quenes gown and hur kyrtell   xvij d.

...

1541–2

BNC   **Alexander Nowell's Notebook**   Bodl.: Brasenose College MS. 31   15
f 45 col 2

...

M*emorandum* to remembre Hunt*es* matt*er* off Oxford, the paynters matter
my play in Englishe

...   20

Magdalen College Liber Computi 1541–2   MC Arch
f 170v   *(Hall costs)*

...

–   Solutu*m* pro candelis consumptis du*m* agere*n*tur   25
commediæ   iiij s. iiij d.

...

f 176   *(External payments)*

...   30
Solutu*m* M*agis*tro redmano pi*o* timpanista   iiij s. viij d.

...

f 176v

...   35
•   Solutu*m* pro merenda data socijs post actas commedias   xiij s. iiij d.

...

4/ Whitsontyde: *5–11 June 1541*
6/ Ocke tyde: *25–6 April 1541*

New College Hall Book   NC Arch: 5530
f [167]   *(24–30 December)*

...

Mercurij ad pra*ndium* cu*m* soc*ijs* ... duo histriones

...   5

f [168]   *(31 December–6 January)*

...

dom*inica*...
ad ce*nam* cu*m* socijs duo histriones   10

...

Mar*tis* ad pra*ndium* cu*m* socijs ... duo histriones
ad ce*nam* cu*m* socijs ... duo histriones

...

Mercurij ad pra*ndium* cu*m* socijs ... duo histriones   15
ad ce*nam* cu*m* socijs duo histriones

...

Iouis ad pra*ndium* cu*m* socijs ... duo histriones...
ad ce*nam* cu*m* socijs duo histriones...
Veneris ad pra*ndium* cu*m* socijs ... duo histriones   20

f [169]   *(7–13 January)*

...

dom*inica*...
ad ce*nam* cu*m* socijs ... duo histriones   25
lune ad pra*ndium* cu*m* socijs ... duo histriones

...

ad ce*nam* cu*m* socijs ... duo histriones

...

Mercurij...   30

...

ad ce*nam* cu*m* socijs duo histriones

...

ve*neris* ad pra*ndium* cu*m* socijs duo histriones

...   35

4/ Mercurij: *29 December 1541*   20/ Veneris: *6 January 1541/2*
9/ dom*inica*: *1 January 1541/2*   24/ dominica: *8 January 1541/2*
12/ Mar*tis*: *3 January 1541/2*   26/ lune: *9 January 1541/2*
15/ Mercurij: *4 January 1541/2*   30/ Mercurij: *11 January 1541/2*
18/ Iouis: *5 January 1541/2*   34/ ve*neris*: *13 January 1541/2*

f [170]   *(14–20 January)*

Sabbato ... ad prandium cum socijs ... duo histriones
...
dominica... 5
ad cenam cum socijs duo histriones
...

f [173]*   *(4–10 February)*
... 10
veneris ad prandium cum socijs ... duo histriones domine Wylloby.
...

The Queen's College Long Roll   QC Arch: 2P131
single mb   *(1 July–1 July) (External expenses)* 15
...
...Item ad tibicines mensibus Augusti & Iunij xx d....
...

Dedicatory Epistle to Gilbert Smith, Archdeacon of Peterborough 20
Grimald: *Christus Redivivus*
sigs A3v–4*

...Postea uerò quàm uersatus in Collegio doctorum, quod ab Aeneo naso
nomen inuenit, per mensem unum & item alterum istam pro mea uirili 25
Spartam ornaueram, ac fortè fortuna ita, ut fiebat, arderet pubes domestica
theatrum conscendere, quô & suos excitarent animos, & ciuibus imaginem
quandam uitæ spectandam exhiberent: continuò ex paucis, qui meum
cubiculum frequentabant, cœpit multis innotescere, quid molirer, quidque in
manibus haberem. Egit itaque mecum Matthæus Smithus Collegij præses et 30
consanguineus tuus, homo mirifica modestia, liberalitate et sanctimonia
præditus: egit Robertus Cauduuellus, uir perhonestus, et insigni|ter doctus:
egerunt lectissimi atque optimæ spei adolescenteis, ut meam sibi fœturam, in
Scenam producendam concrederem, in eaque re, meam illis operam dicarem ac
deuouerem. Quoniam autem negare eis tum præclara petentibus, tum indole 35
sua digna cupientibus, difficile mihi uisum fuit: permisi sanè, ut eorum auspicijs,
hæc ista Comœdia etiam in eruditissimorum uirorum corona publicitus

3/ Sabbato: *14 January 1541/2*
5/ dominica: *15 January 1541/2*
11/ veneris: *10 February 1541/2*
17/ mensibus Augusti & Iunij: *probably August 1541 and June 1542*
33/ adolescenteis: *for* adolescentes

ageretur. Quod simul ut fama uoce loquaci perstrepens, in aureis tuas effuderat: me non solùm per diligentissimum institutorem meum Iohannem Aërium admonere, sed & ipse tu iterum atq*ue* iterum huius poëmatis êditionem rogare comiter sustinuisti. Atque adeò, quoties egomet admiratione & pudore propè confusus, ad caussas ingeniosus extiti: dicebamq*ue* non posse non in adolescente   5
uiginti plus minus annos nato, undiq*ue* apparere inscientiæ uestigia, habebamq*ue* in obiectis omnia, quæ sunt à me superius adducta: toties præceptor ille meus (quæ sua fuit & tibi obsequendi, & prouocandi mei sedulitas) instabat, & exemplis cùm recentiorum, tum etiam ueterum utebatur, quorum extarent monumenta, id ætatis, haud sine summa laude conscripta....   10

1542–3
Magdalen College Libri Computi MC Arch: LCE/5
f 5 *(Hall costs)*

... 15

Solutu*m* pro candelis cu*m* agerentur Co*m*medie   iiij s.

...

f 9v *(External payments)*

... 20

x Solutu*m* pro biberio dato socijs post actas co*m*medias   xiij s. iiij d.

...

Solutu*m* M*a*g*ist*ro oteley pro tympanista in færijs natalitijs   iiij s. viij d.

...

  25

St Peter le Bailey Churchwardens' Accounts ORO: PAR 214/4/F1/26
mb [1] *(25 November–25 November)* *(Receipts)*

...

It*em* receyued and made of the Hock Ale   iiij s. v d.
It*em* receyued and made of the whitson Ale   xxvj s. viij d. 30

...

1543–4
St Martin Churchwardens' Accounts ORO: PAR 207/4/F1/1, item 6
single mb col 1* *(25 November–25 November)* *(Receipts)* 35

...

It*em* clere for Hogtyde Ale   xj s. x d.
It*em* clere for Whitsontyde Ale   xiij d.

1/ aureis: *for* aures   37/ Hogtyde: *21–2 April 1544*
29/ Hock: *Hocktide was 2–3 April 1543*   38/ Whitsontyde: *1–7 June 1544*
30/ whitson: *Whitsuntide was 13–19 May 1543*

Item off the bequest of the parishioners the Churche ale
at whitsontyde   xxxiij s. ij d.
...

col 2*   5
...

°Item of diuerse persons for the payment of money to Whytsontyde Ale

In primis Iohn Barry Alderman   xx d.
[Item Thomas popyngaye   viij d.] 10
Item Wyllyam Iones   viij d.
[Item Iohn Hore   xij d.]
Item Davy Iohnson   xij d.°

St Michael at the North Gate Churchwardens' Accounts   15
ORO: PAR 211/4/F1/2, item 119
single mb   *(12 March 1543/4–12 March 1544/5) (Receipts)*
...

Item ffor Ale At Whytsontyde ⌈As Apperythe by A byll⌉   xij s. xj d.
Item for the profytt of the Ale At hoktyde Aboue All charges   v s. v d. ob. 20
...

1544–5
Magdalen College Libri Computi   MC Arch: LCE/5
f 22   *(External payments)*   25
...

Solutum timpanistæ Tyllesley pro opera sua in feriis nataliciis   iiij s. viiij d.
...

St Martin Churchwardens' Accounts   ORO: PAR 207/4/F1/1, item 8   30
single mb   *(25 November–25 November) (Receipts)*
...

Item for hoktyde ale aboue all chargys   vij s. viij d.
Item for Whytsontyde ale of the gyft of the paryssheners
as apperythe by a byll of there namys wyth the somes of   35
money partycularly vppon theym   xxxj s. vj d.
...

2, 7, 19/ whitsontyde, Whytsontyde: *1–7 June 1544*
20/ hoktyde: *21–2 April 1544*
33/ hoktyde: *13–14 April 1545*
34/ Whytsontyde: *24–30 May 1545*

single mb dorse*

...

Item the seid Accompteant*es* Axe to be Allowed for bred
meate & drynke p*ro*vydyd by theym At Whytsontyde for
Soper nyght   xiiij s. iij d.   5
Item of certen Som*m*es of money Assessyde vppon dyu*er*s
p*er*sons not payde at Whytsontyde
Wyllyam Kyrman   xij d.
Iamys Clarke   vj d.
x   Wyll*y*am Ioyner   vj d. 10
x   Stefene Iamys   iiij d.
Iohn Northe   viij d.
Iamys Bocher   viij d.
Gerard Plowghe   iiij d.

...   15

St Michael at the North Gate Churchwardens' Accounts
ORO: PAR 211/4/F1/2, item 120
single mb   *(12 March 1544/5–12 March 1545/6) (Receipts)*

...   20

Item for the ⟨...⟩ytt of the Ale At the ffeast of Pentycost
Aboue All charges   xvj s. viij d.
Item for the p*ro*fytt of the Ale At hoktyde Aboue All charges   viij s. ix d.

...

                                                                                                25

St Peter in the East Churchwardens' Accounts   ORO: PAR 213/4/F1/1
single mb   *(8 December–8 December) (Receipts)*

...

Item R*e*cevid and getheryd at ocke tyde   xiiij s. ix d.
Item Recevyd and ⌈made⌉ of the whytson Alle   xlv s. v d. 30

...

1545–6
Magdalen College Libri Computi   MC Arch: LCE/5
f 35v   *(External payments)*   35

...

Solutu*m* p*ro* tympanista in feriis nataliciis ad man*us*
m*agistr*i wodroffe   iiij s. viij d.

...

4, 7/ Whytsontyde: *24–30 May 1545*   23, 29/ hoktyde, ocke tyde: *13–14 April 1545*
21/ Pentycost: *24 May 1545*   30/ whytson: *Whitsuntide was 24–30 May 1545*

St Peter in the East Churchwardens' Accounts   ORO: PAR 213/4/F1/1
single mb   *(8 December–8 December) (Receipts)*

…

Item Receyued and gathered at hocketide   xij s. x d.
Item Receyued and Maide of the Whitson Ayle   xxvj s. viij d.   5

…

St Peter le Bailey Churchwardens' Accounts   ORO: PAR 214/4/F1/27
mb [1]*   *(13 December–12 December) (Receipts)*

…   10

Item receyved for the hoc ale at easter   v s. v d.

…

Item receyved for whitson ale all chardges clery borne   xij s. vij d. ob.

…

                                                                                                               15

c **1546**
Christ Church Cathedral and College Foundation Statutes
ChCh Arch: D.P.vi.b.1
f 183*   *(Chapter 35) (On the disposition of bedrooms)*

…   20

Vt cubicula prudenter ac bene disponantur Statuimus ordinamus et volumus.
Vt vnusquisque nostre ecclesie in suo cubiculo honeste se gerat et modeste, tam
cum suo cubiculario, quam cum alijs vicinis vtque nullum quouis tempore a
somno, quiete, aut studio impediat, per immoderatos clamores, risus, cantica,
strepitus, saltaciones musicorum instrumentorum pulsaciones, sed si aliquando   25
ante ignem aut alibi, animi relaxandi gracia cum alijs libeat conversari
producatur tempus cum moderato silentio, in his que ad virtutem et doctrinam
attinent. neque in his fiant serotine commessaciones aut potaciones, sed
temperate et salubres…

                                                                                                               30

ff 194–4v

…

        48 De mora non trahenda in aula post refectiones
Vt post ventris repletionem et gratiarum actionem literarum studia aut alia
pietatis opera repetantur Statuimus ordinamus et volumus vt singulis diebus   35
post prandium & cenam persoluta deo gratiarum actione canonici omnes et
singuli ecclesie nostre cuiuscumque gradus extiterint sine vllo intervallo ex
aula nostra recedant nisi quando vel consilia vel alia ardua | ecclesie negotia

---

4, 5/ Item: *in display script*   11/ hoc: *Hocktide was 3–4 May 1546*
4/ hocketide: *3–4 May 1546*   11/ easter: *25 April 1546*
5, 13/ Whitson, whitson: *Whitsuntide was*   13/ clery: *for clerly*
    13–19 June 1546

immediate debeant tractari vel lectiones disputati*one*s aut biblie expositiones
co*n*tinuo sequantur Quibus etiam absolutis statim decedant/ vel quando in
festis solemnioribus ad solatium om*nium* inh*a*bitantium ib*ide*m construitur
ignis/ tunc *per*mittimus ecclesie n*os*tre canonicis et alijs pred*icti*s post d*icta*s
refectiones. et potaci*one*s gr*ati*a recreaci*on*is modeste vt decet cl*er*icis in canticis   5
et alijs solatijs honestis in aula moram facere/ necno*n* poemata ac historias et
cetera huius generis literata ocia inter se excercere, conferre, legere et enarrare/.
…

1546–7   10
Merton College Register   MCR: 1.2
f 299
…

® Satrapar*um*
adventus

Pri*m*o die Ianuarij accesseru*n*t ad collegiu*m* satrapæ [villæ] ⌜civi*tatis*⌝ oxon*iæ*
ad c*an*tandu*m* canticu*m* in aula q*u*o finito ex mera ben*e*volen*ti*a socioru*m* dati 15
su*n*t eijs sex solidi cu*m* octo denarijs & grato a*n*imo acceperu*n*t et gratias
age*n*tes recesseru*n*t
…

St Martin Churchwardens' Accounts   ORO: PAR 207/4/F1/1, item 9   20
mb [1]*   *(25 November–25 November)* *(Receipts)*
…

Item for hoktyde Ale Above All Charges	xiij s. viij d.
Item for Whytsontyde Ale on the supper nyght	xx s. ij d.

…   25

(Payments)

Item p*ay*de to A mynstrell At wytsontyd	iiij s. vj d.
Item to a mynstrell on the Shotyng daye	xij d.
Item for A quarturne of Ale	iij s. 30
Item for brede	ij s. viij d.

…

St Michael at the North Gate Churchwardens' Accounts
ORO: PAR 211/4/F1/2, item 121   35
single mb *(12 March 1546/7–12 March 1547/8)* *(Receipts)*
…

Item receyuede for the hoke ale	xj s.

4/ ignis/: *virgule corrected from comma*   24, 28/ Whytsontyde, wytsontyd: *29 May–4 June 1547*
23/ hoktyde: *18–19 April 1547*   38/ hoke: *Hocktide was 18–19 April 1547*

Item Receyued for the wytsondaye ale   xix s. iiij d.

...

1547–8
Exeter College Rectors' Accounts   EC Arch: B.I.16   5
mb 1   *(17 December–24 March)*
...
...Item vj s. viij d. sol*utis* p*ro* expe*n*sis co*m*mædiæ publice p*er*agedæ...
...

10

Magdalen College Libri Computi   MC Arch: LCE/5
f 63v   *(External payments)*
...
Solut*um* p*ro* candelis insumptis tempore tragediaru*m* et fac*ibus*   xix s. viij d.
...   15
Solut*um* pro merenda socioru*m* ante tragedias   x s.
...

1549–50
Magdalen College Libri Computi   MC Arch: LCE/5   20
f 90v   *(External payments)*
...
Solut*um* tympanistæ tempore natalis d*om*ini   iiij s. viij d.
...

25

Merton College Register   MCR: 1.2
f 302v
...

°Satrapæ civitat*is*   Primo die Ianuarij accesseru*n*t ad collegiu*m* satrapæ civitat*is* oxon*iæ* ad
oxon*iæ*°   ca*n*tandu*m* vnu*m* canticu*m* q*uo* finito ex mera ben*e*volentia daba*n*tur eijs sex   30
solidi cu*m* octo denarijs grato a*n*imo accepteru*n*t & gratias age*n*tes recesseru*n*t

c 1550
Christ Church College Foundation Statutes   ChCh Arch: D.P.vi.b.1
f 55*   *(Chapter 35) (On the disposition of bedrooms)*   35
...
Statuimus, ordinamus, et volum*us* vt vnusquisq*ue* Ecclesiæ n*ost*ræ in suo
cubiculo honestè se gerat, et modestè tàm cum suo concubiculario, quàm

Collation with ChCh Arch: D.P.vi.b.1 *(A)* f 138v, *(B)* ff 110–11, and *(C)* ff 155–5v:
37 n*ost*ræ] *A omits*

1/ wytsondaye: *29 May 1547*   8/ peragedæ: *for* peragendæ; *abbreviation mark missing*

cum alijs vicinis, vtq*ue* nullum quouis tempore à somno quiete, aut studio
impediat per immoderatos clamores, risus, cantica strepitus saltationes
musicorum instrumentorum pulsationes./ Sed sj aliquando ante ignem aut alibj
animj relaxandj causa cum alijs libeat conversarj, producatur tempus cum
moderato silentio, in his quæ ad virtutem, et doctrinam attinent, neq*ue* in his   5
fient serotinæ co*m*messationes aut potac*io*nes, sed temperatæ, et salubres…

…

f 60*   *(Chapter 53)*

…   10

De mora non trahenda post refectiones:.

Statuimus et volumus vt singulis diebus post prandium et cænam persoluta
Deo gratia*rum* actione, Canonici omnes et singulj ecclesiæ no*str*æ cuiuscumq*ue*
gradus extiterint sine vllo interuallo ex aula recedant; nisi quando vel consilia   15
vel alia ardua Ecclesiæ negotia im*m*ediatè debeant tractarj, vel lectiones,
disputationes, aut Biblij expositiones continuò sequa*n*tur. Quibus etiam
absolutis statim decedant, vel quando in festis solennioribus ad solatium
omnium habitantiu*m* ibidèm constratur ignis. Tunc permittimus ecclesiæ
Canonicis, et alijs prædictis post dictas refectiones et potationes gra*ti*â   20
recreationis modestè, vt decet Ecclesiasticos canticis, et alijs solatijs honestis
in aula moram facere; necno*n* poemata et historias et cætera huius ge*n*eris
*litte*raria ocia inter se exercere conferre, legere et enarrare; Porro vt nullus
pateat malefaciendj locus Decano et Capitulo authoritatem ordinationes et
decreta co*n*dendj in Ecclesia no*str*a no*n* sine pænis violanda tradendj, modò   25
his no*str*is statutjs non reluctentur.

…

Collation continued: 4 causa] gr*acia A*   5 his quæ] his [fiant] que *A*   6 fient]
fiant *A*   6 commessationes] concessaciones *A*   11 De … refectiones] *chapter numbered*
53 *in left margin of B*   11 trahenda post] trahenda in aula post *BC*   13 prandium]
prandu*m C*   15 ex aula] ex aula no*str*a *BC*   16 vel alia ardua] vel alia vel alia ar *C*
17 Biblij] bibliæ *B;* bibli*æ C*   19 habitantiu*m*] inhabitantiu*m BC*   19 constratur]
construatur *B;* construitur *C*   19 ecclesiæ] ecclesiæ no*str*æ *B;* ecclesi*æ* no*str*æ *C*
21 recreationis modestè] refectionis modest*æ C*   21 Ecclesiasticos] clericos *BC*
21 canticis] in canticis *B;* in Canticis *C*   24 authoritatem] authoritatem dam*us B;*
authoritatem damus *C*   25 in Ecclesia no*str*a] et ecclesi*æ* no*str*æ *C*   25 modò]
mode *B;* modo ne *C*   26 his] hisce *BC*   26 non reluctentur] reluctentur *C*

19/ constratur: *for* construatur
24/ authoritatem: *for* authoritatem damus

1550–1
Exeter College Rectors' Accounts   EC Arch: B.I.16
mb 1*   (c 25 December–7 April)
…

…Item de v s. j d. sol*utis* dolye pingenti ea quib*us* opus erat agendis   5
comædijs: … Item de xviij s. vij d. sol*utis* p*ro* reparationib*us* in domo
lord*es* et p*ro* impens*is* quæ fiebant in peragendis comædijs…
…

Magdalen College Libri Computi   MC Arch: LCE/5   10
f 99v*   (Hall costs)
…

Solut*um* 17 Ianuarij thomæ peckouer pro opera 5. dierum
circa scenam dietim viij d.   iij s. iiij d.
Solut*um* gualtero oven laboranti per ide*m* temp*us* dietim vj d.   ij s. vj d. 15
Solut*um* Roberto pro opera triu*m* dieru*m* circa idem   ij s.
…

Merton College Register   MCR: 1.2
f 305v   20
…

Primo die Ianuarij accesseru*n*t ad collegiu*m* satrapæ civitat*is* oxoni*æ* ad
cantandu*m* canticum quo finito daba*n*tur eijs ex mera benevolentia sex
solidi & octo denarij pro quibus imme*n*sas gratias egeru*n*t & recesseru*n*t
…   25

1551–2
Magdalen College Libri Computi   MC Arch: LCE/5
f 125*   (Hall costs)
…   30
Solut*um* Hix 23º Ianuarij extruenti proscenium p*er* tres
dies cu*m* d*imidio* et p*er* vna*m* nocte*m*   iij s.
Solut*um* pro duabus duodenis lichni ix viij p*ro* q*uo*dlibet
duodena   xix s. iiij d.
Solut*um* pro octo duodenis [cardela] candelaru*m*   x s. 35
Solut*um* 23º Ianuarij Hamonde et filio laborantib*us* p*er*
sex dies in extrue*n*do proscenio xiiij d. pro singulo die   vij s.
…

33/ quodlibet: *for* qualibet

f 131v*   *(External payments)*

Billa

...

Solutum pro epulis consumptis in socios post exactas
comedias vt patet per billam   xlij s. vj d.

...   5

f 132v

...

Solutum timpanistæ in natalitijs   iiij s. viij d.

...   10

1552–3
Magdalen College Libri Computi   MC Arch: LCE/5
f 148v   *(Hall costs)*

...   15

Solutum pro funibus ad vsum agentium tragædias   xiiij d.
Solutum Magistro taynter pro funiculo ad eadem spectante   vj d.
Solutum 28 Ianuarij Wilmot pro opera sua actoribus præstita   iij d.

f 157v*   *(Store costs)*   20

...

Solutum eodem tempore Sutton wilmot erigentibus reponentibus
tabulas et diruentibus scenam per 3. dies   iij s.

...

                                                                                    25

f 159   *(Costs of internal repairs)*

...

Solutum 21 Ianuarij Roberto hammon et filio fabricantibus
scænam quadranti arbores. facienti repositoria in coquina
per 6. dies   vij s. 30

...

Solutum roberto hickes cooperanti cum hammon per
totidem dies   iiij s.
Solutum 28 Ianuarij roberto hammon pro opera sua diruendi
scenam. quadranti arbores per quatuor dies 14 d. dietim   iiij s. viij d. 35

...

Solutum 4º marcij roberto hammon et filio fabricato
mensam et alia in ludo musicali per quatuor dies   iiij s. viij d.

...

16/ funibus: *4 minims in* MS   22/ Sutton wilmot: et *or* & *omitted*
22/ eodem tempore: *28 January 1552/3*   37/ fabricato: *for* fabricantibus

f 160v   *(External payments)*

...

billa   Solut*um* pro epulis insumptis in socios et ceteros post exactas
comoedias vt p*atet* per billam   xxviij s. vj d.

...   5

New College Bursars' Accounts   NC Arch: 7522
mb 7   *(Internal costs)*

...So*lutum* p*ro* purgandis aedib*us* post ludos. iiij d....   10

...

1553–4
Magdalen College Draft Libri Computi   MC Arch: LCD/1
f 43*   15

...

[Solut*um* tibicinis p*ro* 14 dieb*us* in ferijs natalicijs xxvj ⟨...⟩]

...

f 56v   *(Hall costs)*   20

...

Solut*um* Hixe ∧⌈3o februarij⌉ op*eran*ti circa theatru*m* p*er*
sex dies dietim 8 d.   iiij s.
Solut*um* eode*m* tempore hammon cu*m* duobus filijs
operantibus per sex dies circa theatru*m* dietim 15 d.   [7 s. 6] vij s. vj d. 25

...

f 60   *(External payments)*

...

Sol*utum* 9o februarij d*omino* day p*ro* tibicinis tempore   30
natalis d*omi*ni   iiij s.

...

billa   Solut*um* 30 Ianuarij in adventu eiusde*m* ad tragedias
∧⌈per duas noctes⌉ per billas   xlij s. viij d. ob.

billa   Solut*um* p*ro* epulis datis socijs post exactas tragedias   35
p*er* billa*m*   x s. ix d.

...

17/ ⟨...⟩: *MS torn*
33/ eiusdem: *Lord Maltravers*

St Martin Churchwardens' Accounts   ORO: PAR 207/4/F1/1, item 22
single mb*   *(25 November–25 November) (Receipts)*

...

Item for hocketyde Ale	xxv s. viij d.
Item for gyuen to the Churche before Whytsontyde	
⌈by diuers of the paryssheners⌉	xviij s. x d.
Item made At Whytsontyde Wyth the supper nyght	lv s. ij d. ob.

...

St Mary the Virgin Churchwardens' Accounts   ORO: PAR 209/4/F1/1
mb [1]*   *(Rendered 3 January 1554/5) (Receipts)*

...

Item at Hoc tyde	xxxj s. vij d. ob.

...

1554–5
Christ Church Chapter Book   ChCh Arch: D&C.i.b.2
p 93*   *(12 December)*

> A decree made by the Dean and Chapiter the xij^th dey of December
>   in the first & seconde yere of the Reigne of our Soueran Lord
>   and Lady Philipp and Mary by the grace of God Kyng &
>   Quene of Englande ffraunce Naples Ierusalem & Irelande &c.

It ys agreed the xij^th day of december in ∧⌈the⌉ first & second yere of owr said
Soueran Lorde and Lady, and decreed by the said Dean and Chapiter, that
ther shalbe nomore allowed yerely towarde the Charges of the Pastyme in
Christmas and the Plays, of the Costes of the Churche but for two comedies
xx s. a pece, And for two tragedies xl s. a playe./ the summe wherof to be in
the wholle syx poundes. Of the which fowre playes, ther shalbe a comedy
in Latyn And a comedy in greke: And a tragedy in latyn and a tragedy in
greke./ *(blank)* And yf ther be one, ij, or but thre plays playd of the stage
then ther shall be allowed ratably accordyng to the proportio⟨.⟩ above
mentioned of comedies and tragedies and nomore.

Item towardes the Lordes other charges also xiij s. iiij d. yerely to be allowed
and nomore./

                    Summa totalis vj li. xiij s. iiij d.

...

4, 13/ hocketyde, Hoc tyde: *2–3 April 1554*
5, 7/ Whytsontyde: *13–19 May 1554*

Magdalen College Libri Computi   MC Arch: LCE/5
f 187v   *(External payments)*

...

Solut*um* tibicinis in ferijs natalitijs   iiij s. viij d.

...   5

Ponet, Apologie (1555)   STC: 20175
pp ix–x*

...

...Thy boke hath betrayed the Martin/ for thy fondnes/ was not knowen   10
befor it came abrode/ but assone as that shewed it self in mens hands/ they
might easely perceaue/ I that in playnge the Christmas lords minion in new
colledge in Oxford/ in thy fooles coat thow diddest learne thy boldnes/ and
lost thy witt/ and began to put of all shame and to put on all impudencye....

...   15

Martin used yerely to play the fole at Christmas in neuu Colledge in Oxford.

Audited Corporation Accounts   OCA: P.5.1
f 6   *(Chamberlains' payments)*

...

Item payed to the kyng*es* Mynstrell*es*   v s.   20

...

St Martin Churchwardens' Accounts   ORO: PAR 207/4/F1/1, item 25
single mb   *(25 November–25 November) (Receipts)*

...   25

Item at hoktyde aboue all chargys clerelye   xxj s. j d.
Item At Whytsontyd aboue all chargys clerely   l s. v d.

...

1555–6   30
St Michael at the North Gate Churchwardens' Accounts
ORO: PAR 211/4/F1/2, item 126
single mb   *(12 March 1555/6–12 March 1556/7) (Receipts)*

...

Item for Whytson ale   xxv s.   35
Item [f] receyued at hocktyde   xiiij s.

...

26/ hoktyde: *22–3 April 1555*
27/ Whytsontyd: *2–8 June 1555*
35/ Whytson: *Whitsuntide was 24–30 May 1556*
36/ hocktyde: *13–14 April 1556*

1556–7
Magdalen College Draft Libri Computi MC Arch: LCD/1
f 130v *(Hall costs)*

...

Solut*um* 5 februarii hixe opera*n*ti circa theatru*m per* vnu*m* diem et d*imidium*	xij d.	5
Solut*um* eodem tempore ham*m*on opera*n*ti *per* diei dimid*ium*	iiij d.	
°Solut*um pro* semiduodena facu*m*	ij s. iiij d.	
Solut*um pro* fune te*m*pore tragediaru*m*	xij d.°	

...

f 134v *(External expenses)*

...

Solut*um* tibicinis tempore natalis d*om*ini	iiij s.	

...

Cardinal Pole's Statutes Bodl.: MS. Top.Oxon b.5
f 85 *(6 November) (Chapter 17)*

...

Circa aut*em* oppidanos. An sint mulieres inhonestæ Item ludi aleatorij 20
gladiatorij vel saltatorij:/.
An sint qui recipiant Scholares in tabernas, vel domos privatas et ad
Commessationes absq*ue* licentia vel Custodis Collegij, vel Aulæ Præpositi ./.

...

25

Privy Councillors' Letter to the Master of the Revels
Surrey History Centre: LM/41/8
f [1]* *(19 December)*

After our most harty Commend⟨.⟩⌈a⌉tyons, wheras the fellos and scholars of 30
the newe College y*n* Oxford entende thys Chrystmas to sett foorthe a learnyd
Tragedye to the glorie of god and increase of learnyng & for the moore decent
settynge foorth of the same have made sute hyther to boroe out of the Revells
certayne sutes of apparell as be heare vndernethe mentyoned, these be hartyly
to requyre youe the moore at ye contemplatyon of these oure *let*tres to satisfie 35
ye saide felloes and scholars of their so honest a requeste puttynge y*n* lawfull
and sufficiente sureties for ye same to be redelyveryd wyth conuenient spede.
And so fare ye most hartyly well. ffrom the Courte ye xix^th of December.

Your lovyng ffrendes.

(signed) Robert Roches*t*er   Io*h*n Bourne 40
         ffrauncys Englefyld

31/ the newe College: *Trinity College (?)*   35/ satisfie: *first* s *written over* b

Thre sut*es* of Apparell ffor Thre kyng*es*
A garment to were vppon harneyes
two sutes of Apparell ffor two duk*es*
ffor sixe Cowncelers .vj garment*es* ffurnyshed
ffor one quyne one sute, & thre gentylwomen furnyshed   5
ffor one yonge prynce one sute
syxe plumes or more yf you can
one ffayre mask v*iz* syxe maskers & ffowre torche berers ffurnyshid

Audited Corporation Accounts   OCA: P.5.1   10
f 14v   *(Chamberlains' payments)*
...

Item [for] geven to the quenes Mynstrells for a rewarde at
mayster mayres commandemente   iij s. iiij d.
...   15

f 15*
...

Item for a reward to the quenes players yn the Guyldhall   vj s. viij d.
Item for there drynkynge   ij s. v d. 20
...

Item to the Erle of Oxford hys playres   vj s. viij d.
...

St Michael at the North Gate Churchwardens' Accounts   25
ORO: PAR 211/4/F1/2, item 127
mb [1]   *(12 March 1556/7–12 March 1557/8)* *(Receipts)*
...

Item Recevyd at hocktyde   vij s. v d.
Item Recevyd for wytsune alle   iiij s. vj d. 30
...

St Peter le Bailey Churchwardens' Accounts   ORO: PAR 214/4/F1/29
sheet [1]*   *(13 December–12 December) (Receipts)*
...   35
Item receyuyd for hocke ayle   x s. iij d.
...

Item Res*eived* for a w*h*itson ayle all charg*es* payd   xxiij s. j d.
...

29*l* hocktyde: *26–7 April 1557*
30, 38*l* wytsune, whitson: *Whitsuntide was 6–12 June 1557*
36*l* hocke: *Hocktide was 26–7 April 1557*

1557–8
Magdalen College Libri Computi   MC Arch: LCE/5
f 203v   *(Chapel costs)*

...

Solutu*m* [⌈in⌉] die Iouis in cæna domini .12. Symphonistis   xij d. 5

...

f 205   *(Hall costs)*

...

Solut*um* *pro* fune occupato circa theatru*m*   xij d. 10

...

f 213   *(External payments)*

...

Solut*um* Tibicin' tempore natalis domini   iiij s. viij d. 15

...

Magdalen College Draft Libri Computi   MC Arch: LCD/1
f 147   *(Hall costs)*

...   20

Solutu*m* ouen & famulo .9. Ianu*arij* opera*ntibus* circa
theatru*m* alteri dietim x. d. alteri .8. d. p*er* tres dies   iiij s. vj d.

...

St Martin Churchwardens' Accounts   ORO: PAR 207/4/F1/1, item 28   25
single mb*   *(25 November–25 November)* *(Receipts)*

...

Item made at hoctyde clere   xxiiij s. iij d.

...

Item made at Whytsontyde clere to the churche   v li. ix d. 30

...

St Michael at the North Gate Churchwardens' Accounts
ORO: PAR 211/4/F1/2, item 129
single mb   *(12 March 1557/8–12 March 1558/9)* *(Receipts)*   35

...

Item made at whytson Ale clere above all charg*es*   xviij s.
Item made at hoctyde   xv s.

...

5/ die Iouis in cæna domini: *12 April 1558*   30/ Whytsontyde: *29 May–4 June 1558*
28, 38/ hoctyde: *18–19 April 1558*   37/ whytson: *Whitsuntide was 29 May–4 June 1558*

1558–9
Merton College Register MCR: 1.2
f 320v

Datu*m* satrapis
civitat*is* oxon*iæ*
ex mera et
spo*n*tanea
liberalitate

Primo die Ianuarij *id est* die circu*m*cisionis accesseru*n*t ad collegiu*m* satrapæ 5
ciuitat*is* oxon*iæ* ad ca*n*tandu*m* vnu*m* ca*n*ticum, quod q*u*ide*m* suum pensu*m*
min*us* p*er*solvebat, ne*c* tame*n* sine iusta quærela, na*m* q*u*i eorum cecinisset
s*u*bito morbo correptus fuit vt aieba*n*t vno ore o*m*nes, quapropt*er* eijs
ignosce*n*du*m* duxim*us* ac nihilomin*us* ex mera benevole*n*tia dedim*us* sex
sol*i*dos et octo denarios, grato a*n*i*m*o accepem*n*t et gra*t*ias agentes recesseru*n*t. 10
...

The Queen's College Long Roll QC Arch: 2P146
single mb *(7 July–7 July) (External expenses)*
... 15
...Ite*m* tibicinib*us* xvj d....
...

St Martin Churchwardens' Accounts ORO: PAR 207/4/F1/1, item 30
single mb *(25 November–25 November) (Receipts)* 20
...

Item made at hocktyde Clere	xxvj s. ij d. ob.
Item made at whytsontyde Clere to the churche	iij li. x s. vij d.

...

25

c **1559**
AC *Notes on a Trinity College Bursar's Book*
Warton: *History of English Poetry*, vol 2
p 380

30

...In an audit-book of Trinity college in Oxford, I think for the year 1559,
I find the following disbursements relating to this subject. 'Pro apparatu in
comoedia Andriæ, vii li. ix s. iv d. Pro prandio Principis Natalicii eodem
tempore, xiii s. ix d. Pro refectione præfectorum et doctorum magis illustrium
cum Bursariis prandentium tempore comoediæ, iv li. vii d.' That is, For 35
dresses and scenes in acting Terence's Andria, for the dinner of the Christmas
Prince, and for the entertainment of the heads of the colleges and the most
eminent doctors dining with the bursars or treasurers, at the time of acting
the comedy, twelve pounds, three shillings, and eight pence....

22/ hocktyde: *3–4 April 1559*
23/ whytsontyde: *14–20 May 1559*

1559-60
Magdalen College Libri Computi   MC Arch: LCE/6
f 5*   *(Hall costs)*

...

Solutum ouen et famulo operantibus circa theatrum 9o   5
februarij per vndecim dies dietim xix d.   xvij s. vj d.

°et sic plurima
circa theatrum° Solutum webster circa idem occupato per tres dies dietim ix d.   ij s. iiij d.
Solutum Cryspe circa idem versato per idem tempus   ij s. iiij d.
Solutum wryghte et Cutberde ferentibus multa ad idem
theatrum per quinque dies dietim xiiij d.   v s. x d. 10
Solutum welles et heywarde serrantibus varia pro eodem
theatro per quatuor dies dietim xx d.   vj s. viij d.
Solutum Iohanni willows et henrico heywode 26o Ianuarij
pro eodem theatro per tres dies cum dimidio serrantibus
varia dietim xx d.   v s. x d. 15
Solutum eodem tempore pro duabus duodenis facum   viij s.
Solutum alkot et welles remouentibus theatrum   x d.
Solutum hix reparanti scanna et mensas post æditas commedias   viij d.

...

                                                                              20

f 8*   *(Internal repairs)*

...

Solutum 28 Ianuarij Ouen et famulo per quinque dies et
dimidium circa fenestram magistri Atkinson et in aula
theatrum versatis dietim xix d.   viij s. viij d. 25

...

f 8v*   *(External payments)*

...

+   Solutum domino presidi pro expensis in filios dominorum   30
tempore spectaculorum   liij s. iiij d.

...

Solutum tibicinibus tempore natalis domini   iiij s.

...

                                                                              35

Magdalen College Draft Libri Computi   MC Arch: LCD/1
f 183

...

°Solutum° dedimus tibicinibus in partem Solutionis
maioris summæ   xiij s. iiij d. 40

...

25/ theatrum: *for* circa theatrum *(?)*

Merton College Register   MCR: 1.2
f 322v

…

Primo Ianuarij accesserunt satrapæ ciuitatis oxoniæ ad cantandum canticum
quo peracto ex mera benevolentia dedimus eis sex solidos et octo denarios.   5

…

Audited Corporation Accounts   OCA: P.5.1
f 26*   *(Chamberlains' payments)*

…   10

Item geven to my lorde Roberte Dudleys players   vj s. viij d.
Item bestowed vpon the said players at mr Cogans house   vj s. iiij d.

…

St Mary Magdalen Churchwardens' Accounts   ORO: PAR 208/4/F1/2   15
single mb   *(Rendered 11 May 1561) (Receipts)*

…

Item Received and made of the churche ale att
wytsontyde declaro   xlv s. iij d. qua.

…   20

St Mary the Virgin Churchwardens' Accounts   ORO: PAR 209/4/F1/2
single mb* *(Receipts)*

…

Item recevyd at Hoctyde clere althinges discharged   xiij s. vij d. 25

…

1560-1
Magdalen College Libri Computi   MC Arch: LCE/6
f 17*   *(Hall costs)*   30

…

xx   Solutum Ioyner pictori, depingenti nomina heræsium in
spectaculo, quod choristarum moderator ædidit   iij s. iiij d.

…

                                                                               35

f 21   *(External expenses)*

…

x   Solutum Tibicinibus tempore natalis domini   iiij s.

…

19/ wytsontyde: *2–8 June 1560*
25/ Hoctyde: *22–3 April 1560*

Audited Corporation Accounts   OCA: P.5.1
f 29v   *(Chamberlains' payments)*

...

Item geven to huchins the bereward   iij s. iij d.

...   5

f 30*   *(Reparations)*

...

Item payed to Quenes Iester   ij s.

...   10

Item to the Quenes bereward   vj s. viij d.
Item spent vppon hym   x d.

...

St Mary Magdalen Churchwardens' Accounts   ORO: PAR 208/4/F1/3   15
mb [1]   *(Rendered 3 May 1562) (Payments)*

ffyrst payde to the mynstrylls att wyttsontyde last   iiij d.

...

                                                                                      20

St Michael at the North Gate Churchwardens' Accounts
ORO: PAR 211/4/F1/2, item 130
single mb   *(12 March 1560/1–12 March 1561/2) (Receipts)*

...

Item recevyd for the hock Ale   ix s. x d. ob. qua. 25

...

St Peter le Bailey Churchwardens' Accounts   ORO: PAR 214/4/F1/31
single sheet*   *(15 December–14 December) (Receipts)*

...   30

Item for Hoc ale   x s.
Item for Whitsontyde ale   xvj s. viij d.

...

1561–2   35
Magdalen College Libri Computi   MC Arch: LCE/6
f 35v*   *(Hall costs)*

...

Solutum vltimo Ianuarij Squiar et filio serrantibus varia pro
theatro per quinque dies cum dimidio dietim xx d.   viij s. iiij d. 40

18, 32/ wyttsontyde last, Whitsontyde: *25–31 May 1561*   40/ viij s. iiij d.: *for* ix s. ij d. *(?)*
25, 31/ hock, Hoc: *Hocktide was 14–15 April 1561*

Solutum eodem tempore Ouen et famulo conficientibus varia ad
spectacula ædenda per .6. dies dietim xviij d.   ix s.
Solutum 7º februarij Squiar et filio serrantibus varia
pro theatro per 4ᵒʳ dies dietim xx d.   vj s. viij d.
Solutum 8º februarij Ouen et famulo erigentibus theatrum et   5
conficientibus varia pro spectaculis per 5ᵉ dies dietim xviij d.   vij s. vj d.
Solutum eodem tempore wryxon et white collaborantibus per
totidem dies dietim xviij d.   vij s. vj d.
Solutum Showsmythe emendanti vitreas fenestras ex pacto   vj s. viij d.
Solutum eidem in regardo pro vitro in spectaculis fracto   iij s. iiij d. 10
Solutum pro candelis spectaculorum tempore insumptis   vj s. viij d.

...

f 40   (External payments)

...   15

Solutum tibicinibus tempore natalis domini   iiij s.

...

billa   Solutum pro epulis datis Magistro Winchecombe et alijs
tempore spectaculorum vt patet per billam   xj s. x d.

...   20

Magdalen College Draft Libri Computi   MC Arch: LCD/1
f 222   (6 February)

...

°Solutum° dedimus mutuo domino Brasbridge 6º februarij   25
⌈pro coma muliebri iij s.⌉   iij li. x s.

...

f 223v

...   30

Solutum pro 2ᵃᵇᵘˢ duodenis facum ⌈ad spectaculo præbenda⌉   viij s.

...

Merton College Register   MCR: 1.2
f 326   35

liberalitas
collegij in
satrapas villæ
oxoniæ

21º octobris magister Iones satraparum villæ oxoniæ facile princeps recepit de
magistro gifford burssario loco magistri Attwood qui 19. eiusdem [socius]
mensis socius diutius esse sua sponte recusavit, vj s. et vj d. ob., idque ex
consensu domini custodis et seniorum quam summam se suosque nullo iure,   40
sed ex mera collegij liberalitate habere non solum fatebatur dictus Iones verum

31/ spectaculo: *for* spectacula

etia*m* profitebatur *p*resentibus marshall vic*ecustode* et gifford burs*ario*
…

f 326v

…

Satrapæ hoc
a*nno* nos no*n*
viseru*nt*

In die circu*m*cisionis, satrapæ villæ oxoni*æ* huc ad nos a pra*n*dio no*n* veneru*nt*
omni*n*o, quod miru*m* videri possit, cu*m* ante hac quæ collegiu*m* n*ostru*m in
illos spo*n*te & vltro co*n*tulerit, [aui] auidissime captare solebant

…

Chancellor's Court Inventories   OUA: Hyp/B/10
f [1]   *(17 October)* *(Inventory of Ralph Allen of Balliol College)*

…

It*em* a gytterne the brydge beyng off

…

Letter of John Foxe to Laurence Humphrey   BL: MS Harleian 416
f [1v]*   *(January?)*

Qui*n* neq*ue* minus ⌈etia*m*⌉ reip*ublicæ* [etiam] literariæ [⌈publica⌉] causa
gratula*n*dum existimo, ⌈no*n* minima sane pars specta⟨.⟩⌉ ad qua*m* [potissi⟨…⟩
spectat], ⌈huius⌉ quicquid ex hac tua dignitate spera*n*dum est lucri et vtilitatis.
⌈Cæteru*m*⌉ Dum haec ad ₍ₐ₎⌈te⌉ scriberem, pluraq*ue* ⌈vellem⌉ [cogitare*m*], [de
eadem] in hac [grt] gratula*n*di mate⟨…⟩ ⟨…⟩ latissimo, lætissimoq*ue* scribe*n*di
campo versatus, commodu*m* super uenit Robertus noster Edouardi tui
famulus [, Iuuenis] que*m* ut semper ₍ₐ₎⌈ego⌉ ob rara*m* pietatis modestiæq*ue*
indolem Basiliæ olim, ut scis adamaui: it⟨.⟩ [et] ⌈nu*n*c⌉ dignu*m* puto, cui et
tu pro tua hac vberiori ⌈facultate⌉ [fortuna] benefacias. Post eu*m* [super]
sequutæ et tuæ literæ [mihi per M*agistrum* Goodallum redditæ] veteris
laurentij mei, no*n* manum solum, sed et totum pectoris candorem referent⟨..⟩
Quibus ego literis ⌈ut aliquid responde*am* [quonia*m* omni*n*o tacere no*n* licet]⌉
[etsi no*n* habea*m* in præsentia quo satisfacia*m*, attame*n*] quonia*m* tacere no*n*
siu*er*it officiu*m*. ⌈De spectaculo quod scribis⌉ [De] Christ*us* triumphantes
⌈eis⌉ [quod scribis constituisse] ⌈si ita decreueru*n*t⌉ Magdalenenses, precor ut
bene ⌈illis⌉ vertat Christus, omniu*m* bonaru*m* actionu*m* choragus. [Hoc ⌈Id
uero⌉ unu*m* miro arbitror, Hoc vnu*m* scio, Quu*m* aute*m* tot] veru*m* quu*m*

p 105, l.37–p 106, l.1/ 21º … bursario: *entry written in blank space at top margin of page*
20/ literariæ: *second* r *altered from* æ
29/ M*agistrum* Goodallum: *bursar of Magdalen College in 1562*
33/ Christ*us*: *corrected from* Christo
33/ triumphantes: *for* triumphans
36/ Quu*m*: Q *corrected from* q

tot si*n*t in manib*us* com*æ*diæ latinæ, græcæ, sacræ et prophanæ, in quib*us* tanto
[⌈potera*n*t in illis⌉ illis vtiliore*m* opera*m* ⌈nauare⌉ possent insumere,] miror
[quu*m* hac ad age*n*du*m* proponere.] ∧⌈eoru*m* in huius defensibus rationem⌉
potera*n*t illi in alijs vtiliore*m* fortasse opera*m* nauare. [Cæteru*m*] Sed qua*n*do
sic ipsis visu*m*   5
[Certe si q*uae* accommoda ⌈sit⌉ esset ad pietate*m* materia,] Mihi etsi spectatori
esse [pr] no*n* licet per negotia, ⌈non deero⌉ [ero] tame*n* inter eos qui [pl]
præclaris Magdalene*n*sium conatibus [lube] semper applaudu*n*t lube*n*ter.
Interim de comitate tua, qui ta*m* ama*n*ter me ⌈istuc⌉ inuitas[q*ue*], ingentes
habeo gratias. De pauli conuersione inijcienda, no*n* du*m* certum habeo quid   10
pollicear, [aut quidares] quidue respo*n*deam. Petit eni*m* ille cui negare no*n*
licet. Sic aut*em* distineor [reb*us* quib*us*dam] impræsentia negotijs, ut [omn*ium*]
sup*ra* vacet etsi velim. Spero tame*n* ⌈ante paucos dies⌉ [p breui] ⌈me⌉ [me]
fusius [de] de hoc negotio ad te scripturu*m* permite*n*te Christo triu*m*phatore
nostro.   15

Audited Corporation Accounts   OCA: P.5.1
f 33*   *(Chamberlains' payments)*

...

Item payd to Dorden the trumpeter when he came home   20
w*i*th m*aste*r mayre   iij s. iiij d.

...

Item geven to my of warwykes players when they playd in
the guyld hall theight day of Iune   vj s. viij d.
Item spent vpon them the same tyme   xvj d. 25

...

Item payd to my Lord Rober*tes* players   vj s. viij d.

...

f 33v*   *(Reparations)*   30

...

Item payd to wilson the mynstrell for playeng & singyng at
dyner on thelleccion day   iiij s.

...

3/ eoru*m* ... rationem: *some or all of this may have been intended for cancellation*
3/ defensibus: *written over another word now illegible*
4/ in: *i corrected from* a
10/ quid: *corrected from* quod
12/ [omn*ium*]: *probably intended to be replaced by* non (?)
23/ my of: *for* my lord of
33/ thelleccion day: *14 September 1562*

St Mary Magdalen Churchwardens' Accounts   ORO: PAR 208/4/F1/3
mb [1]   *(Rendered 3 May)* *(Receipts)*

...

Item Reseived for hock mony   ij s. x d. ob.

...   5

Item Reseived for an olde saye coot of grene wyche was
made for the lord for wettsontyd   xij d.

...

1562–3   10
Magdalen College Libri Computi   MC Arch: LCE/6
f 59v   *(External payments)*

...

Solutum Tibicinibus tempore natiuitatis Christi   iiij s.

...   15

Audited Corporation Accounts   OCA: P.5.1
f 38*   *(Chamberlains' payments)*

...

Item paid for a Rewarde to ye quenes berward vpon   20
Sainte tedwardes daye   v s.

...

Item payd for a reward to the quenes gester the thursday
before St Andrews day   ij s.

...   25

ff 39v–40*   *(Mayor's dinner expenses)*

...

Inprimis payd for xxij dosen of bred   xxij s.
Item payd for v quaerters of ale   xxiiij s. iiij d. 30
Item for a kylderkyn of beere   iiij s. iiij d.
Item for a quarter of xvj   ij s. viiij d.
Item for powder beef   xxvj s.
Item for Rostinge beef   xxvj s. viij d.
Item for vj geese   vj s. 35
Item for xv pygges   xv s.
Item for sewett   viij s.
Item for veale   xvij s.
Item for xix capons   xix s.

4/ hock: *Hocktide was 6–7 April 1562*
21/ Sainte tedwardes daye: *probably the Translation*
   of Edward the Confessor, 13 October 1562

23/ thursday: d *corrected over another letter*
23–4/ thursday ... day: *26 November 1562*

Item for xxxij copull of conys   xviij s. ⟨...⟩
Item for Mutton   ij s.
Item for butter   v s.
Item for egge*s*   iij s. iiij d.
Item for chese   viij d.   5
Item for peres   viij d.
Item for appell*es*   viij d.
Item for whyte sache   iij d.
Item for a lode of wood   v s. iiij d.
Item for faggott*es*   iij s. iiij d. | 10
Item payd for flower   vij s. iiij d.
Item payd for wyne   xviij s.
Item for Spyce   xxvj s. iij d.
Item for the laborers   vj s. vj d.
Item for feaskett*es*   viij d. 15
Item for two cokes   v s. iiij d.
Item to the mynstrells   ij s. vj d.
...

1563–4   20
Balliol College Register   BC Arch: First Latin Register
p 93

A note of diuerse customes by report vsed °1564°
...   25
8 It*em* on midsomear eve*n* seynt peters eve*n* magdalin eve*n* and Saynt Iames
eve*n* the M*aste*r and felowes wear wont by a laudabel custom to haue an
honest drinkinge & [good] fyne cak*es* and good ale and wear wo*n*t being then
together to sing som himpen or anthe*m*
...   30

The Queen's College Long Roll   QC Arch: 2P150
single mb   *(7 July–7 July)* *(External expenses)*
...
...Item tibicini vj d....   35
...

St Peter le Bailey Churchwardens' Accounts   ORO: PAR 214/4/F1/32
single sheet*   *(12 December–10 December)* *(Receipts)*
...   40
Item for the hoc Ale   xx s.

4/ egge*s*: e *corrected over another letter*   41/ hoc: *Hocktide was 10–11 April 1564*

Item Receyued for the Whytson ⟨...⟩ Ale   xxxv s.

...

c 1564–74
Bunny, A Briefe Answer (1589)   STC: 4088   5
pp 151–3*

...

Isaac was but a
child with him,
when he was
fortie yeeres
old. Pagina 16.

...what time as Isaac went foorth to | meditate, as you alledge, you make him
then to bee but a childe: and if wee ioine your woordes togither, that there
stande but a little a sunder, a little childe. And this (we are sure) was no bodies   10.
els but onely your owne: because it is not in the former Booke, but onely in
this latter, of your owne trimming vp. But I feare it is you that was the child,
and not he: because the Scripture (in the next chapter after) doth plainely
witnesse, that he was at that time vpon fortie yeeres olde. Whence you shuld
haue this conceit of yours, I cannot tell. Howbeit hereby you make me to call   15
to remembrance a much like matter that was saide to bee doone in Oxfoord,
about the same time that you were there (if you bee the same that I heare that
you are:) or at least not so long before, but that a fresh report thereof might
very well reach vnto you. A certaine company of country plaiers came thither
to play: they made it knowne what they did meane; and, as the maner is, drew   20
in a companie soone vnto them. Among other thinges they had to deale with
the storie of Isaac: both of his sacrificing, when he was but a childe; and of his
marriage, when after he came to riper age. They were not so wel stored of
persons to furnish their partes, but that one boy must play Isaac, both in his
childhood, and manhood also: but as the boies own face serued their turne   25
for Isaacs childhood; so had they for him a faire long beard, to resemble his
manhood. But all the cunning was to hit the time when he should haue his
beard on, and when | he should not. What will you? there was no more but
right and wrong. When therefore hee came foorth as a childe to bee sacrificed,
hee had on his beard: and when after he was to be married, then as a child he   30
had it off, and onely his owne boyes face to shut vp the matter. But I hope
you were neuer so mad, as to take it thence....

...

1564–5   35
Magdalen College Libri Computi   MC Arch: LCE/6
f 97   (External payments)

...

Solutum tibicinibus tempore Natiuitatis Christi   iiij s.

...   40

1/ Whytson: *Whitsuntide was 21–7 May 1564*

Solut*um* Tibicinib*us* die pentecostes ex mandato vice*p*residis   xij d.
…

Trinity College Bursars' Books   TC Arch: I/A/1
f 66v   *(External expenses)*   5
…

Solut*um* p*ro* spectaculo edito in festo trinitatis sc*ilicet* quercu
[&] in damario posit*o*   vj s. vj d.
…

                                                                            10

Audited Corporation Accounts   OCA: P.5.1
f 43*   *(Chamberlains' payments)*
…

It*e*m paid to the Quenes bereward and Drynckynge w*i*th him   vij s. ij d.
…   15

ff 44v–5v*   *(Election dinner expenses)*
…

In primis paid to mr Sweatt for fyue quarters of ale and
A quarter of Syxtens   xx s. 20
Item paid to master Carpenter three kynderkyns of bere   x s.
Item paid to master Burnett for fouretene dossen of
[brea.] bread   xiiij s.
Item paid for Rostinge beffe & boyllinge beffe   lvj s. vj d. |
Item paid for foure neat*es* toung*es*   xvj d. 25
It*e*m paid for ix Legs of motton   iiij s. ij d.
It*e*m paid for veall   xij s. vj d.
Item paid for fyue pound of shwett   xj s. viij d.
Item paid for sixtene pyges   xviij s. ij d.
Item paid for fowre geesse   iij s. viij d. 30
Item paid for seven copell of Caprons   xij s. xj d.
It*e*m paid for eight cople of Checkyns   vj s. iiij d.
Item paid for [xix]ᴧ⌈xxix⌉ cople of Connyes   xvij s. vj d.
Item paid for a hundereth and a half of egs   iiij s. iiij d.
Item paid for fowretene pound of buttyre   iij s. ij d. ob. 35
Item paid for a dossen of pygeons   xij d.
Item paid for three bushells and half a peck of flowre   xj s. xj d.
Item paid for Spyce   xxxij s. iiij d. ob.
It*e*m paid to the keper of wodstoke parcke and to one
that fett the ven*i*son   iiij s. iiij d. 40

1/ die pentecostes: *10 June 1565*   7/ trinitatis: a *corrected from* is
7/ in festo trinitatis: *17 June 1565*

Item paid to the stewardes ffraunches dynner for wodd
and other necessaryes in the hall   iij s. iiij d.

Item paid for three quarters of coles   iij s. vj d.

Item paid to Thomas kyrby for a Lode of wodd and
charriadge of the same   v s. iiij d.   5

Item paid to burrnett for heatinge his oven   viij d.

Item paid for a Chese   ix d.

Item paid for peres and damsons   x d.

Item paid for a gallon and three quarters of Creame   ij s. xj d.

Item paid for a pecke of apples   iij d.   10

Item paid for a howpe for a powederinge covere   iiij d.

Item paid for a pecke of barley for Caprons   iij d.

Item paid for a pounde of candills   iij d.

Item paid to mr Spencer for seven gallons of gasscune
wyne and a gallon of Ceke   xj s. iiij d.   15

Item paid for a bushell of baye salt   ij s.

Item paid to Iohn Gylbert Coocke   iij s. |

Item paid to William Haukyns   iij s.

Item paid to Iohn Gylbert for the Lone of fowre dossen
of vessell   viij d.   20

Item paid to William Essex and hewe cooke   ij s. ij d.

Item paid to three tourne broches   xij d.

Item paid to William Thackame and his wyff   ij s. iiij d.

Item paid to Rychardson for healping in the kytchen   xviij d.

Item paid to three pore folckes that fett vessell and carryed   25
them agayne   viij d.

Item paid to a man and a boye that ⟨.⟩ealped in the Kytchen   viij d.

Item paid for flagons   viij d.

Item paid to my Lord of Wynsors Mynstrels   iij s. iij d.

               Summa   xiiij li. xiiij s. vij d.   30

...

St Martin Churchwardens' Accounts   ORO: PAR 207/4/F1/1, item 37
mb [1]   *(25 November–25 November)* *(Receipts)*

...   35

Item receaved at hocktyde clere   xxx s.

Item mad clere at Whitsontyde   v li. vj d.

...

14/ gasscune: *5 minims in MS*
36/ hocktyde: *30 April–1 May 1565*
37/ Whitsontyde: *10–16 June 1565*

St Mary Magdalen Churchwardens' Accounts   ORO: PAR 208/4/F1/6
single mb   *(Rendered 25 May) (Receipts)*

…

R*eceived* of the hoocke mony clere   x s.

…   5

St Mary Magdalen Churchwardens' Accounts   ORO: PAR 208/4/F1/7
single mb   *(Rendered 19 May 1566) (Receipts)*

…

It*em* R*eceived* at wyttsontyde of the ale   liij s. iiij d. 10

…

1565–6
Christ Church Expenses for the Royal Visit   Bodl.: MS. Rawlinson C.878
ff 1–9*   15

Expenses of Christeschurche
⸕ by Occasion of ye Quenes Ma*ie*sties
co*m*minge thither .21. Iul*y* 1566.

                                                                                                              20

21 Iuly	Imprimis to Thom*as* donyel for squaringe 7 tonne of tymber after xvj d. the tonne, & for viij [d.] kirfes viij d.	x s.
	It*em* to Austen Myles & his man for sawinge iij C. di. of elme borde after xviij d. the C.	v s. iij d.
24	It*em* to eight laborers helpinge [to ridd⟨.⟩ &] ∧⌐to¬ make [cleane] ⌐ready¬ the Qu*enes* seller: by Ellys	iij s. v d. 25
+	It*em* to Rich*arde* Wynkle for makinge newe wardes & a new springe to a locke of a door there, & a boy workinge there aboue the seyde eight	xij d.
	It*em* for six lodes of grauell to water deue for the same place	ij s. 30
	It*em* to Iohn Smyth & his man taking downe the partitions & makinge othere necesaries there	ij s. iiij d.
26.	It*em* to Thom*as* donyel for squaringe 8 tonne of tymber & vij kirfes	xj s. iij d.
4. Aug*ust*	It*em* to water dewe for iiij lodes of tymber, & ij lodes of borde cariage for s. Margarets well after xvj d. the lode, & for drawinge two peces of tymber there to the sawe pitte	viij s. viij d. 35
	It*em* to two couples of Sawyers for sawinge 900 of borde after xviij d.: by Rich*arde* Brem*ton*	xiij s. vj d.
	It*em* to Thom*as* donyel for squaringe fyue tonne of tymber	vj s. viij d. 40

4/ hoocke: *Hocktide was 30 April–1 May 1565*   10/ wyttsontyde: *10–16 June 1565*

+   Item to Richarde wynkell for hinges etc. by byll   xix s. ⟨...⟩
                    Summa iiij li. iij s. v d. ob. Exoneratur |
+   Item to Richarde Bremton & william pickouer for six dayes
      ˏ about the dore to mr walleys steares   x s.
      Item to water dewe for drawinge our tymber at s. Magaretes well   5
      out of the groue into Tattersals medowe & bringinge home one
      lode of tymber iij s. & for bringinge home six lodes more viij s.   xj s.

10. August To Austen Myles, Andrewe Myles, & their men for sawinge
      one M. of borde   xv s.
      To Thomas donyell for hewinge fyue tonne of tymber & iiij kirfes   vij s.   10
      To hughe williams & his man for sawinge halfe a day, &
      Edmunde wyuolde one day   xxij d.
      To Robert hart a carpenter for ij dayes worke   xx d.
+   To Richarde Smyth for lockes & staples to [⟨d⟩] ij dores:
      by byll   ij s. vj d.   15
      To Richarde Bremton & william pickouer for vj dayes makinge
      dores & other neccesarie[s] alterations   x s.
                    Summa lix s. Exoneratur |
+   To Beryll & his laborer for vj dayes whytynge the kitchin
      ⌈after xviij d.⌉   ix s.   20
+   To william Steuens for iiijˣˣ fote of drye elme bordes to lyne dores iiij s.
      To Thomas Symson for iiij dayes di. after xij d. & to Thomas howes
Masons   for v dayes after x d., & to one laborer v dayes after viij d. the daye
      takinge downe the harth in the hall & makinge it vp agayne   xij s.
      To Iohn huet, william fyshe, & Iohn Clarke after viij d. the day   25
laborers   for v dayes, & one of them for vj   x s. viij d.
17. August To Richarde Sutton for ij lodes of lyme   xxvj s. viij d.
      To Iohn horton for 500 double ten penny nayles viij s. iiij d.:
      3000 single tennes xxv s.: 8000 sixes xl s.: 5000 fyues xx s.
      x d.: 8000 foures xxvj s. viij d.: 12000 busshell nayles xvj s.:   30
      12000 lathe nayles xvj s.   vij li. xij s. x d.
                    Summa x li. xv s. ij d. Ex⟨.⟩ |
      To Iohn froste, peter freese, Iohn Crare ioyners for viij dayes
Ioyners   workinge on a porche for the Quenes entrance into the greate
[Memorandum chamber after viij d. the daye beside their borde   xvj s.   35
to aske
allowance for   for 250 quarter borde after vj s. the hundred [⟨...⟩] by
bording]   Iohn Crare   xv s.
      for ij greate plankes for the porche by Iohn Crare   v s.
Ioyner   To Owen Gylney for iiij dayes workinge about the sayd porche
      after xij d. the daye   iiij s. iiij d.   40
      To Thomas donyell for squarynge fyue tonne of tymber at
      s. Margarettes well   vj s. viij d.

17. Aug*ust*	To Iohn kirton for the hyer of an horse one day goinge to	
	woodstocke with the comm*iss*ion ⌈& for his expenses there⌉	xvj d.
	Sum*ma* xlviij s. iiij d. Ex*o*neratu*r* |	
17. Aug*ust*	It*em* to Ed*munde* wyuolde, & hughe will*ia*ms, & their men	
	for vj dayes sawinge of tymber	xx s. 5
	It*em* to Iohn wyens & his man for iij daies di. sawinge tymber	v̄ s. x d.
	It*em* to Tho*mas* Symson for v dayes di. v s. vj d. & to Iohn Stele	
Masons	& his sonne for [six] ⌈seuen⌉ dayes x s. vj d. & to Tho*mas* howes,	
	& Rob*er*t Matthewe for six dayes xij s.	xxviij s.
	It*em* to Rob*er*t hart for v dayes & di., [& to will] v s. vj d., & to	10
	will*ia*m pickouer for vj dayes vj s., & to water Ouen & his man	
Carp*enter*s	for ij dayes di., iiij s. vij d., & to Rich*ard*e pickouer, & Thomas	
	Smyth & their men for v dayes xx s.	xxxvj s. j d.
	It*em* for one hundred, quart*er*, & v fote of oken borde by	
	will*ia*m pickouer	vij s. x d. 15
	It*em* for halfe an hundred of elme borde by the same	ij s. iiij d.
	It*em* to Augustyne Myles ⌈& his fellowes⌉ for sawinge 1600	
	of borde	xxiiij s.
[+]	[It*em* to Rich*ard*e Tayler makinge a key to m*aste*r deanes	
	larder dore	vj d.] 20
+	It*em* to Berell & his man for vj dayes about peckwaters inne hall,	
	& m*aste*r deanes gallery & the greate hall ⌈& for heare⌉	ix s. ij d.
	It*em* to will*ia*m fyshe, Iohn Clerke, Rafe rogers, & Iohn huet	
laborers	for six dayes, & to Thomas Whynyarde, Iohn dewe, & will*ia*m	
+	hollande for v dayes after viij d. the day [struinge] masons [&	25
	leuelinge the quadrantes]	xxvj s.
	Sum*ma* pag*ine* vij li. xix s. iij d. Ex*o*neratu*r* |	
+	It*em* to Rob*er*t Wood for iiij dayes, & Rich*ard*e farre for	
	v dayes ⌈about ye same⌉	vj s.
	It*em* to water dewe for cariage of eleuen lodes of tymber &	30
	borde fro*m* s. Margaretes well	xiiij s. viij d.
	It*em* [for d*i*] to the same for drawinge ix peces of tymber to the	
	sawe pitte, & for cariage of xij lodes of grauell & cley after iiij d.	vij s.
	It*em* to the same for cariage of iiij lodes of stone from Osney	
	after vj d. ⌈the lode⌉	ij s. 35
	It*em* to Guy dewe for cariage of xiij lodes of grauell & cley	iiij s. iiij d.
	It*em* 25. Aug*ust* to mr Rich*ard*e flaxney for iiij C. of	
	borde after iiij s. iiij d. the hundred, & to Iohn Tattleton	
	for vij C. di. after iiij s. viij d. the hundred	lij s. iiij d.

1/ day: d *corrected over* g
36/ Guy: *underlined*

[v s. by pick]   Item to Augustine Myles, & his three men for sawinge iij M.

[Item x s.]   & iij of an hundred borde at s. Margaretes well after xviij

    the hundred   xlvj s. j d. ob.

    Item the 27 of August to william Benson & his boy for 7 dayes,

Masons   x s. vj d.; & to Richarde Bernarde for v dayes, v s.,   xv s. vj d. 5

25 August   Item to Owen Gylney for vj dayes, vj s. vj d., & Iohn Crare, &

Ioyners   peter freese for vj dayes viij s., & Edwarde Spike for iiij dayes,

    iiij s. iiij d., & to Iohn froste for ij dayes xvj d.   xx s. ij d.

            Summa pagine viij li. viij s. j d. ob. Exoneratur |

    Item 30. August to Iohn Clarke for the cariage of one lode   10

    of byrche   vj s. viij d.

Sawyers   Item to Nicholas Bladen, & Clement pemberton, & their menne

    for fyue dayes worke, & for sawinge a few rafters in the morning   xviij ⟨…⟩

    Item to william Browne, & Iames Orcharde for iij dayes workinge

    on master dr kennalles walle & their men as longe ⌜°for my lorde   15

    lecestre°⌝   x s.

    Item to Beryll & his man for x dayes pargettynge & suche like   xv s.

+   Item for a busshell of heare & besomes & pricke madame   viij d.

    Item to Thomas donyell for ix dayes & his boye after hewinge

    of tymber at s. Margaretes   xiij s. vj d. 20

    & for makinge a sawe pitte & a pece of worke more   xij d.

    Item to phillip ponde for x[⟨.⟩] dayes, Nicholas Bowelles

laborers   for v dayes, powell Evans for viij dayes, Robert henson

    for vj dayes, william Buston for vj dayes di., George   xxx s. iij d. caryage

    Goghe iiij dayes, Iohn doxe vj dayes   of [rub] ruble &c. 25

+   Item to Nicholas Noke for ij lockes & ij staples for master deane   iij s.

    Item to william [hollak⟨.⟩] holland for x dayes labor   vj s. viij d.

    Item to Iohn Style & his sonne for v dayes vij s. vj d., & Geffrey

Masons   whyte for v dayes v s., & Robert Matthewe for vij dayes, vij s., &

    his boye[s] [i]ij dayes [ij s. vj d.] [xvij d.] ⌜xij d.⌝   xx s. vj d. 30

            Summa pagine vj li. v s. iiij d. ob. Exoneratur |

⟨…⟩ns   Item to Thomas howes for x dayes, & his laborer   xvj s. viij d.

⟨.⟩ewell   31 August to Iohn Sewell for a locke, a staple & a payre of

    crosse garnettes ⌜for the quenes chamber,⌝ iij s. viij d., &

    for a locke & ij staples for the chaundry, ij s. iiij d.   vj s. taken a way 35

    Item to water Ouen for xj dayes, xj s., & Iohn neuell xij dayes

    xj s., & Roger Bennet for viij dayes vij s. iiij d., & to Richarde

    Bremton for one day xij d., to Thomas Gybbons for iiij dayes

    [xij] iiij s., to Iohn Marshe [for] & kellam hadley for x dayes xx s.,

Carpenters   to Roger & william parnell, & Roger w⌜h⌝eler & his boye for   40

2/ xviij: for xviij d.

v dayes di. [xxxiij s. viij d.] xx s. ij d. to Iohn Stanton for
v dayes v s. [⟨da.⟩] to willi*am* phillippes iiij dayes iiij s. &
Tho*mas* pilkinton for ij dayes ij s., to Rich*arde* pickouer &
his man for xij dayes xxiiij s., to Tho*mas* Smyth & his man
for xij dayes xxiiij s.   vj li. xiij s. vj d.   5

Carpenters

It*em* to Tho*mas* Shepperde for v dayes di., v s. vj d., to Rob*ert*
hart for xij dayes xij s., to Rich*arde* brygus iiij dayes di. iiij s. vj d.,
to Rich*arde* ha⌐r⌐wode & Simon Garlande for ix dayes xviij s.,
to William pickouer for xij dayes xij s., to Iohn, & dauid horne,
& their iiij menne for vj dayes xxxij s., & for wo⌐r⌐kinge in   10
the night xij d.   iiij li. iiij s.

            Sum*ma* pag*ine* xij li. ij d. Exonerat*ur* |
It*em* to Iames dodwell for ij C. & fyue fote of elme borde
ix s. viij d., & for xij oken peces xv s., by wat*er* Ouen   xviij s. viij d.
It*em* to Rafe Rogers, & Rich*arde* Kent for watchinge one night   15
⌐in the tymber yarde⌐   xvj d.
It*em* to hughe willi*ams* & his [three] man for xij dayes, xx s.,
& to hym for one other couple of sawyers, xj dayes, xviij s.

Sawyers

iiij d., to Edmunde wyuolde & his man for xij dayes xx s.,
to hughe Tynsley & his man for six dayes x s., to Edwarde   20
hall for iij dayes di., v s. x d.   iij li. xiiij s. ij d.
It*em* to Iohn dewe for x dayes vj s. viij d., to Iohn Clerke for
xij dayes, viij s., to Rich*arde* Atwode for ix dayes vj s., to Iohn

Laborers

huet for xij dayes viij s., to Tho*mas* legroue for ix dayes vj s.,
to Tho*mas* Glynne for vj dayes iiij s., to Tho*mas* whynyarde for   25
xij dayes viij s., to willi*am* fyshe for xij dayes viij s., to Rich*arde*
kent for vj dayes iiij s., to   lviij s. viij d.
To mr Coggan for xvj C. of elme borde & some odde iij li.
xv s., & great quarters v s. iiij d. to mr whitthington for one
hundred xvij fote of elme borde v s., to willi*am* furne[⟨.⟩]s   30
for viij C. xxviij fote of elme borde xxxviij s., all by willi*am*
pickouer   vj li. iij s. iiij d.
            Sum*ma* pag*ine* xiiij li. xvj s. ij d. Exonerat*ur* |
It*em* to willi*am* kinge for viij dayes, v s. iiij d., to Iohn Nicols
for one day viij d., to Rob*ert* Matthewe for one dayes masonry   35
xij d. [It*em* to] & his laborer one day vj d.   vij s. vj d.
[It*em* to Guy dewe for cariage of xxij lodes of tymber, plankes ⟨…⟩]

8, 20/ &: *corrected from* f
17/ for: f *corrected from* x
37/ [Item … plankes ⟨…⟩]: *largely illegible 4-line entry either written over for correction or entirely cancelled*
    with scribbling

Item to Robert Mooneson for plumbe worke as by byll
[xxx⟨.⟩] [appeareth] ⌜loke for this in the end of the boke⌝   [xxxviiij viij d.]
[Item for iij C. ⟨...⟩ quarterne ix li. of leade spent about the
hall stares & the churche yle ther⟨...⟩ three shillinges   xxxiij s.]
+ Item to Richarde winkell for Smyththery worke as appeareth   5
by byll   iij li. xij s.
Item to Richarde Emans & Thomas Tydder for one dayes labor
⌜a pece almoste⌝   x d.
7. September   Item to Iohn ley, for iij dayes labor before the Quenes comminge   ij s.
Item to Richarde farre for xij dayes [worke] labor before the quenes   10
comminge viij s., & for [hym] one nightes watche viij d.; & to
Robert wodde for xij dayes labor ye same tyme viij s., & to Iohn
Ellys for vj baskettes viij d.   xvij s. iiij d.
+ ⌜[Item to Iohn] Nicols for one nights watche with same
at the steres   viij d.⌝ 15
9. September   to Richarde Greene for cariage of xxij lodes of grauell
⌜of Marston⌝   vij s. iiij d.
Item to Guy dewe for xlij lodes of grauell   xiiij s.
Item to Iohn Syre, & Richarde wyllys for cariage of xiiij lodes
of grauell   iiij s. viij d. 20
Summa viij li. v s. Exoneratur |
10. September Item to Anne More, Richardsons mayde, & Courtyardes mayde
+ for swepinge ye chambers before ye Quenes comminge   xij d.
Item to Robert Bote for diuers women makinge garlandes &
gatheringe Iuye, as by byll   iij li. vij s. x d. 25
Item to the Queenes carpenter as by byll   xix s. x d.
+ Item to dayly payntinge kinge henryes name in golde & the
tables etc. ⌜by byll⌝   xij s. x d.
12. September to Robert Burton & his boy for v dayes after xvj d. the day,
& William Carter, & Robert hart, & Ouens man as longe after   30
x d. ye day takinge downe ye scaffolds, stage, porche, & settinge
vp partitions beaton downe before   xix s. ij d.
Item to Iohn Noke for a locke for master deanes mannes chamber
that was taken awaye   xij d.
14 September   to phillip ponde a laborer for six dayes after vij d.   35
ye daye iij s. vj d., & for a boule loste iiij d., to
Thomas Berell, Thomas house, [Thomas Stele]
pargetters, & to Iohn Nicols, Rafe Rogers, [⟨.⟩]
their laborers for six dayes xvij s., To Iohn huet,
Iohn Doxe for six dayes laborers, vij s., & to   40

11/ for: *corrected from* to   40/ &: *corrected over letter* t

Tho*mas* Berell, Thomas house, Iohn Nichols, Rafe
Rogers, Iohn huet, Rich*arde* Yemans ⌜Iohn Nichol*s*⌝
as laborers for one daye the laste weke; all takinge
downe the stage, & settinge vp partions iij s. vj d.,
& to Iohn farre ⌜by Iohn Nichols⌝ for iij dayes about   5
the same xxj d., & to house & Rogers his laborer[s]
mendinge the range & the sinke in the kitchins in the
time of the Quenes beinge here xvij d., to Iohn huet
for labor at diuers tymes extraordynary viij d., to
Berell for iiij dayes labor about the playes & alterations   10
of the stage ij s. iiij d.

                                        [xxvij s. vj d.] xxxvij s. vj d.
              Sum*ma* viij li. [⟨.⟩j s. ij d.] xiiij d. Exo*neratur* |
16 Sep*tember*   To water dewe for cariage of xxiiij lodes of tymber, plankes, &
             bordes fro*m* s. Margar*etes* well after xvj d. the lode xxxij s., & for   15
             drawinge xij borde stockes to the sawe pitte iiij s., & for cariage
             of nyne lodes of grauell iij s., & for cariage of diuers bordes &
             tymber out of the towne to o*ur* house [at] xvij iorneys v s.   xliiij s.
        +   To harry Thatcher for two women makinge cleane the churche
             & singinge breade   v d. 20
             To Ouen for hymselfe & his man helpinge to take downe the
             stage & scaffolde the saturday after the Quenes departure xx d.,
             [& to willi*am* pickouer for one]   xx d.
             To mr hartox for ij C. xl^tie foote of elme borde after iiij s. viij d.,
             by Ouen   xj s. ij d. 25
E.R.   +   To Edyth Robson & Margaret Wymatt for makinge cleane
             m*aster* deanes chambers after ye Quenes departure   viij d.
             To Robert Wood [hel] laborer for v dayes about the takinge
             downe of the scaffoldes & stages etc.   ij s. xj d.
17.   To [Iohn S] Rich*arde* Sutton for fyue lodes of lyme to make   30
             up [that was] ⌄⌜partitions & walles⌝ throwen downe   iij li. vj s. viij d.
             To George franklyn[g]e for drawinge ij bor̸de stockes out
             of ye tymberyarde to the farre pitte   vj d.
[⟨.⟩ s.]   [It*em* to Thomas Tymberley for makinge 5000 [& 900] of
             lathe after ij d. the hundred   viij s. iiij d.] 35
             It*em* for 5000 lath after xij d. the thousande made by
             Tho*mas* Tymberley   l s.
                    Sum*ma* viij li. xviij s. Exo*neratur* |
19 [Au]   To mr Gilbert for one pece of elme bought of ladyman v s., for
⌜Sep*tember*⌝ two peces bought of leonard ⌜ye⌝ barbar viij s. iiij d. for ij peces   40

4l partions: *for* partitions

Memorandum
to spek to
m*aste*r deane
⟨…⟩ of the laste
of elme & iiij peces of oke bought of Guy pennyngton
xxvj s. viij d., for ij elmes bought of mr dodwell x s., &
for iij peces to Bagwell xv s.   iij li. v s.
To mr Gylbert for tymber as by byll   v li. vj s. ix d.

20 Sep*tember*   to Iohn horton for 1000 of double tenne penny nayles xvj s.   5
viij d., 3000 single tennes xxv s., 4500 of sixes xxij s. vj d.,
4000 fyues xvj s. viij d., 4000 threes x s., 4000 busshel nayle
v s. iiij d., 18000 lath nayle [x s. viij d.] xxiiij s., 7000 sprigges
viij s. ij d. spent in the Quenes worke   vj li. viij s. iiij d.
to ye same for 2000 lath nayle more   ij s. viij d.   10
It*em* to Edwarde Tanner for xlj lodes of grauell spent at the
Quenes com*m*inge   xij s. viij d.
[It*em* to George Bradstocke for fellynge & sawinge ij lodes
of tymber to make lath with viij d., & for cariage of the same
fro*m* Chaundese to Christeschurche [x] iij s.   iij s. viij d.]   15
+   To Rich*ar*de winkell by byll ⌈for lock*es* &c.⌉   iij s. viij d.
To Rich*ar*de Bremton & willi*a*m pickouer for vj dayes settinge
vp partitions; takinge downe ye stayres, mendynge o*ur* gat*es*,
& bridge   x s.
To willi*a*m pickouer for one day more   x d.   20
            Summ*a* xvj li. x s. xj d. Exoneratu*r* |

20. September   To Ed*war*de Tanner for vij lodes of grauell at the earle of
Ley*cester*s com*m*inge   ij s. iiij d.

20 Sep*tember*   To goodwife dauis for di. C. of borde [&] ij s. iiij d. & for
studdes about the houses of ye stage ij s. viij d., & to mr   25
Coggan for di. C. of borde ij s. iiij d., & for cariage of iij
lodes of borde xiij d. all by willi*a*m pickouer   viij s. iiij d.
To Geffray white for vj dayes di. vj s. vj d., & to Iohn Style

Masons   for vij dayes vij s., & for his boy as longe iij s. vj d., about
the wall of the steares & stoppinge up mr Siddalles dore &   30
to Geffray white for his laborer iij dayes di. ij s. ij d.   xix s. ij d.
To Thomas Steele for viij dayes & his man as longe xj s. iiij d.,
& to Thomas Berill & his man for v dayes vij s. j d., & for ij
quarterne di. of heare [&] vj s. viij d., & for ij busshells of

parget*ters*   heare lyme x d. by Iohn Ellys, & to Thomas house for iij dayes   35
ij s. vj d., & to Rafe Rogers & doxey for iij dayes iij s. vj d., &
to Iohn huet for v dayes ij s. xj d., & to Willi*a*m Wymarke for
iij dayes di. ij s. [pa] laththinge, pargettinge, & preparinge stuffe
to pargett ye partitions throwen downe   xxxvj s. x d.

1–3m/ *Memorandum* … laste: *written over original, largely illegible text of memorandum referring to*
    gylbert *and a sum of money*
37/ to¹: t *corrected from* I

To [Guy] ⌈wat*er*⌉ dewe for cariage of ix lode of stone fro*m*
Osney to make up diuers walles iij s. vj d. & for vij lodes
about the house xxj d., & for carienge iiij lodes to the broken
bridge xij d., & for ij lodes of grauell & one of cley xij d., &
for cariage of one lode of lyme out of ye towne iiij d. ⌈& for   5
ij lodes of street fenne iiij d.⌉   viij s. xj d.

22. Sep*tember* +   to fyshe kepinge the woodyarde the daye ye Quene departed   viij d.
                          Sum*ma* iij li. xvj s. iij d. Ex*oneratu*r |

28 Sep*tember*   [to Iohn Typpinge in rewarde to helpe vs to the woode
                   appoynted us by the Clerkes of the Greene cloth   v s.] 10
                   It*em* to Robert bote for diuers thinges spent by byll   iij li. iij s. j d.

28 Sep*tember* +   to Geffray white & his laborer for iij dayes after xix d. the
                   daye & stile & his boy for ij dayes after xviij d. the daye
                   makinge an ende of the steres walle ⌈by white⌉   vij s. ix d.
                   To mr Barsdale for viij busshels of here ij s. viij d. & to Thomas   15
                   house, Rafe Rogers, for iij dayes after [ij s.] ⌈xvij d.⌉ the daye iiij s.
                   [i]iij d., & to Thomas Stele & his laborer for ij dayes ij s. x d., &
By Beryll   to [Thomas] ⌈Iohn⌉ Doxey, & Iohn huet, for ij dayes ij s. iiij d.,
                   & to Thomas Beryll & Iohn Nicolles for vj dayes after xvij d.
                   the day makinge an end of pargettynge the partitions, & whyte   20
                   lyminge some, & makinge vp d*r* kennalles wall ⌈viij s. vj d.⌉   xx s. vij d.
                   To wat*er* dewe for one Lode of cley & an other of grauell cariage
                   ⌈by I*ohn* Ellys for⌉ d*r* kennalls wall   viij d.
        +   To Nicholas Noke for mendinge ij lockes in mr Bernard*es* chamber,
                   & for ij square staples in the Quenes chamber [xx d.] xviij d., &   25
                   for a key for the Quenes buttery iiij d., & for mendinge a locke &
                   makinge a key for m*aste*r deanes buttery viij d.   ij s. vj d.
        ♂   It*em* for xxvij tonne of tymber cutt at s. Margaret*es* well
                   ⌈after vij s. iiij d. ye tonne⌉   ix li. xviij [d.] s.
                          Sum*ma* xiiij li. xij s. vij d. Ex*oneratu*r | 30
        ♂   It*em* for three ioyners borde ij wekes di.   xxv s.
122 li./ 12 s./   [*Memorandum* that in this is not counted viij li. xj s. ix d. which Iones allowed
10 d./   mr Gilbert]
                   3. Sep*tember* to the Clerkes of the greene clothe for [sparinge us]
                   ⌈unburdeninge⌉ at o*ur* requeste the vniuersitie & us of the lightes   35
                   & russhes, iij payre of gloues   xvij⟨...⟩
        +   4. Sep*tember* to the gentleman ussher one payre of gloues   iiij s. iiij d.
        +   To the Qu*enes* porters   x s.
        +   To the yeoman of the woodyarde for helpinge us to a reco*m*pence
                   of o*ur* woode & cole spent   x s.   40
                   It*em* for (blank)

18/ Doxey: D *corrected over* B

+ Item 2. October to Richarde Smyth for makinge one key &
settinge on[e] ij lockes in master deanes lodginge   viij d.
[To Richarde Winkel for makinge a key to one of my dores]
4. October to Richarde Winkell for viij newe clampes for the
+ wall at the hall steares ij s. iij d., & for a newe bolte & a staple   5
to the larder dore vj d.   ij s. x d.
6. October   To Sewell ye smyth by byll   xxj d.
11.   [To Michael Herne for makinge the Quenes armes to sett on the porche]
13.   To Robert Mooneson & his seruaunt & his ∧⌈boye⌉ for ij dayes
stoppynge of the holes made in the roofe of the hall for lightes   iiij s.   10
Item to Berell & Iohn Nicolls for three dayes whit[h]inge my
lodginge & mr dayes   iiij s. iij d.
Summa iiij li. x d. Exoneratur |
26. October to Thomas Beryll for v dayes w⟨.⟩ytinge ouer mr
dayes lodginge agayne & mr Siddalles   iiij s. ij d. 15
⟨...⟩ To Iohn Bolten for ij dayes settinge ⟨...⟩ mr dayes portalles
with other thinges & one of myne   ij s.
16. Nouember to Richarde Bremton & william pickauer for
one daye a pece makinge a bere yat was broken at the playes
xx d. & to pickauer for one other day settinge vp master deanes   20
portalles x d., & to them both for one halfe day about mr dayes
study x d.   iij s. iiij d.
8. December to henry Towe for glasinge worke
done by reason of the Quenes Maiesties beinge
in Christeschurch; by byll   xiiij li. iiij s. vj d. ob. qua. 25
9. To Richarde Bremton & william pickauer for one
day mendinge master dr Calfhille stable altered &
disordered by the yeoman of the larder; & remouinge
to their places ij dores in master deanes chamber   xx d.
Item for one other lode of byrche not yet payed for, but   30
dewe to our woodman of South stoke   vj s. viij d.
Summa pagine xv li. ij s. iiij d. ob. qua.
Summa totalis Cxlviij li. ij s. j d. ob. qua. Exoneratur
To Robert Mooneson for castinge iij C. of leade v s. vj d., &
for iij dayes for hym & his iij men layenge the sayde leade ouer   35
ye Quenes stayres, & takinge downe the olde viij s., & for hym
& his [i]ij men hanginge vp lightes iij dayes v⟨...⟩ s.   xxj s. vj d.

Christ Church Expense Sheet   Bodl.: MS. Top.Oxon c.22
single sheet*   40

Item worke downe at Crystescherche ageneste the quines magestyse
comminge thether

Item Resseved of *Master* tresurar in owlde Leade feyve hundarthe thre
quar[fefe]
Item delyvered In new Leade vj hundarthe iij quartarnes
Item dely⟨...⟩ed more in new Le⟨.⟩de for the yelde in the chirche ij
hunda⟨...⟩   5
Item delyv⟨...⟩d more in new Leade to make cappse ov*er* the hall/   xvj li.
Item delyvered more to make candelsticke in the hall   xxj
so in new Leade I have delyvered ix hundarthe   x[j] li.
for the castinge of the same aftar xxij d. the hundarthe com*m*se to ⟨...⟩
Item delyvered more in new Leade then I have ressevved owlde   10
Leade by iij hundarthe [xj li.] ⌈one quartarne⌉   ix li.
Item for one dayese worke for mey selfe and mey ij men   ij s. vj d.
Item for tow dayese and aholfe when mey man swept the hall   ij s. j d.
Item for Swipinge the hall iiij dayese more ⌈°by an other man°⌉   ij s. viij d.
Item another daye for my and mey tow men abowt the hall   ij s. vj d. 15
Item mey selfe and mey tow men iij dayese more for [makyn]
hanginge vpp Lyghtts in the hall   viij s.
Item for one dayese worke more for ij of mey men for takinge
downe Lede of the steres in the hall   xx d.
Item for iiij dayese worke more in swipinge of the chirche   ij s. viij d. 20
     Some [xxx xxix xxxix s. x d. viij d.]
     Sum*ma* xxxviij s. viij d.
°casty*n*ge leade iij C. v s. vj d. iij days lay*n*ge the leade v s. iij. days for hy*m*
& hys too men hagy*n*g vj lyghtes viij s.°

                     25

Corpus Christi College Bursars' Accounts CCCA: C/1/1/4
f [9]* *(External expenses)*
...
Item bindinge the booke of verses made in the Quenes com*m*inge   xxij d.
...   30

Lincoln College Computus LC Arch: Computus 6
f 34 *(21 December–21 December) (Necessary internal expenses)*
...
Item ffor making cleane the streates at my lord of Lecest*er*s   35
com*m*yng   iij d.
...

7/ xxj: li. *omitted in* MS *(?)*
12/ vj d.: *corrected from* vij d.
16/ mey¹: *tear in* MS; *the beginning of* e *and a portion of* y *are visible*
24/ hagyng: *for* hangyng

f 35

Item for paper and ynck to make the Secound book at the queens
being heare   ij d.
Item ffor rushes for the chappell at the same time   xiij d.   5
Item to my lord of Lecesters mann at suche time as he brought
a booke   iij s. iiij d.

…

Magdalen College Libri Computi   MC Arch: LCE/6   10
f 106   (Chapel costs)

…

Solutum Shewsmyth emendanti fenestras ex pacto   vj s. viij d.
Solutum eidem reparanti fenestras pilis et tempore spectaculorum
confractas   iij s. iiij d.   15

…

f 106v   (Hall costs)

Solutum oven et 2bus famulis operantibus circa Theatrum in   20
ferijs natalitijs varijs temporibus .6. dies   xiiij s.

…

Solutum oven et 2bus famulis operantibus circa theatrum per
6. dies   xiiij s.
Solutum Rixon et Morryse idem facientibus per 4or dies   vj s.   25
Solutum squyer et famulo serrantibus varia pro eodem opere
.4. dies   vj s.

…

billa.   Solutum Magistro Brasbrig pro Expensis in Comædia   vij s. x d.
…   30
billæ.   Solutum pro varijs ad Spectacula pertinentibus
per billas   xiij li. vij s. xj d. ob.
Solutum pro Candelis tempore Spectaculorum insumptis   xv s.
Solutum oven et famulo operantibus circa Theatrum per
tres dies   vij s. vj d.   35
°Solutum pro carbonibus ibidem insumptis   iiij li.°

…

f 108v   (Groundskeeping costs)
…   40
Solutum oven et 2bus famulis dolantibus meremium pro
nouo theatro per tres dies   vij s. vj d.

Solut*um* Squyar et fa*mu*lo serra*n*tib*us* eode*m* tempore p*ro*
qui*n*que dies   viij s. iiij d.
…

f 109v   *(External payments)*   5
…
Solut*um* Tibicinib*us* tempore natiuitatis Chr*ist*i   iiij s.
…
Solut*um* cuidam affere*n*ti literas a co*n*siliarijs Reginæ   v s.
…   10
Solut*um* p*ro* expe*n*sis te*m*pore progressus Reginæ   vj li.
…

f 110
…   15
°Solut*um* p*ro* epulis datis g*e*nerosis te*m*pore spectaculor*um*   xvij s. iiij d.°
…

Magdalen College Draft Libri Computi   MC Arch: LCD/1
f 293   *(Memoranda)*   20
…
°Solut*um*° dedim*us* p*re* manib*us* tibicinib*us*   xxxxiij s. iiij d.
…
dedim*us* p*re* manib*us* bachalarijs ad p*re*benda spectacula   iij li. xj s. viij d.
…   25

Letter of Guzmán de Silva to the King of Spain
Archivo General de Simancas: Estado, legajo 819
f [2v]   *(6 September)*
…   30
Esta Reyna a sido Rescebida e*n*esta V*n*iuersidad d*el*a manera, que los principes
suelen serlo enlos lugares q*ue* los desean con todo, aplauso y. Regocijo hizieron
le quatro oraçiones en diuersos lugares a su entrada tres en latin y vna en griego
en las quales alabaron sus Virtudes y letras. mostrando el regocijo yalegria de su
Venida quean tenido, los dias queaqui a estado sea hallado en los. actos publicos 35
deletias que sean hecho entodas ciencias y las noches en comedias y trajedias en
lengua latina y. Inglesa, Ayer fue el Vltimo dia en el qual seacauaron. y la Reyna
les dio las gracias en lengua latina con buenas y graues palabra⟨.⟩ no sea tratado
en los actos comedias ni disputas ninguna materia de Religion sino/ ordinarias
aunque en el Vltimo acto, que fue de teolugia/…   40
…

38/ palabra⟨.⟩: *letter lost due to deterioration of page edge*

Miles Windsor's Narrative   CCC: MS 257
f 115*

The Gestes of ye Quenes Maiesties
receavinge in oxfourde   5
1566
Anno domini 1566.
The Receavinge of ye Quenes
Maiestie into Oxford

10

ff 116v–17v*   *(31 August)*

...

ix of ye clocke/   This ˄⌜daye⌝ beinge Saterdaye ye Quenes maiestie cam from woodstocke...

At ye vttermoste parte of ye vniuersitye liberties besydes a village named   15
woolvercott ij myle from oxfourde ye Earle of leycester with iiij doctours
⌜in scarlet gownes & hoodes⌝ vz. dr Kenall comissarye, dr vmphry dr
godwyn, dr whyte [wente to] met[e] ye Quenes maiestie with viijᵗʰ masters
of arte beinge heddes of howses, & iij esquyer bedels which delyvered vpp
there staves to ye Chauncelor & by hym to ye Quenes maiestie whoo   20
delyvered ye same to ye bedels agayne/ Then an oracion was there made
by one mr marbecke of Christechurche enduringe [a] ⌜one⌝ quarter of an
hower which was lyked verye well, ⌜of her maiestie sayinge⌝ [& ye Quene
sayde master Secretarye you thincke there be no eloquente men] but in
Cambridge, & to mr marbecke I shee sayde wee haue harde of you before   25
but nowe wee knowe you ⌜& ye spanishe embassadoure sayde hic non
pauca multis sed multa paucis complecens est/ Sayinge⌝ & then gaue
hym her hande to kysse, & ⌜so⌝ to ye reste of ye doctours & sayde to

Collation with CCC: MS 257 *(F)* ff 104–14:   4–6 The Gestes ... oxfourde 1566]
F, f 104, omits   13m ix of ye clocke/] *F, f 105v, omits*   17 gownes & hoodes]
F, f 105v, omits   17 comissarye] vichauncellor *F, f 105v*   19 arte] Artes *F, f 105v*
20 ye¹] our *F, f 106*   20 by hym to ye Quenes maiestie] hee to ye Quene *F, f 106*
21 there] *F, f 106, omits*   22 one¹] *F, f 106, omits*   22 Christechurche]
Christeschurche *F, f 106*   23 lyked verye well] verye well lyked *F, f 106*   23–5 [&
ye Quene ... mr marbecke I shee sayde] *F, f 106, omits*   25 wee haue harde of
you] shee had heard of hym *F, f 106*   26 wee knowe you] shee knewe hym *corrected*
to wee knowe you *F, f 106*   26 &] *F, f 106, omits*   26 hic] cunctis *F, f 106*
27 Sayinge & then gaue] The Quene gave *F, f 106*   28 & sayde] sayinge *F, f 106*

23–5/ of her maiestie ... in Cambridge: *incomplete cancellation and revision (?)*
26–7/ hic ... est: *'Here he is grasping not a little with much but much with a little'*
27/ complecens: *for complectens*

m*aste*r doctoure vmphrey me thinckethe yis gowne becu*m*meth you verye
well & I m*a*ruell y*a*t you ar so straighte laced in thes poynt*es* but I ca*m* not
nowe to chyde & so gaue hym her hande to kysse, This beinge done shee w*i*th
her nobilitye & these of ye vniu*er*sitye aforenamed w*i*th ye iij esquyer bedels
[⟨.⟩] ⌈carynge there staves⌉ cam rydinge w*i*thin a myle of oxfourd where ye   5
mayior named mr wylliams w*i*th his ald*er*men ⌈& Burgesses 13 besyd*es* ye
maior⌉ in scarlet gown*es* xiiij in nu*m*ber [w*i*th ye rest of ye citisens] ⌈&
c*er*tayne other cytizens⌉ receaved her maiestye & ye mayior delyvered vpp
to her his mace w*h*ich was delyvered to hym agayne & yen he made a shorte
oracion [to her] in englishe ⌈lattyn⌉ & presented [to] in ye name of ye whoole   10
citye a cupp of sylver double gylte in valewe x li., in ye w*h*ich cupp was aboute
xl li. in olde golde [as yt was thoughte] Afterwarde [when shee entered]
⌈entringe in ryall ma*ie*stie⌉ into ye citye of oxfourde ⌈[abou] betwene v &
vj of ye clocke⌉ at ye northegate called bocardo (from ye w*h*ich place vnto
Christechurche haull doore all ye vniu*er*sitye standinge in ord*er* accordinge   15
to yer degrees fyrste schollers of ye w*h*ich ij in ye name of ye reste exhebeted
to ye Quene an oracion in wrytinge & c*er*tayne verses, yen batchelars of ye
w*h*ich ij dyd in lycke sorte/ afterwarde m*a*sters of arte amonge [ye w*h*ich]
⌈whome⌉ mr Penson & mr Bereblocke [an] ⌈delyvered ij⌉ orations [to ye
Quene in lyke sorte] vnto whome ye Quene sayde Gratias habeo vobis ⌈[⟨..⟩e]⌉   20
ingentes/ & laste of all doctors everye degree in his habite & hood/) ⌈At ye
entringe of ye Schollers abovte northgate⌉ a shorte oracion was made vnto her
by a scholler named deale, from I whence shee cu*m*mynge passed throughe ye
streete where ye schollers in order knelinge cryed vivat regina w*h*ich she
takinge verye thanckfullye w*i*th a ioyfull countenance sayde oftentymes   25
syttinge in an honorable riche [cowche] ⌈lytter⌉ Gratias ago/ [When shee
cam to ye topp of] ⌈At her co*m*minge to⌉ Carfoxe al*ia*s ⌈Catervies the noble
mounte & cheife place of ye Citie dep*a*rtinge 4 fayre & statelie street*es*⌉

Collation continued: 1 m*a*ster doctoure] dr *F f 106*   1 gowne] gowne & habite
F f 106   3 so] then *F f 106*   4 ye iij] three *F f 106*   6 his] the *F f 106*   / in
scarlet gown*es* … of ye citisens] *F f 106, omits*   8–9 & ye mayior delyvered vpp
to her] the Maeor delyveringe vpp *F f 106*   9 &] *F f 106, omits*   10 ⌈lattyn⌉]
F f 106, omits   11 cupp²] *F f 106, omits*   12 in] of *F f 106*   12 Afterwarde]
Afterward*es F f 106*   13m ye] *F f 106, omits*   14m stewarde] Steward of the Citie
F f 106   15 Christechurche] christ*e*schurche *F f 106*   17 to ye Quene] *F f 106,
omits*   17 yen] Then stood the *F f 106*   18 afterwarde] Then *F f 106*   18 arte]
Art*es F f 106*   20 vnto] to *F f 106*   20 sayde] ⌈gaue thanck*es* hartelielie yn
thies word*es*⌉ *F f 106*   21 &] *F f 106, omits*   22 vnto her] *F f 106, omits*
23 cu*m*mynge] *F f 106, omits*   24 she] her Ma*ie*stie *F f 106*   26 [cowche] ⌈lytter⌉]
Chariot ⌈lytter or coche⌉ *F f 106v*   27 Catervies] Catervoyes *F f 106v*

6/ mr wylliams: *Thomas Williams*   20–1/ Gratias … ingentes: *'I am very grateful to you'*

beinge ye chefeste place of ye cItye an oration was made [vnto her] in greeke
by [one] mr Lawrence publicke reader of ye greeke lecture aboute a quarter of
an how*er which* shee verye well accepted & gaue hym thanck*es* in ye greeke
tounge & after sayde yt was ye beste oracion y*at* ever shee harde in greeke, wee
[wyll] woulde answere you presentlye but w*ith* yis greate co*m*panye wee ar   5
su*m*what abashed wee wyll taulke more w*ith* you in o*ur* chamber/

ffrom thence passinge styll throughe ye schollers shee cam to ye hauledoore
in Christechurche where an other oracion was made vnto her by one mr
Kyngsmell orator of ye vniu*er*sitye whome shee thanked for his paynes &   10
sayde you woulde haue done well yf you hadd ⌈a⌉ good matter [& ⟨...⟩] [wee
here say y*at* you are kyn to one whome wee loue verye well]

f 118*

...   15

There were sett vppon ye colledge gat*es* ye haule doore & wall*es* adioyninge
thervnto where ye Quene entered dyvers verses in lattyn & greeke & at ye
greate gat*es* a large scroll of verses made by m*aster* dr Perse.

           Inclyta fæminei V*ir*go que gloria sexus
           & gen*us* & dec*us* es gentis Regina Bryta*n*ne   20
           grata venis nobis, p*er*fectaq*ue* gaudia portas,
           imp*er*fecta tui subiens monumenta Pare*n*tis

   ...

The players appoynted afore her ma*iest*ie m*ar*beck &c by whome [saythe]

Collation continued: 1 beinge ... cItye] *F, f 106v, omits*   1 in greeke] in Greeke
ₐ⌈verses⌉ *F, f 106v*   2–3 aboute a quarter of an how*er*] a quarter of an hower *in left
margin of F, f 106v*   4 wee] sayinge further wee *F, f 106v*   8 styll throughe ye
schollers] *cancelled and corrected to* awaye by the Bachelors & M*asters F, f 106v*
9 vnto her] *F, f 106v, omits*   10 for his paynes] *F, f 106v, omits*   11 ⌈a⌉] *F, f 106v,
omits*   16–17 adioyninge thervnto] thearto adioyninge *F, f 107*   18 large] longe
F, f 107   18 dr Perse.] dr Perse. Among other thies verses weare made by M*aster
dr* calfehill. *F, f 107*   24 The players ... m*ar*beck &c] Actors in the Playes./ Marbeck./
Banes./ Badger./ Rook*es*./ Ball./ Buste./ Glasyer./ Bristoo./ Thornton./ Penson./ Pot*es*
senior./ Pot*es* iunior./ Mathewe./ Dalaper./ Danet./ Mauncell./ Iones./ Argall./
Suo*m*mers./ Townesende.// Wyndsor./ Twyne./ Raynold*es*./ Dorcet./ Grey./ Egerton./
Carew./ Poll./ Younge./ ffourd./ Iutsam./ Dalapers boye./ Smythe nutrix./ *F, f 107*

5/ with: *corrected from* we
19–22/ Inclyta ... Parentis: *'Famous virgin, glory of the female sex, queen of the British race, who are both its
noble offspring and ornament, you come as one welcome to us and you bring complete joys, as you enter your
father's incomplete monuments'*
24/ The players ... &c: *listed on f 123v; see p 135, ll.14–18*

[playinge ye parte] of ⌈by⌉ Palamon saythe the Queene*s* ma*i*estie I warrante
hym hee dalyethe not in love when hee was in love in deede and by [Banes]
⌈Arcyte⌉ hee was a righte marciall knighte whoe had in deede a swarse &
manlye Cowntenance. and by [dalap*er*] ⌈Trevatio⌉ beinge owte of his p*ar*te &
missinge his kewe ⌈&⌉ offringe his servise to ye ladyes swearinge by ye masse   5
or Gote*s* blutt I am owte. [Gode*s* pitty] & lyke to m*aste*r Secretarye whistelinge
vpp a hornepype in verye good measor [Goo thy waye] Gode*s* pitty saythe ye
Quene what a knave it tis & lykewise m*aste*r Secretarye goo yi wayes thowe
art wider owte thowe mayste be lowde to playe ye knave in any grownde in
england. [It*em* duke] ⌈By⌉ Perithous [castinge] ⌈in⌉ ye ⟨.....⟩ of ye funerall fyer   10
throwinge in wi*th* Theseus Palamon & Ladye Emilia everye one a Iewell or
token of love Gode*s* wounde*s* saythe a stander by ⌊what mean ye⌋ will ye burn
ye K*ing* Edward cloake ⌈in ye fyer⌉ goo yi wayes saythe [Edwarde*s*] ⌈goo foole⌉
hee [playeth] ⌈knowethe⌉ his part kyndeste the player hym selfe to one y*at*
would haue stayed hym by ye arme wherfore sayeth hee ar yei sent to keepe   15
ye fyer. & the Queene*s* ma*i*estie her selfe said what aylyt ye let ye gentleman
alone hee [doth] playethe his p*ar*te let ye likewise yem doo theirs. And
lykewise at ye devise in ye Quadrante of Dr K*enn*alls hownde*s* wi*th* a trayle
at a ffox when ye ladyes in ye wyndowe crydd nowe nowe & hallowed oh
excellent said ye Quene*s* ma*i*estie those boyes ar readye to leape oute of ye   20
windowe to folow ye hownde*s* whi*ch* in treuthe was so kyndleye set owte
y*at* nider Praxiteles Polycletes nor Apelles divine patroniste of ven⟨..⟩s, veile,
nor lyne*s* wi*th* penn or pensell then y*at* was set owte by sens⟨..⟩e affection

Collation continued: p 128, l.24–p 129, l.1 by whome … ma*i*estie] By Palamon
shee sayde *F, f 110v*   2 hym] *F, f 110v, omits*   2–3 and by [Banes] ⌈Arcyte⌉] By
Arcyte *F, f 110v*   3 whoe had in deede] havinge *F, f 110v*   3–4 a swarse & manlye
Cowntenance] a swarse countenance & a manlye face *F, f 110v*   4–10 and by
[dalap*er*] ⌈Trevatio⌉ … england] By Trevatio, Gode*s* pitie what a knave yt is./
F, f 110v   10–17 [It*em* duke] ⌈By⌉ Perithous … doo theirs.] By Perithous
throwinge K*ing* Edwarde*s* riche Cloake into the ffunerall fyer whome a stander by
woulde haue stayed by the arme wi*th* an oathe goo foole hee knowethe his parte./
F, f 110v   17–19 And lykewise … hallowed] At the Crye of the hownde*s* in the
Quadrante vppon the trayle of a ffox in the huntinge of Theseus when the boyes in
the wyndows hallowed & cryed nowe nowe: *F, f 110v*   21–3 whi*ch* in treuthe …
affection] *F, f 110v, omits*

1/ [playinge ye parte] of: *incomplete cancellation (?)*   12/ ⌊what mean ye⌋: *written interlinearly with no*
4–6/ beinge owte … I am owte.: *underlined*   *mark of insertion; positioning here only conjectural*
6–7/ & lyke to … good measor: *underlined*   17–23/ doo theirs … affection: *written in top margin*
8–10/ & lykewise m*aste*r … in england.: *underlined*   *of f 118v in continuation of f 118*
10/ ⟨.....⟩: *one word written over another; both illegible*   18/ of: *written over by or vice versa*

whome ye Queene afterwardes made her scoller by these wordes askinge of my
Lord windsor what hee was wher answeringe hym to be his cousen shee said
I thot him to a gentleman by his courage & cowntenance & with hye thanckes
gaue hym her hand to kisse when shee had ridd before on chiltryne hilles in ye
cold a longe howr by torche lighte. & ye Lord Shefeild & ye Lord windsor with   5
master Secretarye with verye good wordes did signifie yat yt was her maiesties
pleasor yat hee shoulde be her scoller.

which was so well lyked afore ye Quenes maiesties comminge beinge playd by
ye players in there gownes in Mr marbeckes lodging yat shee sayde yt sur passe   10
damon & Pythias yen ye which nothinge could be better & others lykewise
sayd yf hee did anye more afore his deathe hee woulde runne mad where in
deede yt was ye laste & ye beste yat Edwardes dyd

f 118v*   (1 September)   15

...

This daye in ye morninge ye Quenes maiestie kepinge her chamber [one] mr
peter Carewe ⌃⌜a fyne boye⌝ made an oracion to her in lattyn with ij greeke
verses in ye ende which ye Quene lyked so well yat shee sente for master
Secretarye & wylled ye boye to pronownce yt agayne ye seconde tyme &   20
sayde before he began I praye god my boye thowe mayste say yt so well as
thou dyddeste to me/ & when he hadd ended she sayde yis boye doothe as
well as manye masters of cambridge

This nighte was playde in ye [common] ⌜greate⌝ haull at Christechurche vppon   25
a fayre lardge scaffolde with ⌜princelie⌝ lightes of wax princelick ye Chaundrye
wroughte nighte & daye & lightes yat were provyded for v nightes woulde

Collation continued: 1–7 whome ye Queene ... shoulde be her scoller.] F, f 110v,
omits   9–13 which was so well lyked ... Edwardes dyd] This beinge but repeated
afore certayne Cowtiers in Mr Marbeckes Lodginge by the Players in theire Schollars
gownes before the Quenes Comminge was so well lyked, that they sayde yt far passed
damon & Pythis: then the which nothinge cowlde be better/ lykewise some sayde yf
hee dyd anye more afore his deathe hee woulde ronne mad/ wheare in deede this was
the laste./ neyther dyd hee lyve manye Monethes after./ F, f 110v   18 her] the
Quene F, f 107v   19 ye Quene lyked] lyked her F, f 107v   22–3 & when ... of
cambridge] F, f 107v, omits   25 at] of F, f 107v   26–7 princelick ye Chaundrye
wroughte nighte & daye] curiouslie wrought F, f 107v

1–7/ whome ye Queene ... shoulde be her scoller.:   9–13/ which ... Edwardes dyd: written in left margin
    written in left margin of f 118, presumably in   of f 118v, presumably in reference to the performance
    reference to Perithous, ie, Miles Windsor   of Palamon and Arcite
3/ to a: for to be a   22–3/ & when ... cambridge: underlined

serve but one nighte/ a lattyn playe named marcus geminus [at ye which] made
& sett oute by one mr mathewe ⌜& oother ye studentes of Christchurche/⌝
wherat was presente all ye nobilitye & ye Spanishe embassadoure which
commended ye same highlye to ye Quene insomuche yat her grace sayde yat
shee harde so good reporte of ther doinges yat shee would Loese no more   5
sporte & ye Spanishe embassadoure sayde multa vidi *sed* haec sunt admiranda
⌜et sic referam vbi patriam venero⌝ & my ladye Cycell commended yt very
muche [⟨...⟩ after] ⌜The Spanish Embassador⌝ at Bradnam at ye Lord Windsors
howse hee said in ye presence greate chamber at supper Profecto memorabilia
sunt oxoniensium spectacula.   10

ff 119–19v*   *(2 September)*

...

This daye ye Quenes maiestie woulde haue harde disputacions in Christechurche
haull [but for] ⌜in ye afternone⌝ & fowrmes were thyther broughte & provision 15
there made but for ye stage [shee] yt coulde not bee |
The same daye [me] mr neele ⌜ebrewe reader⌝ gaue vnto ye Quenes maiestie
⌜a booke of all⌝ [a translation] ⌜[comment]⌝ of ⌜all⌝ ye prophetes oute of
ebrewe, & a lyttle booke of verses contayninge ye description of [v] everye
colledge with ye antiquitye of them. memorandum ye verses to be insirted here. 20

This daye [beinge mundaye] ⌜at nighte⌝ ye Quene harde ye fyrste parte of

Collation continued: p 130, l.27–p 131, l.1 & lightes yat ... but one nighte]
Lightes provyded for 5 nightes woulde serve but one nighte *in left margin of F f 107v*
1–2 [at ye which] ... of Christchurche] *F f 107v, omits*   3 was] weare *F f 107v*
4 highlye] so highlie *F f 107v*   4 insomuche] *F f 107v, omits*   4–6 yat shee ...
sporte &] shee woulde lose no more sporte for the good reporte shee heard of their
doinges./ *F f 107v*   7 & my] The *F f 107v*   7–8 very muche] greatelie *F f 107v*
8 Bradnam at] Braddenhoun *F f 107v*   9 hee said] *F f 107v, omits*   9 at supper]
at supper on saterdaye folowinge spake thies wordes [follow] *F f 107v*   9 Profecto
memorabilia] Memorabilia Profecto *F f 107v*   10 spectacula] Spectacula./ Heervnto
accordethe her Maiesties owne wordes ratyfinge & approvinge with ryall assente before
her Nobles & the [whole] assemblye of the whole vniversitie all that was done & sayde:
Ex quo Oxonium veni, multa vidi, multa audivi, probavi omnia. Erant et prudenter
facta et eleganter dicta./ *F f 107v*   15 &¹] *F f 108, omits*   16 there] was *F f 108*
18 [a translation] ⌜[comment]⌝ of ⌜all⌝] *F f 108, omits*   20 with ye antiquitye ...
insirted here.] in Lattyn verses *F f 108*

p 130, l.26–p 131, l.1/ ye Chaundrye ... but one
  nighte/: *underlined and written interlinearly*
6–7/ multa ... venero: *'I have seen many things, but*
  these are to be wondered at, and I will say so when
  I return to my country'

8/ Bradnam: *Bradenham, Buckinghamshire*
9–10/ Profecto ... spectacula: *'The spectacles of the*
  people of Oxford are memorable indeed'

an englishe playe named palamon & arcyte made by one mr Edwardes of ye
chappell & playde in ye common haull in Christechurche, & at ye ende therof
ye Quens maiestie called mr Edwardes & gaue hym ⌜greate⌝ thanckes/ sayinge
hee showlde not wante his reward.

At ye begynninge of yis playe there were by mischaunce iij slayne (a scoller   5
mr pennye   of St Marye haull named Walker/ ye oother a cooke of Corpuschristi colledge
named Ihon gylberte & ye thirde a brewer named mr Pennye/ & v more
hurte by ye presse of ye multitude whoo thruste downe a peece of the syde
wall of ye steyre vppon yem/ my Lord Chamberlayne when he harde yt yat
yei were dedd sayde burye yem/ The Quene vnderstandinge therof sente   10
furthe ⌜vicechamberlen/⌝ her one surgions to helpe yem but for all yat [s⟨…⟩]
⌜mischaunce⌝ shee laughed full hartelye afterwarde at sum of ye players/ The
Actors ⌃⌜notwithstanding⌝ performed their partes so well yat the Quene
laughed hartelie

                                                                         15

f 120v*   *(3 September)*

…

This nighte shoulde haue byn playde ye oother parte of palamon & arcyte but
yt was so late afore ye Quene cam from disputations yat [yt was] shee sente
worde yf yei woulde playe ye nobilitye shoulde be there presente but shee   20
coulde not cum vnto whome mr Edwardes made supplication yat yt meight
be dyfferred vnto ye nexte nighte which ye Quene grawnted oute of hande/

…

Collation continued: 1 one] *F, f 108v, omits*   1 ye] her Maiesties *F, f 108v*   2 in²]
of *F, f 108v*   2 &²] *F, f 108v, omits*   2 therof] heerof *F, f 108v*   3 maiestie]
F, f 108v, omits   3–4 sayinge hee … reward] *F, f 108v, omits*   5 mischaunce]
mischaunce of a wall fallinge downe *F, f 108v*   5 a scoller] *vz.* a Scholler *F, f 108v*
6–7 ye oother … Pennye/ &] a Brewer named Mr Pennye./ & the third a Cooke
of Corpus Christi Colledge named Iohn Gylberte/ *F, f 108v*   8 hurte] weare
hurte *F, f 108v*   8–9 the syde wall] the same wall *F, f 108v*   9–10 of ye steyre
… burye yem] *F, f 108v, omits*   11 furthe] furthe[lie] presentlye *F, f 108v*
11 ⌜vicechamberlen/⌝] Master Vicechamberlayne & *F, f 108v*   11–14 but for all
yat … laughed hartelie] The Actors notwithstanding so well perfourmed their partes
that the Quene lawghed afterwardes hartelie./ *F, f 108v*   19–20 [yt was] shee sente
worde] worde was sente *F, f 109v*   22 oute of hande/] *F, f 109v, omits*

3–4/ sayinge hee … reward.: *written at end of line, interlinearly, and underlined*
5–7/ (a scoller … mr Pennye/: *no closing parenthesis*
6/ Walker: *followed by a caret connected by a line to* mr pennye *in left margin*
9–10/ my Lord Chamberlayne … burye yem/: *underlined*
11/ ⌜vicechamberlen/⌝: *written above* her one *but with no mark to indicate point of insertion*
22/ oute of hande/: *underlined*

f 121*   *(4 September)*

This daye at nighte ye Quene was presente at ye oother parte of ye playe [called]
⌈of⌉ Palamon & arcyte in Christechurche in ye common haull & when all ye
playe was done shee [promysed] ⌈called⌉ Mr Edwardes the maker therof [a   5
rewarde for his paynes/] ⌈& gaue hym greate thanckes with promyse of reward.⌉
And afterwarde her maiestie gaue vnto one Ihon Raynoldes a scholler of
Corpuschristi colledge which was a player in ye same playe viiij olde angels
in rewarde/ The ladye Emilia for gatheringe her flowers pretelie in ye garden
& singinge sweetelie in ye pryme of maye receaued 8 angelles for a gracious   10
reward by her maiesties Commandment
…

f 121v*   *(5 September)*

                                                                            15
This daye [ye Quene] vppon Comminge owte of her maiestie to St maries
mr Etheridge sometyme Greeke reader to ye vniversitie presented a booke of
greeke verses contayninge ye noble artes of h⟨..⟩ Graces ffather/ mr Edwardes
standinge by sayd madam this was my master wherto ye Queene spake yat
hee gaue hym not whippinge ynoughe./   20
…

f 122*

Mr Etheridges booke gyven to her of greeke verses   25
Mr Edwardes sayde madam this was my master to whome answered he was
to blame for not whippinge hym more/

This daye at nighte was playde before ye Quene in ye common haull at
Christechurche a tragedye in lattyn named Progne made by master Dr Caulfyll 30
…

(6 September)
This daye beinge frydaye Dr Perse made a sermon in lattyn before dyner in

Collation continued: 4 in ye common haull] hall *F, f 109v*   4–5 & when all ye
playe was done] When the Playe was all ended *F, f 110v*   7–9 And afterwarde …
angels in rewarde] *F, f 110v, omits*   16 Comminge] the comminge *F, f 111v*
18 h⟨..⟩] her *F, f 111v*   30 a tragedye in lattyn] a Lattyn Tragedy *F, f 112*

16–20/ This daye … ynoughe./: *written in top margin of f 121v*
26/ to whome answered: *for* to whome shee *or* the Quene answered *(?)*
30/ tragedye: g *written over* d

Christechurche dyvers of ye nobilitye & oothers beinge presente but ye
Quenes maiestie was not there by reason of late watchinge at disputacions
& at ye playe…

This daye ye [commissarye] ⌈vicechancellor⌉ & ye ij proctors in ye name   5
of ye hoole vniversitye presented vnto ye Quenes maiestie [in ye name of ye
vniversitie] vj payer of ∧⌈verye⌉ fyne gloves, & to dyvers of ye noble men &
to ye officers of ye Quenes howse sum ij payre sum one which were accepted
verye thanckfullye

                                                                          10

f 123*

This daye after dyner at ye departure of ye Quene oute of Christechurche
mr mathewe made an oracion before her maiestie ⌈at ye haull doore to whome
her maiestie gaue yat lykinge yat shee nominated hym her scholler of her owne   15
chusinge⌉ ye which done shee with her nobilitye & verye manye gentlemen
orderlye cumynge from Christechurche over Carfox & so downe by St Maryes
(where dyvers sheetes of verses were sett vpp on ye doores & walles [vpp] &
lykewyse vppon ye doores & walles of colledges as shee passed bye) ye schollers
standinge in order from St maryes to ye Easte gate iiij doctors [of ye vniuersitye]   20
vz. dr Kenall ye commissarye. dr Godwyn. dr vmphreye. dr Whyte rydinge
before her in scarlet gownes & hoodes with footecloathes & viij masters of
arte rydinge in blacke gownes & hoodes, & ye bedels rydynge before them
(the mayior with xiiij of his brethern rydinge before [her] in yer scarletes to
ye ende of magdalen bridge where yer liberties endethe which beinge tolde   25
to ye Quene by yer Stewarde Sir francis Knolles shee bydd yem farewell with
thanckes) even to Shotouver a myle & sumwhat more oute of oxfourde where
vnderstandinge by ye Earle of leycester Chaunceler of ye vniuersitye yat ye
vniuersitye liberties ended there after an oracion made [by] ⌈to⌉ ye Quene by
mr marbecke shee gaue hym her hande to kisse & with thanckes to ye hoole   30
vniuersitye bydd yem farewell/ ⌈by these wordes⌉ a lyttle after yis a scholler

Collation continued: 1 Christechurche] Christeschurche F, f 112v
13 Christechurche] Christes Churche F, f 113v   14 at ye haull doore] F, f 113v,
omits   14–16 to whome … owne chusinge] whome shee nominated her Scholler
F, f 113v   16 ye which done] which done F, f 113v   17 Christechurche] Christes
Churche F, f 113v   18 &²] F, f 113v, *omits*   21 commissarye] vichauncellor F,
f 113v   22–3 with … hoodes,] F, f 113v, *omits*   24 xiiij of his brethern] his 13
Burgesses & bretherne F, f 113v   26 yer Stewarde Sir francis Knolles] Sir francis
Knolles their Steward F, f 113v   26 bydd] bad F, f 113v   27 where] where the
Quene F, f 113v

5/ vicechancellor: *John Kennall*   5/ ye ij proctors: *William Leche, William Stocker*

named deale made an oracion vnto her which shee accepted verye thanckfullye
& so roade yat nighte to Rycott to mr Norrys howse viij myles from oxfourde

by these wordes confirminge ⌐by these wordes⌐ with riall assente ffarewell
[of the] the worthye vniversitye [of Oxf] & ffarewell my good subiectes &   5
scollers of oxford

Item ye Gentlemen of oxfordshire standinge at ye sowthe syde of ye streete she
gaue mr Browne greate [service] for his good service there enquiringe thryse
whose men yei weare   10

f 123v*
…

marbecke/ Banes/ Badger/ Rookes/ Ball/ Buste/ Bristoo/ Penson/ mathewe/
Potes/ thornton/ Pottes/ Iones/ Summers/ argall/ dalaper/ danet/ edwardes/   15
mancell/ wynsor/ Twyne/ Rainoldes/ Pryn/ Egerton/ Carewe/ Poll/ Yonge/
dalapers boye/ Townsend/ glasyer/ dorset/ graye/ fourde/ Romans/ Iutsam/
Smithe/ nutrix/
…

                                                                               20
Nicholas Robinson's 'Of the Actes Done at Oxford'
Folger Shakespeare Library: MS V.a.176
f 154

Of the Actes Done at Oxford when the Quenes Maiestie was there so collected   25
and noted by Nicholas Robinson at Oxforde: Nowe being Bishop of Bangor.

f 158v   (1 September)
…

Hunc diem clausit historia quædam Gemini cuiusdam quam historiam studiosi   30
quidam Collegij Christi in formam redegerant comœdiæ, sed oratione soluta,
qui eandem in scena peregerunt in Aula eiusdem collegij, vbi omnia erant ad
splendorem & ornatum satis illustria, sumptibus regijs & adiumento magistri
Edwards, qui duobus fere mensibus in Academia mansit ad opus etiam quoddam
Anglicum conficiendum, quod sequenti nocte edidit./ Huic historiali Comœdiæ 35
interfuerunt Consiliarij regij, nobiles viri ac fœminæ vna cum Legato Regis

Collation continued: p 134, l.31–p 135, l.2 ⌐by these wordes⌐ … from oxfourde]
F f 113v, omits   4 by these wordes confirminge … assente] with thies words F f 113v
8–10 Item … weare] F f 113v, omits   14–18 marbecke … nutrix/] F f 107 (see
collation note to l.24 on p 128), presents the names in a different order, specifies Potes
senior and iunior, and omits edwardes, Pryn, and Romans

Hispan*iae/*. aberat Regina vel egritudinis metu vel alijs impedita negotijs.
Sonuerat ia*m* prima a media nocte cu*m* huic spectaculo esset Impositus finis./
…

f 159   *(2 September)*   5

…

Vt superiori nocte sic et ista theatru*m* exornatu*m* fuit splendide, quo publicè
exhiberetur Fabula Militis (vt Chaucer*us* no*m*i*n*at) e Latino in [grae] anglicu*m*
sermone*m* translata p*er* M*a*gist*rum* Edwars, alios⌊que⌋ eiusde*m* Collegij
alu*m*nos. *(blank)* postea qu*am* ingressa fuerat Reg*ia* maie*s*t*as* in theatru*m*,   10
clausiq*ue* essent o*m*nes aditus: nescio q*u*o casu, nec qua ratione, cecidit muri
cui*us*dam pars, qua in aulam itur, oppressitq*ue* scholarem aul*ae* Be*atæ* Mariæ,
et oppidanu*m* no*m*ine penny, qui ibidem mortui su*n*t ac [esse] etia*m* alteri*us*
cui*us*dam scholaris crus fractum fuit: Cociq*ue* vru*m*que crus conquassatu*m*,
faciesq*ue* confecta [vul] quasi vulnerib*us* fuit lapidu*m* ruina. veru*n*tame*n* non   15
fuit intermissu*m* spectaculu*m*, sed ad media*m* nocte*m* prorogatu*m*.
…

f 161v   *(4 September)*

…   20

Hac nocte quod erat reliquu*m* de historia vel fabula Palemonis et Arcis,
actitatu*m* est, Regina ipsa in scena presente./
…

ff 164v–5   *(5 September)*   25

…

…postea | Reg*ia* maie*s*t*as* in Aula*m* deducitur accensis tædis cereis, q*uod*
octaua ia*m* hora sonuerat./
    In hui*us* noctis sile*n*tio in scena exhibetur, quo*m*o*d*o Tereus Rex commedit
filiu*m* necatum apparatu*m*q*ue* ab vxore Progne ob stupratam sorore*m* suam./ 30
o*m*nia certe provt oportebat su*m*mo apparatu, cultuq*ue* vere regio./ Cum hæc
Tragœdia plausu*m* suu*m* accepit, itu*m* est cubitum.
…

Bereblock's Commentary   Bodl.: MS. Rawlinson D.1071   35
pp 13–15   *(1 September)*

…

…Nocte adueniente spectacula apparatissima data sunt, qu*ae* non|nullis

---

9/ Edwars: *for* Edwards   14/ vru*m*que: *for* vtrumque

qui eadem otiosi tota die expectarant, pro mercedis cumulo claritate sua
fuerunt. Nihilque iam pretiosius vel magnificentius excogitari potuit illorum
apparatione atque instruccione. Primo ibi ab ingenti solido pariete patefacto
aditu procestrium insigne fuit, ponsque ab eo ligneus pensilis sublicis impositus
paruo et perpolito tractu per transuersos gradus ad magnam Collegij aulam   5
protrahitur. festa fronde, caelato pictoque vmbraculo exornatur vt per eum
sine motu et perturbatione prementis vulgi, regina posset quasi equabili
gressu ad preparata spectacula contendere. Erat aula laqueari aurato, et picto,
arcuatoque introrsus tecto granditate ac superbia sua veteris Romani Palatij
amplitudinem, et magnificentia imaginem antiquitatis diceres imitari, parte   10
illius superori qua occidentem respicit theatrum excitatur magnum et erectum,
gradibusque multis excelsum iuxta omnes parietes podia et pegmata extructa
sunt, subsellia eisdem superiora fuerunt multorum fastigiorum, vnde viri
illustres ac Matronae suspicerentur, et populus circum circa ludos prospicere
potuit Lucernae, lichni, candelaeque ardentes clarissimam ibi lucem fecerunt, 15
tot luminaribus ramulis ac orbibus diuisis, totque passim funalibus, inaequali
splendore, incertam praebentibus lucem, splendebat Locus, vt et instar diei,
micare et spectaculorum claritatem adiuvare candore summo visa sint, ex
vtroque scenae latere comoedis ac personatis magnifica palatia aedesque
apparatissimae extruuntur. Sublime fixa sella fuit, puluinaribus ac tapetijs   20
ornata, aureoque | vmbraculo operta, Reginae destinatus locus erat verum
illa quidem certe hac nocte non adfuit cum omnia iam hoc ordine preparata
fuerunt domusque erat bene plena et completa licuit statim in scæna Geminum
Campanum inspicere, a Duillio et Cotta apud Alexandrum seuerum invidia
ac aemulatione falso accusatum, servos agricolas, et rusticos corruptelarum   25
illecebris irretitos, testes introductos, nihilque tum magis ridiculum quam
istos contemplari tanquam in certa victoria sordide triumphantes, de Gemini
supplicio decernentes, de facultatibus diuidendis rixantes, adeoque inter
se pugnantes, deinde suum infortunium lamentis muliebriter lachrimisque
deplorantes, vbi satis ita lusum est libertini postea honestiores introducuntur 30
quos nec paena, nec praemium, ad iniuriosam accusationem potuit deducere.
Istorum ergo Chirographa testificaciones indicia, questiones, rem manifestam
fecere, serui igitur tum accusatores imperatoris mandato cruci affiguntur,
Duillius et Cotta debite plectuntur. Libertini remunerantur. Geminus absoluitur,

Collation with Bodl.: MS. Additional A 63 *(B)* ff 5–6, 7v–8v, 11v, 13–14, 17v, 18v
and Folger Shakespeare Library: MS V.a.109 *(F)* ff [5v–6v], [8–9], [12v], [14–15],
[18], [19v]: 1 sua] fua *F*   7 et] ac *BF*   11 superori] superiori *BF*   12 et] ac *F*
14 circum] cirum *B*   16 inaequali] in aequali *F*   18 spectaculorum] spactaculorum *F*
20 ac] at *F*   30 ita] *B omits*

11/ superori: *for* superiori   26/ nihilque: *corrected from* nihil
19/ comoedis: *for* comoedijs

magnus ex omnibus plausus excita*ur* Quo finito cubitum disceditur.
…

pp 19–21   *(2 September)*

…Nocte adveniente ad preparata spectacula conveniunt, Quorum magnificus
apparatus cultusq*ue* elegantia ˄incredibili opinione sua ita omniu*m* animos
[⟨..⟩ere] auresq*ue* compleuerat, vt eo infinita ac in*n*umerabilis hominu*m*
multitudo i*m*mensa et i*m*moderata videndi cupiditate confluxerit. Principis
etia*m* presentia qua iam biduo destituti sunt [ita omniu*m*] tantum sui
desideriu*m* omniu*m* me*n*tibus addiderat, vt inde fuerat numerus longe auctior
et infinitior. vix iam cum p*r*oceribus, viris primarijs regina ingressa est
sellaq*ue* sublimiori consederat, cum tanta omnes | concursac*io*ne ad theatri
aditus convolarent (aula ea collegij fuerat) gradusq*ue* iam a plebe completi
sunt, vt violentia sua co*m*mune gaudium foeda strage contaminaveri*n*t Murus
quida*m* fuerat ex lapidibus quadratis, ingentibus, gradibus, ex vtroq*ue* latere
p*r*opugnaculum opponebatur, ad ascendentiu*m* impetus sustine*n*dos, co*n*cursus
freque*n*tior fit, impetus gra*n*dior murus tametsi firmior sustinere non potuit,
ex vno graduu*m* latere concidit, ruina tres oppressi sunt, totidem vulnerati
[s] ex oppressis qui diutissime supervixit, non vltra biduu*m* vixit vulnerati
adhibitis medicame*n*tis breui co*n*ualuere Hoc malum qua*m*vis potuit,
commune*m* laetitiam co*n*taminare nihilominus tame*n* eandem commaculare
non potuit. Ad spectacula itaq*ue* omnes alieno ia*m* periculo cautiores [iam]
revertuntur. Duos ibi contemplari licuit adolescentes regios, Arcitu*m*, et
Palamone*m*, quos eadem terra concordes diu habuerat, quos idem vit*a*e
periculu*m* carcerq*ue* co*m*munis connexerat, quos affinitatis co*n*iunctio ac
iusiura*n*dum fratres reddiderat, vna*m* isti eande*m*que virgine*m* Emiliam
sorore*m* Ducis Athenarum misere deperierunt Hic tum in illis fas erat
perspicere animos retro contrarioq*ue* motu pulsu ac impulsu huc illuc agitatos,
ac in carcere vix satis concordes appetitu veheme*n*tiori perturbari. pugnare,
digladiari, quid multis? mandato p*r*ohibentur, non curant mandatum:
incarcera*n*tur: erumpunt: exulant: amor non sinit longius | p*r*ogredi, biduu*m*

5

10

15

20

25

30

Collation continued: 1 disceditur] deceditur *B*   9 multitudo] multiduo *F*   9 et]
ac *BF*   10 sui] suu*m BF*   12 et] ac *B*   13 consederat] considerat *B*   14 iam
a plebe] ia*m* ita *B;* a plebe ia*m* ita *F*   15 contaminaveri*n*t] contaminarint *B*
16 fuerat] fuit *BF*   16 gradibus] grandibus *B*   17 p*r*opugnaculum]
propugugnaculu*m F*   19 vno] vino *F*   26 carcerq*ue*] idemque carcer *BF*   29 ac]
et *BF*

1/ magnus: u *corrected from* i *(?)*
7/ incredibili: *written in right margin and marked with caret for insertion here*
32/ erumpunt: *first* u *corrected over* i *(?)*

nimium est triduum ferre non potest. Regius itaque adolescens capitale
supplicium non curat, habitu indecentiori reuertitur, ex Arcito mutato nomine
Philostrates fit, ad omne genus officij seipsum instruit, nullum tam vile munus
quod non exequitur, nihil tam a natura molestum quod non E⌐mi⌐lie presentia
suave illi et iucundum facit, sine ista iucundissima quaeque laboriosa, grauia,   5
odiosa sunt. Palamon interea custodem potione fallit, ex difficultatibus elabitur
Nocte fugit interdiu silvis latitat, fratri tandem fit obvius. Novos hic tumultus
Emilia commovet, adeoque vehementes amor iam fecerat, animi concitaciones
ac offensiones vt mox demicarent, verum statim interventu Thesei pugna
sedatur. Docet tum Palemon qui sint, quo proposito pugnaverint nec tamen   10
mortem, quamvis grauiter deliquerit deprecatur. Dux illarum prece commotus
quae tum forte illi inter venandum aderant, Duellum statuit, iubet pugnam
in quadragesimum diem parent, praemium victori virginem pollicetur. Dici
non potest quanta iam voluptate et laetitia adolescentes decesscet. nos etiam
postquam deo ab omnibus pro principe conclamatum erat [dicessimus] ea   15
nocte dicessimus.
...

p 29   (3 September)
                                                                                          20
...nulla spectacula hac nocte data sunt quod Regina longiori antea disputacione
impedita non potuit eisdem sine salutis suae aliquo discrimine adesse.
...

pp 33-4   (4 September)   25

...Hac nocte Ludis intermissis instaurativi constituti sunt. Theatrum ergo
iam summa contentione alta nocte repetimus regina proceresque invitantur
spectaculo, invitati accedunt Consedere omnes, ingens silentium consequuutum
est Iam tum in scaena milites ambo, Arcitus et Palamon ad diem certum   30
presto fuere, firmissimo presidio vterque septus. Erat ab vno latere Emetrius
Indorum rex cuius in tutela Arcitus fuit, Hunc centum milites sequuti
sunt totidem habebat ex altera parte Threicius Licurgus, cuius virtuti, fidei,
foelicitati commendatus est Palamon. visum est Theseo pugnam singulari
certamine, agi oportere cum illo virginem futuram cum quo victoria fuerit.   35

Collation continued: 2 indecentiori] inde recentiori B; inde°centiori°[tiori] F
5 et] ac BF 8 commovet] commovit BF 14 decesscet] discessere B; dicessere F
16 dicessimus] discessimus B 27 instaurativi] instauratim B 30 et] F omits
34-5 pugnam ... futuram] B omits

14/ decesscet: *for* decessere   27/ instaurativi: *final* i *corrected over another letter*

Haud displicet consilium regibus, nec fratres recusant, fiunt igitur in silvis
septa marmorea, tria ibi extruuntur religiosissima altaria, ad vnam, quae
Dianae fuerat su‸⌈p⌉plex accedit Emilia, hic tum illa vitae solitudinem et
perpetuam castimoniam precatur, Infoelix nimium non potuit exorare, dea
matrimonium predixit, ex altera parte Arcitus ab eo cuius sint in tutela   5
presidia bellicae virtutis victoriam petijt, continuo ei Mars intonuit victoriam
Venerem Palamon altari suo pro virgine precatur cui illa statim virginem
pollicetur. Hic iam inter | Deos contentio facta est, eam disrumpit Saturnus
interea vterque princeps armorum curationem pro suo milite suscepit, quo
finito tubarum cantus strepitusque audiuntur, consertis deinde manibus   10
ferocius pugnant vt primo statim concursu increpuere arma, micantesque
fulsere gladij, horror ingens spectantes perstringit et neutro adhuc inclinata
spe bis lassitudine defatigati pugnantes requiescunt, tertio cum iam non
motus tantum corporum agitatioque anceps telorum, sed vulnera quoque et
sanguis spectaculo omnibus erant corruit Palamon, et victori obijcitur fratri   15
Arcitum gaudio omnes conclamant ovantes gratulantesque accipiunt, Palamonem
exanimatum spes iam tota, non tamen cura deseruerat. Quamobrem altiori
iam oratione actioneque ardentiori furit et venerem cui ab infantia seruiverat
quasi nullius iam aut voluntatis aut potestatis execratur, non tulit indignantem
venus nec potuit aequo animo Martem sibi prepositum ferre suam causam   20
lamentis agit muliebriter, fletuque; Eius lachrimis commotus Saturnus victorem
insigniori laurea triumphantem igne ferit subterraneo, ita confestim Arcitus
moritur ingens tum apparatus sepulturae fuit, publico honestatur funere
subeunt lecticam optimates, sequuntur reges, corpus solemniori pompa
crematur Postremo, regio consilio communique omnium consensione   25
Palamoni virgo traditur idque factum frequentissimo iam theatro incredibili
spectatorum clamore et plausu comprobatum est, atque hac ista nocte
proposita spectacula fuerunt.

p 43   *(5 September)*   30

...Hic sextus ab adventu principis dies in ciuitatem fuit, Is iam quartam in
theatro [nostro] noctem ludorum nostrorum dedit tum munus amplissimum
et apparatissimum quod communis expectacio desiderabat, communi opera

---

Collation continued: 2 quae] qua *BF*   4 castimoniam] testimonium *B; partly*
corrected to tastimoniam *by B or B1*   4 dea] *B corrected by B or B1 to* dea; Deam *F*
5 sint] sunt *F*   15 spectaculo] spactaculo *B*   15 erant] erat *F*   19 nullius iam
aut] *B omits* aut; iam nullius *F*   20 Martem] *B omits*   20 prepositum] propositam *B*
22 insigniori] insigniorem *B*   23 publico] publica *possibly corrected to* publico *B*
25 consensione] consensu *B*   32 ciuitatem] ciuitate *BF*

27/ clamore: *corrected from* clamorem

restituitur, Eius eligantia ac [sc⟨.⟩*aema*] scen*ae* magnific*en*tiae Regina *proceresque*
mirum in modu*m* ac impense admodu*m* delectati sunt. Fabula*m* sexto
humanaru*m* conuersionu*m* libro Ouidius dedit ex eo libet qua*ntum* possum*us*
eande*m* referat....

5

pp 45–6
...

Eratq*ue* spectaculum istud in prauis actibus insignis humani generis similitudo
fuitq*ue* intue*n*tibus | quasi fabula qu*ae*dam illustris, eoru*m* omniu*m* qui, vel
amori vel iracundi*ae* nimiu*m* indulge*n*t quoru*m* vtrumq*ue* etia*m*si ad meliores   10
veniu*n*t. inflam*m*ant tame*n* appetitione nimia, eosq*ue* longe q*uam* antea
ferociores impotentioresq*ue* reddunt, atq*ue* voce vultu spiritu, dictis et factis
a temper*an*tia et moderatione plurimu*m* disside*n*tes, finito spectaculo cum
iam populus ascensioni princepis nomine plausu*m* atq*ue* probatione*m* dedisset,
domu*m* festi*n*antes reuertimu*r*.   15

...

Stow, Chronicles (1570)   STC: 23322
ff 408v–9*

20

The Quenes Progresse to Oxeford.

   The 31 of August the Queenes maiestie in her progresse came to
thuniuersitye of Oxeforde, and was of all the Studentes, which had loked
for her cominge thether ii. yeres, so honourably and ioyfullye receyued, as
eyther theyr loyalnes towards the Queenes maiestye or thexpectation of
their friendes did require. Co*n*cerninge orders in disputacions, and other   25
Academical exercises they agreed much with those whych thuniuersitie of
Cambridge had vsed ii yeares before. Comedyes also and Tragidies were set
foorthe by thuniuersitie, and playde in Christs church, where the Quenes
highnes lodged. Amongest the whyche, the Comodie entituled Palemon
and Arcet, made by master Edwardes of the Quenes Chappell, had such   30

Misfortune.

Tragicall successe, as was lamentable. For at that time by the fall of the
syde wale and a payre of stayres, and great presse of ye multitude 3. men
were slayne. The fifth of September after disputacions the Queenes
Maiestye at the humble sute of certayne her nobilitie and the King of

Collation continued: 1 ac] et *BF*   1 magnific*en*tiae] magnificentia *BF*   2 sexto]
sexta*m B*   3–4 ex eo ... referat] *B omits*   4 referat] referre *F*   12 et] ac *F*
13 et] ac *B*   13 disside*n*tes] discede*n*tes *F*   14 populus] populus ingenti *BF*
14 ascensioni] assentione *BF*   14 princepis] principis *B*   14 nomine] nome*n B*
14 probatione*m*] approbatione*m BF*

1/ eligantia: i *written above* e   10/ etia*m*si: *corrected from* etiam
4/ referrat: *for* referre   11/ nimia: *4 minims for* m *in* MS

Spaynes Embassadour, made a bryefe Oracion in Latine to the vniuersitie, but
so wise and pithie | as Englande may reioyce, that it hath so learned a Prince,
thuniuersities maye triumphe that they haue so noble a patronesse, and
forraine countryes maye wonder to behold such excelencie in that sere. The
6 of September after dinner her grace comming from Christs church ouer   5
Carfox, and so to saint Maries, (the Scolars standing in order accordinge to
theyr degrees euen to the East gate) certayne Doctors of the vniuersitie dyd
ride before her in their Skarlet gownes and Hoodes, and maisters of Arte in
blacke gownes and Hoodes: the Maior also with certayne of his brethern dyd
ryde before her in Scarlet to the ende of Magdalene bridge, wher their liberties   10
ended: but ye Doctors and Maisters went forward stil to Shotouer a mile and
more out of Oxeforde, because their liberties extended so farre, and ther after
oracions made, her highnes wyth thankes to the whole vniuersitie, bad them
farewell, and rode that nighte to Ricote:

…   15

Camden, Annales (1615)   STC: 4496
p 103

…

Elizabetha in agros iam exspatiata animi relaxandi causa, vt se non minùs   20
propitiam Musis Oxoniensibus, quàm Cantabrigiensibus candidè inter se
æmulis præberet, ad Academiam Oxoniam deflectit, vbi magnificè excepta,
septem dies substitit loci amænitate, Collegiorum pulchritudine, studiosorum
ingenijs, & doctrina exquisitissima inprimis oblectata, qui noctem ludis
theatralibus, dies eruditis dissertationibus protruserunt, de quibus singulari   25
Orationis suauitate Latinè gratias cumulatè egit, & benignissimè valedixit.

…

Emily's Lament from Palamon and Arcite   BL: MS Additional 26737
f 106v col 1*   30

An Elegie on
the death of a
Sweetheart.

Come follow mee ye Nymphes,
    whose eyes are never drye:
Augment your waileinge numbers now
    with mee poore Emelie.   35
Give place yee to my plaintes,
    whose ioyes are pincht with paine:
My love, alas, through fowle mishapp,
    most cruell death hath slayne.

40

What witt can will, alas,
    my sorrowes to indite?

I wayle & want my new desire
   I lacke my new delight.
Gush out my tricklinge teares,
   like mighty floudes of rayne:
My Knight, alas, through fowle myshap   5
   most cruell death hath slayne.

col 2*

Oh hap, alas, most hard   10
   oh death why diddst thou so?
Why could not I embrace my ioy?
   for mee that bidd such woe:
ffalse fortune out, alas,
   Woe worth thy subtill trayne: 15
Whereby my love through fowle myshap
   most cruell death hath slayne.

Rocke mee asleepe in woe,
   you wofull Sisters three: 20
Oh, cutt you of my fatal threed,
   dispatch poor Emeley.
Why should I live, alas,
   and linger thus in paine?
ffarewell my life, syth that my love   25
   most cruell death hath slayne.

          The songe of Emelye per Edwardes.
...

       30

Audited Corporation Accounts   OCA: P.5.1
f 51v*   *(Chamberlains' payments)*

Item paid to the quenes Berward   vj s. viij d.
Item paid for bredd and wyne for his breckfast   ij s. 35
...
Item paid to the quenes players   x s.
...

28/ The songe ... Edwardes.: *centred at foot of verse across the 2 columns*

f 54v*   *(Keykeepers' accounts)*

...

Item delyuered to mr williams the xij^th of Iune to Delyver to
mr Taylor to by v oxen to present the Quenes grace   xxx li.

...   5

Item paid to Redshawe to Ryde to master Recorder agaynst
the Quenes Cominge   v s.

Item paid the xth of august to the Quenes Harreldes   xxvj s. viij d.

Item paid to master Mayor for the Queines offycers   xlj s. viij d.

...   10

St Martin Churchwardens' Accounts   ORO: PAR 207/4/F1/1, item 39
mb [1]   *(25 November–25 November) (Receipts)*

...

Item receaved cleare at Hocktyde   xj s. iiij d. 15

...

(Payments)

Item paid to the rynggers for rynggyng when the Queene
came into the citie & went forthe agayne   ij s. 20

...

1566-7

Letter of the Dean and Chapter of Christ Church to the Chancellor
Pepys Library: MS 2502/15   25
f [1]*

Our humble dewtie remembryd to your honor, whereas the Quenes Maiesties
repaire to the vniuersitie, and her abode with vs: In the discharge of our
Dewties in generall, grewe privatly to be moste charge vnto vs more then our   30
Churche is able to beare or well forbeare, as your Lordshipes wisdome well
vnderstandeth. These are moste humblye to beseche your honor so farr to
extende your goodnes towardes vs, that in respecte howe her highnes camme
not particulerly to vs, but to the whole vniuersitie, and therefore as summtyme
your lordshipe curteously did affirme vnto vs, that althoughe the monye were   35
layde out only by vs, yet shulde the whole vniuersitie be likewise partakers of
the burthen and charge: ye will addresse your lettres to the convocacion, that
accordingly we maye be vnburdened of the same either out of the Common
hutch, yf it be able to supplye the lacke, or by the Colledges proportionably,

---

3/ mr williams: *Thomas Williams, mayor*   19/ rynggers: *first r corrected over another letter*
15/ Hocktyde: *22–3 April 1566*

the whole charge thereof be borne, wherein we refuse not to answere our
portion. And whether of these wayes it shall please your honor to take,
Accordinge to your wisdome & promised good will, we shall thinke our
selffes for our present releif, muche bounde vnto your goodnes, and Rest
hereafter alwayes att your Lordshipes commaundement. And thus we committe   5
your lordshipe vnto god prayinge for contynuaunce of your health with
muche encrese of honor. ffrom Christes churche Oxon. the xth daye of
December 1566.

...

                                                                                                10

Episcopal Visitation to Corpus Christi College
Hampshire Record Office: 21M65/A1/26
f 24*   (17 October) (Charges of Jerome Reynolds, fellow, against Thomas
    Greenway, president)

                                                                                                15

...Item he hath in progress as I have hard minstrells and women to the
infamy of our Colledge & diminution of our goodes. Item he resorteth to
bullbeytinges and bearebeytinges in London and commenndeth his man to
put yt on another score. Item in Christmas last past he cumming drunck from
the Towne sat in the hall amongest Schollers vntill j of the Clocke totering   20
with his Legges, tipling with his mouth, and hering bawdy songes with his
eares as, my Lady hath a prety thinge, and suche like, In thende drawinge to
bed cold not be perswaded that yt was yet ix of the clock where indeade yt was
past ij/ And in like sorte at Candlemas last he was notoriously drunck....

                                                                                                25

f 25v   (Thomas Greenway's reply)

...Yf ever I had minstrells in progresse yt was in an Inne, where I being with
others cannot conveniently repell them, And yet I neuer remember that euer
anie came into vs but once,/ I was never in my liff to my remembrance in   30
Parris garden or anye other suche place in London at anye other berbaytinges
but once And that was by occasion of a Gentleman with whom I had then
to doe that was there, Where yt ys obiected that I am a common drunkerd
yf yt may appeare by the Testimony of anye honest man that I was ever sene
druncke than I yeld to this accusation...   35

Merton College Bursars' Accounts   MCR: 3932d
single mb   (22 November–21 March) (External expenses)
...
...tibicinibus ex consensu quo tempore fabulam egerunt scholastici in domo   40

31/ Parris garden: *Paris Garden, bear garden and playhouse*

Custodis v s.... tibicinibus quo tempore comœdia*m* dederunt Scholastici in domo Custodis v s....

...

Merton College Register   MCR: 1.2
f 347

® Comoedia.   Tertio die Ianuarij acta est Wylie beguylie Comoedia anglica, nocte, In ædibus Cust*od*is, *per* scolares, pr*a*esentibus vic*ecustode*, magistris, baccalaureis cum *o*mnibus domesticis et nonnullis extraneis: meritò Laudandi rectè agendo pr*ae* se tulerunt su*m*mam spem.

...

f 348

...

® Comoedia.   Septimo Die Februarij agebatur Evnuchus Terentianus in ædibus Custodis *per* scholares, pr*a*esentibus o*m*nibus Domesticis et non*n*ullis extraneis.

...

Episcopal Visitation to New College
Hampshire Record Office: 21M65/A1/26
f 55*   *(18 March)*   *(Charges against Martin Colepeper)*

...Quodqu*e* idem mag*ister* Culpeper nequiter h*a*bet seu saltem h*a*buit ludibrio Psalmos Daviticos an*tedictos* app*ellando* eos*dem* Robin whodes Ballad*es*. Et continuo....

f 56v   *(Charges against Bartholomew Bolnye, Christopher Diggles, and William Browne)*

Item Q*uo*d pr*e*fatus Bartholomeus Bolnye *contra* formam statutor*um* dicti Coll*e*gij vtitur pug*n*acione, Quodque saltandi c*au*sa, singulis fere diebus a prand*io* confert se in oppidum locaq*ue* suspecta ... Item q*uo*d dicti Chr*is*toferus Digles et will*el*mus Browne simili modo co*m*mu*n*iter frequentant oppidu*m* et loca suspecta pr*edic*ta saltandi gr*at*ia...

Vice-Chancellors' Accounts   OUA: WP/β/21(4)
p 65   *(21 December–21 December)*

...

Solut*um* Decano et Cap*itu*lo ecclesiæ Chr*is*ti pro tertia p*ar*te expensaru*m* suaru*m* a*n*no elapso pro receptione Regia, vigore decreti cuiusda*m* Convocati*on*is editi ad contemplatione*m* Li*tte*raru*m* Comitis Lecestriæ Cancell*ar*ij istius Vnivers*itatis* vt

5

10

15

20

25

30

35

40

*pat*et *p*er billa*m* Doctoris westfaling thesaurarij ib*ide*m pro 3ª
*p*arte maremij venditi coll*egio* Co*r*poris Chri*s*ti 4 li. 3 s. 4 d.
et pro expensis prædictis in receptione principis 33 l. 4 s. 8 d.
in toto   xxxvij li. viij s.

                                                                                                 5

Chancellor's Court Inventories   OUA: Hyp/B/15
single sheet   *(16 February)* *(Inventory of Richard Ludbye)*
...

                              Booke*s*

...   10
A virginal book[*es*]   j d.
...

Wardrobe of the Robes Day Book   PRO: C/115/L2/6697
p 23*   *(January)*   15
...

It*em* there was occupied and worne at Oxforde in a pleye before her ma*i*estie
certeyne of the Apparrell that was late Quene maryes in the chardge of the
said Rauf hope at what tyme there was lost one foreq*ua*rter of a Gowne
withowte sleves of purple vellat with Satten grounde &c.   20

Audited Corporation Accounts   OCA: P.5.1
f 59*   *(Chamberlains' payments)*
...
Item for two shellinges paid to the Quenes Gester   ij s. 25
...

St Martin Churchwardens' Accounts   ORO: PAR 207/4/F1/1, item 41
single mb   *(25 November–25 November) (Receipts)*
...   30
It*em* rec*eived* clere at hocketide   xxxvj ε. ij d.
...
It*em* rec*eived* clere at Whytesonetide   iiij li. ij d.
...

                                                                                                 35
St Mary Magdalen Churchwardens' Accounts   ORO: PAR 208/4/F1/8
single mb   *(Rendered 21 May 1568) (Receipts)*
...
Item R*eceived* at Wyttsontyde cawlyd the churche ale   xxxij s. x d.
...   40

31/ hocketide: *7–8 April 1567*
33, 39/ Whytesonetide, Wyttsontyde: *18–24 May 1567*

St Michael at the North Gate Churchwardens' Accounts
ORO: PAR 211/4/F1/2, item 135
single mb   *(12 March 1566/7–12 March 1567/8)   (Receipts)*
…

Item Recevyd at Hoctyd	xxj s.	5
Item Recevyd of ye yownge men at mayday	iiij s.	
Item Recevyd at wyttsontyde	xxxiiij s. xj d.	

…

1567–8   10
All Souls College Bursars' Accounts   Bodl.: MS. D.D. All Souls c.283
mb 6   *(2 November–2 November)   (Various expenses)*
…

Et de ij s. datis ly waites ad natalem domini

…   15

Magdalen College Libri Computi   MC Arch: LCE/6
f 129v   *(Hall costs)*
…

Solutum oven et duobus famulis occupatis circa theatrum		20
per diem	ij s. vj d.	

…

Solutum oven et duobus famulis operantibus circa scanna confracta		
in comœdia exhibita per .6. dies dietim singulis x d.	xv s.	
Solutum eisdem idem agentibus et alia ibidem per 4or dies		25
dietim ut supra	x s.	

…

f 135v   *(External payments)*
…   30

Solutum Tibicinibus tempore Natalis Domini	iiij s.

…

Merton College Bursars' Accounts   MCR: 3932e
single sheet*   *(21 November–20 March)   (External expenses)*   35
…

…tibicinibus & scholasticis agentibus fabulam, Damon & Pithias, in domo
Custodis x s. alijs tibicinibus pulsantibus in magna aula in die Circum꜀ci꜀sionis
ij s. tibicinibus & scholasticis quo tempore dederunt comœdiam Menechmi
x s.….   40

…

5/ Hoctyd: *7–8 April 1567*   7/ wyttsontyde: *18–24 May 1567*

Merton College Register   MCR: 1.3
p 3

...

Comœdiæ. Vicesimo primo die Ianuarij, nocte, in aula, acta est Menechmus, comœdia
Plauti *per* scholares: cùm ante paucos dies ijdem egissent in *a*edibus Custodis,   5
tragicocomœdiam Damonis et Pythiæ Anglicè, *pra*esentibus Magistris,
baccalaureis, et alijs domesticis cum no*n*nullis extraneis.

...

Audited Corporation Accounts   OCA: P.5.1   10
f 66v*   *(Chamberlains' payments)*

...

Item paid to the quenes mai*esties* bereward that brought
the whit bere   iij s. iiij d.

...   15

f 67

...

Item paid to the quenes players   x s.
Item paid to the quenes mai*es*ties   xx s.   20

...

Tailors' Wardens' Accounts   Bodl.: MS. Morrell 9
f 33*   *(Rendered 7 July) (Payments)*

...   25
for the mvsisiones   xij d.

...

St Mary Magdalen Churchwardens' Accounts   ORO: PAR 208/4/F1/8
single mb   *(Rendered 21 May 1568) (Receipts)*   30

...

Item R*eceived* at hoctyde   xiij s.

...

St Mary Magdalen Churchwardens' Accounts   ORO: PAR 208/4/F1/9   35
single mb   *(Rendered 15 May 1569) (Receipts)*

...

Item R*eceived* att wytsontyde cawled the [w]
churche ale   iij li. xiij s. vj d. ob.

...   40

20/ maiesties: *no word or blank after* maiesties   38/ wytsontyde: *6–12 June 1568*
32/ hoctyde: *26–7 April 1568*

1568-9
Letter of Thomas Cooper, Dean of Christ Church, to the Chancellor
Pepys Library: MS 2503/273
f [1]*   *(5 May)*

5

After most humble thankes for your honorable purpose and determination
to all our great comfortes to see your Vniuersitie, as I am informed, the
fiftenth of this present moneth, I haue thought it my dewtie to lette your
Honour vnderstande what exercises there is to that purpose praepared, that
if it shall seme good to your wisedome you may alter them as it ⌈you⌉   10
shall thinke best.... We haue also in readinesse a playe or shew of the
destruction of Thebes, and the contention betwene Eteocles and Polynices
for the gouernement therof. but herein I thinke we shall be forced to
desyre your Honours fauorable healpe for prouision for somme apparaile
and other thinges needefull. What order we shall vse in these exercises we   15
know not because we doe not yet heare how longe it shall be your honours
pleasure to remaine heere. I woulde be humble shutour[⟨.⟩] to your
Lordeshipe that it may be no lesse then two dayes and that it may please
you[r] [Lodgeinge] to take Lodgeinge both for your selfe and my *Lord*
the Cardinall in Christchurch....   20

Corpus Christi College Bursars' Accounts   CCCA: C/1/1/4
f [7]   *(29 September–25 December)* *(Buttery expenses)*
...

for wyne at Christmas	iij s. 25
To the mynstrell*es*	ij s. vj d.
for wyne on Twelffeday	iiij d.

...

Magdalen College Libri Computi   MC Arch: LCE/6   30
f 144   *(Hall costs)*
...

Solutu*m* ha*m*mon et famulo repara*n*tibus scan*n*a et
remove*n*tib*us* theatru*m* per 3es dies   iiij s.

...   35

f 147v   *(External payments)*
...

Solutu*m* tibicinibus te*m*pore feriar*um* nativitatis
do*mi*ni   iiij s. 40

...

St John's College Computus Annuus SJC Arch: Acc.I.A.l
p 6*   *(25 December–25 March) (Internal payments)*

...

Imprimis for x dossen pound of great candels for ye plaies
at iij s. ∧⌈iiij d.⌉ dossen   xxxij s. 6 d.   5

...

Item for 4 stapls to stay ye selinge in ye haul againste ye plaies   ij d.

...

Item paied to my lord at ye appointment of Mr *president* &
ye companie towardes ye charges of ye plaies in Christmas   xl s.   10
Item to Elie for his charges in prouidinge ye apparell   xiiij s. x d.

...

p 7   *(Repairs)*

...   15

Imprimis to ye carpenters for squaringe timber & other thinges
for ye stage againste Christmas   x s. viij d.

Audited Corporation Accounts OCA: P.5.1
f 74v*   *(Chamberlains' payments)*   20

...

Item payed to the Quenes bearward ye vj^th of march   vj s. viij d.
Item Spent vpon hym the same tyme./   xij d.

...
                                                                      25

St Martin Churchwardens' Accounts ORO: PAR 207/4/F1/1, item 17
mb [1]*   *(Receipts)*

...

Item Recevid at hoctide   xxiiij s.

...   30

St Mary Magdalen Churchwardens' Accounts ORO: PAR 208/4/F1/9
single mb   *(Rendered 15 May 1569) (Receipts)*

...

Item *Received* att hocktyde that the churche ⟨...⟩   35
men gathered   xv s. iiij d.

...

5/ iiij d.: *interlineation smudged; possibly for* iij d.
29, 35/ hoctide, hocktyde: *18–19 April 1569*

St Mary Magdalen Churchwardens' Accounts   ORO: PAR 208/4/F1/10
single mb   *(Rendered 7 May 1570)* *(Receipts)*
…

Item R*eceived* in the churche that we gathered at wettsontyde   xxvj s. x d.
…   5

St Michael at the North Gate Churchwardens' Accounts
ORO: PAR 211/4/F1/2, item 136
single mb   *(12 March 1568/9–12 March 1569/70)* *(Receipts)*
…   10
Ite*m* R*ecevyd* at hoctid clear   xviij s. viij d.
…

1569–70
Magdalen College Libri Computi   MC Arch: LCE/6   15
f 168   *(External payments)*
…
Sol*utum* p*ro* tibicinib*us* tempore natalis do*mi*ni   iiij s.
…

                                                                                          20
Chancellor's Court Inventories   OUA: Hyp/B/12
f [1v]   *(18 April)* *(Inventory of John Dunnet)*
…
Ite*m* a Lute   iij s. iiij d.
…   25

Audited Corporation Accounts   OCA: P.5.1
f 81v*   *(Chamberlains' payments)*
…
Ite*m* to the Quenes players the 7th of december 1569   vj s. viij d. 30
…
Ite*m* to the Earle of Leycesters players the 4 of Maye   vj s. viij d.
…

Lease of St Aldate's Parish House   ORO: MS. DD. Par. Oxford St Aldate c.24/1 35
single mb

This indenture made the xxx^th daye of Ianuarye in the xij yeare of the rayne
of o*ur* souerayne ladye Elyzabeth by the grace of god quene of England
ffraunce and Ireland defendores of the fayth etc. Betwine Thomas Smithe   40

4/ wettsontyde: *29 April–4 May 1569*   38/ This indenture: *in display script*
11/ hoctid: *18–19 April 1569*

of the parish of sant Tolles within the cytye of oxon. bearebruer william Barton
of the same Bucher William Toveye of the same Tanner Iohn ffurnes of the
same Baker Thomas Willson of the same bucher Edward Barkesdall of the
same tanner Edward kyrbye of the same bocher and Richard smith of the
same chaundeler of the onne parte ad Rychard Williams of the cytye of Oxon.   5
gentleman of the other parte Witnessethe that the sayde Thomas William[s]
ₐ⌈William⌉ Iohn Thomas Edward Edward ad Rychard with the whole assente
will consent a⌈n⌉d agreamente of all the parisheners of the ₐ⌈said⌉ parish haue
deuised granted and to ferme letten and by theys presentes do deuise grante &
to ferme lett to the sayd Rychard Willms the house next to the est side of the   10
church yearde of the church of the sayd parishe ₐ⌈of⌉ saynte Tolles comonly
called the church house together with all cotages or houses & a gardayne
ground theareto adioyninge with all and singuler the appurtenaunces except the
ocupacyon ₐ⌈of þe said⌉ church house for the space of fifteine dayes yearely at
or aboute the feaste of Penthecost yf church ale or whiteson ale for the whole   15
parish of saynte Tolles aforesayde shalbe at the sayde feaste Penthecost there
be kept in the same house...

...

St Mary Magdalen Churchwardens' Accounts   ORO: PAR 208/4/F1/11   20
single mb   *(Rendered 27 May 1571) (Receipts)*

...

Item Recevyd in the parrishe for wytson ale   xxv s. viij d.

...

25

St Michael at the North Gate Churchwardens' Accounts
ORO: PAR 211/4/F1/2, item 137
single mb   *(12 March 1569/70–12 March 1570/1) (Receipts)*

...

Item receaved at Hocktyde cleare   xviij s. iij d. 30

...

1570–1
Chancellor's Court Inventories   OUA: Hyp/B/13
f [1]   *(10 March) (Inventory of Robert Harte)*   35

...

Item a payer of virgynalles   xx s.

...

1, 11, 16/ sant Tolles, saynte Tolles: *ie, St Aldate*
5, 7/ ad: *for and*
6/ Witnessethe: *in display script*

10/ Willms: *for Williams; abbreviation mark missing*
23/ wytson: *Whitsuntide was 14–20 May 1570*
30/ Hocktyde: *3–4 April 1570*

Audited Corporation Accounts   OCA: P.5.1
f 92*   *(Chamberlains' payments)*
...
Item geven to the Quenes berward   vj s. viij d.
...   5

St Michael at the North Gate Churchwardens' Accounts
ORO: PAR 211/4/F1/2, item 138
single mb   *(12 March 1570/1–12 March 1571/2) (Receipts)*
...   10
Item *R*eceyued at hoctyde cleare   xv s. xj d.
...

1571–2
The Queen's College Long Roll   QC Arch: 2P156   15
single mb   *(7 July 1572–7 July 1573) (Expenses)*

...Item Tibicinibus Reginae 27 Augusti x s....
...
                                                                         20
Chancellor's Court Inventories   OUA: Hyp/B/10
single sheet verso   *(23 March) (Inventory of William Battbrantes of
    Christ Church)*
...
iiij singing bookes   iiij d. 25
...

Chancellor's Court Inventories   OUA: Hyp/B/18
single sheet   *(10 June) (Inventory of William Smalwood)*
...   30
Item a payre of virginall*es*   xx s.
Item a payre of clavecolles   iiij s.
...

Audited Corporation Accounts   OCA: P.5.1   35
f 97v   *(Chamberlains' payments)*
...
Item paid to the Quenes players   vj s. viij d.
...
Item geven to the Quenes Trumpeters   x s.   40

11/ hoctyde: *23–4 April 1571*

Item wyne & suger the m*aste*r mayor gave them   ij s. vj d.

…

1572–3

All Souls College Bursars' Accounts   Bodl.: MS. D.D. All Souls c.284   5
mb 4   *(2 November–2 November)* *(Various expenses)*

…

Et de iij s. vj d. datis ly Wayght*es*

…

10

Corpus Christi College Bursars' Accounts   CCCA: C/1/1/5
f [8v]   *(25 December–25 March)* *(Buttery expenses)*

…

for wine gevin to my lord straunge and others at the plaie   ij s. iiij d.

…   15

f 35v   *(29 September–25 December)* *(Internal expenses)*

…

for linckes at the scholars plaie   xij d.
for the musicions   iiij s. 20

…

gevin to the carpenters at the scholars plaie   vj d.

…

Magdalen College Libri Computi   MC Arch: LCE/6   25
f 205v*   *(Hall costs)*

…

Solut*um* oven et 4*or* famulis fabricantib*us* & remoue*ntibus*
theatr*um* spect*aculis* edendis   xxviij s.
Solut*um* diversa serrantib*us* eodem tempore pro eodem theatro   ix s. viij d. 30
Solut*um* M*agist*ro lister pro 2.*bus*. C. asserum   x s.
Solut*um* M*agist*ro Gylberd p*ro* 7.*em* quarterijs ad p*redict*um
theat*rum*   iij s. iiij d.
Solut*um* You*n*ge p*ro* 2.*bus* C. asseru*m* ad idem opus   x s.
Solut*um* pro candelis in spectaculis insumptis   x s. 35

…

f 209   *(External payments)*

…

Solut*um* tibicinib*us*   v s. 40

…

1/ m*aste*r mayor: *William Levinz*

Merton College Bursars' Accounts   MCR: 3944c
single mb   *(21 November–20 March)*   *(External expenses)*

...

...Musicis villa Oxon*ie* xij d....

...   5

The Queen's College Long Roll   QC Arch: 2P156
single mb   *(7 July–7 July)*   *(Internal repairs)*

...

...It*em* pro fabricatione scene in aula ad tragicam comediam enarrandam   10
iij s. viij d....

...

(Expenses)
...It*em* in expensis tragic*ae* comedi*ae* in natali chr*ist*i vij s. v d....   15

...

Chancellor's Court Inventories   OUA: Hyp/B/14
f [3]   *(2 August)*   *(Inventory of Henry Hutchinson)*

...   20
A lutinge booke.

...

Audited Corporation Accounts   OCA: P.5.1
f 105   *(Chamberlains' payments)*   25

...

Item geven to my Lorde Chamb*er*lens playe in the Easter weke   x s.

...

St Peter le Bailey Churchwardens' Accounts   ORO: PAR 214/4/F1/34   30
single sheet   *(14 December–13 December)*   *(Receipts)*

...

Item Receyued at Hoctyde   x s.

...

                                                                          35

1573–4

BC ***Persons, Briefe Apologie (1601)***   STC: 19392
ff 194v–5*

A notorious bad
dealing of M*r*
Bag*shaw* vvith   ...
Fr *Persons*
           Fr Persons being gone to Lo*n*don at Christmas tyme, M*r* Bagshaw allured   40

27/ playe: *for* player *or* players (?)   33/ Hoctyde: *30–1 March 1573*
27/ Easter weke: *22–8 March 1573*

vnto him a very proper youth called Mr Iames Hanley of whome Fr Persons
being tutor, had special care both for his good parts, and for his frends who
lyued in London, and with whome Fr Persons remayned at this tyme. The
manner of drawing him was (as we vnder-|stand) by carrying the said youth
forth by night being of yery tender age, to certayne commedies which Fr   5
Persons had forbidden at his departure, for feare of inconueniences that might
ensue in such throng and hauing committed this fault he persuaded the
youth that Fr Persons would not pardon it, and so when he came home Mr
Bagshaw kept this youth shut vp in his owne chamber, & would not suffer
him to go to Fr Persons when he sent for him, nor yet when he came for him   10

® The story of
Mr Iames
Hanley.

himselfe, vnder pretence of feare that he would punish him ouer rigorously,
and the yong gentleman to this day (whome we heare to be hoth very
vertuous and learned) can testifie wel this act of Mr Bagshaw which act
being expulsion by statute to deny any scholler, to the deane, especially his
owne (for Fr Persons as we vnderstand was deane this yeare, of the house) and 15
he hauing no other remedy (for he perceaued Mr Squire to concurre secretly
in this deuise) he called a publike Chapter of all the fellowes laying open the
iniury done vnto him....

BC   *Ely, Certaine Briefe Notes (1602)* STC: 7628   20
     pp 32-3*
     ...

For Parsons his departure out of Oxon. he telleth a tale vvithout head or feet
that because he vvould haue punished on Mr Iames Hau-|ley his owne
scholler for going to a play, I ioyned vvith the Protestant party, vvhoe vvould   25
needs throw him and all his out of the College the same night, except he
would yeald to departe. If he had not a marueilous conceypt of his ovvne
vvitt, he vvould not vtter such narrations, not onely voyd of substance but
of all probability or colour of truthe. Long tyme he hath bin suffered to
reporte, that he was putt out of Oxon. for his Religion, vvith some touch of   30
credit to me and others, vntill at length his exorbitant grating vpon euery
one vvho stood in his way, gaue some occasion by some insinuation of the
truthe to giue him a caueat, not to be so sawcy in medling vvith other mens
matters, and so far so forget his ovvne imperfections.
     ...   35

1, 13m/ Hanley: *for* Hauley (?)
5/ yery: *for* very
12/ hoth: *for* both
15/ the house: *Balliol College*
24/ on: *for* one
34/ so²: *for* to (?)

Magdalen College Libri Computi   MC Arch: LCE/6
f 218v*   (Hall costs)

...

Solutum Noke fabricanti ostium pro spectaculis	x s. ix d.
°Billa° Solutum Oven conficienti waynscott ibidem °per billam°	xxxvij s. iij d. 5
Solutum fabro pro sera et duobus paribus cardinum	x s. vj d.

...

Solutum Oven et famulis fabricantibus erigentibus et remouentibus Theatrum spectaculis	v li. iij s.

...   10

Solutum Noke et famulo pinnacula erigentibus et confirmantibus quæ spectaculorum tempore vel diruta vel concussa erant	xvj d.

...

15

f 223   (External payments)

...

+ Solutum Tibicinibus		xxv s. v s.

...

20

f 223v*

...

Solutum Buccinatoribus	(blank)

...

25

Magdalen College Draft Libri Computi   MC Arch: LCD/1
f 440v   (External payments)

...

Solutum [Tybicinibus] ⌈Buccinatoribus⌉ Reginæ 30. augusti	xx s. 30

...

Audited Corporation Accounts   OCA: P.5.1
f 112v   (Chamberlains' payments)

...   35

Item for the players of my lorde of leyster	x s.
Item bestowed more of them by the commaundement of master mayer	iij s. j d.

...

18/ xxv s. v s.: xxv s. corrected from xv s.; for xxv s. v d. (?)
38/ master mayer: Roger Hewett

f 113* *(Accession Day expenses)*

...

In primis for two quarters of Ale	x s. iiij d.
Item for iij gallons of whyte wyne	v s.
Item payed to the waytes	v s.

...

Item payed to George ewen	ij s. vj d.
Item payed for iiij dozen of brede	iiij s.

...

Item for brynging the Ale to Carfaxe	iiij d.

...

Item for [iij] two li. & a quart*er* of Sugar	iij s.
Item for An ownce of nutmeges	vj d.
Item iij stone pottes	ix d.

...

Tailors' Wardens' Accounts   Bodl.: MS. Morrell 9
f 37*   *(30 June–29 June)* *(Payments)*

...

Item payde to the musyc*i*ons at Richarde Floyd*es* dynner	xij d.

...

1574–5
All Souls College Bursars' Accounts   Bodl.: MS. D.D. All Souls c.284
mb 5   *(2 November–2 November)* *(Various expenses)*

...

Et de xij d. pro ly torches at the playe
Et de vj s. viij d. dat*is* ly musitions eodem tempore

...

Richard Carnsew's Diary   PRO: SP/46/15
f [4v] col 4*   *(21 December)*

...

deuisid to haue a lorde & determinid of our exercise:.

(24 December)
the chois of o*u*r lorde

(27 December)
newes of a rebellio*n*:.

(31 December)
beseigid the adversaries force:.

col 5*   *(19 December)* *(Expenses)*

...

paid the wait*es* there wagis.   12 s.

...

Audited Corporation Accounts   OCA: P.5.1

f 118v*   *(Chamberlains' payments)*

...

Inprimis payed to the Quenes Beareward   x s.

...

f 119*   *(Accession Day expenses)*

...

Item for wyne & cakes   v s. vj d.
Item payed for two quarter of ale   vij s. iiij d.
Item payed for dozen of breade   iiij s.
Item payed to the waytes   v s.

...

ff 120–20v*   *(Election dinner expenses)*

...

Inprimis for breade   xxv s.
Item for seven quarter of Ale   xxviij s.
Item for bere   iij s. viij d.
Item for drynke for the Cookes   ij s.
Item for wyne for the dynner   xx s. vj d.
Item for boyling byffe & Rosting byffe   iij li. xix s. vj d.
Item for xliiij pounde of Shewett   ix s.
Item for fyftene Legg*es* of mutton   x s. viij d.
Item for two gyese   ij s. vj d.
Item for veale   v s. viij d.
Item for neates toungu*es* & others   iiij s. iiij d.
Item for marybons   ij s.
Item for vj turkeys   x s. viij d.
Item for xiiij copell of capons   xxx s. x d.
Item for xxxij Cheekyng*es*   xiij s.
Item for xix pygg*es*   xxvj s. x d.
Item for xiiij gyese   xviij s. viij d.
Item for iij dozen of conneys   xxvij s.
Item for fyve dozen ∧⌐& a halfe⌐ of pyggeons   viij s.
Item for xij [de⟨...⟩kes] duckes   vj s.
Item for butter   x s. iiij d. ob.

Item for ygg*es*   vj s. iij d.
Item for Creme   iiij s.
Item for cabbyshes & cowcombers   xviij d.
Item for barberyes   vj d. |
Item for Quynses   ij s. viij d.   5
Item for Appells pears nutt*es* & ploumes   iij s. vj d.
Item for cheese   ij s.
Item for a hundrede & a halfe of crafyshe   ij s. iiij d.
Item for onyons   viij d.
Item for fyshinge of the waters   iiij s. viij d. 10
Item for flaggs for the haule   xij d.
Item for vj quarter & a halfe of coles   viij s. viij d.
Item for byllett & faggott*es*   v s. ij d.
Item for spyces to mistris mathewe   xxxv s. vj d.
Item for spyc*es* to Mr Alderman whytington   xiiij s. viij d. 15
Item payed to A carpenter   xx d.
Item payed to godstowe the cooke   vj s. viij d.
Item payed to Iherom the cooke   vj s. viij d.
Item payed to hawkins the cooke   vj s. viij d.
Item payed to whyte the cooke   vj s. viij d. 20
Item payed to perkins   iij s. iiij d.
Item payed to markes   iij s.
Item payed to moundaye & hys wyeffe   ij s. iiij d.
Item payed to godstowes man   ij s. vj d.
Item payed vnto xj Laborers   vj s. 25
Item payed vnto A Smyth for mending the locke of
the buttery dore & for A staple   vj d.
Item payed to geore Ewen for playing   v s.
Item payed for halfe a quarter of wheate   x s.
Item payed for flower & baking   vij s. vj d. 30
Item payed vnto them that brought the veneson   x s.
Item payed for the hyer of vessell*es*   xj s.
Item payed for ij [pl] platters & a dyshe that was Lost   v s.
Item payed for carryinge of bordes that weare borowed
[⟨.⟩] in the towne   xij d. 35
Item payed for Stuffe that made the iij Rackes   iij s.
Item payed for breade & drynke when the masons dyd
make the wale & the cookes Supper   v s. x d.

...

28/ geore: *for* george

St Martin Churchwardens' Accounts ORO: PAR 207/4/F1/1, item 48
mb [1] *(28 November–27 November)* *(Receipts)*
...
Item Received cleare to the Churche at Hoctyde   xxxv s. ij d. ob. qua.
...

St Michael at the North Gate Churchwardens' Accounts
ORO: PAR 211/4/F1/2, item 141
single mb *(12 March 1574/5–12 March 1575/6)* *(Receipts)*
...
Item Receyved for hocke ale & whytson ale   xxvij s. j d.
...

1575-6
All Souls College Bursars' Accounts Bodl.: MS. D.D. All Souls c.284
mb 4 *(2 November–2 November)* *(Various expenses)*
...
Et de ij s. datis ly wayghtes
Et de ij s. vj d. datis ly musicions ad festum natiuitatis et animarum
...

Balliol College Bursars' Accounts BC Arch: Computi 1568–1592
f 43v *(18 October–7 July)* *(Expenses noted)*
...
Item geven to the musitions   ij s.
...

Magdalen College Draft Libri Computi MC Arch: LCD/1
f 456v* *(29 September–25 December)* *(External payments)*
...
+ Solutum Magistro Lilly pro Histrionibus Comitis Leicestriæ [xx s.]   xx s.
...
Solutum Wilson musico pro musica in aula in festo
Anunciationis mariæ   x s.
...

Merton College Register MCR: 1.3
p 49
...
Ignis Regentium [Nouembris vicesimo secundo Ignis Regentium, qui per multos iam annos

---

4/ Hoctyde: *11–12 April 1575*
11/ hocke: *Hocktide was 11–12 April 1575*

11/ whytson: *Whitsuntide was 22–8 May 1575*

cineribus reconditus et penè extinctus iacuit, iterum vires capit: et tanto
prorumpit ardore, vt sine pomis, nucibus, vino, cæteris*que* eius vis retundi
nequibat.]
…

New College Bursars' Accounts   NC Arch: 7553
mb 8   *(External expenses)*
…
…*Solutum* Wilson cytharedo iiij s.…
…

Episcopal Visitation to New College
Hampshire Record Office: 21M65/A1/26
f 110   *(16 January)* *(Charges against Mr Smith)*

…Tunc d*o*mi*ni* obiecerunt *contra* Smith qu*od* turpes Cantilenas solet
decantare et q*uod* dixit se nunq*uam* velle credere p*re*dicatorem aliquem. Et
ipse turpeloquiu*m* negat quoad cetera fatet*ur* that he saide Preachers should
live according to their preaching, els lay men will not beleve them…

Audited Corporation Accounts   OCA: P.5.1
f 128*   *(Chamberlains' payments)*
…
Inprimis payed to the Quenes bearewarde   x s.
…
Item payed to the Earle of Sussex players   x s.
…

f 128v
…
Item payed to George Ewen for playing on the Coronation
daye and at the elleccion dynner   x s.
…

St Mary Magdalen Churchwardens' Accounts   ORO: PAR 208/4/F1/15
single mb*   *(Rendered 24 May)* *(Payments)*
…
Item payd ffor pavynge of the strete at the bull Rynge   *(blank)*
…

32/ elleccion dynner: *17 September 1576*

1576-7
Balliol College Bursars' Accounts   BC Arch: Computi 1568-1592
f 49v   *(18 October-7 July)*   *(Expenses noted)*
...
Item geuen to the musitians comminge to the Colledge   ij s.   5
...

f 50
...
Item mr Bagshawe gaue to musitians   xij d.   10
...

Lincoln College Computus   LC Arch: Computus 10
f 1*   *(21 December-21 December)*   *(Commons costs)*
...   15
to the musitions   viij d.
...

f 1v*
...   20
Twesday master Rector kept cowrt
Geven to a minstrell   vj d.
...
To the musitions   xij d.
...   25

Magdalen College Libri Computi   MC Arch: LCE/6
f 236v   *(External expenses)*
...
+ Solutum musicis in natalitijs christi et alijs temporibus   28 s.   30
...

f 237
...
Solutum Buccinatori domini Shandois in ferijs natalitijs   35
Christi   [18] s.
...

36/ [18] s.: *figure cancelled but not corrected*

Chancellor's Court Inventories   OUA: Hyp/B/18
f [2v]   *(31 August) (Inventory of John Simpson)*

...

Item iij Lutes   iij li.

...

Item a luting boke   iiij s.

...

Audited Corporation Accounts   OCA: P.5.1
f 139*   *(Chamberlains' payments)*

...

Item geven to the Counties of Essex players in money
and a bankett   xvj s.

f 139v*

...

Item payed to the Quenes ma*ies*ties *ser*vaunte that kepeth
her game of beres   vj s. viij d.

...

(Accession Day expenses)
Inprimis for wyne   xij s. x d.
Item for two quarters of Ale   x s.
Item fo a kynderkyne of Bere   iiij s. viij d.
Item for Bread and Cakes   vij s.

...

Item payed to george Yewen   v s.

...

Item payed for [i]ij stone *pottes* loste   x d.

...

St Mary Magdalen Churchwardens' Accounts   ORO: PAR 208/4/F1/16
single mb   *(Rendered 12 May 1577) (Receipts)*

...

Item Receavid in gatheringe at hocktyde, for
the paryshe   xx s. 1 d. ob.

...

24/ fo: *for* for
35/ hocktyde: *15–16 April 1577*

St Mary Magdalen Churchwardens' Accounts   ORO: PAR 208/4/F1/17
single mb* *(Rendered 4 May 1578) (Receipts)*
…

Item we gatheryd at whytsontyde and all thinges
dyscarged   xlvij s. vij d.   5
…

(Payments)
Item payd to Mr Case for the use of his howsse
at Whytsontyde   iiij s.   10
…

St Peter le Bailey Churchwardens' Accounts   ORO: PAR 214/4/F1/35
single sheet *(9 December 1576–15 December 1577) (Receipts)*
…   15
Receyved at hocktyde   xx s.
…

1577-8
All Souls College Bursars' Accounts   Bodl.: MS. D.D. All Souls c.284   20
mb 5* *(2 November 1576–2 November 1577) (Various expenses)*
…
Et de ij s. dat*is* le weat*es*.
Et de ij s. vj d. dat*is* musicians ad festu*m* om*nium* sanctoru*m*
…   25

Chancellor's Court Inventories   OUA: Hyp/B/17
mb 1 *(5 April) (Inventory of Thomas Pope)*
…
Item a cyturne & a olde lute   vj s.   30
…

Chancellor's Court Inventories   OUA: Hyp/B/12
f [1] *(15 October) (Inventory of Giles Dewhurst)*
…   35
Item a Lute   ij s.
…

4, 10/ whytsontyde, Whytsontyde: *26 May–1 June 1577*
5/ dyscarged: *for* dyscharged
16/ hocktyde: *15–16 April 1577*

Chancellor's Court Inventories OUA: Hyp/B/18
f [1] *(21 October) (Inventory of James Reynolds)*

...

Item a payer of virginall*es*   xx s.
Item a Lute   viij s. 5

...

City Council Minutes OCA: C/FC/1/A1/001
f 203v* *(8 October)*

... 10

The delyvering | Att this Counsell came George Ewen & George Bucknall [and] ⌜here⌝
in of the wayt*es* | delivered vpp theire scutchins w*hi*ch theye hadd of this Cytie for to be
Scutchins | theire Wayt*es* And they were at the same counsell w*i*th theire [sl] sureties
dyscharged vntill suche tyme as farther order shoulde be taken by the counsell
of this howse & the scutchins are delyvered to the key kepers 15

Audited Corporation Accounts OCA: P.5.1
f 147* *(Chamberlains' payments)*

...

Item payed to the Quenes bearewardes   vj s. viij d. 20

...

f 149 *(Decayed rents)*

...

Item for Thomas Wilson musition   iij d. 25

...

Keykeepers' Accounts OCA: P.4.1
f 33

... 30

Memorand*um* that the Key kepers are charged frome tyme to tyme with ij
skutchyns of sylver w*hi*ch the waytes had/

...

St Mary Magdalen Churchwardens' Accounts ORO: PAR 208/4/F1/17 35
single mb *(Rendered 4 May 1578) (Receipts)*

...

Item Recevyd w*i*th gatheringe at hocktyde   xij s.

...

38/ hocktyde: *7–8 April 1578*

(Payments)
Item payd for two towelles the w*hi*che we bought w*i*th
o*ur* hocke money for the churche   xij s.
...

St Mary Magdalen Churchwardens' Accounts   ORO: PAR 208/4/F1/18
single mb   *(Rendered 24 May 1579)* *(Receipts)*
...
Item we gatheryd at Wytsontyde and all thinges
dyscharged   xxvj s. xj d. 10
...

1578-9
All Souls College Bursars' Accounts   Bodl.: MS. D.D. All Souls c.284
mb 4   *(2 November-2 November)* *(Various expenses)*   15

Et de v s. to the trumpetters
...

Christ Church Disbursements   ChCh Arch: xii.b.21   20
f 31   *(25 December-25 March)* *(Rewards)*

Ian*uari*j To the Countese of Essex men for paines tak*en* in
the q*u*ire the last holie daies   x s.
...   25

New College Bursars' Accounts   NC Arch: 7556
mb 6   *(Internal costs)*
...
...so*lutum* buccinatorib*us* ad ferias natalitias iij s. iiij d.... so*lutum* musicis 30
die circu*m*cisionis iiij s....
...

Trinity College Bursars' Books   TC Arch: I/A/1
f 222   *(25 December-25 March)* *(External expenses)*   35
...
Solutu*m* latomo laboranti circa [aula] fenestra*m* in aula
ludoru*m* tempore   ij s.
...

3/ hocke: *Hocktide was 7-8 April 1578*
9/ Wytsontyde: *18-24 May 1578*

University College Bursar's Account   UC Arch: BU1/F/171
single mb col 2   *(25 March–25 March)* *(External expenses)*
...
It*em* giuen to the musicions   xij d.
...   5

Chancellor's Court Inventories   OUA: Hyp/B/11
mb 1*   *(19 January)* *(Inventory of Nicholas Clifton)*
...
8 Item a payre of virginales   vj s. 10
...

Audited Corporation Accounts   OCA: P.5.1
f 154v   *(Chamberlains' payments)*
...   15
Item payed to the Countice of Essex players   x s.
...

Tailors' Wardens' Accounts   Bodl.: MS. Rolls Oxon 66, roll 2
mb [2]*   *(Payments)*   20
...
Item for two pottells of wyne at Thomas Collyns dynner   xxij d.
Item geven to the mynstrells the same daye   xij d.
...
                                                                              25

St Martin Churchwardens' Accounts   ORO: PAR 207/4/F1/1, item 55
mb [1]   *(30 November–29 November)* *(Receipts)*
...
It*em* rec*evid* cleare at hoctide cleare all things
Dischargede   xxiij s. iiij d. 30
...

St Mary Magdalen Churchwardens' Accounts   ORO: PAR 208/4/F1/18
single mb   *(Rendered 24 May 1579)* *(Receipts)*
...   35
Item we gatheryd at hoctyde   xij s.
...

10/ 8: *the eighth of 11 items inventoried in the hall*
29/ cleare at hoctide cleare: *dittography (?)*
29, 36/ hoctide, hoctyde: *27–8 April 1579*

St Mary Magdalen Churchwardens' Accounts   ORO: PAR 208/4/F1/19
single mb   *(Rendered 8 May 1580)* *(Receipts)*

…

Item gatheryd at Whytsontyde and all thinges dyscharged   xl s.

…   5

1579–80
All Souls College Bursars' Accounts   Bodl.: MS. D.D. All Souls c.284
mb 4   *(2 November–2 November)* *(Various expenses)*

…   10

Et de ij s. vj d. to the players at Christmas.

…

Magdalen College Libri Computi   MC Arch: LCE/6
f 260v   *(External expenses)*   15

…

Solut*um* Musicis in vigelate et festo Bursarior*um*   16 s.

…

Magdalen College Vice-President's Register   MC Arch: VP1/A1/1   20
f 42v

…

Ite*m* eode*m* tempore D*ominus* Pr*es*es et reliqui 13. seniores simul co*n*sentientes
decreverunt vt p*ro* theatricoru*m* expensis p*ro*bationarij solua*n*t 40 s. ceteri ta*m*
socij, qu*am* comminarij, et semicominarij vna cu*m* reliqua multitudine p*ro*   25
p*er*sonaru*m* et graduu*m* dignitate su*m*ptui relicto complete satisfacient.

…

Trinity College Bursars' Books   TC Arch: I/A/1
f 232v   *(25 December–25 March)* *(External expenses)*   30

…

Solut*um* Musicis festis Natalicijs   ij s. vj d.

…

City Council Minutes   OCA: C/FC/1/A1/001   35
f 221v*   *(17 February)*

…

No players to   Hit ys inacted and agreed at this Counsayle that no Mayor of this Cytie or
playe in the   his deputie frome henceforth/ shall geve leave to any players/ to playe within
Guilde Halls   the Guilde hall or the Lower hall/ or in the Guilde hall courte withowt   40

4/ Whytsontyde: *7–13 June 1579*   23/ eodem tempore: *5 April 1580*

consent of the Counsell of this Cytie first hadd/ vppon payne of forfeyture of
Tenne pound*es*/ for the w*h*ich hit shalbe lawfull for the Bayliff*es* to enter in
to his howsse and distreyne and the same to kepe vntyll the said som*m*e of
Tenne pound*es* be fullie payed/ eight pound*es* to the vse of this Cytie/ And
fortie shilling*es* to the vse of the said Bayliffes for the tyme being   5

...

Audited Corporation Accounts   OCA: P.5.1
f 159v*   *(Chamberlains' payments)*

...   10

Item to the Countice of Essex players   x s.

...

Item to the quenes bearerode   vj s. viij d.

...
                                                                   15

ff 160–60v*   *(Election dinner expenses)*

Inprimis payed to Anthonye the Butcher for
two loyn*es* and two brest*es* ⌈of bieffe⌉   xxiiij s.
Item to Mark*es* for two loynes   ix s. 20
Item to ffoster for two brest*es* of biefe   viij s. viij d.
Item to Butler for two loines two brest*es* and
two Crop*es* of bieffe   xxviij s.
Item to Henrie Hodgis for sixe legg*es* of Mutton   ij s. iiij d.
Item to Butler for x legg*es* of mutton   iiij s. iiij d. 25
Item for xiij^th Geise   xv s. ij d.
Item for vj Cople of Capons   xiij s. x d.
Item for xix piggeons   xx d.
Item for xxvij pound*es* of Butter   vj s. ix d.
Item for ij gallons of sacke   v s. iiij d. 30
Item for vj gallons of Clarett wyne   xij s.
Item for Egges   ij s.
Item for philbeard*es*   iiij d.
Item for peares Apples and plumes   xij d.
Item for three turkeys   vj s. 35
Item for xxx Cople of Cunnyes   xxij s. vj d.
Item for xxj pygg*es*   xxv s. viij d.
Item for Rosewater   xij d.
Item for xij [s] Chickins   iiij s.
Item for viij quarters of Ale   xxix s. iiij d. 40
Item for one quarter of syxtenes   xx d.
Item for a kinderkine of beare   ij s.

Item for xx^{ti} dozen of breade	xx s.
Item for Groserye ware	xxx s.
Item for viij quarter of Coles	x s.
Item for iij busshells of wheate	viij s.
Item for one Busshell and a halfe of flower	vj s. 5
Item for baking of the vennysone	ij s.
Item for baking of the Chewettes at Chapmans	xviij d.
Item for faggottes	ij s. vj d.
Item for iij gallons and a pottle of creame	v s. x d.
Item for a banburie cheise	xij d. 10
Item to iij Master Cookes	xviij s.
Item to ij vnder Cookes	vj s. ij d.
Item for one laborer	xiiij d.
Item to vij turne Spyttes	iij s.	
Item for one Bushell of salte	xxij d. 15
Item to the Cookes for lone of xxix dozen	
of vessell	x s.
Item to the Carpenters for setting vppe the portall	
and for fotyinge of tressells	ij s.
Item for slattes for the haule	xvj d. 20
Item to Thomas Capper and his wiffe for making	
cleane the hawle and setting vppe table	ij s.
Item to two poore women for washinge vppe	
the vessell	xviij d.
Item for viniger	viij d. 25
Item for varges	iij d.
Item for mustard	viij d.
Item for ij li. of Candells	vj d.
Item to the parson and Clarke for sayeng service	xiiij d.
Item for halfe a pecke of meate prickes	ij d. 30
Item for barberies	ij d.
Item for Shewett	v s.
Item for the Cookes dynner on frydaye and	
dynner and Super one Saturdaye	v s.
Item for iij quarte pottes and two pottell pottes	xx d. 35
Item to the waytes for pleainge	iij s. iiij d.
Item to the ale bearers when they brought in	
the ale	viij d.
Item to the kepers when they brought the venyson	x s.
Item for a dishe that was loste	xvj d. 40

Summa xix li. xj s. iiij d.

...

St Martin Churchwardens' Accounts ORO: PAR 207/4/F1/1, items 56–9
mb [1] *(29 November–27 November) (Receipts)*

…

Item recevid at hocketyde allthings discharged   xxx s. vj d.

…   5

St Mary Magdalen Churchwardens' Accounts ORO: PAR 208/4/F1/19
single mb   *(Rendered 8 May 1580) (Receipts)*

…

Item gatheryd at hocktyde all thinges dyscharged   viij s. 10

…

(Payments)
Item payde ffor A Towell and a Comunyon Clothe the
whiche we bought with our hocke money   viij s. iiij d. 15

…

St Mary Magdalen Churchwardens' Accounts ORO: PAR 208/4/F1/20
single mb   *(Rendered 30 April 1581) (Receipts)*

…   20

Item Recevyd at Whytsontyd & all thinges dyscharged   l s. xj d.

…

St Michael at the North Gate Churchwardens' Accounts
ORO: PAR 211/4/F1/2, item 146   25
single mb   *(12 March 1579/80–12 March 1580/1) (Receipts)*

…

Item receaved of the hocktyde money   xij s. vj d.

…

                                                                                                                                30

1580–1

ChCh   ***William Withie's Notebook***   BL: MS Sloane 300
f 51v*

…

Tarleton being hissed at Oxon. potted oute these   35
I am not in that golden land wheare Iason wonn the fleese
but I am in that hissing land wheare freshmen play the geese

…

4, 10, 28/ hocketyde, hocktyde: *11–12 April 1580*
21/ Whytsontyd: *22–8 May 1580*

St John's College Computus Annuus   SJC Arch: Acc.I.A.2

p 73   *(25 December–25 March)* *(Internal and external expenses)*

...

x   Item 11º Martij given vnto the Bachilers in
Consideracon of an interlude   XX S.   5

...

Audited Corporation Accounts   OCA: P.5.1

f 167v   *(Chamberlains' payments)*

...   10

Item payed to the quenes Bearewarde   vj s. viij d.

...

Item to the [mys] musytions   v s.

...

                                                                                  15

St Mary Magdalen Churchwardens' Accounts   ORO: PAR 208/4/F1/20

single mb   *(Rendered 30 April 1581)* *(Receipts)*

...

Item Recevyd at hoctyde and all thinges
dyscharged   x s.   20

...

St Mary Magdalen Churchwardens' Accounts   ORO: PAR 208/4/F1/21

single mb   *(Rendered 20 May 1582)* *(Receipts)*

...   25

Item Recevyd at Whytsontyde & all thinges
dyscharged   lij s.

...

St Michael at the North Gate Churchwardens' Accounts   30

ORO: PAR 211/4/F1/2, item 147
single mb   *(12 March 1580/1–12 March 1581/2)* *(Receipts)*

...

Item Receaued at hocketyde   xij s.

...   35

5/ Consideracon: *for* Consideracion; *abbreviation mark missing*
19, 34/ hoctyde, hocketyde: *3–4 April 1581*
26/ Whytsontyde: *14–20 May 1581*

1581–2
Christ Church Treasurers' Account   Bodl.: MS. Top.Oxon c.23
f 46

...

Et in ex*pensis* circa Comed*ias* et Traged*ias* hoc A*nn*o   5
vt p*atet per* ib*idem*   vij li.

...

Christ Church Disbursements   ChCh Arch: xii.b.24
f 28*   *(25 December–25 March)*   10

...

Comedies &   .15. febr*uarij*. To mr browne & mr heton toward the
trag*edies*   charges of setting forth one comedie & three tragedies   vij li. °Ex*oneratur*°
                              °Agnoscimus nos recepisse per
                                        billam amissam.   15
          (signed)   Martin Heton°

...

f 34v   *(Internal repairs)*

...   20

17. Ianuar*ij* To will*ia*m pichaver for w*o*rke done in m*a*ster
[deanes] ⌐subdeanes⌐ house & oth*er* places, as by bill   xv s. x d.
5. febr*uarij* to him for worke done in the walkes about
the stage ⌐by bill⌐   ix s. viij d.
The stage.   9. febr*uarij* to Iohn Essex for w*o*rke done at worton for   25
the stage ⌐by bill⌐   viij s.
eod*em* to will*ia*m pichaver for worke done there for the
same businesse as by bill   xv s. j d.
19. febr*uarij* to him w*o*rking about the stage, as by bill   lvj s. ij d.
eod*em* to horton for the same w*o*rke of sixe penie nayles 3000   30
xv s. five penie nayles 1000. iiij s. ij d. tenne penie nayles 1000.
viij s. iiij d. fourepenie nayles 1000. iij s. iiij d. threepenie nayles
2000. v s. bushel nayles 4000. v s. iiij d. gret hookes 150 xviij d.
& small hooke*s* 500. xv d.   xliij s. xj d.
1. martij, to will*ia*m pichaver ending the stage worke, as by bill   xxxij s.   35
3. m*a*rtij. to the smith for worke done about the stage,
p*er* billa*m*   ix s. v d.

...

6/ vt p*atet per* ib*ide*m: *for* vt patet ibidem *or* vt patet per librum
6/ ibidem: *if correct, an unidentified* liber *mentioned in the first entry of the account*
14–15/ Agnoscimus ... amissam: *'We acknowledge that we have received (this) by a bill (now) lost'*
25/ worton: *Worton, a village near Cassington, Oxfordshire*

Christ Church Computi   ChCh Arch: iii.c.6(b.)
mb 2

…

Et in expensis circa Co*mm*ed*ias* et Traged*ias* hoc a*nn*o
vt p*atet* ib*i*d*e*m   vij li.   5

…

Magdalen College Draft Libri Computi   MC Arch: LCD/2
f 3v   *(External payments)*

…   10

Solut*um* Musicis tempore Spectacul*orum*, & pro vigilate   13 s. 4 d.

…

Solut*um* Musicis d*omi*no fox Domina*n*te   10 s.

…

Solut*um* Musicis in festo Bursarioru*m* et p*ro* vigilate   13 s. 4 d.   15

St John's College Register   SJC Arch: Admin.I.A.1
f 204*

…

An order for ye
solemnysation
of her ma*ie*sties
coronation day.

Also it was agreed the same time, that ⌜at⌝ the solemnising of the day of the   20
Queenes Coronation ∧⌜with divine service⌝ there shall be ordinary gaudyes
kept, as vpon other ⌜lesser⌝ feastes day, ⌜to⌝ the valew of vj s. viij d. ∧⌜&
a fire in the hall & ye charge of ye gaudyes⌝ w*hi*ch shall be alowed out of
other gaudye dayes, w*hi*ch may well be omitted by the opinion of m*aste*r
President & the officers./   25

…

f 209v*

…

order for ye
playes

M*emoran*dum it was graunted concluded and agreed by the President & x   30
seniors that the rest of the charges over & above xxvj li. viij s. iiij d. collected
amongst the studentes towarde the charges of two tragedies & a com*œ*dy
played in the Colledge publickly the xviijth xixth, & xxth of february 1581.
shall be borne by the Colledge, & payd by the Bousars out of the com*m*on
coffers. In wittnesse wherof we the President & felowes have subscribed o*ur*   35
names the xxvijth of february 1581.

…

5/ ib*i*d*e*m: librum Thess*au*rij *mentioned earlier in the roll*
20/ the same time: *27 November 1581*

St John's College Computus Annuus   SJC Arch: Acc.1.A.3

f 24   *(25 December–25 March)*   *(Internal and external expenses)*

…

Item ye charges of one comedye & two tragœdies playd by
the studentes of the Colledge 18o, 19o. 20o Februarii 1581   5
with the repayring of the ruines by reason therof, ouer &
aboue xxvj li. viij s. [⟨.⟩]iiij d. borne by the studentes   xx li.

…

ye charges of ye particulers &c is set downe in a byll which remayneth in ye thresure howse

f 28v   *(25 March–24 June)*   *(Repairs)*   10

…

x   Item for a borde to repare Sir Kites windowe which was broken
at the plaies   xiiij d.

…

x   Item for reparing Mr Lees steres [&⟨..⟩] being broken at the plaies   xij d. 15

…

OUM   **Laurence Humphrey's Ash Wednesday Sermon (1582)**   STC: 13961
pp 163–5*   *(28 February)*

                                                                               20

DE FERMENTO
vitando, Laurentij
Humfredi, Concio.

Matth. 16. Mar. 8. Luc. 12.   25
Iesus dixit illis (Discupulis) Videte & Cauete à
fermento Pharisæorum & Sadducæorum.

® Comaediæ & Tragaediae Oxoniae in fine Februarii

Satis iam satis (Auditores) Theatricis spectaculis aures & oculos oblectauimus:
satis laruarum ac lemurum, vidimus, audiuimus: satis & risui Comico, &   30
luctui Tragico indulsimus: nunc hæc dies, hoc festum quasi Cineritium, alios
mores, aliam diaetam, aliam personam ab vnoquoque nostrûm postulat: vt
quæ a tergo sunt obliti, porrò pergamus, & quæ ante oculos, & quæ prae
manibus sunt, agamus sedulò: vt à ludicris ad seria, à socco ad saccum, à
Cothurno ad Cineres, à prophanis ad sacra, à fabulis ad ipsam veritatis   35
inuestigationem & disciplinam transeamus: quandoquidem omni quantumnis
apparatissima scena nostra veritatis imago est illustrior, & Græcorum Helena
pulchrior & amabilior est Christianorum veritas. Nam si, vt rectè placet

® Veritas cognoscenda.

® Augustinus.

6m/ a byll: *now lost*
25/ Matth. 16. … Luc. 12.: *cp Mt 16.6, Mk 8.15, and Lk 12.1*
29/ Satis: *large embellished initial S*

36/ quantumnis: *for* quantumuis
37m/ Augustinus: Epistola 40.4.7: *'Incomparabiliter enim pulchrior est veritas Christianorum, quam Helena Graecorum'*

Philosophis vestris, contraria se ita habent, vt nosse alterum non posses, nisi |
vtrumq*ue* cognoueris: cùm iam per aliquot dies & noctes fabulis iucundis illis
quidem & laudabiliter actis, fabulis tamen operam dederitis: multo certè
maius studium in veritatis cognitione & contemplatione ponendum: & ita

2. Veritas
amanda.

ponendum, vt illas spectasse tantùm & intellexisse suffecerit: hanc amare &   5
amplecti oporteat. Vt enim Ignoti nulla cupido: sic postquam nouimus,
concupiscendum, desiderandum, amandum est. At non amat qui amat frigidè:

3. ardenter

non amat qui non feruet, qui non ardet, non deperit. In amore hæc inest vis,
omnisq*ue* zeli boni mali, co*n*siderati cæci, hæc est natura, hæc proprietas, vt
nisi vehemens, intensus ince*n*sus fuerit, omnium verè amatoru*m* sententia,   10
amor gelidus aut omnino nullus esse iudicetur. Quod etiam in illis vestris
fabulis vidisse & animaduertisse vos arbitror: in quibus Amoris flamma sic

Fabulæ in
coll*egiis* D*iui*
Ioannis,
Christi, M*ariae*
Magd*alenae*

apparuit & erupit, vt non amor sed amaror, non feruor sed furor esse videretur.
An non meministis Euclione*m* sic ollam suam, Antonium sic Cleopatra*m*,
Alexandru*m* sic Bagoam suu*m* Eunuchum, Philarchum sic Phædram suam,   15
Meleagrum suam Atalantam, & Menechmu*m* Plautinu*m* meretrice*m* Erotium,
Oedipum etiam matre*m* Iocastam, Iulium Cæsarem sic imperium deamasse,
vt regni causa iusiurandum imò omne ius violandu*m* censeat? Et nos amore
Christianæ veritatis non flagrabimus, cuius faciem, ac forma*m*, si oculo mentis
vestræ paulisper intueri | libeat, mirabiles profectò amores sui excitabit?   20
…

pp 175–6*
…

®6 Cultus
diuinorum.

Offerunt Iesuitæ non Deo soli sed Diuis aliis cultu*m*, inuocationem; A   25
Pharis*a*eis haustu*m* est, qui defunctos colueru*n*t, sanctorum mortuorum
sepulchra ornarunt, & memoriam celebrarunt, | & quorum superstitum
sermones ipsorum patres ferre non poterant, eorum corpora omni suppliciorum
immanitate diuexarunt. Romanistæ vt sibi omnes diuos placarent, nullum
offenderent, offa quasi iniecta omnibus, omnium Sanctoru festu*m* instituerunt,   30
& Romæ Pantheon Ethnicu*m* in horum omniu*m* memoriam verterunt:
deterriti, credo, miserando Oenei regis Exemplo, qui cùm omnibus Diis sacra

Sophocl*es*

fecisset, Dianam solam pr*ae*teriisset, neglecti officii pœnas dedit ipse, vxor,
liberi, vt vobis Scena Tragicè repr*ae*sentauit.
…   35

pp 180–1*
…

Opera aliis
perniciosa.

At sunt publicum bonum, Ecclèsiæ, alijs vtilitatem afferunt? Quibus?

2/ iucundis: *corrected from* ineundis *in Errata list*
30/ Sanctoru: *for* Sanctoru*m*

Num viduis? earum domos deuorant, ijs prætextu longarum precum,
confessionum, exhortationum, aniles fabulas inanissimè & sophisticè
Mulierculæ.   insusurrant. Sic Pharisæi in Euangelio & Alexandra Regina ab illis sic
infatuata, & Circeo quasi poculo dementata est, vt mirabilis imò monstrosa
facta sit Metamorphosis fœminæ: non sicut in Theatro audiuistis Oenei   5
Iosephi Belli   filias tres in aues transformatas, sed Regina in seruam & mancipium
Iudaici libri I.   Pharisæorum commutata est: vt quae alijs omnibus optimatibus imperauerat,
capitulo 4.   Pharisæis morem gerere | & famulari videretur.

...
                                                                                          10

Richard Madox's Diary   BL: MS Cotton Appendix 47
ff 3–3v*   (6–8 January)
...

6   ♄ epiphanie I supt at master maiors & af⟨...⟩ wasseld with mr Brush ye
chamberlayn/   15

7   ☿ .G. I dyned with mr marvin at Trinyty colle⟨.⟩ge wher with my brother
& ye 2 paulets & others we concluded a clubbyng on ye moroe. we supt at
[trynyty colledge] lyncoln colledg

®clubbin⟨.⟩   8   ☾ we went a clubbyng owt of al howses in ye town some abowt 400. with
drome bagpipe & other melody at nyght we cam some with ⟨.....⟩ torches   20
and at Vnyversytie College Latwar⟨.⟩ of St Iohns welcomed vs in verse with
a f⟨...⟩ oration in ye name of kyng aulrede crown vs with 2 fayr garlonds &
offered ye third but I answering his oration gave hym y⟨.⟩ third & crowned
hym poet lawreat. so marched we vp to carfox wher sir Abbots of bayly
colledg had an oration in prose co⟨...⟩ vs for taking ye savage who did ther   25
an⟨...⟩ & yelded his hollyn club being with his ⟨...⟩ al in yvye, so went we
to trynyty ⟨...⟩ | & at ye gate sir wurford received me with an oration &
my brother had an other of sir poticary, then at ye entry mr marvin had
one by sir (blank) we supt at ye presidents lodging & after had ye supposes
handeled in ye haul indifferently.   30

...

f 5*   (4 February)
...

4   ☉ .G. knyght of corpus christi preched & did wel mr den, lankford, pryce   35
& short dyned with vs at nyght. we had musycians & went vp with them &
20 clubs to carfox

...

6–8m/ Iosephi ... capitulo 4.: *Josephus,* Bellum   14/ master maiors: *William Noble's*
  Judaicum *1.5.2–3 (1.110–16)*   16, 35/ .G.: *dominical letter*
8m/ 4: *for* 5   22/ aulrede: *for* alurede

Epilogue to Caesar Interfectus   Bodl.: MS. Top.Oxon e.5
p 359*

> Epilogus Cæsaris interfecti, quomodo in scenam prodijt ea res acta
> in ecclesia christi Oxoniæ, qui epilogus a Magistro Ricardo Eedes et   5
> scriptus et in proscenio ibidem dictus fuit.°1582.°

Egit triumphum Cæsar de Republica Brutus de Cæsare; nihil ille magis potuit,
nihil iste magis voluit; nihil aut ille, aut iste minus debuit: Est quod vtrique
laudi tribuam; est quod vtrique vitio vertam; male Cæsar qui occupauit
Rempublicam benè, qui sine cæde & sanguine occupauit: rectè Brutus qui   10
libertatem restituit; improbè, qui interfecto Cæsare, restituendam censuit;
illius facinoris turpitudini victoriæ moderatio; quasi velum obduxit; huius
facti gloriæ ingrata crudelitas tenebras offudit; ille se gessit optimè in causa
pessima; hic pessimè in optima. Sed neque defuerunt qui hos tam illustres
viros, alterum regni, alterum libertatis studiosum, velut admotis facibus   15
concitârunt. Antonius Cæsari, subiecit igniculos, Bruto Cassius: Cæsari
Antonius regium diadema ita optauit, ut offerret; Cæsar ita recusauit; vt
cuperet. Quicquid voluit, valde voluit Brutus; nimium Cassius: tanto certè
quidem Dux melior quanto vir Brutus: in altero major vis, in altero virtus:
Brutum amicum habere malles; magis inimicum timeres Cassium: odio habuit   20
ille tyrannidem, hic tyrannum: Cæsarem secuta est fortuna iusta, si tyrannidem
spectemus; iniusta si hominem: sed neque tyrannos Dij immortales licet
optimos ferunt; et illi quasi in mercedem tantæ virtutis datum est, ut videret;
non ut caveret interitum./

25

Gager, Meleager (1592)   STC: 11515
sig A2*

> ILLVSTRISSIMO AC NOBILISSIMO HEROI, Roberto Essexiæ
> Comiti, aureæ Periscelidis sodali, equorumque regiorum Magistro,   30
> fœlix faustumque noui anni auspicium precatur.

Annus iam penè vndecimus agitur, Nobilissime Comes, ex quo Meleager
primum, octauus ex quo iterum in Scenam vênit ac primùm quidem volens,
ac sponte suâ; triennio pòst, inuitatus, publiceque euocatus, secundùm   35
prodiit; assidentibus, ac spectantibus clarissimis Comitibus, Penbrochiensi, ac
Lecestrensi, Cancellario tum nostro, vnà cum nobilissimo Philippo Sidnæo,
nonnullisque illustribus Aulicis. Quâ tum approbatione acceptus sit, nec iam
memini, nec magni vnquam feci; satis ad laudem Meleagro fuit, si qua tamen
ea laus sit, quòd politissimarum aurium discrimen bis subierit, nullo sanè   40

6/ 1582.: *underlined; added in a later hand, possibly Anthony Wood's*

insignis fastidii dehonestamento. Ecce iam tertium exit, non quidem in
Scenam, sed in lucem id est conspectum tuum...

St Aldate Churchwardens' Accounts
ORO: DD Par. Oxford St Aldate c.15/11 5
mb [1]   *(4 February 1581/2–4 February 1582/3) (Expenses)*
...

Item p*ai*d to the Ale bearers at hocktyde   j d.
...

10

mb [2]   *(Receipts)*
...

Rec*eyv*ed at hocktyde   xxiiij s.
...

15

St Martin Churchwardens' Accounts   ORO: PAR 207/4/F1/1, item 63
mb [1]   *(26 November 1581–2 December 1582) (Receipts)*
...

It*em* rec*evi*d at hoctyde allthing*es* discharged   xxxv s. v d.
...   20

St Mary Magdalen Churchwardens' Accounts   ORO: PAR 208/4/F1/21
single mb   *(Rendered 20 May) (Receipts)*
...

It*em* Recevyd at hoctyde and all thinges dyscharged   xij s. 25
...

St Peter in the East Churchwardens' Accounts   ORO: PAR 213/4/F1/1
single mb col 1   *(8 December–8 December) (Receipts)*
...   30

It*em* for hock money at hocktyde   xxx s.
...

1582–3
Christ Church Disbursements   ChCh Arch: xii.b.25 35
f 48   *(25 March–24 June) (Rewards)*

5. Ianuarij. To a tru*m*peter by co*n*sent of mr deane & oth*er* dining
in the hall, w*hich* should haue bin entered the last quarter   ij s.
...   40

8, 13, 19, 25, 31/ hocktyde, hoctyde: *23–4 April 1582*

f 51v*   *(Internal repairs)*

...

eod*em* To Alexander nichols & his fellow sawyres for 6. dayes
sawing timber agaynst the co*m*ming of palatine laskie for div*er*s
purposes at xviij d. pence the day   ix s.   5

...

f 52*

1. Iunij To Edmu*n*d daniel for 6. dayes worke hewing timber   10
for the sawiers, & preparing the kitchin in pecke waters Inne,
for the vse of the companie, x d. a day   v s.

...

10. Iunij To Rich*a*rd west for felling 4. timber trees at
Chandense for the heaven & oth*er* new building on the   15
stage, 3 d. a tree xij d. for felling 3. oth*er* lesse trees, 2 d.
a tree vj d. for squaring of one tree xvj d. for dressing 3.
trees [xi d.] x d. for cariage of 2. lode of the same timber
iij s. In all   vj s. viij d.

...   20

f 66v   *(Extraordinary expenses)*

...

To the vniv*er*sitie by order towa*r*d the charges for the
entertaynem*en*t of palatine laskie, a polonian, as by bill   xxv li.   25

...

To the vniv*er*sitie agayne by order of the delegates for
th'entertaynem*en*t of the foresayd palatine, as by bill   xv li.

...

                                                                      30

f 69v   *(Internal repairs)*

19. Iunij To mr willis & mr Randoll by mr maxie for nayles
remayning after the pulling downe of the stage, vid*elicet* 700
of single tennes v s. x d., at x d. the 100. ₍ᴧ⌜[⟨...⟩]⌝ & for 300.   35
of sixepenie nayles at vj d. the 100. xviij d. & 3000 of
fivepenie nayles at 4 s. 2 d. the thowsand xij s. vj d.
fourepenie nayle [2075.] ⌜2750.⌝ at 3 s. 4 d. the thowsand
ix s. ij d. threepenie nayle 5000. at ij s. vj d. the thowsand
xij s. vj d. Bushel nayles tenne thowsand, at xvj d. the   40

3/ eod*em*: *1 June 1583*   5/ xviij d. pence: *dittography*

thowsand xiij s. iiij d. lath nayles tenne thowsand at xvj d.
the thowsand xiij s. iiij d.   lxviij s. ij s.
       (signed)   Emanuell Maxey:
...

22. Iunij To Iohn Elles for worke donne, espeaciallie at the   5
comming of palatine laskie ⌈by bill⌉   xv s.
...

(24 June–29 September)
29. Iunij To Robert mallet Ioyner for [32] 43 foote of crest,   10
set vp in the hall, beyng broken downe at the playes, at
ij d. ob. a foote   viij s. xj d. ob.
eodem to him for 4. new pendentes at the entrie into the
quire, & fastening the other, xviij d. & for fastening old
crestes in the hall vj d. ob.   ij s. ob. 15
       (signed)   by me robart mallet
...

f 89*

                                                   20

[Monie paid & delivered in respect of the playes & intertaynement
          of the palatine laskie etc
Receaued by me °George Peele° the xxvj^th day of May anno 1583 at the
handes of mr Thomas Thornton Treasurer the some of xx li. I say the
somme of twenty poundes.   25
       (signed)   George Peele]

William Gager's Commonplace Book BL: MS Additional 22583
f 63v*   *(26 September)* *(List of deans, prebendaries, masters, and students*
  then at Christ Church)   30
...
                 Mr Leonardus Hutton.
Seu scribenda siet Comædia seu sit agenda,
   Primum, Huttone, potes sumere iure locum.
...   35

f 64*

                 Mr Ihoannes Kinge.
Sunt laudi tragicæ tibi partes Kinge furentes: 40

1/ tenne: *first* e *written over* h

Quantâ spe iuuenis? quantaque stella domus?
                    Mr Thomas Crane.
Indolis egregiæ, et Romæ spes altera nostræ
    Te persona magis Comica, Crane, decet.
...   5

Corpus Christi College Bursars' Accounts   CCCA: C/1/1/6
f [10]   *(25 March–24 June) (Internal expenses)*
...

To the apoticarie for a perfume prepared for the librarie   10
against the duke of Polonia his comming.   xiij d.
...

New College Bursars' Accounts   NC Arch: 7563
mb 7   *(Internal expenses)*   15
...

...Solutum to the musitians vppon Twelthe daye v s.... Solutum for bindinge
the booke of verses geven the Duke of Polonia xviij d. Solutum to the
musitians x s....
...   20

St John's College Computus Annuus   SJC Arch: Acc.I.A.4
f 19v   *(25 December–25 March) (Internal and external expenses)*
...

Item 10 of ffebruarie to ye musitions & for linkes at which   25
time ye studentes had a commodie & Tragœdie   vij s.
...

f 22v   *(25 March–24 June)*
...   30

Item 13. Iunij paid for a bankett prepared for ye Palatine
a lasco of Polonia, & other ye nobilitie of Englande with
ye musicke   xx s.
Item paid by order of ye convocation house towardes the
charges of ye entertayninge of ye said Palatine &c. 10. 11,   35
12, 13º of Iune 1583   vij li. x s.
...

f 24v   *(24 June–29 September)*
...   40

Item given in reward to ye musitians at Middsommer   x s.
...

Register of Congregation and Convocation   OUA: NEP/Supra/L
f 234v   *(13 May) (Letter from the earl of Leicester to the vice-chancellor)*
...

To my very louinge friendes the vicechauncellor and the rest of
the conuocacion of the vniuersitye of Oxon.   5

After my right hartie commendacions The Queenes maiestie hath will me to
signifye vnto you yat the Palatin Laskey the noble man yat is now heare owt
of Polonia mindeth shortlye to cum downe to the vniuersitye of Oxfourd
and that her highnesse pleasure thearfore is yat he be receuid of you with   10
all the curtesey and sollenitye yat you may I mind my selfe to accumpanye
him thether the time we apoint to be theare shall be one mundaye the xth
daye of Iune & theare to remaine yat daye all twseday and all wensdaye and
on thursdaye morninge to depart: you must vse all sollennitye of disputations
oracions & readinges as you did at her maiesties beinge with you Youre   15
scaffoldes must allso be sett vpp for disputations as they weare for so wold
her highnesse haue it I wish lattin sermons to be prouidid for wheare of the
first to be made by Master dr Mathewe and so leuinge the rest to youre good
consideracions Not doubtinge but you will carefullye applye youre selues to
the satisfinge of her maiesties pleasuer in this be halfe and with yat regard   20
which the respect of your one reputacion requiret in such a case I thus bid
you right hartelye fare well from the court the xiij^th of Maye 1583//
I do thinke it fitest for him to lye in Christes Church and do praye you to
call for youre most able and sufficient men of the vniuersitye yat be a brode
against that time and doubt not but you will be carefull to haue all youre   25
actes for learninge to be as well dunn as possiblie maye for he is well learnid
him selfe & of greate iudgement: Youre verye louinge friend & chauncellor
Robert Leycester
...

                                                                                 30

f 19v*   *(17 May) (Orders for plays for royal visitors)*
...

Item statutum est duo theatra ædificanda vnum in ecclesia Sanctæ Mariæ pro
disputationibus publicis alterum in ecclesia Christi pro ludis theatricis et vt
nullus ex Academia nec alius quisquam (peregrinis solummodo excepetis)   35
theatra ascendere praesumat sub poena incarcerationis per spacium vnius
mensis, et solutionis quadraginta solidorum vniuersitati et procuratoribus...
...

Item vt ludi theatrici constituantur in aula ecclesiæ Christi per discretionem
decani thesaurariorum vel vnius eorum et bursarij simul cum consensu   40

7/ will: *for* willed   35/ excepetis: *for* exceptis

vicecancellarij doctoris Humfrey doctoris Dalober Magistri Willis Magistri Eds
procuratoris vel consensu duorum supra nominatorum tam de argumento
quam de actoribus et expensis eorundem

...

Vice-Chancellors' Draft Accounts   OUA: WP/β/S/1
sheet 1, ff [1–2]   *(10 June)*

The Accountes of all the expences defrayed & disbursed in the Entertaynment
of the Duke Palatyne Laskye aswell for his diett & such as came to the
Vniuersitye with him as also for the Playes guifts and all other chardges
duringe the tyme of his beinge heare which was fowre dayes./ Six Meales

Imprimis for [the] the three suppers breakfastes and drinckinges at Christchurch as appeareth by the perticular accomptes of Mr Harrison & Mr ffoster	lxxxij li. vj s. x d. ob.
Item for the dinner att Magdalen Colledge as appeareth by the Accomptes of Mr Hearne Manciple there	xxxj li.
Item for the dinner att Newe Colledge as appeareth by the Accomptes of Mr Kitchin Manciple there	xxxviij li. xvij s. j d. ob.
Item for the dinner att Allsoules Colledge as appeareth by the Accomptes of Mr Iackson Manciple there	xxx li. xv s. vj d.
Item for halfe a tunne of Gascoigne wine vz. clarett and white and for an Hogshead of Rennish wine and for a great Runlett of sacke containinge xxij^ty Gallons provided at London as appeareth by the Merchaunts byll vz. Mr Anthony Radcliffe	xvj li. ij s. vj d.
Item for lv pounds of sugar provided att London by the saide Mr Radcliffe, wherofe xl pounde is att x d. per pounde and xv pounde att xij d. ob. the pounde	x li. ix s.
Item for xv gallons of wine fott from Ioseph Barnes in Oxon. & spent in the said colledges att the seuerall dinners as appeareth by the sayd Ioseph his bill and for three Runlettes of wine	xl s.
Item payd by Mr Harrison for the carriadge of wine Cates apparrell for the playes and all other carriadges from London to Oxon. as appeareth by his bill	v li. v s. l
Item for Iourneys to the court and to London to make provision as appeareth by Mr Harrisons and mr Smythes accomptes	vj li.
Item the chardges of a Comedye and a Tragedye and	

1/ vicecancellarij: *Robert Hovenden*

a shewe of fire worke as appeareth by the perticuler
billes of Master Vicechauncelor Mr Housone Mr Maxie
and Mr Pille.   lxxxvj li. xviij s. ij d.
Item for a Bible bounde in Veluet, & gilted which was
geven to the Duke   lvj s. iiij d.   5
Item for newe bindinge and trimminge Master
Vicechauncelors booke of his office   iiij s.
Item for Gloues geven to the Duke and the Lordes and
the rest of his companye   vij li. viij s.
Item geven to the vj Beedelles toward the provision of   10
their liverye gownes   x li.
Item payd to the Clarcke of the Vniuersitie for his chardges
and travayle in trimminge vpp of St Maryes church and the
Divinitye schoole   xxij s.
Item geuen in rewardes to Sir Henrye Leighs manne for   15
his paynes in bringinge a brase of Buckes & for the chardges
of bringinge the warrante to Sir Henrye Leigh.   viij s.
Item for enlarginge the Stage in St Maryes church as
appeareth by Master Randolls bill   lvij s. iiij d.
Item payde to Greenwood for fetchinge of fowre Buckes   20
from Whichwood his horse and him selfe as appeareth
by his bill   xxxv s. viij d. |
Item geven in rewardes to the fowre Mancipls and to
Sir Christopher Brownes ⌊°Bromes°⌋ mann   iij li.
          Summa totalis   CCCxxxj li. v s. vj d. 25
Whereof to be allowed out of the Vniuersitie coffers
according to the agreement of the delegates   Clxv li. xij s. ix d.
Remaynethe to be gathered aboue .106 li. 11 s. 3 d.
levied vppon the Colledges the summ of   lix li. xviij d.
          the which is to be answered   30
     from Christchurch   xv li.
     from Magdalen colledge   xvj li.
     from Newe colledge   xviij li.
     from Allsolls colledge   v li.
And more from Christchurche for nayles & tymber   35
of thuniuersities   v li. x s.
          Summa   lix li. x s.
...

sheet 2, ff [1–2]   40

The accountes of mr Robert Hovenden Doctor of diuinitie, and Vichauncellor
of the Vniuersitie of Oxforde of suche monye as he hathe receiued and laied

out by decree of Convocation for the interteynment of Palatine Lasky a noble
man of Polonia, and others directed to the vniuersitie by her maiestie the
xth daye of Iune in the yere 1583. where they continewed fower dayes, and
receiued vj meales.

5

Recepta	Inprimis receiued of thuniuersitie treasure the sume of	Clxv li. xij s. ix d.
	Item receiued of Christchurche	xl li.
	Item of Magdalen colledge	*(blank)*
	Item of New colledg	xij li. x s. 10
	Item of AllSoles colledg	xij li. x s.
	Item of Merton colledg	iiij li. xv s.
	Item of Corpus Christi	v li. x s.
	Item of St Iohns	vij li. x s.
	Item of Brasennose	iij li. x s. 15
	Item of Quenes colledg	xl s.
	Item of Trinitie colledg	iij li. xv s.
	Item of Excester colledg	iij li. xv s.
	Item of Oriell colledge	lvj s. iij d.
	Item of Lincoln colledg	l s. 20
	Item of Vniuersitie colledg	xxv s.
	Item of Baylioll colledg	xxv s.
	Summa totalis	CClxx li. iiij s.

Expensa	Inprimis payed to Richarde Garbrand for a bible in quires	25
	wasshed and ruled to be given to the Lasky	xiij s. iiij d.
	Item to Dominicke Pynnart for bindinge the same bible	xliij s.
	Item payed to the bedles by order of the committies for newe liueries	x li.
	Item to mr Smithe the bedle for his charges going to my	30
	Lord of lecester with letters	xviij s. viij d. |
	Item payed to Cavie for newe binding the vichauncellors [⟨…⟩] ∧⌜booke⌝ adding parchment therto	iiij s.
	Item to Cavie for dressing the churche and scholes	xij s.
	Item payed to Welles the glover for gloves geven to the	35
	Duke and others	vij li. viij s.
	Item to mr Phillip Rondell principall of Hart haule for enlarging the stage in St maries churche	lvij s. iiij d.
	Item to Woodsonne the Bedle for sedg and russhes to strew in the churche	x s. 40
	Item to mr Peele for prouision for the playes at Christchurche	xviij li.
	Item to mr Howson for charges concerninge the same playes.	xix li. xj s. ij d.

Item to mr maxie for charges about the stage and
other necessaries for the same playes.   xxiij li. xiij s.
Item to George House and Iohn Esard of London,
for dressing the stage, and other deuises about the
playes.   xvij li. xvij s. xj d.   5
Item to master President of St Iohns for wine, sugar etc.
prouided from London   xx li. xiiij s. vj d.
Item to edward ffoster manciple of Christchurche for
cates spent there for three suppers   xliiij li. vj s. x d.
Item mr harrison for iornyes cates et cetera spent at   10
Christchurche   xlvij li. xvj s. ij d.
Item to Henrie Iackson manciple of Allsoles colledg
for a dinner for the Palatine, the lordes Russell, Gray,
Chandos, sir phillip Sydnye, sir william Russell & others   xxxij li. v s. vj d.
Item to the Bursers of New colledg towardes there   15
charges for the Palatines dinner there   xv li.
Item to Magdalen colledg for the Palatines dinner there   (blank)
Item to Sir Henrie Leas man bringing veneson from
woodstocke   v s.
Item to morgan and Pagett two of the cookes hyred   20
at Christchurche   xxx s. |
Item to Tyffin an other cooke hyred there   xx s.
Item to .v. laborers helping in the kitchin there   vij s. x d.
Item to the Cookes for the hyer of vessell at
Allsoles colledg   ix s.   25
Item for half an Oxe prouided by master president
of St Iohns, & master prouost of Oriell colledg spent
at this tyme   iiij li.
Item for engrossing this account   iij s.
Item to the Cook for hier of vessell   xlj s. viij d.   30
Item to mr Smith vt patet per Billam   xxij s. vj d.
Item to Daniell the Carpenter   xxxvj s. j d.
         Suma totalis expensorum   CCLxxvij li. vj s. vj d.

…

°The dynner
ther came to
xxxj li. att ther
owne coste and
charges wh(.)lys°

35

Visit of the Prince of Siradia   Folger Shakespeare Library: MS L.b.606
single sheet – single sheet verso

The entertaynment of the Polonian was in this wise as followeth.

40

when he came neer Oxford master Dr westfaylinge accompanyed with 4 or 5
other doctors went forth to meete hym at his entraunce in to the lybertyes
whear master Doctor westfaylinge did byd him welcome with a little short

oration after he was outsid the towne the mayor and his brethren presented
him with gloues and byd him welcome also by the mouth of theyr towne
clarcke, from whome he passinge to the midst of the towne and agaynst St
maries which ys the vniversytie church he was agayne in lyke saluted in the
name of the vniversytie by the orator therof, and presented with a booke and   5
gloues by the vicechauncellour in the behalf of the vniversytie also thence he
lastly came to Christchurch where he was wellcomed by a master of Art in
the name of that priuate house wheare the supped and lodged that night
ₐ⌜when about one of clok were made ⟨..⟩ay fyre wourkes in quadrant⌝ the
next day ... he was brought to Christchurche to supper [which ended he]   10
⌜and afterward⌝ heard a comedy in the hall and so to bedd. | The next day in
the morning being wedensday there was a sermon ... which ended he went
to supper to Christchurch and [after] after was a tragedy and so to bedd.

Holinshed, Third Volume of Chronicles (1587)   STC: 13569   15
p 1355 cols 1–2   *(June)*
...

    Touching the interteinement which he had at Oxenford, and how the
vniuersitie did congratulate his comming, it is somewhat worth the noting.
In the moneth of Iune, the said Albertus de Lasco coming from the marriage   20
of the lord Norris his daughter, with sir *Amias* Paulets eldest sonne at Ricot,
he put himselfe on the waie to Oxenford; wherof the vniuersitie (doctor
Houendon then vicechancellor, & maister Leison with maister Edes proctors)
hauing intelligence, prouided for his conuenient receiuing: insomuch that in
the waie to Oxenford, there met him doctor Westfailing, who greeted him   25
with a pithie salutation. In like sort did the maior and his breethren, in whose
behalfe for the whole citie, the towne clerke a worshipfull maister of art,
pronounced his short and sententious speech in Latine, not without some
gratulatorie gift from that corporation. On the east gate wherat he entered,
stood a consort of musicians, who for a long space made verie sweet harmonie,   30
which could not but mooue & delight:
           Inscia plebs populúsque arrectis auribus astat,
           Dulciferúmque rudi suscipit aure melos.

The
welcomming
of Albertus to
the vniuersitie
of Oxenford,
with a partile
description
of his
interteinment.

    All vp the high street vnto saint Maries church, on either side the waie, were
decentlie marshalled scholers in their gownes & caps, batchelors and maisters   35
in their habits and hoods. At saint Maries the orator of the vniuersitie (notable
in his facultie) presented him a booke, in which were closelie couched verie
rich and gorgeous gloues. From thense he marched to Christs church, where
he was whilest he abode in the vniuersitie most honourablie interteined. And

<hr>

1/ the mayor: *Edward Bennett*
32–3/ Inscia ... melos: '*The ignorant populace and people stand there with their ears pricked up, And receive
sweet honey with an uncivilized ear*'

the first night being vacant, as in which he sought rather rest in his lodging than recreation in anie academicall pastimes, strange fire works were shewed, in the great quadrangle, besides rockets and a number such maner of deuises. On the second daie, his first dinner was made him at Alsoules college, where (besides dutifull receiuing of him) he was solemnelie satisfied with scholerlie 5 exercises and courtlie fare. This night & the night insuing, after sumptuous suppers in his lodging, he personaly was present with his traine in the hall, first at the plaieng of a pleasant comedie intituled Riuales; then at the setting out of a verie statelie tragedie named Dido, wherein the queenes banket (with Eneas narration of the destruction of Troie) was liuelie described in a 10 marchpaine patterne, there was also a goodlie sight of hunters with full crie of a kennell of hounds, Mercurie and Iris descending and ascending from and to an high place, the tempest wherein it hailed small confects, rained rosewater, and snew an artificiall kind of snow, all strange, maruellous, & abundant. 15

Raine of rosewater, and haile of sugar confects, &c.

Most of the actors were of the same house, six or seauen of them were of saint Iohns, & three or foure of other colleges & hals.... At afternoone the fourth & last daie, he went towards Woodstocke manour, and without the north gate by the waie he was inuited vnto a banket at saint Iohns college, where the gates & outward wals ouercouered with thousands of verses, & 20 other emblematicall poetries then offered him, argued their hartie goodwils: but his hasting to his iournies end caused him not to tarrie the delicat banket; yet onelie staieng the deliuerie of a sweet oration and his owne quicke wittie replie therevnto, he departed immediatelie, accompanied for a mile or two with the most of those reuerend doctors and heads of houses all on 25 horssebacke, where the orator againe gaue him an orators farewell. And this is the summe of his interteinement, not deliuered in such sort as the dignitie of the same requireth; howbeit sufficient for a sudden remembrance.

...

30

Camden, Annales (1615) STC: 4496

p 344

...

Albertus Alasco Polonus in Angliam venit.

E Polonia Russiæ vicina hac æstate venit in Angliam, vt Reginam inuiseret, Albertus Alasco Palatinus Siradiensis, vir eruditus, corporis lineamentis, 35 barba promississima, vestitu decoro & pervenusto, qui perbenignè ab ipsa nobilibus*que* magno honore & lautitijs, & ab Academia Oxoniensi eruditis oblectationibus, atq*ue* varijs spectaculis exceptus, post quatuor menses ære alieno oppressus clàm recessit.

...

40

14/ artificiall: *col 1 ends after first* i

Hannisters' Registers   OCA: A.5.3
f 17*   *(12 August)*

...

Willelmus Gybbons musition admissus est in libertatem huius Ciuitatis eisdem
die et Anno/ et solvit iiij s. vj d. pro feodis officiariorum eiusdem Ciuitatis et   5
Iuratus/

...

City Council Minutes   OCA: C/FC/1/A1/001
f 259   *(6 August)*   10

...

William
Gybbons
admitted and
to [the] have
the Scutchins

Hit is furthermore agreed at this Counsell/ That William Gybbons musition
was admitted into the freedome of this Cytie and to beare the [Schutch]
Scuttchins of oure Waytes/ not havinge any certen fee of this Cytie for the
same/ So that he enter in bande with one sufficient suretye that at his   15
departure or leavinge of the same scutchins with chayns of sylver to the
valewe of fower poundes better then theye nowe be/

...

Audited Corporation Accounts   OCA: P.5.1   20
f 181v   *(Chamberlains' payments)*

...

Item for gravell stones and workmanshippe at the est
bridge agaynst the dukes comynge   xij s. x d.
Item payed two poore fokes for carrienge awaye the   25
mucke before the yeld hall the same time   viij d.

...

St Martin Churchwardens' Accounts   ORO: PAR 207/4/F1/1, item 65
single mb   *(2 December–1 December) (Receipts)*   30

...

Item Recevid at hoctide allthings dischardged   xxiij s. ij d.

...

St Mary Magdalen Churchwardens' Accounts   ORO: PAR 208/4/F1/22   35
single mb   *(Rendered 24 May 1584) (Receipts)*

...

Item Received at Whytsontyde and all thinges
dyscharged   x s.

...   40

32/ hoctide: *8–9 April 1583*   38/ Whytsontyde: *19–25 May 1583*

St Michael at the North Gate Churchwardens' Accounts
ORO: PAR 211/4/F1/2, item 148
single mb *(12 March 1582/3–12 March 1583/4) (Receipts)*
…

Item receaued at hoctide and whitsontide   liij s.   5

…

St Peter in the East Churchwardens' Accounts   ORO: PAR 213/4/F1/1
single mb col 1   *(8 December–8 December) (Receipts)*
…   10

Item rec*eived* hocke mony at hocktyde   xxiij s. iiij d.

…

1583–4
Christ Church Computi   ChCh Arch: iii.c.6(c.)   15
mb 2
…

Et in xp*ensis* commediar*um* et tragediar*um* hoc
Anno fact*arum*   n*il* li.

…   20

Lincoln College Computus   LC Arch: Computus 7
f 43   *(21 December–21 December) (Necessary internal expenses)*
…

Ite*m* towardes ye expe*n*ces and receavinge of ye   25
duke palatine   l s.

…

Ite*m* geve*n* to ye Hungarian   vj s. 8 d.

…
                                                                                                            30

f 62

…

Ite*m* to the musicians on shroveso*n*day   iij s.

…
                                                                                                            35

Merton College Register   MCR: 1.3
p 94
…

Comedia acta.   Vicesimo primo eiusdem Portionistæ in aula d*omi*ni Custodis ageban⟨.⟩

5, 11/ hoctide, hocktyde: *8–9 April 1583*   33/ shrovesonday: *1 March 1583/4*
5/ whitsontide: *19–25 May 1583*   39/ Vicesimo primo eiusdem: *21 January 1583/4*
18/ xp*ensis*: *for* expensis

Plauti quanda*m* comediam, quæ vocatur Captivus. D*o*minus autem custos
donavit ⟨...⟩ viginti solidis.

...

New College Bursars' Accounts   NC Arch: 7564   5
mb 9   *(Internal expenses)*

...

...so*lutum* waites et musicians twelve day x s....

The Queen's College Long Roll   QC Arch: 2P161   10
single mb   *(7 July–7 July) (External expenses)*

...

...Item tibicinibus in festo Circumcisionis xviij d.... It*em* dat*um* tibicinibus 2°
februarij x s....

...   15

St John's College Computus Annuus   SJC Arch: Acc.i.A.5
f 21   *(25 December–25 March) (Internal and external expenses)*

...

Ite*m* to the musitions on Newyers daye at nighte   iiij s. 20

...

Register of Congregation and Convocation   OUA: NEP/Supra/L
f 241v*   *(24 July) (Statutes in answer to royal complaints)*

...   25

3   Item decretum est no*n* licere vicecan*cellarij* veniam histrionib*us* concedere vt
suos ludos theatricos habea*nt* infra p*r*ecinctu*m* vniu*er*sitatis nisi ex speciali
gratia co*n*uocationis

...

                                                                                       30

f 242*

Statuts prouided for all such disorders as lately haue bin co*m*planed of by her
m*a*ie*s*tie and so certified vnto vs by the Right honorable the Earele of Leycester
o*u*r Chauncellor, in his last le*tt*ers co*n*cerni*n*ge the reformacio*n* of ab∧⌈u⌉ses in 35
this Vniu*er*sitye

...

2/ ⟨...⟩: *word lost in binding, probably* illis
2/ solidis: *for* solidos

f 242v*

Item vppon consideracion of sicknesse wheare with this vniuersitye of late hath
often times bin greuoslye visited by reson of the extraordenary concurse of
poeple at vnsesonable times of the yeare to see stage playse and games it hath   5
bin thought a matter most conuenient as well for the maintaninge of health
amounge ˄⌈vs⌉ as allso for the detaninge of the younger sort from extraordinary
spendinge more then theire smale exhibicion will beare & most of all that
they maye not be spectators of so manye lewde and euill sportes as in them
are practised, that no common stage players be permitted to vse or do anye   10
such thinge with in the precincte of the vniuersitye And if it happen by
extraordinarye meanes yat stage players shall gett or obtane leaue by the maior
or other wayse yet it shall not be lawfull for anye master bachiler or scholler
aboue the age of eighteene to repaire or go to see anye such thinge vnder paine
of imprisonment And if any vnder the age of eighteene shall presume to   15
do anye thinge contrarye to this statute the partye so offendinge shall suffer
open punishment in St Maries Church according to the discrecion of the
vichauncellor or Proctors

...
                                                                                        20

      The confirmacion of thease statutes aboue specified by the right
      honorable the Lord of Leycester our Chauncellor by his one hande

As I like and alowe all thease statutes and articles aboue written and namelye
in the fiuth article do thinke the prohibicion of common stage players very   25
requisite so wolde I ˄⌈not⌉ haue it meant theare bye theat the tragedies
commodies & other shewes of exercises of learninge in that kinde vsed to be
sett foarth by vniuersitye men should be forbedden but acceptinge them as
commendable and greate furderances of learninge do wish them in anye wise
to be continuid at set times and incresed [and the] and the youth of the   30
vniuersitye by good meanes to be incurragid to the decent and frequent
settinge fourth of them
                                                                        Robert Leycester

City Memorandum Book   OCA: D.5.2   35
ff [1–1v]*   *(21 December)*

Nouerint universi per presentes me Willelmum Gibbon de Ciuitate Oxonie
mynstrell teneri et firmiter obligari Willelmo ffrere de ciuitate Oxonie predicta

3/ Item: *the numeral 5 originally stood in the margin*   29/ anye: y *altered from* i
  before this entry but has been cropped   31/ decent: *written over another word*
26/ theat: *for* that

armigero in ducentis libris bone et legalis monete Anglie soluend*is* eid*em*
will*el*mo ffrere aut suo certo att*ornato* hered*ibus* vel assign*atis* suis ad quam
quidem soluc*ionem* ben*e* et fidel*iter* fac*iendam* obligo me heredes executor*es* et
admin*istratores* meos firm*iter* p*er* p*re*sentes sigillo meo sigill*atas* Dat*as* vicesimo
primo die Decembris anno regni d*omi*ne n*ost*re Elizabethe dei gr*aci*a Anglie   5
ffraunc*ie* et Hib*er*nie Regine fidei defens*oris* &c. vicesimo sexto./
Sealed & deliu*er*ed in the p*re*sens of
(signed) Rob*er*t Crasse Henry Beaumont
        Phi*lip* Coles   [h⟨...⟩] hod
                  wal⟨...⟩ | 10

The Condicion of this obligacion is suche that if the within bounden william
Gibbon his executors administrators & assigns shall well & trulie performe
fulfill observe & kepe all & singuler suche coue*n*auntes graunt*es* artycles
paymentes condicions and agreament*es* as are conteyned specified & declared   15
in certen Indentures bearing date the daie & yere of thes p*re*sent*es* made
betwene the within named will*ia*m ffrere on thone parte & the said Will*ia*m
Gibbon on thother parte whiche on the parte of the said Will*ia*m Gibbon his
executors admin*istrators* & assignes are & oughte to be performed & kept
according to the forme effect & true meaninge exp*re*ssed in the said Indentures 20
That then this obligacon to be void & of none effect orelse to stand in full
power & vertue/

Keykeepers' Accounts   OCA: P.4.1
f 45v   25
...
One bande of will*ia*m Gibbons for the Scuttchins
...

St Martin Churchwardens' Accounts   ORO: PAR 207/4/F1/1, items 67–9 30
mb [1]   *(1 December–29 November) (Receipts)*
...
It*em* rec*ev*id at hoctide Clearlye   xxxviij s.
...
                                                        35
St Mary Magdalen Churchwardens' Accounts   ORO: PAR 208/4/F1/22
single mb   *(Rendered 24 May 1584) (Receipts)*
...
Item R*eceived* at hoctyde and all thinges dyscharged   ix s.
...   40

21/ obligacon: *for* obligacion; *abbreviation mark missing*
33, 39/ hoctide, hoctyde: *27–8 April 1584*

St Mary Magdalen Churchwardens' Accounts   ORO: PAR 208/4/F1/23
single mb   *(Rendered 16 May 1585) (Receipts)*

…

Item R*eceived* at Whytsontyde and all thinges dyscharged   x s.

…   5

c 1584
Letters of Complaint Regarding Abuses at Magdalen College
MC Arch: MS 655a
p 321   *(Complaint of Edward Gellibrand)*   10

…

Bursariorum   Transgressed by spending money on plaies, entertainment of great men, and
Electio   not on such uses only as Statute seemeth to allow.

…

                                                                                      15

p 322*

Sine licentia non   Broken by resorting to tavernes, Cookeshouses, spectacles, and such other
divillandum   plaies forbidden.

Quod no*n*   Broken by having dogges, hounds, greyhounds. Dice, cardes usual in chambers, 20
exerceant ludos   at ye accustomed time of ye yere. Lords of misrule, stonebowes, playing at ball
inhonestos   against ye church windowes, coursing of dogges, singing of roundes, throwing
                      of stones, in the night, to ye trouble of study and sleepe.

…

                                                                                      25

p 331   *(Complaint of William Cooke)*

…

19   our schollers demyes some of them haue resisted their censors and no
     punishment could be inflicted m*aste*r President taking the matter into his
     owne hand: to the great emboldning of others in the like dissolutenes. also   30
     there is one m*r* Green w*hich* was once demy of this house that doth still
     abyde about the same, and is the author of all misorder amongst youthe, of
     singing all the night long round about the cloysters, and throwing stones
     w*ith* many moe such abuses: and yet for all this he is p*er*mitted to lye w*ith*in
     the Colledge and haith been this long tyme. I am p*er*suaded he doth corrupt   35
     very many towardly youth in this house.

…

p 339   *(Complaint of Simeon Pett)*

…   40

…Sir Browne togither with his scholler Whitton have kepte evill rule in the

4/ Whytsontyde: *7–13 June 1584*   28m/ 19: *ie, item 19*

night tyme, singing in the cloisters and disturbing the whole colledg. Mr.
Stroud, Mr. Chitty, testes. He went forth 2 without leave of the dean, wherof
the one tyme was since the visitation was published. Mr. Atkins and I can
testefye this.

...   5

1584–5
Christ Church Disbursements   ChCh Arch: xii.b.27
f 30*   *(25 December–25 March)* *(Rewards)*

...   10

23o Ian*uarij* to ye musicians at my L*ord* of Leycesters beinge
here for theire paynes at supper and at ye tragedie, and whe*n*
ye comedie was ferst played   xx s.

                       (signed) Henr*icus* Hayes

To Ed*ward* Foster w*hi*ch he payde to mr Maxie for cariadge   15
of stuffe fro*m* ye reuills and backe agayne whe*n* my L*ord* of
Leycester came hether   xvj s.

                       (signed) Edward foster

...
                                                                                   20
f 31   *(Expenses)*

...

Expenses for Tragedies and co*medies*

To Henrie Clinche, Raph Clinche, and Roger More for
payntinge eych of them 2 dayes 2 night*es* and halfe a day at
xvj d. ye day, and as muche ye night, to eych of them ∧⌜vj s.   25
in all⌝   xviij s.
(signed)   By me henry Clynche   Raulfe Clynch   Roger Mor⌜e⌝
12o Ian*uarij* to m*aste*r Subdeane layde out in my absence
as by bill   xxj s.
Eode*m* to willia*m* Pickhauer ye carpenter for one cople of   30
sawiers 5 dayes and an halfe about ye stage at 18 d. ye day   viij s. iij d.
+
Eode*m* to Cakebreade ye smith for 15 li. of candles for ye
comedie at 3 d. ye pound w*hi*ch he bought at m*aste*r subdeanes
appoyntme*nt*   iij s. ix d. 35
to him more for 16. dish candlestickes bought of ye turner
at m*aste*r subd*eanes* appoyntme*nt*   xx d.
to him more for his owne woorke 2 dayes about ye candlestickes
and his laborers one day   ij s. iij d.

2/ 2: *for* 2 *times (?)*
32/ +: *presumably Pickhaver's personal mark; resembles an X*

+

To Iohn Daniel for woorke donne about ye stage *per* billa*m*	xxij s. xj d.
13o Ian*uarij* to mr Maxie as layed forth by him p*er* billa*m*	ix li. iij s. x d.
Eode*m* to mr Lilies ma*n* for ye lone of som*me* apparell ex	
co*n*sensu ˄⌈Decani et capituli⌉	xx s.
Eode*m* to Nightingale for ye lone of apparell and his charges	
hether ex consensu Decani et Capituli	iij li. vj s. viij d.
Eode*m* to Tipslowe for ye like cause wi*t*h ye like co*n*sent	iij li. v s.
Eode*m* to his wyfe more for ye lone of a cloke	v s.
Eode*m* to Tipslowe for ye Reuels p*ro*mised by mr Maxie,	
and allowed by m*aste*r Deane and ye chapitre	v li.
Eode*m* to George ye Paynter for his paynes ex co*n*sensu	
vt supra	xxxiij s. 4 d.
Eode*m* for gloues sent to mr Lilie for his curtesie in lendinge	
som*me* appara*l*l ex co*n*sensu Decani et Subdecani	vj s. viij d.
Eode*m* to mr Ed*war*d Browne p*er* billa*m*	iiij s.
14o Ian*uarij* to mr Maxie layde forth by him whe*n* ye comedie	
was played ye seconde tyme p*er* billa*m*	iiij s. ij d.
To William Pickhauer for worke donne about ye stage	
˄⌈p*er* billa*m*⌉	xix s. ij d.
To willia*m* Pickhauer for 1980 foote of elme borde bought	
of mr Milwarde and others for ye stage at v s. ye hundreth	iiij li. xix s.
To him more for Mosses ma*n* woorkinge 2 dayes wi*t*h him	
about ye stage	xx d.

+

To Person ye plumber for his woorke and an others in hanginge	
vp and takinge downe ye candlestickes in ye haull	ij s.

+

To mr Heyse for ye musicians at m*aste*r Subdeanes appoyntme*n*t	v s.
(signed) Henr*icus* Hayes	

34 li. 13 s. 4 d.   Summa xxxiiij li. xiij s. iiij d.

...

f 49v   *(25 March–24 June)*

...

Tragedies and
Com*edies*

4o Maij payde to Iackso*n* by m*aste*r Subdeane in my absence	
for small necessaries at ye playes not the*n* demaunded vt patet	
p*er* billa*m*	xxiij d.

...

1/ +: *presumably Cakebread's personal mark; resembles an inverted U*
25/ +: *presumably Pickhaver's personal mark again*
28/ +: *presumably Persons' personal mark; resembles a double O*

Magdalen College Draft Libri Computi   MC Arch: LCD/2
f 20v col 1*   *(Charges of external payments)*

...

Solut*um pro* ludis theatricis in adventu comitis
Lecestre*nsis*   3 li. 19 s. 5 d.   5
Solut*um pro* epulis in adventu eiusdem   10 li.

...

The Queen's College Long Roll   QC Arch: 2P162
single mb*   *(7 July–7 July) (External expenses)*   10

...

...It*em* dat*um* Maurisio in festo Circu*m*cisionis Christi xij d. It*em* dat*um*
tibicinibus iussu Præpositi x s....

...

15

St John's College Computus Annuus   SJC Arch: Acc.I.A.6
f 21   *(25 December–25 March) (Internal and external expenses)*

...

It*em* to ye Musitians at Candelmas   iij s. iiij d.
...   20
It*em* paid to ye intertainment of my Lord of Lecester
in ye vniu*er*sitie   l s.
...
It*em* to ye Musitions sett one in Battells   xvij s.
...   25

Trinity College Bursars' Books   TC Arch: I/A/1
f 276   *(25 December–25 March) (External expenses)*

...

Solut*um* pro ludis   xx s.   30
...

Register of Congregation and Convocation   OUA: NEP/Supra/L
f 282v*   *(Visit of Lord Leicester, chancellor)*

...   35

Hora prima post meridie*m* die supradicto ven*erabiles* viri delegati a ven*erabili*
domo convocat*ionis* secu*n*d*um* delegatione*m* sibi co*m*missa*m* convenerunt in
*a*edibus ven*erabi*lis viri do*c*toris Vnderhill vicecan*cellarij* et Com*m*uni consensu
decreverunt contiones habendas et disputationes in singulis facultatibus ac
etia*m* ludos theatricos in ecclesia chris*ti* et Coll*egio* Magdalanensi p*ro* quor*um*   40

36/ die supradicto: *2 January 1584/5*

expensis allocabunt viginti minanas æqualiter dividen*das* dat*as* inter
Collegia pr*e*dicta.

...

Gager, Meleager (1592)   *STC*: 11515   5

See 1581–2

Audited Corporation Accounts   OCA: P.5.1
f 196v*   *(Chamberlains' payments)*   10
...
Item for removinge of the Bull ringe and a stone of
Mr Massyes   viij d.
...

                                                                            15

f 197
...
Item for the Erle of Oxfordes musytions   vj s. viij d.
...

                                                                            20

Keykeepers' Accounts   OCA: P.4.1
f 47v
...
One bande of Will*i*am Gibbons and others for the Schutchins./
...   25

St Martin Churchwardens' Accounts   ORO: PAR 207/4/F1/1, item 73
single mb   *(29 November–28 November) (Receipts)*
...
Item Rec*eived* at Hoctyde all things discharged   xxv s. iij d. 30
...

St Mary the Virgin Churchwardens' Accounts   ORO: PAR 209/4/F1/12
single mb*   *(30 November–30 November) (Receipts)*
...   35
Item Cleerlye at Hoketyde and all thinge Dyschardge   xxxj s.
...

1/ minanas: *for* minas
30, 36/ Hoctyde, Hoketyde: *19–20 April 1585*

St Mary Magdalen Churchwardens' Accounts   ORO: PAR 208/4/F1/23
single mb   *(Rendered 16 May 1585) (Receipts)*

...

Item R*eceived* at hoctyde and all thinges dyscharged   xiij s. iiij d.

...   5

St Mary Magdalen Churchwardens' Accounts   ORO: PAR 208/4/F1/24
single mb   *(Rendered 8 May 1586) (Receipts)*

...

Item R*eceavyd* at Whytsontyde and all thinges dyscharged   xvj s. q*u*a. 10

...

1585–6
Christ Church Disbursements   ChCh Arch: xii.b.28
f 64   *(24 June–29 September) (Rewards)*   15

...

13o Iulij to musitians p*er* manus m*agist*ri Edes at the hall   xij d.

...

Exeter College Rectors' Accounts   EC Arch: A.II.9   20
f 105*   *(Memorandum)*

...versus expensas ludi in aula nostra. x s....

The Queen's College Long Roll   QC Arch: 2P163   25
single mb   *(7 July–7 July) (External costs)*

...

...It*em* musicis febr*u*arij 2o. xij d....

...   30

Walton, 'Life of Henry Wotton' in Reliquiae Wottonianae   Wing: W3648
sig b4v

...

   And that he might be confirmed in this regularity, he was at a fit age
removed from that School, to New-Colledge in Oxford, both being founded   35
by William Wickham Bishop of Winchester.
   There he continued till about the eighteenth year of his age, and was then
transplanted into Queens Colledge, where within that year, he was by the
Chief of that Colledge, perswasively injoyned to write a Play for their

---

4/ hoctyde: *19–20 April 1585*   35/ that School: *Winchester College*
10/ Whytsontyde: *30 May–5 June 1585*   37/ eighteenth year of his age: *1585–6; Wotton*
34/ he: *Sir Henry Wotton*   *was born in 1568*

private use, (it was the Tragedy of Tancredo) which was so interwoven with
Sentences, and for the method and exact personating those humours, passions,
and dispositions, which he proposed to represent, so performed; that the
gravest of that Society declared, he had in a slight imployment, given an
early and solid testimony of future abilities. And though there may be some   5
sower dispositions, which may think this not worth a Memoriall, yet that
wise Knight Guarina Baptista (whom learned Italy accounts one of her
Ornaments) thought it neither an uncomely, nor an unprofitable imployment
for his age.

　　But I passe to what wil be thought more serious.   10

…

City Council Minutes   OCA: C/FC/1/A1/001
f 284v*   *(11 May)*

…   15

Hit is agreed at this Counsell that the right honorable the Earle of Essex
men shall playe onlie at this tyme in the Guylde Hall Courte of this Cytie/
notwithstandinge an acte heretofore made to the contrarie/ the xvij^th of
februarie in the xxij^th yeare of the quenes maiesties Raigne that now ys/
And that the same acte shalbe dispensed withall onlie for this tyme/ and   20
afterwardes to be and remayne in his former strengthe and vertue./

…

The Earle of essex men to playe in the yeld hall Courte/

Audited Corporation Accounts   OCA: P.5.1
f 203*   *(Chamberlains' payments)*   25

…

Item paid to the Quenes Maiesties players   x s.

…

Item to Mr Pryme for makinge the Sermon in the daye of
Tryvmphe & to the musytions   xj s. 30

…

f 203v

…

Item paid to the Erle of Lecester mvsytions   vj s. viij d. 35

…

Keykeepers' Accounts   OCA: P.4.1
f 49v

                                                                                40

One bande of Mr Gibbons the musition, for the Scutchens. of this Cytie.

…

St Martin Churchwardens' Accounts   ORO: PAR 207/4/F1/1, item 74
mb [1]   *(28 November–27 November) (Receipts)*
...
Item Rec*ey*ved at Hoctyde clearlye   xxj s. vj d.
...   5

St Mary Magdalen Churchwardens' Accounts   ORO: PAR 208/4/F1/24
single mb *(Rendered 8 May 1586) (Receipts)*
...
Item R*ecea*vyd at hoctyde & all thinges dyscharged   xj s. vj d. 10
...

St Michael at the North Gate Churchwardens' Accounts
ORO: PAR 211/4/F1/2, item 149
single mb   *(12 March 1585/6–12 March 1586/7) (Receipts)*   15
...
R*eceiv*ed at hoctyde & all charges borne   xiij s. ij d.
...

1586–7   20
Christ Church Disbursements   ChCh Arch: xii.b.29
f 46v   *(25 March–24 June) (Extraordinary expenses)*
...
To mr King and mr Crane Censors towards theyr
expences in a comedy ex decreto capit*uli*   xx s. 25
                                                    (signed) Iohn Kinge.
...

Magdalen College Draft Libri Computi   MC Arch: LCD/2
f 36v col 1   *(Charges of external payments)*   30
...
Solut*um* tibicinib*us* in festo burs*ariorum*   6 s. 8 d.
...

The Queen's College Long Roll   QC Arch: 2P164   35
single mb   *(7 July–7 July) (External costs)*
...
...Item Morisio tybicini in festo Circu*m*cisi*on*is xij d....
...

4, 10, 17/ Hoctyde, hoctyde: *11–12 April 1586*

St John's College Computus Annuus SJC Arch: Acc.I.A.8
f 19   *(25 December–25 March)* *(Internal and external expenses)*
…

Item geve*n* to the studente*s* toward*es* their chardg*es* of
the shewe   iij li. vj s.   5
…

Audited Corporation Accounts OCA: P.5.1
f 210v*   *(Chamberlains' payments)*
…   10

Item to Rowlande Barber at M*aste*r mayors Request,
to geve the Lord Admyralls players   xx s.
…

Keykeepers' Accounts OCA: P.4.1   15
f 52
…
One obligac*i*on of Mr Gibbons for the Scutchins of this Citie/

St Aldate Churchwardens' Accounts   20
ORO: DD Par. Oxford St Aldate c.15/15
single mb col 2   *(2 February 1586/7–2 February 1587/8)* *(Expenses)*
…

It*em* Receive*d* of ye wemen at Hoctide all thinges discharged
clere to ye churche   x s. 25

St Mary Magdalen Churchwardens' Accounts   ORO: PAR 208/4/F1/25
single mb   *(Rendered 21 May 1588)* *(Receipts)*
…

It*em* R*e*ceavid at whytsontyde and all thinges dyscharged   iij li. vij s. 30
…

St Michael at the North Gate Churchwardens' Accounts
ORO: PAR 211/4/F1/2, item 150
single mb   *(12 March 1586/7–12 March 1587/8)* *(Receipts)*   35
…

Item receaved at hoctide and Whitsontide   xx s.
…

11/ M*aste*r mayors: *William Levinz's*
24, 37/ Hoctide, hoctide: *24–5 April 1587*
30, 37/ whytsontyde, Whitsontide: *4–10 June 1587*

St Peter le Bailey Churchwardens' Accounts   ORO: PAR 214/4/F1/37
single sheet*   *(11 December–10 December)*   *(Receipts)*

...

Item receaved at Hocktide all thinges beinge discharged   xxij s. vij d. ob.

...

1587–8
Vice-Chancellors' Accounts   OUA: WP/β/21(4)
p 111   *(17 July–16 July)*   *(Extraordinary expenses)*

...

Solut*um* Histrionibus Comitis Lecestriæ vt cu*m* suis ludis
sine maiore Academiæ molestia discedant   xx s.
Solut*um* Histrionibus Honoratiss*imi* D*omi*ni Howard   xx s.

...

Chancellor's Court Inventories   OUA: Hyp/B/12
mb 1   *(1 May)*   *(Inventory of Robert Dowe)*

...

Item his songe books Valu*e*   vj s. viij d.

...

City Council Minutes   OCA: C/FC/1/A1/001
f 302v*   *(14 September)*

...

George
Buckner to
have the
Scutchins and
appoynted/
Waytes

Hit is moreover agreed at this Counsell that George Bucknall beinge appoynted
to be the Waite*s* for this Cytie/ shall have the three scuttchins Delivered vnto
hym/ w*hi*ch mr Gybbons brought in/ And the said George shall make one at
his owne charges/ And where mr Gybbons is to make one more to be likewise
Delivered to the said George/ The said George shall fyne two suerties for the
redeliverie of all the same scuttchins at suche tyme/ as they shalbe Demaunded
by M*aste*r Mayor/ or any his Successor/ M*aste*r Chamberlen Goode gave his
worde &c/

Audited Corporation Accounts   OCA: P.5.1
f 218v   *(Chamberlains' payments)*

...

Item to m*aste*r mayor the xj^th of December to geve to
the Earle of Lecesters players   vj s. viij d.

...

4/ Hocktide: *24–5 April 1587*
26/ Waite*s*: *for* Waite
29m/ Wayt*es*: *for* Wayte

29/ fyne: *for* fynde
31/ M*aste*r Mayor: *Thomas Rowe*

Keykeepers' Accounts OCA: P.4.1
f 54v

...

One obligac*i*on of Mr Gibbons for the Scutchins of this Cytie./

...   5

St Mary Magdalen Churchwardens' Accounts ORO: PAR 208/4/F1/25
single mb *(Rendered 21 May 1588) (Receipts)*

...

It*em* R*e*ceavid at hoctyde and all thinges dyscharged   x s. iiij d. 10

...

St Mary Magdalen Churchwardens' Accounts ORO: PAR 208/4/F1/26
single mb *(Rendered 4 May 1589) (Receipts)*

...   15

It*em* reaceaued at whitsontide all thinges discharged   iiij li.

...

St Michael at the North Gate Churchwardens' Accounts
ORO: PAR 211/4/F1/2, item 151
mb [1] *(12 March 1587/8–12 March 1588/9) (Receipts)*   20

...

Item receiued at hoctide and whitsontide   liij s. iiij d.

...

                                                                                      25

St Peter in the East Churchwardens' Accounts ORO: PAR 213/4/F1/1
single mb col 1* *(8 December–8 December) (Receipts)*

...

Item R*e*ceived at hoctide   xxxviij s.

...   30

St Peter le Bailey Churchwardens' Accounts ORO: PAR 214/4/F1/38
single sheet col 1 *(10 December–10 December) (Receipts)*

...

It*em* gotten at Hocktide clere   xxxv s. 35
It*em* at whitsontide likewise   xv s.

...

10, 23, 29, 35/ hoctyde, hoctide, Hocktide: *15–16 April 1588*
16, 23, 36/ whitsontide: *26 May–1 June 1588*

c **1588–96**
Daniel, Whole Workes (1623)   STC: 6238
pp 253–4*

...

The Apology.   5

The wrong application, and misconceiuing of this Tragedy of Philotas,
vrges me worthy Readers, to answere for mine innocency, both in the
choice of the subiect, and the motiues that long since induced me to write it,
which were first the delight I tooke in the History it selfe as it lay, and
then the aptnesse, I saw it had to fall easily into act, without interlacing   10
other inuention, then it properly yeelded in the owne circumstances, we
were sufficient for the worke, and a lawfull representing of a Tragedy. Besides
aboue eight yeares since, meeting with my deare friend D*r* Lateware, (whose
memory I reuerence) in his Lords Chamber, and mine, I told him the
purpose I had for Philotas, who sayd that himselfe had written the same   15
argument, and caused it to be presented in St. Iohns Colledge in Oxford,
where as I after heard, it was worthily and with great applause performed.
And though; I sayd, he had therin preuented me, yet I would not desist,
whensoeuer my Fortunes would giue me | peace, to try what I could doe in
the same subiect, wherevnto both hee, and who were present, incouraged   20
me as to an example worthy of note. And liuing in the Country, about
foure yeares since, and neere halfe a yeare before the late Tragedy of ours,
(whereunto this is now most ignorantly resembled) vnfortunately fell out
heere in England, I began the same...

...   25

1588–9
Christ Church Disbursements   ChCh Arch: xii.b.31
f 28   *(25 December–25 March)* *(Rewards)*

     30

To ye Musitians on friday in ye audit ex consensu dec*ani*   v s.
...

Magdalen College Libri Computi   MC Arch: LCE/7
f 15   *(Charges of external payments)*   35
...
Musicis in festo bursariorum.   6 s. 8 d.

...

11/ we: *for* which

Vice-Chancellors' Accounts   OUA: WP/β/21(4)
p 114   *(10 July 1588–16 July 1589)*   *(Extraordinary expenses)*

...

Solut*um* Histrionibus ne ludos inhonestos exercerent infra
Vniversitatem   *(blank)* 5

...

Robert Ashley's Autobiography   BL: MS Sloane 2131
ff [3–3v]*

...   10

...Anno ætatis vicesimo tertio inchoato et mense Decembri cum feriæ
Natalitiæ Redemptoris approquinquarent celebrandæ [cum] ⌈et⌉ solennis
in Collegio mos [esset] ⌈inolevisset⌉ vt aliquis e primarijs Iuvenibus [⟨.⟩]
∧⌈inter socios⌉ ∧⌈eligeretur quem ceteri vt Dominum præcoijs ac laudibus
venerarentur et efferent⌉ cuius tanquam [Domini et] Principis auspicijs   15
cetera turba in triumphis tripudijs et choræis moderatretur: ob spem et
expectationem quam de me concitaveram Ego Dominus ac Princeps Iuventis
sum salutatus me in regno illo claustrali humeris evehunt, in solio constituunt
[Panegyricis] ∧ Encomijs ac Orationibus ∧⌈ornant⌉ condecorant; Ego tam
flagrantium adolescentum in me propensionem grato animo recognoscere;   20
modeste de meipso ac humiliter sentire, illorum de me Iudici*um* et
existimatione*m* magni facere vt | mos erat brevi oratiuncula significare
satago: Dein*de* regno, triumpho.

...

                                                                                     25

Audited Corporation Accounts   OCA: P.5.1
f 227   *(Chamberlains' payments)*

...

Item [to] geven to the quenes ma*iesties* players   x s.

...   30

Keykeepers' Accounts   OCA: P.4.1
f 57v

...

One Obligac*i*on of mr Gibbons for the Scutchins of this Cytie/   35

...

11/ Anno ... Decembri: *underlined*
12/ approquinquarent: *4 minims for* uin *in* MS; *for* appropinquarent
14/ præcoijs: *for* præconijs
16/ moderatretur: *for* moderaretur
17–18/ Ego ... salutatus: *underlined*
17/ Iuventis: *for* Iuventutis

St Aldate Churchwardens' Accounts
ORO: DD Par. Oxford St Aldate c.15/17
mb [2]   *(4 February 1588/9–4 February 1589/90) (Receipts)*
...
Item rec*eived* at Whitsontide for our Church ale   xliij s. iiij d.   5
...

St Martin Churchwardens' Accounts   ORO: PAR 207/4/F1/1, item 77
single mb   *(1 December–30 November) (Receipts)*
...   10
It*em* Rec*evid* at hoctyde declarow   xxiij s. v d.
...

St Mary Magdalen Churchwardens' Accounts   ORO: PAR 208/4/F1/26
single mb   *(Rendered 4 May 1589) (Receipts)*   15
...
It*em* reaceaued at hoctide althinges discharged   xij s.
...

St Michael at the North Gate Churchwardens' Accounts   20
ORO: PAR 211/4/F1/2, item 152
single mb*   *(12 March 1588/9–12 March 1589/90) (Receipts)*
...
Item receaued at hocktide and whitsontide
ou*er* & aboue all charge*s*   iij li. xiij s. iiij d.   25
...

St Peter in the East Churchwardens' Accounts   ORO: PAR 213/4/F1/1
single mb col 1   *(8 December–8 December) (Receipts)*
...   30
It*em* at the mens hocking: at hocktide   vj s. v d. ob.
...
It*em* Receaued of the wemens hocking   xxvij s.
...
                                                                                        35
St Peter le Bailey Churchwardens' Accounts   ORO: PAR 214/4/F1/39
single sheet col 1   *(15 December(?)–14 December) (Receipts)*
...
Item got at hoctide cleare all thinges discharged   xxxvij s. viij d.
...   40

5, 24/ Whitsontide, whitsontide: *18–24 May 1589*
11, 17, 24, 31, 39/ hoctyde, hoctide, hocktide: *7–8 April 1589*

Item for Drainge of ij quarters of Aell at witsontide   iij s. iiij d.

...

1589–90
Christ Church Disbursements   ChCh Arch: xii.b.32   5
f 12   *(Rewards)*

To ye [Kings] Queenes players by m*aster* Do*ctor* Kennalls
commaundeme*nt* p*er* burs*arium*   x s.

...   10

Magdalen College Draft Libri Computi   MC Arch: LCD/2
f 44v col 2   *(Charges of external payments)*

...
Solut*um* Tibicinibus in festo Bursariorum   6 s. 8 d. 15

...

The Queen's College Long Roll   QC Arch: 2P165
single mb   *(7 July–7 July)* *(External costs)*

...   20

...It*em* Mauritio et socio eius tibicini festo circu*m*cisionis xij d....

...

Vice-Chancellors' Accounts   OUA: WP/β/21(4)
p 116   *(16 July–10 July)* *(Extraordinary expenses)*   25

...
Solut*um* Histrionibus Reginæ vt sine molestia ab Academia
discerent   xx s. 0 0

...

                                                                          30

Audited Corporation Accounts   OCA: P.5.1
f 234v*   *(Chamberlains' payments)*

...
Item to the quenes players   x s.
Item to my lord Admyralls men   vj s. viij d. 35

...

f 235v*

...
Item for wyne and suger for the Earle of Essex men   iiij s. vj d. 40

...

1/ witsontide: *18–24 May 1589*   28/ discerent: *for* discederent

Keykeepers' Accounts   OCA: P.4.1
f 60*
...
One obligac*i*on of Mr Gibbons for the Scutchins of this Cytie/
...   5

St Martin Churchwardens' Accounts   ORO: PAR 207/4/F1/1, item 81
mb [1]   *(30 November–29 November) (Receipts)*
...
It*em* rec*evi*d at hoctide. dilaro   xxij s. 10
...

St Mary Magdalen Churchwardens' Accounts   ORO: PAR 208/4/F1/27
single mb   *(Rendered 9 May 1591) (Receipts)*
...   15
It*em* Receaved at Whitsontyde and all thinges Discharged   lvij s. x d.
...

St Michael at the North Gate Churchwardens' Accounts
ORO: PAR 211/4/F1/2, item 153   20
mb [1]   *(12 March 1589/90–12 March 1590/1) (Receipts)*
...
Item receaued at the hockale   xx s. ix d.
...

                                                                                    25
St Peter in the East Churchwardens' Accounts   ORO: PAR 213/4/F1/1
single mb col 1   *(8 December–8 December) (Receipts)*
...
Item receyved in Hocke money   xxix s. vj d.
...   30

St Peter le Bailey Churchwardens' Accounts   ORO: PAR 214/4/F1/40
single sheet col 1   *(14 December–13 December) (Receipts)*
...
Item made at hoctyde and all Charges borne   xxx s. ix d. ob. 35
...

10, 35/ hoctide, hoctyde: *27–8 April 1590*
10/ dilaro: *for* diclaro
16/ Whitsontyde: *7–13 June 1590*
23, 29/ hockale, Hocke: *Hocktide was 27–8 April 1590*

1590–1
Christ Church Disbursements ChCh Arch: xii.b.33
f 28v* *(25 December–25 March) (Expenses)*

...

Expenses in
comoed*iis* &
tragoed*iis*

To the Bachilers when they played octavia   xx s. 5

...

Magdalen College Libri Computi MC Arch: LCE/7
f 26v *(Charges of external expenses)*

...   10

x Solut*um* pro Cinctura Librj Carminum
Reginæ exhibitj   10 s.

...

f 27   15

...
Solut*um* Tibicinibus in festo Bursariorum   6 s. 8 d.

...

Merton College Bursars' Accounts MCR: 3.1   20
f 24v *(20 November–19 March) (External expenses)*

...
...Musicis Oxon*iæ* ex consensu vj s. viij d....

New College Bursars' Accounts NC Arch: 7576   25
mb 8 *(25 December–25 March) (External expenses)*

...
...so*lutum* to ye Musitians vj s. viij d....

...

     30

Vice-Chancellors' Accounts OUA: WP/β/21(4)
p 118 *(16 July–16 July) (Extraordinary expenses)*

...
Solut*um* per D*octorem* Eedes vicecan*cellarij* locum tenenti
quibusda*m* Histrionibus vt sine p*er*turbatione et strepitu   35
ab Academia discederent   x s. 0

...

34/ tenenti: *for* tenentem

Audited Corporation Accounts   OCA: P.5.2
f 1*   *(Chamberlains' payments)*
...

Item to George Bucknold for playinge on the quenes daye   v s.
...   5

f 1v
...

Item geven to the queenes players   xiij s. iiij d.
Item geven to the Lord Admyralls players   x s. 10
...

Keykeepers' Accounts   OCA: P.4.1
f 63

...   15
One obligacion of Mr Gibbons for the Scutchins/.

St Martin Churchwardens' Accounts   ORO: PAR 207/4/F1/1, item 82
mb [1]   *(29 November−29 November) (Receipts)*
...   20
Item Recevid at hoctid declaroe   xvij s. vij d.
...

St Mary Magdalen Churchwardens' Accounts   ORO: PAR 208/4/F1/27
single mb   *(Rendered 9 May 1591) (Receipts)*   25
...
Item Receaved at Hoctide an(.) all thinges Discharged   xv s. x d.
...

St Mary Magdalen Churchwardens' Accounts   ORO: PAR 208/4/F1/28   30
single mb   *(Rendered 30 April 1592) (Receipts)*
...
Item Receved at Whitsontyde and all thinges discharged   xxvij s. ij d.
...

                                                                                 35
St Peter le Bailey Churchwardens' Accounts   ORO: PAR 214/4/F1/41
single sheet*   *(13 December−12 December) (Receipts)*
...
Receaved of Hocktide all thinges beinge discharged   xxij s. vij d.
...   40

21, 27, 39/ hoctid, Hoctide, Hocktide: *12−13 April 1591*
33/ Whitsontyde: *23−9 May 1591*

1591–2
All Souls College Bursars' Accounts   Bodl.: MS. D.D. All Souls c.286
mb 11*   *(2 November–2 November)*   *(Various expenses)*
...

et de ij s. vj d. to the Trumpeters at pes comp*utorum*   5
...

mb 13
...

et de xx s. geaven to Quenes Trumpeters geaven when the *Queen* was heare   10
...

Christ Church Disbursements   ChCh Arch: xii.b.34
f 8   *(Rewards)*
...   15
To the musitions that played when the bohemian was here   ij s.
...

f 24
       20
To the fower musitians in the audite   v s.
...

f 85*
       25
[anno Reg*ni* Regine Elizabeth 34o
Delivered to mr Hammon & mr Hayewoode towards the furnishinge
of one comedie and too tragedies this 4 of february fivetie shillings for
the house
          (signed) Thomas Hammond   30
          (signed) Raphael Heywood]
m*emorandum* crossed vpon mistakinge this sum*m* of xl s. for thother of xl s.
wherto there nams be in like sorte/.
...

[Delivered to mr Hammonde and mr Haywood by m*aste*r Deans appointmente   35
towardes the payemente of the su*m*me of fiue pownds sixitene shillings sett
vpon diverse of the students names towards ye furnishinge of playes fourtie
shillings. 12 feb*ruary* 1591
          (signed) Thomas Hammond.
          (signed) Raphael Heywood]   40

...

Christ Church Computi   ChCh Arch: iii.c.6(f.)
mb 2

...

Et in exp*ensis* Commediar*um* et tragediar*um* hoc A*nno*
h*abitarum* vt p*atet* ib*idem*   n*il* li.   5

...

Exeter College Rectors' Accounts   EC Arch: A.II.9
f 134v   *(1 November–1 November)*

...   10

Item de solut*is* regijs buccinatoribus, cum ad collegium nostrum accederent;
p*ro* honestate Collegij xx s.

...

Lincoln College Computus   LC Arch: Computus 8   15
f 29   *(Internal expenses)*

...

Ite*m* to the Queenes Trumpeters   xiiij s. vj d.

...

                                                                                  20

Magdalen College Libri Computi   MC Arch: LCE/7
f 38v   *(Charges of external payments)*

...

Tibicinibus D*omini* Howarde   0 6 8
...   25
Pro lichnis in festo Epiphani*ae* pro ludis   0 4 0

...

Tibicinibus in festo bursarior*um*   0 5 0
Pro rata parte collegij in adventu D*ominæ* reginæ   18 10 s.

...   30

MC   ***Letter of Nicholas Bond to Lord Treasurer Dorset***
Centre for Kentish Studies: U269 C1
f [1v]

                                                                                  35

My humble dutie to yo*ur* Lordshi*p* premised. I haue receiued y*our* Lordshi*ps*
le*tt*res for venison, and haue deliuered some of to m*aste*r deane of Christ
Church, who of the rest of the Heades only remaines in the Towne. It ys to
be feared that fewe of them wilbe sped, bycause the season of Buckes wilbe

---

5/ ibidem: *referring to the formula at the top of the*   18/ Queenes: Q *written over* qu
    membrane, vt p*atet* per librum Thess*aurij*   37/ some of: *word or words omitted in* MS

past before the Queenes cominge. Howbeit howsoever it fall oute, we must all
acknowledge & reuerence your Lordships honorable care & paines takinge as
well in this as all other thinges appertayninge. We haue sent vp two to procure
furniture for our Playes with your Lordships lettre to the Master of the Reuels,
whom we vnderstande not to be in London & therefore we must craue of your   5
Lordship that these parties may haue accesse vnto your Lordship & vse your
help as occasion shall serue. Your Lordships comminge is greatly expected &
will exceedingly be missed yf you should not come. Mr Sauile is gone to the
Courte to try whether their purposes doe houlde. Yf there be any alteracion
your Lordship shall heare of it on Thursday. In the meane time I humble take   10
my leaue, recommendinge your Lordship to Gods eternall prouidence ffrom
Magdalen College in Oxon. 11o Die Septembris 1592./.

...

Merton College Register   MCR: 1.3   15
p 158*

...

<table>
<tr><td>Reginæ
aduentus ad
Academiam.

Taxatio
Collegiorum.</td><td>

Ad hæc tempora nuntium accepimus Serenissimam Reginam academiam
nostram mense Septembri inuisuram. Plurimæ tum publicè tum priuatim
habitæ sunt deliberationes de officio tum ab Academica, tum singulis Collegijs   20
Regiæ maiestati pro nostris fortunis cumulatissimè prestando. Cuius rei causa
petijt vicecancellarius a singulis collegijs vt pro ratione census et redituum
ad publicos Academiæ sumptus faciendos certas pecuniæ summas conferrent.
Statuunt vero Præfecti ac socij collegiorum vt pro quolibet centenario librarum
reditus antiqui, numerentur vniuersitati in vsus publicos viginti solidi. Census   25
vero vniuscuiusque collegij ad vicecancellarium delatus erat huiusmodi
</td></tr>
</table>

Christchurch	2000. lib.	Magdalen colledge	1200. lib.
New colledge	1000. lib.	Alsouls	500. lib.
Merton colledge	400. lib.	Corpus christi	500
Sct Ihons	400	Queenes Colledge	260
Brasennose	300	Trinity colledge	200
Exeter	200	Oriell	200
Lincolne	130	Baliol	100
vniuersity colledge	100:		

°7490. li.°   (line 30)

35

<table>
<tr><td>Allocatio facta
Custodi pro
2bus ferculis ad
refectiones
aulicorum</td><td>

A nobis priuatim decernitur quod Regia Maiestate hic commorante, Custos
duo fercula singulis refectionibus apparari faciat in gratiam æquestris ordinis
aulicorum, commode instructa: Impensarum vero in hoc apparatu factarum
pars 3ª. a Custode penditur Reliquæ. duæ a Collegio. Firmarij de Kibworth
</td></tr>
</table>

10/ humble: *for* humblie *(?)*
39/ Kibworth: o *written over* e; *the manor of Kibworth, comprising Kibworth Beauchamp and Kibworth*
       Harcourt, Leicestershire

Barkby Cuxam Ibston wolford Margaret stratton varijs opsoniorum generibus
has epulas instruunt.

...

xxij[j]º Septembris ad Academiam accessit Regina. recessit xxviijº

Prandium
Consiliarijs
regijs ac
nobilibus
institutum a
collegio.
ac habitæ
disputationes.

xxvº Septembris Regiæ Maiestati a secretioribus consilijs omnes nobiles, ac in   5
aula existentes Heroes Comites Barones singuli a nobis inuitati ad prandium
accedant, concomitati insignioris notæ aulicis omnibus: hique omnes [ad
numerum 60 hominum] sexaginta numero in alta aula ad vnam mensam
per vniuersam aulam extensam accumbentes epulas laute satis ac magnificè
apparatas sumunt. Finito prandio habitæ sunt disputationes, Magistro Cuffe   10
Grecæ linguæ professore Regio respondente, opponentibus Magistris French
Traford wilkinson Mason moderante Magistro Sauile tunc temporis procuratore.
questio. An dissentiones ciuium sint vtiles reipublicæ. Finitis disputationibus
Consiliarij Regij de rebus ad Rempublicam Spectantibus cum legato Galliæ
qui vna conuiuio interfuit acturi ad cubiculum Magistri Colmer secedunt.   15

Regina ad
Academicos
orationem
habet.

Conuocatis Academiæ primoribus alijsque ad exercitia prestanda designatis,
Regina in suo discessu orationem habuit cuius exemplum pagina 160 extat.

Oriel College Treasurers' Accounts   OC Arch: S 1.C.1
f 49   *(External expenses)*   20

...

Item buccinatoribus reginæ   x s.

...

f 49v   25

...

Item vniversitati in adventum reginæ   iij li.

...

The Queen's College Long Roll   QC Arch: 2P167   30
single mb   *(7 July–7 July) (External costs)*

...

...Item buccinatoribus comitis Cumbriæ ex iussu præpositi v s.... Item Moritio
et filijs suis tibicinibus in die circumcisionis ij s. Item tibicinibus ⟨...⟩mo post
purificationis beatæ Virginis, x s.... Item buccinatoribus ij s....   35

...

1/ Barkby: *Barkby, Leicestershire*   4/ Academiam: c *corrected over* a

1/ Cuxam: *Cuxham, Oxfordshire*   8/ sexaginta numero: *underlined*

1/ Ibston: *Ibstone, Buckinghamshire*   13/ Finitis: *final* i *corrected over* o

1/ wolford: *Great or Little Wolford, Warwickshire*   34/ ⟨...⟩mo: MS *torn; probably* die proximo

1/ Margaret stratton: *Stratton St Margaret, Wiltshire*

Register of Congregation and Convocation OUA: NEP/Supra/L
f 258v   *(17 August)*

…

Decrees and ordres set downe by the delegates concerning
her M*aies*ties entertainment*es*   5

1. Inprimis that the Vicechancell*o*r D*r* yeldard D*r* Cole D*r* Iames D*r* hovenden
   D*r* Lylly D*r* Culpeper, w*i*th theyr skarlet gownes and footclothes, both the
   Procters the President of St Johns the warden of Merton college the Rector of
   Lincolne college the principall of Brasenose the Principall of Magdalen hall Mr   10
   Purefey Mr Beaumont Mr ffarrar Mr Buffalde & Mr Singleton accompanied
   w*i*th the three Esquier Bedels vpon footclothes shall meete her M*aies*tie at the
   confines of our liberties: And that an oration shalbe pronounced before her,
   by one of the Procters

2. Item that every man shall stande to entertaine her M*aies*tie as shee passeth by   15
   according to the order following .1o. the Doct*or*s at Christchurch gate .2o. the
   bacchilers of Divinitie .3o. Masters of Art*es* & bacchilers of Lawe 4o. bacchilers
   of art*es* then the schollers of houses in theyr schollers gownes and cappes.
   Lastlie the Gentlemen and Halliers as farre as they will reache vnto St Gyles./

3. Item that they shall stand there quietlie w*i*thout removing from theyr places   20
   [as] and as soone as the traine is past pr*e*sentlie to departe to theyr severall
   howses.

4 Item that at the toppe of Quartuorvoice the Greeke reader shall make a greeke
   oration before her M*aies*tie

5. Item at her M*aies*ties alighting in Christchu⟨..⟩h the orator shall entertaine her   25
   with an oration.

   …

ff 259–9v

…   30

14. Item there are appointed to oversee and provyde for the playes in Christchurch
    M*aste*r Deane of Christchurch M*aste*r Subdeane D*r* Dalavere. D*r* Gager. D*r*
    Martin Mr Purifey Mr Hutton Mr Gwin Mr Dochen vna cu*m* vice*cancellario*
    et proc*uratoribus*

    …   35

16. Item there are appointed to see the street*es* well ordred and prepared as also to
    keepe order amongst the graduat*es* and schollers for theyr placing when the
    Queene cometh in D*r* Robinson D*r* Bust D*r* Beale D*r* Edwardes the President
    of St Johns ˄⌈mr Singleton, mr wharton mr Browne⌉ w*i*th the M*aste*rs of the
    street*es* vic*echancellor* and Procters./   40

    …

7/ Vicechancell*o*r: *Nicholas Bond*   8–9/ the Procters: *Thomas Savile, Ralph Winwood*

19. Item that the colleges may be rated for contribution to the charges, according
     as the Heades shall agree/

20. Item that the Vicechancellor master deane of Christchurch master Dr Cole
     Dr yeldard Dr Hovenden Dr Lilly Dr Hollande Dr Culpeper & all other
     Doctors of Divinitie & Heades of Colleges, that be Doctors shall provyde   5
     them skarelet gownes and hoodes sutable for the honor of her Maiestie &
     the credit of theyr degrees
     …

22. Item that the heades of every Howse, shall call theyr companies before them
     at or before the sixt of September and examine whether they be provyded of   10
     gownes hoodes and other apparrell according to this order and shall deliver the
     names of so manie as are vnfurnished without parcialitie to ye Vicechancellor
     …

34. Item if anie actor shall fall sicke or otherwise necessarilie be letted then another
     shalbe appointed by the vicechancellor & Procters and the maior parte of the   15
     delegates of the same facultie.

                Advertismentes for heades of howses to deliver with greate charge
                                vnto theyr companies.

                                                                                      20

1.   Inprimis that they admonish all Doctors and graduates, scholler fellowes and
     probationers to provyde gownes hoodes and cappes according to the statutes
     of their howses and that all commoners & halliers Doe weare rounde cappes
     and such coulours and fashions in theyr apparrell as the statute proscribeth

2.   Item that whosoever shalbe taken or seene by the vicechancellor or Procters   25
     or other overseers to be appointed by the said delegates in the streetes or anie
     publique place, During the Queenes Maiesties abode otherwise apparrelled
     then the statutes of the Vniversitie Do appoint for everie degree shall presentlie
     forfeit x s. and suffer imprisonment at the discreation of the said officers the
     said forfeiture to be levied by the Vicechancellor. or whome he shall appoint   30
     and to be imployed towardes the Defrayinge of the charges for her Maiesties
     entertainment./ |

3.   Item that vpon the daie when the Queene cometh all graduates shalbe readie
     at the ringing of St Maries bell to come in theyr habites and hoodes according
     to theyr degree and all schollers in theyr gownes and cappes and to stand   35
     quietlie in such order as shalbe appointed vntill her Maiestie be passed into
     Christchurch and the trayne being past every man to resort to his owne college.
     …

7.   Item that the schollers which cannot be admitted to see the playes Doe not
     make any outcries or vndecent noyse about the haule staires or within the   40

14m/ 34: *for* 24

Quadrancle of Christchurch, as vsuallie they were wont to doe vpon paine
of present imprisonment and other punishment according to the discretion
of the Vicechancellor and Procters

8   Item that they warne theyr companies to provyde verses to be disposed or set
vpon St Maries and other places convenient and that those verses be corrected   5
by the Deanes or some other appointed by the heades.

9   Item that a short oration be provyded at every severall colledge to entertaine
her Maiestie if her pleasure be to visit the same and verses set vp.

10.   Item that Vniversitie Colledge, Allsoules, Magdalen: do set vp verses at
her Maiesties departure, vpon such places soe as they may be seene as she   10
passeth by.

…

Vice-Chancellors' Accounts   OUA: WP/β/21(4)
p 119   *(16 July–13 July) (Extraordinary expenses)*   15

…

Solutum Histrionibus quibusdam vt sine strepitu et molestia
ab Academia discederent   x s.

Treasurer of the Chamber's Account   PRO: E/351/542   20
mb 166d

…To the same Symon Bowyer for ye Allowaunce of himself, and ye foresaide
number of yeomen, and gromes for makinge readie Christchurch Colledge in
Oxforde for her maiestie by ye space of viij dayes Mensis September 1592 as   25
appeareth by a Bill signed by ye Lord Chamberlaine *Summa* vij li. xvij s. iiij d./
To the saide Symon Bowyer for ye Allowaunce of himself, and ye Like number
of yeomen, and gromes for makinge readie the Hall at Christchurch in Oxford
for her maiestie by ye space of fower dayes mensis September 1592 as appeereth
by a Byll signed by ye Lord Chamberlaine *Summa* lxxviij s. viij d./…   30

Harvey, Four Letters (1592)   STC: 12900
pp 28–9*

…Flourishing Mr Greene is most-wofully faded, and whilest I am bemoaning   35
his ouer-pittious decay; & discoursing the vsuall successe of such ranke wittes.
Loe all on the suddaine, his sworne brother, Mr Pierce Penni-lesse … in a
raving, and franticke moode, most desperately exhibiteth his supplication to
the Diuell. A strange title, an od wit, and a mad hooreson, I warrant him:
doubtles it wil proue I some dainty deuise, quiently contriued by way of   40

23–4/ ye foresaide number: *ie, three*   40/ quiently: *for* queintly

humble Supplication To the high, and mighty Prince of Darkenesse: not
Dunsically botched-vp, but right-formally co*n*ueied, according to the stile,
and tenour of Tarletons president, his famous play of the seauen Deadly sinnes:
which most-dealy, but most liuely playe, I might haue seene in London: and
was verie gently inuited thereunto at Oxford, by Tarleton himselfe...   5

Harington, Metamorphosis of Ajax (1596)   *STC*: 12779
p 119*

...

® This Comedy
was playd at
her Maiesties
last being at
Oxford.

Seco*n*dly tel me pretty Wil, what is a nown substantiue? That that may   10
be seene, felt, heard, or vnderstood. Very wel, now I wil ioyne issue with
you on this point, where shall we trie it? Not in Cambridge you will say, for
I thinke they will bee parciall on my side. Well then in Oxford be it, & no
better Iudge then M. Poeta, who was cheefe Captayn of all the nownes in that
excellent comedie of Bellum gramaticale. For without all perauenture, whe*n*   15
he shal here that one of his band & so nere about him, is brought to that
state, that he is neither to be seene, smellt, hard, nor vnderstood, he wil
swere gogs nowns he wil thrust him out of his selected band of the most
substantiall substantiues, and sort him with the rascal rableme*n*t of the most
abiect adiectiues....   20

Narratives by Cambridge Men
Cambridge University Library: MS Additional 34
ff 4v–5*   *(Philip Stringer's account)*

25

A brefe of the entertainment giuen to Queene Eli*z*abeth by the
uniuersity of Oxford: in An*n*o 1592

On ffryday beinge the 22th of September An*n*o 1592 about three of the clock
in the afternoone of the same daye the Queenes most excellent Ma*i*estie entred
into the bound*es* or precinct*es* of the vniu*er*sity of Oxford at a place called   30
Godstowbrige much about a mile from the City of Oxford where hir highnes
was attended for by the viceChancellor & the rest of the do*ct*ors head*es* of
Colledges with the Proctors & Beadles of the vniu*er*sity beinge all then on
foote in gownes. The do*ct*ors in Scarlet the rest otherwise as was answereable
to their degrees and place.   35

Vpon intelligence of the viceChan*cellor* beinge ready w*i*th the rest to present
their dutyes vnto hir highnes, hir Ma*i*estie was pleased to haue the Coach
stayed wherein she was notw*i*thstandinge ye foulnes of the weather: wherevpon
the viceChan*cellor* deliuered vp vnto his highnes the beadles staues w*hi*ch were

4/ dealy: *for* deadly
30/ or: r *corrected over* f
30, 33/ vniu*er*sity: *2 minims for* ni *in* MS

immediatly redeliuered vnto him by hir selfe with the significacion of hir
gratious pleasure to stay the heareinge of a speach wherewithall they were
prouided (as hir highnes vnderstood) so that it were not too longe which beinge
knowen mr Sauill the senior Proctor beinge then vpon his knees with the
rest of the company did presently enter into a short speach wherein he first   5
signifyed what greate ioy the vniuersity had conceiued by hir Maiesties
approchinge so nere vnto them & then that in ye name of the whole body
for the better manifestinge of their dutifullnes he was to yeld vp vnto hir
Maiestie the libertyes priuiledges howses Colledges temples goodes with
themselues also and whatsoeuer they were by hir Maiesties goodnes possessed   10
of with their most instant & dutifull prayers for the longe & blessed
preseruacion of hir highnes./ |
This done hir Maiestie with the nobillity & the rest of hir royall traine goinge
towardes the City was within halfe a mile receiued by the Maior of Oxford &
his bretheren with a short spech deliuered by their Recorder & from thence   15
passinge by St Iohns Colledge was there presented with a priuate speech in the
behalfe of that Colledge (as vnto me it seemed)/ From whenc enteringe into
the City she passed thorow the streetes the schollers standinge in order on both
the sydes of the same till hir highnes came to the place which is called Carfax
or Cater foyse where she was pleased to heare an oration in the Greeke tonge   20
which was offered vnto hir by mr (blank) then the greeke reader from whence
she passed alonge to hir Lodginge which was prouided for hir highnes in
Christes Church the schollers standinge on both sydes ᴧ⌜of⌝ the street in their
order as is already sayd and in their gownes hoodes & Capps answerable to
their seuerall degres in Christ Church goinge here in the end of the Minster   25
(before hir highnes goinge vp to the roomes prouided for) she was receiued
with an Oration by mr Smyth in the behalfe of that Colledge (as I then
conceiued of it) the deane thereof and the Company attendinge there for the
performacion of that dutye./
...   30

f 6v*   *(24 September)*

...

At night there was a Comedy also acted before hir highnes in the hall of that
Colledge and one other on tuesday at night beinge both of them but meanly   35
performed as we thought and yet most gratiously and with greate patience

6/ vniuersity: *2 minims for* ni *in* MS   34–5/ that Colledge: *ie, Christ Church*
16/ passinge: p *corrected over* b   36/ we: *Philip Stringer and Henry Mowtlowe, 2 official*
17/ enteringe: t *written over* d   *observers sent by Cambridge*
25/ goinge: *5 minims in* MS
26/ goinge: *4 minims in* MS

heard by hir Maiestie the one beinge called Bellum gramaticale & the other
intituled .Riuales.

…

f 8*   *(26 September)*   5

…

It must not be forgotten that this day betweene the howers of x and xj of the
Clock in the forenoone it pleased hir Maiesty to heare an Oration made by
the viceChauncellor in the chamber of presence presentinge hir highnes
with two bibles the one in Greeke and the other in Latine in the name of   10
the whole vniuersity./

…

(27 September)
There was also at the same time a Lecture in Musicke with the practise thereof 15
by Instrument in the Common Schooles.

f 9*   *(28 September)*

On Thursday hir Maiesty about ten of the Clock in the forenoone of this day   20
made an Oration to the viceChanceller the doctors &c. in hir highnes Chamber
of presence in most gratious manner deliueringe her acceptance of that which
they had done &c. as appeareth by the Oration at which we were not beinge
then in the attendance vpon our honorable Chancellor at his lodginge in an
other part of the Court./   25
Hir highness departed from the vniuersity this day about xj of the Clock in the
forenoone in hir open and princly Carriadge and heard lastly a longe tedious
oration reade vnto hir by the iunior Proctor of the vniuersity about a mile from
the City in the very edge of their boundes or Libertyes towardes Shotover./

                                                                            30

City Council Minutes   OCA: C/FC/1/A1/001
f 337v*   *(10 August)*

…

The eleccion
dynner not to
be kept

A cupp and
[⟨..⟩] lx angells
to present the
quene/.

Hit is agreed at this Counsell That the chardges for the election Dynner for
this yere, shalbe ymployed towardes the entertaynment of the quenes maiestie   35
and the Steward of this Citie/ yf hit shall please her maiestie to come hither
[⟨.⟩] And that A Cuppe of silver ∧⌈gilt⌉ to the valewe of twenty poundes shalbe

---

15/ the same time: *9:00 AM*
23/ we: *Philip Stringer and Henry Mowtlowe, 2 official observers sent by Cambridge*
24/ our honorable Chancellor: *Sir William Cecil, Lord Burghley, chancellor of Cambridge*
26, 28/ vniuersity: *2 minims for* ni *in* MS

provided at the chardg*es* of this Citie to pr*es*ent her maiestie at her Com*m*inge, and threescore Angells w*i*thall And in the meane tyme, that Penyles benche

Repa*r*acions to be don./

and the gat*es* and other necessarie places about the Citie shalbe decentlie repayred and amended at the chardg*es* of this Citie in suche sorte as M*aste*r Mayo̊r and his brethren or the more parte of them shall thinke most Convenient And that the mayor the thirtene and bayliff*es* w*i*th the rest of

certen appointed to receaue her ma*ies*ty

the better sorte of the Citizens shall prepare them selves for receaving her maiestie at the place and suche attyer as at her maiesties last being here was done/.

...   10

f 338*   *(13 August)*

...

money lent to the Citie by the Citizens

Hit is agreed at this counsell That everie one of the thirtene Associat*es* and the Townclarke shall lend to the vse of this Citie fyue pound*es* apeece/   15 everie one that hath ben bayliffe fforty shilling*es*/ everie one that hath ben Chamberlayne Thirty shilling*es*/ everye of the Com*m*on counsell twenty shilling*es*/ And all and everie such other com*m*oner As m*aste*r mayor and the rest of the thirtene associat*es* or the more p*ar*te of them shall thinke best able/ twenty shilling*es* apeece/. The same money to be brought to the   20 Office and paid to m*aste*r mayor on [the] monday next by nyne of the clocke in the forenone of the same daye to be ymployed in the behalfe of the Citie, against her ma*ies*ties Com*m*inge hither/. And that the same money shalbe repaid by this Citie to everie p*er*son lending the same, w*i*thin one yere nowe next ensuynge/. And hit is ordered by the whole consent of   25 this howse That yf any of the p*er*sons aforesaide shall not bring in and pay their money as abovesaid/ That then hit shalbe lawfull for this howse, to put everie one of this howse (not doing the same) from the roome and place he now hathe w*i*thin this Citie And to choose another in his place yf neede be/ And everie ‸⌈Com*m*oner⌉ that shalbe thought able as aforesaide   30 (not p*er*forming the same) to be disfraunchesed/.

f 339   *(1 September)*

...

gloves to be geven to noble men/

Hit is also agreed that certen gloves shalbe provided to be geven to Noble   35 men and others at her ma*ies*ties com*m*inge hither (at the chardg*es* of this Citie) suche and so many as M*aste*r Mayor and the most parte of the thirtene associat*es* shall thinke good/./

...

4–5/ M*aste*r Mayor: *Richard Browne*

Audited Corporation Accounts   OCA: P.5.2

f 8v   *(Chamberlain's payments)*

…

Item for a proclamacion at the quenes being here	iij s. iiij d.

…   5

f 12*   *(Keykeepers' accounts)*

…

Item for A Cuppe geven to the queenes maiestie at her	
Comming Hither 25 September 1592	xix li. xj s. ij d. 10
Item to the Carrier for bringing the same Cuppe from London	ij s. vj d.
Item geven lx angells in the said Cuppe to her maiestie	xxx li.
Item geven to diuerse of her maiesties officers at her highnes	
beinge here 26 September 1592	xv li.
Item paid to the [pains] painters for worke donne in diverse	15
places for the citie against her maiesties Comming hither	xij li.
Item deliuered to the Stewardes of the dinners for the Lordes	
of the counsell/ 3 October 1592	lxxv li.
Item to Henry Wilkes for gloves geven to certen Noble men	
at her maiesties being here	lij s. 20

…

Item for newe gilding and burnishinge the greate Mace	
against her maiesties comming	xxvj s. viij d.
Item to Edward Shisson for gloves at her maiesties being	
here which were geven away	xviij s. viij d. 25

…

Item to mr Wells for gloves which were geven [awa] to	
certen Noble men at her maiesties being here 1592	vij li. xij s.
Item to mr Barton for gloves for her maiestie and other	
gloves geuen to certen noble men at the same tyme	viij li. xvj s. 30
Item for Torches and other thinges at the same tyme	xvj s. x d.

f 12v

…

Item to mr Carpenter for his chardge to the Courte diuers	35
tymes whiles her maiestie was in progresse	x s.
Item [fo] geven by the Citie towardes the repairing of Bolt	
Shipton waye against her maiesties comming hither/ which	
was deliuered to mr Browne	xl s.
Item to Iohn Willis Phillippe Cover and Richarde Griffin	40
for post horses whiles her [maiesties] maiestie was in her	
progresse in this Countrey	iiij li. iiij s. viij d.

…

Item for Carrieng a packett of lettres to the Courte and for a
horse hier for mr Sydnam to the Courte and for sarcenet for
the quenes gloves   iij s. viij d.

...
                                                                                                        5

Keykeepers' Accounts   OCA: P.4.1
f 68

...

One band of mr Gibbons for the Scutchins/

...   10

f 70v*

...

Thomas
Mundye

Item they are charged with the somme of eight powndes and
seaven shillinges which was remayning of the money which   15
was delyuered by Mr Mundy to the Stewardes of the Dynners
for the lordes of the Counsell at the quenes being here   viij li. vij s.

Tailors' Wardens' Accounts   Bodl.: MS. Rolls Oxon 66, roll 3
mb [2]*   *(Payments)*   20

...

Item for wyne and suger at Dobsons dynner   iij s. xj d.
Item to the musicions at the same tyme   iij s.

...

Item for wyne and suger at Osweld Beltes Dynner   ij s. j d. 25
Item to the musitions then   ij s.

...

Item for wyne and suger at Pearsons Dynner   iiij s. x d.
Item to the musitions then   ij s. vj d.

...   30

Item to the musitions at the masters Dynner   v s.

...

St Aldate Churchwardens' Accounts
ORO: DD Par. Oxford St Aldate c.16/1   35
mb [2]   *(4 February 1591/2–4 February 1592/3) (Expenses)*

...

Item payd to ye ringers at ye Queenes cominge   iij s. vj d.

...

Item payd to ye ringers when ye Queene went awaie   iij s. iiij d. 40

...

31/ masters: *Thomas Harris'*

St Mary Magdalen Churchwardens' Accounts   ORO: PAR 208/4/F1/28
single mb   *(Rendered 30 April 1592) (Receipts)*

...

Item Receved at Hoctyde and all thinges discharged   xvj s. j d. ob.

...   5

St Peter in the East Churchwardens' Accounts   ORO: PAR 213/4/F1/1
single mb   *(8 December–8 December) (Payments)*

...

Item to the Ringers when the Queene came to Oxforde   iij s. 10
Item ffor Ringinge att her Departure   xviij d.

...

1592–3
All Souls College Bursars' Accounts   Bodl.: MS. D.D. All Souls c.286   15
mb 13   *(2 November 1591–2 November 1592) (Various expenses)*

...

et de ij s. to the Musicions on Allsoules daye

...

                                                                                               20

mb 17*   *(2 November 1592–2 November 1593) (Rewards)*

...

et de v s. geven to Trompeters on Candlemas Daye

...

                                                                                               25

Balliol College Bursars' Accounts   BC Arch: Computi 1592–1614
f 1v   *(7 July–18 October 1593) (Expenses noted)*

...

Item for ye entertaynemente of the quene when the college was
awarded to paye and toward the charges of the vniversitye   xxx s. 30

...

Item geven the quenes Trompeters when the court was here   x s.

...

Christ Church Disbursements   ChCh Arch: xii.b.35   35
f 27*   *(25 December–25 March)*

...

Comedies &   to mr hammon towards the furnishinge of too tragedies
tragedies   & one comedie at shorfetyde laste 1592 by master deans
              appointmente & not accompted   l s. 40
                        (signed) Thomas Hammond

4/ Hoctyde: *3–4 April 1592*   39/ shorfetyde laste 1592: *5–7 February 1591/2*

to daniell for settinge vp ye stage & taking hit downe
& for boords at ye same time   lvij s.
to the Smith for an yron rodd & rings for the stage ix s.
vj d. & for an iron barr for the hall doore yet standinge
there, & boltes & saple at ⌈ix s. v d. in all⌉   xviij s. xj d. 5

6 li. 5 s. 11 d./   °Summa   vj li. v s. xj d. Exoneratur°

...

f 28   (Rewards)

...   10

to the musicions this avdite the firste sondaye   v s.

...

To mr goodman for writinge out of our bills of
demaunds to the Vniuersitie by occasione of the
queens entertainmente   ij s. vj d. 15

...

f 46v   (Extraordinary expenses)

...

expended in the entertainmente of her maiestie   20
in the yeare 1592 besids that was alowed by ye
Vniuersitie as appeireth by an especiall note in the
ende of this booke   Cxxvij li. x s. ix d.

...

25

f 97

Expenses in the intertainment of her Maiestie cummynge hether
the xxij^th day of September 1592 & stayinge here vij daies./
Imprimis for a Canope   liiij li. iij s. vj d. 30
Item in stage & towardes plaies   xxxj li ij s. ij d.
Item in rewardes   [lx.] xix li. v s.
Item in repare & translatinge of lodginges   lxxj li. xij s. ij d.
Item in iourneis for messages   xxvij s. xj d.
                        Summa Clxxvij li. x s. ix d. Inde deducted as   35
                        allowed by the Vniuersitie l li. And so this churche
                        is clerelie charged with Cxxvij li. x s. ix d. which is
                        allowed in the title of extraordinarie charges in the
                        third quarter of this boke 1593.

5/ saple: for staple (?)
14/ Vniuersitie: 2 minims for ni in MS

Lincoln College Computus   LC Arch: Computus 8
f 59v   *(21 December–21 March)* *(Internal expenses)*

...

Given to the trumpeters at candlemasse besides that which
was gathered   ij s. iiij d.   5

...

Magdalen College Libri Computi   MC Arch: LCE/7
f 48   *(External payments)*

...   10

Tibicinibus in festo bursariorum   6 s. 8 d.

...

Buccinatoribus diversis temporibus   12 s.

...

15

Merton College Bursars' Accounts   MCR: 3.1
f 33v   *(28 July–24 November 1592)* *(External expenses)*

...

...tubicinibus Regijs ex iussu Custodis xx s....

...   20

The Queen's College Long Rolls   QC Arch: LRA
f 3   *(7 July–7 July)* *(External costs)*

...

...Item buccinatoribus regijs ex iussu præpositi 20 s.   25

...

Item buccinatoribus quibusdam ex iussu præpositi 3 s. 4 d. Item tibicinibus
de Oxonia 10 s....

...

30

Register of Congregation and Convocation   OUA: NEP/Supra/L
ff 262–2v*   *(Privy council letter)*

...

    To our verie loving freindes The Vicechancellor of the vniuersitie
of Oxenforde and to the Maysters and heades of the several houses   35
and colleges within the same.
After our verie hartie commendacions wheras the two vniversities of Oxford
and Cambridge are the Nurseries to bring vp youth in the knowledge and fere
of god in all manner of good learning and vertuous education wherby after
they may serve theyr prince and countrie in divers callings for which respect a   40
special care ys to be had of those two Vniversities that all meanes may be vsed

to further the bringing vp of youth that are bestowed there in all good learning
Civill education and honest manners whereby the state and Common wealth
maie receaue hereafter greate good And lyke care ys to be vsed that all such
things as may allure and entyce them to lewdnes folly and vitious manners
(whervnto the corruption of mannes nature ys more enclyned) may (in no
wyse) be vsed or practysed in those places that are the schooles of learning and
good nouriture; Wee therfore as Counsailors of Estate to her Maiestie amongst
other things concerning the good goverment of this Realme cannot but have a
more especiall care of these principal places being the fountaynes from whence
learning and education doth flowe, and so ys deryved into all other partes of
the Realme. And for that cause vnderstanding that common playe‸⌈r⌉s do
ordinarily resort to the Vniversitie of Oxford there to recyte interluds and
playes some of them being ful of lewde examples and most of vanity besyds the
gathering together of multitudes of people whereby ys greate occasion also of
divers other inconveniences; wee have [th] thought good to Require you the
Vicechancellor with the assistance of the heads of the colleges, to take speciall
order that herafter there may [be] no plays or interluds of common players be
vsed or set forth eyther in the | vniversitie or in anie other place within the
compasse of fyve myles, nor any shewes of vnlawfull games that are forbidden
by the statuts of this Realme And for the better Execution herof, you shall
communicate these our lettres to the Maior or Maiors of the Cittie of Oxford
for the tyme being with there of the Iustices of the peace inhabiting within
fyve myles to the sayd Cittie and that no other Iustices may give them licence
to the contrary whoe shall lykewyse by vertue hereof be Required as wel as you
to see the tenor of these our lettres put in due execucion, everie one of you
in your severall Iurisdiccions/ ... So Requiring you to have care from tyme
to tyme, that these good orders may be observed according to this direction,
wee bid you ⟨.....⟩ verie hartely farewel from the Court at Otelandes the 29th
of Iulie 1593

Your verie loving freinds

(signed) Iohn Puckeringes William Burgly. Esscx. Howard.

Thomas Buckehurst

Robert Cecyll, Iohn Wolley.

...

Vice-Chancellors' Accounts OUA: WP/β/21(4)

p 122   (13 July 1592–17 July 1593) (Extraordinary expenses)

...

Solutum diversorum Nobilium Histrionibus
vt sine strepitu et molestia ab Academia
discederent   xx s.

...

Vice-Chancellor's Proclamation   OUA: SEP/T/7/g
f [2]   *(August)*

Edmund Lillie *Doctor* of divinitie & Vicechauncelor of the Vniuersitie of
Oxford Henrie Dodwell Maior of the Citie of Oxford to all the inhabitant*es*   5
w*i*thin the said Vniu*er*sity, [&] Citie & Suburbs of the same greetinge, ffor
so much as it hath pleased god to visit divers Cities townes & villages of this
Realme w*i*th most dangerous & infectioues sicknes ⌈so⌉ [&] y*a*t this place
like wise w*i*thout especial care [&] good [goveremt] goverment & god*es* great
mercy is likely to feele the misery thereof wee therfore as well by direction   10
from the lord*es* ⌈of⌉ her M*a*ie*s*ties moste Hon*orable* privie Counsel vnto vs
given, as also of our owne authoritie doe straightly charge & com*m*aund these
orders by vs heer set downe for the generall safety of the whole vniu*er*sity &
Citie by you & every of you wel & truly to be observed & kept vpon payne
of imprisonment & such forfeiture & punishment as in everie article ensuing   15
is specified & declared

[(.)]   It*em* yt shall not be lawfull for any ⌈man⌉ w*i*thin this vniu*er*sity [&] Citie [&]
ₐ⌈or⌉ subvrbs of the same to keepe ⌈or vse⌉ any daunsing schoole fensyng
schoole or vautinge schoole vpon payne of v li. [for everie tyme offending]   20
⌈& iij moneths imprisonme*nt*⌉ or ⌈keepe⌉ to vse any forbidden game vpon
payne to encur such pennaltie [or pennalties] as by the lawes of this Realme
[are all ready] ⌈on that behalfe is provided⌉ etc downe on such offenders
…

5   It*em* it shall not be lawfull from henceforth for any com*m*on players to publish   25
or write any enterludes or playes w*i*thin this vniuersity city or suburbs of the
same vppon payne of x li. for eury tyme herein offending.

Camden, Tomus Alter Annalium (1627)   STC: 4496.5
p 53   30
…

℞ Regina
Academiam
Oxoniensem
inuisit

Regina æstiuis mensibus rus profecta per Oxoniam iter habuit, vbi
politissimis orationibus, Ludis Scenicis eruditis disputationibus oblectata
aliquot dies hæsit, opiparis conuiuijs à Buckhursto Academiæ Cancellario
excepta. Discedens oratione Latina valedixit, in qua professa est se   35
perspectissimum Academicorum amorem cæteris omnibus oblectationibus
licet gratissimis longe præponere. Pro quo gratias cumulate persoluit,
votum vouit & consilium dedit. Votum erat, vt nihil magis optauit quam
vniuersi Regni salutem cum fælicissima securitate & honore, ita etiam &
Academia, vt quæ alterum Regni lumen, splendidius indies inclaresceret   40
& æternum effloresceret. Consilium erat vt Deum imprimis colerent non
ad exquisita quorundam ingenia sed ad Leges Dei & Regni, Leges non

præirent, sed sequerentur, non disputarent an meliores possint præscribi
sed præscriptas obseruarent, superioribus obedirent & postremo fraterna
pietate & concordia se inuicem complecterentur.

...

Audited Corporation Accounts   OCA: P.5.2
f 14*   *(Chamberlains' payments)*

...

Item geven to the wait*es*   v s.

...

Item geven to the queenes players 25 ffebruar*ie*   x s.
[Ith] It*em* geven to the lord Strang*es* players the vj^th
of October   vj s. viij d.

Keykeepers' Accounts   OCA: P.4.1
f 72v

...

One band of mr Gibbons for the Scutchins

...

St Martin Churchwardens' Accounts   ORO: PAR 207/4/F1/1, item 85
single mb   *(3 December–2 December) (Receipts)*

...

It*em* Recevid at hocktid declaroe   xxij s. iij d.

...

St Mary Magdalen Churchwardens' Accounts   ORO: PAR 208/4/F1/29
single mb   *(Rendered 5 May 1594) (Receipts)*

...

Item Receaved at Whitsontyde and thinges
discharged   v li. vj s. ij d. ob.

...

St Michael at the North Gate Churchwardens' Accounts
ORO: PAR 211/4/F1/2, item 154
single mb   *(12 March 1592/3–12 March 1593/4) (Receipts)*

...

It*em* gathered & collected at Hocktyde   xxviij s.

...

24, 38/ hocktid, Hocktyde: *23–4 April 1593*   30/ Whitsontyde: *1–7 June 1593*

St Peter le Bailey Churchwardens' Accounts   ORO: PAR 214/4/F1/42
single mb   *(10 December 1592–16 December 1593) (Receipts)*

...

Item Receaved at Hocktide, all thinges being
discharged   xxv s. ij d.   5

...

1593–4

Magdalen College Libri Computi   MC Arch: LCE/7
f 57   *(Charges of external payments)*   10

...

Tibicinibus in festo Bursarior*um*   0 5 0

...

Buccinatoribus in natali D*omini*   [5] 5. 0

...   15

Merton College Bursars' Accounts   MCR: 3.1
f 40   *(23 November–22 March) (External expenses)*

...

...Musicis ex consensu vj s. viij d....   20

...

NC   ***Robert Townshend's Expenses***   NC Arch: PA/L2
single sheet–single sheet verso*   *(December–March)*

...   25

Inpr*imis* his battelings one ye buttery Book together
with Com*m*on servaunts wages, decrements and
salting money.   xlj s. ix d. ob. q*u*a.

...

It*em* to his Instructor in singing: x s.   30

...

It*em* a Singing paper book.   xij d. |

...

It*em* given to ye musitians.   vj d.

...   35

NC   ***Letter of Arthur Lake to Lady Townshend***   NC Arch: PA/L2
single sheet   *(3 April)*

Madame by y*at* le*tt*re w*hich* was last sent fro*m* y*our* Lad*yship* I vndrestond   40

4/ Hocktide: *23–4 April 1593*   20/ vj: j *altered from* i

yat you request a note of *your* sonnes expenses; *which* according to *your*
expectation I have sent herin inclosed; whereby *you* shall *per*ceive allso what
I have receaved, what layd out, and what remaineth w*i*th mee to bestowed
for him this next quarter.... As for his chamber I have not provided any
severall fro*m* his Cousin. because I see no reason why wherefore they shall   5
reast together, god willing, untill some be offered. especially seeing it is
greatly for their good, & my ease, to say nothing that it will also diminish
much their expence: w*hi*ch hath bene ∧⌜this⌝ quarter the greater, by reason
of the charge of fuel & other winter provision, & moreover their Lenten
diet. & their singing schoolmastres allowance....   10
...

The Queen's College Long Rolls   QC Arch: LRA
f 5 col 2   *(7 July–7 July) (External payments)*
...   15
It*em* Tibicinib*us* de Oxon*ia*   10 s.
It*em* buccinatorib*us* iussu m*agist*ri Ayraie locum tenent*is*   3 s. 4 d.
...

St John's College Computus Hebdomalis   SJC Arch: Acc.v.E.1   20
f 6   *(4–10 February)*
...
Sett on for the musitians [xxij s.] ⌜xviij s.⌝ iiij d. M*emoran*d*um* the musitians
had in toto xxx s.
...   25

Keykeepers' Accounts   OCA: P.4.1
f 76   *(Bonds and bills not summed)*
...
One bond of mr Gibbons for the scutchins   30
...

f 77*
...
Iohn Willyams It*em* they are chardged w*i*th fower shilling*es* Receaued   35
               of mr Good for Torches deliu*er*ed him when her ma*i*esty
               was here at Oxon.   iij s.
               ...

5/ wherefore: w *corrected over another letter*

St Mary Magdalen Churchwardens' Accounts   ORO: PAR 208/4/F1/29
single mb   *(Rendered 5 May 1594) (Receipts)*

...

Item Rec*eaved* at Hoctyde and all thinges
discharged   xv s. v d. ob. q*u*a.   5

...

St Mary Magdalen Churchwardens' Accounts   ORO: PAR 208/4/F1/30
single mb   *(Rendered 25 May 1595) (Receipts)*

...   10

Item Receavid at Whitsontide and all things discharged   iij li. ij s.

...

St Michael at the North Gate Churchwardens' Accounts
ORO: PAR 211/4/F1/2, item 155   15
mb [1]   *(12 March 1593/4–12 March 1594/5) (Receipts)*

...

It*e*m Receaved at Hocktide ou*er* & above all Charg*es*   xxx s.

...

                                                                                           20

St Peter le Bailey Churchwardens' Accounts   ORO: PAR 214/4/F1/43
single mb   *(16 December–15 December) (Receipts)*

...

It*e*m at Hocktyde clerely gotten & all thinges
being dischardged   xxij s.   25

...

1594-5
Magdalen College Libri Computi   MC Arch: LCE/7
f 68   *(Internal payments)*   30

...

Tibjcinibus in Festo Bursariorum   0 5 s. 0

...

Merton College Bursars' Accounts   MCR: 3.1   35
f 44   *(22 November–21 March) (External expenses)*

...

...Musicis ex consensu vj s. viij d....

...

4, 18, 24/ Hoctyde, Hocktide, Hocktyde: *8–9 April 1594*
11/ Whitsontide: *19–25 May 1594*

Robert Townshend's Expenses   NC Arch: PA/L2
single sheet–single sheet verso   *(December–March)*

...

Item for his instructor in singeinge   x s.

...   5

Item Stringing Bandes   ij d. |

...

Item the Musitians   xij d.

...

                                                                                                            10

The Queen's College Long Rolls   QC Arch: LRA
f 7 col 1   *(7 July–7 July)* *(External expenses)*

...

Item datum cuidam Musico Ianuarij 1o   2 s.

...   15

Item datum buccinatoribus de Oxonia   10 s.

...

St John's College Computus Hebdomalis   SJC Arch: Acc.v.E.1
f 19v   *(17–23 February)*   20

...

Impositi pro Musicis 36 s. 6 d.

...

Vice-Chancellors' Accounts   OUA: WP/β/21(4)   25
p 124   *(12 July 1594–5 August 1595)* *(Extraordinary expenses)*

Solutum Histrionibus Dominæ Reginæ vt sine strepitu et
molestia ab Academia discederent   xx s.

...   30

Solutum Histrionibus Domini Morley vt sine molestia ab
Academia discederent   x s.

...

Audited Corporation Accounts   OCA: P.5.2   35
f 26v   *(Chamberlains' payments)*

...

Item geven to the Lord Morleys players   vj s. viij d.

...

Item geven to the Lord Admiralls players   x s. 40

...

f 27

...

Item geven to the queenes players   xx s.

...

Keykeepers' Accounts   OCA: P.4.1
f 78v   *(Bonds and bills not summed)*

...

One bond of mr Gibbons for the scutchins

...

St Aldate Churchwardens' Accounts
ORO: DD Par. Oxford St Aldate c.16/4
mb [1]   *(4 February 1594/5–4 February 1595/6)   (Receipts)*

...

Item 5 ⌈o⌉ maij gotten by hocking   xiij s. iiij d.
Item by menes hocking   iiij s. ob.

...

St Martin Churchwardens' Accounts   ORO: PAR 207/4/F1/1, item 89
mb [1]   *(1 December–30 November)   (Receipts)*

...

Item Received at Hoctide declarowe   xix s. ij d.

...

St Mary Magdalen Churchwardens' Accounts   ORO: PAR 208/4/F1/30
single mb   *(Rendered 25 May 1595)   (Receipts)*

...

Item Receavid at Hocktide and all things
discharged   xiij s. ix d.

...

St Mary Magdalen Churchwardens' Accounts   ORO: PAR 208/4/F1/31
single mb   *(Rendered 16 May 1596)   (Receipts)*

...

Item receavid at whitsontide all thinges
discharged   v li. viij s.

...

16/ hocking: *Hocktide was 28–9 April 1595*
23, 29/ Hoctide, Hocktide: *28–9 April 1595*
36/ whitsontide: *8–14 June 1595*

St Peter in the East Churchwardens' Accounts   ORO: PAR 213/4/F1/1
single mb col 1*   *(8 December–8 December) (Receipts)*

…

Item receyved for hockinge   xliiij s. vij d.

…   5

St Peter le Bailey Churchwardens' Accounts   ORO: PAR 214/4/F1/44
single mb   *(15 December–14 December) (Receipts)*

…

Item R*eceaved* Clear at hoctyde & all Charges borne   xv s.   10

…

Item R*eceaved* of the Childrens Gaynes at Whitsontyde   xv s. x d.

…

1595–6   15
Magdalen College Libri Computi   MC Arch: LCE/7
f 79   *(Internal and external payments)*

…

Solut*um* Buckner musico in festo burs*ariorum*   5 s.

…   20

Merton College Bursars' Accounts   MCR: 3.1
f 48v   *(21 November–19 March) (External expenses)*

…

…Musicis ex consensu vj s. viij d.…   25

…

The Queen's College Long Rolls   QC Arch: LRA
f 8v col 2   *(7 July–7 July) (External expenses)*

…   30

It*em* tibicinibus in festo Circu*m*cisionis   2 s.
It*em* tibicinibus de Oxoni*a* Ianu*arij* 26   10 s.

…

St John's College Computus Hebdomalis   SJC Arch: Acc.v.E.1   35
f 31   *(5–10 January)*

…

Sett on for tom tu*m*bler   v s. iiij d.

…

4/ hockinge: *Hocktide was 28–9 April 1595*   12/ Whitsontyde: *8–14 June 1595*
10/ hoctyde: *28–9 April 1595*   19/ Buckner: *George Buckner*

f 33   *(23–9 February)*

…

Sett on for Geordg & his Company the towne Musitions   xxxj s. v d.

…

Vice-Chancellors' Accounts   OUA: WP/β/21(4)
p 128   *(5 August–17 July)* *(Extraordinary expenses)*

Solut*um* Histrionibus D*omin*æ Reginæ vt abstinerent
a pub*li*ca Actione   0 ₁₀

…

Audited Corporation Accounts   OCA: P.5.2
f 33   *(Chamberlains' payments)*

…

Item geven to the Lord Admiralls players   x s.
Item geven to the earle of Darbies players   xx s.
Item geven to the earle of Pembrookes players   x s.

…

Keykeepers' Accounts   OCA: P.4.1
f 83   *(Bonds and bills not summed)*

…

One bond of Gibbons for the scutchins

…

Tailors' Wardens' Accounts   Bodl.: MS. Rolls Oxon 66, roll 4
mb [2]*   *(Payments)*

…

Item for wyne and suger at Thomas Ewens Dynner   ij s. viij d.
Item to the musitions at the same time   xviij d.
Item for the election dynner [at] on the sonnday before
the elec*c*ion day   £v
Item to the musitions at the same tyme   v s.

…

St Aldate Churchwardens' Accounts
ORO: DD Par. Oxford St Aldate c.16/5
mb [1]   *(4 February 1595/6–4 February 1596/7)* *(Receipts)*

…

Item at hocktide by hocking   xxij s.

3/ Geordg: *ie, George Buckner*   41/ hocktide: *19–20 April 1596*

Item receuid at Whitsuntid for ale   xx s.
...

St Mary Magdalen Churchwardens' Accounts   ORO: PAR 208/4/F1/31
single mb   *(Rendered 16 May 1596) (Receipts)*   5
...
Item receavid at Hocktide all thing*es*
discharged   xx s.
...

                                                                       10

St Mary Magdalen Churchwardens' Accounts   ORO: PAR 208/4/F1/32
single mb   *(Rendered 1 May 1597) (Receipts)*
...
Item rec*eavid* at whitsontide and all thing*es*
discharged   v li. xij s. vij d. 15
...

St Michael at the North Gate Churchwardens' Accounts
ORO: PAR 211/4/F1/2, item 158
mb [1]   *(12 March 1595/6–12 March 1596/7) (Receipts)*   20
...
Item Rec*eaved* At Midsomm*er* for Church ale then
kept in the p*a*rishe, above all Charges   xx s.
Item Rec*eaved* At hocktide above all Charges   xxvj s. viij d.
...   25

St Peter in the East Churchwardens' Accounts   ORO: PAR 213/4/F1/1
single mb col 1   *(8 December–8 December) (Receipts)*
...
Item receiued for hocking   xxxviij s. 30
...

1596–7
Magdalen College Libri Computi   MC Arch: LCE/7
f 91v   *(Internal and external payments)*   35
...
Tibicinib*us* in festo bursario*rum*   5 s.
...

1, 14/ Whitsu*n*tid, whitsontide: *30 May–5 June 1596*
7, 24/ Hocktide, hocktide: *19–20 April 1596*
30/ hocking: *Hocktide was 19–20 April 1596*

Merton College Bursars' Accounts   MCR: 3.1
f 53   *(19 November–18 March)* *(External expenses)*
...
...Musicis ex consensu vj s. viij d....

5

The Queen's College Long Rolls   QC Arch: LRA
f 11v col 2   *(7 July–7 July)* *(External expenses)*
...

Item Moritio alijsque fidicinibus   2 s.
Item Tibicinibus de Oxonia   10 s.   10
...

St John's College Computus Hebdomalis   SJC Arch: Acc.v.E.1
f 42v*   *(8–14 November)*
...   15
Set on for Maio ye fidler   14 s.
...

f 43v   *(27 December–2 January)*
...   20
Sent for a Commedye   x s.
...

f 45*   *(7–13 February)*
...   25
Sett on for the towne musetions   xxx s. vij d.
...

(14–20 February)
for Mayo the fydler   vij s. x d.   30
...

Vice-Chancellors' Accounts   OUA: WP/β/21(4)
p 129   *(17 July–14 July)* *(Extraordinary expenses)*
...   35
Solutum Histrionibus quibusdam vt sine strepitu ab
Academia discederent   xx s.

Hannisters' Registers   OCA: L.5.1
f 245v*   40
...
Georgius Bucknell musition admissus est in libertatem Ciuitatis [pro] predicte

xx s.   d*icto* xxiiij° die Novembris Anno xxxix° supra*dicto* Et soluit viginti solid*os* ad
vsu*m* d*icte* ciuit*atis* et iiij s. vj d. p*ro* feod*is* offic*iariorum* Et Iur*atus* &c/

Leonardus Maior musition admissus est in li*ber*tate*m* Ciuitatis p*redicte* eodem
xxiiij° die Novembris Anno xxxix° supra*dicto* Et soluit xx s. ad vsu*m* d*icte* 5
ciuit*atis* et iiij s. vj d. p*ro* feod*is* offic*iariorum* Et Iur*atus* &c

...

Audited Corporation Accounts OCA: P.5.2
f 38   *(Chamberlains' payments)*   10

...

It*e*m geven to one of the earle of Essex players   vj s. viij d.

f 39*

...   15

It*e*m geven to the quenes players   x s.

...

f 39v*

...   20

It*e*m geven to the quenes players   x s.

...

Keykeepers' Accounts OCA: P.4.1
f 86   *(Bonds and bills not summed)*   25

...

One bond of Gibbons for the scutchins

...

St Mary Magdalen Churchwardens' Accounts ORO: PAR 208/4/F1/32 30
single mb   *(Rendered 1 May 1597) (Receipts)*

...

Item rec*eavid* at hocktide all things discharged   xx s. vj d. q*u*a.

...   35

St Mary Magdalen Churchwardens' Accounts ORO: PAR 208/4/F1/33
single mb   *(Rendered 21 May 1598) (Receipts)*

...

Item rec*eavid* at whitsontide all thing*es* discharged   xxxvij s. viij d. ob.

...   40

33/ hocktide: *4–5 April 1597*   39/ whitsontide: *15–21 May 1597*

St Michael at the North Gate Churchwardens' Accounts
ORO: PAR 211/4/F1/2, item 159
single mb   *(12 March 1596/7–12 March 1597/8) (Receipts)*

…

Item R*eceved* at hoctide in money All   5
Charges borne   xv s. viij d.

…

St Peter in the East Churchwardens' Accounts   ORO: PAR 213/4/F1/1
single mb col 1   *(8 December–8 December) (Receipts)*   10

…

Item for hockinge   xxv s.

…

1597–8   15
All Souls College Bursars' Accounts   Bodl.: MS. D.D. All Souls c.287
mb 11   *(2 November–2 November) (Rewards)*

…

Et de ij s. vj d. to the Lorde of Darbye his trumpeters

…   20

Christ Church Computi   ChCh Arch: iii.c.7(a.)
mb 4*

…

Et in exp*ensis* Comediar*um* et tragediar*um* hoc   25
An*n*o fact*arum*   n*il* li.

…

Lincoln College Computus   LC Arch: Computus 8
f 135v   *(21 December–21 December) (Necessary internal expenses)*

…   30

Given to the trumpeters   ij s. vj d.

…

Magdalen College Libri Computi   MC Arch: LCE/7   35
f 105   *(Internal and external payments)*

…

Tibicinibus in festo Bursarior*um*   0 5 s. 0

…

5/ hoctide: *4–5 April 1597*
12/ hockinge: *Hocktide was 4–5 April 1597*

Merton College Bursars' Accounts   MCR: 3.1
f 59v   *(18 November–24 March)* *(External expenses)*

...musicis ex consensu vj s. viij d....

...   5

New College Bursars' Accounts   NC Arch: 7586
mb 6   *(Internal expenses)*
...
...so*lutum* Georgio Bucknar musico vj s. viij d....   10
...

The Queen's College Long Rolls   QC Arch: LRA
f 14 col 1   *(7 July–7 July)* *(External expenses)*
...   15
It*em* Ianu*arij* 2º. Moritio fidicini   2 s.
...
It*em* Febr*uarij* i6º tibicinib*us* de Oxon*ia*   10 s.
...
                                                                  20

St John's College Computus Hebdomalis   SJC Arch: Acc.v.E.1
f 57v   *(16–22 January)*
...
A tragedy of Astiages/
Acted post 30ª ⟨...⟩os in   25
aedib*us* Praesidentis
...

f 58   *(23–9 January)*
...   30
Eade*m* tragœdia
Astiagis publice acta
in Aula/
...
                                                                  35
f 59   *(27 February–5 March)*
...
Impositi pro Musitia*ns*   xxj s. ix d.
et p*ro* alteris   v s. vj d.
...   40

25/ Acted: Ac *written over 2 other letters, possibly* Ba

Chancellor's Court Inventories   OUA: Hyp/B/19
f [1]   *(31 July) (Inventory of Christopher Tillyard)*
...

5 Singinge bookes   12 d.

...   5

OUM   **Report of the University to the High Steward of Oxford**
Hatfield House Library: Cecil Papers MS 62/16
single sheet*

                                                                        10
    A true Reporte of all that happened betweene the Schollers of the
    Vniuersitye of Oxforde and Townsmen there the xxviijth of May last./

Vppon the twoe Sondayes next goeinge before the Ascention day laste paste,
and also vpon Ascention day A greate nomber of the inhabitantes of Oxeforde, 15
boyes woemen and men assembled themselves together early in the morninge
of theis dayes with drome and shott, and other weapons, and men attyred
in woemens apparrell and brought into the towne a woeman bedeckte with
garlandes and flowers named by them the Queene of May. They also had
morrish daunces and other disordered and vnseemely sportes, And intended 20
the next sonday in like manner to contynew the same abvses:

To prevent the said intended disorders on satterday at nighte, Mr Bellingham
one of the Proctors accompanyed not with so many as is vsuall in that case
did keepe anight watch personally himselfe until twoe of the clocke in the 25
morninge.

Then beinge weary and willinge to take some rest, hee deputed mr daniell
a Preacher and master of Artes to supplye his roome, which is vsuall and
warrantable by the ordinaunce of our vniuersitye.   30

After the Proctors departure, betweene three and 4 of the clocke in the
morninge beinge the 28th of May and the sabaoth day, the said mr daniell
did heare a drome sounded in the streete, wherevpon accompanyed with the
Proctors twoe knowne servantes and no more went to see and knowe the 35
cause thereof./

He founde there assembled a great nomber, a great parte of them beinge boyes
and not men furnished with holbertes and shott, soundinge theire drome,

14/ twoe Sondayes ... laste paste: *14 and 21 May 1598*   23/ satterday: *27 May 1598*
15/ Ascention day: *Thursday, 25 May 1598*   24/ the Proctors: *Edward Gee, Henry Bellingham*
21/ the next sonday: *28 May 1598*

shootinge of their peeces, and preparinge themselues to goe out of the towne
to bringe in a showe for the honoringe of a Marriadge, as they pretended to
be solempnized that day.

Mr daniell perceivinge them still as before to contynew in prophaninge of   5
Sabaoths, and to disturbe and disorder the studientes of the vniuersitye at
such vnseasonable tymes tooke their drome & intreated them peaceably to
goe home yat day.

This disordered company notwithstandinge determyninge to proceide in their   10
vnruly sportes, forced vpon the said mr daniell, intendinge as yt seemed to
take the drome agayne from him, and therevpon he did with his hand strike
a boy of the company who vsed himselfe malepertly, and tooke from him
an holberte, and because he would not therewith be quieted, threatened the
boy with ymprisonment and whippinge, and in fyne comitted him to one of   15
the Proctors men, and carryed the drome and holbert into his colledge./

The Proctors man was hindered by the company to carry this boy to prison;
which beinge signifyed vnto mr daniell at his retorne he layde holde of the
same boy the second tyme, whome to reskewe annother boy of that companye   20
drew his dagger, and proffered yt vnto the said mr daniell; and another one
ffornass son to the maior of oxforde that now is bent his peece at his bosome.
vpon which occasion, and because he ment to ymprison the disordered boy,
which he could not because the company so pressed vpon him, he drewe a
Scottish dagger the only weapon that he then had, & called for a sowrde where   25
vpon the company gave Rome and mr daniell caried the boy to prison.

The same sonday morninge about five of the clocke worde was brought vnto
mr Gee one of the Proctors, that mr daniell the Proctors deputye (if he were
not assisted) was in daunger to be slayne.   30

Mr Gee accompanyed with his man went to see the truth of this Reporte, and
to keepe peace if any tumulte were towarde.

At the East gate of the Cittye, the said master Proctor Gee mett with the   35
disordered assembly and kyndly intreated them to leave of their shootinge, or
at least quietly without soundinge the dromme (thereby to draw concourse
of people) to goe to the markett place, and there once to dischardge their
peeces & so to departe wherevpon some of the best advised of the company
at least in speech agreed./   40

22/ the maior: *William Furness*   32/ man: a *corrected over another letter*

Not withstandinge they did not accordingly but dischardged diuers voleyes
of Shott vsed sedetious speeches, went vp[on] & downe the streetes stil
dischardginge their peeces especially before the Colledge where the vice
Chauncellor for that tyme was, in contempte as it seemed./

when the Proctor perceived that his kynde intreaty tooke no better effect, he
singled one of the vnruliest in the route and carryed him vnto prison, and
also because he sawe great concourse both of Townsmen and Schollers and
feared the event thereof, he comaunded the dromme to be taken away, and
layed yt vp in a house there; he also intreated one Baker that florished with
a naked sowrde like a whifler to goe aside into a house, and there tooke from
him his sowrde, accomptinge as indeede yt fell out, that the departure of
that Baker would dissolve the company.

The Redelivery of all theis the thinges taken away as a foresaid hath byn
proffered to the maior Towneclark if ether he or any other would have fetched,
or sent for the same.

This broyle thus pacifyed master Doctor Maisters the deputye vnto the
vicechauncellor desyringe that theis discontentmentes might be examyned,
and such corrected as did deserve punishmente at the afternoone of the same
day appoynted with the maior, a tyme for conference the next day followinge
between the Governors of the towne & vniuersitye, but afterwardes hearinge
that master Vicechauncellor himselfe, woulde shortly retorne who might
better reform theis abvses and correct the malefactors if any had offended
with the likinge of master Maior differed the tyme of meetinge vnto master
Vicechauncellors retorne, And in the meane tyme to take away all occasions
of greevances released those out of prison which were comitted:/

Master vicechauncellor retorninge on friday then next followinge, on satterday
morninge sente to intreate the Maior to give him meetinge ether that day, or
any tyme else by himselfe to be chosen, To the which message the said Maior
did make a frivolous and dilatory aunsweare, and in the meane tyme preferred
as it seemeth by the letters of our honorable Chauncellor; a most vniust and
slanderous complaynte against the Vniversitye.

3–4/ vice Chauncellor: *Thomas Ravis*
22/ the next day followinge: *Monday, 29 May 1598*
30/ friday ... followinge: *2 June 1598*

This premisses to be true, and all that was don we the Principall agent*es* herein are reddye to Iustefye vpon *our* oathes./

OUM *Letter of the Mayor and Aldermen of Oxford to the High Steward of Oxford* Hatfield House Library: Cecil Papers MS 62/14   5
f [1] *(3 June)*

Right honorable our verie good Lord and Steward: duringe the tyme of your goverment of vs wee haue forborne to Complayne to *your* Lordshipp of any wronges done to vs by Schollers of the Vniu*er*sytie, for that wee   10
hoped suffrance woulde in the end worke the end of there wronginge of vs, speciallye for that youre *Lordshi*pp a knowen honorable Patron of learninge and learned men, hath taken the protection of vs against there Iniuryes, for which wee ever acknowledge our selves most bound to your honor. At all tymes it is our dutie to be Careful that some of our Citizens be trayned and   15
made fitt soldyers and speciallye nowe in respect of your honor, to whom in any ymploym*ent* of yours wee would present men expert and able to serve. The fault was by *p*articuler *p*ersons Commytted and therefore our Complaynt shalbe of them and not of the Vniu*er*sytie in gen*er*all, thoughe the Magistrates slacknesse of punisheinge the Offendors dryve⟨...⟩ Complayne   20
in the Starrchamber, Yf it maye stande w*ith* yo⟨...⟩ allowance thereof, wherein as in all thing*es* els wee humb⟨...⟩ our selves to your *Lordshi*pp*es* pleasure, beseechinge Your hono⟨...⟩ and direction, and still prayeinge for the prosperouse suit ⟨...⟩ Your honorable Actions.

25

All your *Lordshi*pp*es* to be Commaunded
most redie and Assured.

The Maior Aldermen & Commynalty
of the Cytie of Oxon. 30

Audited Corporation Accounts OCA: P.5.2
f 45v* *(Chamberlains' payments)*

Item paid to the Queenes Ma*ie*sties Berwode   x s. 35

...

Keykeepers' Accounts OCA: P.4.1
f 89v *(Bonds and bills not summed)*

...   40

One bond of Gibbons for the scutchins

...

Tailors' Wardens' Accounts   Bodl.: MS. Rolls Oxon 66, roll 5
mb [2]*   *(Payments)*

...

Item for the masters allowance towards his dynner for
the company   £v   5
Item to the musitions at the same tyme   v s.

...

St Martin Churchwardens' Accounts   ORO: PAR 207/4/F1/1, item 94
mb [1]   *(27 November–26 November) (Receipts)*   10

...

Item of the wemen which the got at Hocktide   xiiij s. vj d.

...

St Mary Magdalen Churchwardens' Accounts   ORO: PAR 208/4/F1/33   15
single mb   *(Rendered 21 May 1598) (Receipts)*

...

Item receavid at hocketide all thinges discharged   xij s.

...

                                                                    20

St Mary Magdalen Churchwardens' Accounts   ORO: PAR 208/4/F1/34
single mb   *(Rendered 13 May 1599) (Receipts)*

...

Item receavid at whitsontide all thinges discharged   iiij li. viij s. ij d.
...   25

St Peter in the East Churchwardens' Accounts   ORO: PAR 213/4/F1/1
single mb col 1*   *(8 December–8 December) (Receipts)*

...

Item ⟨..⟩r money gotten at Hocktyde   xxvj s. 30
Item ⟨..⟩r money that we gott at Wyts⟨..⟩tid   l s.

...

St Peter le Bailey Churchwardens' Accounts   ORO: PAR 214/4/F1/45
single mb   *(11 December–10 December) (Receipts)*   35

...

Item gotten at hocktide clerly   xv s.

...

12/ Item: *in display script*
12, 18, 30, 37/ Hocktide, hocketide, Hocktyde, hocktide: *24–5 April 1598*
24, 31/ whitsontide, Wyts⟨..⟩tid: *4–10 June 1598*

1598
Hentzner's Travels in England   Hentzner: *Itinerarium*
p 214

...Conspiciuntur in angulo quodam oppidi rudera arcis satis amplæ, sed   5
penitus dirutæ. In cœnâ fuimus excepti, Musicâ excellentissimâ, variis &
diversis ex instrumentis concinnatâ.
...

1598-9   10
Christ Church Disbursements   ChCh Arch: xii.b.43
f 8   *(29 September–25 December) (Rewards)*
...
To George Buckenar comming this audit [& offering]
to sing & play, by consent   iij s. iiij d. 15
...

Christ Church Computi   ChCh Arch: iii.c.7(b.)
mb 3d
...   20
Et in exp*ensis* Comediar*um* et tragediar*um* hoc
Anno fact*arum*   n*il* li.
...

Magdalen College Draft Libri Computi   MC Arch: LCD/2   25
f 91 col 1   *(Charges of internal and external payments)*
...
Tibicinibus in festo Bursario*rum*   5 s.
...
                                                                           30
Merton College Bursars' Accounts   MCR: 3.1
f 65v   *(24 November–23 March) (External expenses)*

...Musicis ex consensu vj s. viij d....
...   35

The Queen's College Long Rolls   QC Arch: LRA
f 16 col 1   *(7 July–7 July) (External expenses)*
...
Item fidicinibus oppidanis   10 s. 40
...

St John's College Computus Annuus   sJC Arch: Acc.I.A.10
f 20v   *(25 December–25 March)*   *(Expenses)*

…

Item geuen to the schollers for the chardg of the
sporte on twelfnight   xviij d.   5

…

Item for the expences of a Comedie & a tragedye
publickely acted 23 et 24 ffeb alowed by Master
President and ye officers   iij li. v s. ix d.

…   10

Item ye chardg of the schollers exercise [against]
⌜on⌝ Newe Yeares Day   ij s.
Item to them on twlf night payd to Tuer
and Groome   ij s. vj d.

…   15

f 27   *(Requests for payment)*

…

Item to the Schollers chardges of their exercise
17o Nouember   vj s. viij d.   20

…

St John's College Computus Hebdomalis   sJC Arch: Acc.v.E.2
f 5v   *(15–21 January)*

…   25

Tenantes with
Neweyearsgift

Impositi pro spectaculis   22 d.

…

f 6   *(29 January–4 February)*

…   30

An interlude

…

f 6v*   *(19–25 February)*

…   35

Sett on for Mais the Studentes fydle
the holydayse   xxij s. iij d.

…

13/ twlf: *for* twelf
36/ Mais: *probably for* Maio

f 7v   *(5–11 March)*

…

Imposit*i* p*ro* Commœdia et tragœdia
acta p*er* Scholares et conuictores   54 s.
°Allocat*i* for many Strangers intertayned at the playes & otherwyse°   5

…

Sett on for the yearely Musitions of the Cyty   xlij s. ij d.

Vice-Chancellors' Accounts   OUA: WP/β/21(4)
p 134   *(18 July–17 July)* *(Extraordinary expenses)*   10

…

Solut*um* Histrionibus Regijs et alijs vt
sine strepitu et molestia ab Academia
discederent   XXV s.

…   15

Letter of Dudley Carleton to John Chamberlain   PRO: SP/12/270
f [3]   *(3 April)*

I find no change at Oxford saue onely that all the Colledges especially   20
Christchurch are full of very very pretty wenches. [insomuch that at] vppon
which at Shroftide last in [cho] steede of chusing an Emperor w*h*ich was
wont to be theyr Annuall solemnitie they mad⟨.⟩ a pretty boy an Empress
and they ⟨…⟩ were sutable maskes and mum*m*inges ⟨…⟩…

…   25

Audited Corporation Accounts   OCA: P.5.2
f 50   *(Chamberlains' payments)*

…

It*e*m paid to the Queenes mai*e*sties plaiers   X S. 30

…

Keykeepers' Accounts   OCA: P.4.1
f 92v   *(Bonds and bills not summed)*

…   35

One bond of Gibbons for the Scutchins

…

22/ Shroftide last: *20 February 1598/9*

Tailors' Wardens' Accounts   Bodl.: MS. Rolls Oxon 66, roll 6
mb [2]   *(Payments)*
...
Item for the masters allowance for his dynner   £v
Item to the mvsitions at the same tyme   v s.   5
...

St Martin Churchwardens' Accounts   ORO: PAR 207/4/F1/1, item 96
single mb   *(26 November 1598–2 December 1599) (Receipts)*
...   10
Item of the wemen which the got at Hocktyde   xxxj s. j d.
...

St Mary Magdalen Churchwardens' Accounts   ORO: PAR 208/4/F1/34
single mb   *(Rendered 13 May 1599) (Receipts)*   15
...
Item rec*eavid* at Hocktide all thing*es* discharged   xxxiij s. ij d.
...

St Mary Magdalen Churchwardens' Accounts   ORO: PAR 208/4/F1/35   20
single mb   *(Rendered 27 April 1600) (Receipts)*
...
Item Receued at Whitsontyde all things beinge discharged   iij li.
...

                                                                                         25

St Michael at the North Gate Churchwardens' Accounts
ORO: PAR 211/4/F1/2, item 162
single mb   *(12 March 1598/9–12 March 1599/1600) (Receipts)*
...
Item Rec*eived* at Hocktide & all thing*es* discharged   xvj s.   30
...

St Peter in the East Churchwardens' Accounts   ORO: PAR 213/4/F1/1
single mb col 1   *(8 December–8 December) (Receipts)*
...   35
Item Recea⟨.⟩ed for hockinge   xlviij s.
Item for *our* Whytson Ale   xix s.
...

4/ masters: *Owen Jones'*   36/ hockinge: *Hocktide was 16–17 April 1599*
11, 17, 30/ Hocktyde, Hocktide: *16–17 April 1599*   37/ Whytson: *Whitsuntide was 27 May–2 June 1599*
23/ Whitsontyde: *27 May–2 June 1599*

St Peter le Bailey Churchwardens' Accounts   ORO: PAR 214/4/F1/46
single mb   *(10 December–9 December) (Receipts)*

…

Item receiued at hocktide at whitsonetide clereley
& all things discharged   v li. vj s. vij d.   5
Item receiued for ye bower and ye Sapplins   xij s.

…

1599–1600
All Souls College Bursars' Accounts   Bodl.: MS. D.D. All Souls c.287   10
mb 11   *(2 November–2 November) (Rewards)*

…

et de vj s. to Trumpeters diuersis temporibus.

…

15

Christ Church Disbursements   ChCh Arch: xii.b.44
f 23   *(25 December–25 March) (Rewards)*

…

To the Trumpeters [for] sowndinge in the hale in ye
Christmas hollidayes by consent of the Table   ij s. vj d. 20
                                                                    Leonard 〈…〉

f 37v   *(25 March–24 June) (Rewards)*

…

Aprilis. 25. geuen to the Trumpetters by consent of the table   ij s. 25

…

Magdalen College Libri Computi   MC Arch: LCE/7
f 117v*   *(Internal and external expenses)*

…

30

Buccinatoribus Comitum Southampton et Nottingham
in regardo: 0 6 s.

…

Tibicinibus in festo Bursariorum   0 5 s.

…

35

Merton College Bursars' Accounts   MCR: 3.1
f 70v   *(23 November–21 March) (External expenses)*

…

…Musicis ex consensu vj s. viij d.….   40

…

4/ hocktide: *16–17 April 1599*   4/ whitsonetide: *27 May–2 June 1599*

New College Bursars' Accounts   NC Arch: 7588
mb 7   *(Internal expenses)*

...

...So*lutum* buccinitor*ibus* in regard*is* iiij s....

...   5

Oriel College Treasurers' Accounts   OC Arch: S I.C.1
f 93   *(Internal expenses)*

...

Item Buccinatoribus D*om*ini Mowntioye festo nativitatis   10
per concensu*m*   v s.

...

The Queen's College Long Rolls   QC Arch: LRA
f 18 col 1   *(7 July–7 July) (External expenses)*   15

...

de*cembris* 29.   It*em* deliberat*i* buccinatoribus   2 s.
de*cembris* 31   It*em* Clarionib*us*   2 s.

...

Ian*uarij* 1o   It*em* Mauritio fidicini   2 s. 20

...

Ian*uarij* 17   It*em* Tibicinib*us* Oxon*ie*   10 s.

...

St John's College Computus Annuus   SJC Arch: Acc.I.A.10   25
f 47   *(29 September–25 December) (Expenses)*

...

x   Item for the schollers chardge of an exercise 17o Nouember*   vj s. viij d.

...
                                                                      30

St John's College Computus Hebdomalis   SJC Arch: Acc.v.E.2
f 17   *(19–25 November) (Allowances)*

...

Allocat*i* 17o November vj s. viij d.

...   35

An interlud the Quenes night

...

f 18v   *(7–13 January)*

...   40

et p*ro* tubicinib*us*   ij s. vj d.

...

An interlud vpon New yearesday

f 19v   *(4–10 February)*

...

Set on for musitians xxiiij s. xi d.

...

5

f 23   *(5–11 May)*

...

Impositi pro tubicinibus De Mountegle   2 s.

...

10

Baron Waldstein's Diary   Biblioteca Apostolica Vaticana: Reg. lat. 666
f 167*   *(12 July)*

...

   Die ♄ 22. Iulij.
Initium Comitiorum Oxoniensium: manè lectiones habitæ à singulis   15
Professoribus: nos interfuimus lectioni Theologicæ cuiusdam Holandi viri
doctissimi. A meridie disputationes Theologicæ et declamationes egregiæ de
Peregrinatione. Windishgracij nos conveniunt, cum quibus vesperi navicula
cum Musica exspatiamur

...   20

Audited Corporation Accounts   OCA: P.5.2
f 55v*   *(Chamberlains' payments)*

...

Item to Baldwyn Hedges to geve the players   x s. 25

...

f 56v*

...

Item to Iohn Greene for Lodging my Lordes men   ij s. iij d. 30

...

Item geven to diuerse noble mens mucisions And to
Mr Mores men   xx s.

...

Item geven to the botmen when master mayor Ryde   35
the ffranches   xviij d.
Item to the Trumpeter at the same tyme   x s.

14/ 22. Iulij: *New Style, ie, by Gregorian calendar*   35/ master mayor: *Isaac Bartholomew*

Keykeepers' Accounts   OCA: P.4.1
f 95v   *(Bonds and bills not summed)*

...

One bond of mr Gibbons for the Scutchins

...   5

St Mary Magdalen Churchwardens' Accounts   ORO: PAR 208/4/F1/35
single mb   *(Rendered 27 April 1600) (Receipts)*

...

Item Receued at hoctyde all thinges beinge discharged   xxvij s. 10

...

St Michael at the North Gate Churchwardens' Accounts
ORO: PAR 211/4/F1/2, item 163
single mb   *(12 March 1599/1600–12 March 1600/1) (Receipts)*   15

...

Item Rec*eued* at hoctyde all thynges beinge discharged   xxj s. viij d.

...

St Peter in the East Churchwardens' Accounts   ORO: PAR 213/4/F1/1   20
single mb col 1   *(8 December–8 December) (Receipts)*

...

Item Receaued for hockinge   xxxij s.

...

                                                                              25

St Peter le Bailey Churchwardens' Accounts   ORO: PAR 214/4/F1/47
single mb   *(9 December 1599–14 December 1600) (Receipts)*

...

In primis Rec*eived* at Hoctide   xviij s. x d.

...   30

AC   *Proceedings Regarding George Buckner*   Bodl.: MS. Twyne-Langbaine 3
ff 121–1v*   *(20 August)*

Proceeding of the court held before Thomas Edwards and Robert Master, the   35
vice-chancellor's deputies

...

® This Buckner   Processus sup*er* Bonis Georgij Buckner felonis de se excerpt*us* ex libro
was one of   Actor*um*, scil*icet* inter Acta termini Trinitatis a*n*no D*om*ini 1599, et Acta
ye Towne
musitians

10, 17, 29/ hoctyde, Hoctide: *31 March–1 April*   23/ hocking: *Hocktide was 31 March–1 April 1600*
1600   29/ In primis: *in display script*

® See ye Act
books of that
year

termini s. Mich*ael*is eiusd*em* anni in magna vacatione, mense Augusti
...

Quib*us* die et loco dicti vener*abiles* viri Thomas Edwards et Robertus Maister
Deputati vener*abilis* viri antedicti accedentes ad domum cuiusdam Georgij
Buckner felonis de se, nomine vni*u*ersitatis oxon*iensis* possessionem capiebant   5
Domus seu cuiusdam tenementi in p*a*rochia s. Mariæ Magdalenæ extra portam
Borealem Ciuitatis oxon*iæ*, omn*i*umque et singulor*um* bonor*um* Iurium et
creditor*um* in dicta domo seu tenemento existen*tium* seu quouismodo ad
eund*em* Georg*ium* Buckner tempore vitæ et mortis pertinen*tium* forisfact*orum*
vni*u*ersitati et ad eand*em* spectan*tium* ratione priuilegiorum et chartar*um*,   10
quib*us* conced*u*nt*ur* dictæ vni*u*ersitati om*n*ia et singula bona Iura et credita
quar*um*cumq*ue* personar*um* infra pr*æ*cinctum vni*u*ersitatis pr*æ*dictæ
Inhabitantium, violentas manus sibi inferen*tium* et se occidentiu*m*: | quorum
intuitu, quoniam pr*æ*dictus Georgius, manus violentas in se intulit, et felo
de se existebat a*n*no Dom*i*ni. 1598. mense Ianuarij vltimo elapso pr*æ*dicti   15
venerabiles viri [venerabilis viri] Thomæ Thornton pr*æ*dicti Deputati, vacuam
possessionem eiusd*em* Domus et tenementi nup*er* pr*æ*fati Georgij intrantes,
capiebant no*m*ine q*u*o supra, et insuper nomine bonor*um* iurium et creditor*um*
eorundemq*ue* possessionis in domo pr*æ*dict*a* capiebant de manu vrsulæ Buckner
pr*æ*fati Georgij relictæ, a certaine cupp or nutt, laide about w*i*th syluer, ye w*hi*ch   20
they did take & carry awaye to ye vse of the saide vni*u*ersitie.

In pr*æ*sentia m*a*gist*r*i Thomæ French Notarij publici et
Iohan*n*is wodson dictæ vni*u*ersitatis ⟨...⟩

Then followeth an Inventary of ye goodds of ye saide George Buckner: 25
amountinge to ye su*m*me of xviii. li. 19 s. x d.
  praysed by ⎰ Rich*ar*d Lloyd
         ⎱ Io*h*n Leonard
         ⎱ Leonard Maior
...   30

c 1600–5
A Letter to Mr T.H. from Sir Edward Hoby (1609)   *stc*: 13541
p 12

...   35

  That famous Colledge of Christs Church in Oxford, which you haue ill
repaied, for the sweete milke which you haue sucked out of her breasts, hath
not yet forgotten how you were euer stained with Puritanisme, how violently
aduerse you were to all such, as were suspected to fauour the Romish Sea.
She doth yet smile to think, what paine you took, being Censor of the house,   40
in putting your hand to the sawing downe of a poore harmelesse May-pole,
because you thought it came out of a Romish forrest....

Theophilus Higgons' Answer to Sir Edward Hoby (1609)   STC: 13452
pp 4–5

...

11.   First then (Sir Edward) vnto your first; I confesse the fact, which you
alleadge, I deny the cause, which you assigne. For the originall, and proper   5
motiue of my disconceipt against the harmelesse Maypole (wherof I was the
Aduersary, & you the Aduocate) was, because it came out of the Colledge
grounds; I taken thence by stealth, and erected (with scorne) neere vnto our
walls, wthout our consent; and this also to justify a former wrong, lately
offered in the same kind. This was the cause (as many can yet remember)   10
first moouing me vnto that enterprise; which, though it were not expedient
for me then to vndertake, yet (being a wooden proof in your behalf) it was
not conuenient for you to mention at this time.

...

15

1600–1
All Souls College Bursars' Accounts   Bodl.: MS. D.D. All Souls c.287
mb 10   *(2 November–2 November)*   *(Rewards)*
...

et de v s. to ye Queens Trumpetters   20
...

et de v s. given to ye Queenes trumpeters.
...

Christ Church Disbursements   ChCh Arch: xii.b.45   25
f 27v   *(25 December–25 March)*   *(Rewards)*
...

To the Trumpetters on Christmas daye sowndinge
in ye hale. by consente   ij s. vj d.
...   30

f 59v   *(24 June–29 September)*   *(Rewards)*
...

Septembris 14. geuen by master Subdeane to
the queenes Trumpetters when the queene was   35
in progresse, & I absent   xx s.
            (signed) Iohn wryght
...

9/ wthout: *for* without

Christ Church Computi   ChCh Arch: iii.c.7(c.)
mb 3d

...

Et in expen*sis* Comediar*um* et Tragediar*um* hoc
A*n*no fact*arum*   n*il* li.   5

...

Magdalen College Libri Computi   MC Arch: LCE/7
f 130*   *(Internal and external payments)*

...   10

Buccinatoribus regijs 20 s. do*m*ini Compton 5 s.   1 li. 5 s.

...

Musicis in festo bursarior*um*   0 5 s.
Promo pro festo ducis Bauariæ *per* billam   10 li. 10 s. 9 d.

...   15

Merton College Bursars' Accounts   MCR: 3.1
f 76   *(21 November–20 March)* *(External expenses)*

...

...musicis ex consensu vj s. viij d....   20

New College Bursars' Accounts   NC Arch: 7590
mb 5*   *(25 December–25 March)* *(Internal expenses)*

...

So*lutum* for the binding of a booke & stringes for the Duke of Bavare   25
ij s....

(24 June–29 September)
...So*lutum* buccinatorib*us* in regar‸|do| ij s. v s.

...   30

The Queen's College Long Rolls   QC Arch: LRA
f 19v col 2   *(7 July–7 July)* *(External expenses)*

...

Decemb*ris* 26⁰.   buccinatoribus ex iussu P*re*pos*iti*   2 s. 6 d. 35

...

Ian*uarii* 1⁰   Moricio tibicini   18 d.
Ian*uarii* 29⁰   Tibicinib*us* de Oxon*ia*   10 s.

...

St John's College Computus Annuus   SJC Arch: Acc.I.A.10
f 77v   *(25 December–25 March)* *(Expenses)*

…

Item geuen to the schollers towardes their chardges
in the Enterlude   ij s. vj d.   5

…

f 83v   *(Requests for payments)*

…

Item geuen to a Harper at the Audytt   xij d.   10

…

St John's College Computus Hebdomalis   SJC Arch: Acc.v.E.2
f 31v   *(5–11 January)*

…   15

An Interlud vpon ye Newe [year first] yeares fyrst day *per* scholares et
conuictores inter prandend*os*

f 33   *(16–22 February)*

…   20

Impositi *pro* minoribus tibicenib*us*   xxj s. iiij d.

…

f 33v   *(23 February–1 March)*

…   25

An exercyse of the Student*es* in Latin V*erse* acted in M*aster* p*res*ident*es* Lodging
Impositi *pro* maiorib*us* tibicinib*us*   37 s. [⟨.⟩ d.]

…

St John's College Computus Hebdomalis   SJC Arch: Acc.v.E.3   30
f 23   *(16–22 February)*

…

Set on for the fidlers xxj s. iiij d.

…

35

f 24   *(23 February–1 March)*

…

In Decrementis xxxix s. x d. q*u*a.
The reason of these Decrement*es* grew by entertayning most of the Head*es*
of Colledg*es* &/   40

17/ prandend*os*: *for* prandentes (?)

Set on for the ffidlers al*i*as musitians xxxvij s.

...

Audited Corporation Accounts   OCA: P.5.2
f 64v*   *(Chamberlains' payments)*   5
...

Item to the Music*i*ons at the bakers dinner   v s.

...

Item to three Companies of players   xxx s.
                                                                              10

f 65

...

Item to the Queenes Trumpeters   xx s.

...
                                                                              15

Keykeepers' Accounts   OCA: P.4.1
f 98v   *(Bonds and bills not summed)*

...

One bond of Gibbons for the Scutchins/
...   20

St Martin Churchwardens' Accounts   ORO: PAR 207/4/F1/1, item 98
single mb   *(30 November–29 November) (Receipts)*
...

Item of the wemen w*hi*ch they got at Hocktyde   xix s. iiij d. 25

...

St Peter in the East Churchwardens' Accounts   ORO: PAR 213/4/F1/2
single mb   *(8 December–8 December) (Receipts)*
...   30

Item for monie gotten at hocktyde   xxx s.

...

St Peter le Bailey Churchwardens' Accounts   ORO: PAR 214/4/F1/48
single mb   *(14 December–13 December) (Receipts)*   35

...

Item receaved at Hocktyde, and all thinges
dischardged cleerly   xxj s. ij d.

...

25, 31, 37/ Hocktyde, hocktyde: *20–1 April 1601*

1601–2
Christ Church Computi   ChCh Arch: iii.c.7(d.)
mb 3*

...

Et in expen*sis* Comediar*um* et Tragediar*um* hoc A*nno* fact*arum*   n*il* li.   5

...

Magdalen College Libri Computi   MC Arch: LCE/7
f 141   *(Internal and external payments)*

...   10
Musicis in festo Bursario*rum*   0 5 s. 0

...

Merton College Bursars' Accounts   MCR: 3.1
f 81v   *(20 November–19 March)* *(External expenses)*   15

...

...musicis ex consensu vj s. viij d....

The Queen's College Long Rolls   QC Arch: LRA
f 21v col 2   *(7 July–7 July)* *(External expenses)*   20

...

Item buccinatorib*us* Regin*æ*   20 s.

...

Ia*nuarij* 28   Item tibicinib*us* de Oxon*ia*   10 s.
Item Mauritio tibicini   18 d. 25

...

St John's College Computus Annuus   SJC Arch: Acc.I.A.10
f 110v   *(25 December–24 March)* *(Expenses)*

...   30
x   It*em* geven to the Chardg*es* of the exercyse that was
in the hall on new-yeares daye   v s. iiij d.

...

x   Item for two Torches for the Comm*e*dye in the hall on
twelf night   ij s. 35

...

f 112v   *(24 March–24 June)*

...

x   Item alowed by the howse toward the Tragedye ouer   40
& aboue iiij li. put on the student*es* head*es*   iij li. xij s. iiij d.

...

St John's College Computus Hebdomalis   SJC Arch: Acc.v.E.2
f 45   *(11–17 January)*
…

An Interlude at dinner vpon Neweyaresday & a commedy vpon twelfnight
…   5

f 46v   *(22–8 February)*
…

Impositi *pro* Musitions   40 s. 4 d.
…   10

(1–7 March)
A Tragaedye Acted publickly by the studentes vpon St Mathyes Euenl

Keykeepers' Accounts   OCA: P.4.1   15
f 101v   *(Bonds and bills not summed)*
…

One bond of mr Gibbons for the Scutchins
…
                                                                           20

St Martin Churchwardens' Accounts   ORO: PAR 207/4/F1/1, item 99
single mb   *(29 November–28 November) (Receipts)*
…

Item of the women at Hocktyde   xix s. iiij d.
…   25

St Mary Magdalen Churchwardens' Accounts   ORO: PAR 208/4/F1/36
single mb*   *(Rendered 29 May 1603) (Receipts)*
…

Item Receued at whitsontyde all thinges beinge   30
discharged   iij li. j d.
…

St Mary the Virgin Churchwardens' Accounts   ORO: PAR 209/4/F1/18
single mb*   *(30 November–30 November) (Receipts)*   35
…

Item receiued at Hocketide   xxvij s.
…

13/ St Mathyes: *ie, St Mathias'*
24, 37/ Hocktyde, Hocketide: *12–13 April 1602*
30/ whitsontyde: *23–9 May 1602*

St Michael at the North Gate Churchwardens' Accounts
ORO: PAR 211/4/F1/3, item 165
single mb *(12 March 1601/2–12 March 1602/3)* *(Receipts)*
...

Item receiuede at hoctide and all thing*es*   5
dischargede   XXV s.
...

St Peter le Bailey Churchwardens' Accounts   ORO: PAR 214/4/F1/49
single mb*   *(13 December–12 December)* *(Receipts)*   10
...

Item gotten at Hocktide aboue all expenses   xxij s. x d. ob.
...

Item gotten at o*ur* shooting daye   x s. xj d.
Item gotten at Whitsontide   xx s. 15
...

1602–3
All Souls College Bursars' Accounts   Bodl.: MS. D.D. All Souls c.288
mb 7   *(2 November–2 November)* *(Rewards)*   20
...

de ij s. vj d. to the trumpeters at Chri*st*mas
...

de xiij s. iiij d. giuen to the Kinges trumpeters when the Court was at
woodstocke   25
...

Exeter College Rectors' Accounts   EC Arch: A.II.9
f 179v   *(1 November–1 November)*
...   30
Item de solutis & dono datis buccinatorib*us* regijs   20 s.
...

Magdalen College Libri Computi   MC Arch: LCE/7
f 151v*   *(Internal and external payments)*   35
...

Buccinatoribus d*omi*ni Richard*i* Lucey in regardo   0 6 s. 0
...

5, 12/ hoctide, Hocktide: *12–13 April 1602*
15/ Whitsontide: *23–9 May 1602*

Merton College Bursars' Accounts MCR: 3.1
f 86v *(19 November–18 March)* *(External expenses)*

...

...Musicis ex consensu 6 s. 8 d....

5

Merton College Register MCR: 1.3
p 202

...

Eodem tempore consensum *est* ut bursarius de more solveret tibicinib*us*, qui
ad nos manè ventilant, sex solidos octo denarios.

10

...

New College Bursars' Accounts NC Arch: 7593
mb 4* *(25 December–25 March)* *(Internal expenses)*

...

15

...So*lutum* buccinitorib*us*. 3 s.... So*lutum* Leonardo et socijs Musi*cis* vj s. viij d....

(24 June–29 September)
...So*lutum* Buccinitorib*us* in regardijs

x s.

...

20

The Queen's College Long Rolls QC Arch: LRA
f 23v col 1* *(7 July–7 July)* *(External expenses)*

...

It*em* Moritio tibicini

18 d. 25

...

It*em* tibicinibus Oxon*iæ*

10 s.

...

St John's College Computus Annuus SJC Arch: Acc.I.A.10
f 137 *(29 September–25 December)* *(Expenses)*

30

...

x It*em* to the Actors for y*er* Chargesse in y*er* wassall

iij s. vj d.

...

35

f 138 *(25 December–25 March)*

...

It*em* giuen a trumpeter

vj d.

...

x It*em* allowed toward ye Showe att Newyears tide

v s. 40

...

9/ Eodem tempore: *10 February 1602/3*

f 140   *(24 June–29 September)*

…

It*em* giuen to ye King*es* trumpeters   xiij s. iiij d.

…

                                      5

f 143*   *(Requests for payment)*

…

x   It*em* allowed to Henry Harbart for vizard*es* and other
furniture for a play 1601 in full payment   x s.

…   10

St John's College Computus Hebdomalis   sjc Arch: Acc.v.E.2
f 59*   *(10–16 January)*

…

Tenant*es* with Neweyeasgyft*es*   15
2 Commeydies.
Mr Langley.
Som*me* strangers/

f 60v   *(14–20 February)*   20

…

dat*i* maiorib*us* tibicinib*us* xlij s. vj d.

…

A Twelfth Night Play at St John's   Bodl.: MS. Rawlinson poet.212   25
f 82*

A Twelfe night merriment: an*n*o 1602.

Interloquutores.   30

1 Tyresias   6 Eccho
2 Cephisus   7 Lyriope
3 Narcissus   8 Florida
4 Dorastus   9 Clois
5 Clinias   10 The well   35
          11 Porter.

f 81v

Enter ye porter at ye end of supper   40

15/ Neweyeasgyft*es*: *for* Neweyearsgyftes

Porter: Master & Mistris with all your guests
                God save you, heerin ye matter rests
                Christmas is now at ye point to bee past
                Tis giving vp ye ghost & this is ye last
                And shall it passe thus without life or cheere   5
                This hath not beene seene this many a yeere
                If youl have any sporte, then say ye woord
                Heere come youths of ye parish yat will it affoord
                They are heere hard by comminge alonge
                Crowning their wassaile bowle with a songe   10
                They have some other sport too out of dowbt
                Lett mee alone & I will finde it out
                I am your porter & your vassaile
                Shall I lett in ye boyes with their wassaile
                Say: they are at doore to sing they beginne   15
                Goe to then, ile goe & lett them in./.
                        Enter ye wassaile, two of them bearinge ye bowle, &
                        singinge ye songe & all of them bearing ye burden

...

                                                              20

f 67*

...

                      Enter ye porter as Epilogue.
Are these ye ladds yat would doe ye deede
They may bee gone & God bee their speede   25
Ile take vpp their buckett but I sweare by ye water
I have seene a farre better play at ye Theater.
Ile shutt them out of doores tis no matter for their larges
Thinke you well of my service & ile beare ye charges./
If there bee any yat expecte some dances   30
Tis I must performe it for my name is Frances.
                Finis.

f 84

                                                              35

A speech made for ye foresaid Porter, who pronounc't it in ye hall before
most of ye house and Master Praesident yat had sconc't him 10 groates for
lettinge ye fidlers into ye hall at Christmas

...

29–30/ Thinke ... dances: *these lines separated by a rule*
32/ Finis.: *followed by a rule*

ff 83v–2v

...Sub nocte silenti (i) in nocte vel paulo ante noctem cum spectatur in
ignibus aurum; when you might have seene gold in ye fier, ye fier shin'de so
like gold, Ecce per opaca locorum. came ye fidlers creeping alonge, densa   5
subter testudine casus; their instruments vnder their arms in their cases, &
at lenghe, Itum est in viscera terrae; broke open into ye harte of the hall:
neither when they were there could they bee content to warme their | fingers
by ye fier & bee gone, though I would have persuaded them thereto, but
Iuvat vsque morari et conferre gradum: they would needes staye & ye youth   10
daunce: But oh to see, woe to see, yat pleasure is but a pinch & felicitye but
a phillippe: when as Iuvat ire per altum. some were cutting capers aloft in
ye ayre [and] Canit similiter huic; & they likewise with their Minstrelsey
fitting it to their footing all on a suddaine, subito I may say to them but
repente to mee, their sporte was spoild their Musicke marrd their dauncinge   15
dasht with a, vox hominem sonat, with a voyce, with an awefull voyce,
Haeccine fieri flagitia; ar these ye fruites of ye fires; statur a me (i) sto, statur
ab illis (i) stant, They that even now scrap't so fast with their stickes fell now
to scraping faster with their leggs their fum fum was turn'd to Mum Mum
& their pleasaunt melodye to most pittifull making of faces; But when they   20
look't yat their fiddles should have flyen about their eares, their calveskin
cases, about their calveshead pates, as ye sunne shines brightest through a
shower, so did softnes in ye midst of severitye, there was noe more said to
them, but, Teque his ait eripe | flammis; they were best, since they had made
many mens heeles warme with shakinge, to coole their owne by quaking   25
without doore But ye more mercy was shewed before ye lesse was left for mee,
had I beene dealt with soe mercifullye, I had not neede to have come, with
this exclamation, or had it beene but gratia ab officio, but a groat out of mine
office I should not have stonied ye stones nor rented ye rockes, with my
dolorous outcryes, But when it shall come to denarij dicti quod denos,   30
when tenn groats shall make a muster togeather & sitte heavy on my head,

3/ Sub nocte silenti: 'Under the silent night'; Virgil, Aeneid 4.527; 7.87

3–4/ cum ... aurum: 'when gold is seen in fire'; cp Ovid, Tristia 1.5.25

5/ Ecce ... locorum: 'Behold, through the shadows'; cp Virgil, Aeneid 2.725

5–6/ densa ... casus: 'under their compact shield (bearing) chances'; cp Virgil, Aeneid 9.513–14

7/ lenghe: for lengthe

7/ Itum ... terrae: 'They went into the bowels of the earth'; Ovid, Metamorphoses 1.138

10/ Iuvat ... gradum: 'It delights (them) to linger and match step'; Virgil, Aeneid 6.487–8

12/ Iuvat ... altum: 'It delights (them) to go up in the air'; cp Ovid, Metamorphoses 15.147–8

16/ vox ... sonat: 'the voice sounds human'; cp Virgil, Aeneid 1.328

17/ Haeccine ... flagitia: 'that these scandals occurred'; cp Cicero, Pro Sex. Roscio 9(25)

24/ Teque ... flammis: "And snatch yourself from the flames," he says'; Virgil, Aeneid 2.289

30/ denarij ... denos: 'denarii are so-called because (they are worth) ten'; cp Varro, De lingua latina 5.173

actum est ilicet, ye porter perijt. O weathercoke of wretchednes y*at* I am,
seated on ye may-pole of misfortune, whither shall I turne or to whome shall I
looke for releife? shall I speake to my minstrells for my money? why they have
allready forsaken mee to ye verifieng of ye ould pr*o*verbe: Quantu*m* quisq*ue*
sua nu*m*moru*m* servat in arca: tantu*m* habet et fidei; As long as a man hath   5
money in his purse so long hee shall have ye fidlers: What is to bee looked for
of them, y*at* will doe nothing w*i*thout pay & hard-mony for their harmonye.
Shall I speake to my frends? why: Nullus ad amissas ibit amicus opes:

Looke for more
ye last leafe of
this rule

ff 43–2v   10

Oh then lett mee runne to ye speare of Achilles (recorded by auncient
Phillosophers) wh*ich* first hurt mee & last can heale mee; lett my penitencye
find pittye, and my confession move compassion; if you will live according
to rule, ever after pænitet, tædet, lett miseret miserescit succeede. That they   15
came in it was a fault of oversight in not overseeing my office; If any should
slinke by Cerberus out of hell, it weare a thing to bee wondred at & yet wee
see there doth ther are so many spirritts walking: if any should steale by Ianus
into heaven, it weare much woorthy of marvaile, & yet wee see there doth,
there are soe many of Iupiters Le*m*mans; if anye should skippe in or out by   20
mee it is not to bee admired; for why? Cerber*us* ye Porter of hell hath 3 heads,
Ianus hath two, & I yo*ur* poore Colledg porter have but one. That they weare
not putt out of ye Colledge when they weare in, it was a fault; but a fault of
Curtesie; for who could find in his hart when hee seeth a man acco*m*panied
with Musicke, Musis comitantib*us*, to bidd him, Ibis Homere foras, gett   25
you home for an Asse: But though my breast (I must | confesse) weare then
somew*ha*t moved with their Melodye, yet heerafter my breast shall bee
Marble when they warble; Nemo sibi Mimos accipere debet favori, I will
never lett in Minstrells againe vpon favour; for yo*ur* selves I can say no more
but profit: & when (after this Christmas cheere is ended) you fall againe to   30
your studdies, I could wish that Hippocrene may bee Hippocrise ye Muses
Muskadine & ye Pierides, pies every day for your sakes & as for my tenn
groates if it will please you to remitte it, I will give you: decies decem Mille
Gratiaru*m*.

Dixi.   35

1/ actum … ilicet: *'It's done. It's all over';* Plautus, Cistellaria *685 (4.2.15)*
4–5/ Quantu*m* … fidei: *'A person has as much faith as they keep money in their chest';* Juvenal, Saturae *3.143–4*
8–10m/ Looke … rule: *written vertically in left margin and marked with an asterisk for insertion after* opes
8/ Nullus … opes: *'No friend will approach lost wealth';* Ovid, Tristia *1.9.10*
25/ Musis comitantib*us*: *'With the muses accompanying';* cp Ovid, Ars Amatoria *2.279*
25/ Ibis … foras: *'You will go outside, Homer';* Ovid, Ars Amatoria *2.280*

City Council Minutes   OCA: C/FC/1/A1/002
f 85*   *(14 April)*

...

An act
touching ye
Musicions

It is also agreed That Order shalbe sett downe by master Maior & thaldermen
touching the inhibitione of all Musicions playing within this Cytie & suburbes   5
other then the Wayghtes of this Cytie And that Order to stand and be allowed
for ever/ And if any Musicions (other then the Waytes) of this Cytie) shall
play in any other sort to be imprysoned toties quoties by the Maior or any
other alderman in his Warde

...   10

f 85v*   *(11 May)*

...

Iohn Baldwyn
musicion
admitted free

It is agreed At this Counsell That Iohn Baldwin Musicion shall from
henceforth be free of this Cytie paying to this Cytie Twenty shillinges &   15
providing himself a Scutchin of silver worth Twenty shillinges at his owne
Chardge/ Which Scutchin after his death or removall from hence he shall
leave vnto the vse of this Cytie/ which he graunted to doe/ & he hath paid
iiij s. vj d. for thofficers fees & ij s. vj d. for a leather buckett/ & is sworne.

...   20

Audited Corporation Accounts   OCA: P.5.2
f 76v*   *(Chamberlains' payments)*

...

Item to the Towne Waytes at the proclamacion   25
of the King   x s.

...

f 77

...   30
Item to the Kinges Harbinger & his Trumpetters   xl s.

...

Keykeepers' Accounts   OCA: P.4.1
f 104   *(Bonds and bills not summed)*   35

...

One bond of mr Gibbons for the Scutchins/.

...

7/ (other ...Waytes) of this Cytie): *duplication of closing parenthesis*

St Aldate Churchwardens' Accounts
ORO: DD Par. Oxford St Aldate c.16/10
mb [2]   *(4 February 1602/3–4 February 1603/4)* *(Receipts)*
...

Re*ceiu*ed over pluse for whitsun and hockinge all   5
thing*es* dyschardgid   vij li. ij s.
...

St Martin Churchwardens' Accounts   ORO: PAR 207/4/F1/1, item 100
single mb   *(28 November–27 November)* *(Receipts)*   10
...

I*tem* receaved of the weomen at Hocktyde   xxx s.
I*tem* the clere gaynes made at Whitsontyde all manner
of chardges deducted is   ij li. x s. ij d.
I*tem* more for a tree at the same tyme   v s. vj d. 15
...

St Mary Magdalen Churchwardens' Accounts   ORO: PAR 208/4/F1/36
single mb*   *(Rendered 29 May 1603)* *(Receipts)*
...   20
Ite*m* Rece*ued* at hoctyde all thinges beinge discharged   xvij s.
...

St Mary the Virgin Churchwardens' Accounts   ORO: PAR 209/4/F1/19
single mb   *(30 November–30 November)* *(Receipts)*   25
...

Item received at Hocktide   xxxij s.
Item gained at o*ur* Midsomer sporte and for our Wood   xxviij s.
...

                                                                                    30
St Michael at the North Gate Churchwardens' Accounts
ORO: PAR 211/4/F1/3, item 166
single mb*   *(12 March 1602/3–12 March 1603/4)* *(Receipts)*
...

received at hoctide & all thing*es* discharged   xx⌈s.⌉ iiij s. 35
...

5/ whitsun: *Whitsuntide was 12–18 June 1603*
5/ hockinge: *Hocktide was 2–3 May 1603*
12, 21, 27, 35/ Hocktyde, hoctyde, Hocktide,
   hoctide: *2–3 May 1603*

13/ Whitsontyde: *12–18 June 1603*
35/ xx⌈s.⌉ iiij s.: *possibly an incomplete correction for*
   xx s. iiij d. *(?)*

St Peter in the East Churchwardens' Accounts   ORO: PAR 213/4/F1/2
single mb*   *(8 December–8 December) (Receipts)*

…

Item Receaved for hocking   xl s.

…   5

St Peter le Bailey Churchwardens' Accounts   ORO: PAR 214/4/F1/50
single sheet   *(12 December–11 December) (Receipts)*

…

Item receued at hocktide an all thindes   10
discharged   xxxv[j] s. iij d. ob.
Item receued for the bouer   xiiii d.

…

Item ⌜receued⌝ for a sapling that should haue
mad a sumer pole   xii d. 15

…

1603–4
Christ Church Computi   ChCh Arch: iii.c.7(e.)
mb 3*   20

…

Et in expen*sis* Comediar*um* et Tragediar*um* hoc
A*nn*o fact*arum*   n*il* li.

…

                                                              25

Magdalen College Libri Computi   MC Arch: LCE/7
f 163   *(Internal and external payments)*

…

Tibicinibus in festo bursario*rum*   0 5 s.

…   30

Merton College Bursars' Accounts   MCR: 3.1
f 93   *(18 November–23 March) (External expenses)*

…Symphoniacis ex consensu 6 s. 8 d.…   35

…

4/ hocking: *Hocktide was 2–3 May 1603*
10/ hocktide: *2–3 May 1603*
10/ thindes: *for* thinges
11/ iij d.: iij *corrected over* v

Merton College Register   MCR: 1.3
p 209
...

Tunc etiam consensum est ibidem, vt publicis Academiæ oppidique musicis,
bursarius sex solidos octo denarios, more solito, elargiretur.   5
...

New College Bursars' Accounts   NC Arch: 7595
mb 5   *(25 December–25 March)* *(Internal expenses)*
                                                                                                10
...Solutum musicis oppidanis vj s. viij d....
...

The Queen's College Long Rolls   QC Arch: LRA
f 25v col 1*   *(7 July–7 July)* *(External expenses)*   15
...
Item Mauritio tibicini   18 d.
Item tibicinibus de Oxonia   10 s.
...

                                                                                                20
St John's College Computus Annuus   SJC Arch: Acc.I.A.10
f 164v*   *(29 September–25 December)* *(External and internal expenses)*
...
x   Item allowed to Henry Harbart for vizardes & other
furnitur for a play 1601 in full paiment   x s. 25
...

f 165   *(25 December–25 March)*
...
x   Item layd out for diuers shewes and for the appurtenances   30
at Christmas   xlvj s. v d.
...

St John's College Computus Hebdomalis   SJC Arch: Acc.v.E.2
f 72v   *(16–22 January)*   35
...
pro Tibicinibus   v s. ij d.
...

4/ Tunc: *5 February 1603/4*

f 73v   *(20-6 February)*

...

A tragedy of Hippolitus acted publickly. 13º Fe*br*uarij
Impositi *pro* expensis in tragedia et musicis in toto anno   iij li. vij s. v d.
p*ra*eter pecunias   5
Vnde soluti musicis 43 s. p*ra*eter 9 s. 6 d. in pecunijs

Vice-Chancellors' Accounts   OUA: WP/β/21(4)
p 148   *(23 July-14 July)* *(Extraordinary expenses)*
...   10
Solut*um* Buccinatoribus Regis existent*ibus* Wodstocke   xx s.
...

p 149
...   15
Solut*um* histrionibus Reginæ vt sine strepitu discederent   xl s.
...

Audited Corporation Accounts   OCA: P.5.2
f 82v*   *(Chamberlains' payments)*   20
...
Item to mr Niccolls for the king*es* players   xx s.
...

Keykeepers' Accounts   OCA: P.4.1   25
f 108   *(Bonds and bills not summed)*

...

One bond of mr Gibbons for the Scutchins
...
                                                                                                          30

St Aldate Churchwardens' Accounts
ORO: DD Par. Oxford St Aldate c.16/11
single mb*   *(Rendered 2 April 1605)* *(Receipts)*

In primis Rec⟨....⟩d by hocking   xxxviij s. 35
Item at Whitson⟨...⟩d   iiij li. v s.
...
Item for our pole   iiij s.
...

35/ Rec⟨....⟩d: *hole in parchment*   36/ Whitson⟨...⟩d: *27 May-2 June 1604*
35/ hocking: *Hocktide was 16-17 April 1604*

St Martin Churchwardens' Accounts   ORO: PAR 207/4/F1/1, item 102
single mb*   *(27 November 1603–1 April 1605) (Receipts)*

...

Itim receued of the women at hocktyde	xxx s.
Itim receued the clere gaine at whitsontyde all	5
charges deducted	xxx s.

...

St Mary Magdalen Churchwardens' Accounts   ORO: PAR 208/4/F1/37
single mb   *(Rendered 5 May 1605) (Receipts)*   10

...

Item Rec*eued* at Whitsontyde all thing*es*	
beinge discharged	iij li. x s. ob.

...

15

St Michael at the North Gate Churchwardens' Accounts
ORO: PAR 211/4/F1/3, item 167
single mb   *(Rendered 4 April 1605) (Receipts)*

...

Item receaved at Hocktyde all thing*es* beinge	20
discharged	xx s.
Item gotten at Whitsontyde	xx s.

...

St Peter le Bailey Churchwardens' Accounts   ORO: PAR 214/4/F1/51   25
single sheet*   *(21 December 1603–10 April 1605) (Receipts)*

...

Item rec*eyved* at Hocktyde and all thing*es*	
dischardged	xiiij s. ij d.

...

30

1604–5
All Souls College Bursars' Accounts   Bodl.: MS. D.D. All Souls c.288
mb 7   *(2 November–2 November) (Various expenses)*

...

35

Et de xv li. payd to the vicechancelor toward*es* the vniversity charges, for the
kings entertainment.

...

4, 20, 28/ hocktyde, Hocktyde: *16–17 April 1604*
5, 12, 22/ whitsontyde, Whitsontyde: *27 May–2 June 1604*
36/ vicechancelor: *George Abbot*

Balliol College Bursars' Accounts   BC Arch: Computi 1592–1614
f 68v   *(18 October–7 July)* *(Expenses noted)*

...

Item giuen to trumpetors at Chrismas   iij s. vj d.

...   5

f 70v   *(7 July–18 October)*

...

Item allowed towardes the publike Charge of the
Vniuersitie at the King beyinge heere more then   10
allowed in the butterye   27 s.

...

Item to trumpeters   7 s.

...

15

Christ Church Treasurers' Accounts   ChCh Arch: iii.c.1
f 124

...

Et in expensis Comediarum et [Trad] Tragediarum hoc
Anno factarum   nil li. 20

...

Christ Church Disbursements   ChCh Arch: xii.b.49
f 43   *(25 March–24 June)* *(Extraordinary expenses)*

25

Towards Musick and lyghtes one the kings day att
the Comedie by consent   xx s.
              (signed)   Receaued by me William Pearce.

...

30

f 60*   *(24 June–29 September)*

...

Expended att the Kings comminge this yeare as
more particularly appeares in a note in the ende
of this booke one hundred seuentie seauen pounds   35
six shillings six pence halfpenny   177 li. 6 s. 6 d. ob.

...

20/ factarum: c *altered from* t
34–5/ note ... booke: *the* note *is missing*

Exeter College Rectors' Accounts   EC Arch: A.II.9
f 187v   *(1 November–1 November)*

...

Item de Datis tubicenibus regijs	10 s.

...

Lincoln College Calculus 1604–5   LC Arch
f 10v   *(21 December–21 December) (Internal expenses)*

...

Item in mony against ye Kynges comming to Oxford	iiij li. x s.

...

Item to ye Trumpeters	ix s.

...

Magdalen College Libri Computi   MC Arch: LCE/7
f 170 col 1   *(Internal and external payments)*

...

Buccinatoribus Dominj Gulielmi Munson:	0 6 s. 0.
Buccinatoribus Dominj Crumwell: in regardo	0. 5 s. 0.

...

Domino Doctorj Abbot Vicecancellario pro Contributione Collegij in adventu Regis	36 li. 0 0

...

Pro duobus paribus Chirothecarum pro Principe et pro vno pro Domino Chancellario de Oxonia:	10 li. 15 s. 0

...

Musicis Regis et Principis in regardo.	2 li. 0. 0.
Satellitibus Principis in regardo	2 li. 0 0

...

Magistro Castilion conficientj Commediam in adventum Principis pro Candelis et potu in tempore repititionis:	0. 10 s. 0.

...

col 2

...

Doctorj Hood afferentj Globos a Nobilissima Heroina Domina Arbella in regardo	2 li. 0 0
Billingsley pro Chirothecis datis Dominæ Arbellæ	2 li. 10 s. 0

4/ Datis: Da *corrected over other letters*
37/ Nobilissima: N *corrected over another letter*

Musicis in festo Bursariorum   0. 5 s. 0.

...

Merton College Bursars' Accounts   MCR: 3.1
f 98v   *(23 November–22 March)* *(External expenses)*   5

...

...Musicis publicis ex consensu 6 s. 8 d....

...

New College Bursars' Accounts   NC Arch: 7596   10
mb 4   *(25 December–25 March)* *(Internal expenses)*

...Solutum Musicis oppidanis vj s. viij d....

(25 March–24 June) *(External expenses)*   15
...Solutum to Master ViceChancelour for the Vniversity expences xxx li....

...

Solutum Buccinatoribus regijs x s....

...

                                                                                       20
Oriel College Treasurers' Accounts   OC Arch: S 1.C.1
f 119   *(External expenses)*

...

Item Vicecancellario pro sumptibus in Regis adventu
factis secundum vniuersitatis decretum, et consensu   25
præpositi et societatis   vj li.

...

f 120v   *(Internal expenses)*
                                                                                       30
Item buccinatoribus Regijs   x s.

...

The Queen's College Long Rolls   QC Arch: LRA
f 27 col 2   *(7 July–7 July)* *(Internal expenses)*   35

...
December 25   Item tibicinæ Morrice   2 s.

...

f 27v col 1   40

...
Julij 3   Item deliberatum pro tuba & vectura a London & emendatione   28 s.

...

f 28 col 1*   *(External expenses)*

...

Item Tibicinibus de Oxon*ia*	10 s.
Item Buccinatorib*us* de Barnecastle	3 s.
Item Clarionib*us* tribus	3 s. 5

...

f 30 col 2*   *(7 July 1605–7 July 1606)*

...

August 1º Item deliberatu*m* Vicechancellario in adventu*m*   10
Serenissi*mi* Regis   7 li. 16 s.

...

Item Clarionib*us* sex   3 s.

...

25 Item deliberatum *pro* 2b*us* paribus cheritheca*rum*   15
Serenissi*mæ* Reginæ   14 li. 10 s.

...

Item Clarionib*us* Serenissi*mi* Regis   20 s.

...
20

St John's College Computus Hebdomalis   sɪc Arch: Acc.v.E.4
f 6v   *(18–24 February)*

...

Shrouemunday The tragœdy of Lucretia publickly acted xjth of ffebruary wi*t*h good
co*m*mendacon   25
And dyuerse strangers interteyned in respect thereof/

f 7   *(25 February–3 March)*

...

Imposit*i pro* tragœdia Lucretjæ 3 li. 17 s. 8 d. pr*æ*ter 22 s. 4 d. in   30
pecunijs solut*is*
     In Decrementis xj s. ix d. ob.

...

(4–10 March)   35
Imposit*i pro* musicis *pro* toto
A*n*no et *pro* 2º noctib*us*   iij li. ij s.
Vnde solut*i* musicis   iij li.

...

4/ Barnecastle: *Barnard Castle, Durham*
15m/ 25: *25 August 1605*
25/ commendacon: *for* commendacion; *abbreviation mark missing*

prœter xj s. vj d. in pecunijs dat*is* ipsis musicis

...

   In Decrementis xxxij s. ix d. ob. q*u*a.

f 13   *(12–18 August)*   5

...

Imposit*i* sup*er* capit*a* Conuictor*um* ex decreto conuocationis in aduent*u* Regis
vid*elicet* filij Equitis 3 s. 4 d. filij Ar*migeri* xx d., Generosi 12 d., Plebeij 4 d.
in toto liij s. iiij d.
Vnde solut*i* vniuersit*ati* ⌜°p*er* G.R.°⌝ 40 s. et p*er* Coll*egium* v li.   10

...

f 13v   *(2–8 September)*

...

In decrementis. xxxv li. xiiij s.   15

Mr Iones.   The cause of this decrement*es* was by reason that the King*es* M*a*iesty the
Queene and Prince was 3 dayse in the Vniversity And that the L*ord* Admirall
& the L*ord* of Effingha*m* with the Ladyes did lye in M*aste*r Præsident*es* his
lodging 7 dayse.   20

Vice-Chancellors' Accounts   OUA: WP/β/21(4)
p 152   *(14 July 1604–17 July 1605) (Extraordinary expenses)*

...

Solut*um* Buccinatoribus Regijs existentibus Woodstock   xx s. 25

...

Orders of the Delegates of Convocation for the Royal Plays
OUA: WP/γ/19/1
f 1v*   *(18 July)*   30

     decrees & orders sett downe by ye delegates co*n*cer*n*inge
       his M*a*iesties entertaynme*n*te
1   Imp*rimis* y*a*t the Vicechancell*or* the dean of Christch*ur*ch d*r* Hovenden lilly
[Reynoldes] bond Reynoldes holland *(blank)* Rives Singleton Eglienby Howson 35
bluirch ∧⌜with⌝ ther Scarlett gownes and hoodes both the procters ye p*re*sident
of St Iohns the principalls of brodgates, Glocester hall, hart hall, Alborne hall,
∧⌜St Mary Hall⌝ M*aste*rs boughton Russell, [baw⟨...⟩n,] Ewer, Gower, holme,
Osborne, accompayned with the three Esquier beedles, vppon foote clothes,

10/ G.R.: *probably George Rainsbie*
36/ the procters: *Richard Fitz-Herbert, John Hanmer*

shall meet his maiestie att ye confines of the vniuersitie liberties, and that
master Vicechancellor att ye confines or boundes shall entertayne his maiestie
with an oration at what tyme he doeth deliver vpp vnto his ∧⌈maiestie⌉ the
insignes of his office, and shall withall deliver vnto his maiestie such a present
as master Vichancellor with the delegates shall thinke to be fitt [betweene   5
this present]

2 Item yat everie man shall stand to entertayne his maiestie as he passeth by
   according to the order followinge: first the doctors att Christchurch [⟨.⟩] gate
   Secondly ye bacchilers of divinitie; thirdly masters of Artes and batchilers of
   Lawe, fourthly batchilers of Artes, then the schollers of houses in schollers 10
   gownes & square capps, lastlie ye commoners of Colleges & halls, & all other
   schollers not of the foundation of any colledg in ther rounde cappes: and all
   these to stand on one side of the stret as farre as they will reach vnto St Giles

3 Item yat they shall stand there quietlie without removinge from ther places and
   assoone as the trayne is past presentlie to depart to yer severall houses   15

4 Item yat att ye topp of Quartervois ye greeke professor shall make a very breife
   and short oration in greeke not exceedinge twentie lynes to his maiestie./

5 Item at his maiesties alightinge in Christchurch the Orator of the vniuersitie
   shall entertayne him with an oration very breife & shorte

   ...   20

ff 2v-4*

Item ther are appoynted to see the streetes well ordered & prepared as also to
keepe order amongst ye graduates and scholers master doctor Buste master   25
president of St Johns, mr Boughton, mr Braddell, mr wharton, mr ffarrar mr
hugh llyd of Iesus Colledge mr master mr wright of christchurch with the
masters of the streates ye Vicechancellor & procters
Item that the heades of everie Colledg shall call yer companies befor them
and examine whather they be provided of gownes hoodes & other apparell   30
accordinge to the orders sett downe & shall make certificate & deliuer ye
names of soe many as ar vnfurnished to master Vicechancellor & this to be
donn without parcialtie at or befor the first of August next.
Item that if any actor shall fall sick or otherwise necessaryly be letted then an
other shalbe appoynted by master Vicechancellor & procters and ye maior part 35
of the delegates.
                    Concerninge ye stage & playes.
It is concluded three playes to be made in Lattin. viz. ij comodies & a tragedie.
And christchurch hath vndertaken ye performance of one comodie & Magdalen
Colledge new Colledge & St Iohns haue vndertaken ye performance of one   40
other comedie & on tragedie havinge authoritie to make choyce of Actors &
pen men to helpe to penn them, out of the whole vniuersitie; and that the

heades of the aforesaid three houses. vid*elicet*. Magd*alen* Coll*edge* New Coll*edge* & St Iohns shall choyse delegates out of the aforsaid [h] three houses vnto them whoe shall ioyntly order all matters co*n*cerni*n*ge ye aforesaid playes.

It is agreed that ther shalbe a co*n*tribution co*n*cerni*n*ge ye playes and all thinges app*er*teyni*n*ge therv*n*to (except the matter & fabrick of the stage) and money 5 to be brought in to m*aste*r Vicech*ancellor*, and by him to be delivered to certen stew*ar*d*es* of the vniv*er*sitie to be appoynted and sworne by the delegat*es* to make a iust & p*ar*ticular accompt to be hard & allowed by ye aforesaid delegat*es*. p*ro*vided allwayes y*at* if any new tymber shalbe necessarie to be bestowed for ye inlardginge of ⟨...⟩ stage ye co*n*sideraci*o*n therof shalbe 10 referred to the stew*ar*d*es* of the vniv*ers*⟨....⟩ appoynted to y*at* ende & to be brought in vppon yer accompt*es* |

It is agreed that m*aste*r Vicech*ancellor* shall call vnto him m*aste*r dean of christch*urch* m*aste*r president of magd*alen*. m*aste*r warden of new Colledg ⌐& m*aste*r president of St Iohns¬ and after co*n*sultation had [after] to send vpp 15 ij to S*i*r Thomas Chaloner yer to take direction from him what [advise] he will advise ye vniv*er*sitie co*n*cerni*n*ge ye fashion of yer stage and y*at* m*aste*r Vicech*ancellor* in the name of ye vniv*er*sitie shall geue S*i*r Thoma very great thankes for his loue and care toward*es* ye vniv*er*sitie

It is agreed & co*n*cluded y*at* all the Colledges shalbe rated according to ye 20 old rate of yer land*es* xxx s. in everie hundred pound*es* and ye Com*m*oners in Colledges and halls to be rated accordinge as they pay in ye matriculation booke by ye heades of Colledges & halls.

It is agreed that ye rate of money aboue mentioned to be payd by the Colledges and halls shalbe gathered and delivered to m*aste*r vicech*ancellor* by the first 25 of August next ensuing & that this be doon*n* by the bursers of Colledges & manciples of halls.

	ye steward*es* appoynted by ye delegates	
1 d*r* Hovenden	6 m*aste*r president of St Iohns	
2 d*r* bond	7 m*aste*r principall of Gloc*ester* Hall	30
3 d*r* Aery	8 m*aste*r principall of new Inne	
4 d*r* Ketle	9 mr Boughton	
5 d*r* Howson	10 mr browne of Vniversitie Coll*edge*	
	11 mr floyd of Allsoules	

Collation with Bodl.: MS. Twyne 17 *(T)* pp 181–3 and Cambridge University Library: MS Additional 34 *(CU)* ff 28–9:   4 agreed] agreed & co*n*cluded *T*   6 by him] so *T*   7 certen] ye *T*   7 to be] *T omits*   7 the²] those *T*   12 yer] ye *T*   13–19 It is agreed that ... vniv*er*sitie] *T omits*   20 It is] It*em* it is *T*   24 agreed] agreed & concluded *T*   25 m*aste*r vicech*ancellor*] m*aste*r vicech*ancellor* for ye time beinge *T*

7/ by: b *written over* ye   18/ Thoma: *for* Thomas

It is agreed & concluded yat the stewardes aboue named shalbe named to
make a faythfull accompt of all ye money by them receaved & disbursed for
and in ye behalf of ye vniversitie concerninge ye kinges comminge and yat
ye aforsaid stewardes shall make yer accomptes within on moneth next &
immediatlie followinge after ye kinges departur and that master Vicechancellor   5
shall haue power to call before him the aforesaid stewardes as often as occasion
shalbe offered and lastlie yat the money aboue mencioned shalbe receaved &
disbursed by ye aforesaid delegates or by the maior part of them.
It is agreed yat the three yeomen bedles shall provide them new violett gownes
garded with a gard of velvett or a fayre billament of lace and yat ye stewardes   10
shall geue them ix li. viz. iij li. a peece towardes ye providinge of them.
It is concluded yat ther shalbe two orations made to our honorable chauncellor
ye one by master Vicechancellor ye other by the Orator of the vniversitie att
such places as his honor shall appoynt. |

                                                                                  15
            Advertismentes for the heades of houses to delivere with
                        great chardge, vnto yer companies.

  1 Imprimis that they admonish all doctors and graduates fellowes probationers
     & schollers to provide before ye first day of August next gownes hoodes &   20
     capps according to the statutes of ther howses and orders of the vniversitie
     & that all Comoners & halliers doe weere round capps and such colours &
     fashions in ther apparell as the statutes doe prescribe
  2 Item yat whoesoever shalbe sene by the Vicechancellor and proctors or other
     overseers appoynted by the said delegates in the streetes or any publick place,   25
     duringe ye kinges maiesties aboad otherwise apparelled then ye statutes of yer
     house or of ye vniversitie doe appoynt for yer degree shall presentlie forfeit x s.
     and suffer inprisonment at ye discretion of ye said officers, ye said forfeiture
     to be levied by master vicechancellor or by whome he shall appoynte & to be
     imployed towardes the defrayinge of ye chardges for his maiesties entertaynment   30
  3 Item yat vppon ye day when the kinge commeth all graduates shalbe readie
     at ye ringinge of St Maries bell to comm in ther habites and hoodes according
     to yer degrees and all schollers in ther gownes & capps and to stand quietlie in
     such order as shalbe appoynted vntill his maiestie be passed into Christchurch;

Collation continued: 1 named²] sworne *T* 4–5 within on … after] before All
hallowtide next followinge *T* 5 master Vicechancellor] master Vicechancellor for ye
time beinge, *T* 6 aforesaid] saide *T* 6 as often] *T omits* 9 agreed] agreed &
concluded *T* 10 of²] *T omits* 13 master Vicechancellor] master vicechancellor
then beinge, *T* 19–20 fellowes probationers & schollers] scholler⟨.⟩ fellowes and
Probationers *CU* 24 and] or *CU* 25 said] *CU omits* 25 streetes] streete *CU*
28 forfeiture] forfeit *CU* 29–30 master vicechancellor or by … entertaynment] the
Vicechancelor or whome he shall appointe *CU*

and ye trayne being past everie man to resort to his owne Colledge.

...

7   Item yat ye Schollers which cannot be admitted to see ye playes doe not make
any outcryes or vndecent noyse about ye hall stayres or within ye Quadrangle
of christchurch, as vsually they weare wont to doe vppon of present   5
imprisonment & other punishment accordinge to the discretion of ye
Vicechancellor and procters.

8   Item that they warne ther companies to provide verses to be disposed or sett
vppon St Maries or other places convenient & yat those verses be corected by
the Deanes or some other appoynted by the heades. | 10

9   Item yat a short oration be provided [be provided] att every severall Colledge
to ⟨..⟩tertayne his maiestie if his pleasure be to visitt ye same & verses sett vpp

10 Item yat vniversitie Colledg, Allsoules and Magdalen doe sett vpp verses att
his maiesties departure vppon such places, soe as they may be seene as he
passeth by   15

11 Item yat the fellowes and Schollers of the bodie of each Colledge be called
home and not permitted to goe abroad vntill his maiestie be gone from the
vniversitie and that they be at home by the first of August, and soe continewe
vntill his maiestie be gone.

Redditi Assessionum Collegiorum		ye Colledges rated after xxx s. in the hundred vnde super totum sequitur	
	Christchurch	2000 li.	xxx li.	
+	Magdalen Colledge	1200 li.	xviij li.
+	New Colledge	1000 li.	xv li.
+	Allsoules	500 li.	vij li. x s.
+	Merton Colledge	400 li.	vj li.
+	Corpus christi Colledge	400 li.	vj li.
+	St Iohns	400 li.	vj li.
+	Brasnose Colledge	300 li.	4 li. x s.
+	Queens Colledge	260 li.	iij li. xviij s.
+	Trinity Colledge	220 li.	iij li. vj s. 200 li. Received 3 li.
+	Exeter Colledge	200 li.	iij li.
+	Oriell Colledge	200 li.	iij li.
+	lincoln Colledge	150 li.	xlv s.

(line numbers 20, 25, 30, 35 in right margin)

Collation continued: 3m 7] 6 *CU*   4 hall stayres] hall, stayers *CU*   5 as
vsually ... doe] *CU omits*   5 vppon of] upon paine of *CU*   8m 8] 7 *CU*   11m 9]
8 *CU*   11 Colledge] howse *CU*   13m 10] 9 *CU*   16m 11] 10 *CU*   16 Colledge]
howse *CU*   18 they be] they maye be *CU*   18–19 and soe continewe ... gone]
CU omits   20 Collegiorum] Collegiorum per annum *T*   20 ye Colledges rated]
Rates payable by ye Colledges *T*   22 vide ... sequitur] *T omits*

5/ vppon of: *for* vppon payne of

+ bayley C*olledge*   100 li.   xxx s.
+ vniversitie Coll*edge*   100 li.   xxx s.

                                   Su*mma* Cxj li. ix s./

It is agreed y*at* d*r* Howson mr Thornton m*aste*r p*re*sident of St Iohns mr
boughton mr Sachewerill of new coll*edge* shall haue ye overesight of ye stage   5
att Christchurch.

...

ff 4v–5*

...   10

It*em* it is con*c*luded ye senior proctor to moderate in morall phylosoph because
mr sydney is sicke att london and the Iunior proctor to make an oration to the
kinge att his departure att ye bound*es* of ye vni*ver*sity liberties
It*em* y*at* m*aste*r principall of St Mary hall may ride on a footcloth as some
other head*es* of halls doe to meet ye kinge   15
It*em* y*at* the xl li. gathered out of the Colledges & halls as a stock to sett ye
poore a worke and hath layne now longe in d*r* Rives and d*r* Howsons hand*es*
shall be incontine*n*tly delivered to m*aste*r vicech*a*ncellor to be bestowed toward*es*
ye charge of ye king*es* cominge: but of this so*m*me & thirtie pound*es* more to
be delivered to m*aste*r vicech*a*ncell*er* [⟨...⟩] ⌜out⌝ of ye vni*ver*sitys chest, ther   20
is an A*rti*cle of Convocation.

...

It is agreed y*at* m*aste*r vicech*a*ncellor shall bestowe gloves vppon ye kinge,
Queene, Prince, and my L*ord* Tresurer vppon ye vni*ver*sitie purse accordinge
to his owne discretion   25
It is agreed and con*c*lueded y*at* all ye Colled⟨.⟩es shalbe once agayne rated
accordinge to the old rate of yer Lands vj d. xxx s. in every | hundred pound*es*
and ye Com*m*yners in Colledges & halls to be agayne rated accordinge as they
pay in the matriculation ∧⌜books⌝ by the head*es* of ye Colledges & halls
wh*e*are they are, and this money to be brought in by ye bursers of Colledges   30
& Manciples of halls as before hath been doon*n* by saterday next beenge ye
xxiiii^th of this *pre*sent August w*i*thout fayle

...

Collation continued: 3 Su*mma* ... ix s./] Su*mma* 7430. Su*mma* C.xj li. 9 s. *under
cols 2 and 3 in T*   4–6 It is ... Christchurch.] *preceded by* July. 29. *T*   5 mr
Sachewerill] mr Sacheuorill subwarden *T*   5 haue ye overesight of] ou*er*see ye
orderinge of *T*   11 It*em* it is] It is *T*   12 and the Iunior proctor to make] y*at* ye
Iunior *pro*ctor shall make *T*   13 liberties] *T omits*   14 Item] It is concluded *T*
14 may ride] shall ride *T*   14–15 as some ... kinge] at ye king*es* co*m*minge *T*
16–32 It*em* y*at* the xl li. ... w*i*thout fayle] *T omits*

11/ phylosoph: *for* phylosophy   20/ delivered: red *written over* d

Costumes and Props for the Plays for King James   OUA: WP/β/P/5/3
sheet [1], f [1]*   *(17–20 August)*

2 long white beard*es* and hayres the one in lockes for a sea god, the other for
old nestor to the girdle.   5
1 flexen or yellowe hayre to the shoulders for Apollo
Tuckes and Tresses of hayre to hange lose browne black flexen and all colors
for [1]20 nymphes.
1 long black beard and hayre vncurreled for à magitia*n*
fachions of Antique fashio*n* 20. or 30. or 40.   10
8 ⌜or 10.⌝ rich robes for King*es* of cloth of gold or embrodred velvett. *wi*thout
sleaves to hange onlye downe behind.
20 mantles of severall coulors
2. black robes ∧⌜one⌝ of velvett thother of saten or sylke.
2 or 3 black saten habit*es* to gyrd [to the] close vnder robes.   15
4. rich garment*es* lose for wome*n* of gold tyssue or the best can be gott
20 lose garment*es* of severall colors sylke and saten for nymphes.
1. hunting suite of greene.
[Apparell for sheppard*es* long r]
6 suites for morrice dancers all lyke *wi*th garters of bels. 2 for everye one.   20
1 lose Hermit*es* gowne of browne or black cloth. or otherwyse
1 habit for an old woma*n* lose & black.

sheet [1], ff [2–2v]*
                                                                                                          25
for 10 satyrs goates beard*es* and pols of short hayre of [⟨.⟩] goates color.
for 2 or 3 woode me*n* ∧⌜vel⌝ sylvanes. suites greene close to the bodye.
120 torches
120 Tapers, or waxe candles
60 pownd of cotton candles. dutch lyght*es*. a yeare old yf maie be.   30
[f]lether for 20 payre of buskins.
Plumes of feathers. of necessitye.
6 payre of longe stoking*es* of severall colors to sett vp *wi*th à short hose.
1 foote cloth.
    delyvered mathew ffox. att the signe of the ffox ⟨..⟩ th'old Bayley xx s.   35
            Receaved the some of xx s. of
                Bernard Banger ⟨..⟩
                part ⟨.⟩ payment.
                (signed) by me mathew ffox

11/ cloth: cl *corrected over other letters*   15/ gyrd: y *corrected over another letter*
11–12/ without … behind.: *added later, probably in*   30/ 60 pownd … be.: *this line followed by horizontal*
    same hand   *stroke across left quarter of page*

Receaved of Bernard Banger the 16th of August 1605 in
part of payment for the lending of furniture to furnishe
the playes att Oxford 36 s. I saye receaved   36 s.
          (signed) by me Thomas Kendall |
Receaved more in part of payment 24 s. the 17th of August   5
(signed) by me Thomas Kendall   24

sheet [2], ff [1–1v]

    x   2: Longe White Beardes and hayres, the one in lockes for à sea god, the other 10
for old nestor downe to the gyrdle.

    x   1. fflexen or yelowe hayre to the shoulders, for Apollo.

    x   20 Tuckes & Tresses of hayre to hange loose of browne, black, fflexen or anye
colors, for 20 nymphes.

    x   1. longe black beard and hayre vncurled for à magitian.   15

        20. ffachions of Antique fashions. 4. provyded.

    ⊕ 8 Rich Robes for Kinges of cloth of glold or embrodered velvett.

    ⊕ 20. mantles of severall coulors. 10 provyded.

        2. black robes the one of Saten or sylke th'other of velvett.

        2. or 3. blacke saten habit*es* w*i*th or w*i*thout sleeves, to gyrte close vnder 20
Robes. 1 provyded

    ⊕ 4. Rich garment*es* loose for women of gold, Tissue, or the best can be gotten.

12 provided   20 loose garment*es* of severall coulors of sylke and saten for nymphes.

    x   1. huntinge suite of greene.

    x   6. Suites for morrice dancers all lyke w*i*th garters of bels.   25

        1. loose Heremit*es* gowne of browne or black cloth.

        1. habite for an old woman loose and blacke

    x   10. goates beard*es* and pols of short hayre of goates color for Satyres.

        3 suites of greene close to the bodye for sylvanes. |

    x   one cassock of crimson velvett w*i*th twist of gold   30

    x   one cosseck of cloth of gold lyned w*i*th purple saten.

    x   on cosseck of cloth of Tyssue, [lyned] carnatio*n* ground lyned w*i*th
crimsen saten.

    x   one ⌐casseck⌐ of cloth of gold ground purple, embrodered round w*i*th à border
of purple velvet & sylver lyned part w*i*th saten and part w*i*th taffatye   35

    x   one cape cloake of cloth of sylver stripped w*i*th wthite velvett embrodered
w*i*th two gard*es* ∧⌐of white velvett⌐ round about of gold lyned w*i*th white
velvett.

17*l* glold: *for* gold
25*l* morrice: c *corrected from* s
36*l* wthite: *for* white; *corrected from* with; *the first* t *is superscript*

x   Item one cape cloake purple cloth of gold embrodered with one gard of
purple velvett with gold ro⟨.⟩nd about lyned with purple velvett

sheet [3], f [1]*

5

of mr Kyrkham.
x x   Syxe antique suites of cloth of gold
x x   Syxe payre of breeches 3 of ⟨...⟩ cloth of gold three of sylver.
x x   Syxe capps of cloth of gold with white feathers. 1 wanting
x x   One Robe for Apollo of cloth of Tissue blewe.   10
x x   Three mantles of cloth of gold Orenge coulor.
x x   Three mantles of cloth of sylver branched with purple and Orenge tawnye
x x   2 mantles of carnation and sylver branches
                        18th of August.
                        of mr Kendall the 20th of August 1605.   15
x x   one hunting suite of greene embrodered lyke starrs.
x x   8 greene Robes of taffatye waved with frenge
x [x] [1 orenge tawnye and] white Robe of Taffatye. habet.
x x   1 cloudye taffatye Robe of severall colors of [taffatye]
        [10 heades and six beardes for satyrs.]   20
x x   14. Antique vizardes.
x x   20 [⟨. .⟩] long hayres for nimphes
x x   2 mens hayres the one for Apollo th'other blacke.
x x   1 blewe hayre and beard for neptune.
x x   1 blacke smooth hayre and beard for à magitian.   25
x x   1 white hayre and beard for nestor
x x   1 Rounde white hayre.
x x   2 heremits beardes the on graye thother white. white deest
x x   3 beards one Red one blacke thother flexen.
x x   10. satyrs heades & berdes [th'one] and one suite for Pan.   30
x x   14. Antique vizardes.

sheet [3], f [2]

        Receaved more of mr Kyrkham the: 20th of August 1605.   35
x   Inprimis foure vpper garmentes of sea greene saten with sleeves
x   Item foure payre of [greene] wachet bases, all lymned.
x x   Item foure payre of sea greene bases all lymmed. 1 wanting.

1/ embrodered: *written around large ink blot*	18/ habet.: *added later, probably in same hand*
9, 38/ 1 wanting: *added later, probably in same hand*	21/ 14: *4 blotched or written over another number*
15/ of mr ... 1605.: *added later, probably in same hand*	22/ 20 [⟨. .⟩]: 20 *written at left of cancelled number*
28/ white deest: *added later, probably in same hand*

Receaved more of mr Kendall the 26th of August 1605.

x   14 vizardes

x   7 longe hayres

x   4 berdes

5

sheet [4], ff [1–1v]

Receaved of mr Kendall to the vse of the vniversitye of Oxford
the 20th of August 1605. these thinges followinge.

Inprimis one Hunting suite of greene embrodered with sylver stars.   10

Item eyght greene Robes of Taffatye waved with ffrenge.

Item one Orenge Tawney Robe of Taffata

Item one Robe of cloudye taffata of severall coulors

Item one suite of goates skinnes for Pan

Item 28 Antique vizardes   15

Item 20 longe hayres for nymphes.

Item 2 mens hayres the one for Apollo the other black

Item one blewe hayre and beard for neptune

Item one black smoth hayre & berd for à magitian.

Item one white hayre & beard for nestor   20

Item one Rounde white hayre.

Item fyve other beardes of severall coulors

Item Ten Satyres heades and berdes

Item 4 other beardes for Heremites |

25

Brought more by mr Kendall for the Englysh Pastorall vppon
mr Daniels lettres [⟨...⟩]

Inprimis 4 Sheppardes coates of Taffata of severall coulors.

Item 7 Hattes of Taffata

Item 7 Sheepe Hookes.   30

Item 3 velvett nightcaps with borders of hayre.

Item one yelowe Taffata Robe.

sheet [5], f [1]

35

x   1 Inprimis one Iupe and safegard of murrey saten imbrodered over with
gold & sylver

x   2 Item on round Kirtle of Ashecoulor Saten imbrodered all over with gold
& sylver

x   3 Item on round Kirtle of Tawnye satyn imbrodered all over with gold and   40
sylver lyke wheate eares.

41/ lyke: l *corrected over another letter*

x   4 Item on Kirtle of peace coulor saten embrodered with gold and sylver &
coulored sylke lyke greate branches

x   5 Item on round Kirtle of cloth of gold of Turkye worke

x   1 Item on lose gowne of carnation saten abowtye strip with sylver.   5

x   2 Item one lose gowne [with] of white sylver tabine with workes lyke dropps
& flower deluces.

x   3 Item on lose garment of white spanish Tafatye with workes lyke slyps of
gold sylver ∧⌈colored⌉ & sylke.

x   4. Item on lose gowne of carnation vncutt velvett florished all over with sylver.   10

x   1 Item one lose gowne of Ashcoulor saten florished ⌈all⌉ over with sylver
lyke flames

x   2 Item on lose gowne of Isabella coulor saten laced round with sylver lace
lyke cloudes   15

x   3. Item on lose gowne of sylver chambled with ⌈[great]⌉ [gold] ∧⌈great⌉
branches of gold

x   4. Item o⟨.⟩ lose gowne of murrey saten cutt and cuffed with a narrowe
border embrodered round about with gold & sylver

                                                                                         20

sheet [5], ff [2–2v]

x   Item on lose gowne of black saten embrodered all over with gold and sylver
lyke slyps of Roses

x   Item on lose gowne of Bee color velvett embrodered all over with Oaes of   25
gold and sylver with 27 buttons.

x   Item on lose gowne of sylver Tabine with workes of hayre color velvett faced
with orenge color and white spotted shag.

x   Item on lose gowne of pinck colored saten with à gold and sylver spang lace
round about   30

x   Item a longe cloake of Hayre colored saten lyned with ash color plushe.

x   Item one mantle with à Trayne of white Tiffanye stripe with sylver & workes
of colors lyke cloudes

x   Item on lose gowne of Ash color nett worke florished all over with gold and
sylver and somme small black bugles without sleeves.   35

x   Item on lose gowne of sylver Tynsell printed with flowers all over of ∧⌈sylke
of⌉ needle worke.

3/ 5 Item on round … worke: *this line followed by a*   10/ 4. Item on lose gowne … with sylver.: *this line*
    horizontal rule across the page   *followed by a shorter horizontal rule*
3/ of³: *corrected over other letters*   26/ sylver: *altered from* saten

x   Item on lose gowne of black ‸⌈nett⌉ worke florished all over with gold &
    sylver and workes lyke fethers without sleeves.

x   Item on lose gowne of black nett worke florished all over with sylver in workes
    lyke [brances] slypes

x   Item on lose gowne of color de roye, nett worke floreshed downe right with   5
    waves of gold.

x   Item on lose gowne of black nett worke florished all over with gold and
    sylver and sylver buttons. |

x   Item on dublett of pinck colored nett worke florished with gold and sylver
    and workes of sylke lyke byrdes and fyshes.   10

x   Item on dublett of white taffatye cutt all over embrodered with gold and
    sylver lyke roses & panses & sylver oaes.

x   Item one dublett of Orenge colored saten embrodered ‸⌈all⌉ over with sylver
    and drawen out with white tyffanye.

x   Item one dublett of white saten stripe with gold [lace] plate all over.   15
              This stuff to be folded vp with the threed not agaynst the threed.

Master of the Revels' Annual Engrossed Account   PRO: AO/1/2046/11
sheet [3]   *(1 November–31 October) (Purchases and provisions)*
...   20
Tape threede and woorkmanshipp of the garmentes sente to
Oxforde at the Kinges beinge there   XX s.
...

Letters of the Venetian Ambassador Nicolò Molen to the Doge   25
Archivio di Stato: Senato, dispacci ambasciatori Inghilterra, filza IV
f 72   *(10 August)*
...
Andai martedi otto di mattina li .2. del presente a tro⟨.⟩ar sua Maesta à Tibals
luogo del signor Sicil conforme all'ordine...   30

f 72v

...il Re ... entrò poi à discorrermi del suo uiaggio, et mi inuitò di andar' à
oxfort, che è, Città di studio, doue preparano quei Dottori, et scolari molte 35
disputationi, et comedie per dar trattenimento alla Maesta sua, la quale non
hauendo più ueduto quella Città, hà però piacere di esser riceuuta con molte
feste, et solennita, et con ogni termine di honore....

f 82   *(14 September)*   40
...
    Son stato questi giorni passati à oxfort inuitato dalla Maestà sua, come con

altre mie scrissi à Vostra Serenità di douer fare, entrò il Re con la Regina
Principe, et tutta la Corte con molta pompa nella Città il martedi .6. del
corrente, doue si è trattenuto tre giorni, li. quali si sono consumati tutti in
comedie la sera doppo cena, et il giorno in diuerse disputationi...

5

Letter of Robert Burton to his brother, William Burton
Staffordshire Record Office: D649/1/1
paper fragment*

...heare is no newes but praeparation for the kinges cominge, who will-be   10
heare on Teusday come forthe nighte. playes ∧⌈verses⌉ etc, that parte of ye
play which I made is very well liked, espetially those scenes of the Magus, and
I haue had greate thantkes for my paynes of .Dr. Kinge our newe Deane....
the xjᵗʰ. of August./ 1605

                      Ille ego qui quondam.   15
              (signed) Robertus Burton./

Letter of Sir Thomas Bodley to Sir John Scudamore
PRO: C/115/M20, no 7594
ff [1–1v]*   (20 September)   20

...since I came from Oxon., at ye kinges being there, I neither sawe London,
Courtier, nor Court, that I can tell you very litle of forrene occurrences. The
king was muche delited there, with ye sight of ye Librarie, and with ye number
and order of placing ye bookes: for which he gaue me ye choise of all his   25
manuscriptes and other bookes in his Libraries: which will I proue a princely
gifte, if I may be well dealt withall in ye deliuerie. There was nothing
perfourmed in ye Vniuersitie exercise; but ye king did grace it euery way,
both with his countenance and construction. Their tragedie and Comedies
were very clerkly penned, but not so well acted, and somwhat ouer tedious,   30
one onely excepted....

William Ayshcombe's Memoirs   Huntington Library: MS HM 30665
f 2v

   ...   35

Anno Domini   I returned to Oxforde & there liued about the space of a yeare in studyes.
.1605.   The king & queene came to Oxford & lay at Christchurch, where there were

12/ those: o corrected from e
13/ thantkes: for thankes
13/ Kinge: K altered from k

playes latin & english, the prince Henry at magdalen Colledge, where there
were likewise playes & orations. there was an Acte kepte in St maryes.

...

Narratives by Cambridge Men   5
Cambridge University Library: MS Additional 34
f 28*

The preparac*i*on at Oxford in August 1605. against the com*m*inge
thither of king Iames w*i*th the quene and Younge Prince, together w*i*th   10
the thing*es* then and there done, and the maner thereof./

...

ff 30–30v*

15
Against the king*es* Com*m*inge to Oxford, it was provided that all rayles, Post*es*,
Barrs of Windowes, Casement*es*, and Pumpes were newlie paynted and all
Armes were newlie tricked the like was done alsoe in all the street*es* of the
Citye, and all the severall gates of the Citye w*i*th dialls & such like, the street*es*
were verye fynely paved & cleane swept./   20
Iouis 22º. Augusti 1605./
This daye at 6. in the afternoone, I came to Oxford, (bringinge w*i*th mee
from the king*es* Attorney gen*er*all a booke ready for his Ma*i*est*i*es Signature
for two Parsonages given to the Vniuersitie for the benefite and better
mayntenau*n*ce of our two Readers in divinitye) there I fownd the Earles of   25
Wor*c*ester Suffo*lk*, and Northampton. w*i*th the Lo*rd* Carye who had bene
to viewe St. Maryes and Christchurch, the lodging*es* there for his Ma*i*estie
and the Quene, and the Princes lodginge in Magdalen Colledge.
They (but especiallie Suffo*lk*) vtterlie disliked the stage att Christchurch, and
above all, the place appointed for the Chayre of estate because yt was no higher. 30
and the K*i*nge soe placed that the Audit*or*y could see but his Cheeke onlie.
this dislike of the Earle of Suffo*lk* much troubled the Vicechancelor, and all the
workmen, yet they stood in defence of the thinge done, and maynteyned that
by the art p*er*spective the Kinge should behould all better then if he sat higher/
Their Chauncelor also after his com*m*inge, tooke part w*i*th the vniuersitie, and   35
on the Sondaye morninge the matter was debated in the Councell chamber,
in the end the place was removed, and sett in the midst of the hall, but too
farr from the stage. (vizt.) xxviij. foote, soe that there were manye longe speeches
delivered, which neyther the Kinge nor anye neere him could well heare or
vnderstand./   40

24/ the Vniuersitie: *ie, Cambridge*

The stage was built close to the vpper end of the Hall, as it seemed at the
first sight, but indeed it was but a false | wall fayre painted and adorned with
statelie pillers which pillers would turne about, by reason whereof with the
helpe of other painted clothes, their stage did varrie three tymes in the
Actinge of one Tragedye. Behind the foresaid false wall there was reserved   5
5. or 6. paces of the vpper end of the Hall which served them to good vses
for their howses, and receipt of their Actors and souldiors &c./
...

ff 32–4*   10
...

Martis 27. Augusti. 1605./

In the fore noone all things were performed as on the daye before, at one of the
clock in the afternoone the Vicechauncelor & doctors went to their Chauncelor
at New Colledge, and from thence presently to meete the Kinge in maner   15
followinge (viz.) ffirst 3. esquire Beadles rode on foote clothes in fayre gownes
with gold Cheines in velvett capps carrienge their staves as att other tymes,
but bare headed (as did the serieant of the Mace) who rode next behind them
ymediatelie before their Chauncelor, he rode talkinge with the vicechauncelor
the Vicechauncelor beringe back about half the length of his horse. After   20
them 6. or 8. doctors alsoe in Scarlett two by two vpon their foote clothes,
then the two Proctors in their Civill Hoodes and after them 10. or 12. in
black gownes and Civill hoodes vpon their footecloathes ridinge two by two.
Theis were some of them heades of Halles and some of them Auncient
Bachelors in divinity all theis vniuersitye men did weare square Capps. They   25
stayed first at a place called Aristotles Well being about a mile from the citye
but for that it was narrowe place much anoyed with dust the lord Chamberleyn
sent them word to come a litle forward into a fayre meadowe where they all
savinge the Serieant of the mace, alighted from their | horses and stayed a
litle beside the high waye, expectinge the kinge.   30
In the meane tyme the Maior of the Citye, 12. Aldermen in Scarlett, and
some six score Commoners in black Coates guarded with velvett and layd on
with billament lace passed forward of them some fortie score whereat the
vicechauncelor & doctors were much discontented and made knowne their
greif to their Chauncelor, who presentlye called his Serieant at Armes and   35
willed him to tell Master Maior and his bretheren that they had forgott
themelves to proceed beyond their bowndes, and that he required them vpon
their perill to come back agayne behind him and the vniversitye and not
to dare to speake to the kinge till they had first done. The Mayor sent two
of his Aldermen who alighted from their horses and came on foote to the   40

31/ the Maior: *Thomas Cossam*   31/ 12. Aldermen: *ie, the council of Thirteen*

Chauncelor craving pardon & excusinge the matter. ffirst for that they were
sent for, by the Lord Chamberleyn to come forward out of the dust and
secondlye for that they did not see his honor as they passed by/
To whome the said Chauncelor answered I thinke wee should vnderstand the
Lord Chamberlens mind as well as you, he sent vs word to staye here, and you   5
were not best presume to goe before vs. Soe the Mayor and his companye
retourned back behind the Chauncelor about some twentye score./
Imediatlye after the Kinge came rydinge on horseback with his queene one
his left hand, and the | Prince before them, the Duke of Lynox carrienge the
Sword. The Nobilitye attendinge the kinge was verye great and richlye attired   10
in every respect, the kinge came somewhat neare them, and then stayed his
horse, the Chauncelor went towardes his maiestie 5. or 6. paces, and then
kneled downe, but what he sayd I could not heare, the kinge gave him his
hands and pulled him vpp, he [vttered] retired to the Vicechauncelor by whome
three beadles stood, and the kinge comminge a litle nearer, the vicechauncelor   15
began his speech which he delivered vpon his knee with good grace, and
cleare voyce, in which speech hee highlye commended their vniuersitie, and
preffered yt before all others in the world racione celi et soli antiquitatis
pulchritudinis edeficiorum multititudinis Collegiorum Studentium et
doctorum virorum and last of all that it pleased his highnes to vouchsafe   20
first of all to come & see the same, and soe ended within lesse then a
quarter of an hower, that done the Beadles delivered vpp their Staves to
their Chauncelor, who delivered them to the kinge kneelinge. The kinge
puttinge them back with his hand smylinge, bad him take them agayne./
After that they presented to his Maiestie a Greeke testament in folio washed   25
and Ruled and bownd vpp in darke murrey velvett without eyther Claspe or
stringe and two payre of Oxford gloves with deepe fringe of gold, the turne
overs beinge wrought with Pearle they cost as I [vnderstand] ‸⌈was informed⌉
vj li. a payre; They also gave vnto the queene two paire of gloves much like
the former, and a paire vnto the Prince./ | 30
Soe they went a litle forward, the beadles bearing thcir staves before the kinge
with the Armes vpward, and next them went 3. Serieants at Armes, then the
Swordbearer who was that daye (as I sayd) the duke of Lenox, then the Prince,
king, and queene, and all the Nobilitye. Soe they came to Master Mayor and
his brethren, the Towne Clerke (in the absence of the Recorder) made a long   35
speech in englishe extollinge highlye the late queene and her governement the
great feare at her death, the exceeding ioye and infallible hope that succeeded
vpon [t] it./
After this the Mayor surrendred his Mace to the kinge, who putt yt vpon

18–20/ racione … virorum: 'by reason of the climate and land, its antiquity, the beauty of the buildings, the
    multitude of colleges, students, and learned men'

him agayne, and then the Mayor gave the kinge after their Oration done, a
fayre standinge Cupp havinge 50 li. of gold in yt both worth 100 li.; alsoe to
the queene they presented another, worth 40 li. and to the Prince another
standinge Cupp guilt & covered worth 30 li./
So then they marched on slowlie towards the citye next before the Sword   5
bearer rode the 3. Serieants, then the Kinge att Armes on his Coate Armour,
and on his right hand the vicechauncelor, and on his [right] ^⌈left⌉ hand the
Mayor of the Citye carrienge their Mace on his shoulder which was verye neare
as fayre as the kings Maces, next before them rode the doctors in Scarlett and
square Capps, and before them the Proctors, and before them, some 6. heades   10
of Halls, no doctors, and 6. or 8. more auncient Bachelors in divinitye, all in
black, and next them the 3 Esquier | Beadles then the Aldermen And so the
Burgers the best next the kinge and the meanest formost. The Chauncelor went
next before the kinge with the Lord Chamberlaine not as Chauncelor but as
Treasurer, I marveyled why the Beadles rode so farr from the Vicechauncelor,   15
and further from the King, the Proctors and some others answered, they went
before the vniuersitie, and secondlye that their Chauncelor was there in person./
This being done he rode on vntill he came to St. Iohns Colledge, where,
comminge against the gate, three youghes in habitt and attire like Nimphes
confronted him, representing England, Scotland and Ireland, and talking   20
Dialogue wise eche to other of their state, at last concluded, yelding vpp
themselves to his gracious governement.
The Scollers stood all on one side of the street, and the Strangers of all sortes
on the other, the Scollers stood first, then the Bachelors, and last the masters
of Artes./ (blank) At Carfax the greeke reader standinge in one of the answerers 25
seates with a deske before him made an Oration in greeke with good accion
and elocucion and as (doctor Hamond sayd) in good familiar greeke, the
kinge heard him willingly and queene much more because she said she never
heard greeke.
ffrom thence to Christchurch, where, at the Hall staires foote, the vniversitie 30
Orator made a good oration onlie preferringe their vniuersitye because the kinge
came thether first and passed over all other matters without comparison./
…

f 35*   (27 August)   35

The Comedie began between 9. and 10., and ended at one, the name of
yt was Alba, whereof I never saw reason, it was a pastorall much like one
which I have seene in Kinges Colledg in Cambridge, but acted farr worse,
in the actinge thereof they brought in 5. or 6. men almost naked which   40

19/ youghes: for youthes   27/ as (doctor … sayd): for (as doctor … sayd)

were much disliked by the Queene and Ladyes, and alsoe manye rusticall
songes and daunces, which made it seeme verye tedious in soe much that
if the Chauncelors of both the Vniuersityes had not intreated his Maiestie
earnestlye, he would have bene gone before half the Comedie had bene
ended./ 5

…

f 37* *(28 August)*

…The same daye after supper about 9. of the Clock they began to act the 10
Tragedye of Aiax flagellifer, wherein their stage varried 3. times, they had all
goodlie anticke apparrell, but for all that yt was not acted soe well by many
degrees as I have seene yt in Cambridge, the kinge was verye weary before
he came thither, but much more wearied by that, and spake manye wordes
of dislike/ 15

…

f 39v* *(29 August)*

That night after supper about 9. began their Comedie called Virtumnus verye 20
well and learnedly penned by Doctor Guynn, it was acted much better then
eyther of the other, and cheifly by St. Iohns men, yet the kinge was soe
overwearied at St Maryes that after a while he distasted it, and fell a sleepe,
when he awaked, he would have bene gone, sayinge I marvell what they
thinke mee to be, with such other like speeches shewinge his dislike thereof, 25
yet he did tarrye till they had ended yt, which was after one of the clock.
The queene was not there that night.

Veneris 30. Augusti 1605.

There was an english playe acted in the same place before the queene and
yonge Prince with all the Ladyes and gallantes attendinge the Court, It was 30
penned by Mr. daniell and drawne out of fydus pastor which was sometimes
acted by kinges Colledge men in Cambridg, I was not there present, but
by report it was well acted and greatlye applawded./ It was named Arcadia
reformed….

35

f 41* *(30 August)*
…

After 9. the kinge came to veiwe their librarye vpon whom attended a great
part of the nobillitye, amongst whome were the Lord Chamberlayne, and our
Chauncelor who were, by Sir Henry Savill entreated to staye their Coach and 40
come into the Convocacion, which they willingly did….

…

ff 42v–3v*

...

In the tyme of this Convocacion (vizt) about 9., the kinge came to the
Librarye, and from thence returned by brasen nose Colledge where he heard
an oration came out of his Coach and walked about the square, veiwed   5
their Colledg and comended their gardein within the square, which at that
tyme was finely kept, from thence he went by Alsowles Colledge where he
heard an oration, and from thence to Magdalen Colledge, and there heard
an oration, and from thence returned to Christchurch to dynner, where in
tyme of dinner doctor Lillye of Baylioll Colledge made vnto him a learned   10
oration but too too longe, After the kinge had dyned, there was postinge to
horse, at the Stayres foote where the kinge entred into the Court the Iunior
proctor made a short oracion | and delivered yt with good audacitye, that
done, their Chauncelor havinge the graunt of the perpetuitye to the vniuersitye
for the vse of the kinges Reader delivered yt to his Maiestie in a longe box,   15
who tooke yt in his hand and gave yt to the vicechauncelor, but said litle
or nothinge that I could learne, only hee and the queene gave their handes
to be kissed of the vicechauncelor and the rest of the doctors, and bad them
farewell and trouble themselves no further, who otherwise had their horses
and footeclothes ready to have carried him out of their liberty. Then the   20
Kinge queene and prince went all into one Coach, and passed through the
Towne by Magdalene Colledge not stayinge anye where./
The Mayor and 12 in scarlett with their Serieant Towne Clerk and 4. or 5. in
black (who I think were baylies, or such like officers) rode before his Maiestie
through the towne to the further end of the bridge, and there stayed, the   25
Mayor carried the Mace as he did at his Maiesties enteringe./
There were verses sett vpon the walls of such Colledges as were on his waye
(vizt.) Alsoules, Copus Christi, & Magdalens, which the kinge seemed not
to see, or not | to regard neyther did a man stepp out of the trayne to veiwe
or read anye of them, soe they were by the boyes rudelie pulled downe.   30
The scollers stood alonge by their Colledges, some orderlye in the hoodes
and habittes fitt for their degrees, some more confusedly and disorderlye
without any such respect./

...

35

f 44*   *(Other things observed)*

...

All men were vncovered in St. Maryes while the Kinge was in presence, both
at the disputacions, and att the Commodyes in Christchurche/

...   40

23/ 12 in scarlett: *ie, the council of Thirteen*   28/ Copus: *for* Corpus

ff 44v-5v*

…

It was reported crediblye and expected that the playes should be acted againe
the weeke followinge to give satisfaction to the vniuersitie, which before could
not see them acted./ But on the Saterdaye at night, I heard of a certain that the   5
Apparrell was packed vpp to be sent awaye, and there was an end./
ffor the better contrivinge and finishinge of their stages, seates, and scaffoldes
in St. Maries and Christchurch, they intertayned two of his Maiesties Master
Carpenters, and they had the advise of the Comptroler of his workes.
They also hired one Mr. Iones a great travellor who vndertooke to further them   10
much and furnish them with rare devises, but performed very litle to that
which was expected, he had for his paynes as I heard yt constantly reported
50 li./
The money to defray all theis charges was levyed vpon the heades of the
studentes accordinge to everye mans place and abilitye, I as for example, in   15
a litle poore hall the head was assessed to pay xx s.; and the pencioners of
the same 4 li., and yet they made accoumpt that they should have a second
assessment/

…

The Lord Treasurer their Chauncelor stayed till mondaye next after the kinges 20
departure. He sent to the disputers and Actors 20 li. in money and 5. brace
of Buckes, soe he sent to every Colledge and Hall veneson and money, after
this proportion (vizt.) to I Brasen-nose Colledge 5. Bucks and 10. Angells to
St Edmondes hall 4. Redd deere Pies, and 4. Angelles./

…   25

Nixon, Oxfords Triumph (1605) STC: 18589
sigs A4-B2v*

…

    For vpon Tuesday the 27. of August laste, his Maiestie comming from   30
VVoodstocke to Oxford, the Earle of Dorset Lord Chauncelor, accompanied
with the Vice-Chauncelor, the Doctors, Proctors & certaine Senior Masters,
rode foorth vpon their foote-cloath Horses, verie richlye furnished to meete
the King, whome they expected about Aristotles Well, where hauing intention
that the Vice-Chauncelor should first salute his Majestie with a speech, Maister 35
Maior with his company passed by without regard to them, purpo-Ising
indeed that his Orator should first speak, which when the Lord Chauncelor
perceiued, he presently sent to the Maior, and charged him to surcease his
purpose till the Vice-Chauncelor had finished his Oration to the King: with
which message the Maior was litle pleased, yet his mends were small, for hee 40
retired with speede, and had no better excuse for himselfe, then to say hee
did not see them, notwithstanding they were hard by him, and all in their
Scarlet Gownes.

After this, his Maiestie drawing neere, the Lord Treasorer and the Vice-chauncelor repayred vnto him, who stayed his course, and rayned his Horsse of State whereon he rode: the Vice-chaunccllor presenting him-selfe with his speech vnto his Highnes, surrendring vp the Keyes of the Vniuersitye, and the Beadles deposing their Staues, and laying them downe at his Majesties feet: 5
Further deliuering vnto him the New Testament in Greeke, very fairely bound, and richly guilded: vnto the Queene a Purse, & to the young Prince a paire of gloues. With which Oration at his | first meeting, and the seuerall guiftes presented vnto them, the King, Queene and Prince, were so well pleased and delighted, that the whole Vniuersitie receiued much content & comfort.   10

After the Lord Chauncelors, and the Vniuersites salutation, Maister Maior addressed himselfe towards the King: and by the mouth of the Townes Orator, he & his bretheren pronounced an English speech to his Majestie, and presented three seuerall Cuppes: the one to the King, another to the Queene and another to the Prince. Maister Maior rendring vp his Mace, striued with   15
himselfe to doe all duetifull obeysance that might be accepted, which the King discouering, verie graciously encouraged, and gaue him great and heartye thankes for his good will and louing duetie towards him.

This finished, his Majestie passed along till hee came before Saint Iohns Colledge, where three little Boyes comming foorth of a Castle, made all of   20
Iuie, drest like three Nimphes, (the conceipt wherof the King did very much | applaude) and deliuered three Orations: first in Latine to the King, then in english to the Queene and young Prince; which beeing ended, his Majestie proceeded towards the Eastgate of the Citie, where the Townes-men againe deliuered vnto him another speech in english.   25

That speech ended, the King with all his traine of Noble men and others, entred the Cittie, where in the after noone about one of the clocke, by the ringing of a Bell at Saint Maries Church, the Schollers in their formalities according to their seuerall degrees, were gathered together and repaired towards Christe-Church gates, where they began to be placed and rancked. They stood   30
all of one side of the streete without any intermixion eyther of strangers, Townes-men, or any others that were not Schollers of the Vniuersitie, and were of the left hand of the King as he passed by. Next to the gates of Christ Church (where his Majestie was receiued) stood the Doctors of Diuinity in their Scarlet: next them the Doctors of Phisick, & then the Doctors of | Lawe: 35
next them the Batchelors of Diuinitie, and the Senior Maisters of Arte in their silke hoodes: then the Batchelors of Law, and the Regent Masters in their Miniuer Hoods, and then the Batchelors of Arte. All which graduates, reached from Christes Church to aboue Carefax. Next to those Graduates, stood the vnder Graduates, whoe rancke thus placed in this seemely decorum, reached   40
to St. Giles.

31/ intermixion: *for* intermixtion

His Maiestie still passing along into the Cittie by the Easte gate of it, where
(as is before remembred) the Townes-men deliuered a speech and the Schollers
gaue him a viuat.

From the Easte gate, his Majestie marched along till he came to Carefax,
where Doctor Perin was placed in a Pue, and saluted him with a Greeke   5
Oration, which while hee was pronouncing, the Queene asked the King once
or twise what hee said? and he answered her, that he spake verie well and
learnedly.

From Carefax, the King with the Queene on his left hand, & the young
Prince next before them (all on their seueral great horses) marched downe the   10
streete, till they came to Christ-|Church, where at the gates, the Vniuersityes
Orator made an Oration vnto to him.

…

The Prince hauing accompanied the Kings Majestie vnto the Chamber
of Presence, departed: and betaking himselfe to his Coach, went straight to   15
Magdalen Colledge, where the President standing in the Gates, receiued him
with all joyfull reuerence and duety…

…

sig B3*   *(27 August)*   20

…

After Supper his Majestie, the Queene, and Prince, with the Noblemen,
had a Comedie played before them in Latine in Christ-Church Hall, which
continued the space of three houres and more.

                                                                             25

sig C1v*   *(28 August)*

…

Vpon Wednesday at night after supper, there was a Tragedie set out by
Magdalen Colledge men, acted before his Majestie in Christ-Church Hall,
which was verie long, for it continued from nine till one of the clocke, The   30
subiect whereof was of Aiax and Vlisses, But the deuice was so costly and
curious in setting the same foorth, that it was not thought teadious, but the
King shewed himselfe verie well pleased, and content with it.

sigs E1v–2*   *(29–30 August)*   35

…

Where vppon Thursdaie at nighte after supper there was a Comedie plaied
by saint Iohns men before his Maiestie. The subiect whereof was the foure
Complexions. This comedie was so richlie set foorth and beautified, with
such curious and quaint conceipts and deuices, as that it made his Maiestie   40
pronounce himselfe as muche delighted therewith, as with anie sight (of the

37/ Where: *Christ Church*

like nature) at anie time heretofore presented vnto him.

The next morrowe, beeing Fridaie, the thirtieth daie of August, was the daie
of his | Maiesties departure from Oxforde, and as soone as the Sunne had
vailed the curtaine of the night, he got vp, carrieng the opinion of Cæsar.

Lucani libro 2. in fine.   5

Nil actum credens, cum quid superesset agendum.
That he had done nothing, when any thinge was left vndone: and mounted
himself with diuers of his Nobles to see the Vniuersities Librarie, which is in
length all ouer the Diuinty Schoole....

...   10

sigs E3–3v*

Whilst his Maiestie was thus busied in taking of this suruey of the librarie;
the queen and Prince were in the meane space, as much delighted with an   15
English Comedie, presented and plaide before them in Christ-church hall,
by certaine Schollers: which was as richlie set forth and perfourmed, as with
as great | applause, and commendation as any of the rest that had beene
before since the Kinges comming to Oxford.

...   20

sigs E4v–F*

Thus when his Maiestie had viewed the Chappell, he was forthwith
conducted into the Cloysters, and from thence into the squadrant Court   25
within the Cloysters, where he staied a good space, taking a thorow view of
all such seuerall Pictures as were there set vp round about, and now against
this entertain were newly trimmed and painted, which caused his Maiestie
to demande the meaning of them, wherein the President and others fully
resolued him.   30

From thence he returned backe to Christ church againe vnto the Queene
and younge Prince, and in the waie (as is credibly reported) he woulde needes
be guided to Brazen Nose Colledge gate, that he might be made an eie-
witness to that, of which he hadde so often heard, and that whereof the
Colledge carrieth the name.   35

And both as he passed forth of Magdalen Colledge gates, and so vpwardes
all along, the Schollers cried Viuat, uiuat, &c. and the others of the multitude,
with a loude voice, God saue king Iames, &c. |

Much about twelue of the clocke the same day he tooke his leave, and left
the Vniuersite, addressing his course towardes Windsore Castle....   40

5/ Lucani ... fine: *Lucan, Bellum Civile 2.657*   24/ the Chappell: *of Magdalen College*

Wake, Rex Platonicus (1607)   *STC*: 24939
pp 18–19*   *(27 August)*

...

   Fabulæ ansam dedit antiqua de Regia prosapia historiola apud Scoto-
Britannos celebrata, quæ narrat tres olim Sibyllas occurrisse duobus Scotiæ   5
proceribus Macbetho & Banchoni, & illum prædixisse Rege*m* futurum, sed
Regem nullum geniturum, hunc Regem non futurum, sed Reges geniturum
multos. Vaticinij veritatem rerum eventus comprobavit: Banchonis enim è
stirpe Potentissimus Iacobus oriundus. Tres adolescentes concinno Sibyllarum
habitu induti, è Colle|gio prodeuntes, & carmina lepida alternatim canentes,   10
Regi se tres esse illas Sibyllas profitentur, quæ Banchoni olim sobolis imperia
prædixerant, jamq*ue* iterum comparere, vt eâdem vaticinij veritate prædicerent
Iacobo, se iam, & diu regem futurum Britanniæ felicissimum & multorum
Regum parentem, vt ex Banchonis stirpe nunquam sit hæres Britannico
diademati defuturus. Deinde tribus Principibus suaves felicitatu*m* triplicitates   15
triplicatis carminum vicibus succinentes, veniamq*ue* precantes, quòd alumni
ædium Divi Iohannis (qui præcursor Christi) alum*n*os Ædis Christi (quo tu*m*
Rex tendebat) præcursoriâ hâc salutatione antevertissent, Principes ingeniosâ
fictiunculâ delectatos dimittunt; quos inde vniversa astantium multitudo,
felici prædictionum successui suffragans, votis precibusq*ue* ad portam vsq*ue*   20
civitatis Borealem prosequitur.

...

pp 45–8*

...   25

i Huius pars gra*n*dis (cum hîc *Domina* Elizabetha an*n*o 1566. spectaculo
interesset) decidit ex infinitæ multitudinis confluxu & pondere. Cuius ruinâ
permulti partim enecti, partim me*m*bris miserandè contusi, quum toto iam
Regiæ commorationis tempore (deo sic propitio) nemo aut hîc aut vllibi, (quod
in tanta frequentia perrarum est) vel levissimam læsiunculam pateretur. †   30
   Sed vt instituto pergam: dum ista in Collegio Magdalensi peraguntur, alius
Academicos labor avocat, theatrico apparatui (quo Principes à cœna excepturi |
erant) intentos. Locus Scenæ præstitutus erat Aula Ædichristiana, quia &
spatiosissima, & cœnaculis Augustalibus vicina. Habent enim vtraq*ue*i
Propylæum commune, quo duplici latissimorum graduum ordine ascenditur,   35
quod propter Turris, arcuumq*ue* sublimem amplitudinem, column*æ* vnic*æ*

Collation with *STC*: 24939.5 *(B)* pp 27–8, 71–5, 121–3, 171–2, 216–19; *STC*:
24940 *(C)* pp 27–8, 71–5, 121–3, 171–2, 216–19; *STC*: 24941 *(D)* pp 29–30,
75–9, 128–9, 180–1, 227–31; *STC*: 24942 *(E)* pp 29–30, 75–9, 128–9, 180–1,
227–31; *STC*: 24942.5 *(F)* pp 29–30, 75–9, 128–9, 180–1, 227–31:   4 historiola]
hostoriola *C*   16 carminum] terminum *EF*   31 in] *EF omit*

incumbentium, peritissimos Architectonices attonitos tenet. Interiora Aul*e*
dubiu*m* ampliora sint loci spatio, an Fundatoris sumptu, an artificum solertiâ.
Fenestræ octodecim opere picturato amplæ, & sublimes; Aulæ totius ambitus
supernè,

k Manil*ij* libr*o* I.   *k*Seu nitet ingenti stellarum balteus orbe,   5
quasi continuis fasciis desculptoru*m* artis Heraldicæ ancylium præfulgidus:
laquearium pensilia triplicatis intervallis deaurata, omniumq́*ue* emblematum
varietate rutilantia: Ista (si alia hîc spectacula non essent) satis essent spectaculo.
Partem Aulæ superiorem occupauit scena, cuius Proscenium molliter decliue
(quod actoru*m* egressui, quasi è monte descendentium, multum attulit   10
dignitatis) in planitiem desinebat. Peripetasmata Scenicaq́*ue* habitacula,
machinis ita artificiosè ad omnium locorum rerumq́*ue* varietatem apparata, vt
non modò pro singulorum indies spectaculorum, sed etiam pro Scenarum vnâ
eâdemq́*ue* fabulâ diversitate, subitò (ad stuporem omnium) compareret nova
totius theatralis fabricæ facies. Machinæ, quibus ista omnia latè obtegebantur, 15
tam artifici manu & suspensæ erant & depict*æ* motantibus quasi nubibus,
vt eas, Sole Britannico statim ingressuro, aufugientes putares, ipsumq́*ue* cœlum
videre crederes, nisi Cynthiam & sydera mox inferiùs fulgentia contuerere. Ab
infimis Aulæ tabullatis vsq*ue* ad summa laquearium fastigia cunei parietibus
ingenti circuitu affiguntur; mediâ caueâ thronus Augustalis cancellis cinctus 20
Principibus erigitur, que*m* vtrinq*ue* optimatum stationes communiunt:
reliquu*m* inter thronum & theatrum interstitium Heroinarum Gynæcæum
est paulò depressius. Rege Reginâq́*ue* ingressis, vnà cum Henrico Principe (qui
illuc à cœna essedo advectus est) incredibiliq́*ue* omnium ordinum multitudine
cuneos caveamq́*ue* occupante (adeò vt ipsi spectatores essent spectaculo) ab 25
eiusdem Collegij alumnis (qui & cothurno tragico & socco comico principes

Collation continued: 1 tenet] *BCDEF add* Multiplices aute*m* illius Turris
concamerationes, Wols*æ*us totidem scholas esse voluit, linguarum triumq*ue*
facultatum, septèmq*ue* etiam Artium Liberalium, & Philosophiæ professoribus. Nec
enim hîc tam Collegium, quam alteram ferè Academiam in Academiâ co*n*stitutere
pr*æ*stituerat; eumq*ue* in finem lectissimum totius Vniversitatis florem delibatum huc
transtulit; non nullos etia*m* Cantabrigiâ, vbi literis non infeliciter operam dederant;
sed quum propter fortunarum inopiam, studiis persequendis pares non erant,
Cardinalis supplicibus eorum precibus, & amicorum ṣolicitationibus permotus hic
inter suos sedem subsidiumq*ue* munificè concessit. Quin Aulam ingredimur? Turba
adstantium impedit; perrumpimus, sudamus, intus sumus. *with CDEF reading*
magnificè *for* munificè *B*   16 motantibus] morantibus *DEF*   17 Sole] *preceded by*
an a *in BCDEF, which add marginal note* Iacobo Rege *in reference to* Sole Britannico
18 Cynthiam] *preceded by a* b *in BCDEF, which add marginal note* Reginam Annam
cum Heroinis *in reference to* Cynthiam & sydera   21 communiunt] communium
DEF   23 Rege] Regi *BCD*

5m/ Manil*ij* libro I: *cp, Manilius,* Astronomica *1.679*

semper habebantur) Vertumnùs, Comœdia faceta ad Principes exhilarandos
exhibetur. In qua tres rivales Pomonæ amorem ambiunt, Chærilus poeta vanus,
Sylvanus bene potus, & Vertumnus: hic multiformi illam fuco aucupatur:
primò piscatorem, deinde Aulicum, tertiò militem induens, vt eam in amorem
pelliciat: sed hisce dolis voti minimè compos, postremò virum exuit, & mulier   5
mulierem aggreditur, illâ*que* sub specie mirabiles amores sui apud Pomonam
concitat; quo facto, seipsum prodit, & Vertumnus ipse ipsâ potitur Pomonâ.
Cui fabulæ quum deesset nihil ingenuaru*m* deliciarum quibus aut aures aut
oculi deliniri cuperent (quod eruditi ex ipso argumento coniectabunt, et si è
prælo, quod speratur, emerserit, facilè intelligent) tum nihil Academicis, &   10
Aulicis omnibus iucundius esse potuit, quàm quod in principum pectora
(vnde, propitio Deo, omnia nostra gaudia promanant) lætitiæ rivulos vicissim
refluere tam liquidis testimonijs animadverterent. Qui enim ingentes Regum
molestias non intelligunt, ijs ingenia videntur valde stupida; sed | qui tantis
molestijs sua solatia, & quasi avocamenta necessaria esse non intelligunt, eos   15
nihil intelligere quivis intelligat. Illud autem, etsi fortuitum, non tamen
prætereundum, quòd cum columbæ aliquot (fabula sic exigente) è transenna
emitterentur,
     (Aspicis vt veniant ad candida tecta columbæ.)
Earum vna Reginam (pectus verè candidum, & columbinum) petijt, ejus*que*   20
cathedræ insedit, vt multos columbam aut arte fictam (vti illam Architæ) aut
arte doctam,[k] vt illam Mahometis asseuerantes audierim. Quid multis? omnia
placebant omnibus, nisi qui aut non intelligerent, aut somnium potiùs quàm
sales appeterent. Rex autem in serijs semper, iam etiam ludis vigil, postquam
luculento manuum applausu, vocisq*ue* testificatione omnia comprobásset,   25
quem deinde Regina, Princepsq*ue* cæteriq*ue* subsequuntur, discedunt omnes
vt oculos (media enim nox erat) in crastinæ diei spectacula refocillarent.

pp 78–9   *(28 August)*
...   30
    Sed breuis est intermissio voluptatis, quam statim à Cænâ renovant
periucunda Tragœdiæ spectacula, & quasi seri*ae* antegress*ae* disputationis
condimentum. Fabulæ (quam delecti ex vniuersa Academia adolescentes
egerunt) nomen AIAX FLAGALLIFAR, titulo ex Sophocle mutuato, sed re, tam
diversa, quàm idiomate. Cujus argumenti factus est delectus, non tantùm   35
quòd splendidâ, pomposáq*ue* representationum varietate, tantis spectatoribus

k Quam
Mahometes ex
aure sua grana
tritici rostro
excipere
edoctam, postea
auriculæ
frequentiùs
rostrum
inijcientem,
fingebat
spiritum fuisse
sanctu*m*, qui ei
esset à Deo
nu*n*cius,
omniaq*ue* ei
insusurraret.

Collation continued: 1 Vertumnus] *marked with an asterisk in D, which adds*
marginal note Huius Comædiæ author Dr Gwin Iohannensis *in reference to* Vertumnus
8 deesset] deesse *DEF*   19 columbæ.] columbæ? *BC;* columbæ; *DEF*   23 somnium]
somnum *BCDEF*   26 omnes] omne *B*   32 periucunda] per jucunda *EF*

19/ (Aspicis ... columbæ.): *Ovid,* Tristia *1.9.7*

delectationem affluente*m* ministraret; sed quòd materia etiam videretur Aulicis, Academicis*que* auribus, animis*que* perquàm accomodata. Celebris enim representatur illa de Achillis defuncti armis contentio, quæ sibi pro militaris virtutis præmio vendicauit Aiax sed obtinuit Vlysses, prudentiæ meritò, & literatæ facundi*a*e. Victus miles theatrum, circum*que* omnem furioso complet   5
boatu; Furias euocat; ᴅeos homines*que* execratur; nihil pr*a*eter minas, & vindictam spirat. Sed et vanæ iræ, sine viribus, & vires sine prudentia; in*que* domini perniciem cedit ferocia, quam non literarum, & doctrinæ cultura temperat. Post va|ria furibundi hominis facinora, ovium grege, ducum Græcorum vice contrucidato, ingenti ariete pro Vlysse immaniter flagellato,   10
menti tandem restitutus sibi mortem consciscit, dementior quàm quum demens. Domini mortem miserrimè luget Tecmessa, sed exultat Vmbra Hectoris, qu*a*e Aiaci insensissima, Chori pr*a*ebebat vice*m*. Quæ omnia, quàm mirificâ, & aures, & oculos varietate pascerent, facilè non est dicere; eo*que* magis, quòd pro materiæ varietate, tota Scenæ fabrica, & artificiosus   15
peripetasmatum apparatus, iterum at*que* iterum, mirantibus omnibus, innouaretur: vbi modò Troiæ, & littoris Sigæi Jdeam viuam co*n*spexeras, mox syluas, & solitudines, horrenda antra, & furiarum domicilia: his*que* subinde vanescentibus, Tentoriorum Naviumqúe faciem jucundissimam inexpectatò contuereris.   20

pp 112–13   (*29 August*)
...

Sed à cœnâ, ad scenam properandum est; quâ loco sueto, Principibus à Iohannensibus representatur ᴀɴɴᴠѕ ʀᴀᴄᴠʀʀᴀɴѕ; fabula socco Comico, sed   25
pede Tragico, Tragicis enim senarijs ad nouitatem scripta. Scena in formam Zodiaci exactissimè efficta, et Sole omnia Dodecatemorij signa splendido artificio pertra*n*seunte. Cuius decursu quatuor anni tempestates, quatuor æ|tatis humanae progressus, quatuor humorum corporis varietates, et si quæ vspiam sint varietates aliæ, aut fortunarum, aut ingeniorum, aut amorum,   30
aut ludorum, omnes delectabili harmoniâ in theatrum productæ, & in Microcosmo representat*a*e, adolesce*n*te primùm Academico, aliarum deinde omnium conditionum varietatem experiente. Sed quid ego ista? quum ipsa iam è prælo emerserit festiuissima Comœdia: Incepta est, Sole Arietem ingrediente, finita quum Pisces Solis igne coquerentur. Digna quidem quæ toto vertente   35
anno duraret; sed ideo zodiacum suum festinantiùs Sol visus est transiisse, vt Principibus, multo istius diei tædio lassis, quiescendi otium concederetur.

pp 134–6   (*30 August*)
...   40

Academici aute*m*, qui huc vsq*ue* quicquid aut dictu*m* erat, aut factum, ad

Collation continued: 41 huc] hinc *DEF*

teretem illam & magni Arbitri eruditam aurem omnia limâssent, vt etiam
hominum minùs eruditorum, & inprimis illustrium fœminarum auriculis
aliquid darent, quales inter tot Phœbes nostræ fulgentes stellas, fuisse
aliquas non poterant non suspicari, in Sydnæi nostri, Chauceríque scriptis
frequentiores, quàm Plauti aut Aristotelis (nec enim omnes aut Arabellæ   5
sunt, aut Luciæ) hoc tempus maximè iudicârunt opportunum, quo Sacram
Annæ Clementiam, & cum Henrico Principe totam Aulici Gynaecaei
pulchritudinem demulcerent; idque auenâ, non patriâ modò, sed & pastorali,
quâ ARCADIAM RASTAVRATAM, Isiacorum Arcadum lectissimi cecinerunt; vnóque
opere, Principum, omniúmque spectantium animos immensâ, & vltra fidem   10
affecerunt voluptate, simúlque patrios ludiones, etsi exercitatissimos, quantùm
intersit inter scenam mercenariam, & eruditam docuerunt. Arduum dicere,
actionis maior gloria, an Poëseos. Quantum autem omnium aures fascinaverit,
non arduum iudicare: Alteram enim & Aula, & Academia loquitur; ac ita
loquitur, quasi loqui nunquam satìs posset: alteram res ipsa loquitur, liberque   15
omnium iam manibus attritus:
    Nostra nec erubuit Syluas habitare Thalia:
Præsertim Danielis nostri sylvas, quibus nec vrbes ipsas censebis magis vrbanas.
Cuius ex ingenij arcâ diâ ARICADIA, NOSTRA, cæteraque laudatissima scripta
tanta cum laude evolârunt, quantam alumno suo Academia nostra gratulatur   20
meritò; eóque magis, quòd is saltem sit, cuius exemplo, Poetæ coætanei,
posteríque omnes ediscant, tantum non esse inter ingenij acumina, &
paginarum castitates bellum, quin possint, debeántque se mutuô amplecti.
    Si quis Anglicè non callens, Arcadiæ huius velit ex me conditionem
cognoscere, recolligat ipse, quicquid aut fraude, aut philtro fieri possit, quo   25
amores mali conglutinentur; quicquid aut calumnijs, aut Zelotypijs, quo
amores etiam boni veríque dissuantur; quicquid, quo adolescentuli ad
libidinem virgines ad mentium, ornatúsque lasciuiam ardescant; & intelligat
quantum ganeonum lasciuorum, lenarúmque corruptricium facibus
conflagravit Arcadum respublica; istis manum medicam adhibere studuerunt,   30
qui pristinam Arcadiæ integritatem per ætatem reminisci, per virtutem
exoptare, per authoritatem, prudentiámque restituere, optimè poterant:
Jstísque malis artibus aliæ non minùs perniciosæ Arcadiam invaserant,
sacrorum rituum corruptelæ nefariæ, prætextu pietatis; Circulatorum fumosæ
imposturae honorifico medicorum nomine, habitúque simulato; Leguleiorum   35
deníque fæces decem-drachmariæ, qui inter opiliones se iactitant Jurisperitos,
inter Jurisperitos ne opilionum quidem æstimatione habentur. quorum dum

---

Collation continued: 1 aurem] auram *DEF* 3 inter] ⟨.⟩on *D* 13 Quantum]
Qa⟨.⟩ntum *D* 15 satìs] sacis *F* 18 Præsertim] ⟨....⟩ertim *D* 22 ingenij]
ingeniorum *BCDEF* 26 aut¹] *DEF omit* 36 iactitant] jactent *DEF*

17/ Nostra … Thalia: *cp Virgil,* Eclogues *6.2*

omni*um* fuci represent*an*tur, pristináq, Reipublic*æ* formâ revocatâ, legibus,
pœnis*que* expi*an*tur, si Reginæ, Principi, cæterís*que* spectatoribus vniversis
mirificè dixero placuisse, id tantu*m* dixero, quod Regina, Princeps, & vniversi
spectatores, & magnifico tum applausu præ | se tulerunt, & etiam dum
mirificâ laude contestantur.   5

Quanquam quid fluxis istis voluptatum, gloriolæ*que* nominibus fatuus
capior? quum nemini sit iniucundius infortunia pati, quàm felicitatis apicem
experto; aut quid Arcadiæ Vtopicæ gloriam restitutam iactem, quum Jsiacæ
Arcadiæ gloriam meram*que* voluptatem abeuntem contueor? Sic omnia humana
posita sunt in theatro; Comœdiâ*que* lætitiæ nostræ finitâ breuiusculâ, Tragœdia, 10
luctús*que* imminens Academiam expectorat. Si enim*f* maiores nostri meritò
lugendum censuerunt, planctú*que* cœlum concutere, quum Solis, Lunæve
vultum lucidum evanescentem cernerent; qua*n*tus nos manet dolor, qui Sole,
Cynthiâ*que* & Iulio lucido sydere, nobis splendoris sui præsentiam iam iám*que*
subducturis, eò grauioribus tenebris obruemur, quò præcellentiori luce   15
circumfulsimus? At sistite deliciae nostrae, sistite, quam diu nos non ingratos,
non inofficiosos hospites censueritis, tam autem diu si manseritis, hîc aeternùm
manebitis. Sed qui istos maiorum luctus pij imitamur eorum superstitionem
frustra experimur; lux enim nostra planctibus revocari non potest, nec
quicquam nobis restat, nisi, vt quam lucem ipsi videre no*n* possumus, eande*m* 20
alijs qui possunt, invideamus.

…

f Germanis hoc
esse solenne
narrat Boemus

Vertumnus Plot Synopsis   Inner Temple Library: Petyt MS 538, vol 43
ff 293–3v   25

The yeare about. as it was acted and plaide at oxeford before the Kings
and Queenes Maiesties, the Prince and Nobilitie, deuised and written
by Doctor Gwinne.

Actus 1. Scena 1.   Vertunnus (God of the yeare) brings forth the foure Seasons; placeth them in 30
their foure quartes for all the playe-while: goeth forth without speache, and
streight turnes out the Calender, appareled in the tuelf signes; who wondreth
seing his foure quarter-lords mett at once, enquireth the cause of their meeting,
which being to shewe their Maiesties the sport's of the yeare, they laye the
charge on Calender to shewe their force on Man (called Microcosme or the   35

Collation continued: 4 magnifico tum] magnificorum *DEF*   6 gloriolæ*que*]
gloriæqu*e DEF*   19 experimur;] experimur? *CDEF*

1/ pristináq: *for* pristiná*que; abbreviation mark missing*
11/ expectorat: *for* expectat

little world) in his foure ages: to which purpose they ioyne to him the foure
humor's. Lustie-blood; Hottspurre; Mallicoly; Milksop.

Scena 2 Theis foure leape-in at-once, hauing awhile in their seuerall kindes plaide the
merie knaue's on with another, they receiue their charge, and badges: the first
a Butter-flye, the 2. a Grasse-hopper; the 3 a Batt, and the fourth a Dormouse. 5
So are they sett to serue man, or rather to be his Maisters.

Scena 3 Calender dismissing them, receiue's a new command of onelie Iests', and
seeke's farther instruction of vertunnus.

Scena 4. Returning, he takes doune the seasons, and with them makes the prologue
to their Maiesties.   10

Actus 2 The stage being fairelie framed to the forme of a compleate Zodiake,

Scena 1 Lustie-blood describe's the spring by the signes. et cetera

2 Man (a yong scholler) with his tutor, and parasite debate of booke's, of hound's,
of horses, of plaies and games fitt for the season.

3 He groweth acquainted with Tracqitanto, a strange traueller, to learne   15
fashions of him, and growe greate friends:

4 The toune-hockwomen meete with him going on hunting; well used by the
scholler, ill and churlishly by the stranger.

5 The Goddesse of the season with Euphrosine and other Nimph's being at
their sporte's, are found by theis hunters.   20

6 Euphrosine beloued of Man is caught in a barlie-breake, for which

7 sauciness he is chidd awaie by Flora, but there is the beginning of their
mutuall loue.

Actus 3. Scena 1 Hottspurre describes the summer by moneths and signes.

2 Yong man hottlie pursues his loue, disputing with his Tutor and seruant of   25
loue and such lyke:

3 And for his first takes on him the habit of a sheapheard, faining to be stung
in his lip by a bee, praing help of his nimph by a charme,

4 which while she useth, he discloseth his loue, and therfore is driuen awaie
by Flora.   30

5 The Nimphs goe to bathe them. The bragart traueler wooes Corna, who
seemes to yeald, but deceiues him; she hides, and he seekes.

6 The Nimphs relate how Euphrosine bathing had lyke to haue bin droun'd,
but was saued by Man disguised.

7 They sett to Summer-sport's, a Morice-dance, in which is Man, and would   35
haue his friend ioyne; who skorning it, is hoist, and caried awaie

8 to be duckt. Man is putt in better hope of his loue.

9 while a Nimph is asleepe, the Bragart would oppresse hir, she is waked by a
noise; he flyes upon hir outcrye, and is pursued. |

27/ first: *ie, first disguise*   36/ his friend: *ie, the traveller (?)*
34/ disguised: *as a fisher*   36/ hoist: *2 minims in* MS

The yeare about.

Actus 4. Scena 1   The Autumne is described by Mallicolie. Man discourseth how he is profited
in Artes by loue. Enquireth of the kindes of Fantastikes, and seauen question
therof.

2   The seruant sent to his Mistrisse, with the Traueller conspires to bring Man   5
into Ielousie. They take occasion of it by bearing hir in heate

3   of haruest calle for the Sowthwest wynde to coole hir.

4   She is tempted by the Bragart, but flyes from him, leauing by chance hir
scarf behind hir: wherby he accuseth hir to hir loue of

5   falsehood, who disguised lyke an Indian marchant would corrupt hir, but   10
is refused.

6   Afterward lykewise in Bacchus his sportes, he lyke one of his Priests

7   getteth confession of hir, that she hath loued foure, a gentleman, a sheapherd,
a fisher, and a dancer. All proued to be him-self.

8   Moreouer, of the Marchant and this Priest, as also of the Bragart; wherupon   15
he and the seruant are discarded.

Actus 5. Scena 1   winter is described by Milksop. Man being growen olde becoms miserablie
couetous. Consults with his Tutore how to be ritch,

2   which skorned by him, he is counselled by his seruant to keepe his wife short,
to putt awaie seruants, and his Tutor, which is donne.   20

3   Complaint made by the Tutor, the Mistriss with hir olde woman: The olde
man is called forth, and putt in hope upon amendment to haue a pot of golde
leaft him by his mother; which he finde's

4   to be earth, and therfore chargeth hir and his olde Tutor with felonie: But by
another pott found by hir is satisfide. So sett they to Christmasse sporte's, and   25
with Calender doe conclude.

…

Gwinne, *Vertumnus* (1607)   STC: 12555
sigs B3–4   30

Ad Illustrissimum Montgomeriæ Comitem, Dominum
PHILIPPVM HERBART, Thalia.
Regi chare Philippe Comes, cui Messis in Herba,
Te Montgomeriæ Comitem tibi grata Thalia   35
Patronum inuitat, recolit, resalutat, adorat.
Illa verecundo rogat interfusa rubore,
Quæ placuit spectata semel, relegenda placebit?
Illam spectarunt (meminit, memoratque triumphans)
Deliciæ humani generis, decora vrbis & Orbis,   40
In terris superi, clarissima lumina mundi:
Rex, instar Iouis Augustus, Ioue digna propago

Princeps, hic iuuenum miraculum, at ille virorum.
Spectàrunt Comites (Comitatus Apolline dignus)
Musarum inprimis Præses Dorsettus Apollo.
Inde Houardorum tria nomina (numina dicam)
Consilio, imperio insignes, & munere summos   5
Northantona, Notinghamia, & Suffolcia norunt:
Portubus ille præest, hic nauibus, ædibus alter.
Inde (sed in versus, veniam date, si cadat ordo
Inuersus, scenæ vix sedit in ordine quisquam)
Intererat magis, an præerat (nam chara præesse   10
Cura dedit) cui clara dedit Worcestria nomen.
Moribus antiquis Rutlandius adfuit illis.
Comberlandius hîc aderat peramicus, at illum
Mars magis, an Musæ deflent; quòd amicus obiret.
Inde Trisantoninus; & inde Deuonius Heros;   15
Illum Dij superesse velint; hunc abstulit æther:
Hic fuit, ille manet (maneatque) columna Poetæ. |
Mecænas exinde meus, frater tuus, altèr
Phœbus, Pembrochius, cui chartula seria quondam
Ante annos tredecim, Medicinam ex more legentis,   20
Talia de Mundo scripsit maiore, minore,
Qualia nunc scenæ retulit ludendo Thalia.
Tu Comes ante omnes comis, quasi Cyprin Adonis,
Lætus spectasti, audisti (nisi fallor amore)
Lætus; at affectu (verum qui monstret amorem)   25
Ne placeat dubius, donec placuisse videres.
Hoc inter plures animo Danuersius Heros,
Atque Effinghamius, spectasse, audisse notati.
Ignoscant alij maiores, siue minores,
Scoti, Angliue; Duces, Comitesue; Barones,   30
Siue Equites; clari censu, sensuuè; fauentes
Musis, quos Musæ recolunt, celebrantque vicissim;
Si quos non nôrit, reticet venerando Thalia.
Ignoscant pariter Comitissæ, sydera vestra,
Et desideria, et nostri spectacula cœli,   35
Et domina Illustres animorum (dicam?) an amorum,
Spectari magis, vt dignæ, an spectare paratæ,
Si quas ignorat, sileat pudibunda Thalia.
Præ reliquis, orbes velut inter Luna minores,

36/ domina: *for* dominæ

Inter Ephydriadas Thetis, inter numina Iuno,
Vnio, gemmarum gemma, et Dea prima Dearum,
Anna, antè et retrò, velut annulus, instar amoris,
Regibus orta, parens Regum, Regina Britanna,
Expectata, vtinam spectasset, læta: sed illam   5
Melpomene pridiè lassârat, læserat Aiax,
Postridiè Euterpe expectans deliniit Arcas,
Illa Latina minus, magis vt vernacula mallet;
Illa licèt magis, hæc minùs apta Scholaribus essent.
E reliquis simili de causa absentibus, ille   10
Ille Sarisberiæ Comes, Hermes Angligenarum,
Lingua, caput, cor, mens, manus; à Ioue proximus Heros; |
Illa, illa excellens Bedfordia Lucia, lumen
Fæmineum, Musis columen, patrona Poetæ,
Spectassent vtinam: nam si quibus arte placere   15
Nostra Thalia cupit, cupit illis illa placere
Quamuis vix vllis queat illa placere, nec illis.
Nec te Summe silere potest, cum narrat amicos
Musarum illustres, ô Cancellarie: nam se
Debet Egertono, et sua quantulacunque Poeta.   20
Sed nec adesse tulere negotia maxima Regni,
Nec grauitas, tanto leuis vnde Thaliæ placeret.
Tum placuisse tamen Tu testis, an author, an actor;
Nam placuisse tibi tribuit: sed enim rogat vltrà,
Quæ placuit spectata, audita, legenda placebit?   25
Te tacitura Thalia iubente, iubente legetur.

Thalia, cur non comico versu, rogas?
Heroa, par, heroico metro roget

                                                                30

sig C2v

...

   Aptum Proscenium ad Tempestates quatuor. Palma in medio ramis
duodecim, lucernis totidem. Ὑπερσκενιον ad formam Zodiaci, Solis
imagine per Dodecatemoria, tria ad actus singulos postremos, percurrente.   35
Vox, actio, persona, gestus, scripto non possunt exprimi, Imaginare.

sigs H3-3v*   *(27 August)*

   Ad Regis introitum, è Ioannensi Collegio extra portam Vrbis Borealem   40
     sito, tres quasi Sibyllæ, sic (vt é sylua) salutarunt.

® Reges
Scotorum
Duncan Angliæ
Canut. Walliæ
Llhewelyn ap
Sitsylht.

1. Fatidicas olim fama est cecinisse Sorores
Imperium sine fine tuæ, Rex Inclyte, stirpis.
Banquonem agnouit generosa Loquabria Thanum:
Nec tibi Banquo, tuis sed sceptra nepotibus illæ
Immortalibus immortalia vaticinatæ: 5
In saltum, vt lateas, dum Banquo recedis ab Aula.
Tres eadem pariter canimus tibi fata, tuisque,
Dum spectande tuis, e saltu accedis ad Vrbem:
Teque salutamus: Salue, cui Scotia seruit.
2. Anglia cui, salue. 3. Cui seruit Hibernia, salue.   10
1. Gallia cui titulos, terras dant cætera, salue.
2. Quem, diuisa priùs, colit vna Britannia, salue.
3. Summe Monarcha Britannice, Hibernice, Gallice, salue.
1. Anna parens Regum, soror, vxor, filia, salue.
2. Salue Henrice Hæres, Princeps pulcherrime salue.   15
3. Dux Carole, & perbelle Polonice Regule, salue.
1. Nec metas fatis, nec tempora ponimus istis;
Quin Orbis regno, famæ sint terminus astra:
Canutvm referas regno quadruplice clarum:
Maior Auis, æquande tuis diademate solis. | 20
Nec serimus cædes, nec bella, nec anxia corda:
Nec furor in nobis: sed agente calescimus illo
Numine, quo Thomas Whitvs per somnia motus,
Londinensis Eques, Musis hæc tecta dicauit:
Musis? imo Deo, tutelarique Ioanni.   25
Ille Deo charum, & curam, propè prætereuntem
Ire salutatum, Christi Præcursor, ad Ædem
Christi pergentem, iussit. Dictâ ergo salute,
Perge, tuo aspectu sit læta Academia, perge.
                                        M.G.   30

...

Poem on the Royal Visit   Bodl.: MS. Ashmole 36, 37
f 259 col 1*

                                                                                                    35

1   To Oxenford our king is gone, with all his noble peers
who hath maintaind this relme so long, from all popish fryers
Such a king he hath bene, as ye like was never seene
knights did ride by his side evermore to be his guide
A 100 knights a 1000 knights of 40 pownds a yeare   40

2   The king approching neare ye towne ye chancellor did ride

with many a reverent *Docto*r attending on ech side
All they on horses gray ride to meet ye king y*a*t day
Beadles 6 w*i*th guilded sticks pranse & make their horse ⌄⌐shew tricks⌐
That they therby might testifie y*a*t all ye beasts ther were glad:

                                                                                5

3   These men I say whose naggs did play by some are called bedles
But from ye tipstaffs they do beare some other called the*m* peadles
But I did looke pedu*m* in my book*es* & found it was a shepherds ⌄⌐crooke⌐
wherefore I might certanely affirme ech of them mistooke
They were rather, called bedle of their forfather, because they do bid & warne. 10

4   And when ye King to Oxford came, they hard a brave o⌐r⌐ation
wh*i*ch in ye barands iudgement then did passe all expectation
w*i*th such faces & such graces & such passing eloquence
such a stile all ye while as passed all intelligence   15
That all ye men y*a*t stood ⌄⌐by⌐ them [by] stampd & stard for ioy.

5   The speech being made ye chancellor, did give ye king a book
guilded Steven testament wheron ye king did looke
This booke tis tould was never sould for lesse the*n* 20 marks in ⌄⌐gould⌐   20
& wel might be for I did see t'was guilded all most curiously
yet they were so kind to Shewe their loving minde
they would give it ye king for nothing.

6   This guift they say they gave ye king who gratefully it tooke   25
& it received at their hands w*i*th a most loving looke
Then ye clowns of ye towne in yer red & scarlet gowns
gave the king such a thing as passed all imagining
even a payre of glovs to testifie their loves
that they to their prince did beare.   30

7   A paire of gloves they gave ye king of stronge and stiffe staggs ⌄⌐lether⌐
I say a paire of hunting glovs to keepe out wind & weather
some relate they gave him plate & a purse stufft full of gould
then said I y*a*ts a lye as soone as ever I hard it told   35
for why said I, should they so give their gould away
when ye king had inough of his owne.

8   when this was done ye chancellor ye king againe did greete
& then ye heralds com*m*anded all to march vp through ye streete   40
ye court in Oxford led ye way w*i*th trowps of horse in good aray
& next to the*m* ye citizens, ye Maior & all ye aldermen
together by 2 & 2 like loving brethren.

9   Close at their heels in martiall sort, came ye beefe eating gua_∧⌐rd⌐
who with their staring countenance ye country pesants scarde
These huge fatt dolts, ware bows & boults, sword & buckler
by their side
Ech man I say in his palphray clad in all his best aray   5
whan these were past ther came at one blast
          Tom trumpetor & his man.

10   Next them ye lordly chamberlaine vpon a milke white steed
accompanied with lord treasarer in order did proceed   10
when these were gone ye deane came on
who bare his sword for his maiestie
And then was seene ye king & [q] queene & all their royall progeny
who with a rout were compassed about
          with many a noble man.   15

col 2*
…

13   When to ye towne ye king was come, we were not for to seeke
but straight ye cheife professor did make a speich in greeke   20
wherin he most earnestlye beseiched ye king yat he would _∧⌐be⌐
Courteous & kind & in his mind, protect ye muses progeny
To which presentlye ye king did reply, yat he would favor their _∧⌐Muse⌐

14   With yat ye publique orator vpon his bended knee   25
did make a speich in latine yeir doctors standing by
Not therfore yat he could do no more then ye rest had done befor⌐e⌐
but that therby ye king might spye, their learning & industry
That they were not to seeke for la_∧⌐tt⌐ in & for greeke
          Yf they were put to it of a sudd⟨…⟩   30

15   which speech because its ech way dekt, with figure & with trope
Ile here this memory, as time shall give me scope
He did say this is ye day, for which we longe before did pray
for we did deeme & eke esteme, yat for to see ye king & queene   35
would be a ioy indeed, yat farr would exceede
          all ioyes vpon ye Earthe.

16   And though ye wished day were come wherin we should be glad
Yet had they this occasion for which they might be sad   40
Yat all this rabble ware _∧⌐not⌐ able, for to give you worthy thanks

28/ learning: *6 minims in* MS   30/ sudd⟨…⟩: *final letters written over or cancelled*

& at this word thus he ⌈stayed⌉ stood, & pointed to ye learned ranck*es*
Yet nere ye lesse they knew his gentlenes did not regard such ₄⌈matter⌉

17   for even as great Iove above, so princes wh*i*ch do beare
Ye p*er*son of a Iove on earth, ought never for to care   5
nor to measure mans good pleasure by ye bounty of their tre⌈asure⌉
but to requite ye poore mans right, w*i*th many a great benefit
& iudge of ye thing wh*i*ch mortall men do bring
            according as they were able.
                                                                                                      10
18   And yet they doubted not but yf ye king should search the ⌈Ear⟨..⟩⌉
y*a*t he should see how ye love of him, possesse ye greater pa⟨.....⟩
And he should find yf he would winde, into ye botto*m*e of their minds
A shrine to be im*m*ortally erected to his maiesty
before wh*i*ch all they did burne both night & day   15
            ye frankensense of their love.

19   Next y*a*t they went to Ch*ri*sts Church straight, a Coll*ege* of worthy fa⟨..⟩
where ye subdeane did him receive, I have forgot his nam⟨.⟩
then they all went to ye hall fagg & rag both greate & small   20
Bells did ring boys did sing evermore god save ye Kinge
& send his grace to runne his race, in pleasure o*n* Royston ⌊downe⌋

20   The hall was hung w*i*th vearses round
            a glorious sight to see.   25
for all were willed for to make
            verses in their degree
Some of ye trade y*a*t had made
            verses called Æsclypead
Here might he find in everie kind   30
            verses fitting to his minde
here an Hexameter, ther a Pentameter
            Sapphycks scazons too. |

f 259v col 1*   35

21   And when ye King in reading the*m* [ye day] had ₄⌈almost⌉ past ye day
            at night he was advertised y*a*t he should see a play
ther in ye hall emongst the*m* all was plaid a pleasant pasto₄⌈rall⌉
            emongst ye rest wh*i*ch pleasd him best, one plaid a rustick ₄⌈hobbinall⌉   40
Beshrew my hart he plaid so well his part, he would make a horse breake
his halter.

22   The play being done gigg & all, ye king forth with was led
to a chamber hung with painted cloths, wherin stood a bed
& a sheet so white, stretched out so right plaid ye canopy ∧⌈yat night⌉
ther he lay as some say till ye breaking of ye day
then he rose & pluckt on his close   5
& called for his breakfast straight.
…

Verses on the Comedians at Oxford and Cambridge   Bodl.: MS. Malone 19
pp 125–8*   10
…
One the Comædians of Oxford & Cambridge.

Now Cambridge is a merry towne
And Oxford is another,   15
The King was wellcome to the one
And far'd well at the other.

And is not this strange, & is not this strange
That both exceeded, neyther needed   20
Ffoole for foole to change.

So as I know not vnto which,
The King is most a debtour;
Though Oxford made him passing cheere   25
Yet Cambridge store was greater.
And is not this strange. &c

In gay aray the Oxford men
Receiue him man by manna,   30
And Cambridge spent in butterd beere
Three pound to sing Hosanna.
And is not this. &c.

Oxford had good pleasing songes   35
And some of them wear wittye. |
And soe had Cambridge by my fayth
And tweare not for the dittye.
And is not .&c.

                                                                                                                       40
Oxford had good Comedyes
But not such Benefactors

ffor Cambr*idge* Byshops whiflers had
And preachers for the Actors.
And is not—

Oxford cryed God saue the Kinge   5
And blesse to cryed some,
But Cambr*idge* cryed more learnedly
Behold the King doth come.
And is not this—

                                                                  10
Cambr*idge* is a witty Towne
And Oxf*ord* is as wise,
But neythers Logick could discerne
Spectators fro*m* ye skyes.
And is not—   15

Oxf*ord* shee a *Christ* Church had
To entertayne the Kinge
And Cambr*idge* had a Trinitye
And scarce one [b⟨.⟩elt] ∧⌈wise⌉ the*re*in.   20
And is not this— |

Most Iacob Charles thow wellcome art
Did Cambr*idge* crye to vs,
An Oxf*ord* boy must haue vntrust   25
If he had cryed thus.
And is not this—

Oxford her Vice=chancellor
Exceeded in a Muffe,   30
But Cambr*idge* in a Iacke of blew
And in a fringed Ruffe.
And is not—

Oxf*ord* her Vice=chancellor   35
Did take his vsuall place,
But Cambr*idge* lay vppon the stage
At pawne for bett*er* grace.
And is not—

                                                                  40
Oxford had King, Queene, & Prince

And all the*re* royall trayne,
Camb*ridge* had the K*ing* & Prince
But god knowes who did gayne.
And is not this—

Ox*ford* her Vice=chancellor
No ent*er*taynment spar[e]'d,
Nor Camb*ridge* with a good fatt hen
Ffor to bumbast ye guard. |
And is not this strange—

Ox*ford* Comicke iesters had
Camb*ridge* a Lawyer foole
Who Ignoram*us* christened was
By name of the*re* owne schoole.
And is not this—

Yet will his grace review the same
And awake himselfe will keepe
God graunt they please him then not worse
Then when he was a sleepe
[And is not]
Or else it would be strange, ore else, &c—
That he his rest, for such poore Iestes
Of Dollman would exchange.

But Oxford as of Winter Fruite
Of Camb*ridge* sport*es* may say
They did but budd the 7th of March
And blossome at mıd=May.
And is not this strange, &c
That he his rest. &c

Yet howsoeuer I thus conclude
And friend to eyth*er* place
Both shalbe fooles vntill they striue
Each oth*er* to disgrace.
And is not, &c. And is not this strange, that
Bothe exceeded, neyth*er* needed,
Ffooles for fooles to change.

City Council Minutes   OCA: C/FC/1/A1/002
f 101*   *(7 June)*

…

An acte
touching ye
intertaynement
of ye King//.

It is agreed at this Counsell/ That whereas the Kinges Maiestye the Queene &
the young prince (as it is thought) will comme to this Cytie in August next/   5
Provision shalbe made for their receyving as may be for the worshippe of this
Cytie both in giving the cuppe already provided, to his maiestye/ some

This act is in
some part
altered the first
of August next

costly gloues to the Queene & some Cuppe vnto the prince/ And the Maior
Aldermen, the residewe of the Thirteene & the Bayliffes for the yeare to
ryde with foote clothes in Scarlett, And some Threescore of the bayliffes   10
Chamberlayns Common Counsell, & others of the most sufficient commoners
to be appoynted that shall ride in comely blacke coates in like sort as When
the late Queene was here/ And other the provision & order for the commlynes
to be taken as shalbe thought fitt by Master Maior, thaldermen & the
Thirteene/ And money to be borrowed to support the Charges according   15
as thexpence shall arryse//.

…

ff 101v–2*

                                                                                    20

                Orders sett downe how the Citizens shalbe apparrelled at
                ye meeting of ⌊ye⌋ King & in what sort they shall ryde

how ye mayor
shall ryde with
4 footemen

It is ordered by master Maior, the Aldermen & the Thirteene That at the
Kinges Comminge the Maior shall ryde alone before Thaldermen in his   25
scarlett gowne, Velvit coate & Velvit hose with foure foote men to attend
[thym] him & with his foote cloth//.

how thaldermen
shall ryde

Item That the residue of thaldermen shall likewise ryde with their foote
Clothes in scarlet gownes/ Velvit Coates & velvit hose/.   30

how ye xiijteene
shall ryde

Item That the residue of the Thirteene shall ryde in Scarlet gownes/ sattyn
doublettes/ Velvit hose & Typpettes as the Maior & Aldermen must doe/.

how ye bayliffes
shall ryde

Item That the Bayliffes for Ye yeare shall ryde in their Scarlet gownes sattyn   35
doublettes & velvit hose on their foote Clothes eyther of them having a
white rodd in his hand/

Thaldermen,
xiijteene & ye
bayliffes to haue
one footeman
apiece

Item for That thaldermen and the residue of the Thirteene must ryde two
& two & likewise the Two bayliffes/ everye one of then must provide one   40
footeman in comely sort//.

How eu*er*y one yat hath been bayliffe or chamb*er*len shall ryde

Item That eu*er*ye one That hath beene bayliff or Chamb*er*len shall ryde in garded coat*es* & sattyn doublett*es*, w*i*th com*m*ely hose handsomely booted & spurred

how ye com*m*on counsell & comon*er*s shall ryde

The Com*m*on Counsell & other able Com*m*oners That shalbe appoynted to ryde, all of them shall ryde in blacke coat*es* all of them layd [one] on w*i*th velvit lace in blacke doublet*es* & com*m*ely hose handsomly booted & spurred/
…

(13 June)

Certeine appointed to call in ye Cyties debt*es*/

It is agreed that all pawnes for money lent vnto any man by this Cytie shalbe speedily redeemed by the owners or els to be sold & money made ready/ And likewise all debt*es* to be called in & obliga*ci*ons & bills for money owing to be put in suite if ye debters will not pay p*re*sent money for the p*re*sent necessitie of the Cytie against the King*es* Com*m*inge/ And M*aste*r Bayliff Potter & Mr Wright are appoynted by this howse to call in all the said debt*es* & to sell the pawnes if the owners bring not in money w*i*th speed// |

(20 June)

The penaltie of them y*at* make default at ye meeting of ye king

It is agreed by the Whole consent of this Howse that eu*er*y person appoynted to ryde as a Citizen to meete the King when M*aste*r Maior & thaldermen doe ryde shall p*ro*vide themselves w*i*th handsome horses & comely apparell, booted & spurred to meete ye King at y*at* tyme vppon payne that eu*er*ye one making default either in not com*m*ing or not being p*ro*vided as is already sett downe by M*aste*r Maior and thaldermen/ Everie of the thirteene shall forfeit to the vse of this Cytie fyve pound*es*/ everye one having a bayliff*es* place/ Three pound*es*/ every one having a Chamb*er*lens place forty shilling*es*/ every of the Com*m*on Counsell & Com*m*oners that are appoynted to ryde Thirty shilling*es* w*i*thout any pardon or remission & to be imprysoned untill they pay the money/ And if any of the Com*m*on Counsell shall p*re*pare himself in better apparell then is appoynted for his degree he is to ryde in order w*i*th those y*at* are so appoynted to be apparelled after the Iunior Chamberlayns//.
…

(25 June)

An act to lend money to ye Cytie or to pay interest for money borrowed

It is agreed At this Counsell That Whereas money is to be borrowed against the King*es* com*m*inge, eu*er*ye one of the Thirteene Bayliff*es*/ Chamb*er*laynes Com*m*on Counsell & eu*er*ye able Com*m*oner shall lend the Cytie for a yeare so much money as by an act of com*m*on Counsell the xiij^th of August in ye xxxiiij^th yeare of her late Ma*ie*stye was agreed vppon or els the Cytie borrowing the money eu*er*ye one shall pay for the interest of such money for one yeare

after the rate of Tenne pound*es* the hundred as the interest of the money w*h*ich
he should haue lent vnto ye Cytie should com*m*e vnto//

f 103* *(29 July)*

...

It is agreed that Mr Iohn Poole & Mr Pigott togeather w*i*th m*aste*r
Chamb*er*laynes shall cause such places w*i*thin the Cytie to be paynted &
washed, as at the Northgate & Pen*n*ylesse benche & other places as shalbe
appoynted by m*aste*r Maior & the most p*a*rte of thaldermen/ And money
to be deliu*er*ed unto them from the Cytie for that m*aste*r chamb*er*layns
haue expended more then they haue receaued//.

...

(1 August)

...

Guift*es*
appoynted for
ye king queene
& prince

Item it is agreed that at the meetinge of the Kinge when he com*m*yth into
our lib*er*ties His Ma*i*estie shalbe p*rese*nted w*i*th a Cuppe and xl*tie* Aungells/
The queene w*i*th a [cuppe] ⌈pursse⌉ & fyftie Aungells The prince w*i*th a
cuppe and xx*tie* Aungells/ notw*i*thstanding the act made in the xiij*th* of
Iune last.

Those wh*i*ch
are bound
for money
borrowed to be
saued harmles

Item it is agreed That such men as are or shalbe bounde for money borrowed
to the Cyties vse shalbe saued harmles by this Cytie:/

...

(12 August)

c*er*teine to be
saued harmles
being bounde
for the Cytie

Item it is agreed That M*aste*r Alderman Levinz M*aste*r Alderman Goode M*aste*r
Alderman Bartholomew & Mr Hollway the Townclarcke shall haue securitie
by obligac*i*on from the Cytie vnder the Cities seale to be saued harmelesse from
all such bond*es* as they haue already entred into for money borrowed for
the Cyties vse or shall enter into for money [borrowe] to be borrowed for
the Cytie//.

Audited Corporation Accounts OCA: P.5.2

f 86* *(Chamberlains' receipts)*

...

Item receaued of mr Will*ia*m Potter being p*a*rcell of the
debt*es* belonging to the Cytie wh*i*ch he was appoynted to
gather vpp against the King*es* Com*m*ing   xx li.

...

f 87   (Chamberlains' payments)

…

Item paid to the Ioyner for amending Pennyles bench
against the Kinges Comminge   xvj d.
Item for Whiting of the seeling of the bench   xviij d.   5

…

f 88v

…

Item for making the bridge cleane At the kinges Departure   xvj d.   10

…

Item paid to Iohn Maior for the Caryage of gravell to be
spread at Northgate against the kinges Comming   ij s. vj d.

…

15

f 89   (Keykeepers' accounts)

…

Item they Dischardge themselues by deliuerye of a cupp
given to the king by the Cytie valued at   xxv li. v s. iij d.

…

20

f 89v*

…

Item deliuered to Mr Niccolls the xx^th of August 1605
to be put into the kinges cupp queenes purse & princes   25
cupp in gould   l li.
Item deliuered to Mr Niccols which was disbursed for
the Cytie   v li.
Item paid to William Tyrer & Iames Twayte late Chamberlens of
the Cytie of Oxon. by thandes of Mr William Potter/ imployed   30
in the repairing amending and paynting of Diuerse places of the
Cytie against the kinges comming in August 1605   xx li.
Item paid the xxj^th day of August 1605 for rewardes given to
the kinges Officers & for gloues given to Noble men and for
diuerse other thinges   xl li. 35
Item Deliuered By Master Alderman Bartholomew being one
of the Keykeepers for thexchaung of fiftye poundes of money
into gould to Mr William Wright gouldsmith the xxij^th of
August 1605   xvj s.
Item given to the Lord Chamberlens man   vj s.   40

36/ Deliuered By: *corrected over* receaued of

Item deliuered to Mr Niccolls The xxvjth of August to be
putt into the kinges cupp   v li.

Item paid to Iohn Willis for two dayes ryding to the Court
with Master Alderman Bartholomew & Mr Harris when
the king was at Woodstocke in August 1605 & for other   5
Consideracions   viij s.

Item paid the vth day of September 1605 to Mr William
Wright goldsmith for the Cupp given to the young prince   xiiij li. xiiij s.

...

                                                                              10

Keykeepers' Accounts   OCA: P.4.1
f 110

...

In plate in the chest
Inprimis the great Cuppe provided for the King valued at   xxv li. v s. iij d. 15

f 110v   *(Bonds and bills not summed)*

...

One bonde of mr Gibbons for ye Scutchins

...   20

f 112v   *(Total receipts)*

...

Whereof they dischardge themselues Vz.

...   25

By deliuery of the kinges cupp   xxv li. v s. iij d.

...

St Aldate Churchwardens' Accounts
ORO: DD Par. Oxford St Aldate c.16/12   30
single mb*   *(31 March 1605–20 April 1606) (Receipts)*

...

Item Receved by hockinge   xliij s. iij d.
Item Receved by whitsontyde   iiij li. xij s. 9 d.

...   35

Item Received by Mr Royce by hocking   xij s.

...

33, 36/ hockinge, hocking: *Hocktide was 8–9 April 1605*
34/ whitsontyde: *19–25 May 1605*

St Martin Churchwardens' Accounts ORO: PAR 207/4/F1/1, item 103
single mb *(Rendered 23 April 1606) (Receipts)*
...
Item in the boxe at hocktid   xxxiiij s. j d.
...   5

St Mary Magdalen Churchwardens' Accounts ORO: PAR 208/4/F1/38
single mb *(Rendered 22 April 1606) (Receipts)*
...
Item Rec*eued* at Hoctyde all thinges beinge discharged   xxxij s. 10
Item Rec*eued* at Whitsontyde all thinges beinge discharged   iij li. xviij s.
...

(Payments)
Item p*ay*d to the Ryngers at his ma*i*esties Com*m*inge to oxon.   iij s. iiij d. 15
...
Item p*ay*d for an Amercemente in the forreste for our tree
at Whitsontyde   iij s. iiij d.
...
                                                                                            20

St Mary the Virgin Churchwardens' Accounts ORO: PAR 209/4/F1/21
single mb* *(30 November 1604–20 April 1606) (Receipts)*
...
Item gayned and received at Hocktyde   xxxij s.
...   25

St Michael at the North Gate Churchwardens' Accounts
ORO: PAR 211/4/F1/3, item 168
mb [1] *(Rendered 23 April 1606) (Receipts)*
...   30
Item Receaved at Hocktyde   xl s.
Item receaved at Whitsontyde   xl s.
...

(Payments)   35
Item payed to five Ringers when the kyng*es* ma*i*estie
came to the Citie   iiij s. vj d.
...

4, 10, 24, 31/ hocktid, Hoctyde, Hocktyde: *8–9 April 1605*
11, 18, 32/ Whitsontyde: *19–25 May 1605*

St Peter in the East Churchwardens' Accounts   ORO: PAR 213/4/F1/2
single mb   *(3 April 1605–23 April 1606) (Receipts)*
...
Item at 〈..〉 Hock tyde   xliiij s.
...   5

St Peter le Bailey Churchwardens' Accounts   ORO: PAR 214/4/F1/52
single mb*   *(Rendered 27 April 1606) (Receipts)*
...
Item rec*eyved* for Hockinge   xix s.   10
Item gotten at Whitsonetide   xxiij s. vj d.
Item rec*eived* for *our* wood and bowes   xiij s. iiij d.
...

(Payments)   15
Item for Musicke to yonge Charles on *our*
Shootinge daie   viij d.
...
Item for fetchinge in the Tree and the bowes   xj s. ij d.
...   20

c 1605–8
Armin, A Nest of Ninnies (1608)   STC: 772.7
sig A2*
                                                                                            25

To the most true and rightly compleat in all good gifts and graces, the
generous Gentlemen of Oxenford, Cambridge, and the Innes of Court.
Ro*bert* Armin greeting.
...
...I haue seene the stars at midnight in your societies, and might haue   30
Commenst like an Asse as I was, but I lackt liberty in that, yet I was admitted
in Oxford to be of Christs Church, while they of Al-soules gaue ayme, such
as knew me remember my meaning. I promised them to proue mad, and
I thinke I am so, else I would not meddle with Folly so deepely, but similis
similem, &c....   35
...

4/ Hock tyde: *8–9 April 1605*
10/ Hockinge: *Hocktide was 8–9 April 1605*
11/ Whitsonetide: *19–25 May 1605*

1605–6
Christ Church Disbursements ChCh Arch: xii.b.50
f 25v *(25 December–25 March)*

...

Tragedies and
Comedies

To mr Iuxkes and mr Blundell for the English com̅medie   5
per billam   v li. x s.
(signed) Simon Iucks. *(signed)* Francys Blundell.

6.1.0.

For lightes and torches att the scholers comedie   xj s.
                (signed)   Thomas Baughe.
                        Sum̅ma   vj li. xij d. 10

...

Christ Church Computi ChCh Arch: iii.c.7(g.)
mb 3d*

                                                                              15

Et in expensis Comediarum et Tragediarum hoc
Anno factarum   vj li. xij d.

...

ChCh ***Letter of Bishop of Llandaff to Sir Thomas Lake*** PRO: SP/15/37   20
f [1]* *(3 November)*

After our very hearty Com̅mendacions: whereas ther is one Thomas Godwyn
a Com̅oner of Christchurch in Oxford a very towardly youth that in diuers
exercises as namely in a Com̅edy before his maiestie in Oxford hath giuen   25
proofe of his likelyhoode to be com̅e a learned man and a profitable member
of the Com̅on wealth: we haue thought it not amisse to recom̅mende hym
vnto your good fauour, earnestly intreating, yow would be pleased, to be a
meanes vnto his maiestye, for his gratious lettres vnto the Deane and Chapter
of Christ Church, for his placing in the roome of a scholler there. wee shall 30
account our selues much beholding vnto yow for the same and be ready to
requite it in any good office we may. wherof desyring yow to rest assured we
Com̅itt yow to [God] the protection of Almighty God./ London november
3. 1605....

                                                                              35

ChCh ***Letter of King James to Christ Church*** PRO: SP/15/37
single sheet *(14 November)*

Trusty &c. We haue receaved so good testymonie of the [good disposition
and] forwardnes in learning ˄⌈honest conversacion & other rare quallities⌉ of 40
Thomas Godwyn now Com̅oner of that our Howse, called Christchurch
in [that] our Vnyuersitie of Oxford, as We [[h] are pleased to addresse

these o*ur* le*tt*res vnto you in his behalf requiring you to admitt him a]
ᴧ⌐thinck him worthy of the place of a⌐ Scholler of that Colledge ᴧ⌐and do
therfore require you hereby to make choice⌐ of him before any other and at
ye next election to ᴧ⌐admitt him to be a Scholler of that howse⌐ and after his
placing in the same roome to allowe vnto him all such dueties and allowances   5
as are or shalbe due and incident to the same place. Your conformitie to
yeeld vs satisfaction herein we will thanckfully accept.

Memorandum of the Dean and Chapter of Christ Church
ChCh Arch: D.P.ii.c.1, item 6   10
single sheet*   *(4 January)*

Memorandum That whereas an hundred & ffyve pownd*es* ᴧ⌐Clare⌐ was gyven
to the Deane & Chapter to Ease their Chardges at the King*es* Com*m*ynge
to Oxon*ia* A*n*no d*om*ini 1605/ Lxxxxiij li. ix s. ob. of that monye went to   15
acquite a Bond of debte vnder the Chapter Seale for the buyldinge of the
Newe Lodging*es* in Peckwater Inne and the Remaynder thereof, viz. xj li. x s.
xj d. ob. was Charged in the Style of Extraordynarye Receipt*es* eod*em* Anno/
Script*a* quarto die Ianuarij A*n*no tercio Iacobi Reg*is* 1605/
…   20

Magdalen College Libri Computi   MC Arch: LCE/8
f 3v col 2   *(Internal and external payments)*
…
Musicis in festo Bursarioru*m*   5 s.   25
…

Merton College Bursars' Accounts   MCR: 3.1
f 102   *(26 July–22 November) (External expenses)*
…   30
…D*om*ino Vicecancellario in aduentu Regis ex consensu, 12 li.…
…

f 103   *(25 November–25 March) (External expenses)*
…   35
…Musicjs publicjs ex consensu 6 s. 8 d.…

3/ of him … and: *written in left margin and marked by asterisks for insertion here*
4/ admitt … howse: *written above the line and marked by caret and symbol* ⊖ *for insertion here*
31/ D*om*ino Vicecancellario: *George Abbot*

New College Bursars' Accounts   NC Arch: 7599
mb 5   *(25 December–25 March)* *(Internal expenses)*

...

...So*lutum* Musicis oppidanis vj s. viij d....

...   5

The Queen's College Long Rolls   QC Arch: LRA
f 30v col 1*   *(7 July–7 July)* *(External expenses)*

...

Item Mauritio fidicini   2 s. 10

...

Item Tibicin*us* de Oxon*ia*   10 s.

...

St John's College Computus Hebdomalis   SJC Arch: Acc.v.E.4   15
f 15v   *(14–20 October)*

...

Imposit*i* p*er* decretu*m* Conuocationis 2⁰
p*ro* Expensis vniuersitatis in aduent*u* regiis
maiestatis   lvij s. 4 d. 20

...

f 18v*   *(13–19 January)*

...

Set on for o*ur* Christmas-Lord   iij li. xvj d. 25

...

f 19   *(27 January–2 February)*

...

Set on for o*ur* Christmas-Lord   ij s. 30

...

f 19v   *(17–23 February)*

...

for virtue his playe.   9 s. 35
& for ye musitions.   3 li. 16 s.

19/ vniuersitatis: *altered from* in adve
19/ regiis: *for* regiæ

Vice-Chancellors' Accounts   OUA: WP/β/21(4)
p 154   *(17 July–17 July)* *(Extraordinary expenses)*
…

Solut*um* pro residuo pecuniæ expositæ in receptione
Ser*enissimæ* Regiæ Ma*iestatis*   Clj li. ix s. vj d.   5
…

Letter of John Chamberlain to Ralph Winwood
Boughton House: Winwood Papers, vol 4
f [1]*   *(12 October)*   10

S*ir* after so longe silence I am out of my bias, and know not where to begin,
neither know I what is new or what is old to you, for the Kinges intertainment
at Oxford must nedes be stale, whence I make no question but you had so many
large aduertisements that nothing could scape vntoucht: yet at all aduentures   15
I will shoote my bolt, and geue a short censure. the disputations for the most
part were well performed and pleased the Kinge excedingly, for he had a great
part in them, and spake often and to the purpose, but he was so continually
interrupted w*ith* applauding that he could not express himself so well, as he
wisht, yet he found taste in that distast and was nere a whit offended. but the   20
playes had not the like successe, specially magdalens tragedie of Aiax, w*h*ich
was very tedious and wearied all the companie. but the day of departure an
english pastorall of Samuell Daniells (presented before the Quene) made
amends for all, being indeed very excillent, and some parts exactly acted.…

25

Hannisters' Registers   OCA: L.5.1
f 275   *(9 December)*
…

Ioh*annes* Smyth nup*er* apprenticius Leonardi Maior de Ciuitate Oxon*ie* musition
admiss*us* est in lib*er*tat*em* Ciuitatis p*re*dicte Nono die decembr*is* Anno Tertio   30
supra*dicto* et soluit feod*a* Offi*ciariorum*, et ij s. vj d. p*ro* sitella Corp*or*ata et Iur*atus*l.
…

City Council Minutes   OCA: C/FC/1/A1/002
f 106*   *(11 December)*   35

Certeine
allowau*nces*
made to m*aster*
Alderm*an*
Cossam
touching his
accompt*es*

…

It is agreed at this Counsell That m*aster* Alderman Cossam shalbe allowed
in his accompt the [twenty pound*es*] Sixteene pound*es* laid out at the
repairing of the Southbridge/ Highe bridge and the Castle bridge/ and the
Nyneteene pound*es* and six pence given to the Kinge*s* officers at the kinge*s*   40

37/ It is: *in display script*

being here/ although he much blamed for laying out the money for the Bridg*es*
without the Consent of this howse/ and for exceeding in giving excessiue ffees
to thofficers/ And this howse doth disallowe his accompt of the Tenn pound*es*
that was in the princes Cuppe and the thirty shilling*es* in the Queenes purse/
vnles m*aste*r alderman cann make *p*roofe that the money was given according   5
to the Cyties appointment*es*/ and when he shall make p*r*oouufe at any tyme
hereafter That the same Eleaven pound*es* tenn shilling*es* was duly given/ Then
he shalbe againe allowed the same vnto him/ and for his elec*ci*on dinner the
howse denyeth to make him any allowaunce thereof/ And touching the Offall
tymber & Chipp*es* at the amending of the Bridge/ the howse will haue fforty   10
shilling*es* allowed to the Cytie as the auditors haue adiudged the same//.

...

f 109*   *(18 September)*
                                                                                15
It is agreed That Iohn Harrington shall haue a Lease of the Tenem*ent* and
garden ground in his tenure & of the daunsing schoole for five pound*es*
sixteene shilling*es* yearely rent for the tearme of one & thirty yeares so that
he agree w*i*th Iohn Bossely for his int*er*est therein/.

...   20

Audited Corporation Accounts   OCA: P.5.2
f 91v   *(Chamberlains' payments)*
...
Item given to ye king*es* players ye ix^th day of Octob*er* 1605   x s. 25
...

f 92*
...
Item for wine & suger & other thing*es* on ye xxiiij^th of march vz....   30
ffor a pottle of muscadine for ye Se*r*geant*es* & Musitions   ij s.
...
Item given to ye Queenes trumpetters   ij s. vj d.
...
                                                                                35
f 93*
...
Item given to ye Earle of Hartford*es* players ye ix^th of Iuly
by m*aste*r mayors appoyntm*ent*   x s.
Item given to ye Princes Servaunt*es* the xvij^th day of Iuly   xx s. 40
...

1/ much blamed: *for* is much blamed   16/ It: *in display script*

Item given to the kinge*s* players   xx s.

...

f 93v

...   5

Item paid the xix^th Day of August for two boat*es* when

m*aste*r Mayor rode the ffranchises of the Citie   iij s.

Item given to the Musitions at the same tyme   v s.

...

10

Keykeepers' Accounts   OCA: P.4.1

f 115   *(Bonds and bills not summed)*

...

One bonde of mr Gibbins for the scutchins

...   15

All Saints Churchwardens' Accounts   ORO: PAR 189/4/F1/1, item 1

single mb   *(23 April 1606–8 April 1607) (Receipts)*

...

Item for hockinge mony   l s. 20

...

St Aldate Churchwardens' Accounts

ORO: DD Par. Oxford St Aldate c.16/13

mb [1]   *(Rendered in April 1607) (Receipts)*   25

...

Item Receyved vpon Maye daie and at Hocktyde   iij li. vj s. iiij d.

Item Receyved at Whitsontyde   xxx s.

...

30

St Martin Churchwardens' Accounts   ORO: PAR 207/4/F1/1, item 105

single mb   *(Rendered 8 April 1607) (Receipts)*

...

Item in the boxe at hocketide   xxxij s. ix d.

...   35

7/ m*aste*r Mayor: *Richard Bryan*
20/ hockinge: *Hocktide was 28–9 April 1606*
27, 34/ Hocktyde, hocketide: *28–9 April 1606*
28/ Whitsontyde: *8–14 June 1606*

St Mary Magdalen Churchwardens' Accounts   ORO: PAR 208/4/F1/39
single mb   *(Rendered 7 April 1607) (Receipts)*
…

Item Receued at hoctyde all thinges beinge discharged   xxxiij s.
Item Rec*eued* at Whitsonetyde all thinges beinge discharged   iij li. xij d.   5
…

St Michael at the North Gate Churchwardens' Accounts
ORO: PAR 211/4/F1/3, item 169
mb [1]   *(Rendered 9 April 1607) (Receipts)*   10
…

Item receaved at Hocktyde, all thing*es* beinge Discharged   xxx s.
…

St Peter in the East Churchwardens' Accounts   ORO: PAR 213/4/F1/2   15
single mb   *(23 April 1606–10 April 1607) (Receipts)*
…

Item recevid for hockinge   xxxiiij s.
…

                                                                                        20
St Peter le Bailey Churchwardens' Accounts   ORO: PAR 214/4/F1/53
single mb   *(Rendered 12 April 1607) (Receipts)*
…

Item gotten at may daye at hoctyde and at our suppers
[all thinges beinge discharged]   xxxiij s.   25
…

1606–7
Christ Church Computi   ChCh Arch: iii.c.8(a.)
mb 3d   30
…

Et in expens*is* Comediar*um* et Tragediar*um* hoc a*nno* fact*arum*   n*il* li.
…

Christ Church Battells Books   ChCh Arch: x(i).c.43   35
f 26   *(6–12 February) (Extra expenses)*
…

…the Musitians vij li. x s.…
…

4, 12, 24/ hoctyde, Hocktyde: *28–9 April 1606*   18/ hockinge: *Hocktide was 28–9 April 1606*
5/ Whitsonetyde: *8–14 June 1606*

Magdalen College Draft Libri Computi   MC Arch: LCD/2
f 142   *(Repairs)*

…

pro expens*is* spectaculoru*m* habitis hoc anno   22 li. 19 s. 8 d. ob.

…   5

(Internal and external payments)
Musicis in festo Bursarioru*m*   0 5 s. 0 0

…

Buccinatoribus domin*orum* Oxoni*æ* et Compton in regardo   0 5 s. 0 0   10

…

Merton College Bursars' Accounts   MCR: 3.1
f 109v   *(21 November–20 March)* *(External expenses)*

15

…Musicis ex co*n*se*n*su 6 s. 8 d. in ipsor*um* cæna*m* 2 s.…

…

New College Bursars' Accounts   NC Arch: 7600
mb 8   *(25 December–25 March)* *(Internal expenses)*   20

…

…So*lutum* buccinatoribus in regardijs iij s.
So*lutum* musicis oppidanis vj s. viij d.…

…

25

The Queen's College Long Rolls   QC Arch: LRA
f 32 col 2*   *(7 July–7 July)* *(External expenses)*

…

Item Tibicin[is]*ibus*   10 s.

…   30

Item Mauriceo Tibicen*i*   1 s. 6 d.

…

St John's College Computus Hebdomalis   SJC Arch: Acc.v.E.4
f 34   *(16–22 February)*   35

…

Set on for ye Musitions. iij li. ij s.

…

f 34v   *(23 February–1 March)*   40

…

Set on for the ffidler*es* xix s. ij d.

…

Audited Corporation Accounts OCA: P.5.2
f 98 *(Chamberlains' payments)*

…

Item given by master mayor the fourteenth of August to
the Queenes Players   xx s. 5

…

Item given to the Kinges players the vijᵗʰ day of september   xx s.

…

f 98v   10

…

Item paid for Wine for the Waytes of the Cytie the vᵗʰ
of August   xvj d.

15

Keykeepers' Accounts OCA: P.4.1
f 118v *(Bonds and bills not summed)*

…

One band of Gybbyns for the scutchins

20

St Aldate Churchwardens' Accounts
ORO: DD Par. Oxford St Aldate c.16/14
single mb *(Rendered April 1608) (Receipts)*

…

Item receaved Clere at Whitsontide   vj li. xiij s. iiij d. 25

…

St Michael at the North Gate Churchwardens' Accounts
ORO: PAR 211/4/F1/3, item 170
mb [1] *(Rendered 31 March 1608) (Receipts)*   30

…

Item receaved at Hocktyde, All thinges being discharged   xxviij s.

…

St Peter in the East Churchwardens' Accounts ORO: PAR 213/4/F1/2 35
single mb *(10 April 1607–31 March 1608) (Receipts)*

…

Item Receyved at hoctide   xxxij s.

…

4/ master mayor: *Richard Good*   32, 38/ Hocktyde, hoctide: *13–14 April 1607*
25/ Whitsontide: *24–30 May 1607*

St Peter le Bailey Churchwardens' Accounts   ORO: PAR 214/4/F1/54
mb [1]   *(Rendered 2 April 1608)*   *(Receipts)*

…

Item Rec*eived* at Hocktid and Whitsontyd all expences paied   xxiiij s.

…   5

1607–8
All Souls College Bursars' Accounts   Bodl.: MS. D.D. All Souls c.289
mb 14   *(2 November–2 November)*   *(Rewards)*

…   10

Et de v s. to the Kinges trumpeters

…

Christ Church Disbursements   ChCh Arch: xii.b.52
f 28   *(25 December–25 March)*   15

…

Comedyes &   Ianuarij. 29. To the Censors ⌈towardes⌉ [for] defrayinge
trag*edies.*   of the charge of a Comedy   vj li. xij s. iiij d.
                    (signed)   Simon Iucks
                    (signed)   Willi*am* Osbolston.   20

…

Christ Church Computi   ChCh Arch: iii.c.8(b.)
mb 3d

…   25

Et in expens*is* Com*a*ediar*um* et Tragediar*um* hoc A*n*no
fact*arum* vt p*atet* ib*ide*m   vj li. xij s. iiij d.

…

Christ Church Battells Books   ChCh Arch: x(i).c.44   30
f 26   *(12–18 February)*   *(Extra expenses)*

…

…to the Musitians & set on. vij li. vij s.…

…
                                                                                          35

Lincoln College Calculus 1607–8   LC Arch
f 5*   *(7 December–6 March)*

            festu*m* purificationis Mariae   xviij d.

…   40

4/ Hocktid: *13–14 April 1607*   18/ the: t *written over* C
4/ Whitsontyd: *24–30 May 1607*

musitia*ns*   domus vij s. j d.

...

f 14   *(Internal expenses)*

...   5

Ite*m* for ye Kings trumpeters   x s.

...

Magdalen College Draft Libri Computi   MC Arch: LCD/2

f 149v   *(Internal and external payments)*   10

...

Buccinatoribus D*o*mini Regis in regardo   10 s.

...

f 150   15

...

Musicis in festo Bursario*rum*   5 s.

...

Merton College Bursars' Accounts   MCR: 3.1   20

f 115v   *(20 November–18 March)* *(External expenses)*

...Musicis ex consensu vj s. viij d: in ipso*rum* caena*m* ex consensu
xviij d....
...   25

New College Bursars' Accounts   NC Arch: 7603

mb 6   *(25 December–25 March)* *(Internal expenses)*

...

...So*lutum* musicis oppidanis in regard*is* 6 s. 8 d.   30

(25 March–24 June)
...So*lutum* to a set of trumpeters 3 s.

(24 June–29 September)   35
...So*lutum* to the king*es* trumpeters in regardijs .6 s....

...

12/ Buccinatoribus: ib *written over* is

The Queen's College Long Rolls   QC Arch: LRA
f 35 col 1*   *(7 July–7 July)   (External expenses)*

...

Item buccinatoribus de Oxonia   10 s.

...   5

St John's College Computus Hebdomalis   SJC Arch: Acc.v.E.4
f 46v   *(18–24 January)*

...

Set on for Musick   7 s. 10

...

f 48*   *(22–8 February)*

...

Set on for an end of our Christmas sportes   vj li. iij s. 15

...

f 48v   *(14–20 March)*

...

Set on for ye Musitians.   iij li. x s. 20

...

St John's College Christmas Prince   SJC Library: MS 52
pp 5–10*   *(Election of the Prince)*

25

A true, and faithfull relation of the risinge, and fall of THOMAS
TVCKER Prince of Alba Fortunata, Lord St Iohns &ct. With all
the Occurrents which happened through-out his whole Domination

It hapned in the yeare of our Lord 1607, the 31 of October, beinge All-Sayntes 30
Eue, that at night à fier was made in the Hall of St Iohn Baptist's Colledge in
Oxon., accordinge to the custome, & statut's of the same place; at which time
the whole companye or most parte of the Studentes of the same house mette
toogether to beginne their Christmas, of which somme came to see sports to
witte the Seniors as well Graduates, as vnder-graduates, others to make sport's, 35
viz Studentes of the seconde yeare whom they call Poulderling's, others to make
sporte withall of this last sorte were they whome they call Fresh-menn Punies
of the first yeare, who are by no meanes admitted to be agent's or behoulders of
those sports, before themselues haue binne patient perfourmers of them. But
(as it often falleth out), the Freshmen, or patient's, thinkinge the Poulderling's 40
or Agentes too buysie and nimble, They them too dull and backwarde, jn theyr
duety, the standers by findinge both of them too forwarde & violente, the

sportes for that night for feare of tumultes, [for] weare broken vpp, euerye
mann betakinge himselfe to his reste.

The next night followinge beinge the feast of All-sayntes at nighte they
mett agayne together; And wheras yt was hoped à night*es* sleepe would haue
somewhat abated theyr rage, it contrarywise sett a greater edge on theyr furye,   5
they hauinge all this while but consulted how to gett more strength on agaynst
another, and consequently to breed newe quarrells and contradictions, jn so
much that the strife & contentions of youthes & Children*n* had like to haue
sett Men*n* together by the eares, to the vtter annihilatinge of all Christmas
sportes, for the whole yeare followinge.   10

Wherfore for the auoydinge both the one, and the other, some who studied
the quiet of all mentioned the choosinge of a Christmas Lord, or Prince of the
Revells, who should haue authorytie both to appoynt & moderate all such
games, and pastimes as should ensue, & to pun*n*ishe all offenders w*h*ich should
any way hinder or interrupte the free & quiet passage of any auntient and   15
allowed sporte.

This motion (for that the person of a Prince or Lorde of the Revells had
not bin*n*e knowen amongst them for thirty | yeares before, & so consequentlye
the danger, charge, and trouble of such iestinge was cleane forgotten*n*) was
pr*e*sentlye allowed, and greedilye apprehended of all; Wher vpon 13 of the   20
senior-Vndergraduates (7 of the bodye of the House, & 6 Com*m*oners, Elector's
in such à case) w*i*thdrew themselues into the Parlor, where after longe debatinge
whether they should chouse a Graduate, or an Vnder-Graduate, thinkinge the
former would not vouchsafe to vndertake yt at theyre appoyn*n*tmentes, ye
later should not be vpheld & backed as yt was meete & necessary for such a   25
place, they came forth rather to make triall what would be don*n*e, then to
resolue what should be don*n*e: And therfore at their first entrance into the
Hall meetinge S*i*r Towse a younge man*n* (as they thought) fitt for the choyse,
they layed handes on him, and by maine strength liftinge him vpp viua voce
pronounced him Lord. But hee as st$_\wedge$⌈r⌉ongelye refusinge the place, as they   30
violentlye thrust it vpon him, shewinge w*i*th all reasons why hee could by no
meanes vnder-goe such a charge they gott onlye this good by their first attempt,
that they vnderstood heer-by how that ye whole Colledge was rather willinge
a Senior Batchelour at least, yf not a junior Ma*ste*r should be chosen in to the
place, rather then any Vndergraduate; because they would rather an earnest   35
sporte, then à scoffinge jest should be made of it. Wherfore the Elector's
retourninge againe jn to the Parlor & shuttinge the dore close vpon themselues
beganne more seriously to consult of the matter; and findinge some vnable,
some vnwillinge to take the place, at length they concluded to make the 2
assay, but w*i*th more formalitie, and deliberation, resoluinge, yf they were not   40
now seconded of all handes, to meddle no more w*i*th yt. Wherfore entringe ye
second time in to the Hall they desired one of the 10 Seniors & one of the

Deanes of the Colledge to hould the Scrutinye and the Vice-Præsident to sitt by
as ouer seer; who willingly harkninge to their request sate all 3 downe at the
highe Table; Then the Electors went vp one by one in senioritye to giue. their
voyce by writinge. In the meane time there was great expectation who should
bee the Mann: Somme in ye lower ende of the Hall to make sport had theyr   5
Names loudest in their mouthes, whome they least thought of jn their mindes,
& whome they [kw] knewe should come I shortest of the place. At length all
the voyces beinge giuen, and, accordinge to the custome, the Scrutinie at large
beinge burned, the Vice-præsident with the rest stoode vpp, and out of the
abstract the Deane read distinctly in the hearinge of all present as followeth   10
        Nominantur in hoc Scrutinio duo quorum
        ⎧ 1us Ioannes Towse, habet suffragia sex.
        ⎩ 2us Thomas Tucker, habet suffragia septem./
These wordes were not out of his mouthe, before à generall and loud ˄⌈crie⌉
was made of Tucker, Tucker, Viuat, Viuat, &ct. After which all the younger   15
sorte ranne forth of the Colledge crieinge the same jn the street's: Which Sir
Tucker, beinge then howsde not farr from the Colledge, ouer hearinge, kept
himself close till the companye were past, and then as soone and secretly as he
could gott him to his Chamber; Where (after he had binne longe sought for
abroad in the Towne, and at home jn ye Colledge, haste, and desire out-   20
runninge it self, and seekinge there last where it might first finde) He was in
à manner surprised, and more by violence, then any will of his owne taken
vpp, and with continuall and ioyfull outcries, carried about ye Hall, and so
backe to his Chamber, as his owne request was; where for yat night he rested
dismissinge ye Company, and desiringe some time to thinke of their loues and 25
goodwill, and to consider of his owne charge and place

(The Prince's private installation)
    About 3 or 4 dayes after, on the 5 of Nouember the Lord Elect with the
Batchelours, and some of the Senior Vnder-graduates came into ye Hall where 30
euery mann beinge seated in his order many speaches were made by diuerse of
diuerse matters, some commendinge a monarchicall state of Gouermente, and
ye sometimes suddayne necessitye of Dictators, others discommendinge both:
Some agayne extollinge sportes and réuell's, others mainely disallowinge
them, all of them drawinge some conclusion concerninge ye like or dislike of 35
ye gouerment newly begunne, and like for a little space to continue amongst
them; In ye ende the Lord Elect himselfe to conclude all, deliuered his owne
minde jn manner followinge
        Quæ beneficia (Viri Electores clarissimi) plus difficultatis atque oneris
        apportant collocata, quam debitè administrata poterunt honoris, cautè   40
        magis primo jn limine credo excipienda quam aùt immensæ dignitatis
        expectatione appetenda auidè, aut boni incogniti cæco appetitu

apprehendenda temere. Quoru*m* jn albo (Electores conscripti) cu*m*
sempèr dignitates istiusmodi seriò retulerim, Vos (pace dica*m* vestræ
diligentiæ) non tàm mihi videmini gratias debere expectare, quà*m* ipse
istud onus suscepturus videor promereri. Na*m* illud demùm gratijs
excipitur beneficiu*m*, (pro temporu*m* ratione loquor.) quod nec   5
sollicitudo | vrget, nec officiu*m*. Infinitæ autèm adèo sunt anxietates
quæ vel istam dominatus ἀνατύπωσιν circumcingunt, vt pauci
velint ipsas cu*m* dominatu lubentèr amplecti, nulli possint euitare,
nulli sustinere. Na*m* vbi veri imperij facies est repræsentanda,
expectanda sempèr est aliqua curaru*m* proportio. Veru*m* cùm dignitas   10
Electoria, amicitia suffragatoria, populi applausus, o*mnium* consensus
Democratiæ tollendæ causâ ad primatum euocauerint, lubens animi
nostri strenuè renuentis temperabo impetu*m*, et sedulò impenda*m*
curam, vt Reip*ublicæ* (si vobis minùs possim singulis) totj satisfacia*m*.
Hic ego non ità existimo opportunu*m*, progressuu*m* nostroru*m*   15
aduersarijs, cura*m* imperij promiscuam et jndigestam collaudantib*us*
respondere, aut stat*us* Monarchici necessitate*m* efferentib*us* assentari:
Disceptationu*m* vestraru*m* non accessi judex, accersor jmperator;
Amori vestro (Viri nobis adprimè chari) lubens tribuo gloriæ nostræ
ortu*m*, progressu*m* augustu*m* atq*ue* gloriosum à vobis ex officio vestro   20
exigere, prætèr amore*m* nostrum fore no*n* arbitror. Tyrannidem
non profiteor, jmperiu*m* exercebo. Cujus fæliciores processus vt
promoueantur, atq*ue* indiès stabiliantur æris magìs quàm oris debetis
esse prodigi. Quarè primitias amoris, atq*ue* officij vestri statuo extemplò
exigendas, nè aut ipse sine authoritate imperare, aut imperium sinè   25
gloriâ capessisse videar. Πολιτείαν Atheniensem sequimur, cujus ad
normam Ego ad munus regiu*m* jàm suffectus, Mineruæ, Vulcano et
Prometheo sacra cu*m* ludorum Curatorib*us* prò moris vsu, primâ
meâ in his sacris authoritate fieri curabo. Interìm vero (Viri nostrâ
authoritate adhùc majores) juxtà prædictæ Reipublicæ jmagine*m*   30
choragos, seù adjutores desidero, qui no*n* tantùm ludis præponantur,
sed et liberalitate prò opu*m* ratione in Rejpublicæ impensas vtentes,
ex ære publico præmia parti*m* proponant, partìm de suo jnsumant,
hoc nomine quod illoru*m* sint præfecti. Quæ alia vestri sunt officij,
moniti præstabitis, quæ amoris, vltrò (vtì spero) offeretis.   35

This was counted sufficient for his priuate jnstallmente, but w*i*thall it was
thought necessary y*a*t some more publicke notice hereof should be giuen to
the whole Vniuersitie, with more solemnitie, and better fashion; yet before
they would venter to publish their priuate jntendements, they were desirous
to knowe what authoritie & jurisdiction would be graunted them, what   40

14/ totj: *corrected from* totus

money allowed them towards the better goinge thorough with that they had begun*n*e, And not longe after the | whole company of the Batchelours sent 2 bills to the *Maste*rs fire, ye one crauinge duety and alleageance, ye other money & maintenance, jn man*n*er & forme followinge:

The coppye of a Bill sent by ye Lord Elect, and ye whole company of   5
ye Batchelours to ye *Maste*rs fire, crauinge their duety, and alleageance
Not doubtinge of those ceremonious and outward duetyes, which your selues (for example sake) will perfourme, Wee Thomas Tucker, with ye rest of ye Bacchelours are bold to entreat, but as Thomas Lord Elect with ye rest of our Councell are ready to expect, that no Tutor, or Officer whatsoeuer, shall at any   10
time, or vpon any occasion jntermeddle, or partake with any Scholler, or youth whatsoeuer, but leauinge all matters to the discretion of our selues, stand to those censures and judgementes [wich] which Wee shall giue of all offenders y*a*t are vnder our gouer*n*mente in causes appertaininge to our gouernment; Allwayes promisinge a carefull readinesse, to see schollerlike exercise perfourmed,   15
and orderly quietnesse mayntained in all sortes; This as Wee promise for our owne partes, so Wee would willingly desire y*a*t you should promise the perfourmance of ye rest for your partes, accordinge to y*a*t bountye & loue which allready you haue shewed Vs

Yours   20
Thomas Tucker

Ioseph Fletcher	Thomas Downer
Iohn Smith	Rouland Iuxon
Richard Baylye	Iohn Huckstepp
Richard Holbrooke	Iames Bearblocke 25
Iohn Towse	Iohn English

This Bill subscribed with all their handes was seene & allowed by all the *Maste*rs, who promised rather more then lesse, then that which was demaunded. But concerninge ye other Bill for Subsidyes it was answered, that it was not in their power to graunt it without ye Præsident, whose com*m*inge [w]home was   30
euery day expected: against which time it was prouided, and deliuered vnto him; Who, together with the 10 Seniors, was loath to graunt any thinge till they were certified what sportes should bee, of what quality, & charge, that so they might ye better proportion ye one to ye other, ye meanes to the matter: They were allso willinge to knowe what particular Men*n* would take vpon   35
them ye care of furnishinge particular nightes For they would by no meanes relye vpon generall promises | because they were not ignorant how that which concerneth all in generall is by no man*n* in speciall regarded. Wherfore they beinge somewhat allthough not fully satisfied in their [mindes] Demaundes by some of ye *Maste*rs, whom they seemed [wholly] ⌈cheefly⌉ to trust with ye   40
whole businesse the Bill was againe perused, and euery man ceazed in manner and forme followinge

(Subsidies granted)

      The coppye of an auncient Act for taxes and subsidyes made in ye
      raygne of our Prædecessor of famous memorye in this Parliament,
      held in aula regni, ye vjth of Nouember 1577. and now for Our self
      newly ratified and published, anno regni j° Nouembris 7°. 1607.   5
Because all louinge & loyall Subjects, doe owe not onely themselues, but allso
their landes, liuinges, goodes, and what soeuer they call theirs, to ye good of ye
Commonwealth, and estate, vnder which they peaceably enjoy all. It is farther
enacted that no mann dissemble his estate, or hide his abilitye, but be willinge
at all times to pay such duetyes, taxes, and subsidies as shall be lawfully   10
demaunded, & thought reasonable without ye hinderance of his owne estate,
vpon payne of forfettinge himself, and his goodes whatsoeuer.

...

pp 11–13*   *(Privy seals sent forth)*   15
...

Though ye whole company had thus largely contributed towards ye ensuinge
sports, yet it was found that when all thinges necessary should be layed
toogether a great somme of money would be wantinge; and therfor a course
was thought vpon of sendinge out priuie Seales to able & willinge Gentlemenn 20
which had binne sometimes Fellowes or Commoners of ye Colledge, yat it
would please them to better ye stocke, and out of their goodwill contribute
somwhat towardes ye Princes Reuelles. ye forme of this writt was in manner
followinge

             The Superscription   25
      To our trustye, and welbeloued, N: N
          Knight, or Esquier |

Trusty and welbeloued wee greet you well. Allthough there bee nothinge
more against our minde then to be drawne into any course that may burden 30
our loyall Subjects, Yet such is our estate, at this time in regard of ye great
and vrgent occasions fallinge and growinge dayly vpon vs, without time or
respiration, as wee shalbe forced præsently to disburse greater sommes of
money then is possible for vs to prouide by any ordinarye meanes, or to
want without great præjudice. Seing as well ye fame of our Kingdome in ye 35
entertaynment of forraine Princes & Embassadours, as ye safetie of our owne
person, and ye whole Common wealth for the præuentinge of warrs and
tumultes, likely to ensue, consisteth in ye wealth of our coffers, as much as in
any one meanes whatsoeuer. In which consideration, wee thinke it needlesse
to vse any more argumentes from such a Prince to such a Subiect, but yat as 40

25–7/ The Superscription ... Esquier: *followed by illustration of Prince's seal, top of p 12 in* MS

our necessitie is ye only cause of our request, so your loue, and duety must be
ye cheife motiue of your ready perfourmance and helpe in furnishinge these our
wantes, not only with your person, but with your purse in your owne absence;
A matter wherof we make no doubt, beinge fully perswaded of your seruice &
fidelitie. Therfore our will and pleasure is that præsently vpon ye receipt hereof   5
you cause a somme of money accordinge to your abilitie, & greatnesse of your
loue, to bee deliuered to Thomas Clarke whom we haue appointed to be our
Collector in ye County⌈e⌉ of Middlesex; the lone wherof only we desire to be
vntill ye next great yeare of Plato, then to be jmmediatly repayd by vs or our
successors to you or your Assignes yat shall then demaund it.   10

   Giuen vnder our priuye Seale at our Pallace of St | Iohns in Oxen', the
seuenth of December in the first yeare of our rayne 1607.

   The names of those who were serued with this writt, and who most
willingly obeyed vpon the receipt *thereof, were these followinge.

*Others were
serued, and
bragd of it as
though they
had giuen but
sent nothing

Sir Robert Chamberlen who contributed	ij li.	Mr Lydall	xx s.	15
Sir William Paddye	iij li.	Mr Barklye	xx s.	
Sir George Wright	xx s.	Mr Kiete	xx s.	
Master Doctor Perin	xx s.	Mr Hugh, May	xx s.	
Master Doctor Searchfield	xx s.	Mr Martin	x s.	
Master Doctor Warner	x s.	Mr Wilmont	x s.	20
Mr Hawlye	xx s.	Mr Bowstred	x s.	
Mr Whitlock	xxx s.			

Summa xvj li. x s.

   For all these Subsidies at home, and helpes abroad, yet it was founde yat in
ye ende there would rather be want (as jndeed it hapned) then any superfluitye;   25
and therfore ye Prince tooke order with the Bowsers to send out warrantes
to all ye Tenantes & other frendes of ye Colledge, yat they should send in
extraordinary prouision against euery Feast, which accordingly was perfourmed;
Some sendinge money, some Wine, some Venison, some other prouision, euery
one accordinge to his abilitye   30

   All thinges beinge thus sufficiently (as it was thought) prouided for; ye
Councell table, with ye Lord himself mett together to nominate Officers, &
to appoynt the day of ye Princes publike installment which was agreed should
be on St Andrews day at night; because at that time ye Colledge allso was to
chouse their new officers for ye yeare followinge   35

   Now for yat they would not playnely & barely jnstall him without any
farther ceremonies, it was thought fitt that his whole ensuinge Regiment (for
goode lucke sake) should be consecrated to ye Deitie of Fortune, as ye sole
Mistres & Patronesse of his estate, and therfore a Schollerlike deuise called
Ara Fortunæ was prouided for his installment; which was perfourmed in   40
manner and forme followinge.

40–1/ in manner ... followinge: Ara Fortunae, pp 14–26 in ms pp 26–39*

…

    This Showe by our selues was not thought worthye of a stage or scaffoldes, and therfore after supper ye tables were onlye sett together, which was not done without great toyle & difficullty by reason of ye great multitude of people   5 (which by ye default of ye Dore-keepers, and diuers others, euery mann bringinge in his freindes) had fild ye Hall before wee thought of it. But for all this it beganne before 8 of clock, and was well liked by ye whole audience, who, how vnrulye so euer they meante to bee afterwardes, resolued I thinke at first with their good applause and quiet behauiour to drawe vs on so farr as   10 Wee should not bee able to retourne backwardes without shame & discreditt. They gaue vs at ye ende 4 seuerall & generall plaudites; at ye 2 wherof ye Canopie which hunge ouer ye Altare of Fortune (as it had binne frighted with ye noise, or meante to signifie that 2 plaudites were as much as it deserued) suddenly fell downe; but it was cleanly supported by some of ye standers by   15 till ye Company was voyded, yat none but our selues tooke notice of it

    Some vpon ye sight of this Showe, (for ye better ennoblinge of his person, and drawinge his pedigree euen from ye Godes because the Princes name was Tucker, and ye last Prince before him was Dr Case) made this conceipt yat Casus et Fortuna genuerunt Τυχερον Principem Fortunatum, So ye one his   20 Father, and ye other his Mother;

    Another accident worthy obseruation, (and which was allso then obserued) was yat ye Foole carelesly sittinge downe at ye Princes feete brake [in] his staff in ye midst; whence Wee could not but directly gather a verye ill omen, yat ye default | and follye of some woulde bee ye very breaknecke of our ensueinge   25 sports, which how it fell out, I leaue to the censures of others; our selues (I am sure) were guilty to our selues of many weaknesses and faultes, ye number whereof [weah] were encreased by ye crossinge vntowardnesse, and backwardnesse of diuers of ye Princes neerest followers, nay ye Prince himself had some weaknesses which did much præiudice his state, whereof ye cheifest   30 weere his opennesse, and familiaritye with all sortes, beinge vnwillinge to displease any, yet not able to please all But to proceede; On St Thomas day at night ye Officers before elect were solemnly proclaimed by a Sergeant at armes, and an Herauld, ye trompetts soundinge beetwixt euery title. This Proclamation after it was read, was for a time hunge up in ye Hall, yat euery man might ye   35 better vnderstande ye qualitie of his owne place, and they yat were of lower, or no place might learne what duety to perfourme to others;

           The manner wherof was as followeth |

3/ This Showe: *Ara Fortunae*
39/ The manner … followeth: *heraldic sketch precedes proclamation of Prince and officers, top of p 28 in* MS

(Proclamation of the Prince and officers)

Whereas by ye contagious poyson, and spreadinge malice of some ill disposed
persons, hath binne threatned, not onelye ye daunger of subuertinge peaceable
& orderlye proceedinges, but ye allmost vtter annihilatinge of auncient &
laudable customes, It hath binne thought conuenient, or rather absolutely   5
necessarye for ye auoydinge of a most daungerous ensuinge Anarchie a more
setled order of gouerment for the better safetye of all well meaninge Subiects,
and curbinge of discontented, headstronge persons should bee established. And
whereas through wante of good lawes by wise & discreet Magistrates to bee
duely and truely executed, a giddye conceipt hath posses't ye mindes of manye   10
turbulent spirites, of endueringe no superiour, hardly an æquall whereby ye
Commonwealth [might] might growe to bee a manye-headed monster. It
hath binne prouided by ye staide and mature deliberations of well experienc't
gouernours | and prouident Counsellours, yat one whose highe desert's might
answere his highe aduauncement should bee sett ouer all to ye rulinge and   15
directinge of all; Therefore by these præsentes bee it knowne vnto all of what
estate or condicion soeuer whome it shall concerne yat Thomas Tucker an
honorable wise & learned Gentlemann to ye great comeforte of ye weale-
publique from hence-forth to be reputed, taken and obayed for ye true, onely
& vndoubted Monarche of this reuellinge Climate, whome ye generall consent   20
and ioynte approbation of ye whole Common-wealth hath inuested and
crowned with these honours & titles followinge:

   The most magnificent, and renowned Thomas, by ye fauour of
   Fortune, Prince of Alba Fortunata, Lord St Iohns; high Regent of ye
   Hall, Duke of St Giles, Marquesse of Magdalens, Landgraue of ye   25
   Groue, County Palatine of ye Cloisters cheife Bailiffe of ye Beaumonts,
   high Ruler of Rome, Maister of the Mannor of *Waltham, Gouernour
   of Gloster greene, Sole Commaunder of all Tiltes, Turneaments, and
   Triumphes, Super-intendent in all Solemnities whatsoeuer |

Now because they whom ye vnknowne cares, & vnweildie burdens of a   30
sole regiment shall relie vpon, neede extraordinary helpe in yeir more then
ordinarye affaires, Hee hath as well for ye better discharge, & ease of those
royall duetyes (as it were) which attend on his place, as for ye auoidinge ye
odious & ingratefull suspition of a single dominion, and priuate Tyrannye,
selected and chosen vnto himself a graue, and learned assistance both for   35
Councell and gouernment, whom, and euery of which, his Princely will is
shall in yeir seuerall places & dignities bee both honored and obeid, with no
lesse respect and obseruance then if himself were there præsent in person.
And that carelesse ignorance may bee no lawfull excuse for ye breach of his
will therin hee hath appointed their seuerall names, and titles, with their   40

® *Walton

22/ these honours … followinge: *heraldic sketch precedes proclamation of Prince's title, middle of p 29 in* MS

.

subordinate Officers and Deputies to be signified & proclaimed to all his
louinge and leige Subjects, in manner followinge

The right Gracious Iohn Duke of Groue-land, Earle de Bello-Monte, Baron
Smith, cheife Ranger of ye Wood's & Forrest's, great Master of ye Princes   5
game, Hath for his subordinate Officers.
    Sir Frauncis Hudson, Keeper of ye Parkes, & Warder of ye Warrens.
    Sir Thomas Grice, Forrester, & Sargeaunt of ye Wood-howse. |

The right honourable Rowland Lord Iuxon, Lord Chauncelour, Keeper of ye   10
great Seale, Signer of all publicke Charters, allower of all Priuiledges, hath for
his subordinate Officers.
    Sir William Dickenson, Master of ye Requests, & ye Princes
    Remembrances;
    Sir Owen Vertue, Clarke of ye Signet, and Chafer of Waxe.   15

The right honourable Thomas Lord Downer, Lord high Treasurer Receauer
generall of all Rents, Reuenewes, Subsidies, belonginge by Nature, custome, or
accident to ye Prince; ye great Payemaster of all necessary charges appertayninge
to ye Court hath for his subordinate Officers.   20
    Sir Iohn Williamson Steward of ye Howsehold, Disburser for ye Familye.
    Sir Christopher Wrenn Cofferer, and Clarke of ye Exchequer |

The right honourable Ioseph Lord Fletcher, Lord high Admirall: great
Commaunder of all ye narrow seas, floods, and passages; Suruayer of ye   25
Nauye, Mayster of ye Ordinance, hath for his subordinate Officers.
    Sir Stephan Angier, Warden of ye Cinque Port's, and Victualer of ye Fleet;
    Sir Anthony Steeuens Captayne of ye Guarde

The right honourable Richard Lord Baylie, Lord high Marshall, Præsident of   30
all Tiltes, and Turneament's, Commander in all Triumphes, Suppressor of
suddayne tumultes, Supervisor of all games, and publique pastimes, hath for
his subordinate Officers.
    Sir William Blagroue Master of ye Reuells:
    Sir Iohn Hungerford, Knight Marshall, seuere Commaunder of ye Wayes   35
    for ye Princes passage |

The right honourable Iohn Lord Towse, Lord high Chamberlayne, Purueior
for ye [Lords] Princes pallace; Ouerseer of all feast's, and banquet's, furnisher
of all Chamber's, and Galleries, Examiner of all priuate pastimes, hath for   40

2/ in manner followinge: *heraldic sketches precede each of the 9 proclamations of officers' titles, pp 30–4 in* MS

his subordinate Officers,
  Sir Richard Swinerton }
  Sir William Cheyney   } ye Princes Ward's & Squier's of his bodye.
  Mr Edward Cooper, Groome-Porter.

The right honourable Richard Lord Holbrooke Comptroller generall cheife
ouer-seer of all Purseauantes, Orderer of all howsehold Seruauntes hath for
his subordinate officers
  Sir Thomas Stanley } Sergeauntes at Armes, & Gentlemen
  Mr Iohn Alford   } Vshers ∧⌈to ye Prince⌉.
  Mr Brian Nailor, Master of ye Robes of state, Keeper of ye Wardropp, and
Surveior of ye Liueries |

The right honourable Iames Lord Berbloke, principall Secretarye, Lord priuye
Seale, designer of all Embasies Drawer of all Edictes and Letters, Scribe to ye
State, hath for his subordinate Officers,
  Sir Thomas Clarke Master of ye Roles & Prothonotarye
  Mr Marcheaumount Nedham Clarke of ye Councell-Table

The right honourable Iohn Lord English, Lord Cheife-Iustice Examener of
all causes capitall; Sessor vpon life & death, Iudge of controuersies criminall,
hath for his subordinate Officers
  Sir Iohn Alder, Attourney generall, & ye Princes Sollicitor
  Mr Iohn Sackevile Baylife Erraunt |

(Decrees and statutes)
  Now because good Gouernours with-out good lawes, carefull Magistrates
with-out wholesome Statutes, are like dumme (though paynted) Images, or
vnweapon'd Souldiers, Hee of his absolute authoritye, conferred vpon him in
ye late free Election, doth ratifie, and establish all such Decrees, and Statutes,
as Hee now findeth, wisely, and warely ordayned of his famous Prædecessor;
promisinge onelye by a full, and seueare execution to put life in their dead
remembrance, Addinge moreouer some few cautions to [.]bee obserued in his
ensuinge Triumphe, as followeth
First Wee will and commaund yat no Forreyner, or home-borne Subject, of
what estate, or condicion soeuer presume to disturbe Vs in our priuate Walkes,
and Galleries, much lesse to pester our Chamber of Præsence, either by
themselues or others, vpon perill of our displeasure and certaine imprisonment,
for ye night present; Which fault because it is too common, and very
præjudiciall to our State, Wee charge our Officers appointed for yat purpose
to see punnisht with all rigour & severitye respectinge no mans person, but
such as shall be thought necessarye and allowed by speciall Prærogatiue of
ye Prince himself

Secondly because lowlinesse, and vndervaluinge humilitie in the judgement
of ye Sage haue bin*n*e allwayes præfer'd before high pride & ouertoppinge
arrogance, wee thinke it most reasonable, y*a*t for ye better freedome of all
mens sight, and auoydinge ye abvse of engrossinge of our sportes, y*a*t the
meanest and lowest of our Subjects enjoy ye former places, y*a*t if they offende   5
they may bee easily ouer-look't by their Superiours, whom Wee will haue
stand behinde for ye same purpose vpon perill of displacinge, or loosinge
their hatt*es* if not yeir head's

Thirdly for pr*e*ventinge ye malice of detractinge tounges, and y*a*t Wee may   10
seeme to com*m*aund no thinge w*h*ich ye most parte of our Subject's shall not
bee most willinge to obserue, Wee will & strayghtly charge, y*a*t nothinge
either priuately or publickly shalbe perfourmed at w*h*ich there shall not bee
som*m*e, and perhaps just exception taken; w*i*thall vpon o*u*r Princely bountye,
licensinge them w*h*ich knowe least to except most   15

Fourthly out of o*u*r open*n* liberalitye wee graunt free libertye to all
wandringe Spies, & Knight's errant y*a*t shall visitt o*u*r Court to furnish
yemselues w*i*th any necessarye y*a*t themselues shall like, or first lay hand's
on: All-wayes prouided, y*a*t beinge forreiners, and jn a strange place, their   20
carriadge be cleanely & warye vpon payne of beeinge discried, & so taken
for plaine theeves, w*h*ich otherwise might passe for howse-hold purveiors,
& allowed taker's |

Fiftly because out of diuersities of opinion ye best may bee chosen, and y*a*t ye   25
multitude of objections most discouer trueth, Wee further will and com*m*aund,
that no man*n* com*m*e to any of o*u*r consultations w*i*thout some objection
readye; and that no two ᴀ⌈agree⌉ jn one and ye same opinion: but w*i*thall
warninge them y*a*t they be as willinge to be answered, as to oppose, vpon
perill of talkinge jdlely, & by consequence not to bee hearde   30

Six[l]tly because nothinge is more for ye enrichinge of a Kingdome, then
Merchandize & com*m*erce w*i*th other Nations; Bee it therefore enacted for
ye maintenaunce of ye same trade in veluet*es*, Satin's Sylkes Rashe, and other
Stuff*es* as fitt for tearinge, as fine for wearinge, y*a*t none of his Highenesse   35
Subject*es*, of what Degree or State soeuer com*m*inge to visitt his Court at
time of Revells, shall pr*e*sume to hinder or finde fault w*i*th nayles, tenter-
hookes, haspes-latches, splinter's, chinkes, or such like put in trust by his
Highnesse to teare out good clothes, and to keepe Markett*es* quicke, vnder
payne of beinge accounted miserable, and to base to followe ye Courte.   40
Prouided allwayes y*a*t no Subject be forced to such willfull prodigallitye
as to rente good clothes, if hee can*n* keepe them whole; any thinge to the
contrarye in this Act notw*i*thstandinge.

Seauenthly because it is farr from ye Princes purpose to ouer-burdenn any
of his louinge and leige People, or to take too much of any free or forwarde
spirite, readye to doe him all loyall and laudable seruice, Bee it therefore lawfull
for manye which shall freely, and of their owne accorde, without any constrainte,
or jnuitation, make their personall attendance at ye Princes Reuells, to see more   5
then they knowe, and to heare more then they vnderstand Yea, and (yf need be,
and yeir owne occasion so require) to vnderstand more then yei heare; that is
to say to mistake, and misconstrue any thinge accordinge to their owne will
and purpose, vpon [⟨.⟩] payne of beinge thought to judicious for ye one, and
to jngeniouse for ye other, and so consequently vnfitt to liue in this criticall,   10
and censorious age. Allwayes prouided that euery one may see and heare as
much as hee cann I vnderstand as much as hee is able, anythinge in this Statute
to the contrary not withstandinge

Eyghthly, and lastly, for yat ye Princes will and pleasure is that one Subject may   15
liue by an other, and yat ye greater and stronger sorte of People may not too
much wronge, and oppresse ye weaker, which hath from time to time bredd
much clamour, and lamantable outcryes, euen within his owne Pallace,
therefore for ye auoydinge of all such oppression, his Highnesse strayghtly
chargeth and commaundeth all such as at any time cannot gett in, to stande   20
without vpon paine of beinge thought foolish & desperate for attemptinge
more then is possible; Prouided allwayes yat no mann bee constrained to
comme so late that hee must needes be shutt out, or so soone yat he must
need's be thrust out: but that yei which are within may bee conueniently
prouided for, and they that be without may quietly prouide for themselues,   25
and not striue to enter by indirect meanes, as climebinge of wall's, breakinge of
windowes, and such like; when as ye doores, and gates euer doe, or shall lie
open for yem, All which his Highnesse will haue perfourmed vpon paine of
beinge troublesome to no purpose
  Giuen at our Manor of Whites-Hall   30
  December ye 21th, in ye first of our Raygne I

(The advancement of Henry Swinnarton)
The same night the Prince, with the rest of his Councell meetinge at the
high table in the Hall; a Bill was præferred by the Lord Treasurer for the   35
aduauncement of Mr Henery Swinartonn to ye [l] Earldomme of Cloyster-
sheere, and ye ouerseeinge of ye Princes great Librarye: what ye Particular
woordes of this Bill were is vncertaine; onlye it beinge subscribed with a Seruus
tibi deuotissimus. *Henricus* Swinartonn the Prince pervsinge it, was heard to
say, Seruus tibi deuotissimus, et tanta quærit? Are his woordes so lowely, and   40
his request so highe? Yet it beinge further prest for him by ye whole Councell,

---

31/ Raygne: *followed by sketch of crown, bottom of p 37 in* MS

who pleaded that it came vnto him by a kinde of right, and lineall descent, for
that his Chamber was directly vnder the Librarye and joyninge to ye Cloysters,
ye Prince at length graunted ye request, and his title was presently drawne by
ye Clarke of ye Councell-table, and pronounced in manner followinge

5

The right Honorable Henery Lord Swinartonn Earle of Cloister-Sheer Barronn
of ye Garden, cheife Master of ye Presse, and ouerseer of ye Princes great
Library hath for his Subordinate Officers
    Mr William Rippin Surveior of ye Walkes
    Mr Christopher Riley Corrector of ye Printe   10

(The Prince's service and attendance)
From this time forward, and not before, the Prince was thought fully to be
enstal'de, and ye forme of gouernement fully established, in-so-much that
none might or durst contradict any thinge which was appoynted by himself,   15
or any of his Officers:
The Holy-Dayes beinge now at hand his priuye-Chamber was prouided and
furnisht, wherein a Chayre of State was placed vpon a carpett with a cloth of
State hangde ouer it, newly made for ye same purpose.
On Christ-mas day in ye morninge he was attended on to prayers by ye whole 20
companye of ye Bacchelours, and some other's of his Gentlemenn Vshers bare
before him At dinner beinge sett downe in ye Hall at ye high table in ye Vice-
Præsident's place (for ye Præsident him-self was then allso present) hee was
serued with 20 dishes to a | Messe, all which were brought in by Gentlemenn
of ye Howse attired in his Guard's coat's, vsher'd in by ye Lord Comptroller, 25
and other Officers of ye Hall. The first messe was a Boar's Head which was
carried by ye tallest and lustiest of all ye Guard, before whom (as attendant's)
wente first, one attired in a horseman's coate with a Boars-speare in his hande,
next to him an other Hunts-man in greene with a bloody fauchion drawne;
next to him 2 Pages in tafatye Sarcenet each of yem with a messe of mustard,   30
next to whome came hee yat carried ye Boares-head crost with a greene silke
Scarfe, by which hunge ye emptye Scabbard of ye faulchion which was carried
before him; As yei ent'red ye Hall He sange this Christmas Caroll ye three last
verses of euerye Staffe beinge repeated after him by ye whole companye
    1.   The Boare is dead,   35
        Loe heare is his head,
           What mann could haue done more;
        Then his head of to strike
        Meleager like
           And bringe it as I doe before   40

4/ in manner followinge: *heraldic sketch precedes proclamation of Swinnarton's title, middle of p 38 in* MS

2.   He liuinge spoyled
    Where good-men toyled
        Which made kinde Ceres sorrye;
    But now dead and drawne,
    Is very good brawne,   5
        And here wee haue brought it for you.

3.   Then sett downe ye Swineyard,
    The foe to ye Vineyard,
        Lett Bacchus crowne his fall,
    Lett this Boares-head and mustard   10
    Stand for Pigg, Goose & Custard,
        And so you are welcomme all

At this time, as on all other Holy-Dayes, ye Princes allowed Musitions (which
were sent for from Readinge, because our owne Towne Musick had giuenn vs
the slipp, as yei vse to doe, at that time when wee had most need of them)   15
played all Dinner time, and allso at Supper; The Prince as ofte as he satt in ye
Hall was attended on by a Commoner, and Scholler of ye Colledge in tafaty
Sarcenett. After Supper there was a private Showe perfourmed in ye manner
of an Inter-lude, contayninge the order of ye Saturnall's, and shewinge the first
cause of Christmas-Candles, and in the ende there was an application made   20
to the Day, and Natiuitie of Christ. All which was perfourmed jn manner
followinge

pp 47–9
...   25
This shew was very well liked of our selves and the better ffirst, because itt
was the voluntary service of a younge youth Nexte, because there were no
straungers to trouble vs.

St Steevens day was past-over in silence, and so had St Iohns day also: butt   30
that some of the Princes honest neighbours of St. Giles's presented him with
a maske or morris which though it were but rudely performed, yet itt being
so freely | and lovingly profered, it could not but bee as lovingly received

The same nighte the twelve daies, were suddenly and as it were extempore   35
brought in, to offer their service to the [service] Prince, the holy-daies speaking
Latine and the working-daies English, the transition was this.
    Yee see these working-daies, they weare no satten.
    And I assure you, they can speake no Latten.

14/ Readinge: *Reading, Berkshire*
21–2/ jn manner followinge: Saturnalia, *pp 41–7 in* MS
26/ This shew: Saturnalia

> But if you please to stay a-while
> Some shepheard for them will chaunge the style.

After some few daunces the Prince, not much liking the sporte (for that most
of them were out both in there speeches and measures, having but thought
of this devise some few houres before) rose, & lefte the Hall, after whose   5
departure an honest fellow to breake of the sportes for that night, and to void
the Company made suddenly this Epilogue

> These daunces were *per*form'd of yore
> By many worthy Elfes
> Now if you will haue any more   10
> Pray shake your heeles your selues.

The next day being Innocen*tes* day, it was expected & partly determined by
*ou*r selues, that the Tragedy of Philomela. should haue bene publikely acted
w*hi*ch (as wee thought) would well haue fitted the day by reason of the   15
murder of Innocent Itis. But the Carpenters beeing no-way ready w*i*th the
stage or scaffold's (whereof notwithstanding some were made before Christmas,
wee were Constrained to differre it till the nexte day w*hi*ch was the 29 of
December.

At which time in the morning *Maste*r President, sending for one of ye   20
Deanes, to know whether all thinges were in a readines, it was aunsweared
that the Prince himselfe who was to play Tereus, had gott such an exceeding
Cold, that it was impossible for him to speake, or speaking to bee heard.
Wherefore they Consulted to differre the acting of it, yet longer, but then
Considering that all the straungers were already invited, and all other thinges   25
in readines that was ₐ⌜not⌝ thought so fitt. And therefore Casting againe in
their mind*es* what might bee done, many Courses were thought vpon but all
disliked, att length, itt was Concluded (in Case the Prince should not hould
out) that then the Authour of the [shew] Tragedy, who was best acquainted
with it, & Could say most of the verses, should goe forward, where the Prince   30
was Constrained to leave, and to that purpose both were ready in apparell,
and there | for the better Conveiaunce fowre verses were thought vpon, to
bee said by the Prince att the end of the first Sceane of the seconde Acte. The
verses were these.

> Terea tyrannum pace Fortunæ exuo   35
> Elinguis esse pergo Fortunæ modo
> Sic muta sequitur, pœna, pro muto malo
> Suffectus alius Tereus placeat precor.

This Conceipte was ₐ⌜so-⌝well liked of all them that heard of itt, that
manye sayde that itt was pitty itt was not put in practise, though there were   40

17/ (whereof … Christmas,: *comma for closing parenthesis*
40/ manye sayde: *written in left margin*

noe need of itt, but yet for all that, wee thought plaine dealing, better then
a Cunning shifte.

Now for that itt was thought not to stand with the Princes state, barely to
bee an act*ou*r with others, itt was Contriued that hee should first enter like
him selfe, w*i*th his traine, and so take his chaire as the Cheife spectat*ou*r.   5
and then ffortune his only patronesse, should appeare and find faulte with
his still looking on, and doeing nothing himselfe wheruppon bothe for the
more Solemnity should take vppon them to bee Act*ou*rs in the ensueing
Tragedy, all w*hi*ch was *p*erformed in manner followeing.

10

pp 83–5
…

At the end of this Tragedy when fortune and the prince were ready to enter
the stage, it was remembred that there was never an epologue to desmisse
the I Company and therefore suddenly this one verse was made and put in   15
fortunes mouth to speake
                    Et si ista place⌈a⌉nt vel deæ plausum date
And so this begging of a plaudity for a god sake seru'd for other compliment
which was not mist because it was thought no more was intended.

20

The whole play was wel acted and wel liked, the princes voyce held out
wel, but the best and most judicious sort sayd in merryment that there was
one great fault – and that was the losse of Philomelas voyce who (as long as
the history gave her leave to speake) spake so sweetly and acted so smothly
that the audience could have found in their hartes that the story should   25
have rather beene falsified then so good a voyce lost. But it pleased us well
that they should rather desire to heare more, then bee weary of that which
they hard.

Itys was much wondered at for speaking Lattin because he was so
little in his long coates that hee was taken to bee but a child of 7 or 8   30
yeares ould.

Other accidents were observed as the fall of the prince which was so great
that they say'd hee stood like a prince and fell like a prince, majesticke in the
one and terrible in the other.

35

New-yeares eue was wholy spent in preparation for the princes triumphs,
so that nothing was done or expected that night.

Next day in the morning (beeing new-yeares day) the prince sent Mr

9/ in manner followeing: Philomela, *pp 50–83 in* MS
13/ this Tragedy: Philomela
17/ Et si … date: *'And if these matters please (you), then applaud for the goddess (ie, Fortune)'*

Richard Swinnerton on of the Squires of his body to *Maste*r Præsident with a
paire of gloves charging him to say nothing but these two verses.

> The prince and his councell in signe of their loves
> Present you their Præsident with these paire of gloves.

There was somewhat elce written in the paper which covered them but what   5
it is uncertaine.

   At night were celebrated the princes triumphs, at which time onely and
never before nor after he was carryed in full state from his pallace to the
hall where in the sight of the whole Vniuersity a supplication was presented
unto him by time and seconded with a shew call'd times complaint, which   10
wee should bee ashamed heere | heere to insert, if wee thought it would
please no better in the reading then it did in hearing, but (bee it as it will)
wee entend the worse should bee knowne as well as the best though to
speake the truth w*i*thout boasting wee our selves thought not so ill of it as
others nether will future times wee hope judge it so vile as the present did   15
howsoeuer it was perform'de in manner and forme following

pp 111–16

It hath beene observed if they which performe much in these kinde of   20
sportes must needs doe something amisse, or at the least such is the daunger
and trouble of them that something in the dooing will miscarry, and so bee
taken amisse, and such was our fortune at this time. for the Prologue (to
the great prejudice of that which followed) was most shamefully out, and
having but halfe a verse to say, so that by the very sence the audience was   25
able to prompt him in that which followed, yet hee could not goe forward,
but after long stay and silence was compelled abruptly to leave the stage
whereuppon beeing to play another part hee was so dasht, that hee did
nothing well that night.

                                                                                 30

After him Good-wife Spiggot, comming forth before her time, was most
miserably at a non Plus at made others so also whilst her selfe staulked in the
middest like a great Harry-Lion (as it pleased the audience to terme it) ether
saying nothing at all or nothing to the purpose.

                                                                                 35

The drunken-man which in the repetitions had much pleased and done very
well was now so ambitious of his action that he would needs make his part
much longer then it was, and stood so long upon it all that hee grew most

---

11/ heere | heere: *dittography (?); first* heere *does not
   appear to be a catchword*
16/ in manner ... following: *Time's Complaint,
   pp 86–110 in* MS

23/ the Prologue: *of* Time's Complaint
31/ comming: *8 minims in* MS
32/ at²: *for* it *or as (?)*

tedious whereuppon it was well obserued and sayd by one that – – – – –
        twas pitty there should bee
        In any pleasing thing satiety.

To make up the messe of absurdityes the company had so fild the stage that   5
there was [notes] no rome to doe any thing well to bee sure many thinges were
mistaken and therefore could not [bee] but bee very distastfull. for it was
thought that particuler men were aymed at and discipherde by the drunken-
man and Iustice Bryar though it was fully knowne to our selves, that the
author had no such purpose.   10

In fine expectation the deuourer of all good indeuours had swallowed more in
the very name and title of the interlude, then was ether prouided or intended
in the whole matter for wee onely proposed to our selves a shew but the
toune expected a perfect and absolute play so that all things mett to make us   15
unhappy that night and had not time him selfe (whose lines and actions were
thought good) somewhat pleased them they would never have indured us
without hissing, howsoeuer in the end they gaue us two or three cold plaudites
though they departed no way satisfyed, unlesse it were in the shew about the
quadrangle wherein the prince was carryed to his chamber in the same state   20
that hee came from thence in the beginning (as is above mentioned) the [his]
whole company of actors beeing added to his traine | traine who immediatly
followed him before the guard in this order
First Time alone attended with two Pages and lightes.
Next Veritas alone likewise attended.   25
Then Error and Opinion which all the way they went pull'd Veritas by
the sleeue on by one and the other by the other but shee would not harken
to them.
After these came Studioso and Philonices both pleading the case on upon his
fingers and the other with both his hands.   30
Then came Manco the lame [Sh] souldiour and Philonices his man the
souldiour haulting without his Chruch the other beating him with the cruch
for counterfeyting
After these came Clinias and Bellicoso houlding the halter betwixt them
which Bellicoso had found in Clineas his pocket.   35
Last after these came Humphry swallow and goodwife Spiggot hee reeling
uppon her she pulling and hayling him for the mony he ought her.
After these came the guard as before and so the prince in full state was
conveyed to his pallace.

          40

Here wee were ∧⌈all⌉ [al]so discouraged that wee could haue found in our

22/ traine | traine: *dittography (?); first* traine *does not appear to be a catchword*

hearttes to have gone no farther. But then consulting with our selues wee
thought it no way fitt to leave when thinges were at the worst and therefore
resolved by more industry and better care of those things which should follow,
to sue out a fine of recouery for our Credites. Whereuppon the Comedy which
was already afoote and appoynted to bee done on 12 day was revewed and   5
corrected by the best judgments in the house & a Chorus by their direction
inserted to excuse former faults, all which was a cause that twelfe eue & twelfe
day past away in silence because the Comedy beeing wholy altered could not
bee so soone acted neyther could any ₐ⌈other⌉ thing bee so suddenly provided
to furnish those nights. | 10

(Bill of expenses)
Heere the Lord-tresurer made a complaint to the King and the rest of his
councell that his treasure was pore and almost exhausted so that without a
fresh supply or new subsedy nothing more could bee doone. And that this   15
might not seeme an idle complaint a bill of some of the particulars and cheife
expences was exhibited wherein it might appeare how costly the presedent
revels had beene, which bill (for better direction and warning of others
heere after how they medle with such sportes) was thought good heere to
bee inserted   20

The Bill of expences.

Imprimis for 40 dozen of Linkes	4 ll.	10 s.	0 d.
Item for 10 dozen of torches.	4 ll.	10 s.	0 d.
Item for one dozen of great waxe tapers	0 ll.	15 s.	0 d. 25
Item for a shute of tawny tafety for the prince	4 ll.	0	0
Item for a goune for Philomela	3 ll.	0	0
Item for 80 yardes of [Ph] flannel for the guardes coates	5 ll.	6 s.	8 d.
Item for buckarum to make Iackets for Lackeys &			30
other necessaryes to the number of 40 yardes	1 ll.	13 s.	4
Item for two Long-womans-heyres	1 ll.	0	0
Item for beardes and mens-heades of heyre	0	13	0
Item for fethers, spangles, roses, etc*ætera*	1 ll.	10	0
Item for a coate for Itis	0	13	4 35
Item for 2 hundred yardes of Incle	0	8	4
Item for 4 thousand of pinnes	0	3	0
Item for past-boardes	0	8	0
Item for councellours staues and white wandes	1 ll.	0	0
Item for blew silke ribbens and Iewells	0	12 s.	0 40
Item for buskins and pomps	1 ll.	1 s.	0
Item for the princes seale	0	6 s.	8
Item for waxe	0	3	4

Item for a sett of musitians entertayned for the 12 dayes	5 ll.	0	0	
Item for a trumpeter	1 ll.	0	0	
Item for the painter	3 ll.	10	0	
Item to the Taylours besides dyet	2 ll.	0	0	

Item to the Carpenters for setting up the stage scaffolds
twise and lending boardes etcætera   5 ll.   0 s.   0 d.   5
Item for nayles   1 ll.   0 s.   0 d.
Item aloud the prince for his table besides guifts and
his owne great charges   2 ll.   0 s.   0 d.
Item aloud for actors suppers beside that was giuen   3 ll.   0   0   10
Item for butter beere at severall times   1 ll.   0   0
Item for Thomas Clarke for his journey to London   0   13 s.   4
Item for diuers others for journeys [and] for apparrell   0   12   0
Item for guiftes and gratuities   1 ll.   10   0
Item for takeng downe glasse windoes and mending   15
others which were broken at seuerall times   3 ll.   0   0
Item for hyering of apparrell, vizards, cottens, etcætera   2 ll.   10   0
Item pay'd to Labourours for remouing the snow, for stuffing
the hall windoes & such like offices at sundry times   0   16 s.   0
            Summa totalis   lxiiij li.   v s.   0   20

(New privy seals sent forth)
This bill beeing seen⌈e⌉ and allow'd they begane to cast about for more
mony, whereuppon a new privy seale was drawn in Latin in manner and
forme following.   25

Cum maximorum semper Principum majestati neutiquam offecerit, quod
amicos plures, eorumque operam et subsidium non semel desiderârint;
cumque nobilissimus quisque peculiari quodam priuilegio plurimum debere
consueuerit: Ego, ne in minimo majestatis titulo deficere, aut quovis nobilitatis   30
priuilegio viderer non frui plurimis impulsus angustijs et coactus, (quas nec
pro more Principum explicare satis honorificum aut officio tuo exquirere
judicamus satis tutum) has ad te mitto literas mandatorias, quarum virtute
exigitur summa pecuniæ, quam extemplò nostro huic Collectori, pro amoris
tui ratione et censu exhibebis. Quam quidem tibi aut hæredibus tuis obligo me   35
et successores meos ad Græcas Calendas fideliter sine omni fraude aut dolo
malo persoluturos. Datum et sigillatum | sigillatum sigillo nostro priuato,
ex aulâ candidâ Albæ Fortunatæ Calendis Februarij. Anno Regni primo.

24–5/ in manner ... following: *sketch of Prince's privy seal, bottom of p 114 in* MS
37/ sigillatum | sigillatum: *dittography (?); first* sigillatum *does not appear to be a catchword*

The name of those which were
serued with this writte and obey'd
uppon the receipt of it were
these that follow./.

Master President contributed	1 ll.	0 s.	0	
Mr Thomas May.	1 ll.	0	0 d.	
Mr Iohn Soane	0	10 s.	0 d.	
Mr Martin Oakins	0	10 s.	0 d.	
Mr William Lawde	0	10 s.	0 d.	10
Mr Richard Andros	0	10 s.	0 d.	
Mr Nicholas Cliffe	0	10 s.	0 d.	
Mr Michael Boyle	0	10 s.	0	

Summa totalis 5 ll.

(New subsidies granted)
This beeing not as yet sufficient there was a new subsedy [leyed] levyed by
the Iunior *Master*s and the rest of the Colledge to the Summe of six poundes
three shillings whereuppon finding themselues againe before hand and
resoluing to saue nothing for a deere yeare they proceeded to new expences
and new troubles. |

The suneday after beeing the last day of the Vacation and tenth day of the
moneth two shewes were priuately performed in the Lodging the one
presently after dinner called Somnium fundatoris vid. The tradicion that wee
have in the præsident his garden
this interlude by the reason of the death of him that made it, not long after
was lost, and so could not bee heere inserted but it was very well liked and
so wel deserued for that it was both wel penned and well acted.

Now because there were diuers youths whose voyces or personages would
not suffer them to act any thing in publicke, yet withall it was thought fitt
that in so publicke a buisnes euery one should doe something, therefore a
Mocke play was prouided called the 7 dayes of the weeke which was to bee
performed by them which could do nothing in earnest, and that they should
bee sure to spoyle nothing euery mans part was sorted for his parson, and it
was resolued that the worse it was done, the better it would bee liked, and
so it fell out. for the same day after supper it was presented by one which
bore the name of the Clarke of St Gyleses, and acted priuately in the lodging
in manner & forme following.

40/ in manner … following: The Seven Days of the Week, *pp 119–28 in* MS pp 129–30   *(Term prorogued)*

Nothing throughout the whole yeare was better liked and more pleasaunt then
this shew insomuch that allthough it were more priuately done before our
selves onely or some few friends yet the report of it went about all the towne   5
tell it came to the Vicechauncellors and my *Lord* Cliffords eares, who were
very desyrous to see it acted againe and so it was as heereafter shalbee specifyed.

The next day beeing Munday the 11 of Ianuary the terme should have begun
in the house, but because of the extreame cold and froast which had now   10
continued full six weekes and better withowt any intermission as also by
reason the hall was still pestered with the stage and scaffolds which were
suffered to stand still in expectation of the Comedy therefore it was agreed by
the President and the officers that the terme should bee [per] prorogued for
7 dayes longer in which time it was agreed the Comedy should bee publickely   15
acted on frieday the 15th day of Ianuary.

But heere the President and some of the Seniors in abundance of care were
affray'd to put any thing againe to the publicke veiw of the Vniuersity because
their last paines at the Complaint of Time had so ill thriuing. Besides the   20
season was so feirce and tempestuous with wind and snow which had continued
somedayes without ceasing and the complaint of the poore was so greiuious
for want of wood and meate which by this time were growne very scant and
deere that they urged it was a time rather to lament and weepe then make
sport's in whereupon a streight inhibition was sent out from the officers that   25
no man should thinke of playing that night or any time after tell the weather
should breake up and bee more temperate for they thought it no way fitt
puplickly to revell it a time of such generall wo and calamity.

But yet because all thinges were in a readinesse and the expectation of the   30
whole Toune was set uppon that night the younger men of the Colledge went
forward with there buisnes intending to take no notice of what the officers
had aggreed [up] uppon, wherefore some of the officers were fayne to come in
parson to forbid the worke-men and to undo some things which were already
done to the great greife and discouragment of all the youth who though the   35
weather was extreame cold were themselues most hotte uppon the matter in
hand resoluing now or neuer to recouer their loste credit. |

And as though the heavens had favoured their designes so it happened that
about noone the weather brake up and it begann to thaw whereuppon the   40

4/ this shew: The Seven Days of the Week   28/ it: *for* at *(?)*

President was agayne importun'd by the prince himselfe and his councell for
the performance of the Comedy that night, Who (seeing [T] they were all so
earnest) did not so much graunt as not deny them their request whereuppon
they begann againe to sett forward the buisnes and what they wanted, in time,
they made up by their willingnesse and paynes so that for all these crosses they 5
begann the play before 7 a clocke and performed it in manner following.

pp 169–78   *(Description of the Prince's castle)*

This play was very well acted, but especially the Chorus, the stage was 10
never more free, the Audience neuer more quiet, and Contented, so that
they went away many of them crieing Abundè Satisfactum est, itt was so
well liked and applauded of all that saw itt
Here the stage & scaffold were pul'd downe w*hich* had stood from Cristmas,
and it was resolued that vpon the Chaunge of the weather, the terme should 15
begin on the munday followeing.

But in the meane time on Sunday nighte being the Seventeenth of Ianuary
the Vicechancelo*ur* and the L*ord* Clifford, w*ith* many other D*octo*rs and
Gentlemen, were inuited to Supper in the Præsident*es* lodging, where after 20
supper they were entertained with a shew before mentioned, to witt, the 7
Daies in the Weeke, to which by this time there was somewhat added, but
not much, all was most kindely accepted, and the nighte was spent in great
mirth. For the straungenes of the matter, and rarity of the fashion of their
action pleased above [mentioned] expectation. 25
At the end of this shew for the more rarity, there was one brought in my
Lord's Stockes, w*ith* this speech made vppon itt.
My Lord, I w*hich* am the lowest, am now become the lowdest though
(I hope) not the lewdest of your Lor*dshippes* seruauntes. And though
I come pridie Calendas, before I am Cald, yet (I hope) my audacity 30
shall have audience, and my faithfulnes fauour. I am yo*ur* Lor*dshippes*
Elephaunt and heere is yo*ur* Castell, so that where other Lords are
broughte to their Castells, heere yo*ur* Castell is brought to you. Est
locus in carcere, there is a locke vpon yo*ur* Lor*dshipps* Castell, which
was Committed vnto my trust, how faithfull I have bene therein, they 35
Can tell who haue ∧⌈taken⌉ an exact measure of my office by the foote,
the matter of w*hich* your Castell is builded is so precious, that there
is none amongst Company, but is Contented to weare of it w*ithin* his

2/ the²: h *corrected over another letter*
6/ in manner following: Philomathes, *pp 131–68*
in MS

10/ This play: Philomathes
16/ the munday followeing: *18 January 1607/8*

buttons, the end for which it was builded is very Commendable, that
they may bee kepte in order with Wood, which otherwise wou'd not
bee kepte in order, heere is fons latus pedibus tribus, a fountaine to
washe three mens leges that they which haue bene Aurium tenus,
ouer shooes, heere may bee Crurum tenus over bootes too, This your   5
Lordshippes Oracle or *Tripos*, out of which malefactours tell the truth
and foretell of their amendment. Nay I wilbee bould to Compare
itt to your Lordshippes braine, for what is there designed is heere
executed. In these sells or ventricles are fancy, vnderstanding, and
memory. ffor such as your Lordshipp doth not fancy are put in the first   10
hole such as were dull and without vnderstanding were put in the
second hole, but such as your Lordshipp threatned (remember this) or
I'le remember you, were put in the last and lowest dungeon. Cum
nemini obtrudi potest itur ad me. When they Cannot bee I led
otherwise they are brought vnto mee, and my entertainement is   15
Strato discumbitur ostro, they straite sett downe att this oister table,
where they are fast and doe fast. ffor Viuitur exiguo melius, they
make small meales, till the flames of Clemency, doe mitigate the
Salamander of your Lordshipps severity. Now my Lord, since I have
told you what I am, I will bee bold to tell you what you may bee.   20
You are mortall. Ergò you must die, the three sisters will not spare
you, though you were there owne brother, and therefore while you
have your good witts about you. Fac quid velis. Make your will, that
wee may know amongst so many well deseruing men, that doe lay
Claime to this your Castell, to whome as rightfull heire itt shall   25
lawfully descend, that so all Controuersies being ended, before your
Lordshipps deceasse, hereafter your bones may ly, and wee your
subjectes live, in all rest and quietnes.
                              Dixi.

                                                                        30

   To make an end of this nightes sporte, all departed merry and very well
pleased, the actours were much Commended, and the[ir] terme for their
sakes prorogued one day longer.

(The Prince's visitation to Christ Church)   35
   On the Thursday following, the Prince was solemnely invited by the
Canons of Cristchurch[urch] to a Comedy called Yuletide, where many
thinges were either ill ment by them, or ill taken by vs but wee had very
good reason to thincke the former, both for that the whole towne thoughte
so, and the whole play was a medley of Christmas sportes, by which occasion   40

36/ the Thursday following: *21 January 1607/8*

Christmas Lords were much jested at, and our Prince was soe placed that
many thinges were acted vpon him, but yet, Master Deane himselfe then Vicechancelour very kindly sent for the Prince and some others of our howse, and
laboured to satisfie vs protesting that no such thing was mente, as was reported,
wherevpon wee went away contented, and forbore the speaking of many   5
things, which otherwise were afterwards intended, for aunswering of them
in their owne kind.

(The vigilate)
On Candlemas Nighte it was thoughte by our selves, and reported in   10
the Towne, that the Prince should resigne his place, but nothing being in a
readines for that purpose itt was differred, but yet, least nothing should bee
done. There was a Vigilate (as they terme it) a watching nighte procured by
the Prince and his | Counsell, and graunted by the Officers of the Colledge,
which ∧⌐was⌐ performed in manner following.   15
The Vigilate.
First, about eighte of the Clocke (for then itt was to begin, and to Continue
till fowre in the Morning) the Colledge gates were shutt, and all the students
summon'd by the sounding of a Trumpett three times, to make their personall
appearaunce in the greate Hall, where after they were all Come together, that 20
the Princes pleasure might bee the better knowne, this proclamation, was
publikely pronounced by a Serjeant att Armes, in the hearing of them all.

The high and mighty Thomas by the fauour of ffortune Prince of Alba
Fortunata, Lord St *Iohns*, High Regent of the Hall. &c. To all the Presidentes, 25
Vicepresidentes, officers Readers, Masters, Batchelours, ffelowes, Schollers,
Commoners, Vnder-commoners, Seruauntes, Seruitours. sendeth greeting.

Whereas of late by the turbulent spirites of seditious minded persons hath
bene bu[z]zed into the [hee] eares of many of our louing and leige [subjectes] 30
subjectes, a fearefull and dangerous report of our sudden downefall, which
according to their libelling speeches should att this nighte fall vpon vs. Wee
haue thought it necessary, not somuch for [owne] our owne feares which
are none at all, as for satisfieing and strengthening our welmeaning freinds,
in their love and duty to publish, and by these presentes to all our loyall   35
subjectes of what state and Condicion soever, that they make their personall
appearaunce, to the setting and furnishing of a most strong guarde, and |
Carefull watch as well for their security as the safety of our owne Royall
person, & the whole Common wealth, In the which generall-watch for
the ∧⌐better⌐ Comfort and ease of all men, our selfe with our Honourable   40

22/ all.: *followed by sketch of Prince's privy seal, middle of p 171 in* MS

privy Counsell, and the rest of our Nobility intend to bee personally present

But because wee are no way minded to oppresse any man above his power, on our Princely bounty, wee giue licence to such, as (for age or infirmity) are not able to performe that duty, to forfaite for their absence. yf they pleade age ij s. vj d., if infirmity xij d. towardes ye furnishing of his Highnes with a tall   5 and sufficient watchman.

Now because that ‸⌈which⌉ wee haue wisely thought, and for our peace and safety may not prooue the Cause of new troubles and dissentions, wee haue thought good to adjoine some few cautions, in way of admonitions to bee obserued.   10

First, for that the disorders of an vnruly and mutinous watch doe often open as it were the gate of danger and outrage, our Princely will and pleasure is, that each man keepe his station without murmuring performing Cheerefully all such offices and duties, as shalbee lawfully enjoin'd by vs, or our offices, vpon paine of forfeiting ij s. vj d. as for age.   15

Seacondly because sloth is a kind of disease in a well-ordered Common-wealth, wee further Charge and Command, by the vertue of our absolute authority that no man bee found winking or pincking or nodding, much lesse snorting vpon paine of forfaiting twelve-pence as for infirmity

Thirdly for the auoiding of a sudden dearth, or lingring famine which may   20 ensue and justly follow the free an vndoubted liberty of a riotous and luxurious time, yt is by vs thought necessary that no man should in huggermugger eate or drincke more then is publickly seene and allowed by the face of the body Civill and Politicke, vpon paine of paieing twise, for such is in a manner stolne prouision and the second paiment to bee arbitrary.   25

> Given att our Mannour of
> Whites-hall the seacond of
> ffebruary and in the first of
> our Raigne. |

     30

This proclamation beeing read and set up in the great hall the prince called for his officers and seruants about him charging every man carefully to execute his office. ffirst the steward and buttler (who for their auncient fidelity kept their places according as they had long before beene appointed by the colledge) were commaunded to bring their bookes, and by them to call up all the howse   35 whereupon (every one beeing first charged to awnswere to his name it presently appeared who were present and who were absent

              After this the Master of the Revels and the knight Marshall were willed to appoint severall sportes that no man might bee seene idle upon

---

21/ an: *for* and (?)
29/ Raigne.: *followed by sketch of crown, bottom of p 172 in* MS
36/ (every … name: *closing parenthesis omitted*

payne of the princes high displeasure whereupon presently some went to cardes, some to dice, some to dauncing every one to some thing

Not long after for more variety sake there was brought in a maske the devise was sudden and ex tempore vide*licet* A litle page attired in Itys long coats with these six verses which were spoke as soone as he entred 5 the hall.

> These are six carpet knights, and I one page
> Can easily bring in six that bee of age
> They come to visite this your highnes court
> And if they can to make your honour sport 10
> Nay this is all for I haue seene the day
> A richer maske had not so much to say.

After these maskers had finished the measures, and some few other daunces the said page waued them forth with his wan, and spake these two verses. 15

> There are three they say would shew you an anticke
> But when you see them you'l thinke them ffranticke

Then there came in three in an anticke which were well attyred for that purpose and daunced well to the great delite of the beholders.

After these had stollen away one by one as the manner is it 20 pleased the prince to aske what was a clocke, it beeing aunswered almost twelue hee presently calld in for supper. But first the bill of those which were before noted to bee absent was call'd to see whether any of them would yet appeare, and the prince would deale favorably with them. It was also examined whether any of those which were present before were now gon to bed, and 25 accordingly authority was given by the prince to the Marshalls of the hall and other officers to search the chambers for sleepers, and where they made aunswere to aske the reason of their slothfull neglect or wilfull contempt of the princes commaund, and if they pleaded ether infirmity or age to take there fine, and so quietly to depart, first causing them faithfull to give their worde*s* 30 that they harboured no other idle or suspicious parsons. [⟨.⟩] But if they knoct at any of the chambers of those that were absent and nobody would answer then they had full authority to breake open the dores and to make a privy search, and if they found any abed they tooke them as they were in their shirts and carryed them doune in state to the hall after this manner | 35

ffirst went the Marshals with lights to make rome

Then came on squire carrying the goune of him whome they brought and another that carryed his hatt & band.

Then came two other squires whereof one carryed his dublet the other his breeches. 40

Then came two with lights

30/ faithfull: *for* faithfully (?)

Next came he that was in his shirt carryed by two in a chaire and covered with a blancket

Last behind came one squire more that carryed his shoes & stockings. &c.

All these beeing entred the hall, the squires made their attendance about him with great observance, every one reaching him his apparrell as it pleased 5 him to call for it, and then also helping him on with it. And this was the punishment of those that were found a bed.

Others which were found up in their chambers & would not answer were violently brought downe with bills and staves as malefactors and by the knight Marshals appointment were committed close prisoners to the princes castle 10 vide*licet* the stocks which were placed upon a table to that purpose that those which [we] were punished might bee seene to the [tt] terrour of others

By this time supper was ready and the sewer call'd to the dresser whereupon the buttery bell was presently rung as it uses to bee at other ordinary meales besides a trumpet was sounded at the kitchen hatch to call the wayters together. 15

After the first messe was served in, the prince with the rest of his councell satt downe, then all the rest of the hovse in seniority

Towardes the end of supper two gentlemen of the second table fell out wee could neuer distinctly know about what, it was verely supposed themselves scarsly knew, but from wordes they fell suddenly to [blowes,] blowes, and ere 20 any man was aware on of them had stabbed the other into the arme with his knife to the great præjudice of the mirth, which should or would haue followed that night. But the offender was presently apprehended (and (though a gentleman of some worth) put into my Lords stocks, where hee lay most part of that night with shame and blame inough. And yet for all that 25 punishment the next day he was convented before the officers of the Colledge, and there agayne more greivously punished. for the fault was much aggravated by the circumstances of the time, place, and person that was hurt, who was a very worshipfull knights sonne and heyre.

After this the prince with some of the better sort of the howse[s] beeing 30 much disconted with the mischaunce that had happened retyred themselves into the President lodging, where priuatly they made themselues merry, with a wassall called the five bells of Magdalen church, because it was an auncient note of those bells that they were almost neuer silent. This shew for the better grace of the night was performed by some of the *Maste*rs and officers 35 themselues in manner following |

Enter the clarke of Magdalens alone.

Your kind acceptance of the late devise
Presented by St Gyles clarke my neighbour 40

23–4/ (and (though ... worth): *initial parenthesis redundant*
31/ disconted: *for* discontented

Hath hartned mee to furnish in a trice
This nights up [s.⟨.⟩tt] sitting with a two hovres labour.
    ffor any thing I hope though [never] ne're so naghty
    Wilbe accepted in a Vigilate
I have observed as your sportes did passe all   5
(A fault of mine to bee to curious)
The twelfe night slipt away without a wassall
A great defect to custome most iniurious.
    Which I to mend have done my best indeavour
    To bring it in, for better late then never.   10
And more for our more tuneable proceeding
I have ta'ne downe the five bells in our towre
Which will performe it if you give them heeding
Most musicaly though [an an h] they ring an hovre
    Now I go in to oyle my bells and pruin them   15
    When I com downe Ile bring them downe & tune them.   Exit
   After a while he returned with five others presenting his five bels and tyed
with five bel-ropes which after he had pulled one by one they all began a
peale, and sang in Latin as followeth.
                  Iam sumus lætis dapibus repleti   20
                  Copiam vobis ferimus fluentem
                  Gaudium vobis canimus jocose
                            Vivite læti
                  Te deum dicunt (venerande Bacche)
                  Te deam dicunt (reverenda mater)   25
                  Vos graves vobis removete luctus
                            Vivite læti.
                  Dat Ceres vires hominumque firmat
                  Corpora, et Bacchus pater ille vini
                  Liberat curis animos molestis   30
                            Vivite læti.
                  Ne dolor vestros animos [fastige] fatiget
                  Vos jubet læta hæc removere curas
                  Turba, lætari ferieque suadent
                            Vivite læti. | 35
                  En Ceres lætæ segetis creatrix
                  Et pater vini placidique Somni
                  Pocula hæc vobis hilares ministrant
                         Sume   { monarcha.
                                 { magister   40

Bibunt omnes ordine dum actores hæc ultima carmina sæpius repetunt,

Mox singuli toti conventui sic ordine gratulantur.

Tenor
      Reddere fælicem si quemquam copia possit
            Copia fælicis nomen habere jubet.
      Copia læta jubet tristes depellere curas
            Copia quam cingit Bacchus et alma Ceres.   5

Counter Tenor
      Quem non delectant moderatè pocula sumpta?
            Cujus non animum dulcia vina juvant.
      Dulcia vina juvant, dulcem dant vina soporem
            Magnificas ornant dulcia vina dapes.   10

Meane
      ffrugibus alma Ceres mortalia pectora nutrit
            Exornat campum frugibus alma Ceres.
      Si cuiquam desint Cerealia dona, nec illi
            Lenæi patris munera grata placent.   15

      Nec vobis Cereris nec Bacchi munera desint
            Annuat et votis Iupiter ipse meis

Treble.
      Alma Ceres vestris epulis lætatur et ecce   20
            Copia cum Baccho gaudia læta canunt
                Mox omnes cantantes Exeunt

Me⟨.⟩
            Gaudium lætum canimus, canemus
            Hoc idem semper nec enim dolere   25
            Iam licet lætæ feriæ hic aguntur
                Vivite læti
      Sæpius nobis feriæ revertant
            Sæpius vinum liceat potare
            Sæpius vobis hilares canamus   30
                Vivite læti. Exeunt. |

    This shew was suddenly and ex tempore clapt together for want of a better but notwithstanding was as willingly and chearefully receaved as it was profered.

35

    By this time it was foure a clocke and liberty was given to every one to goe to bed or stay up as long as they pleased. The prince with his councell brake up their watch so did most of the Maisters of the hovse. [Soe] But the younger sort stay'd up till prayers time, and durst not goe to bed for feare of one-another. for some after they had licence to depart were fetcht out of their beds by their 40 fellowes and not suffered to put on their clothes till they came in to the hall. And thus the day came & made an end of this nights sport

(A private masque)

On the sixt of february beeing egge satterday it pleased some gentlemen schollers in the towne to make a dauncing night of it. They had provided many new and curious daunces for the maske of Penelopes woers but the yeare beeing far spent and lent drawing on and many other thinges to bee   5 performed the prince was not able to bestow that state upon them, which their love & skill deserved. But their good will was very kindely receiued by the prince in this nights private travels. They had some apparell suddenly provided for them and these few Lattin verses for their induction

  10

> Isti fuere credo Penelopes proci
> Quos justa forsan ira Telemachi domo
> Expulit Vlyssis |

After all this sport was ended the prince entertayned them very royally   15 with good store of wine and a banquet where they were very merry and well pleased all that night.

(The Princes resignation)

Against the next tuesday following beeing shrouetuesday the great stage was   20 againe set up and the scaffoldes built about the hall for the princes resignation which was performed that night with great state and solemnity in manner and forme following.

pp 206–8   25
...

Many straungers of all sortes were invited to this shew, and many more came together, for the names sake only of a resignacion to see the manner and solemnity of it, for yat it was reported (and truly) that there was nothing els to bee done or seene beside the resignacion, and no man thought so-much could   30 haue beene said of so litle matter

The stage was never so oppressed with company, insomuch that it was verely thought itt [⟨.⟩] Could not bee performed that night for want of roome. but the Audience was so favourable as to stand as Close and yeeld as-much backe as was possible: so that for all tumultes it began about 7 a Clocke, and was   35 very well liked of all

Only some few more vpon their owne guilty suspicion then our plaine intention thincking themselves toucht at that verse of Momus.

20/ the next tuesday ... shrouetuesday: *9 February 1607/8*
22–3/ in manner ... following: Ira Fortunae, *pp 179–206 in* MS
27/ this shew: Ira Fortunae
29/ it²: t *corrected over another letter*

Dixi, et quem dederat cursum fortuna peregi.
Laboured to raise an hissing, but it was soone smothered, and the whole
Company in the end, gave vs good applause, and dep*a*rted very well pleased

After the Shew was ended, the sometimes Lord was Carried in state to his
owne private Chamber after this manner.   5

    ffirst went two Squires w*i*th light*es*
    Next Euphemia and Tolmæa
    Then 2 other Squires w*i*th lightes |
    Next Minerva and Fortuna

Then came 4 other Squires with lightes, and in the mid'st of them 4   10
Schollers bearing on their shoulders a tombe or Sepulcher adorned with
Scutchions and litle flagges, wherein all the Princes honours had bene buried
before

After this came the Prince alone, in his Schollers gowne and hood as the
cheife mourner.   15

Then all the rest of his Counsell and Company likewise in blacke gownes
and hoodes, like mourners two by two

All these were said to goe to the Temple of Minerva there to Consecrate
and erecte the sepulcher, and this State was very well liked of all that saw itt.

Heere wee thought to have made an end of all, and to have puld downe   20
the scaffold*es* and stage, but then many said that so much preparac*i*on was
to much for so small a shew./ Besides there was an English Tra[gedy]gedy
almost ready which they were very earnest should bee p*er*formed, but many
argument*es* were alledged against it. ffirst, for the time, because itt was neere
Lent and Consequently a season vnfitt for plaies. Secondly, the stile for that 25
itt was English, a language vnfitt for the Vniuersitie, especially to end so much
late sporte w*i*thall. Thirdly the suspic*i*on of some did more hinder it then all
the rest, for y*a*t it was thought that some p*ar*ticulers were aimed att in the
Chorus, which must needes bee distastfull. Lastly, the ill lucke w*hi*ch wee had
before w*i*th English made many very loth to have any thing done againe in 30
that straine

But these objections being aunswered as well as might bee, and faithfull
p*r*omise being made and taken, y*a*t if any word were thought p*er*sonall, it
should bee presently put out: the Stage was suffered to stand, and the scaffolds
somewhat enlarged against the Saturday following. Att which time such a   35
concourse of People from all places, and of all sort*es* Came together presently
after | dinner, that itt was thought impossible, any thing should have beene
done that night for tumult*es*. Yet in the beginning such order and Care was
taken (every one being willing att the last cast to helpe towardes the making
a good end) that the stage was kepte voide of all Company and the scaffoldes 40

1/ Dixi … peregi: *'I have spoken and I have*   35/ the Saturday following: *13 February 1607/8*
  completed the course that Fortune gave (me)'

were reserved for straungers and men sorte, better then ever they were before so that it began very peaceably somewhat before six a Clocke, and was performed in manner followeing.

pp 210–11   *(Periander, before Act 1)*   5

M*aste*r of the Reue*lls*	Come quickly, quickly: you'l stay all nighte heer: you rogue are these to be hang'd vp nowe? we shall n'ere haue done with these foolish plaies. I thincke you take a greate deale of paines for a little thanckes.
Boy	Faith S*i*r, if there were none heer, but those we take paines for, our kinde 10 freind*es*, and honest good fellowes, our thankes would be large enough.
M*aste*r of the Reue*lls*	Well and what's your play nowe?
Boy	Faith S*i*r a poore tragedy, a tragedy
M*aste*r	Tragedy? I thought so, these boyes are neuer well but when they may mouth it. I haue not seene them yet in the true streyne and turninges of a Comedy. 15 But I haue no iudgment. Let be as may be, any thinge, any thinge, since my Lorde and his freindes will haue it. But what is't, what is't? what Tragedy? The hanging vp of Polycrates? or the whipping of time?
Boy	ffaith S*i*r y'haue ghest well. The fortunes of Polycrates were thought on, and they would haue suted his Lordships declination exceeding well. And the 20 whipping of Time was not forgotten, but that t'was to lowe a subjecte, and to poore an obiect: and indeed had to much vnpleasing reference.
M*aste*r	And what? is't English or Latin?
Boy	Nay honest English S*i*r, plaine English.
M*aste*r	fy, fy fie, starke nought, starke nought: to bad, to bad: schollers? sham'd your 25 selues in English already; and nowe againe? In prose to I warrant.
Boy	ffaith little better S*i*r, plaine blanke [S*i*r] verse.
	Detraction among the Spectators †
	Hisse − − − − −
M*aste*r	Howe nowe? who's that? 30
Det*rac*tion	Poxe: begin your play, and leaue your pratinge.
M*aste*r	Why what are you sir?
Det*rac*tion	As good as you, sir.
M*aste*r	Pray gentlemen heaue him vp, this fellowe would be knowne.
Det*rac*tion	I am well where I am sir. 35
M*aste*r	You shalbe better S*i*r and't please you.
Det*rac*tion	I'le not take your word S*i*r.
M*aste*r	I would a quieter fellowe had yo*u*r place sir.
Det*rac*tion	ffaith t's no matter who ha'st for any thinge he shall gett by it. I haue heard your play repeated man, tis not so worshipful stuffe as is expected. 40
M*aste*r	T'is to good for you sir.

3/ in manner followeing: Periander, *pp 209–56 in* MS

Detraction	And to bad for this Audience.
Master	In what state stand's your desarte then.
Detraction	P'sh: be not your boyes ready yet? I'de faine heare vm whine.
Master	The stockes heer ho, the stockes heere. Pray Gentlemen bestowe him amongst vs: yee see howe he disturbs you. Wee'l do him no harm Ile assure you.

5

Resolution

Resolution	My lorde sends to knowe what noyse this is?
Master	A foolish troublesome fellowe, would be quiet enough, if the play would begin once: for Gods sake let them make hast, and come away.	
Resolution	What Signeur Detraction? you are deceyu'd Sir, hee's vnquiet now because tis not begun; and when they are at it, hee'l be ten times more vnquiett. You shall heare how hee'l mumble and grin, and turne at euery line to some neighbor, flow't and find fault with all: with – that's absolutely stolne; that's base imitation, (as if he had read all) that's cold, that's tædious, that hangs not together. He is indeed an Epitome of all the fowle mouthe's in a whole vniuersity; then where no men speake better, no men worse: And yet this fellowe thinks the world has not eares and leasure enough to intend him. The noysers, the bellowers, the thrusters, the windowbreakers, the beasts are all his followers.
Detraction	Good *Master* Resolution.
Master	So let them talke it out: I am glad I am deliuer'd of the troublesome foole.

10

15

20

Exit *Master* of Reuells.

Detraction	I haue partly knowne you. I speake ill of all (you say) And you neglect all, scorne all, care for no man.
Resolution	Neglect all: scorne all care for none – of thy kindred; detractors. Will you sit Sir: th'are nowe vppon beginning: hear a scene or 2, or a whole act. You and I'le sit for Chorus.
Detraction	Y'are an asse: ther was but one thing which I thought to speake well of, and that was the Chorus they haue already of the other 6 wise men. Though I had no great hope of their proceedings. There I heard theire seate was appointed.
Resolution	Preethee be contented: Thou and I wilbe Chorus, they shall not hold: they'l speake to grauely for vs, and to wisely for the tyme.
Detraction	Come on, I'le sit, Ile sitt.

25

30

Sedent Resolution et Detraction

35

p 221   (Periander, *between Acts I and II*)

Chorus
Detraction. Resolution.

Detraction	And pray, what thinks your worship of this act?	40
Resolution	What are you falne into the blancke verse to?	
Detraction	I mark't it not and care not whether I do or no.	

Resolution   But twill be farre more pleasing.   *Detraction* t'whom I pray
Whom should I please?   *Resolution* Then you forget your parte
Your aime is nowe peculiar for vs.

Detraction   Ther's no such neede of heedy aiming *Sir*.
Mountayne of grosse absurdity wilbe   5
Which way so ere yea cast a sleeping eye.
In your first scene howe haue ye tumbled vp
Melissa's death, howe little is express'd
Of her Deaths cause? and on howe little spleen
A fire was made for Perianders whores?   10
And what a needlesse story did on tell
Of Rome and Tarquin, and I knowe not who?
ffy their's an heap: beshrewe my memory
That haue not brought my Tables.   *Resolution* Worthy *Sir*.
Some dogs of Custome, not of malice bite   15
But your sharpe iudgement *Sir* ha's hit it right.
I knowe that things beginning should be spun
To a faire length, in th'end more nimbly run.
This in the direct subject I confesse:
But things collaterall may be labor'd lesse.   20
Our main is Perianders discontent
Vppon the turne of age, and life ill spent.
Some touches of his madnes it must shewe
But sodeyn as still Tyraunts passions growe.
That reach to Rome was but a windlasse to   25
To net the Marryners, I could farther goe
And so could many better judgements heere
In true objection: but let all run cleer.

Detraction   Cleere as an Inundation, filthy all

Resolution   Except those streames well from your mouth do fall   30
...

p 229   *(Periander, between Acts II and III)*
...

                       Chorus: Resolution, Detraction   35

Detraction   Nowe iudgement, iudgement, iudgement Gentlemen
Was't not a poore Colde Acte? were not the Princes
A pretty while entring the Citty gates?
Did not the eldest fool it handsomely?
Did not the youngest to too slightly stoope   40
To popularity, and base obseruance?
ffy, ffy; will no man hisse? y'are partiall.

® Sibilantibus e
turba nonnullis
pergit

Where? where? freind*es*, brothers: out w*i*th't, out w*i*th't.
Let's neuer keepe it for a secret fire.
These fellowes haue opinion of themselues

Reso*lution*

What wu't thou breath Detraction? for thy paines
To wrong good iudgements, and kind audience   5
Thou wilt be hi'st away thy selfe anon.
This Acte I'le sweare was reasonable well.
More I presume of none: thy selfe can tell
If all the actors daily paines, and Cost
Hold this proportion tis not meerely lost   10
Silence shall aunswere thy obiections nowe
Thou Catchest where thou canst, yet car'st not howe
Detraction, tis thy Custome faulte to finde,
Where thy skill's none, or where thou Com'st behind.

De*traction*

When impudent opynion beares the name   15
Of Resolution, iudgement beares the shame.
I'le pick my teeth, and heare another Acte.

Reso*lution*

If thou shouldst sleepe too, dreaming thou'dst detract.

p 239   (Periander, *between Acts* III *and* IV)   20
...
                         Resolution, Detraction.

De*traction*

I pray S*i*r tell me do's your story say
That he was watcht thus all the night and day?
Heere's boldnes of a barren poet to,   25
To faine a tempest. Iudgement shall this goe?

Reso*lution*

S*i*r thus the scant, and scattered story saies
That whether, greife and hunger in 4 daies
Did pine, and spend him to a feare of death.
That his industrious freinds successiuely   30
Attempted to releife him: but an eye
ffrom euery Corner flue that kept them by.

De*traction*

Tis very likely that the Citty watch
Should be so sterne.   Reso*lution* There's a iuditious Catch.
Who Cannot say howe peremptory stand   35
The mooueable stated Citizens, when Command
With threatned life flyes to them from their Kinge?

De*traction*

Beside all harpe vppon a Common stringe
The liberty of adding that yee take
Poore imitations of all heapes to rake.   40

1–3m/ Sibilantibus ... pergit: *'He continues while some in the crowd hiss'*

Resolution	There is some stuffe in this objection
	But where discouerd y' imitation.
Detraction	In all Cleane throughe. *Resolution* I'de gladly knowe the man
	That bragge of absolute inuention Can
	But haue you read the story. *Detraction* Troth sir no
Resolution	Then what's inserted *Sir* you cannot shewe
	Ther's not a man in all this Company
	But knowes some parrallel parte of history
	Which yet perhaps we neuer sawe nor heard
Detraction	Nay by no meanes wish I yea should be bar'd
	Of your inuentions praise. *Resolution* Preethee sit still.
	Heare all, then speake with thy best skill or will.
Detraction	Blest be the tyme; y'are ritch in rime.
Resolution	Curst be the season; that rob'd thee of reason.

5

10

15

p 246   (Periander, *between Acts IV and V*)

...

Resolution; Detraction.
Chorus.

Detraction	Sir; y'are beholding to my patience.
Resolution	Would I Could sute it with iust recompence
Detraction	Me thought your Lycophron was quicly gon
Resolution	The hast was wisht alike by Sire, and Sonne.
Detraction	For your Cratæa as in euery Scene
	So in the last Cohærence was but meane
Resolution	Such Consequence as diuers stories giue
	We take, beg pardon, where we do not thriue
Detraction	Yea talke of Conquest ouer Procles got
	But of the manner w'haue not seene a iot.
Resolution	Nowe speakest thou like the Asse of all thy schoole
	Fighting and shewes please women, boies and fooles.
Detraction	O then belike penning, and action
	Is all your glory. *Resolution* No Detraction
	Our little practise and much Idlenes
	Our weakenes in them both bid vs confesse.
	Reward writes well: schollers but learne to speake
	'Mongst whome who better order'd studies breake
	With numb'd ioynts wrighting many hundred lines
	Detraction, with thy numerous affines
	Knowe hee Contemn'd thee in his first of thoughts
	And that some forty of these heere haue wrought
	His willing paines. *Detraction* Come are yea ready, Sirs

20

25

30

35

40

The epilogue is past, who home ward stirs?
I'me sicke; I'me mad with't, whoo'le helpe me out
Resolution   Nay by your fauour wee'le haue one more bout
Detraction   Poxe, whister, nose, face, you.   *Resolution* Prethee be quiet
Thereis no way out.   *Detraction* what's lefte I will not buy it,   5
With the least minutes torment.   *Resolution* Then you shall.
Detraction   By heauen Il'e study to disgrace you all.

pp 255–60   *(Periander, after Act v)*

                                                                                    10
                         Chorus Resolution, Detraction.
Resolution   Howe nowe detraction? howe nowe; howe nowe man?
Detraction   T'was scuruy all.
Resolution   Ho Ingenuity
                Heer's a newe patient.   15
                                        Ingenuity.
Ingenuity   God saue all; lets see.
® pulsum tintat   An Inflammation; and about the braine
                T'would Come to a Phrenitis if a vaine
                Should not bee open'd for reuulsion.   20
                Howe did he talke before this passion?
Resolution   Most strangly, madly, senceles, railingly
Ingenuity   Then in his toungue a vain must opend bee
Resolution   Nature did ill to purge her selfe that way
                The breath 'an'ts venome.   *Ingenuity* t' must be nowe as may   25
                Lets haue him in: losse of a little blood
                And purging once or twise will make all good.
Resolution   Ile helpe to haue him in: But who shall pay
                Your fee.   *Ingenuity* T's no matter I'le nere sett him day
                He is a scholler.   *Resolution* Of what house I pray   30
Ingenuity   Of all and none: for longe he doth not stay
                In any place: he boards in towne: frequents
                All exercise: especially the Lents
                Come talking will not Cure him: helpe him in
Resolution   Hee's scarce worth Curing I: yet to doo't's no sinne.   35
                                                                Exeunt. |

                                        Epilogus.

                Gentlemen welcome: our great promises   40
                Wee would make vpp. your selues must needs confesse.

18m/ pulsum tintat: *'He strikes a ringing blow'*   19/ Phrenitis: *4 minims in* MS

But our small timbred actors; narrowe Roome,
Necessity of thrifte make all short come.
Of our first apprehensions. Wee must keepe
Our auntient customes thoughe wee after creepe.
But wee forgett times limitts; Nowe tis Lente.   5
Old store this weeke may lawfully be spente.
Our former shewes were giu'n to one cal'd Lorde
This and att his request for you was storde.
    By many hands was Periander slaine
    Your gentler hands will giue him liue againe.   10

Finis

A Certain gentlewoman vpon the hearing of those two last verses, made two
other verses, and in way of an aunswer sent them to the Prince, who having   15
first plaied Periander afterwards himselfe also pronounced the Epilogue.
                the verses were these.
    If that my hand or hart him life Could give
    By hand and hart should Periander live.
But it is almost incredible to thincke how well this Tragedy was performed   20
of all parties, and how well liked of the whole, which (as many of them as
were within the hall) I were very quiet and attentiue. But those that were
without and Could not get in made such an hideous noice, and raised such a
tumult with breaking of windows all about the Colledge throwinge of stones
into the hall, and such like ryott that the officers of the Colledge (beeing first   25
dar'd to appeare) were faine to rush forth in the beginning of the play, with
abovt a dozen Whiflers, well armed and swords drawne. whereat the whole
Company (which were gathered together before the Chappell doore to try
whether they Could breake it open) seeing them come behind them out of the
lodging, presently gave backe, and ranne away, though itt was thought they   30
werc not so fcw as 4 oı 500.
The officers gave some faire wordes and some fowle as they saw occasion,
the whiflers were very heedfull to marke who were the ringleaders of the rest,
and having some notice given of them by some of our freindes they tooke
some of them, and Committed them to the Porters lodge, where they lay   35
Close Prisoners till the play was done, and then they were brought forth, and
punished, and so sente home
After this all was quiet only some were so thrust in the hall, that they were
Caried forth for dead but soone recouered, when they came into the aire
The Chorus of this Tragedy much pleased for the rarity of it. Detraction   40
beeing taken from among the company where hee had like to haue bene
beaten for his sawsines (as it was supposed) for nobody at first toke him for
an actour. The Cheifest in the hall Commaunded that notice should bee

taken of him, that hee might afterwards bee punished for his boldnes, But
as soone as it once appeared that hee was an actor their disdaine and anger
turned to much pleasure and Content.

All were so pleased att the whole Course of this | play that there were at
least eight generall plaudites given in the mid'st of it in divers places and to 5
divers persons.

In the end they Clapped their hands so long yat they went forth of the
Colledge clapping

But in the midst of all this good liking wee were neere two mischaunces,
the one from Lycophron who lost a faire gold ring from his finger, which 10
notwithstanding all the hurleburly in the end of the play was soone found
againe; the other from Periander, who going to kill his daughter Eugenia, did
not so Couch his dagger within his hand, but that hee prickt her through
all her attire, but (as God would have it) it was onely [st] a scratch, and so
it passed. 15

The conclusion.

Many other thinges were in this yeare entended which neither were nor
could be performed. As the maske of Penelopes wooer, with the state of 20
Telemachus, with a controversie of Irus and his ragged Company, whereof
a great parte was made. The devise of the Embassage from Lubber-land,
wherof also a parte was made. The Creation of white knights of the order
of Aristotles well, which should bee sworne to defend Aristotle against all
authours. water against wine, footemen against horsemen, and many more 25
such like injunctions. A lottery for those of the Colledge or straungers as itt
pleased them to draw, not for matters of wealth, but | only of mirth and
witt. The triumph of all the ffounders of the Colledges in Oxford, a devise
much thought on, but it required more invention, more cost then the time
would afoord. The holding of a Court Leet and Baron for ye Prince, wherein 30
there should have beene Leasses drawne, Copies taken, surrenders made: all
which were not so much neglected as prevented by the shortenes of time and
want of mony, better wits and richer daies may here after make vpp which
was then lefte vnperfect

Here some Letters might bee inserted and other gratulatory messages from 35
divers freindes to the Prince but it is high time to make an end of this tædious
and fruitelesse relation, vnlesse the knowledge of trouble and vanity bee
fruitefull

Wee intended in these excercises, the practise and audacity ⌐of our youth¬
the Creditt and good name of our Colledge, the love and favour of the 40
Vniuersity, but instead of all these (so easie a thing it is to be deceived in
a good meaning) wee met with peevishnesse at home, peruersnes abroad,
contradictions every where, some never thought themselves entreated enough

to their owne good and creditt; others thought themselves able to doe nothing,
if they Could not thwarte and hinder some-thing: most stood by and gave
aime willing to see much and ⌈doe⌉ nothing, nay perchaunce they were ready
to procure most trouble which would bee sure to yeild least helpe. And yet
wee may not so much grudge at faultes at home as wee may iustly Complaine   5
of hard measure abroad. For insteed of the | love and favour of the Vniuersitie,
wee found our selves (wee will say justly) taxed for any the least errour (though
ingenious spirites would have pardoned many thinges where all thinges were
entended for their owne pleasure) but most vnjustly censured, and envied for
that which was done, (wee dare say) indifferently well so that in a word, wee   10
paid deere for trouble, and in a manner hired and sent for men to doe vs wrong.
Let others herafter take heed how they attempte the like, vnlesse they find
better meanes at home, and better mindes abroad. And yet wee cannot
complaine of all, some ment well and said well, and those tooke good will
for good paiment: good endevours for good performaunce, and such (in   15
this kind) shall deserve a private favour, when other shalbee denied a
common benefit

Seria vix rectè agnoscit, qui ludicra nescit.

20

FINIS:

Chancellor's Court Inventories   OUA: HYP/B/10
mb 1   *(21 February) (Inventory of Nicholas Bond)*
…   25

In the Dynynge chamber

…

Item one presse for instrumentes	vj s. viij d.
Item one paire of Virginalls	xl s.
Item ij Lutes	xl s. 30
Item ij Bandores	xl s.
Item one Cetterne	vj s. viij d.

…

Audited Corporation Accounts   OCA: P.5.2   35
f 102v   *(Chamberlains' payments)*
…

Item given to the Queenes Players by the appoyntment
of master mayor   x s.
…   40

19/ Seria … nescit: *'No one understands anything serious well who does not know about jesting'*

f 103

…

Item paid to the King*es* Trumpetters   xvj s.

…

f 103v

…

Item given to Sixe Trumpetters   iij s.
Item to a Noblemans musitions   ij s.

…

Keykeepers' Accounts   OCA: P.4.1
f 123   *(Bonds and bills not summed)*

…

One bond of Gibbins for the Scutchins

…

St Martin Churchwardens' Accounts   ORO: PAR 207/4/F1/1, item 107
single mb*   *(Rendered 7 April 1609) (Receipts)*

…

Item received at Hocketyde   xviij s. v d.

…

Item rec*eived* cleere gaine at Whitsontid   xxxviij s.

…

St Mary Magdalen Churchwardens' Accounts   ORO: PAR 208/4/F1/40
single mb   *(Rendered 18 April 1609) (Receipts)*

…

Item Receiued at Hocktide all thing*es* beinge discharged   xliij s. viij d.
Ite*m* Receiued at Whitsontide all thing*es* beinge discharged   iij li. v s.

…

St Michael at the North Gate Churchwardens' Accounts
ORO: PAR 211/4/F1/3, item 171
single mb   *(Receipts)*

…

Item receiued at Hocketyde all thing*es* beinge dischardged   ij li. iiij s.
Item receiued at Midsomer all thing*es* beinge dischardged   xxxij s. vij d.

…

21, 29, 37/ Hocketyde, Hocktide: *4–5 April 1608*
23, 30/ Whitsontid, Whitsontide: *15–21 May 1608*

St Peter in the East Churchwardens' Accounts   ORO: PAR 213/4/F1/2
single sheet col 1   *(31 March 1608–19 April 1609) (Receipts)*
…

Item Receaved for hockeinge   xlij s.
…   5

St Peter le Bailey Churchwardens' Accounts   ORO: PAR 214/4/F1/55
mb [1]   *(Rendered 25 April 1609) (Receipts)*
…

In primis Receyved for hocktyd and whitsontyde   10
all thing*es* dischardged   v li. vij s. vij d. ob.
…

1608–9
Christ Church Treasurers' Accounts   ChCh Arch: iii.c.1   15
f 152
…

Et in expensis Comædiar*um* et Tragædiar*um* hoc
anno fact*arum*   v li.
…   20

Christ Church Disbursements   ChCh Arch: xii.b.53
f 24v   *(25 December–25 March)*
…

Com*medies* &   To Mr Iux for ye playes by Consent five po*und*es   v li. 25
Trag*edies*   *(signed)* Simon Iucks.
…

Magdalen College Libri Computi   MC Arch: LCE/8
f 15   *(Internal and external payments)*   30
…

Solutum   Buccinatorib*us* Comitis Pembrocij   6 s.
…

f 15v   35
…

Musicis in festo Bursariorum   5 s.
…

4/ hockeinge: *Hocktide was 4–5 April 1608*
10/ In primis: *in display script*
10/ hocktyd: *4–5 April 1608*
10/ whitsontyde: *15–21 May 1608*

Merton College Bursars' Accounts   MCR: 3.1
f 127v   *(18 November–24 March)*   *(External expenses)*
…
…Musicis ex consensu 6 s. 8 d. et pro ijsdem in Cæna 22 d.…
…   5

Merton College Register   MCR: 1.3
p 229   *(Allowances)*
…
Ianuarij 29no allocavimus de more tibicinibus 6 s. 8.   10
…

New College Bursars' Accounts   NC Arch: 7604
mb 8   *(25 December–25 March)*   *(Internal expenses)*
…   15
…So*lutum* to a sett of Trumpeters iiij s.… So*lutum* Musicis oppidanis vj s.
viiij d.…
…

The Queen's College Long Rolls   QC Arch: LRA   20
f 36v col 2   *(7 July–7 July)*   *(External expenses)*
…
Ite*m* buccinatoribus   2 s. 6 d.
…
Ite*m* regis buccinatoribus   10 s. 25
…
Ite*m* tibicinibus de Oxon*ia*   10 s.
…

St John's College Computus Hebdomalis   SJC Arch: Acc.v.E.4   30
f 59v   *(26 December–1 January)*
…
Set on for Musick v s.
…

                                                                                       35
f 61v   *(20–6 February)*
…
Set on for ye Musitions. 3 li. 11 s. 10 d.
…

f 62   *(6–12 March)*

…

Set on for ye ffidlers. xxxv s. x d.

…

                                                                          5

Vice-Chancellors' Accounts   OUA: WP/β/21(4)
p 160   *(17 July–14 July) (Extraordinary expenses)*

Solut*um* Buccinatoribus Regijs   xx s.
…   10

Keykeepers' Accounts   OCA: P.4.1
f 126v   *(Bonds and bills not summed)*

…

One bond of Gibbins for the Scutchins   15

…

St Aldate Churchwardens' Accounts
ORO: DD Par. Oxford St Aldate b.16/15
single mb   *(16 April 1609–8 April 1610) (Receipts)*   20

…

Item gained at Hocktyde   xxx s.

…

(Payments)   25
Item paid to the vndersherife for the maypoll   xxvij s.

…

St Martin Churchwardens' Accounts   ORO: PAR 207/4/F1/1, item 110
single mb   *(Rendered 7 April 1610) (Receipts)*   30

…

Rec*eiued* for Hocking mony declaro   xl s.

…

St Mary Magdalen Churchwardens' Accounts   ORO: PAR 208/4/F1/41   35
single mb   *(Rendered 10 April 1610) (Receipts)*

…

Item rec*eiued* at Hocktide and whitsontide all thinges
beinge discharged: v li. xiiij s.
…   40

22, 38/ Hocktyde, Hocktide: *24–5 April 1609*   38/ whitsontide: *4–10 June 1609*
32/ Hocking: *Hocktide was 24–5 April 1609*

St Mary the Virgin Churchwardens' Accounts   ORO: PAR 209/4/F1/24
single mb   *(16 April 1609–8 April 1610)* *(Receipts)*

...

Item gayned at Hocktyde   xv s.

...   5

St Michael at the North Gate Churchwardens' Accounts
ORO: PAR 211/4/F1/3, item 172
single mb   *(Receipts)*

...   10

The remaines of: Item there remained of ye mony gotten att hoctide
ye hoctide mony all thinges discharged   xxxvij s. j d.

...

St Peter in the East Churchwardens' Accounts   ORO: PAR 213/4/F1/2   15
single mb   *(10 April 1609–31 March 1610)* *(Receipts)*

...

...Item for hockinge mony   xlij s.

...

                                                                              20

St Peter le Bailey Churchwardens' Accounts   ORO: PAR 214/4/F1/56
single mb   *(Rendered 16 April 1610)* *(Receipts)*

...

Item at Hocktide   xxix s. j d.
Item for the vse of the parishe drum*m*e at Whitsontide   ij s. vj d. 25

...

1609–10
All Souls College Bursars' Accounts   Bodl.: MS. D.D. All Souls c.289
mb 12   *(2 November–2 November)* *(Rewards)*   30

...

Et de ij s. vj d. to the Kings Tru*m*peters

...

Balliol College Bursars' Accounts   BC Arch: Computi 1592–1614   35
f 92v   *(18 October–7 July)* *(Expenses noted)*

...

Ite*m* to S*ir* William Munsons trumpetters   2 s. 6 d.

...

4, 11, 24/ Hocktyde, hoctide, Hocktide: *24–5*   18/ hockinge: *Hocktide was 24–5 April 1609*
   April 1609   25/ Whitsontide: *4–10 June 1609*

f 94v   *(7 July–18 October)*

...

It*em* given to the King his Ma*ie*sties Trumpetters   vj s. viij d.

Christ Church Treasurers' Accounts   ChCh Arch: iii.c.1   5
f 164

...

Et in expens*is* Tragædiar*um* et Comædiar*um* hoc
Anno fact*arum*   n*il* li.

...   10

f 172v

...

Comedies & Tragedies   n*il* li.

...   15

Letter of Henry Jackson to D.G.P   CCC: MS 304
ff 83v–4*

® 10.   D.G.P.   20
   –Postremis his diebus adfuerunt Regis Actores Scenici. Egerunt cum
applausu maximo, pleno theatro. Sed viris piis et doctis impii merito visi
sunt, quod non contenti Alcumistas perstringere, ipsas sanctas Scripturas
fœdissimè violarint. Anabaptistas scilicet vellicabant; ut sub hac persona
lateret improbitas.–   25
   –Theologos nostros, qui (pudet dicere) avidissimè confluebant.–
   –nusquam maiori plausu theatra nostra sonuisse, quam cum intraret
personatus ille nebulo, qui, ut | fictam Anabaptistarum sanctitatem
spectatoribus deridendam proponeret, scripturas impie, et prodigiosè
contaminavit. Habuerunt et Tragœdias, quas decorè, et aptè agebant. In   30
quibus non solùm dicendo, sed etiam faciendo quædam lachrymas movebant.–
   –At verò Desdemona illa apud nos a marito occisa, quanquam optimè
semper causam egit, interfecta tamen magis movebat; cum in lecto decumbens
spectantium misericordiam ipso vultu imploraret.–
                                                        Sept*ember* 1610.   35

Exeter College Rectors' Accounts   AC Arch: A.II.9
f 207v   *(1 November–1 November)*

...

Ite*m* de solutis & datis tubicinis regijs   10 s.   40

...

Magdalen College Libri Computi   MC Arch: LCE/8
f 25v   *(Internal and external payments)*

...

Buccinatoribus Regis in regardo   1 li. 0 0

...   5

f 26

...

Buccinatoribus in regardo   0 6 s. 0
Musicis in Festo Bursariorum   0 5 s. 0 10

...

Merton College Bursars' Accounts   MCR: 3.1
f 132v   *(24 November–23 March)* *(External expenses)*

...   15

...Musicis ex consensu 6 s. 8 d. pro caena eorundem 2 s. 6 d.

New College Bursars' Accounts   NC Arch: 7606
mb 9   *(29 September–25 December)* *(Internal expenses)*

...   20

...Solutum to a sett of Trumpeters v s....

...

(25 December–25 March)
...Solutum Musicis oppidanis vj s. viij d.   25

...

mb 10   *(24 June–29 September)*

Solutum to the Kinges trumpeters xx s....   30

...

Oriel College Treasurers' Accounts   OC Arch: S I.C.1
f 152v   *(Internal expenses)*

...   35

Item Regis Buccinatoribus.   v s.

...

The Queen's College Long Rolls   QC Arch: LRA
f 38v col 1   *(7 July–7 July)* *(External expenses)*   40

...

Item buccinatoribus   2 s. 6 d.

Item Mauritio fidicini   18 d.

...

Item tibicinibus de Oxonia   10 s.

...

The Queen's College Long Rolls   QC Arch: LRB
f 4v col 2   *(7 July 1610–7 July 1611)*   *(External expenses)*

...

Item Regis Buccinatoribus ⌈Augusti 29.⌉   20 s.

...

St John's College Computus Hebdomalis   SJC Arch: Acc.v.E.4
f 75v   *(5–11 February)*

...

Set on for ye ffidlers   xxix s. viij d.

...

(12–18 February)
Set on for ye ffidlers   iiij s.

...

f 76   *(19–25 February)*

...

Set on for ye Musitions   lvjj s. iiij d.

...

City Council Minutes   OCA: C/FC/1/A1/002
f 132v*   *(11 May)*

...

Iohn Bosseley
musition to
haue a new
lease

It is also agreed That Iohn Bosseley Musition shall haue a Lease of the Chamber
At Bocardo now in his tenure for xxxj yeares from our Lady Day last past for
ye yearelye rent of xxvj s. viij d. w*i*th such Covenant*es* for Reparac*i*ons as
shalbee thought fitt by this Howse*l*.

...

f 135   *(27 September)*

...

A Certaine
pro*v*isoe to be
putt into Iohn
Bosseleys Lease

Item It is agreed At this Counsell That a Provisoe shalbee putt into Iohn
Bosseleys Lease nott to lett or sett w*ith*out lycense etc And also not to daunce
nor sufferr any Daunching after tenne of the Clocke in the night nor before
ffyve of the Clocke in the morning*l*

38/ Item It is: *in display script*

Audited Corporation Accounts   OCA: P.5.2
f 111v   *(Chamberlains' payments)*

…

Item paid to him ye same day for the king*es* Trumpetters   xx s.
Item paid to him the same day for the king*es* players   xx s.   5

Keykeepers' Accounts   OCA: P.4.1
f 130   *(Bonds and bills not summed)*

…

One band of Gibbins for the scutchins   10

…

Indentures and Leases Book   OCA: D.5.5
f 180*   *(11 May)*

…   15

Iohn Bosseley his Lease

This Indenture made the Eleaventh Dey of May in the Eight yeare of the
Raigne of our sou*er*aigne Lord Iames by the grace of god Kinge of England
ffraunce and Ireland Defender of the ffaith etc And the Three and ffortith
of Scotland Betweene the Mayor Bayliff*es* and Com*m*ynaltie of the Cyttie of
Oxon. in the Countye of Oxon. of thone p*ar*te/ And Iohn Bosseley of the   20
said Cyttie Musition of thother p*ar*te// Witnesseth That the said Mayor
Bayliff*es* and Com*m*ynaltie of their one assent and Consent for Diu*er*se good
Causes and Considerac*i*ons them therevnto Movinge/ Have Demysed,
graunted and to farme Letten/ And by theis *presentes* for them and their
successors Doe Demyse graunte and to farme lett vnto the said Iohn Bosseley   25
All that their vpper Roome Soller or Chamber called or knowne by ye name
of the Dauncing schoole nowe in the tenure of the said Iohn Bosseley
togeather with the Stayres and passages therevnto accustomed which the
said Roome Soller or Chamber is scytuate lying and beinge neare vnto the
Northgate of the said Cyttie of Oxon. in the Countye of Oxon. and reacheth   30
over p*ar*cells of a Tenem*ent* and howses there now in thoccupation of Iohn
Harrington and extendeth through out the whole length thereof vnder a
certen Cockloft now also in thoccupac*i*on of the said Iohn Harrington and
abutteth sowthward vppon certeyne Roomes heretofore leased by the said
Mayor Bayliff*es* and Com*m*ynaltie vnto one Iohn Stacye// To haue and to   35
hould the said vpper Roome Soller or Chamber and eu*er*ye p*ar*te thereof
togeather with the said Stayres and passages therevnto accustomed vnto him

---

4/ him: *the mayor, Thomas Harris*
4/ ye same day: *5 August 1610*
16/ This Indenture: *with display capitals*
19/ Betweene: *with display capital*

21/ Witnesseth: *with display capital*
23/ Have: *with display capital*
35–6/ To haue and to hould: *in display script*

the said Iohn Bosseley his executors ad*ministrators* and assigns ffrom the ffeast
of Than*n*u*n*cyaci*o*n of our blessed Ladye Sa*in*t Marye the Virgine last past
before the date hereof vnto the ffull end and terme of one and thirtye yeares
from thenceforth next followinge fully to bee Compleate and ended// Yelding
& paying therefore yearely During the said terme vnto the said Mayor   5
Baylyff*es* & Com*m*ynaltie their successors and assignes Twentye six shilling*es*
& eight pence of good and lawfull money of England On the ffeast*es* of Sa*in*t
Michaell Tharchangell and Than*n*u*n*cyaci*o*n of our blessed Ladye Sai*n*t Marye
the Virgine by equall porc*i*ons...

...   10

f 181

...

...Provided ffurthermore and it is conditioned by and betwixt the said partyes
to theis presente Indentures that yf the said Iohn Bosseley his executors   15
administrators or assignes or any of them shall att any time or tymes hereafter
During the said terme willingly or wittingly *per*mitt or suffer his or their
scholler or schollers or any other *per*son or *per*sons whatsoever to daunce in
and vppon the said Demysed Roome Sollere or Chamber or any *p*arte or
*p*arcell thereof betweene the Howres of twoe of the clocke in the afternoon   20
and ffive of the Cloke in the fforenoone That then this *pre*sente Indenture
Demyse and graunte and eu*er*ye article C⌃⌜l⌝ause and sentence herein
Conteyned shall cease and be vtterly voide/ Any thinge herein Conteyned to
the Contrary thereof in any wise notwithstandinge/ In witnes whereof the
*p*artyes first aboue said to their *pre*sent Indentures haue interchangeablie sett   25
their seales/ Dated the day and yeare first aboue written.

St Aldate Churchwardens' Accounts
ORO: DD Par. Oxford St Aldate b.17/1
mb [1]*   *(Rendered 31 March 1611) (Receipts)*   30

...

Item receaved & gotten at Whitsontide
& Hocktide   vj li. ⌜v d.⌝ [viij s.] x d. ob.

...

4–5/ Yelding & paying: *in display script*
14/ Provided: *with display capital*
20/ twoe: *written heavily over an erasure, possibly of the word* ten
24/ In witnes: *in display script*
32/ Whitsontide: *27 May–2 June 1610*
33/ Hocktide: *16–17 April 1610*

St Martin Churchwardens' Accounts   ORO: PAR 207/4/F1/1, item 112
single mb   *(Rendered 7 April 1611)* *(Receipts)*
...

Rec*eiue*d for Hockinge mony declaro   xlj s.
...   5

Rec*eiue*d att Whittsontide Declaro   vij li. xiij s. iiij d.
...

St Mary Magdalen Churchwardens' Accounts   ORO: PAR 208/4/F1/42
single mb   *(Rendered 26 March 1611)* *(Receipts)*   10
...

Ite*m* rec*eiue*d att Hocktide and Whitsontide
all thing*es* beinge discharged: v li. iij d.
...

                                                                                                                    15
St Peter le Bailey Churchwardens' Accounts   ORO: PAR 214/4/F1/57
single mb*   *(Rendered 2 April 1611)* *(Receipts)*
...

Item r*eceiv*ed of Hocke mony   36 s. 2 d.
Item of Rowland Barbor for the dru*m*me for a day   12 d. 20
...

***c* 1610–15**
Poem on Mercurius Rusticans   Bodl.: MS. Wood D.18, Pt 2
f 1*   25

Mercurius Rusticans
Scena Hyncksey vel Hincksie

f 29*   30
...

          Mr Sellar of *Corpus Christi College* in jeere of this play
Of ‸⌈old⌉ leathern thongs
And other mens songs
They patcht us up a play   35
Th'were so often out
We began to doubt
Whether th'were Hincksie men or thay.

4, 19/ Hockinge, Hocke: *Hocktide was 16–17 April 1610*
6, 12/ Whittsontide, Whitsontide: *27 May–2 June 1610*
12/ Hocktide: *16–17 April 1610*
28/ Hyncksey, Hincksie: *Hinksey, Berkshire*

1610–11
Christ Church Treasurers' Accounts   ChCh Arch: iii.c.1
f 178

...

Comædies & Tragedies   *(blank)*   5

...

Magdalen College Libri Computi   MC Arch: LCE/8
f 35v   *(Internal and external payments)*

...   10

Buccinatoribus diuersorum nobilium
in regardo   0 6 s. 0

...

Musicis in festo Bursariorum;   0 5 s. 0

...   15

Merton College Bursars' Accounts   MCR: 3.1
f 140   *(23 November–22 March)* *(External expenses)*

...

...Musicis ex consensu. sex solidos octo denarios. pro cæna eorundem duos   20
solidos sex denarios...

The Queen's College Long Rolls   QC Arch: LRB
f 4v col 2   *(7 July–7 July)* *(External expenses)*

...   25

Item tibicinis de Oxonia   10 s.

...

Item Mauritio Fidicini   18 d.

...

                                                                                                                   30

St John's College Computus Hebdomalis   SJC Arch: Acc.v.E.4
f 90   *(11–17 February)*

...

Set on for a commedie & a tragœdie 7 li. 13 s. 4 d.

...   35

f 91   *(11–17 March)*

...

Set on for ye Musitions. 3 li. 14 s. 6 d.

...   40

Keykeepers' Accounts   OCA: P.4.1
f 132v   *(Other bonds)*
…
One bond of Gibbins for the scutchins
…   5

Tailors' Wardens' Accounts   Bodl.: MS. Rolls Oxon 66, roll 8
mb [2]   *(Payments)*
…
Item Towardes the expences of the masters Dinner   £x 10
Item to the musitions at the masters Dinner   vj s. viij d.
…

St Martin Churchwardens' Accounts   ORO: PAR 207/4/F1/1, items 113–15
mb [1]   *(Rendered 24 April 1612) (Receipts)*   15
…
Receved declaro at hocktyd   ij li. viij s. vj d.
Receved at whitsontyde declaro all Charges boren   xviij li.
…
                                                                         20
(Payments)
payd for a Rickinge which was for gotton at Whittsontyd
after wee had made owr Acownts   vij d.
…
                                                                         25
St Mary the Virgin Churchwardens' Accounts   ORO: PAR 209/4/F1/25
single mb   *(29 March 1611–17 April 1612) (Receipts)*
…
Item gained at Hocktide   xlvj s.
…   30

St Michael at the North Gate Churchwardens' Accounts
ORO: PAR 211/4/F1/3, item 174
single mb   *(Receipts)*
…   35
Item gained at Hocktyde all thinges dischardged   xliij s.
Item at Whitsontyde all thinges beinge discharged   iij li. xj s. iij d.
…

10/ masters: *William Cakebread's*
17, 29, 36/ hocktyd, Hocktide, Hocktyde: *1–2 April 1611*
18, 22, 37/ whitsontyde, Whittsontyd, Whitsontyde: *12–18 May 1611*

(Payments)
Item Thomas Burnham asketh allowance for the
vse of his howse for the Church ale x s.

...

St Peter le Bailey Churchwardens' Accounts ORO: PAR 214/4/F1/58
single mb *(Rendered 14 April 1612) (Receipts)*

...

Item Att hocktide j li. x s. 0

...

Item for the vse of the Drumm 0 iij s.

...

Item Received at Whitsontide (all charges paid) j li. [x s.] ⌈vj⌉ s. viij d.

...

1611–12
Balliol College Bursars' Accounts BC Arch: Computi 1592–1614
f 102v *(18 October–7 July) (Expenses noted)*

...

Item giuen to trumpetors February 17⁰ 5 s.

...

f 104 *(7 July–18 October)*

...

Item to the Prince his trumpeters August 19th 10 s.
Item to the Kings Maiesties trumpeters August 29 6 s. 8 d.

...

Christ Church Computi ChCh Arch: iii.c.8(d.)
mb 2d*

...

Et in expensis Tragœdiarum et Comediarum hoc
anno factarum nil

...

Christ Church Battells Books ChCh Arch: x(i).c.48
f 35 *(17–23 April) (Extra expenses)*

...

...to the Musitians. of the Towne. v li. xx d....

...

2/ Thomas Burnham: *churchwarden*   13/ Whitsontide: *12–18 May 1611*
9/ hocktide: *1–2 April 1611*

Corpus Christi College Bursars' Accounts   CCCA: C/1/1/8
f [9]   *(Internal expenses)*

...

To the Kinges Trumpittors   xiij s. iiij d.

...   5

To the Princes Trumpittors   x s.

...

Exeter College Rectors' Accounts   AC Arch: A.II.9
f 216   *(1 November–1 November)*   10

...

Item de solutis Regis & Principis Buccinatoribus   38 s.

...

Magdalen College Libri Computi   MC Arch: LCE/8   15
f 45   *(Internal and external payments)*

...

Musicis in festo Burs*ariorum*   5 s.

...

                                                                         20

f 45v

...

Buccinatorib*us*, in regardo, regijs   20 s.

...

Buccinatorib*us* principis in regardo   20 s. 25

...

Merton College Bursars' Accounts   MCR: 3.1
f 146v   *(22 November–20 March)* *(External expenses)*

...   30

...Musicis ex consensu 6 s. 8 d. p*ro* cæna eoru*m* 2 s.... Tubicinibus
regijs 6 s....

...

The Queen's College Long Rolls   QC Arch: LRB   35
f 7 col 1   *(7 July–7 July)* *(External expenses)*

...

Ite*m* Tibicinibus de Oxon*ia*   10 s.

...

Ite*m* Mauritio Fidicini   18 s. 40

...

f 9 col 2 *(7 July 1612–7 July 1613)* *(External expenses)*

...

Item Clarionib*us* Regis Aug*usti* 28   20 s.

...

Item Clarionibus principis. Septem*bris* 27   10 s.   5

...

St John's College Computus Hebdomalis   SJC Arch: Acc.v.E.4
f 104 *(17–23 February)*

...   10

Set on for ye Musitions   xlvj s. vj d.

...

Audited Corporation Accounts   OCA: P.5.2
f 121v *(Chamberlains' payments)*   15

...

Item given to the King*es* Trumpettors   XX s.
Item given to ye Prince*s* Trumpettors   XV s.

...
                                                                                                  20

Keykeepers' Accounts   OCA: P.4.1
f 138 *(Other bonds)*

...

One Bond of Gibbins for ye Scutchins

...   25

Indentures and Leases Book   OCA: D.5.5
f 189*

Iohn Bosseley   To all Chri*st*ian People to Whom this pr*esent* writing shall Com*m*e to bee   30
his lycense   seene Reade heard or vnderstoode/ Wee the Mayor Bayliff*es* & Comynaltie of
the Cyttie of Oxon. in the Countye of Oxon. send greeting in our Lord god
eu*er*lasting Whereas Wee the said Mayor Bayliff*es* & Comynaltie by our
Indenture of Lease bearing Date of Eleaventh Day of May in the Eight yeare
of the Raigne of our Sou*er*aigne Lord Iames by the grace of god kinge of   35
England ffraunce and Ireland Defender of the ffaith &c and the Three and
fforteth of Scotland Did of our one assent & consent Demyse graunte and to
farme let vnto Iohn Bosseley of the said Cyttie musition All that our Vpper
Roome Soller or Chamber called or knowne by the name of the Dauncing

30/ To all Chri*st*ian People: *in display script*   33/ Whereas: *in display script*
31/ the Mayor: *Matthew Harrison*

Schoole then and now in the tenure of the said Iohn Bosseley Togeather With
the Stayers and passages therevnto accustomed Which said Roome Soller
or Chamber is scytuate lying and beinge neare vnto the North gate of the
said Cyttie of Oxon. in the Countye of Oxon. and Reacheth over parcells of
a Tenement & howses there then and now [of] in the occupacion of Iohn   5
Harrington and extended throughout the Wholl length thereof vnder certayne
cocklofte then and nowe also in thoccupacion of the said Iohn Harrington
To Haue and to hould the said vpper Roome Soller or Chamber and euerye
parte thereof togeather with the said Stay‸⌈ers⌉ and passages therevnto
accustomed vnto him the said Iohn Bosseley his executors Administrators &   10
assignes ffrom the ffeast of Thanuncyacyon of our blessed Lady St Marie the
virgine then last past before the Date [hereof] of the said receyted Indenture
vnto the full end and terme of one and thirtie yeares from thenchforth next
following fullie to bee Compleate and ended/ Yelding and peying therefore
yearelie During the said terme vnto the said Mayor Bayliffes and Commynaltie 15
their successors and assignes Twenty Sixe shillinges and eight pence of good
and lawfull money of England On the feastes of St Michaell Tharchangell and
Thanuncyacion of our blessed Ladye St marie the virgine by equall porcions./
In and by which said receyted Indenture it is provided That neither the said
Iohn Bosseley his executors or assignes no anie of them shall not att anie tyme 20
hereafter During the said terme Demyse graunte let set assigne or sett over
the said [Demysed] premises by theis grauntes demysed nor anie parte or
parcell thereof nor his nor their estate nor terme of yeares thereby graunted
nor anie parte or parcell thereof to anie person or persons whatsoeuer without
the specyall lycense consent and agreement of vs the said Mayor Bayliffes and 25
Commynaltie or our successors therevnto first had and obteyned in Wryting
vnder our Common Seale As in and by the said receyted Indenture/ emongest
Diuerse other thinges therein conteyned more plainelye and larg it doth
and may appeare now knowe yee That wee the said Mayor Bayliffes and
Commynaltie of our one assent [and] Consent and agreement haue lycensed   30
& aucthorised And by theis presentes for vs and our Successors doe lycense
& aucthorize the said Iohn Bosseley Att anie tyme hereafter during the residue
yet to come of the said terme of Thirtye and one yeares to demyse graunte lett
set assigne [⟨.⟩] or set over the said demysed premisses or his estate or terme
of yeares by the said Indenture graunted or anie parte or parcell thereof to   35
Thomas Charles of the Cyttie of Oxon. aforesaid musition his executors
administrators and assignes/ The said Provisoe or anie other Article Condicion
or Clause in the said indenture conteyned to the Contrarie thereof in anie

8/ To Haue: *in display script*
14/ Yelding: *in display script*
19/ In: *in display script*
29/ now knowe: *in display script*

wyse not with standing In witns Whereof Wee the said mayor Bayliffes and
Commynaltie Haue herevnto set our [handes] Common Seale/ dated the ffifte
Day of Iune in the Tenth yeare of the Raigne of our Soueraigne Lord Iames by
the grace of God king of England ffraunce and Ireland Defender of the ffaith
&c and the ffive and fforth of Scotland//:/./   5

St Aldate Churchwardens' Accounts
ORO: DD Par. Oxford St Aldate b.17/3
mb [1]   *(Rendered 18 April 1613)* *(Receipts)*
...   10
Item gayned at Hocktyde   iiij li. ij s. v d.
Item gained by our Whitson ale   v li. xix s. vij d.
Item received for a Tree   vj s.
...

                                                                                 15
St Martin Churchwardens' Accounts   ORO: PAR 207/4/F1/1, item 116
mb [1]*   *(Rendered 11 April 1613)* *(Receipts)*
...
Item Receaved more declaro at hocktide last   ij li. iij s.
Item made declaro at whitsuntide for the Churche   20
by the whitsun ale last   xj li. iiij d.
...

mb [2]   *(Payments)*
...   25
Item for a reckoning for gotten at whitesontide   xij d.
...

St Mary Magdalen Churchwardens' Accounts   ORO: PAR 208/4/F1/43
single mb   *(Rendered 6 April 1613)* *(Receipts)*   30
...
Item receiued att Hocktide and whitsontide
all thinges beinge discharged   iiij li. vij s. ij d.
...

1/ In witns: *in display script; for* In witnes
5/ fforth: *for* ffortieth
11, 19, 32/ Hocktyde, hocktide last, Hocktide: *20–1 April 1612*
12/ Whitson: *Whitsuntide was 31 May–6 June 1612*
20, 26, 32/ whitsuntide, whitesontide, whitsontide: *31 May–6 June 1612*

St Mary the Virgin Churchwardens' Accounts
Bodl.: MS. Ch. Oxon. a.11, item 192
single sheet   *(17 April 1612–8 April 1613)* *(Receipts)*

...

Item gayned at Hocktyde   li s.   5

...

St Michael at the North Gate Churchwardens' Accounts
ORO: PAR 211/4/F1/3, item 175
single mb   *(Rendered 8 April 1613)* *(Receipts)*   10

...

Item gained at Hocktyde all thinges beinge
dischardged   xxxvj s.
Item by our May-ale gained cleerely   xxxvj s.

...   15

St Peter in the East Churchwardens' Accounts   ORO: PAR 213/4/F1/2
single mb col 1   *(15 April 1612–10 April 1613)* *(Receipts)*

...

Item gained at Hocktyde   xl s. vj d.   20

...

col 2   *(Payments)*

...

Item for a mearcement for the woode at   25
whitson tyde was twelvemonth   vj s. viij d.

St Peter le Bailey Churchwardens' Accounts   ORO: PAR 214/4/F1/59
single mb   *(Rendered 16 April 1613)* *(Receipts)*

...   30

Item gotten at Hocketyde   xxxiiij s. viij d.
Item gotten at Whitsontyde   iij li. iij s.

...

1612–13   35
Christ Church Disbursements   ChCh Arch: xii.b.57
f 24   *(25 December–25 March)* *(Extraordinary expenses)*

...

To Gye the Carryer for ye portage of 2.

5, 12, 20, 31/ Hocktyde, Hocketyde: *20–1 April 1612*
26, 32/ whitson tyde, Whitsontyde: *31 May–6 June 1612*

Dozen of torches for ye playes   ij s.
    (signed)   Alex Hill
...

To M*aste*r Auditor for .2. dozen of Torches for ye playes.   xx s.
    (signed)   Phillipp Kinge   5
...

Christ Church Computi   ChCh Arch: iii.c.8(e.)
mb 2d*
...   10
Et in expens*is* Tragœdiar*um* et Comœdiarum hoc
Anno fact*arum*   Nil.
...

Lincoln College Calculus 1612–13   LC Arch   15
f 6   *(30 January–5 February)* *(Commons costs)*
...
Music*is*   Domus   xij s. ij d. q*u*a.
...
                                                         20

Magdalen College Libri Computi   MC Arch: LCE/8
f 55v*   *(Internal and external payments)*
...
Musicis in festo Bursario*rum*   5 s.
...   25
Solut*um* x   M*agist*ro Otes pro Comm*æ*dia habenda coram principe
palatino p*er* billam   5 li. 9 s.
...

New College Bursars' Accounts   NC Arch: 7611   30
mb 8   *(29 September–25 March)* *(Internal expenses)*
...
...So*lutum* Musicis opidanis vj s. viij d.
...
                                                         35

The Queen's College Long Rolls   QC Arch: LRB
f 9v col 1   *(7 July–7 July)* *(External expenses)*
...
Ian*uarij* 1º   Item Mauritio fidicini   18 d.
...   40
Febr*uarij* 18   Item Tibicin*ibus* de Oxon*ia*   10 s.
...

St John's College Computus Hebdomalis   SJC Arch: Acc.v.E.4
f 116v   *(18–24 January)*

...

Set on for ye Christmas Fidlars   xlij s. ij d.

...   5

f 118   *(1–7 March)*

...

Set on for ye Musitions   iij li. vj s. x d.

...   10

Audited Corporation Accounts   OCA: P.5.2
f 126v*   *(Chamberlains' payments)*

...

Item paid to mr Niccolls for the king*es* players given   15
by m*aste*r mayor   x s.

...

Keykeepers' Accounts   OCA: P.4.1
f 143   *(Other bonds)*   20

...

One bond of Gibbins for the Scutchins.

...

St Martin Churchwardens' Accounts   ORO: PAR 207/4/F1/1, item 118   25
mb [1]   *(Rendered 8 May 1614)* *(Receipts)*

...

Item receaved more declaro at hocktide last   xl s.
Item made declaro at Whitsuntide for the Church by
the Whitsun ale last   viii li. 30

...

St Mary Magdalen Churchwardens' Accounts   ORO: PAR 208/4/F1/44
single mb   *(Rendered 26 April 1614)* *(Receipts)*

...   35

Item Rec*eiu*ed att Hocktyde and Whytsontyde all
thing*es* beinge discharged: xxxviij s. v d.

...

16/ m*aste*r mayor: *Ralph Flexney*
28, 36/ hocktide last, Hocktyde: *12–13 April 1613*
29, 36/ Whitsuntide, Whytsontyde: *23–9 May 1613*

St Peter in the East Churchwardens' Accounts ORO: PAR 213/4/F1/3
f 1* *(9 April 1613–27 April 1614)* *(Receipts)*

...

Item for Hockinge Money   xlvij s.

...   5

St Peter le Bailey Churchwardens' Accounts ORO: PAR 214/4/F1/60
single mb *(Rendered 8 May 1614)* *(Receipts)*

...

Item gotten at Hocktyde   35 s. 10
Item gained at Whitsontyde   3 li. 5 s.

...

1613–14
All Souls College Bursars' Accounts Bodl.: MS. D.D. All Souls c.290   15
mb 12 *(2 November–2 November)* *(Rewards)*

...

De vj s. viij d. to the Kings trumpeters

...

  20

Balliol College Bursars' Accounts BC Arch: Computi 1592–1614
f 114v *(7 July–18 October 1614)* *(Expenses noted)*

...

It*em* to the Kings Trumpiters   0   6   8

...   25

Christ Church Treasurers' Accounts ChCh Arch: iii.c.1
f 198

...

Et in expens*is* Trag*æ*diar*um* & Com*œ*diar*um* hoc   30
Anno fact*arum*   nil.

...

Christ Church Battells Books ChCh Arch: x(i).c.50
f 20* *(7–13 January)* *(Extra expenses)*   35

...

...for playes set on m*r* Browne & Trulicke. xv s....

...

4/ Hockinge: *Hocktide was 12–13 April 1613*
10/ Hocktyde: *12–13 April 1613*
11/ Whitsontyde: *23–9 May 1613*

Christ Church Receipts   ChCh Arch: xi.b.16
f 3*

...

[Lent to mr Lancaster 3 Satyrs Sutes with the 3 hornes.
       (signed)   Francis Lancaster]   5

Exeter College Rectors' Accounts   AC Arch: A.II.9
f 224   *(1 November–1 November)*

...

Item Buccinatoribus Regijs   1   2   0 10

...

Magdalen College Libri Computi   MC Arch: LCE/8
f 63v   *(Internal and external payments)*

...   15

Musicis in festo Bursariorum   5 s.

...

Buccinatoribus regijs   20 s.

...

      20

Merton College Bursars' Accounts   MCR: 3.1
f 155   *(19 November–18 March)* *(External expenses)*

...

...Musicis ex consensu 6 s. 8 d...

      25

New College Bursars' Accounts   NC Arch: 7614
mb 9   *(29 September–25 December)* *(Internal expenses)*

...

...so*lutum* Musico ludenti in aula vj d....

...   30

(25 December–25 March)
...so*lutum* musico xij d.... so*lutum* Musicis oppidanis vj s. viij d.

...

      35

(24 June–29 September)
...so*lutum* to the king*es* trumpetters x s....

...

4–5/ [Lent ... Francis Lancaster]: *the entire entry is in Lancaster's hand*

Oriel College Treasurers' Accounts   OC Arch: S 1.C.1
f 180v   *(Internal expenses)*

...

Item Buccinatoribus regijs x s....

...   5

The Queen's College Long Rolls   QC Arch: LRB
f 11v col 2   *(7 July–7 July)* *(External expenses)*

...

Item Tibicini*bus* de Oxon*ia* Febr*uarij* 4.	10 s. 10
Item Mauritio Tibicini	18 d.

...

f 14 col 1   *(7 July 1614–7 July 1615)*

...   15

Item sept*embris* 18 Regijs tibicini*bus*   20 s.

...

St John's College Computus Hebdomalis   SJC Arch: Acc.v.E.4
f 132   *(21–7 February)*   20

...

Set on for ye Musitions   iij li. xix s.

...

Vice-Chancellors' Accounts   OUA: WP/β/21(4)   25
p 172   *(2 August–27 July)* *(Extraordinary expenses)*

...

Solut*um* Histrionibus D*omi*næ Reginæ   xx s.

...

30

Audited Corporation Accounts   OCA: P.5.2
f 131v   *(Chamberlains' payments)*

...

Item paid the 13 of March 1613 to the Queenes Players   xx s.

...   35

f 132v*

...

Item paid to the kinges swordbearer	xj s.
Item paid to the kinges trumpeters	xxx s. 40

...

Item spent at Mr Brookes at the Redd Lyon when
Master Mayor went the ffranchisies   xviij s. vj d.
Item given to the Trumpiter   v s.
Item for a paire of stayers for Master Mayor and his
company to goe downe from the Easte bridge when   5
the ffranchisies are ridden   v s. vj d.
...
Item spente more for Rydinge the ffranchisies   xlvj s. x d.
...

    10

Keykeepers' Accounts   OCA: P.4.1
f 147   *(Other bonds)*
...
One bond of Gibbins for the Scutchins
...   15

St Martin Churchwardens' Accounts   ORO: PAR 207/4/F1/1, item 119
mb [1]   *(Rendered 11 April 1615) (Receipts)*
...
Item receaved declaro at Hocktide   xl s.   20
Item made declaro of the whitson ale   viij li.
...

St Peter in the East Churchwardens' Accounts   ORO: PAR 213/4/F1/3
f 2   *(27 April 1614–14 April 1615) (Receipts)*   25
...
Item for Hockinge Money   xl s.
...

St Peter le Bailey Churchwardens' Accounts   ORO: PAR 214/4/F1/60   30
single mb   *(Rendered 25 April 1615) (Receipts)*
...
Item for the wood at Whitsontyde   iiij s. vj d.
Item gotten at Whitsontide clearly   xl s. 0
Item gotten de claro at Hocktide   xxv s.   35
...

2/ Master Mayor: *Henry Toldervey*
20, 35/ Hocktide: *2–3 May 1614*
21/ whitson: *Whitsuntide was 12–18 June 1614*
27/ Hockinge: *Hocktide was 2–3 May 1614*
33, 34/ Whitsontyde, Whitsontide: *12–18 June 1614*

1614–15
Christ Church Treasurers' Accounts   ChCh Arch: iii.c.1
f 205

...

Et in expens*is* Tragædiaru*m* & Comœdiaru*m* hoc anno factar*um*   nil.   5

...

Lincoln College Calculus 1613–14   LC Arch
f 19v   *(21 September–21 December 1614)*   *(Internal expenses)*

...   10

Ite*m* for the Kings Trumpetters payd to m*aste*r Rector   x s.

...

Lincoln College Calculus 1614–15   LC Arch
f 5*   *(11–17 February)*   15

...

Musitians   Domus   vj s. iiij d. q*u*a.

...

Magdalen College Libri Computi   MC Arch: LCE/8   20
f 71v   *(Internal and external payments)*

...

Musicis in festo Bursarioru*m*   5 s.

...

                                                                                  25

f 72*

...

M*agist*ro powell pro expensis in com*m*ædia habita in
hospitio D*om*ini presidis   1 li.
...   30
Buccinatorib*us* in Commitijs   5 s.

...

Merton College Bursars' Accounts   MCR: 3.1
f 161v   *(17 March–28 July)*   *(External expenses)*   35

...

...Symphoniacis ex consensu 6 s. 8 d...

New College Bursars' Accounts   NC Arch: 7615
mb 9   *(25 December–25 March)*   *(Internal expenses)*   40

...

...So*lutum* musicis oppidanis vj s. 8 d....

...

The Queen's College Long Rolls   QC Arch: LRB
f 14 col 1   *(7 July–7 July) (External expenses)*

...

Item Ianuarij 1. Iohanni Mauritio Tibicini   18 d.

...

Item februarij 1. tibicinibus de Oxonia   10 s.

...

col 2

Item Iulij 11 Regijs tibicinibus   10 s.

...

St John's College Computus Hebdomalis   SJC Arch: Acc.v.E.6
f 11v   *(9–15 January)*

...

Tenantes with new years giftes.
A commodie & a Tragadie.

...

f 12v   *(13–19 February)*

...

Set on for a Commodie & a Tragœdie   xv li. ij s. viij d.

...

f 13v   *(27 February–5 March)*

...

The Musitions bill   iiij li. viij s. viij d.

...

Vice-Chancellors' Accounts   OUA: WP/β/21(4)
p 174   *(27 July–20 July) (Extraordinary expenses)*

...

Item solutum Buccinatoribus Regijs apud woodstock   xxij s.
Item solutum Servientibus tempore prandij apud woodstock
Domino vicecancellario Doctoribus et procuratoribus   xxij s.
Item solutum Buccinatoribus Regijs tempore Comitiorum
vltimo elapso   x s.

...

36/ Domino vicecancellario: *William Goodwin*   37–8/ tempore ... elapso: *10 July 1615*
36/ procuratoribus: *Henry Dicus, Richard Baylie*

Dr Howson's Interrogation PRO: SP/14/80
ff [3–3v]* *(10 June)*

...

...all the ArchBishops & Bishops of London since I was first a preacher,
all the Chauncellors of our Uniuersityes, all the Heades of our Colledges   5
especially favoured mee, & all went current untill ∧⌈his⌉ Grace, whoe was euer
my professed enemye, came to his dignity; since which tyme I had [⟨...⟩ed]
⌈indured⌉ that which I thinke was neuer offered to any Christian in any
Religion: condemned without Articles, soe I that neither I could knowe howe
to reform my selfe, or others by my example to avoyd the Errors, which are   10
the cheife endes why punishmentes are inflicted &c. To this little was
answeared: but that the Lord Buckhurst our Chauncellor presently after
my Vichauncellor beinge informed by Bishopp Ravis what kind of man I
was, did euer after detest the memorye of mee.

    To which I replyed, that if any Man wronged me to him, it was his Grace   15
which I suspected allsoe was done, att his Maiestys beinge att Oxford: when
I confessed the Lord Buckhurst gaue me noe countenance: but I ascribed
it to his Grace in respect of the [high] ⌈English⌉ pastorall, which I by the
appointment of our Deane & Chapter caused to ∧⌈bee⌉ made & repeted in my
Lodginge. Which I know was very offensiue to his Grace as then appeared   20
euidently....

...

Audited Corporation Accounts OCA: P.5.2
f 136v* *(Chamberlains' payments)*   25

...

Item delivered to Master Mayor for the Princes Players
at Allhollowtyde   xx s.

...

                                                                               30

f 137v

...

Item Laid out [for] at Rydeing of a franchises   lj s.
Item paid for bringing the Venison   xvj s.
Item geven to the Trumpeters   v s. 35
Item for the Boatemans breakfast   iiij s.

6/ ∧⌈his⌉ Grace: *George Abbot, archbishop of Canterbury, 1611–33*
15/ him: *Thomas Sackville, Lord Buckhurst, chancellor of the University, 1591–1608*
16/ his Maiestys beinge att Oxford: *in 1605 when Abbot was vice-chancellor*
18/ ⌈English⌉ pastorall: *Samuel Daniel's* The Queen's Arcadia
27/ Master Mayor: *William Wright*

Item paid to Mr Brookes by M*aste*r Mayors
appoyntm*ent*   xxxix s. vj d.

...

Keykeepers' Accounts   OCA: P.4.1   5
f 151   *(Other bonds)*

...

One bond of Gibbins for the Scutchins

...
                                                                                    10
St Martin Churchwardens' Accounts   ORO: PAR 207/4/F1/1, item 121
mb [1]   *(Receipts)*

...

Item for overplus at whitsuntyde ∧⌜and hocktyde⌝   xx li. v s. 0
...   15

St Mary Magdalen Churchwardens' Accounts   ORO: PAR 208/4/F1/45
single mb*   *(Rendered 2 April 1616) (Receipts)*

...

Ite*m* Recei*ued* att Hocktide and whitsontide all thing*es*   20
beinge discharged: vij li. x s. iij d.

...

(Payments)
Ite*m* p*a*id for the makinge a stillinge in the Church house   25
seller to sett drinke vpon: ij s. ix d.
Ite*m* p*a*id for one paire of tressells in the Church house seller   xviij d.
...

Ite*m* p*a*id for amercement*es* for the good of ye p*a*rishe: ⌊att
Whitsontide for a ttree and trunkes:⌋   ix s. 30
...

St Michael at the North Gate Churchwardens' Accounts
ORO: PAR 211/4/F1/3, item 179
single mb   *(Rendered 1 April 1616) (Receipts)*   35
...

Item Received in hockemoney   iij li. v s.
...

14, 20, 30/ whitsuntyde, whitsontide, Whitsontide: 37/ Item: *in display script*
   28 May–3 June 1615   37/ hockemoney: *Hocktide was 17–18 April 1615*
14, 20/ hocktyde, Hocktide: *17–18 April 1615*

St Peter in the East Churchwardens' Accounts   ORO: PAR 213/4/F1/3

f 3*   *(14 April 1615–5 April 1616)   (Receipts)*

...

Item for hockinge Money	xlviij s.
Item for Whitson ˄⌈ale⌉ Money	xl s. 5

...

St Peter le Bailey Churchwardens' Accounts   ORO: PAR 214/4/F1/61

f [1]   *(25 March 1615–25 March 1616)   (Receipts)*

...   10

Item taken at Whitsontyde 1615 of cleare gaines	2 li. 16 s. 5 d.
Item at hocktide by the women gotten	00 9 s. 6 d. ob.
Item at Hocktide gotten by the men	00 7 s. 2 d. ob.

...

15

1615–16
All Souls College Bursars' Accounts   Bodl.: MS. D.D. All Souls c.291

mb 13   *(2 November–2 November)   (Rewards)*

...

De xxij s. geven to ye Queenes trumpetters.	20
De xxij s. geven to ye Kinges trumpeters.	
De [xxij s.] v s. vj d. geven to ye Princes trumpeters	

...

Balliol College Bursars' Accounts   BC Arch: Computi 1615–1662   25

f 10v   *(7 July–18 October 1616)   (Expenses noted)*

...

Item to ye Kings trumpetters	0 10 0
Item to ye Princes ⟨.⟩rummers	0 2 6

...

30

Christ Church Disbursements   ChCh Arch: xii.b.60

f 22v   *(25 December–25 March)*

...

Comedies &   To mr Iles for ij comedies & one tragedie plaied in   35
tragedies   Christchurche hall ex *consensu capituli*   vj li. xiij s. iiij d. 6 13 4

   (signed) Thomas Iles.

...

4/ hockinge: *Hocktide was 17–18 April 1615* 11/ Whitsontyde 1615: *28 May–3 June 1615*
5/ Whitson: *Whitsuntide was 28 May–3 June 1615* 12, 13/ hocktide, Hocktide: *17–18 April 1615*

Christ Church Computi   ChCh Arch: iii.c.8(f.)
mb 2d

...

Et in expens*is* Tragœdiarum et Comœdiarum hoc
anno fact*arum*   vj li. xiij s. iiij d.   5

...

Corpus Christi College Bursars' Accounts   CCCA: C/1/1/8
f [10]   *(Internal expenses)*

...   10

To the Trumpittors   x s.

...

To the Kinges Trumpeters.   xx s.

...

                                                                       15

Magdalen College Libri Computi   MC Arch: LCE/8
f 80   *(Internal and external payments)*

...

Musicis in festo bursario*rum*   5 s.

                                                                       20

f 80v

...

Buccinatorib*us* Regis   1 li. 2 s.
Buccinatorib*us* Reginæ   1 li.
Timpanist' reginae   10 s. 25

...

Buccinatoribus   5 s.

...

New College Bursars' Accounts   NC Arch: 7617   30
mb 7   *(25 December–25 March)* *(Internal expenses)*

...

...so*lutum* to .5. trumpeters playing in the Halle die Epiphanie ij s.... So*lutum*
musicis oppidanis vj s. viij d....

                                                                       35

(25 March–24 June)
...so*lutum* to a trumpeter vj d....

(24 June–29 September)
So*lutum* to a Companye of trumpeters x s.... so*lutum* to the king*es* Trumpeters 40
the King*es* maie*s*tie being this yeare at woodstocke xj s. So*lutum* to Ryngers Prince
Charles com*m*ing to Oxford and into the Colledge and the king passing that

daye bye toward*es* Rycot v s.... so*lutum* to a corneter playing in the Hall to ye
ffelowes vj d....

...

(29 September–25 December) (External expenses) 5
...so*lutum* to a welche blinde harper playing in the hall vj d....

...

The Queen's College Long Rolls   QC Arch: LRB
f 17v col 2   *(7 July–7 July) (External expenses)* 10

...

Ianuarij 1.   Item fidicinj Gul*ielmo* Morrys   18 d.

...

ffebruarij 24.   Item 4or tibicinibus exteris   5 s.
Martij 2.   Item tibicinibus de Oxon*ia*   10 s. 15

...

f 20v col 2   *(7 July 1616–7 July 1617) (External expenses)*
...

23   Item buccinator' Reginæ   10 s. 20
24   Item buccinatorib*us* Regis   10 s.

...

St John's College Computus Hebdomalis   SJC Arch: Acc.v.E.6
f 27v   *(11–17 March)* 25

...

Set on for ye Musitions   4 li. 15 s.

...

Vice-Chancellors' Accounts   OUA: WP/β/21(4) 30
p 176   *(17 July–17 July) (Extraordinary expenses)*

...

It*em* solut*um* Buccinatoribus   x s.
It*em* solut*um* Histrionibus D*omi*ni Regis   xl s.
... 35

p 179*   *(17 July 1616–17 July 1617) (Extraordinary expenses)*
...

It*em* dat*um* Buccinatoribus D*omi*ni Regis 24º die Augusti 1616   xxij s.
It*em* dat*um* Buccinatoribus Dom*i*næ Reginæ 23º Augusti 1616   xxij s. 40

20m/ 23: *23 August 1616*   21m/ 24: *24 August 1616*

Item dati Tympanistis Domini Regis   [x]xj s.
Item dati Servientibus Illustrissimi Principis Caroli
28º Augusti 1616   xxij s.
...

5

Hannisters' Registers   OCA: L.5.2
f 29v

...

Leonard Mayor   Memorandum quod decimo tertio die Augusti Anno supradicto Edwardus
® Edward   haywood fillius walteri haywood de Cokthropp in Comitatu Oxonie yeoman   10
Heywood   posuit seipsum Apprenticium Leonardo Mayor de Ciuitate Oxonie musition ad
                 artem suam qua vtitur erudiendam et cum ipso more Apprenticij Comoratur
                 et servitur a ffesto sancti michaelis proximo futuro Post datum presentium
                 vsque ad finem et terminum Septem Annorum extunc proximorum sequentium
                 &c Et in fine dicti termini dabit eidem Apprenticio suo duplices vestices tali   15
                 Apprenticio Congruentes &c

Hugh Bosle   Memorandum quod vicesimo quarto die Augusti anno supradicto Rogerus
® Roger Bates   Bates filius Edmundi Bates de Norton in Comitatu Oxonie yeoman posuit
                 seipsum Apprenticium Hugonis Bosle de Ciuitate Oxonie Musition ad artem   20
                 suam qua vtitur erudiendam et cum ipso more Apprenticij Comoratur et
                 servitur a die dati presentium vsque ad finem et terminum septem Annorum
                 extunc proximorum sequentium Et in fine dicti termini dabit eidem Apprenticio
                 suo duplices vestices tali Apprenticio Congruentes et vnam trebalem violam
                 Anglice one Treable vilyn &c   25

Audited Corporation Accounts   OCA: P.5.2
f 145*   (Chamberlains' payments)
...

Item paid our Lady Even for Bread   0   10   0   30
Item paid then to the Musitions   0   2   0
...

Keykeepers' Accounts   OCA: P.4.1
f 157*   (Other bonds)   35
...

One Bond of Gibbins for the Scutchins
...

10/ Cokthropp ... Oxonie: *Cokethorpe, Oxfordshire*
15, 24/ vestices: *for* vestes
19/ Norton ... Oxonie: *Brize, Chipping, or Over Norton (?), Oxfordshire*

St Aldate Churchwardens' Accounts
ORO: DD Par. Oxford St Aldate b.17/4
single mb *(Rendered 27 April 1617) (Receipts)*

...

Item Receaved at Hocktide iij li. x s. 5

...

St Martin Churchwardens' Accounts ORO: PAR 207/4/F1/1, item 123
mb [1] *(Rendered 27 April 1617) (Receipts)*

... 10

Inprimis money gayned [l]at hocktyde 40 s.
Item gott att whitsontyde iij li. viij s.

...

St Mary Magdalen Churchwardens' Accounts ORO: PAR 208/4/F1/46 15
single mb *(Rendered 22 April 1617) (Receipts)*

...

Item receiued att Hocktyde and Whitsontyde all thinges
beinge discharged: v li. x s.

... 20

St Michael at the North Gate Churchwardens' Accounts
ORO: PAR 211/4/F1/3, item 180
single mb *(Rendered 25 April 1617) (Receipts)*

... 25

Item gained and received the Hockmoney xl s.

...

St Peter in the East Churchwardens' Accounts ORO: PAR 213/4/F1/3
f 5 *(5 April 1616–25 April 1617) (Receipts)* 30

. . .

Item for Hockinge Money xl s.

...

A ### Antiquities of Oxford Bodl.: MS. Wood F.29(a) 35
f 8c verso col 2*

...

The Conduit built on ye place where ye bull ring was presented for a

---

5, 11, 18/ Hocktide, hocktyde, Hocktyde: *9–10
    April 1616*
11/ Inprimis: *in display script*
11/ 40 s.: *4 written over an erasure*

12, 18/ whitsontyde, Whitsontyde: *20–6 May 1616*
26, 32/ Hockmoney, Hockinge: *Hocktide was 9–10
    April 1616*

Neusance by ye Towne, but I wond*er* at it, seing they have suffered so many
encroachments more towards [than] quatervois Than any part of ye City –
viz. fro*m* ye two facd pu*m*p to Carfax from ye Crow to Carfax Church, &
sufferinge an house to be built on ye ch*urch* yard – ye houses also from ye
flure de lize to ye Taverne – pennileys bench also...   5

1616–17
All Souls College Bursars' Accounts   Bodl.: MS. D.D. All Souls c.291
mb 11   *(2 November–2 November)* *(Rewards)*
...   10
De xxij s. to the Kinges Trumpetors.
...

Balliol College Bursars' Accounts   BC Arch: Computi 1615–1662
f 14v   *(18 October–7 July)* *(Expenses noted)*   15
...
Ite*m* to the Earle of Essex trumpeters   0 2 s. 0
...

f 16v   *(7 July–18 October)*   20
...
Ite*m* to the Kings Trumpeters.   0 13 s. 4 d.
...

Christ Church Treasurers' Accounts   ChCh Arch: iii.c.1   25
f 212
...
Et in expens*is* Tragoediaru*m* et Comoediaru*m* hoc Anno
h*a*bitarum et f*a*ctarum   nil.
...   30

Exeter College Rectors' Accounts   EC Arch: A.II.9
f 236   *(1 November–1 November)*
...
Item de solutis et datis tibicinib*us* regijs   1 li. 2 s. 0 35
Item de solutis pro emendatione tubj   0 11 s. 5 d.
...

1/ wond*er*: o *corrected from* n
3/ ye Crow: *The Split Crow aka Chequers on South Street*
5/ flure de lize: *Fleur de Luce on High Street*
5/ ye Taverne: *The Tavern in North Street*

Lincoln College Calculus 1616–17   LC Arch
f 13   *(31 May–29 August)* *(Internal expenses)*
...
To yᵉ Kings Trumpeters   x s.
...   5

Magdalen College Libri Computi   MC Arch: LCE/8
f 85v   *(Internal and external payments)*
...
Musicis in festo bursariorum   5 s. 10
...
Buccinatoribus Comitis Essex bis.   10 s.
...
Buccinatoribus Reginæ   10 s.
Buccinatoribus Dominj Regis   1 li. 2 s. 15
...
Musicis et pro suffitu in cæna Episcopj Wintoniæ   5 s. 6 d.
...

f 86   20
...
Hoby pro diversis per billam in tragedia per pauperes scholares   8 s.
...

Merton College Bursars' Accounts   MCR: 3.1   25
f 174   *(21 March–25 July)* *(External expenses)*
...
...Symphoniacis ex consensu vj s. viij d...

New College Bursars' Accounts   NC Arch: 7619   30
mb 6*   *(25 December–25 March)* *(Internal expenses)*
...
Solutum to an old man & his boy that sange in the hall 4 d.... Solutum
Musicis oppidanis 6 s. 8 d....
...   35

(24 June–29 September)
...Solutum to the trumpeters vpon Act Saturday 6 s.... Solutum pro chirothecis
datis Episcopo Wintoniæ 3 li. 2 s.... Solutum buccinatoribus regijs 11 s. Solutum
for the lone of a carpett when the Byshopp of Winchester dined in our hall 40

22/ scholares: e *written over* o   38/ Act Saturday: *12 July 1617*

12 d. So*lutum* to the musitians then 5 s....

…

The Queen's College Long Rolls   QC Arch: LRB
f 21 col 1   *(7 July–7 July)* *(External expenses)*   5

…

Ian*uarij* 1   It*em* Mauritio fidicini   18 d.

…

ffeb*ruarij* 17   It*em* Tibicinib*us* de Oxon*ia*   10 s.
…   10

f 22v col 2   *(7 July 1617–7 July 1618)*

…

Inprimis Clarionibus Regis Septem*bris* .8.   20 s.
…   15

St John's College Computus Annuus   SJC Arch: Acc.I.A.11
f 22v   *(29 September–25 December)* *(External and internal expenses)*

…

Item for furnishing the show at New years tide   ij s. vj d. 20

…

f 23   *(25 December–25 March)*

…

It*em* for acting and furnishing a Comedy and Trag*œ*dy   25
ouer and aboue that w*hi*ch was given by the students   xvj li. xvj s. iij d.

(Allowances)
Imp*ositi* heb*domada* 5ᵃ for a Comedy and Tragedy   xxij li. v s. x d.
…   30
Imp*ositi* heb*domada* 9ᵃ for the Musitians   v li. xij d.

…

f 24*   *(24 June–29 September)* *(External and internal expenses)*
…   35
It*em* to the K*ings* Trumpetters   xj s.
It*em* to the towne Musitians which playd when our
honourable Visitour dined in the hall   xj s.

…

7/ fidicini: c *written over* t   31/ heb*domada* 9ᵃ: *16–22 February 1616/17*
29/ heb*domada* 5ᵃ: *19–25 January 1616/17*   38/ Visitour: *the bishop of Winchester*

St John's College Computus Hebdomalis   SJC Arch: Acc.v.E.6
f 39   *(13–19 January)*

...

Tenant*es* with newyears gift*es*
A Comedie publikely acted.   5

...

(20–6 January)
A Tragedie publikly acted.

...   10

f 39v   *(27 January–2 February)*

...

Set on for a Com*m*edie & a Tragedie.   xxij li. v s. x d.

...   15

f 40v   *(24 February–2 March)*

...

Set on for ye Musitions   v li. xij d.

...   20

St John's College Short Book   SJC Arch: Acc.III.D.1
f 23v*   *(25 December–25 March)* *(Expenses)*

...

Ite*m* for furnishinge ye Showe [at] on New-yeares-daye   ij s. vj d. 25

...

f 24*

...

Ite*m* for actinge & Furnishinge a Comodye & a   30
Trag*e*dye ouer & aboue what ye students allowed   xvj li. 26 s. 3 d.

...

(Allowances)
Ite*m* payde for ye Playes Hebdo*m*ada 5ª   22 li. 5 s. x d. 35

...

Ite*m* ye Musitions Bill
{ ye Dauncers   xviij s. xij d.
  ye Butler & Porter   ij s. xij d.
  ye Musitio*n*s [yem]   iiij li. vij s. ij s.
  other Pare   3 s. ix d. xij d. v s. 40

30–1/ Item ... 3 d.: *in left margin a drawing of a hand with pointing index finger*
35/ Hebdo*m*ada 5ª: *19–25 January 1616/17*

ye sum to bee put in ye yeare book is but   v li. xij d.

…

f 25*   *(24 June–29 September)* *(Expenses)*

…

Item to ye kings Trumpeters	xj s.
Item to ye Towne Musitions ⌜for playinge⌝ [when ⟨..⟩]	
when our Honourable Visitor dines in ye Hall	xj s.

…

(Allowances)

Item to Trumpeters at ye Act	vj s.

…

ff 34–4v*

Recknings about ye Playes

Inprimis receaued of Mr Cliff	x s.
Item receaued of Mr Soane	x s.
Item vppon ye bill	xxij li. v s. x d.

Sum xxiij li. v s. x d.

Item more of Mr Bell	vj s. viij d.

Layde oute

Inprimis to Foelix for goinge to Claphole, & for his horshyre	iij s.
Item for a days worke to ye Ioyner for settinge on ye	
Cornish on ye Screen ⌜& glue⌝	[ij ⟨.⟩] ij s.
Item for send a Messenger for apparrell to Fifeelde	ij s.
Item for sendinge a Messenger to Mr Beake for apparrell	0000
Item for suger candye	vj d.
Item for sendinge to Woluerkote, for Arras, & for horshyre	xij d.
Item to ye Paynters vt patet per billam	30 s. xxviij s.
	⌊vj s. v s.⌋
Item to ye Carpenter for settinge vp ye stage & scaffold	
vt patet per billam	[xl s.] iij li.
Item to ye Imbroderer vt patet per billam	xxj s.
[Item for wine vt patet per billam	000]
Item to ye smithe vt patet per billam	vj s. vj d.

8/ Visitor: *the bishop of Winchester*
8/ dines: *for* dined *(?)*
12/ ye Act: *14 July 1617*
26/ [ij ⟨.⟩]: *figure partially obliterated by an ink smudge*

Item to Richarde Clarke vt patet per billam   ix s. vj d.
Item for ye Intertanement of Newe-College Gentlemen
which sange bothe nights   v s. viij d.
In wine   (blank)
Item more in ye kichin   0000   5
Item for sendinge Back clothes to Fifeelde   ij s.
Item for sendinge back clothes to claphole & to ye mayde   vj s.
Item for 2 pair of black gloues   ij s.
Item for makinge ye 2 Iudges hats   xviij d.
Item towards Sir Sherborns Hat   vj s.   10
Item for wine vt patet per billam   x li. vj s. vj d.
Item for Candles   xx s. vij d.
Item for Taking downe ye Glass & settinge it vp agane,
vt patet per billam   xlix s.
Item to ye Fletcher for a cryers staff. & 2 Counsellors staffes   xviij d.   15
Item to Thomas Wilson a Taylor for makinge one Buckerum
Coate & Other worke in ye Playe-dayes   [xii] ij s.
Item To Thomas Clarke vt patet per billam. for Butterde
beer &c.   xix s. vj d.
Item To Boswell ye Mearcer, vt patet per billam   xiiij li. v s.   20
Item To Chillingeworthe ye Mearcer vt patet per billam
⌊A Cooper⌋   iiij li. xix s.
[Item to Gennings ye Taylor vt patet per billam]
Item for Pins   vj d. |
Item to Gennings ye Taylorse vt patet   xvj s. vj d.   25
Item To Puisy vt patet per billam   vj s.
Item for wifling[e] shuts   ij s. vj d.
Item a quyre of Paper to write ye Tragedye twice   iiij d.
Item To ye Mayde which broughte apparrell from claphole   iij s.
Item for mendinge mine owne Canope vj d. &   30
Mr Bailyes Cannopye   xviij d.
Item for Vizards Lost, and broken & ye Loane of other   xviij s.
        Summa Totalis xl li. viij s. ix d.
From which deduct 23 li. 12 s. vj d. restat   xvj li. xvj s. iij d.

1/ Richarde Clarke: *a joiner*
20/ Boswell: *William Boswell, city bailiff*
21/ Chillingeworthe: *William Chillingworth, city bailiff*
22/ A Cooper: *phrase squeezed between the lines with no indication of intended placement*
23/ Gennings: *William Jennings*
26/ Puisy: *Francis Pusey, tailor*
30/ mine owne: *account unsigned; bursars in 1616–17 were Theophilus Tuer and Thomas Tucker*

AC   ***Peter Heylyn's Memoirs***   Bodl.: MS. Wood E.4
f 22v

...

March. 8. My English Tragedy cald Spurius was acted privatly (as Mr Whites
& Mr Bernards plaies were) in the presidents Lodgings   5

...

Audited Corporation Accounts   OCA: P.5.2
f 156v*   *(Chamberlains' payments)*

...   10

Item paid to the Queenes players by master Mayors appoyntment   xx s.

...

Item to the kinges players by Master Mayors appoyntment   x s.

...

      15

f 157*

...

Item to the Kinges Trumpeters   xxiiij s.

...

      20

St Martin Churchwardens' Accounts   ORO: PAR 207/4/F1/1, item 124
mb [1]   *(Rendered 19 April 1618) (Receipts)*

...

Item gaind att Hoctide   xxxx s.

...   25

St Mary Magdalen Churchwardens' Accounts   ORO: PAR 208/4/F1/47
single mb   *(Rendered 7 April 1618) (Receipts)*

...

Item receaued at Hocktyde and Whitsontyde all thinges   30
beinge disscharged   iiij li. xviij s.

...

St Michael at the North Gate Churchwardens' Accounts
ORO: PAR 211/4/F1/3, item 181   35
mb [1]*   *(Rendered 9 April 1618) (Receipts)*

...

°Item receaved at hocktide, all charges borne   xl s.°

...

4/ Spurius: *underlined*   30/ Whitsontyde: *8–14 June 1617*
11/ master Mayors: *Richard Smith's*   38/ Item: *in display script*
24, 30, 38/ Hoctide, Hocktyde, hocktide: *28–9 April 1617*

St Peter in the East Churchwardens' Accounts   ORO: PAR 213/4/F1/3
f 7   *(25 April 1617–10 April 1618)* *(Receipts)*

…

Item received for Hockinge money   xl s.

…   5

St Peter le Bailey Churchwardens' Accounts   ORO: PAR 214/4/F1/62
f [1]   *(Rendered 3 May 1618)* *(Receipts)*

…

Item, taken at Whitsontide of cleare gaines   1 li. 11 s. 6 d. ob. 10
Item, gotten at Hock-tide, all things discharged   1 li. 12 s. 9 d.

…

City Quarter Sessions   OCA: QSC/A2/001
p 51*   *(30 April)*   15

…

William
Stevenson
Com*m*itted

It is Ordered that Willyam Steevenson App*re*ntice to mr ffulke Emerson
being one of the Actors in the Rydeing Company disguised vpon May day and
passing by the Guild hall in tyme of open Sessions [the] in great Contempt
of the Court & of Com*m*aundm*ent* formerly geven by m*aste*r Mayor to   20
the Contrary shalbe Com*m*itted to Bocardo there to remayne dureing the
pleasure of this Court.

…

p 52*   25

…

Warr*an*ts to be
made out
against diverse
*per*sons of the
Ryders

It is Ordered that warr*antes* shalbe made out vnder the Teste of this Court for
the apprehending of Willyam Stapler *(blank)* ffrost the Cobler Peter Short the
Cuttler *(blank)* Tilcock the paynter & *(blank)* Pigeon the Chymney sweep all
of them being of the vnruly and disordered Company of the May day Ryders   30
in Contempt of m*aste*r Mayors Com*m*aundm*ent* to the Contrary and vpon
their appr*eh*enc*i*on to be brought before some of his Ma*i*esties Iustices of this
Cittie to be punished according to the discretion of such Iustic*es* before whome
they or any of them shalbe brought.

…   35

p 54

…

Ryders

It is Ordered that all the Ryders shalbe sett in the stock*es* in the open m*a*rket

---

4/ Hockinge: *Hocktide was 28–9 April 1617*
10/ Whitsontide: *8–14 June 1617*
11/ Hock-tide: *28–9 April 1617*

for the space of two howers the next market day and haue papers on their
hattes expresseing the Cause of their punishment./

...

1617–18   5
Balliol College Bursars' Accounts   BC Arch: Computi 1615–1662
f 19v   *(18 October–7 July)* *(Expenses noted)*

...

Item to the Earle of Essex trumpetters on
St Katherines day   0 2 s. 6 d. 10

...

Item to Earle of Essex trumpetters   2 s.

...

Christ Church Treasurers' Accounts   ChCh Arch: iii.c.1   15
f 220

...

Et in expensis Tragœdiarum & Comœdiarum hoc
Anno habitarum et factarum   nil.

...   20

Corpus Christi College Bursars' Accounts   CCCA: C/1/1/8
f [14]   *(25 March–24 June)* *(External expenses)*

...

To the Trumpeters   v s. 25

...

Magdalen College Libri Computi   MC Arch: LCE/8
f 93v   *(Internal and external payments)*

...   30

Buccinatoribus Comitis Essex   3 s.
Buccinatoribus quorundam Nobiljum   11 s.

...

Diuersis per billas pro Comædja & Tragædja vltra
22 li. 17 s. 4 d. deductos ex battellis   24 li. 9 s. 5 d. 35

...

New College Bursars' Accounts   NC Arch: 7621
mb 8   *(29 September–25 December)* *(Internal expenses)*

...   40

...Solutum buccinatoribus comitis Essexiæ 2. s....

...

(25 December–25 March)
So*lutum* to an olde man that sange in the hall 4 d....

...

(25 March–24 June) 5
...So*lutum* buccinatorib*us* 12 d....

...

(24 June–29 September)
So*lutum* buccinatoribus 5 s.... 10

...

The Queen's College Long Rolls   QC Arch: LRB
f 22v col 2   *(7 July–7 July)* *(External expenses)*
... 15
Item Mauritio Tibicini   18 d.
Item Tibicinib*us* Oxon*ie* feb*rua*r*ij* 4   10 s.

...

St John's College Computus Annuus   SJC Arch: Acc.I.A.12   20
f 19v   *(29 September–25 December)* *(Internal and external expenses)*
...
X   Item given to a Noyse of Trumpetters Nouemb*er* .25.º   ij s. vj d.
...
X   Item for furnishinge the Newe Yeares Day Shewe   vj s. viij d. 25
X   Item allowed toward*es* the Masque on Tweluth Nyght   x s.
...

f 20   *(25 December–25 March)*
... 30
X   Item allowed toward*es* the shewe on Candlemas night   xiij s. x d.
...

f 20v   *(Allowances)*
... 35
X   Item jmpos*iti* hebd*omada* 9ª for the Musityans   vij li. xiiij s.
...

36/ hebd*omada* 9ª: *16–22 February 1617/18*

f 22   (24 June–29 September)   (Internal and external expenses)

...

X   Item given to Trumpetters att the Act   v s.

...

5

St John's College Computus Hebdomalis   SJC Arch: Acc.v.E.6
f 52   (5–11 January)

...

An allowance for ye newyers day showe.

...   10

f 54   (23 February–1 March)

...

The Musitions bill 7 li. 14 s.

...   15

Vice-Chancellors' Accounts   OUA: WP/β/21(4)
p 181   (19 July 1617–20 July 1618)   (Extraordinary expenses)

...

Item datum Servientibus Regijs attendentibus Dominum   20
Vicecancellarium et Doctores apud Woodstocke tempore
prandiorum   xxij s.

...

Item solutum Buccinatoribus Regijs   xxij s.
Item solutum Citharædis Regijs   v s. 25

...

AC   **Peter Heylyn's Memoirs**   Bodl.: MS. Wood E.4
f 22v

...   30

1617
vide Historiam   November 20 Mr Holt chosen Lord (Christmas Lord of Magdalen college) &
temporis queen   solemnly inaugurated on ye 2d of Ianuary following: In which I represented
marie   the Embassador of the Universitie of Vienna.
vide proximam
paginam   ...

1618   August 31. I began my Latin Comedie called Theomachia & finisht it   35
September 14. It was never acted.

...

3/ the Act: 13 July 1618
20–1/ Dominum Vicecancellarium: William Goodwin
31/ of Magdalen college: written in left margin and marked for insertion by an asterisk erroneously placed
    after Christmas

Holyday

ff 23v–4*

...

August 26. Sunday Mr Holidayes Marriage of Arts which had been acted in christ church hall February 13. anno 1617 with no great applause, was with some foolish alterations acted before the King at Wodstock. wherupon I made a copie 5 of verses which passed by ye name of Whoop Holiday & gave occasion to many | many other copies pro et contra, made by severall men, ye Deane of christ church Doctor Corbet (who loved ye Boyes-play verie well) putting in for one.

...

10

Burton, Anatomy of Melancholy (1624) STC: 4160

p 124

...

aHos non ita pridem perstrinxi, in Philosophastro Comedia latinâ, in Æde Christi Oxoniæ publicè habitâ. Anno 1617. Februarij 16. † 15

+Satura
Menippea

...aPhilosophrastri licentiantur in artibus, artem qui non habent, +Eosque sapientes esse iubent, qui nullâ præditi sunt sapientiâ, Et nihil ad gradum, præterquam velle adferunt....

Robert Burton's Philosophaster Harvard Theatre Collection: MS Thr.10 20

p 8* *(Prologue)*

...

Sciat quod undecim abhinc annis scripta fuit,
Inter blattas et tineas in hunc diem delituit,
Ab authore in aeternas damnata tenebras, 25
Aliorum importunitate nunc in scenam venit.

...

pp 89–90* *(Epilogue)*

... 30

Si quid aberratum aut absoletum quid nimis
offendat aures, præmonimus ab initio

Collation with STC: 4159 (1621) *(A)* p 186:   14 perstrinxi, in] perstrinximus in *A* 16–17m +Satura Menippea] *A* omits 16 Philosophrastri] Philosophastri *A* 16–18 +Eosque ... adferunt] *A* omits
Collation with Folger Library: MS V.a.315 *(F)* pp 3, 9, 84–5:   32 præmonimus] praemonibus *F*

3/ August 26: *26 August 1621*
3/ Marriage of Arts: *underlined*
6/ Whoop Holiday: *underlined*
6–7/ many | many: *dittography (?); first* many *does not appear to be a catchword*

16/ Philosophrastri: *for* Philosophastri
23/ undecim: i *altered from* e

vndecem abhinc annis hanc scriptam fabulam.

...

Plauserunt./
Februarij 16ᵗᵒ./
Æde Cristi
1617. |

Actorum Nomina.

Desiderius Dux. Sir Kinge. ye Bishop of Londons sone
Eubulus Mr Gorges. sir Arther Gorges sonne.
Cratinus Mr Bartlit a gentleman commoner.
Polumathes Sir Bennet. Sir Iohn Bennettes sonne./
Philobiblos Sir Haywood. student. bachelor
Polupragmaticus Mr Goffe master of Artes. student
Æquiuocus Mr Iohnson Master of artes student. [bachelor]
Simon Acutus Sir ffortye. student. bachelor
Lodovicus pantometer Sir Westlye student. bacularius artis
Pontamagus Sir Osboston student bachelor of artes
Amphimacer. Limiter scholler of ye house. student
Theanus Sir Vauhan student bachelor
Pedanus Morly scholler. student
Stephanio Sir Arundall. student bachelor
Polupistos Sir Price. bacularius artis student.
Dromo Hilsinge scholler of ye house.
Sir Ingolsby. Harris. Parsones. 3. Townsmen.
Staphila Benefeilde scholler. of ye house
Camaena Price scholler of ye house.
Tarentilla Stroude scholler of ye house.
Lictor promus Sotton scholler of ye house.
Portry, Blunt, Serle, patientes./
Hersen fidicen a querister./
Acted on Shroeuemunday night 1617. Februarij 16. die lunæ. It begane
about .5. at night and ended at eight./

Auctore Roberto Burton
Linliaco Lecestrense./

line numbers: 5, 10, 15, 20, 25, 30, 35

Collation continued: 11 Bartlit] Barlet F   14 Mr Goffe] F omits
17 pantometer] pantometar F   17 artis] F omits   18 Pontamagus]
Pontomagus F   18 of] F omits   21 Pedanus] pedamus F   22 Sir] F omits
24 Hilsinge] Hiling F   29 Lictor ... house.] F omits   32 lunæ] lunæ
Oxon F   35 Linliaco] Lindliaco F

Holyday, Technogamia (1618)   STC: 13617
sig A2v*   (13 February)   (Prologue)

...

Here the vpper part of the Scene open'd; when straight appear'd a Heauen, and
all the Pure Artes sitting on two semi-circular benches, one aboue another: 5
who sate thus till the rest of the Prologue was spoken, which being ended,
they descended in order within the Scene, whiles the Musicke plaid †
...Our Poet knowing our free hearts
Has here inuited Heau'n and All the Artes
To entertayne His Theater, and does bring   10
What he prepar'd for our Platonique King:
Deeming Your iudgements able to supply
The absence of So Great a Maiesty.
But his free conscience does protest, the mirth
Of this his night was but a Fiue-weekes birth;   15
Yet no Abortiue; if your courteous hands
Shall wrap the Infant in his swathing bands.

...

sig P1   (Epilogue)   20

When the Epilogue was about to be spoken, the pure Arts were ascended to
Heauen, and appeared (as in the Prologue) till the Epilogue was ended, and
then the Heauen closed. †®

25

Hannisters' Registers   OCA: L.5.2
f 401*

...

Iohannes Baldwin filius et nuper Apprenticius Iohannis Baldwyn de Civitate
predicta musitian admissus est in libertate dicte Civitatis vicesimo die Iulij   30
Anno predicto Et Iuratus similiter./

...

St Aldate Churchwardens' Accounts
ORO: DD Par. Oxford St Aldate b.17/5   35
mb [1]   (5 April 1618–28 March 1619)   (Receipts)

...

Item receaved at Hocktide   j li. ix s. vj d.

...

38/ Hocktide: *13–14 April 1618*

St Martin Churchwardens' Accounts   ORO: PAR 207/4/F1/1, item 125
mb [1]   *(Rendered 19 April 1619)* *(Receipts)*
...

Item gained at Hocktide	xxx s. viij d.

...

Item gotten to the Church at Whitsontyde   vij li. xvij s. x d.
...

St Michael at the North Gate Churchwardens' Accounts
ORO: PAR 211/4/F1/3, item 182
single mb   *(Rendered 29 April 1619)* *(Receipts)*
...

Item gained at Hocktyde all thinges
being discharged   xlvj s.
...

St Peter in the East Churchwardens' Accounts   ORO: PAR 213/4/F1/3
f 9   *(10 April 1618–31 March 1619)* *(Receipts)*
...

Item received for Hockinge Money   xl s.
...

St Peter le Bailey Churchwardens' Accounts   ORO: PAR 214/4/F1/63
f [1]*   *(Rendered 25 April 1619)* *(Receipts)*
...

Item, taken at Whitsontide	2 li.	8 s.	0
Item, gathered at Hoc-tide	1 li.	14 s.	5 d. ob.

...

Item, received at Midsomer of the young men	0	18 s.	0
Item, for the wood of the bower, sold to			
goodman Turner	0	10 s.	0

...

f [1v]   *(Expenses)*

Item, laid out for a barrell of beare at
Whitsontide   0   9 s.   4 d.
...

4, 13, 27/ Hocktide, Hocktyde, Hoc-tide: *13–14 April 1618*
6, 26, 37/ Whitsontyde, Whitsontide: *24–30 May 1618*
20/ Hockinge: *Hocktide was 13–14 April 1618*

1618–19
All Souls College Bursars' Accounts   Bodl.: MS. D.D. All Souls c.292
mb 12   *(2 November–2 November)* *(Rewards)*

...

de v s. vj d. giuen to the Queens Trumpeters   5

...

de xxij s. giuen to the Kings Trumpeters at the Kings being at Woodstocke

...

Balliol College Bursars' Accounts   BC Arch: Computi 1615–1662   10
f 24v   *(18 October–7 July)* *(Expenses noted)*

...

Item to the trumpeters of his Maiestyes Nauy   0 2 s. 6 d. 0
Item to the Earle of Essex his trumpeters   0 2 s. 6 d. 0

...   15

f 28v   *(7 July–18 October)*

...

Item to the Kings Maiestys Trumpeters   0 11   0 0

...   20

Christ Church Treasurers' Accounts   ChCh Arch: iii.c.1
f 227

...

Et in expensis Tragædiarum & Comœdiarum hoc Anno   25
habitarum & factarum   nil.

...

Corpus Christi College Bursars' Accounts   CCCA: C/1/1/8
f [11] col 2   *(External expenses)*   30

...

To the Kings Trumpeters   22 s.

...

To the Kinges Trumpeters at Christmas and at the Act
followeing, which was then payed by the Manciple at the   35
appointment of the Præsident and vicepræsident   10 s.

...

34–5/ the Act followeing: *12 July 1619*

Exeter College Rectors' Accounts   EC Arch: A.II.9
f 246v   *(1 November–1 November)*

Item Buccinatoribus regijs	0 11 0.	
…		5

Magdalen College Libri Computi   MC Arch: LCE/8
f 103   *(Internal and external payments)*

…
buccinatorib*us* diuersis temporib*us*	0 16 00	10
Buccinatoribus regis	1 2 0	

…

Diuersis p*er* billas p*ro* tragædjis vltra 18 li. 9 s.
deduct*os* e batt*ellis*	13 li. 18 s. ob.	
…		15
Musicis in festo bursar*iorum*	0 5 0	

…

New College Bursars' Accounts   NC Arch: 7623
mb 5   *(29 September–25 December) (Internal expenses)*   20

…*Sol*utum pauperi cuidam seni cantanti in aula*m* iiij d.…
…

(25 December–25 March)   25
…*Sol*utum buccinatoribus v s.… *Sol*utum Musicis oppidanis vj s. viij d.…
…

(25 March–24 June)
…*Sol*utum buccinatoribus ij s. vj d.…   30
…

(24 June–29 September)
…*Sol*utum Buccinatorib*us* Regijs xj s.…
…   35

Oriel College Treasurers' Accounts   OC Arch: S I.C.1
f 216   *(Internal expenses)*

…
It*em* solut*um* Buccinatoribus regijs	x s. 40
…	

14/ 13 li. 18 s. ob.: *added later, possibly by another hand*

The Queen's College Long Rolls QC Arch: LRB
f 25 col 1* *(7 July–7 July) (External expenses)*

...

Item Mauritio fistulantj	18 d.	
Martij 20. Item tibicinibus de Oxon*ia*	10 s.	5

...

f 27 col 1 *(7 July 1619–7 July 1620) (External expenses)*

...

Aug*usti* 23 It*em* Regijs tibicinibus	20 s.	10

...

St John's College Computus Annuus SJC Arch: Acc.I.A.12
f 47v* *(25 December–25 March) (Internal and external expenses)*

... 15

Item for worke done on Newe Yeares day for the Shewe   xx d.

...

f 48*

... 20

Item for the chardges about the Shewe att Newe-yeares tyde   vj s.

...

(Allowances)

Item Impos*iti* heb*domada* .10ª. for the Musitians.	v li. xij s.	25
Item Impos*iti* heb*domada* eade*m* for the Shewe	xij li. xiij s.	

...

f 50* *(24 June–29 September) (Internal and external expenses)*

... 30

Item given to Trumpetters on Act Munday   ij s. vj d.

...

St John's College Computus Hebdomalis SJC Arch: Acc.V.E.6
f 68 *(1–7 March)* 35

...

The Musitions bill	v li. xij s.
Set on for a maske	xij li. xiij s.

...

10/ tibicinibus: *fourth i written over* a; u *corrected from* yi
25/ heb*domada* .10ª.: *22–8 February 1618/19*
31/ Act Munday: *12 July 1619*

f 70   *(19–25 April)*

...

going to ye wood
& ye charges of a maske.

An Actor's Part Book   Harvard Theatre Collection: MS Thr.10.1
f 2*   *(24 February)*

               memarad*um*
An: beare bee layd in toth tyringe house
          Supper provided for ye Actors
          Mutes provided, woemen, men

Poem by Thomas Goffe
Cheshire and Chester Archives: Tabley MS DLT/B 71
ff 24v–5   *(February)*
...

      An Eigie vppon hoarsness
      occasioned by a sudden, and
      vehement could which tooke
      the representer of
      Amurath when he should
      haue acted.
Voyce, emptie aire soone perrish sounde
why shouldst thou so thy selfe confound
denying not thy strenght to those
which ar but natures staynes and foes
To thy perfection creatures vile
Enioy thee fully which defile
Thy Euphonies, with hideous cry
Vse vices but to terrifie
Blaspheming throats haue Organs free
The tongues of slaues for calumnie
Are ne're chaind vp ∧⌈with⌉ diseses

Collation with Harvard Theatre Collection: MS Thr.10.1 *(H)* ff 71v–2v:
18–23 An ... acted.] A Songe vpon ye loss of an Actors Voyce, beeinge to play a
cheife part in ye Vniversitie: *H*   24 perrish] perisht *H*   26 strenght to] strength:
H   28 perfection creatures vile] perfection. of creatures [worst] ⌈vile⌉ *H*   31 vices]
voy[c]es *H*   32 throats] tounges *H*   33 slaues] Scoulds *H*   34 diseses] such
diseses *H*

9/ memarad*um*: *for* memorand*um*   18/ Eigie: *for* Eligie

A witches charme no hindranc stayes
Shee incantations bouldly sayes
The ominous rauen no horseness knowes
Nor puritane that speakes in the nose
four howers in on day is small 5
for him vnstudied sense to yall
And rore out an vnhollowed dome
Against the monstrous whor of Rome |

O horsnes why shouldst thou not claspe 10
Their mouths vp which at euery gaspe
Vomet an oath or fondly belch
words far more thre⌈a⌉tning then welch
when didst thou stope a lawers tongue
who sw⌈a⌉it in pleading to doe wronge 15
To orpans: whose curst eloquence
blasted the light of truths defence
when did a woman euer brawle
and thou stopp her tongue withall
what [osceen] ⌈common⌉ stager that but trowes 20
his pumpt in woords, and turnes to prose
The most fild lynes was euer vext
with such obstructious tones perplext
but when a concourse of such men
As best know how to speake and when 25
They should iudicious silence finde
To hear a dead poeme in thee lind
Then with an envie dost thou locke
Thy aides all vp and thought thou knocke

Collation continued. 1 no hindranc stayes] is never stayde *H* 2 Shee ... sayes]
Bycause it [cannot] is not fully sayde *H* 5 four] Six *H* 6 sense] senser *H*
7 vnhollowed] eternall *H* 8 monstrous] menstruous *H* 10 O horsnes]
Hoarsness *H* 10 claspe] still clasp *H* 12 fondly] fouly *H* 13 far more
thre⌈a⌉tning] more vntunable *H* 14–17 when didst ... defence] *These lines follow
l.19 in H* 19 thou stopp her tongue withall] thou didst stop her mouth at all *H*
20 [osceen] ... trowes] obscene stager, that but throws *H* 22–3 lynes ... perplext]
lines, [did] with action such As would vnman mee, but to touch With ye least
thought; was ever but With [brest] ⌈harsh⌉ obstructious, town perplext? *H*
26 iudicious silence finde] iudicious ⌈silent⌉ pruue *H* 27 lind] live *H* 29 aides ...
knocke] sounds all vp; and though therin kn⟨....⟩ *H*

16/ orpans: *for* orphans
29/ thought: *for* though

Apollo and all heires beside
Yet are thy barren aides deuide
May we no charme? can we entice
by verse/ or purchase the by [poise] prise
o be thou midwife to my braine   5
For without thee all is but vaine
All proues abortive, what hath cost
So many howers must be lost
Dead e're tw'as borne O most vniust
In this Lucina that we must   10
Preuent *our* birth with dearth an come
In to go out whilst speech is dumbe
But I complayne ⟨.⟩ now and may seeme
Some sullen voyce for to esteeme
But if that nothing can obtayne   15
It' soone returne then I will gayne
This morrall vse and frome woords cease
T''is a great thinge to hould on's peace.

Audited Corporation Accounts   OCA: P.5.2   20
f 166   *(Chamberlains' payments)*
…
It*e*m layd out at the Rydinge of the ffranchises and at
the dinner that day to the Musicke and other charges
incident therevnto   xlix s. iiij d. 25
…

St Aldate Churchwardens' Accounts
ORO: DD Par. Oxford St Aldate b.17/6
mb [1]   *(Rendered between 20–9 April 1620) (Receipts)*   30
…
It*e*m gotten at Hocktide and Witsontide   viij li.
…

Collation continued: 1 Apollo and all heires beside] Minerva's [selfe, and all] ⌈and⌉
her Sonns beside *H*   2 aides] tones *H*   3 we[1]] I *H*   3 we[2]] I *H*   11 dearth]
death *H*   14 Some … esteeme] Somewhat a sill⟨.⟩e mope t'esteem *H*   16 It']
Thy *H*   15–18 But if … peace] *these lines follow l.5 in H*

32/ Hocktide: *5–6 April 1619*
32/ Witsontide: *16–22 May 1619*

St Martin Churchwardens' Accounts   ORO: PAR 207/4/F1/1, item 127
single mb   *(Rendered 24 April 1620) (Receipts)*

...

Item received at Hocktide   1 li. xviij s. 0 d.

...   5

St Mary Magdalen Churchwardens' Accounts   ORO: PAR 208/4/F1/48
single mb*   *(Rendered 18 April 1620) (Receipts)*

...

Item at Whitsontide and Hocktyde   iiij li. x s. x d. q*u*a. 10

...

St Michael at the North Gate Churchwardens' Accounts
ORO: PAR 211/4/F1/3, item 184
mb [1]*   *(Rendered between 17–30 April 1620) (Receipts)*   15

...

°Item for hocke monie clere gainned   iij li. xix d.°

...

St Peter in the East Churchwardens' Accounts   ORO: PAR 213/4/F1/3   20
f 11v   *(31 March 1619–19 April 1620) (Receipts)*

...

Item received for hockinge Money   xvj s.

...
                                                                                 25

St Peter le Bailey Churchwardens' Accounts   ORO: PAR 214/4/F1/64
f [1]   *(Rendered 14 May 1620) (Receipts)*

...

Item received in money that was taken at
whitsontide & Hoc-tide   9 li. 30

...

1619–44
Wallington, 'God's Judgement on Sabbath Breakers'   BL: Sloane MS 1457
p 17*   35

...

And here I will set down these [⟨...⟩] obseruations conserning this fier...

2   Secondly. Obserue that the onely Church that was fired & defaced though not

4, 10, 30/ Hocktide, Hocktyde, Hoc-tide: *5–6 April 1619*
10, 30/ Whitsontide, whitsontide: *16–22 May 1619*
17, 23/ hocke, hockinge: *Hocktide was 5–6 April 1619*

wholly burnt, was Cairfax, Where of Giles Widdows (the same y*at* boasted he
cufft the Diuell in his Studie and wroght the schismaticall puritan) was parson,
and had there in often preached against the obseruation of the Lords day:
Saying That dancing & playing was as necessary as preaching, So that this part
of the Towne being so well taught, were alwaies the most euident prophaners   5
of the Sabbath day by keeping Witsun ales & dancing, amongst whome Lame
Giles himselfe would often put off his Gowne & dance with them on y*at* day
...

1619–20   10
Balliol College Bursars' Accounts   BC Arch: Computi 1615–1662
f 30v   *(18 October–7 July)* *(Expenses noted)*
...

It*em* to his Ma*i*esties Trumpeter	0	2	6	0

...   15

f 32v   *(7 July–18 October)*
...

It*em* to his Ma*i*estys trumpeters on Act Munday	0 4 s. 0

...   20

Christ Church Computi   ChCh Arch: iii.c.9(a.)
mb 4*

⟨...⟩gœdiarum & Comœdiarum hoc Anno habitaru*m*   25
et factarum   nil.
...

Corpus Christi College Bursars' Accounts   CCCA: C/1/1/8
f [11] col 2   *(25 March–24 June)* *(External expenses)*   30
...

To the Kings Trumpeters at the Act	1	0	0

...

Magdalen College Libri Computi   MC Arch: LCE/8   35
f 113v   *(Internal and external payments)*
...

Buccinatorib*us* Comitis Ruttland	2 s. 6 d.
Buccinatorib*us* [Regis Bok⟨....⟩] ⌈Comitis Palatini⌉	2 s. 6 d.

...   40

14/ Trumpeter: *3 minims in* MS   25/ ⟨...⟩gœdiarum: MS *torn*
19, 32/ Act Munday, the Act: *10 July 1620*

Puerulo, qui in aula timpanizauerit. 10 s.
Buccinatoribus Regijs & Buckingham. 11 s.
...
Musicis in festo Bursarioru*m*. 5 s. 6 d.
... 5

Merton College Bursars' Accounts MCR: 3.1
f 189 *(24 March–29 July)* *(External expenses)*

...Symphoniacis ex consensu vj s. viij d.... 10
...

New College Bursars' Accounts NC Arch: 7624
mb 5 *(25 December–25 March)* *(Internal expenses)*
... 15
...So*lutum* Musicis oppidanis 6 s. 8 d. So*lutum* to trumpetters 1 s....

(25 March–24 June)
...So*lutum* to a little boy drummer 2 s....
20
(24 June–29 September)
...So*lutum* to trumpetters 2 s. 6 d....
...

The Queen's College Long Rolls QC Arch: LRB 25
f 27 col 1* *(7 July–7 July)* *(External expenses)*
...
It*em* Mauritio fistulanti 18 d.
februarij 21.   It*em* Regijs Tibicinib*us* profecturis
in Bohemia*m* 10 s. 30
It*em* oxoniensib*us* Tibicinib*us* ∧⌈pro⌉
annuo pencione 10 s.
...

St John's College Computus Annuus SJC Arch: Acc.I.A.12 35
f 75* *(25 December–25 March)* *(Allowances)*
...
X   Item Impos*iti* for the Musitians.
Heb*domada* 9. vij li. xiij s. vj d.
... 40

39/ Heb*domada* 9: *20–6 February 1619/20*

f 76v   *(24 June–29 September)*   *(Internal and external expenses)*

...

Item to the Kings Trumpetters   xj s.

...

St John's College Short Book   SJC Arch: Acc.III.D.1
f 59v   *(25 December–25 March)*   *(Allowances)*

...

Item ye Musitians bill
7 li. 14 s. vj d.

ye Musitians	3 li. 23 s. vj d.	
	xxx s.	
ye Showes	xiij s. ij d.	7 li.
gıuen awaye before	xxj s.	2 s.
To ye Seruants	ij s.	2 d.
To Trumpeters	ij s. vj d.	

...

Vice-Chancellors' Accounts   OUA: WP/β/21(4)
p 185   *(17 July 1619–21 July 1620)*   *(Extraordinary expenses)*

...

Item attendentibus tempore prandij in vicecancellarium
et reliquos Doctores apud woodstock   liij s.

...

Item Buccinatoribus Regijs   xxij s.

...

p 186

...

Item Histrionibus vt discedant ab [Academia] vniversitate   xxij s.

...

AC   **Peter Heylyn's Memoirs**   Bodl.: MS. Wood E.4
f 23

...

November 23. Mr Stonehouse (magdalen college) chosen Lord & solemnely
inaugurated in ye Christmas Holidaies, in which pomp I personated ye Duke
of Helicon, the 1st peere of his principalitie & in Ianuary following, my shew
of doublet, breeches & shirt was presented before them.

...

20/ vicecancellarium: *John Prideaux*

Hannisters' Registers OCA: L.5.2
f 63

...

Leonardus
Maior

® ffransiscus Iones

Memorand*um* qu*o*d Tertio die Novembris Anno Regni Regis Iacobi Angl*ie*
&c decimo septimo Et Scotie Quinquagesimo tertio ffranciscus Iones filius   5
Ioh*ann*is Iones de p*ar*ochia Appleton in Com*itatu* Berk*s*hire husbandman
posuit seip*s*um Apprentic*ium* Leonardo Maior de Civit*ate* Oxon*ie* in Com*itatu*
Oxon*ie* Musico ad artem suam qua vtitur erudiend*am* et Cum ip*s*o more
Apprentic*ij* Comorat*ur* et servitur A festo O*mn*ium *S*anctorum quod fuit
Anno Dom*ini* 1618 vsq*ue* ad finem et Terminum septem Annor*um* extunc   10
p*ro*ximor*um* sequen*tium* et plenarie Complend*orum* et finiend*orum* Et in fine
d*ic*ti Termini Dabit eid*em* Apprenticio suo Duplic*es* Vest*es* tali Apprenticio
Congruen*tes*

...

   15

f 395v

...

Georgius Payne nup*er* Apprentic*ius* Leonardo Maior de Civit*ate* Oxon*ie*
Musitian admissus est in Lib*er*tat*em* huius Civitat*is* secund*um* Consuetud*inem*
vicesimo secundo die Novembris Anno supr*a*dic*t*o Et p*re*stitit sacr*amentu*m   20
suu*m*

...

Tailors' Wardens' Accounts Bodl.: MS. Morrell 9
f 46   *(28 June–26 June)* *(Payments)*   25

...

Item to the Musitians at the Masters dynner   0 6 8

...

St Aldate Churchwardens' Accounts   30
ORO: DD Par. Oxford St Aldate b.17/7
mb [1]   *(Rendered in April 1621)* *(Receipts)*

...

Item receaved att Hocktide and Whitsontide
w*hi*ch was clearely gotten   v li. x s. 35

...

6/ Appleton ... Berk*s*hire: *now Appleton, Oxfordshire*
18/ Georgius Payne: *in display script*
27/ Masters: *Charles Russell's*
34/ Hocktide: *24–5 April 1620*
34/ Whitsontide: *4–10 June 1620*

St Martin Churchwardens' Accounts   ORO: PAR 207/4/F1/1, items 134–6
mb [1]   *(Rendered 12 May 1621) (Receipts)*
...
Item R*eceiv*ed at hockinge Cleare   xxx s.
...   5

St Mary Magdalen Churchwardens' Accounts   ORO: PAR 208/4/F1/49
single mb   *(Rendered 5 April 1621) (Receipts)*
...
Item received at Hocktide   iiij li. 10
Item received at Whitson=tyde   xj li.
...

St Michael at the North Gate Churchwardens' Accounts
ORO: PAR 211/4/F1/3, item 185   15
mb [1]   *(Rendered 6 April 1621) (Receipts)*
...
Item receaved att Hocktyde all Chardges diducted   x li. ix s. ix d.
...
                                                                              20
St Peter in the East Churchwardens' Accounts   ORO: PAR 213/4/F1/3
f 12v   *(19 April 1620–4 April 1621) (Receipts)*
...
Item received for Hockinge Money   lvj s. ij d.
...   25

St Peter le Bailey Churchwardens' Accounts   ORO: PAR 214/4/F1/65
f 1   *(Rendered 6 May 1621) (Receipts)*
...
Item received att Hoc-tide   25 s. 5 d. 30
...

1620–1
All Souls College Bursars' Accounts   Bodl.: MS. D.D. All Souls c.292
mb 9   *(2 November–2 November) (Various expenses)*   35
...
De v s. iij d. to three Trumpeters
...

4, 24/ hockinge, Hockinge: *Hocktide was 24–5 April 1620*
10, 18, 30/ Hocktide, Hocktyde, Hoc-tide: *24–5 April 1620*
11/ Whitson=tyde: *4–10 June 1620*
18/ Item: *in display script*

(Rewards)
De xj d. giuen to ye Princes Trumpeters
De xxij s. to the Kings Trumpeters
...

5

Balliol College Bursars' Accounts   BC Arch: Computi 1615–1662
f 37   *(7 July–18 October 1621)* *(Expenses noted)*
...
Item to the Lady Elizabeths Trumpeters   0   2 s.   6 d.
...   10
Item to the prince his Trumpeters   0   5 s.   0
...

f 37v
...   15
Item the Kinges Trumpeters   0   11 s.   0
...

Christ Church Computi   ChCh Arch: iii.c.9(b.)
mb 3d   20
...
Et in expensis Tragædiarum et Comædiarum hoc Anno
habitarum et factarum   nil.
...

25

Magdalen College Libri Computi   MC Arch: LCE/8
f 120v   *(Internal and external payments)*
...
Buccinatoribus Domini Stanhope. ⟨...⟩
Buccinatoribus in Comitijs. ⟨...⟩   30
Buccinatoribus Principis. ⟨...⟩
Buccinatoribus Regis. ⟨...⟩
...
Musicis in festo Bursariorum   5 s.
...   35

Merton College Register   MCR: 1.3
p 268

Februarij 11 conuocatis in vestiarium post preces vespertinas socijs allocavimus   40

29, 30, 31, 32*l* ⟨...⟩: *amounts missing due to a tear in* MS de more tibicinibus 6 s. 8 d.

...

New College Bursars' Accounts   NC Arch: 7626
mb 6   *(25 December–25 March)*   *(Internal expenses)*   5
...
...So*lutum* musicis oppidanis 6 s. 8 d....
...

(24 June–29 September)   10
So*lutum* to the Kings Trumpetters beinge 12 12 s....
...

mb 7   *(External expenses)*
...   15
So*lutum* to a sett of Trumpetters at the Act 3 s....
...

Oriel College Treasurers' Accounts   OC Arch: S I.C.1
f 226v   *(Internal expenses)*   20
...
It*em* solut*um* buccinatoribus regijs   10 s.
It*em* solut*um* buccinatoribus Principis   5 s.
...

                                                                          25

The Queen's College Long Rolls   QC Arch: LRB
f 29 col 2   *(7 July–7 July)*   *(External expenses)*
...
It*em* Mauritio fistulanti   18 d.
It*em* Tibicinis de Oxon*ia*   10 s. 30
...

f 31v col 1   *(7 July 1621–7 July 1622)*
...
It*em* Aug*usti* 22 Buccinatoribus Principis   20 s. 35
It*em* Aug*usti* 27 Buccinatoribus Regis   20 s.
...

16/ the Act: *9 July 1621*

St John's College Computus Annuus   SJC Arch: Acc.I.A.12
f 100   *(29 September–25 December)* *(Internal and external expenses)*
...

X   Item for furnishinge the [s] new yeares. day shew   vj s. viij d.
...   5

f 101v*   *(25 December–25 March)* *(Allowances)*
...

X   Item Impositi hebdomada 8ª for the musicians   ix li. iiij s.
...   10

f 103   *(24 June–29 September)* *(Internal and external expenses)*
...

X   Item to the Princes trumpeters   xj s.
Item to the Kinges trumpeters   xxij s.   15
...

Trinity College Bursars' Books   TC Arch: I/A/2
f 231v   *(25 March–24 June)* *(Reparations)*
...   20

Item buccinatoribus a Rege   10 s.
Item buccinatoribus a Principe   10 s.
...

Audited Corporation Accounts   OCA: P.5.2   25
f 179v*   *(Chamberlains' payments)*
...

Item to master Mayer for the Kings Trompetters and other
Duties at the Kings and Princes comminge hether   ij li. xij s.
...   30

St Aldate Churchwardens' Accounts
ORO: DD Par. Oxford St Aldate b.17/8
mb [1]   *(Rendered 28 April 1622)* *(Receipts)*
...   35

Item at Hocktide and Whitsontide   vij li. iiij s. vij d.
...

4/ vj s.: *altered from* v li.   36/ Hocktide: *9–10 April 1621*
9/ hebdomada 8ª: *12–18 February 1620/1*   36/ Whitsontide: *20–6 May 1621*
28/ master Mayer: *Anthony Fyndall*

St Martin Churchwardens' Accounts   ORO: PAR 207/4/F1/1, items 138–40
mb [1]   *(Rendered 12 May 1622)* *(Receipts)*
...

Item Recevid at hocktyde by the women	xxx s.
Item then by the men Cleare	v s. iij d. 5

...

St Mary Magdalen Churchwardens' Accounts   ORO: PAR 208/4/F1/50
single mb   *(Rendered 29 April 1622)* *(Receipts)*
...   10

Item at Whitsontid and Hoctide   x li. iiij s. vj d.

...

St Michael at the North Gate Churchwardens' Accounts
ORO: PAR 211/4/F1/3, item 186   15
single mb   *(Rendered 26 April 1622)* *(Receipts)*
...

Item gayned att Hocketyde all thyng*es*
being dischardged   liiij s.
...   20

St Peter in the East Churchwardens' Accounts   ORO: PAR 213/4/F1/3
f 14   *(4 April 1621–24 April 1622)* *(Receipts)*
...

Inprimis received out of the Church   25
⌊& for whisson Aile⌋   xxxvij li. 17 s. 10 d.
Item received for Hockinge money   [iiij li. x s.] v li. x [⟨...⟩] iij d.
...

f 14v*   *(Payments)*   30
...

[Item for pitchinge the place where the
May pole stodd   ij d.]
...

4, 11, 18/ hocktyde, Hoctide, Hocketyde: *9–10 April 1621*
11/ Whitsontid: *20–6 May 1621*
26/ whisson: *Whitsuntide was 20–6 May 1621*
27/ Hockinge: *Hocktide was 9–10 April 1621*

St Peter le Bailey Churchwardens' Accounts   ORO: PAR 214/4/F1/66
f [1]   *(Receipts)*

...

Received to the Church his vse by gaine of
Hocktide & whitsuntide   7 li. 18 s. 0   5

...

1621-2
Balliol College Bursars' Accounts   BC Arch: Computi 1615-1662
f 40   *(18 October-7 July)* *(Expenses noted)*   10

...

Item to the Earle of Oxons. Trumpetters   0   2   6   0

...

f 40v   15

...

Item to the Councells Trumpeters at the Act   0   2   6   0

...

Christ Church Computi   ChCh Arch: iii.c.9(c.)   20
mb 3*

...

Et in expensis Tragædiarum et Comœdiarum hoc
Anno habitarum et factarum   Nil.

...   25

Magdalen College Liber Computi   MC Arch: LCE/9
f 4v   *(Internal and external expenses)*

...

Buccinatoribus comitis de Oxonia   3 s. 30
Buccinatoribus comitis de Essex   6 s.
Buccinatoribus ignotis   2 s. 6 d.

...

f 5   35

...

Musicis in festo Bursariorum   5 s.

...

5/ Hocktide: *9-10 April 1621*
5/ whitsuntide: *20-6 May 1621*
17/ the Act: *8 July 1622*

Merton College Register   MCR: 1.3
p 283

...

concessa musicis Tunc etiam consensum est vt publicis academiæ oppidique musicis bursarius
sex solidos octo denarios e bonis collegij pro more solito traderet.   5

New College Bursars' Accounts   NC Arch: 7629
mb 6   (25 December–25 March)   (Internal expenses)

...

...Solutum Musicis oppidanis 6 s. 8 d....   10

...

(24 June–29 September)
Solutum to trumpeters 2 s. 6 d....

...   15

The Queen's College Long Rolls   QC Arch: LRB
f 31v col 1   (7 July–7 July)   (External expenses)

...

Item Ianuarij 1 Mauricio fistulanti   18 d. 20

...

col 2

Item Martij 11 Tibicinibus de Oxonia   10 s. 25

...

St John's College Computus Annuus   SJC Arch: Acc.I.A.12
f 130*   (25 December–25 March)   (Internal and external expenses)

...   30

x   Item for furnishing the founders show.   xxiij s. iiij d.

...

x   Item for fvrnishing the maske above yat which the students paide   xvij s.

...

x   Item to my Lord of Oxfords Trumpetters & Kendoll Musitians   iiij s. vj d. 35

...

f 130v*   (Allowances)

...

x   Item Impositi hebdomada 3ª for the new yeares shew   xvij s. 40

...

4/ Tunc: 3 March 1621/2   40/ hebdomada 3ª: 7–13 January 1621/2

Item Impositi hebdomada 11ᵃ. for the Musitians   vij li. xvij s. vj d.
Item Impositi hebdomada 12ᵃ for a Maske   ˈlv s.

...

St John's College Short Book   SJC Arch: Acc.III.D.1   5
f 69*

X   Inprimis rest of ye Musitions bill   xvj s.

...

10

f 84*   (25 December–25 March) (Expenses)

...

[paid of ye   Inprimis for Furnishinge ye Showe on
Manciple 17 s.]   New years daye   v s. 3 s. 4 d. ij s. j s. ij s. vj d.

...   15

		Wine	4 s.	
		Paynter	v s. v s. vj s.	
X Item for Furnishinge ye Maske		Lights	xj s.	v
		Dauncers	xvj s. xxj s.	
		ye Turner	ij s.		20

...

Item to my Lord of Oxfords Trumpeters &
Kendall Musitions   iiij s. vj d.

...

25

(Allowances)
Item for so much payde at ye [D] Dolphin
for ye Actors on Newyears-daye   vj s.

...

Item to ye Musitions for theyr bill, &   30
Attendance in Christmas   iiij li. vj s. vj d. xl s. x s. v s./

...

f 85*   (24 June–29 September) (Expenses)

...   35

Item to Trumpeter   iij s. 4 d.
Mr. Blagroue   Item to Trumpeters at ye Act   [vj d.] vj s.

...

1/ hebdomada 11ᵃ: 4–10 March 1621/2
2/ hebdomada 12ᵃ: 11–17 March 1621/2
37/ ye Act: 15 July 1622

Vice-Chancellors' Accounts   OUA: WP/β/21(4)
p 189   *(20 July–18 July)* *(Extraordinary expenses)*

...

It*em* dat*um* attendentibus in D*omin*um Vicecan*cellarium*
et reliquos Doctores tempore prandij apud Woodstock   xl s.   5

...

p 190

It*em* Buccinatoribus Regijs   xx s.   10
It*em* Histrionibus Regijs vt discederent ab Academia
nec luderent   xx s.

...

City Council Minutes   OCA: C/FC/1/A2/2   15
f 115   *(20 August)*

...

Whereas yt hath bene here moved vpon the petition of Thomas Charles as
toucheing a lease to be graunted [to th] of the daunceing schole at Bocardo
[that ⟨.⟩ ⟨..⟩th] which was heretofore lett to Iohn Boseley musitian whoe   20
assigned a moyetie thereof to the petic*ioner* ∧⌜& to ther⟨....⟩ the same
∧⌜⟨.... ....⟩⌝ as Ioynt ten*auntes*⌝ that the said lease maye be renued vnto the
two sonnes of the sayd Boseley & the petic*ioner* to thend they maye [by]
∧⌜be⌝ Ioynt tenant*es* to the Cittie, This howse takeing considerac*i*on of the
petic*ioner* doe hereby enact order & agree that if the sayd Boseley thelder &   25
the petic*ioner* shall soe agree ∧⌜between themselves⌝ and that the old Lease
∧⌜form*er*ly made⌝ [mayd] to Boseley maye be brought in & surrendered; that
then the sayd lease shalbe renued as is desyered by the petic*ioner* but only
with [⟨..⟩] an addition of tyme to make vp the terme in being [th] 21. yeres
for the yerely Rent ⌜[⟨... ...⟩]⌝ of xxxiij s. iiij d. and incase the lessees will   30
agree to pay the yerely Rent of xl s. This howse are well pleased & doe agree
that the lease shalbe renued for the terme of xxxj yeres with such Covenant*es*
for payeing of Capons & gryndeing at the Mills as in other cases is vsuall./

St Aldate Churchwardens' Accounts   35
ORO: DD Par. Oxford St Aldate b.17/9
mb [1]*   *(Rendered 18 May 1623)* *(Receipts)*

...

Item at hocktide & Witsuntide   xlvj s. ix d.

...   40

4/ D*omin*um Vicecan*cellarium*: *William Peirs*   39/ hocktide: *29–30 April 1622*
32/ xxxj: *for* xxj *(?)*   39/ Witsuntide: *9–15 June 1622*

(Payments)
Item payd for a key for the hocking box   vj d.
...

St Martin Churchwardens' Accounts   ORO: PAR 207/4/F1/1, items 141–7   5
mb [1]   *(Rendered 27 April 1623) (Receipts)*
...
Rec*eaued* at Hocktide and whitsuntide De Claro
all Charges payd   xxxj li. iij s. iiij d.
...   10

St Mary Magdalen Churchwardens' Accounts   ORO: PAR 208/4/F1/51
single mb   *(Rendered 17 April 1623) (Receipts)*
...
Item at Hocktyde & Whitsontyde   iiij li. xij ⟨.⟩   15
...

St Michael at the North Gate Churchwardens' Accounts
ORO: PAR 211/4/F1/3, item 187
single mb   *(Rendered 18 April 1623) (Receipts)*   20
...
Item gained at Hocktide all thinges
beinge discharged   ij li. j s. iiij d.
...

                                                                                          25
St Peter in the East Churchwardens' Accounts   ORO: PAR 213/4/F1/3
f 15v   *(24 April 1622–16 April 1623) (Receipts)*
...
Item for Hockinge money   lv s.
...   30

f 16v   *(Payments)*
...
Item for a newe key for [⟨.⟩] ∧⌈on of the⌉
Hockeinge boxes   iiij d.   35
...

8, 15, 22/ Hocktide, Hocktyde: *29–30 April 1622*
8, 15/ whitsuntide, Whitsontyde: *9–15 June 1622*
15/ ⟨.⟩: *right edge of parchment cut off*
29/ Hockinge: *Hocktide was 29–30 April 1622*

1622

A   *Jesus College Statutes*   JC Arch: ST4

p 94   *(Chapter 26)*   *(Weapons not to be carried and hindrances to study to be removed)*

...Volumus etiam, quòd nullus Sociorum, aut Scholarium, sive Servientium dicti Collegij, aut degentium in eo, aliquem cane*m*, vel avem qualemcunq*ue*, seu aliud animal quodcunq*ue*, infra [infra] dictum Collegium, vel extra, ad damnum seu detrimentum Collegij, sive ad nocumentum, inquietationem, aut perturbationem alicujus Sociorum, vel Scolarium ejusdem, nutriat seu custodiat, aut etia*m* cantu, clamore, vociferatione, instrumento Musico, aut quovis genere tumultûs, Socium, aut Scholarem quemcunque dicti Collegij, quo minus Studere, aut dormire valeat, quoquo modo impediat, sub pœnâ à Principale vel, eo absente, Vice-principale, ad arbitrium infligendâ.

1622–3

Balliol College Bursars' Accounts   BC Arch: Computi 1615–1662

f 45v*   *(18 October–7 July)*   *(Expenses noted)*

...

To the Lord of Canterbury and the Lord Stannops
Trumpeters   0 2 s. 6 d.

...

f 47   *(7 July–18 October)*

...

To the Counsells Trumpeters   0 2 s. 6 d.

...

Christ Church Computi   ChCh Arch: iii.c.9(d.)

mb 3d*

...

Et in Expens*is* Tragœdiaru*m* et Comœdiaru*m*
hoc Anno habitar et factar   ni*h*il.

...

Corpus Christi College Bursars' Accounts   CCCA: C/1/1/8

f [11] col 2*   *(25 December–25 March)*   *(External expenses)*

...

Giuen by appointment 40 trumpeters at the acte   v s.

...

11/ custodiat: u *corrected over* a   39/ the acte: *14 July 1623*
33/ habitar et factar: *for* habitaru*m* et factaru*m*

Magdalen College Liber Computi   MC Arch: LCE/10
f 4v   *(Internal and external payments)*

...

Buccinatoribus Domini Stanhope   5 s.

...   5

Buccinatoribus ignotis   5 s.

...

Musicis in festo Bursariorum   5 s.

...

10

New College Bursars' Accounts   NC Arch: 7631
mb 6   *(25 December–25 March)* *(Internal expenses)*

...

...Solutum Musicis oppidanis 6 s. 8 d....

...   15

The Queen's College Long Rolls   QC Arch: LRB
f 34 col 2   *(7 July–7 July)* *(External expenses)*

...

Februarii 8   Item Tubicinibus sive Symphoniacis   20
de Oxonia   10 s.

...

St John's College Computus Annuus   SJC Arch: Acc.I.A.12
f 158   *(25 December–25 March)* *(External and internal expenses)*   25

...

X   Item paid towards the New yeares day shew

...

Item to 5 trumpeters

...   30

f 158v   *(Allowances)*

...

Item Impositi hebdomada 11. for the Maske

...   35

Item Impositi hebdomada eadem for the Musitians.

...

34/ hebdomada 11.: *3–9 March 1622/3*

St John's College Computus Hebdomalis   SJC Arch: Acc.v.E.6
f 123   *(10–16 March)*

...

Sett on for a maske	viij li. vij s. viij d.

...

Impositi { [pro] for [⟨....⟩] the fueller   xxvij d. vj d.
ffor ye Musitians   vj li. xviij s. vj d.
ffor fier   v s. vij d.

St John's College Short Book   SJC Arch: Acc.III.D.1
f 95   *(25 December–25 March)*

...

Item of ye Musitions   ij s.

...

St Aldate Churchwardens' Accounts
ORO: DD Par. Oxford St Aldate b.17/10
mb [1]   *(Rendered 25 April 1624) (Receipts)*

...

Item at Hocktide and Whitsontide   v li.

...

St Martin Churchwardens' Accounts   ORO: PAR 207/4/F1/1, item 148
single mb col 1   *(15 April 1623–30 March 1624) (Receipts)*

...

Item receaued at Hocktide and whitsontide
over and aboue all chardges   xx li. vij s.

...

St Mary Magdalen Churchwardens' Accounts   ORO: PAR 208/4/F1/52
single mb   *(Rendered 30 March 1624) (Receipts)*

...

Item at Hocketide and Whitsontide   vij li. j s.

...

St Mary the Virgin Churchwardens' Accounts   ORO: PAR 209/4/F1/27
single mb*   *(Rendered 5 April 1624) (Receipts)*

...

Item gayned at Hocketyde all thinges dischardged.   xl s.

...

20, 26, 33/ Hocktide, Hocketide: *21–2 April 1623*   39/ Hocketyde: *21–2 April 1623 (?)*
20, 26, 33/ Whitsontide, whitsontide: *1–7 June 1623*

St Michael at the North Gate Churchwardens' Accounts
ORO: PAR 211/4/F1/3, item 188
single mb   *(Rendered 1 April 1624)* *(Receipts)*
…

Item gained at hocktide ⌐37 s.¬ and at whitsontide   5
⌐3 li: 1 s. 8 d.¬ all thinges beinge discharged   iiij li. xviij s. viij d.
…

St Peter in the East Churchwardens' Accounts   ORO: PAR 213/4/F1/3
f 17*   *(16 April 1623–2 April 1624)* *(Receipts)*   10
…

Item received for Hockinge Money this yeare   xl s. vj d.
…

1623–4   15
All Souls College Bursars' Accounts   Bodl.: MS. D.D. All Souls c.293
sheet 14*   *(2 November–2 November)* *(Rewards)*
…

De xxij s. given to the King*es* Trumpeters.
De x s. given to the Prince his Trumpeters.   20
…

Balliol College Bursars' Accounts   BC Arch: Computi 1615–1662
f 52v   *(7 July–18 October 1624)* *(Expenses noted)*
…   25
Impr*imis* to the Concells Trumpeters at the Act: 0   5   0
…
It*em* to his Ma*iesties* Trumpeters   0   10   0
It*em* to the Prince his Trumpeters   0   6 s. 0
…   30

Magdalen College Liber Computi   MC Arch: LCE/11
f 4v   *(Internal and external payments)*
…
Buccinatoribus Regis 1 li. Principis 6 s.   35
Ducis Buckingham 5 s. D*omi*ni Stanhop 1 s. 6 d.   1 li. 12 s. 6 d.
…
Musicis in Festo Bursarioru*m*   5 s.
…

5/ Item: *in display script*   12/ Hockinge: *Hocktide was 21–2 April 1623*
5/ hocktide: *21–2 April 1623*   26/ the Act: *12 July 1624*
5/ whitsontide: *1–7 June 1623*

Merton College Register   MCR: 1.3
p 286

…

Concessa
musicis

Tunc etiam consensum est vt publicis Academiæ oppidique Musicis bursarius
6 s. 8 d. pro more solito solueret.   5

…

New College Bursars' Accounts   NC Arch: 7633
mb 8   *(25 December–25 March) (Internal expenses)*

…   10

…*Solutum* Musicis oppidanis 6 s. 8 d.

…

(24 June–29 September)
Solutum to the Trumpetters Iulij .7o 5 s. *Solutum* to the Princes trumpetters   15
Aug*ustij* 13. 11 s. *Solutum* to the Kings Trumpetters 11 s.…

…

Oriel College Treasurers' Accounts   OC Arch: S I.C.1
f 243v   *(Internal expenses)*   20

…

Item buccinatoribus Regijs et Principis   0 16 0

…

The Queen's College Long Rolls   QC Arch: LRB   25
f 36v col 2   *(7 July–7 July) (External expenses)*

…

ffebruarij 7

Item Buccinatoribus de Oxonia   10 s.
Item Mauritio fistulanti   18 d.

…   30

f 39 col 2   *(7 July 1624–7 July 1625)*

…

Augusti 13

Item Buccinatoribus Principis   10 s.

…   35

25

Item Buccinatoribus Regis   20 s.

…

4/ Tunc: *28 February 1623/4*
36m/ 25: *25 August 1624*

St John's College Computus Annuus sjc Arch: Acc.I.A.12

f 178v *(25 December–25 March) (Internal and external expenses)*

...

x	Item to the Lord Stannup's trumpetters	ij s. vj d.

...
5

f 179 *(25 March–24 June)*

...

	Item to the Earle of Northampton's trumpetters	ij s. vj d.

...
10

(Allowances)

Item Impositi hebdomada 2ª for the Musicians   vj li. vj s.

...

15

f 179v *(24 June–29 September) (Internal and external expenses)*

...

x	Item to Trumpetters	ij s. vj d.

...

x	Item to the Princes Trumpetters	x s. 20
x	Item to the Kinges Trumpetters	xx s.

...

Vice-Chancellors' Accounts OUA: WP/β/21(4)

p 198 *(31 July–27 July) (Extraordinary expenses)*
25

...

Solutum Buccinatoribus regijs et alijs Buccinatoribus
alio tempore   xxv s.
Solutum quibusdam Histrionibus vt non luderent   v s.

...
30

City Council Minutes OCA: C/FC/1/A2/2

f 136* *(13 October)*

...

It is also agreed [that] in Remembrance of the happie & safe Retorne of the 35
Prince ∧⌈recently⌉ home into England that on Symon & Judes day next there
shalbe solempne prayers ∧⌈or communion⌉ and a sermon at Carfax ∧⌈and it
shalbe a skarlett day⌉, & there shall also be a barrell of beere & ten dozen of
bread for the poore such quantitie of wyne & Cakes at the bench for the Mayor
the Aldermen Thirteen and bayliffes with the rest of the Counsell of this Cittie 40

13/ hebdomada 2ª: *5–11 April 1624*

as shalbe fitt, and the trayned band of this Cittie shalbe prepared to come
in comelie aray & marshall manner from New parkes or some such place &
enter into the Cittie & discharge their shott in comely manner & euery
muskateere shall have allowed him halfe a pounde of powder [at] and the
Towne Musick shalbe present at the bench after prayers & sermon, & all   5
these things shalbe at the Cities charge & *(blank)*

St Martin Churchwardens' Accounts   ORO: PAR 207/4/F1/1, item 151
single mb col 1   *(30 March 1624–21 April 1625) (Receipts)*
...   10
Item receaved at Hocktyde & Whitsuntyde
ouer & aboue all chardges   ix li. x s. i d.
...

St Mary Magdalen Churchwardens' Accounts   ORO: PAR 208/4/F1/53   15
single mb   *(Rendered 18 April 1625) (Receipts)*
...
Item received at Hocketide   0   vij s.   0 d.
...
                                                                                     20
St Michael at the North Gate Churchwardens' Accounts
ORO: PAR 211/4/F1/3, item 189
single mb   *(Rendered 21 April 1625) (Receipts)*
...
Item gained at hocktide all thinges being   25
discharged   xxxiij s. iiij d.
...

St Peter in the East Churchwardens' Accounts   ORO: PAR 213/4/F1/3
f 19v*   *(2 April 1624–21 April 1625) (Receipts)*   30
...
Item received of the hocking money this yeare   xlviij s. vj d.
...

f 20   *(Payments)*   35
...
Item payd to the Smith for a key for the hocking box   iiij d.
...

11, 18, 25/ Hocktyde, Hocketide, hocktide: *5–6*   25/ Item: *in display script*
   April 1624   32/ hocking: *Hocktide was 5–6 April 1624*
11/ Whitsuntyde: *16–22 May 1624*

St Peter le Bailey Churchwardens' Accounts   ORO: PAR 214/4/F1/67
single mb*   *(Receipts of Thomas Simpson, churchwarden)*
...

		li.	s.	d.	
Imprimis received of monie at whitsontide	}				
and Hocktide and out of the last yeares accompts	}	6	10	0	5

...

(Receipts of Edward Warland, churchwarden)

		li.	s.	d.	
Imprimis received of monie at whitsontide and	}				
Hocktide and out of the last yeares accompts	}	7	0	0	10

...

1624-5
Balliol College Bursars' Accounts   BC Arch: Computi 1615-1662
f 57   *(7 July-18 October 1625) (Expenses noted)*   15

Inprimis to his maiestys Trumpeters   0 5 0 0
...

Magdalen College Liber Computi   MC Arch: LCE/12   20
f 4v   *(Internal and external payments)*
...
Buccinatoribus Regijs   10 s. 6 d.
...

                                                                           25

Merton College Bursars' Accounts   MCR: 3.1
f 215v   *(19 November-18 March) (External expenses)*
...
...Symphoniacis ex consensu vj s. viij d....
...   30

New College Bursars' Accounts   NC Arch: 7635
mb 8   *(24 June-29 September) (Internal expenses)*
...
Solutum Musicis Opidanis 6 s. 8 d. 0...   35
...

4, 9/ whitsontide: *16-22 May 1624*
5, 10/ Hocktide: *5-6 April 1624*

The Queen's College Long Rolls   QC Arch: LRB
f 39 col 2   *(7 July–7 July)* *(External expenses)*

...

Ian*uarij* 6   Mauritio Fidicini   18 d.

...   5

Febr*uarij* 19   Tibicinib*us* Oxoni*æ*   10 s.

...

St John's College Computus Annuus   SJC Arch: Acc.I.A.12
f 202   *(29 September–25 December)* *(Internal and external expenses)*   10

...

X   Item to M*aste*r Deane Filkins for money laid out at ye showe   xviij d.
X   Item to ye painter for work done at ye show   xij d.
X   Item for Torches, Links & waxe lights at ye newyeares show   vij s.

...   15

f 203   *(25 March–24 June)* *(Allowances)*

...

X   Item heb*domada* 4ᵃ for the Musitions   vij li. xviij s. x d.

...   20

f 203v   *(24 June–29 September)* *(Internal and external expenses)*

...

X   Item to ye King's trumpetters   xx s.

...   25

Vice-Chancellors' Accounts   OUA: WP/β/21(4)
p 200   *(27 July–25 July)* *(Extraordinary expenses)*

...

Solut*um* Musicis in funeribus Iacobi nup*er* Regis etc   xx s. 30

...

Solut*um* Buccinatoribus Regis Iacobi   xxij s.
Solut*um* Buccinatoribus Caroli ia*m* Regis   xxij s.

...

                                                                                                            35

Chancellor's Court Inventories   OUA: Hyp/B/17
f [1]*   *(25 January)* *(Inventory of Ambrose Powell)*

...

Item a base viall w*i*th other instruments   xiij s. iiij d.

...   40

19/ heb*domada* 4ᵃ: *18–24 April 1625*   33/ iam: *ie, since 27 March 1625*

City Council Minutes   OCA: C/FC/1/A2/2
f 159*   *(18 July)*

...

Inprimis it is thought fytt in case the king*es* Ma*ie*stie shalbe pleased to come
to this Cittie in p*ar*liament tyme or otherwise that the Maior, the Aldermen,   5
Associat*es* & both the Bayliff*es* shall pr*o*uide themselves to be in a readynes
to meete him as heretofore hath bene done [to] the ˄⌈[in] tyme of⌉ the Late
Quene Elizabeth & king Iames eu*er*y man in his skarlett gowne & velvett
Tippett, his best Apparrell w*i*th each man A lackey, & to be hansomly &
well horsed [on⟨.⟩] ˄⌈& have each man A footecloth of comely black cloth   10
and⌉ [an] m*as*ter Mayor to have two Lackeys, and the officers of the Cittie
[both] aswell the Towne Clerke and the Mayors Sargeant*es* as also the
bayliff*es* sargeant*es* to be decently apparrelled and to attend [⟨.⟩] & Ryde
in their proper plac*es*
And it is furthermore thought fitt that two fayre peec*es* of plate shalbe   15
pr*o*uided to be in readynes also the one dooble guilt w*i*th a [fayer] Cover
about 30 li. price for the King*es* Ma*ie*stie to be geven vnto him an other
[peece] Cup of dooble guilt also w*i*th a Cover of 20 li. price or thereabout*es*
[for] to be geven to the Quenes Ma*ie*stie in case she happen to come hither
to this Cittie   20
And that [⟨.⟩] 40 of the better sort of the Counsell howse hansomly
apparrelled shalbe elected & chosen out [of] to attend m*as*ter Mayor decently
& orderly at such meeting of the king and Quenes Ma*ie*stie in hansome
black guarded Coat*es*
And that my lord wallingford*es* fee the honorable steward of this Cittie   25
shalbe payed and a fayer p*ar*e of gloves of 1 s. or 3 li. shalbe pr*o*uided &
geven him also.
And that the herauld at Arm*es* shall be solicited to m*ar*shall m*as*ter Maior
& his Company & have his fee of 40 s.

...   30

f 159v

...

And that Reward*es* shalbe geven to the King*es* & Queenes Trompiters
footemen Chariteers &c [shalbe geven] if they both come to this Cittie as   35
hath bene form*er*ly accustomed but as muche moderation to be vsed in
the payment as maye bee

...

5/ the Maior: *Oliver Smith*

City Council Minutes   OCA: C/FC/1/A1/002
f 285v*   *(19 July)*

...

Plate to be
provided for the
king and
Quene if they
Come to the
Cittie, and
money to be
borrowed for
the present

Vpon reading of the orders and agreements sett downe in the office by Master
Maior and the Aldermen and Thirteene the Eighteenth day of this month   5
they weare all well approved and allowed of and the seuerall peeces of plate
shalbe bought and all other the perticulers mentioned in the said order shalbe
performed and for that theise matters will requier the disbursment and laieing
out of a greater somme of money then at this time cann be had out of the
Cittie Chest: It is hereby fullie resolved and agreed and soe ordred and enacted: 10
That soo much money as Master Maior the Aldermen and [so] Assosiats with
both the Bayliffes or a maior parte of them shalbe speedilie borrowed and an
instrument for repaieringe of such some or sommes with the interest thereof
according to the Statute shalbe made and Sealed with the Seale of this Cittie
without anie further mocion   15

...

Master
Recorders to
make a speech
to the Kinge &
Queenes
Maiestie

It is alsoe agreed that Master Recordor and Mr Whistler his deputie shalbe
solicited to provid themselues to make such speeches of congratulacion to the
kings Maiesties and the Queene when they come to this Cyttie as shalbe in
theire wisdoms thought fitt/   20

Audited Corporation Accounts   OCA: P.5.2
f 195v   *(Keykeepers' accounts)*

...

Item delivered to Mr ffletcher these soms hereafter following vizt fiftie   25
shillinges which the Cittie allowes Master Maior for his Wheat Money for
Michaellmas quarter fower shillings to the kings Trumpeters Tenn shillings
to the kings Surveyers of the Waies and Tenn shillings to the black Guard
4 li. 14 s. 00

30

St Aldate Churchwardens' Accounts
ORO: DD Par. Oxford St Aldate b.17/11
single mb col 1*   *(19 April 1625–11 April 1626)* *(Receipts)*

...

Item received for Hockeings and att Whitsontyde   3   10   0   35

...

Item paid to Richard Cooke for mending a drumme
that was lente to the parishe att whitsontyde Laste   0   2   0

5/ this month: *July*   35/ Whitsontyde: *5–11 June 1625*
35/ Hockeings: *s larger, perhaps written over another*   35/ 3: *corrected from 2*
    letter; Hocktide was 25–6 April 1625

St Martin Churchwardens' Accounts ORO: PAR 207/4/F1/1, item 153
single mb col 1   *(Rendered 13 April 1626) (Receipts)*

...

Inprimis receaved at Hocktide and Whitsontide
above all chardges   viij li. vj s. ij d.   5

...

St Mary Magdalen Churchwardens' Accounts   ORO: PAR 208/4/F1/54
single mb   *(Rendered 11 April 1626) (Receipts)*

...   10

Item received at Hocketyde   iij li. x s.
Item receved at Whitsondtyde   iiij li.

...

St Peter in the East Churchwardens' Accounts   ORO: PAR 213/4/F1/3   15
f 21*   *(21 April 1625–13 April 1626) (Receipts)*

...

Item receaued of the hocking money this year   1 li. 12 0

...

                                                                                        20

St Peter le Bailey Churchwardens' Accounts   ORO: PAR 214/4/F1/68
single mb*   *(Receipts of Edward Warland, churchwarden)*

...

Item of the Hocke money   0   13   0

...   25

Item for wood which was gotten for the Church
at our Whitson sports   2   2   0

...

(Expenses of Edward Warland, churchwarden)   30
Item paid vnto goodman Oven for the vse of his house
at Whitsuntyde   0   14   0
    And for setting vp boards where the Trunkes stood
    & taking them downe againe   0   2   0
    And for pitching where the Summer poule stood   0   0   1   35

...

4/ Inprimis: *in display script*
4, 11/ Hocktide, Hocketyde: *25–6 April 1625*
4, 12, 32/ Whitsontide, Whitsondtyde, Whitsuntyde: *5–11 June 1625*
18, 24/ hocking, Hocke: *Hocktide was 25–6 April 1625*
27/ Whitson: *Whitsuntide was 5–11 June 1625*

(Receipts of William Johnson, churchwarden)
Item received of the Hocking money   0   13   0
...

City Quarter Sessions   OCA: QSC/A2/001   5
p 213   *(28 April)*

Taken at a session held at the guildhall before Oliver Smith, mayor; John
Prideaux, STD and vice-chancellor of the University; John Hawley, LLD; John
Whistler, esquire; Thomas Flexney, esquire; Thomas Harris, esquire; and   10
William Potter, aldermen
...

Iohn Day and Nicholas Maris convicted here for abarborous misdemanor for
setting vp a horne at the Churche Doore of the parrishe of St Michell vpon
Consideracion had of the bold attempte. It is ordered that they shall both sitt   15
in the stocke vppon [mund] Sunday nexte at the Same Churche Doore by
the space of haulfe an hower in the foorenoone of the same day in the time
of Divine service/
...

20

1625-6
Magdalen College Liber Computi   MC Arch: LCE/13
f 4v*   *(Internal and external payments)*
...
Buccinatoribus classe nauali reuersis repetit*um* per   25
bursarios superioris anni   3 s. 4 d.
...
Buccinatoribus D*omi*ni Stanhop   3 s.
...
Musicis in festo Bursarior*um*   5 s.   30
...

New College Bursars' Accounts   NC Arch: 7637
mb 8   *(25 December-25 March) (Internal expenses)*
...   35
...So*lutum* Musicis Oppidanis 6 s. 8 d....
...

2/ Hocking: *Hocktide was 25-6 April 1625*
16/ Sunday nexte: *30 April 1625*

Iohn Day and
Nicholas Maris
to sitt in the
Stocks half an
hower

The Queen's College Long Rolls   QC Arch: LRB
f 41 col 1   *(7 July–7 July) (External expenses)*

...

Item Buccinatoribus Regis	20 s.

...   5

Decembris 20.   Item buccinatoribus de classe regia   5 s.

...

Aprilis 1.   Item spondialibus Ciuitatis Oxoniæ   10 s.

...

10

St John's College Computus Annuus   SJC Arch: Acc.I.A.12
f 225   *(29 September–25 December) (Internal and external expenses)*

...

x   Item to a noise of Trumpetters   vj s.

...   15

f 226*   *(25 March–24 June)*

...

x   Item to ye Earle of Essex's trumpetters   v s.

...   20

(Allowances)

x   Item Impositi hebdomada 5ta for ye Musitions   Lvj s. vj d.

...

25

St John's College Short Book   SJC Arch: Acc.III.D.2
p 21   *(29 September–25 December) (Expenses and allowances)*

...

Inprimis to a trumpeter on St. Andrews day   xviij d.

...   30

Vice-Chancellors' Accounts   OUA: WP/β/21(4)
p 202   *(25 July–22 July) (Extraordinary expenses)*

...

Item Buccinatoribus Regijs quando Rex erat woodstochiæ   1 li. 2 s. 0   35

...

p 203

...

Item Regiis Buccinatoribus a navibus venientibus   0 10 s. 0   40

...

23/ hebdomada 5ta: *24–30 April 1626*

Thomas Crosfield's Diary   QC Library: MS 390
f 17*

...

13.   *...litterae* missae & librj .13. *with* .3. maskes & points into ye North.

...   5

Audited Corporation Accounts   OCA: P.5.2
f 198   *(Chamberlains' payments)*

...

Item for Cakes and bread being spent ⟨...⟩dstow			10
when *Master* Maior went the ffranchizes	00	x s.	00
Item paied for a barrell of beare	00	x s.	viij d.
Item paied for a greate Iugge	00	ij s.	vj d.
Item for potts	00	00	vij d.
Item paied to 7 boatemen	00	iiij s.	00 15
Item *paied* to Mr Brooks for 26. mens dinners	00	xvij s.	iiij d.
Item *paied* to ffarr for laieing the bridg in Christ			
Church Mead	00	j s.	00
Item paied to the Two drumers	00	v s.	00

...   20

St Martin Churchwardens' Accounts   ORO: PAR 207/4/F1/1, item 155
single mb col 1   *(Rendered 17 April 1627) (Receipts)*

...

Item rec*eaued* at Hocktide   xxx s. 25

...

St Mary Magdalen Churchwardens' Accounts   ORO: PAR 208/4/F1/55
single mb   *(Rendered 27 March 1627) (Receipts)*

...   30

Item received at Hocktide   liiij s. iiij d.

...

St Michael at the North Gate Churchwardens' Accounts
ORO: PAR 211/4/F1/3, item 190   35
single mb*   *(Rendered 29 March 1627) (Receipts)*

...

Item gained at Hocktide all thinges beinge discharged   xxxj s. ij d.

4m/ 13.: *13 March 1625/6*   11/ *Master* Maior: *Henry Bosworth*
4/ ye North: *Cumberland, one of the counties served*   25, 31, 38/ Hocktide: *17–18 April 1626*
   by The Queen's College

of which money remayneth in Goodwif dew her hand   viij s. viij d.

...

Memorand*um* remaininge in Mr ffletcher his hand of
hock money which was gathered 1625   xvij s. xj ⟨.⟩

...   5

St Peter in the East Churchwardens' Accounts   ORO: PAR 213/4/F1/3
f 22v*   *(13 April 1626–30 March 1627)* *(Receipts)*

...

Item for hockinge money   2 li. 0 0 10

...

City Quarter Sessions   OCA: QSC/A2/001
p 229   *(20 April)*

                                                                              15

Taken at a session held at the guildhall before John Prideaux, STD and vice-
chancellor of the University; Henry Bosworth, mayor; John Bancroft, STD; John
Whistler, esquire; Thomas Flexney, esquire; Thomas Harris, William Potter, and
William Wright, aldermen

...   20

Prohibition of   By express Order of this Court, A Generall Publicac*i*on shalbe made in all
whitson sport*es*   Churches throughout this Cittie and Suburbs to prohibite all Sport*es* at
whitsontide, And all meeteing*es* for this yere vpon such occasions to be
forborne by reason of the tyme of infection and danger, and this to be sent
out to all Ministers and Churchwardens in the seu*er*all p*ar*ishes of this Citty 25
& Suburbs to be p*er*formed wi*th* effect, And if any shall offend against this
Order, vpon notice thereof geven to the next Iustice, all such Offendors
to be bownd over to aunswere the same at the next Sessions after.

...

                                                                              30

1626–9
Burnet, Life of Sir Matthew Hale (1682)   Wing: B5828
p 4

     Great care was taken of his Education, and his Guardian intended to breed 35
him to be a Divine, and being inclined to the way of those then called Puritans,
put him to some Schools that were Taught by those of that party, and in the
17th. year of his Age, sent him to Magdalen Hall in Oxford, where Obadiah
Sedgwick was his Tutor. He was an extraordinary Proficient at School, and for
some time at Oxford. But the Stage Players coming thither, he was so much 40

4, 10/ hock, hockinge: *Hocktide was 17–18 April 1626*   37–8/ in the 17th. year of his Age: *20 October 1626*

corrupted by seeing many Playes, that he almost wholly forsook his Studies. By
this, he not only lost much time, but found that his Head came to be thereby
filled with such vain Images of things, that they were at best Improfitable, if
not hurtful to him; and being afterwards sensible of the Mischief of this, he
resolved upon his coming to London, (where he knew the opportunities of   5
such Sights would be more frequent and Inviting) never to see a Play again,
to which he constantly adhered.

...

1626–7   10
All Souls College Bursars' Accounts   Bodl.: MS. D.D. All Souls c.293
mb 10   *(2 November–2 November)* *(Rewards)*

...

De xx s. to ye Kings Trumpeters

...   15

Balliol College Bursars' Accounts   BC Arch: Computi 1615–1662
f 67v   *(7 July–18 October 1627)* *(Expenses noted)*

...

To the Kinges Trumpeters   0 10 s. 0 20
...

Given to the Lord Stanhop his trumpeters   0 2 s. 0

...

Magdalen College Liber Computi   MC Arch: LCE/14   25
f 4   *(Internal and external payments)*

...

Musicis in festo Bursario*rum*   0 5 s. 0

...
                                                                                     30

f 4v

...

Buccinatoribus Regis   1 li. 2 s. 0

...

Buccinatoribus cujusdam Magnatis   0 2 s. 6 35

...

New College Bursars' Accounts   NC Arch: 7638
mb 8   *(25 December–25 March)* *(Internal expenses)*

...   40

...So*lutum* Musicis Opidanis 6 s. 8 d....

...

(24 June–29 September)
So*lutum* to the Kings Trumpeters 10 s....
...

Oriel College Treasurers' Accounts   OC Arch: S 1.C.1   5
f 262   *(External expenses)*
...
Item Buccinatorib*us* Regis   xj s.
...

10

The Queen's College Long Rolls   QC Arch: LRB
f 43 col 1   *(7 July–7 July) (External expenses)*
...
Item Buccinatoribus regijs   10 s.
...   15

col 2

Item Mauritio Fistulanti   18 d.
Item Buccinatorib*us* Oxon*iæ*   10 s. 20
...

f 44v col 2   *(7 July 1627–7 July 1628)   (External expenses)*
...
Aug*usti* 1   Buccinatoribus Regis   20 s. 25
...

St John's College Computus Annuus   SJC Arch: Acc.1.A.12
f 227*   *(29 September–20 November) (Expenses)*
...   30
X   Ite*m* to a noise of Trumpetters   ij s.
...

f 248   *(25 December–25 March)   (Internal and external expenses)*
...   35
X   Item to Stock towards ye Charges of his shew ut patet &c.   xiij s. vj d.
...

f 248v   *(25 March–24 June) (Allowances)*
...   40
Item 2ª for the Musitians   vij li. vij s.
...

41/ 2ª: *ie, the second week, 3–9 April 1627*

f 249*   *(24 June–29 September)*   *(Internal and external expenses)*

...

Item to ye Kings Trumpetors   XX s.

...

Item to 5 Trumpeters y*at* came fro*m* Portsmouth   v s.   5

...

Thomas Crosfield's Diary   QC Library: MS 390
f 21v

...   10

16   a conuocation for ye carriers as followeth: A conuocation for articles touchinge
Eggerley the carrier whierby he is
enioyned to goe euery weeke once
to London except 2: in ye yeares.
2^ly to keep 12 hackney horses &   15
not to take aboue 6 s. a peice of any
priuiledgd person for the hire. 3^ly to
take one penny onely for carriage of
a letter: & for other things 4 s. a
hundred; & also 4 s. for each p*er*son   20
in the waggon, lesse for children:
scholars to be first serud: Lutes
virginals – as they can agree. deliuer
letters & things w*i*thin a day.

...   25

f 24

...

5.   ...Musick night songs ʌ⌐of⌐ capps, Eccho of a woeman, Charon. generatio*n*s
of temporality & spirituality, lawyers. St George for Engl*and* – An old soldier   30
of ye Queenes. ʌ⌐[euery cap]⌐

...

f 28v*

...   35

29.   ...musike vpo*n* wire strings mr Gibbons./.

...

5/ Portsmouth: *Portsmouth, Hampshire*
11m/ 16: *16 December 1626*
18/ take: t *corrected from* c
29m/ 5.: *5 February 1626/7*
36m/ 29.: *29 July 1627*

Audited Corporation Accounts   OCA: P.5.2
f 202   *(Chamberlains' payments)*

...

Item paid the drumer for goeing the ffrenches   0   v s.   0

...   5

Keykeepers' Accounts   OCA: P.4.1
f 193*

...

One bond of Thomas Charles not to lett mr sett the daunceing schoole   10

...

St Martin Churchwardens' Accounts   ORO: PAR 207/4/F1/1, item 157
single mb col 1   *(Rendered 13 May 1628) (Receipts)*

...   15

Inprimis receaved at Hocktide and
Whitsontide   xiiij li. vj s. vj d.

...

St Mary Magdalen Churchwardens' Accounts   ORO: PAR 208/4/F1/56   20
single mb   *(Rendered 15 April 1628) (Receipts)*

...

Item receyved at Hocktide [⟨..⟩t] by
the woemen   iij li. ix s. x d.

...   25

Item gotten by the men at Hocktide   x s.

...

Item gotten at Whitsontide   vj li.

...

                                                                             30

St Michael at the North Gate Churchwardens' Accounts
ORO: PAR 211/4/F1/3, item 191
single mb col 1*   *(Rendered 17 April 1628) (Receipts)*

...

Item receaued of Iohn Stone the said parishe Clarke for   35
hocking money remayning in the Church boxe   ix s.

...

16/ Inprimis: *in display script*
16, 23, 26/ Hocktide: *2–3 April 1627*
17, 28/ Whitsontide: *13–19 May 1627*
36/ hocking: *Hocktide was 2–3 April 1627*

St Peter in the East Churchwardens' Accounts   ORO: PAR 213/4/F1/3
f 23v*   *(30 March 1627–18 April 1628) (Receipts)*

...

In hocking mony   2   5   0

...   5

Inventory of the Goods of John Stacy   ORO: I 60/1/28
single mb*   *(10 August)*

...

It*em* a base vyoll   0   06   08   10

...

1627–8
All Souls College Bursars' Accounts   Bodl.: MS. D.D. All Souls c.293
mb 9*   *(2 November–2 November) (Various expenses)*   15

...

De xj s. to ye Dukes Trumpeters

...

Balliol College Bursars' Accounts   BC Arch: Computi 1615–1662   20
f 74   *(7 July–18 October 1628) (Expenses noted)*

...

It*em* to his Ma*ie*sties trumpetters. & the
Lord Stanhopps   0   11 s.   0

...   25

Magdalen College Liber Computi   MC Arch: LCE/15
f 4   *(Internal and external payments)*

...

Musicis in festo bursario*rum*   5 s.   30

...

New College Bursars' Accounts   NC Arch: 7640
mb 7   *(25 December–25 March) (Internal expenses)*

...   35

...So*lutum* Musicis oppidanis 6 s. 8 d....

...

4/ hocking: *Hocktide was 2–3 April 1627*

Oriel College Treasurers' Accounts   OC Arch: S 1.C.1
f 268v   *(Internal expenses)*
...
It*em* buccinatorib*us* regijs   0 5 0
...   5

The Queen's College Long Rolls   QC Arch: LRB
f 45 col 1   *(7 July–7 July)* *(External expenses)*
...
Mauritio Fidicini   18 d. 10
...
Februarij 23   Tibicinib*us* Oxon*iæ*   10 s.
...
Buccinatorib*us*   5 s.
...   15

St John's College Computus Annuus   SJC Arch: Acc.1.A.12
f 269   *(29 September–25 December)* *(Internal and external expenses)*
...
It*em* given to an Irish Trumpeter   xviij s. 20
...

f 269v   *(25 December–25 March)*
...
It*em* for ye showe on Newyeeres day   7 s. 25
...

f 270*   *(25 March–24 June)*
...
It*em* to ye Kings trumpeters   x s. 30
...

(Allowances)
Item 7ª for ye Musitians   vij li. xiiij s. vj d.
...   35

Vice-Chancellors' Accounts   OUA: WP/β/21(4)
p 209   *(21 July 1627–26 July 1628)* *(Extraordinary expenses)*
...
Inpr*imis* for Gloues at his Ma*i*esties co*m*ming to Woodstock   xvij li. 40
...

34/ 7ª: *ie, the seventh week, 12–18 May 1628*

Item to the Kings Trumpeters   XX s.

...

Thomas Crosfield's Diary   QC Library: MS 390
f 33*   5

...

March. 17.
1627
From Whitehall
to Westminster

Went to London to see the Pompe of Prince & Peeres. goeing to Parliament in
this Order. 1. Trumpeters. 2. Guard in scarlet. 3. ye 4 masters of ye Chancery
in blacke. 4. Barons. 5. Iudges. 6. Byshops. 7. Vicounts. 8. Earles. 9. King.
10. Duke Buckingham. Earl of Holland....   10

...

f 35v col 2*

...

                                        see an 100 verses of ye sight   15
                                        at Oxon. in ye Act.
                                        paginae sequentes

f 36 col 1*

                                                                            20

Almighty God hath soe composd ye frame
Of things as yat each creature ∧⌈praise⌉ [glorify] his name.
Our after ages may ∧⌈even⌉ things behold
Which in those former tymes were neuer told:
Or what of old Mens wits did meditate,   25
to th' honor of our God we consecrate.
1.   We read in sacred writ of ye beginning
     of all ye world, & of Adams sinninge
     [Of Cains & Abells sacrifice we read]
     He was in paradise with Eue, & all   30
     Beasts, fowles & fishes & ye plants full tall.
     But there his wiffe by th' Serpent was beguil'd,
     In that to eate ye aple she did yeild.
     And not content with that, she gaue it him;
     Who eate thereof; & soe they both did sinne.   35
     And nowe alas what should these sinners doe,
     Who had transgressed Gods commandment soe?
     To fly out of his sight they knew not how;
     When they had done what he did not allowe.

8/ Trumpeters: T *corrected from* ye   16/ ye Act: *14 July 1628*
15–17/ see ... sequentes: *preceded by a drawing of a*   22/ [glorify]: *cancelled by underlining*
   hand with a pointing index finger

2.   Their punishm*en*t ensu'd, & it was this:
    The angell driue them out of Paradise.
    And when they were expell'd y*at* sacred place
    to theirs & all posterities disgrace:
    Then they betooke the*m* to their country trade,   5
    Eue w*ith* her distaffe, Adam w*ith* his spade.
    She span, he delu'd & all in misery,
    occasion'd by ye serpent's | subtilty
                           | treachéry.
    Thus was Gods power ‸⌈mad knowne⌉ [seene] in ‸⌈his⌉ creation
    of all things, for mans owne sole consolatio*n*.   10
    But ‸⌈man⌉ [he] transgress'd his law & soe became
    An exile, by Gods iustice; & a shame
    of all his issue: hence his offspring are
    Vntoward, & perplex'd w*ith* griefe & care.
3.   Abell & Cain were Adams first borne sonnes   15
    And each w*ith* sacrifice to th'altar comes.
    After y*at* th'one had plowed, & th'other fed
    his flocke of sheepe: they then sacrificed.
    Th'one was accepted, soe was not ye other,
    therefore did Cain both hate & kill his brother.   20
4.   Of Abrahams faith ye story next doth showe,
    Howe y*at* to kill his owne son at a blowe
    he spar'd not: but ye Angell stepped in,
    & sau'd poore Isaac, who els slayne had bin.
    Thus Abra*h*ams faith was tri'd, who was ye cheife   25
    ⌈Pater fidelium⌉ [& father counted] for his true beleife.
    Oh what obedience did in both appeare?
    Wh*at* duetie in Isaac ye sonne most deare?
    Their faith & ‸⌈deuout⌉ prayers were both rewarded
    & then appeard fro*m* heauen to be regarded: 30

    col 2*

    Nowe followes ye rela*ti*on of something
    ab‸⌈o⌉ut Nebuchadnezzar y*at* proud King.   35
    His ‸⌈cheife⌉ c[ounsell]ontrouler & his counsell graue
    his secretary & attendants [many] brave

17–18/ After … sacrificed.: *these 2 lines added later, set off in a box extending across col 2 and marked for insertion here*
25/ who: *altered from* he
26/ [& father counted]: *cancelled by underlining*
34/ Nowe: *the section heading* 5. *presumably lost when page cropped*

He had: who did consult & after iudge
it meet for all to worship an image.
A golden gallant Image they erected
for all to worship: & who were suspected
not to adore it, they were iudg'd to dy   5
⌈& in⌉ [into] a fiery furnace cast to fry.
Thus Shadrach, Mesheck & Abednego,
were cast; but yet they were preserued so,
that not a haire was sing'd, nor any harme
Beffell them in ye fire. Thus did ye arme   10
Of God from flames by an angell protect
them, as he's wont to doe vnto th'elect.
And this is all out of th'old Testament.

1. That of ye newe which th'author did inuent,
Succeedeth nowe in briefe for to be told.   15
Where first of all we may Ioseph behold,
Also ye virgin Mary, & ye Babe
At Bethlehem within a stable laid.
⌈Thither then⌉ [Then] ye starre directed ye wisemen,
who did bring presents, & were ioyfull when   20
they sawe ye Lord of glory borne in th'Inne
who came to saue them & all men from sinne.

2. After this happie birth, Ioseph was warn'd
to fly with th'babe to Ægipt, least ye arm'd=
=men of King Herod had martyr'd ye Child   25
as they did many in their fury wild,
Vpon their cruell speares./ then followes next

3. Howe Diues feasted, & howe much perplext
poore Lazarus was, while others had their fill
He crau'd an almes; but they did giue him nil,   30
out of their daintyes; But pray marke ye ends
Of this richefeasting Diues, & his freinds:
With Lazarus, howe ye doggs did li⌈c⌉ke his sores
when he was cast out from rich Diues dores.
And after he was sicke & neare to dying   35
From heauen appear'd an Angell yat came flying
for to receiue his soule, & soe ascended
Againe to heauen, & thus his life was ended.
But nowe rich Diues went another way,
namely to hell, where torments are they say,   40

13/ And … Testament.: *underlined to mark the end of the Old Testament section of the poem*

with howlings, cryings & such hiddeous noyse
contrary quite to all celestiall ioyes.
These heauenly ioyes with Lazarus we doe craue
& hope at length with him ye same to haue.
All this ye sight call'd Chaos doth present   5
Express'd by puppets, which one did inuent
In 17 yeares. & this as 'tis well knowne
In Oxford City hath bene often showne./

f 36v   *(24 July)*   10

…

receiued a lettre from mr Dallam touching a clavicord./

…

St Martin Churchwardens' Accounts   ORO: PAR 207/4/F1/1, item 159   15
single mb col 1   *(Rendered May 1629)* *(Receipts)*

…

Inprimis receaved at Hoctide   liiij s. iij d.

…

                                                                                          20

St Mary Magdalen Churchwardens' Accounts   ORO: PAR 208/4/F1/57
single mb   *(Rendered 7 April 1629)* *(Receipts)*

…

Item receyved at Hocktide by
the weemen   iiij li. ij s. 0   25

…

Item gotten by the men at Hocktide   xv s. ix d.
Item gotten at Whitsontide   vj li. iij s.

…

                                                                                          30

St Peter in the East Churchwardens' Accounts   ORO: PAR 213/4/F1/3
f 25   *(18 April 1628–10 April 1629)* *(Receipts)*

…

Item for Hockinge Money   xxv s.

5–8/ All this … showne./: *written in a box at the bottom of the page, extending across the full width of the page*
18/ Inprimis: *in display script*
18, 24, 27/ Hoctide, Hocktide: *21–2 April 1628*
28/ Whitsontide: *1–7 June 1628*
34/ Hockinge: *Hocktide was 21–2 April 1628*

1628–9
All Souls College Bursars' Accounts   Bodl.: MS. D.D. All Souls c.294
mb 11   *(2 November–2 November) (Rewards)*

...

De xx s. to the Kings Trumpeters   5
De x s. to the Queenes Trumpeters

...

Balliol College Bursars' Accounts   BC Arch: Computi 1615–1662
f 80   *(7 July–18 October 1629) (Expenses noted)*   10

...

Item To his Ma*i*esty's Trumpetters   0   10 s.   0

...

Magdalen College Draft Libri Computi   MC Arch: LCD/3   15
f 80v   *(Internal and external payments)*

...

Musicis in festo bursariorum   5 s.

...

Buccinatoribus regis   1 li. 2 s.   20
Buccinatoribus reginæ   10 s.

...

Merton College Bursars' Accounts   MCR: 3.1
f 239v   *(31 July–20 November 1629) (External expenses)*   25

...

...Buccinatoribus Regijs vj s. Buccina*toribus* Reginae x s....

f 240*

                                                                             30

...pro receptione nobilium, et legatoru*m* ... Musicis eodem tempore x s. pro
receptione serenissimi Regis Caroli, illustrissimaeq*ue* Reginae per billam ix li.
x s.... Musicis eodem tempore x s....

...

                                                                             35

New College Bursars' Accounts   NC Arch: 7642
mb 5*   *(25 December–25 March) (Internal expenses)*

...

...So*lutum* Musicis oppidanis vj s. 8 d....

...   40

mb 6*   *(24 June–29 September) (External expenses)*

...

...So*lutum* Buccinatoribus Regis et Reginæ xx s....

...

5

Oriel College Treasurers' Accounts   OC Arch: S 1.C.1
f 276   *(Internal expenses)*

Item Buccinatorib*us* Regijs   1 li. 0 0

...   10

The Queen's College Long Rolls   QC Arch: LRC
f 3v col 2*   *(7 July–7 July) (External expenses)*

...

Maij. 16.   Item tibicinibus Oxon*iæ*   10 s. 15

...

Item Mauritio fidicini, Ian*aurij* 1   18 d.

...

f 5v col 2   *(7 July 1629–7 July 1630) (External expenses)*   20

...

19   Ite*m* Buccinatoribus Regis   20 s.

...

22   Ite*m* Buccinatoribus Reginæ   20 s.

...   25

St John's College Computus Annuus   SJC Arch: Acc.1.A.15
f 19v   *(25 December–25 March) (Allowances)*

...

Item for ye Musitians   vj li. xvj s. 30

...

f 20v   *(24 June–29 September) (Internal and external payments)*

...

Item for ye King & Queenes Trumpeters   xl s. 35

...

22m/ 19: *19 August 1629*
24m/ 22: *22 August 1629*

Thomas Crosfield's Diary   QC Library: MS 390
f 37v   *(2 December)*

[Foure] ˄⌐Five⌐ delightfull materialls for the taste

1. Comfitts as { coriander / violet / orenge } 2 d. a pound./

2. Candy & paste./

For ye Eares at musick schoole

3. Bread as { muske / Bisket } diet. Almond cakes.

For ye smell Apothecaries Oringe pills in syrup. All kindes of Linnen./

4. dry'd sucketts. & candid Orenge Lemon

5. preserves of cherries, damsell, Barbaries, Aringoes.

…

f 40v   *(7 July)*

…

Receiued directions from mr Wilcox touching ye Virginalls which may all be reduced to three

heades together with sundry instruments appertaining therevnto, vizt. Touching

1. The key { making one a newe / mending one old, either for pinn at ye end }

Clacking by putting in a cloth glued at either end vpon which ye key may fitly fall./

The touch by cleansing & opening ye hole in ye midle or gluing on a peice of wood & make a newe hole: als rubbing with a cloath –

2. The Iack & that for ye

Making & mending, where care must be had with a paire of compasses for a iust measure & proportion of ye tonge, breadth & pin & haire.

Tongue haire & pin & cloth

3. The string which requires

1. a wreste . a pin

2. 2. Skill to { Size / putte / Tune, this must be done by 8ts descending from ye treble from eights to fifts & thirds – }

For preserving ye Instrumentes there must be acquired a boxe or two & a pennar.

3 Care to preserve all from moisture & other nocuous quality

36/ 2. 2.: *dittography*

AC   ***Peter Heylyn's Memoirs***   Bodl.: MS. Wood E.4
      ff 26–6v

October 28. Tuesday & Saint Simon & Iudes day I married my dearest mistress   5
mistris Lettice Heygate in ye church or chapel of Magdalen College which I had
caused to be set out in ye best & richest ornaments ye college had, my [old]
old & true freind Iack Allibond performing ye ceremony, & kept my wedding
dinner in my chamber in ye College, to which, I did invite some of ye Fellowes
of ye College, some Doctors of ye Towne & their wives I I placed her at ye head
of the Table, desiring her to bid her freinds welcome for ye day was hers, &   10
had ye Towne Musick to entertaine her withall, which I had caused to play yat
morning at her chamber dore. which open carriage of ye business made it less
suspected...

...

                                                                                 15

      Hannisters' Registers   OCA: L.5.2
      f 180

...

George Abbott   xxvij° Aprilis 1629.
® Richard   *Memorandum* That then George Abbott sonne of George Abbott late of the   20
Burren./   Cittie of Oxon. limner deceased hath put himselfe Apprentice to Richard Burren
                of the said Citty of Oxon. Musition to learn his Art & him after the manner of
                an Apprentice to serue from the Thirtith day of Aprill next commeing after
                the date hereof vnto the full end & terme of Eight Yeares from thence next
                following fully to be compleate & ended And in thend of the said terme shall   25
                give vnto his said Apprentice double apparrell fitting for such an Apprentice.

...

      f 366v*   *(4 December)*

...   30

Iohn Gerrard, Phillippus Golledge, Richardus Burren et [and] Sampson Stronge
Musicions gratis admissi fuerunt in Libertates huius Ciuitatis Solvendo tantum
feoda officiariorum & ij s. vj d. [pro] quilibet eorum pro sitella Corporata
Et prestiterunt sacramentum suum Corporale prout per Actum ad idem
Consilium factum plenius appareat &c/   35

...

      City Council Minutes   OCA: C/FC/1/A1/003
      f 1*   *(4 December)*

...   40
The nominacion
of the Waytes   Item at this Councell it is agreed That these persons following vizt Iohn
of this Cittie

31/ Iohn ... Burren et: *in display script*

Baldwin thelder & Iohn Baldwin the yonger Iohn Gerrard Phillippe
Golledge Richard Burren & Sampson Stronge shall from henceforth be
the waytes of this Cittie. And that the said Gerrard Golledge Burren &
Stronge being noe ffreemen shalbe admitted free of this Cittie for the
officers ffees & euery one a Buckett sauinge Sampson Stronge who   5
serued as an Apprentice to a ffreeman of this Cittie. And with this
Condicion alsoe That euery one of them that hath not a Scutchen shall
at his owne Chardges provide one before they Collect any Money this
next Christmas And be bound to leave the same Schutchens to this
Cittie at theire deaths And that they alsoe ∧⌈once yearlie⌉ surrender   10
theyre Scutchens to Master Mayor as his Seargeantes doe theire Maces
And ∧⌈it is likewyse agreed⌉ that vppon the death of euery of the said
persons this howse to make Choice of another in his Roome soe dyinge
And that Master Mayor shall not be questioned for moveing this howse
for theyre ffreedom gratis Any Act heretofore made to the Contrary   15
notwithstanding/ Afterwardes the said Musitions soe appointed to be
free came into this howse & were sworne & paid theire ffees & for
three Buckettes to the newe Chamberlins.
...

                                                                          20

Audited Corporation Accounts   OCA: P.5.2
f 208   *(Chamberlains' receipts)*
...
Item received of three Musitions for their
buckettes when they were made free   00 07   6 25
...

f 209*   *(Payments)*
...
Item paid for two Cheses   00 03   0 30
Item paid ffarr for laying a Bridge
Christchurch Meade   00 01   0
Item paid to the Boatemen of Hincksey 4 s.
and to Pemerton for going vpSecoth per
1 s. 6 d. in all   00 05   6 35
Item paid for Mr Carters Dinner   00 01   6
Item paid for ffortie mens Dinner   01 10   6
Item paid to Richard Cooke the
Drummer then and for a new head
to his Drumme   00 12 00 40
...

St Martin Churchwardens' Accounts   ORO: PAR 207/4/F1/1, item 161
single mb col 1   *(Rendered May 1630)* *(Receipts)*

…

Inprimis receaved at Hoctide   45 s. 6 d.

…   5

St Mary Magdalen Churchwardens' Accounts   ORO: PAR 208/4/F1/58
single mb   *(Rendered 18 April 1630)* *(Receipts)*

…

Item gotten at Hoctide by the men   ix s. iij d. ob. 10

…

Item of Richard duckett for the Maypole and Bower   xiij s.

…

St Michael at the North Gate Churchwardens' Accounts   15
ORO: PAR 211/4/F1/3, item 192
single mb col 1   *(Rendered 3 April 1630)* *(Receipts)*

…

Item receaued [of] Att hocktide and Whitsontide   iij li. xiij s. iiij d.

…   20

St Peter in the East Churchwardens' Accounts   ORO: PAR 213/4/F1/3
f 28   *(10 April 1629–2 April 1630)* *(Receipts)*

…

Item for hockinge Monies   xl s. 25

…

1629–30
All Souls College Bursars' Accounts   Bodl.: MS. D.D. All Souls c.294
mb 8   *(2 November–2 November)* *(Rewards)*   30

…

De v s. To the Earle of Warwickes Trumpeters

…

Christ Church Treasurers' Accounts   ChCh Arch: iii.c.1   35
f 276

…

Et in expens*is* Tragediaru*m* et Comediaru*m* hoc
Anno habitaru*m* et factaru*m*   nil.

4/ Inprimis: *in display script*   19/ Whitsontide: *24–30 May 1629*
4, 10, 19/ Hoctide, hocktide: *13–14 April 1629*   25/ hockinge: *Hocktide was 13–14 April 1629*
12/ Richard duckett: *churchwarden*

Magdalen College Liber Computi   MC Arch: LCE/16
f 3v*   *(Internal and external payments)*

…

Musicis in festo Bursariorum	5 s.

…

Buccinatoribus Comitis de Warwick & classe
nauali reuersis   5 s. 6 d.

…

New College Bursars' Long Books   NC Arch: 4200
f [182]   *(25 December–25 March)* *(Internal expenses)*

…

Solutum Musicis oppidanis   6 s. 8 d.

…

f [182v]   *(External expenses)*

…

Solutum Buccinatoribus Vicecomitis Comitatus Oxonie   5 s.

…

The Queen's College Long Rolls   QC Arch: LRC
f 5v col 2*   *(7 July–7 July)* *(External expenses)*

…

Item Mauritio fidicinj   18 d.

…

f 6 col 1

…

Maij 8   Item Tibicinibus Oxoniæ   10 s.

…

St John's College Computus Annuus   SJC Arch: Acc.I.A.15
f 45v*   *(25 December–25 March)* *(Internal and external payments)*

…

x   Item paid towards ye furnishing out of ye ffounders shew   x s. ij d.

…

(Allowances)

x   Item hebdomas 12 for ye Musitians   vij li. xiij s.

…

39/ hebdomas 12:   *15–21 March 1629/30 or 22–8 March 1630 (?)*

St John's College Short Book   SJC Arch: Acc.III.D.2
p 126

...

Item given to my lord of norwiches trumpetters   ij s.

...   5

Vice-Chancellors' Accounts   OUA: WP/β/21(4)
p 214   *(27 July–17 July)* *(Extraordinary expenses)*

...

Item to his Maiesties Trumpetters   1   0   0 10

...

Thomas Crosfield's Diary   QC Library: MS 390
f 47

...   15

vpon ye receipt of ye Harpsichon from mr Sadler I lent him 3 li. and
allowed him 20 s. in ye debt he owed me promiseing to returne to him the
said Harpsichon, if he brought me 4 li. before th'Act otherwise to keepe it./

...

                                                                                 20

f 50v*

...

10. At the act, a prize, a horse race, no players at Franklins...

...

                                                                                 25

Hannisters' Registers   OCA: L.5.2
f 192

...

iij Aprilis 1630:

Mathewe   Memorandum that then Mathewe Bradford sonne of George Bradford late   30
Bradford./   of the Citty of Oxon. Cordwayner deceased hath put himselfe Apprentice
℞ Phillippe   to Phillippe Golledge of the Citty of Oxon. aforesaid Musition to learne his
Golledge   art & him after the manner of an Apprentice to serue from the feast day of
              Thannunciacion of the blessed Lady St Mary the Virgin now last past vnto
              the full end & terme of Seaven yeares from thence next followinge fully   35
              to be Compleate & ended And in thend of the said terme the said Master
              shall giue vnto his said Apprentice double apparrell fitting for such an
              Apprentice and Twenty shillinges of lawfull Englishe Money.

...

23m/ 10.: *10 July 1630*
23/ Franklins: *name written at end of line into the right margin; abbreviation mark missing*

f 199v*

...

xxj° Septembris 1630.

Thomas Curtis./   *Memorandum* that then Thomas Curtis sonne of Luke Curtis of Lacocke
®Iohn Gerrard   in the Countye of Wilts*hire* Musition hath putt himself Apprentice to Iohn   5
Gerrard of the Cittie of Oxon. Musition to learne his art & him after the
manner of an Apprentice to serue from the One and Twentyth day of Aprill
now last past vnto the full end & terme of Seauen yeares from thence next
following fully to be Compleate & ended And in thend of the said terme
the said Master shall giue vnto his sayd Apprentice double app*arr*ell fitting   10
to such an Apprentice, three Pound*es* of lawfull Englishe Money and one
Instrum*ent* w*hi*ch he the said Thomas can best vse.

...

Audited Corporation Accounts   OCA: P.5.2   15
f 213*   *(Chamberlains' payments)*
...
Item paid to the kings Trumpeters   00   05   0
...

                                                                           20
St Martin Churchwardens' Accounts   ORO: PAR 207/4/F1/1, item 163
single mb col 1   *(Rendered 12 June 1631) (Receipts)*
...
Inprimis receaued att Hocktide   3 li. 6 s. 9 d.
...   25

St Mary Magdalen Churchwardens' Accounts   ORO: PAR 208/4/F1/59
single mb   *(Rendered 11 April 1631) (Receipts)*
...
It*e*m receyued at Hocktide: gotten by the me*n*n   xj s.   30
...

St Michael at the North Gate Churchwardens' Accounts
ORO: PAR 211/4/F1/3, item 193
single mb col 1   *(Rendered 26 April 1631) (Receipts)*   35
...
It*e*m receaued at Hocktide   ij li. xvj s. ix d.
...

24/ Inprimis: *in display script*
24, 30, 37/ Hocktide: *5–6 April 1630*

1630–1

All Souls College Bursars' Accounts Bodl.: MS. D.D. All Souls c.294
mb 10* *(2 November–2 November) (Rewards)*
...
De x s. to his Ma*i*esties Trumpett*ers* for the Navy.   5
...
De xx s. to the Kings Trumpett*ers.*
...

Balliol College Bursars' Accounts BC Arch: Computi 1615–1662   10
f 91 *(7 July–18 October 1631) (Expenses noted)*
...
It*em* to his Majesty Trumpeter   0   11   0
...

                                                                         15

Jesus College Bursar's Book JC Arch: BU:AC:GEN:1
p 10 *(30 November–30 November) (Annuities)*
...
To the Kings Trumpetters   00:10:00
...   20

Magdalen College Liber Computi MC Arch: LCE/16a
f 3v *(Internal and external payments)*
...
Musicis in festo Bursariorum   5 s. 25
...
Buccinatoribus Regis et alijs   1 li. 7 s. 6 d.
...

Merton College Bursars' Accounts MCR: 3.1   30
f 247 *(18 March–29 July) (External expenses)*

...Buccinatoribus v s....
...

                                                                         35

Merton College Register MCR: 1.3
p 308
...
AUGUST*I* 2ᵈᵒ   Musicis quibusdam, quos haud ita pridem ab Oppidanis segreges adsciuerat

---

13/ Trumpeter: *4 minims in* MS

Academia, & Academiae insigni ac titulo gaudere perm⟨.⟩serat, XII d. in singulos Socios concessi sunt, & proximo fini deducendi.

…

New College Bursars' Accounts   NC Arch: 7645   5
mb 10*   *(25 December–25 March)*   *(Internal expenses)*

…

…So*lutum* Musicis Opidanis 6 s. 8 d.…

…

10

(25 March–24 June)
…So*lutum* to the Trumpetters of his Ma*i*esties ffleete bound for the streight*es* 5 s.

…

15

(24 June–29 September)
…So*lutum* to his Maiesties Trumpetters 10 s.…

…

Oriel College Treasurers' Accounts   OC Arch: S 1.C.1   20
f 286v   *(Internal expenses)*

…

It*em* Buccinatorib*us* regijs   00 010 00

…

25

The Queen's College Long Rolls   QC Arch: LRC
f 8 col 2   *(7 July–7 July)*   *(External expenses)*

…

Ian*uarij* 1. Mauritio Fidicini   18 d.

…
30

Mar*tij* 7. Tibicinibus Oxon*iæ*   10 s.

…

f 10 col 1*   *(7 July 1631–7 July 1632)*

…
35

Aug*usti* 18   Buccinatoribus Regis   20 s.

…

Mauritio Fidicinj   18 d.

…

1/ perm⟨.⟩serat: *letter lost due to cropping of page edge*

St John's College Computus Annuus   sjc Arch: Acc.i.A.15
f 73   *(25 December–25 March)*
...

Item paid towards ye furnishing out of
ye ffounders shew   x s.   5
...

f 73v   *(25 March–24 June) (Allowances)*
...
X   Item Impositi hebdomada eadem for   10
ye Musicians   viij li. ix s.
...

f 74*   *(24 June–29 September) (Internal and external expenses)*
...   15
Item to Trumpe⟨...⟩
...
Item to ye Kings Trumpeters   xx s.
...
                                                                              20
St John's College Short Book   sjc Arch: Acc.iii.D.2
p 178   *(25 March–24 June)*
...
Item given to trumpeters   v s.
...   25

Trinity College Bursars' Books   tc Arch: I/A/2
f 343*   *(25 March–24 June) (Expenses)*
...
Buccinatoribus regijs   10 s. 30
Tibicinibus nauticis ⌈maij 25⌉   6 s.
...

Thomas Crosfield's Diary   qc Library: ms 390
f 56*   *(20 April)*   35
...
master Provost gaue admonition touching gownes, gates, long haire, battles.
Pitcher sould me a sett of Choice Ms. Song bookes 5 & 6 parts, also Allisons
5 parts & Gibbons 5 parts...
...

10/ hebdomada eadem: *ie, the fourth week, 18–24 April 1631* f 57v*   *(11 July)*

...

Things to be seene for money in ye City 1. Playes: 2. dancing vpon ye Rope
& vaulting vpon ye Sadle. 3. virginalls & organs playing by themselves. 4. a
dutch-wench all hairy & rough vpon her body. 5. The history of some parts   5
of ye bible, as of ye creation of ye world, Abrahams Sacrificing his Sonne,
⌈Nineveh beseiged & taken⌉ Dives & Lazarus. 6. The dancing of ye horse at
ye Starre./

...

                                                                              10

f 58*   *(21 August)*

...

The same day was yer a funerall for mr Paine that dyed mare in Oxon. &
was translated to Abingdon during ye Kings abode at woodstocke whose
Trumpeters demanded some fee from ye towne as due, but it was denyed as   15
ye time also of their being there before, which highly displeased ye Lord
Chamberlane

...

Hannisters' Registers   OCA: L.5.2   20
f 201v*

                        15o die Octobris 1630./
ffrancis Taylor.   *Memorandum* that then ffrancis Taylor sonne of Edward Taylor late of the
®Iohn Gerrard   Citty of Oxon. Taylor deceased hath putt himselfe Apprentice to Iohn Gerrard   25
                 of the Cittie of Oxon. Musition to learne his art & him after the manner of
                 an Apprentice to serue from the feast day of All Saints last past before the
                 date hereof vnto the full end and terme of Seaven yeares from thence next
                 followinge & fully to be Compleate and ended And in thend of the said terme
                 the said Master shall giue vnto his said Apprentice double Apparell fitting   30
                 for such an Apprentice and three Pounds of lawfull English Money.

...

f 210v*

                                                                              35

                         9o July 1631.
Iohn Hancocke   *Memorandum* that then Iohn Hancocke sonne of Thomas hancocke late
                 of Reading in the Countie of Berkshire weauer deceased hath put himself
®Richard Burrin   Apprentice to Richard Burrin of the Citty of Oxon. Musition to learne his art

8/ ye Starre: *Star Inn on west side of North Street*
14/ Abingdon: *Abingdon, Berkshire (now Oxfordshire)*

Twelueth

& him after the manner of an apprentice to serue from the Twelueth day of
this instant Iuly vnto the full end & terme of Seauen yeares from thence next
followinge & fully to be Compleate & ended And in thend of the said terme
the said Master shall giue vnto the said Apprentice double apparrell fitting for
such an Apprentice and Sixe & Twenty shillinges & eight pence in money &   5
the Instrument which the said Iohn can then best vse.
°Memorandum quod vicesimo quarto die [Juni] Maij Anno Regni Regis Caroli
decimo venit tam Christoferus Palmer qui duxit in uxorem Mariam nuper
uxorem dicti Richardi Burrin quam idem Apprenticius et Sampson Stronge
Ciuis & Musition ciuitatis Oxonie coram ffraunsico Harris Armigero maiore   10
eiusdem Ciuitatis & me Timotheo Cartar Clerico communitatis Ciuitatis
predicte Et ₍ᵗᵘⁿᶜ⁾ idem Apprenticius cum consensu dicti Christoferi posuit
se Apprenticium dicti Sampson Stronge pro residuo termini predicti & a fine
eiusdem termini vsque vicesimum quartum diem Maij tunc proximum
Sequentem Et idem Sampson adtunc acceptauit eundem Apprenticium in   15
servicium suum Et assumpsit eidem Apprenticio dare eidem Apprenticio
eodem 24o die Maij post finem dicti termini prout predictus Ricardus Burrin
eidem Apprenticio dare debet & prout specificatur in Irrotulamento predicto
⟨..⟩ Iulij 1631
Item est Timotheus Cartar clericus communitatis Civitatis Oxonie°   20

...

f 361*

...

Robertus Duke & Edwardus Golledge Musicions admissi sunt in libertates   25
huius Ciuitatis xixo die Septembris Anno 7o Caroli Regis ad Consilium tunc
tentum gratis sicut alij antea Et Iurati sunt/

...

City Council Minutes   OCA: C/FC/1/A1/003   30
f 26*   *(9 September)*

...

Robert Duke
& Edward
Golledge
admitted gratis

Item it is agreed that Robert Duke & Edward Golledge being now allowed to be
two of the Towne waytes shalbe admitted free of this Cittie for thofficers fees as
hath beene accustomed for others in the like Case wherevpon the said Duke &   35
Edward Golledge came presentlie into the Councell Chamber & were swurne./

...

1/ Twelueth: wel *written over other letters*
7–20/ Memorandum quod ... Oxonie: *interpolated text begins in left margin and concludes in space below*
    original memorandum
16/ eidem Apprenticio dare eidem Apprenticio: *first occurrence of* eidem Apprenticio *redundant*
25/ Robertus ... Golledge: *in display script*

City Waits' Obligations   OCA: F.5.2
f 51

Nouerint vniuersi *per presentes* me Ioh*ann*em Baldwin Iun*iorem* de Civitate
Oxon*ie* Musition teneri & firmit*er* obligari Thome Cooper Ar*migero* maiori   5
Civit*atis* Oxon*ie* pred*icte* Willelmo Potter Willelmo Wright Oliu*ero* Smyth
Willelmo Boswell & Henr*ico* Bosworth Aldri*mannis* eiusd*em* Civit*atis* in decem
libris legalis monet*e* Anglie Soluend*is* eisd*em* Thome Cooper Willelmo Potter
Willelmo Wright Oliu*ero* Smyth Willelmo Boswell & Henr*ico* Bosworth
aut eor*um* alicui dehinc cert*is* Attorn*atis* execut*oribus* adm*inistratoribus* vel   10
assig*natis* suis Ad q*uam* quidem solut*ionem* bene & fidel*iter* faciend*am*
obligo me hered*es* execut*ores* & adm*inistratores* meos firmit*er per presentes*
Sigillo meo sigillat*as* dat*as* decimo quinto die Nouembris Anno Regni
d*omi*ni n*ost*ri Caroli dei grac*ia* Anglie Scotie ffraunc*ie* & Hib*er*nie Regis fidei
defensor*is* &c Sexto   15

The Condic*i*on of this obligac*i*on is such That whereas thabouebounden Iohn
Baldwin Iun*ior* is admitted to be one of ye waytes of the Citty of Oxon. and to
that purpose hath one of the Scutchens of ye Mayor Bayliff*es* & Comynaltie
of ye same Citty deliu*er*ed vnto him Yf therefore the said Iohn Baldwin shall   20
& doe from thenceforth be obedient & conformable to such reasonable order
acte & decrees as are & shalbe made by the said Mayor Bayliff*es* & Comynaltie
or their Successors touching the waytes or company of Musitions of ye said
Citty for the tyme being And doe yearely vppon the day on wh*ich* the Mayor
of ye said Citty for the tyme being shall first enter into his office of Mayoraltie   25
surrender vpp to the said Mayor his said Scutchen in such mann*er* as the
Sargeant*es* of ye said Citty doe their Maces And lastlie if the executors
adm*in*istrators or assignes of ye said Iohn Baldwin doe w*ith*in one weeke next
after the [death day] ₍day of death₎ of him the said Iohn deliu*er* the said
Scutchen to ye Mayor of ye said citty for the tyme beinge by him to be disposed   30
of to the next p*er*son that shalbe admitted in his roome or place That then
this obligac*i*on to be voyde or els to stand & be in full force & vertue/

Sealed & deliu*er*ed
in the p*re*sence of   35
Timothie Carter
Bernard Lyford/   *(signed)* Iohn balldwyin

M*emorand*um that from henceforth the said Iohn Baldwyn Iun*ior* (by
agreame*nt* betweene M*aste*r Mayor & the Company of Music*i*ons) shall   40

10/ dehinc: *2 minims in* MS

not take nor keepe any more Apprentices then one at one tyme./
(signed) Iohn balldwyin

f 53

Noverint vnuersi per presentes me Sampson Strong de Civitate Oxonie
Musition Teneri et firmiter obligari Thome Cooper Armigero Maiori Ciuitatis
Oxonie predicte Willelmo Potter Willelmo Wright Oliuero Smyth Willelmo
Boswell et Henrico Bosworth Aldermanis eiusdem Civitatis in decem Libris
bone et legalis Monete Anglie Soluendis eisdem Thome Cooper Willelmo
Potter Willelmo Wright Oliuero Smyth Willelmo Boswell et Henrico Bosworth
aut eorum alicui dehinc certis Attornatis executoribus administratoribus vel
assignatis suis Ad quam quidem solucionem bene et fideliter faciendam Obligo
me heredes executores et administratores meos firmiter & per presentes Sigillo
meo sigillatas datas decimo quinto die Novembris Anno Regni domini nostri
Caroli dei gracia Anglie Scotie ffrancie et Hibernie Regis fidei defensoris &c
sexto./ Annoque domini 1630/

The Condicion of this Obligacion is such That whereas thabouebounden
Sampson Stronge is admitted to be one of the waytes of the Cittie of Oxon.
And to that purpose hath one of the Scutchens of the Mayor Bayliffes &
Comynaltie of the same Cittie deliuered vnto him Yf therefore the sayd
Sampson Stronge shall & doe from henceforth be obedient & Conformable
to such reasonable Orders & decrees as are or shalbe made by the said Mayor
Bayliffes & Comynaltie or their Successors touchinge the waytes or Company
of Musitions of the said Cittie for the tyme being And doe yearelie vppon the
day On which the Mayor of the said Cittie for the tyme being shall first enter
into his office of Mayoraltie surrender vp to the said Mayor his said Scutchen
in such manner as the Sargeantes of the said Citty doe their Maces And lastlie
yf thexecutors & administrators or assignes of the said Sampson doe within
one weeke next after the day of the death of him the said Sampson deliuer the
said Scutchen to the Mayor of the said Cittie for the tyme being by him to be
disposed of to the next person that shalbe admitted in his roome or place That
then this Obligacion to be voyde Or ells to stand & bee in full force & virtue

Sealed & deliuered
in the presence of
Timothie Carter & of
Bernard Lyford./   (signed) Sampson Strong

Memorandum that from henceforth the said [Ioh] Sampson Strong (by
agreament betweene Master Mayor and the Company of Musicions) shall

not take nor kepe any more Apprentices then one at one tyme./

(signed) Sampson Stronge

Cordwainers' Minutes   Bodl.: MS. Morrell 20

f 78*   (Rendered 11 November) (Payments at the dinner)

...

Item giuen at the Dynner at old Mr Clarckes for
wyne and Musicke   0   15   0

...

Item for the Dynner   5   3   7

Item to the Musicions at the Dynner   0   6   8

...

St Martin Churchwardens' Accounts   ORO: PAR 207/4/F1/1, item 165

single mb col 1   (Rendered 30 May 1632) (Receipts)

...

Inprimis receaved att Hocktide and Whitsontide
aboue all chardges   xvj li. xvj s. iiij d.

...

St Mary Magdalen Churchwardens' Accounts   ORO: PAR 208/4/F1/60

single mb col 1   (Rendered 3 April 1632) (Receipts)

...

Item receyved of the money that was gotten by
the Whittsontide sport   7 li. 6 s. 7 d.

...

Item received for Hockinge money by the men
and women   iiij ii j ob.

Item received for the woode that made the bower   j viij 0

Item received of money that was gotten by the
Morris dauncers at Whitsontide   0 viiij ij

...

col 2   (Payments)

...

morris   Item paid for a Dinner for the Morris Dauncers and for
flowers and for other necessaries ∧⌈on holy Thirsday⌉   j j 0

...

17/ Inprimis: *in display script*

17/ Hocktide: *18–19 April 1631*

17, 25, 31/ Whitsontide, Whittsontide: *29 May–4 June 1631*

27/ Hockinge: *Hocktide was 18–19 April 1631*

36/ Dinner: *4 minims in MS*

37/ holy Thirsday: *Ascension Day, 22 May 1631*

Item paid ffor bringinge home the wood ffor the bower
and for other thinges belonginge to the Whitson sporte   j ii ij

…

Ecclesiastical Court Proceedings   ORO: MS.Oxf. Dioc. papers Oxon.c.2   5
f 225v   *(28 May)*

Proceedings before Samuel Bardon, deputy judge

Contra Thomam Shade *parochie Sanc*te Ebbe Oxon*iensis* †   10
Gard*ianum* ib*i*dem †
Contra Ioh*an*nem Brookes, *pro* consimili †
Contra Ioannam Renche, *pro* consimili †
Contra Katherinam Bright *pro* consimili †
Citat*ur* &c [Quidem die et loco] for keping Whitson ale *with*out auc*to*ritie   15
against the will & minde of the Churchwardens comp*aruerun*t *omnes* et
consentieru*nt* in [diem] locum et d*omin*o Iudican*ti* [Comparuerunt] quib*us*
d*omin*us inhibuit that they meddle no further w*ith* [the] keping Whitson ale &
that they delyver their beere that is left to Samuell Tame Churchwarden & make
an accompt of 32 s. 10 d. by th*em* receyved & deliu*er* what reamayneth to the   20
said Tame & then the said Sam*uell* Tame to goe forward w*ith* the Church
ale & to take their beere that is left & to discharge them of so much as he shall
receyve & of the charge of their musicke for for time to come

…

       25

*2 s. 11 d. solu*ti
pro Sam*uele*
Tame gard*iano*

1631–2
Balliol College Bursars' Accounts   BC Arch: Computi 1615–1662
f 96v   *(7 July–18 October 1632) (Expenses noted)*

…

Item to the Queenes trumpeters   0   5   0   30

…

Brasenose College Senior Bursars' Accounts   BNC Arch: A.2.41
f 17   *(Gifts and rewards)*

…   35

To a Piper uppon Christmas Day   xij d.

…

Giuen att ye Act to 4. Trumpetters   v s.

…

Paid by Mr Trafford to Musitians in ye Hall   xij d.   40

…

23*l* for for: *dittography*   38*l* ye Act: *9 July 1632*

Brasenose College Junior Bursars' Accounts   BNC Arch: A.8.5
f 21v   *(21 December–25 March)* *(Expenses noted)*

…

14   Item for wine to the musitians vppon Shrovetwesday
.m*aster*. vicep*rincipal*   00 00 08   5

…

Ite*m* for a quart of wine for the musitians   00 00 08

…

f 46   *(25 March–24 June)* *(Several payments)*   10

…

Item to the musitians. hand.   *(blank)*

…

Jesus College Bursar's Book   JC Arch: BU:AC:GEN:1   15
p 18   *(30 November–30 November)* *(Annuities)*

…

Vniversity Musicke   0 10: 0.

…

                                                                     20

p 20   *(Various expenses)*

Trumpeters   0: 2: 6.

…

                                                                     25

Magdalen College Liber Computi   MC Arch: LCE/17
f 3v   *(Internal and external payments)*

…

Musicis in festo Burasariorum   5 s.

…   30

Buccinatoribus   10 s.

…

Merton College Bursars' Accounts   MCR: 3.1
f 250   *(29 July–18 November 1631)* *(External expenses)*   35

…

…Buccinatoribus regijs 10 s.…

…

4m/ 14: *14 February 1631/2*
29/ Burasariorum: *for* Bursariorum

Merton College Register   MCR: 1.3
p 311

…

AUGUST*I* 16º.   De consensu Custodis & Sociorum, vice 6 s. 8 d. quos antiquit*ate* satrapis
Villae soluere solebant Bursarij, nunc Citharaedis Academiae deinceps. X s.   5
numerandi sunt quotannis.

…

New College Bursars' Accounts   NC Arch: 7647
mb 8   *(25 December–25 March)* *(Internal expenses)*   10

…

…So*lutum* Musicis Academ*icis* 6 s. 8 d.…

…

(24 June–29 September) *(External expenses)*   15
…So*lutum* to the Trumpetters in the Act tyme 5 s.…

…

Oriel College Treasurers' Accounts   OC Arch: S 1.C.1
f 292   *(Internal expenses)*   20

…

It*em* buccinatorib*us*   0 5 6 d.

…

The Queen's College Long Rolls   QC Arch: LRC   25
f 10 col 1*   *(7 July–7 July)* *(External expenses)*

…

Fidicinib*us* oxon*iæ*   10 s.

…

30

St John's College Computus Annuus   SJC Arch: Acc.1.A.16
f 21v   *(29 September–25 December)* *(Internal and external expenses)*

…

X   It*em* towards ye furnishing of the
ffounders Show   viiij s.   35

…

6/ quotannis: *second* n *altered from* u
16/ the Act tyme: *9 July 1632*

f 22*   *(25 December–25 March)*   *(Allowances)*

...

Item 7ᵃ. for ye Musitians liveries   xxxiiij s.

...

f 22v*   *(25 March–24 June)*

...

Item eadem for ye Musitians Bill   x li. x s. viij d.

...

Thomas Crosfield's Diary   QC Library: MS 390
f 60v*   *(26 December–6 January)*

...

Cupids whirlegig. a Comedy acted by certaine apprentices to printers
booksellars & other priviledgemen in Oxonia./

Brian Twyne's Notes on the History of the University Music
Bodl.: MS. Twyne-Langbaine 4
ff 105–7*

    °An Exemplification of thinges heretofore done and nowe required
      to be authorized for ye companie of ye Vniuersitie Musitians°
              De Vniuersitatis Musicis, siue Auledis

Ex Registro Vniuersitatis Oxoniensis, siuè libro Actorum .D. pagina 93.1. anno.
Domini. 1501. et anno Regis Henrici 7ⁱ .16º.

[Coram Commissario Thoma Banks Sacrae Theologiae Doctore collegij
Lyncolnensis Rectore
Existente tunc Cancellario Oxoniensis Willelmo Smyth Reverendo in Christo
patre et Episcopo Lyncolnensis Collegij Æneanasensis fundatori] †®
4º Calendarum Iunij venit coram nobis quidam Willelmus Iannys Citherarius
et extraneus; et conquestus est, quod duo viri scilicet Pittes et Hawkinse de
parochia Sancti Michaelis ad portam Borialem suam Citheram iniustè
retinerent; vendicantes ab eo servitium quod nunquam eis debuit, nec promisit.
Et ad hoc probandum induxit Iohannem Huskinse de parochia Sanctæ
Mariæ, qui se promisit et fide iussit hoc idem probare, scilicet quod prædictus
Willelmus non promisit prædictis Pittes et Hawkinse aliquod seruitium, sed

---

3/ 7ᵃ.: *ie, the seventh week, 6–12 February*
    1631/2
8/ eadem: *ie, the third week, 10–16 April 1632*
15/ priviledgemen: led *corrected over other letters*

21–2/ °An Exemplification ... Musitians°: *in*
    Gerard Langbaine's hand
25/ 93.1: *ie, 93 recto*
33/ est: *corrected from* esset *(?)*

promisit seruitium sibi Iohanni Huskinse et socijs eius. Et ideò requisiuit me
tam prædictus Willelmus quàm præfatus Iohannes, ut registraretur, quod
Willelmus sæpedictus promouit causam suam coram Commisario Vniuersitatis,
ne iniustè vexarentur per Villanos Balliuos vel per Maiorem Villæ eo quod
extraneus esset, promittens fide sua se responsurum, pariturum, facturum, et   5
accepturum quod iustitia exigeret, si ad hoc esset conuentus
    Willelmus Iannys, Iohannes Huskinse, Pittes et Hawkinse

Acta hæc erant Coram Magistro Thoma Banks Sacræ Theologiæ Doctore,
Collegij Lyncolnensis Rectore, et Deputato [Commisa] Magistri Willelmi   10
Atwater, Sacræ Theologiæ Doctoris, Reuerendi in Christo patris Willelmi
Smyth tunc Episcopi Lyncolnensis Vniuersitatis Oxoniensis Cancellarij, et
Collegij Æneanasensis fundatoris: Commissarij Generalis.

By this Act it plainely appeareth, that in King Henry ye 7th his time, there   15
were .2. companies of Musitians in Oxford; ye one for ye Vniuersities vse, ye
other for ye Townes vse: and that some of ye Towne companie, would haue
ₐ⌈or did⌉ seaze[d] vppon ye instrument of this William Iannys heere playntife,
(as beinge a stranger) and forbid him to vse his play vnlesse he would playe
in their companie; whereas, some of ye vniuersitie companie, had made   20
some contract with him before (as it seemes) to playe in their companie;
wherevppon this stranger William Iannys was aduized, to make his complaynt
to ye commissary of ye Vniuersitie; and Iohn Huskinse one of ye vniuersitie
companie, came forth & iustified that he had delt with this stranger to playe
with him & in his companie &c: which plainely argueth, that there were then   25
two companies of Musitians in this place, and that this stranger William Iannys
was made free of ye priuiledge companie. |

°Musicians.°

The petition of Iohn Iarratt & his fellowes & seruants to be
ye Vniuersitie Musitians   30

Mr Brookes of
Oriell Colledge

To ye Rightworshipfull Dr Smith Vicechancellour of ye Vniuersitie of
Oxford, ye Rightworshipfull ye Doctors, ye Worshipfull ye proctors,
ye Heades of houses & ye whole companie of ye Masters of Artes
within ye same vniuersitie   35

The most humble petition of your truely deuoted ye Musitians of
ye Vniuersitie of Oxford

Rightworshipfull & Worshipfull   40
You may please to remember yat not longe since out of your good affections
& likinge to ye cause of Musick, you were pleased by your seuerall consentes
then to giue waye for ye erectinge of a companie of skillfull Musitians only

for ye due & commendable seruice & content vnto ye Vniuersitie; And withall
gaue power vnto vs your humble petitioners to elect & chuse so many vnto vs
as might make vp ye compleate number of seauen; which by your speciall
fauours we haue allready made choice of & as we hope to ye good content
of your worshipp & ye rest of your honorable incorporation without [any]   5
preiudice to any person or persons whatsoeuer. And, as for those your ample
fauours conferred uppon vs we are euer bound vnto your worshippes in ye
loyaltie of our best seruices, so we are further emboldned to become humble
suitors vnto your worships that to those your [proceedinge] precedinge seuerall
goodnesses vnto us, you would be pleased to adde this one concludinge fauour,   10
viz, that it would please your wirships some waye to ratifie & confirme vnto vs
what you haue thus aduisedly & with good deliberation begun. And because
that both our presens & ye qualitie of our cause, are of so meane a condition,
as that we cannot without an vniustifiable presumption begg this to be ratified
by your venerable house of Conuocation, we therefore most humbly craue   15
of your worships that it might seeme good vnto you that ye Right worshipfull
Master Vicechancellour, in ye name and power of ye Rightworshipfull ye
Doctors of ye vniuersitie, & the worshipfull master Proctors in ye name [of]
& power of ye Masters of Arts of ye saide vniuersitie, subscribe their names
on these seuerall labelles. And that this Act & monument of your grant vnto vs   20
may be committed vnto ye fidelitie & custodie of ye senior of our companie,
that by this it maye appear as well to succeedinge ages, as to ye present, yat
we are by your publike alloweance, and fauour, made & ratified.
The Vniuersities most humble
& loyall seruants   25
The Companie of Musitions
To this petition in parchment hangeth .3. labelles without any seales or
inscriptions of names. |

To ye Rightworshipfull ye Doctores of ye Vniuersitie of Oxford &   30
ye whole companie of ye Worshipfull ye Masters of Art within
ye same Vniuersitie

® Mr Brookes of
Oriell Colledge

The humble petition of your truely deuoted seruants
ye vniuersitie Musitians   35

Rightworshipfull & Worshipfull
Whereas it hath pleased your Worships out of ye good affection & likinge
to ye cause of Musick to elect & choose vs to be your seruants for ye dutifull
performance of our Musick only vnto ye Vniuersitie, we humbly craue of your   40
worships, that as out of your speciall fauour vnto vs you haue byn pleased to
make vs yours, So out of your particular bountie & goodnesse vnto vs you
would be pleased to owne vs by your gift of Recognisance, the booke with .7.

seales cutt & inammelled in siluer plate & worne before in a fayre siluer chayne.
And as ye charge of seuen of these will not be very great, so we humbly desire
but your moderate benevolence for ye purchasinge of them, that by these
lastinge monuments of your fauours both we and our successours may be
both knowne & honored to be yours, and   5

ye vniuersities most humbly deuoted

Seruantes

The Companie of Musitianes

The beneuolence of ye Rightworshipfull ye Doctors of ye vniuersitie of Oxonia
& ye worshipfull ye whole company of ye Masters of Arts within ye same   10
vniuersitie of Oxonia for ye buyenge of your Recognizance

	li.	s.	d.		
Christchurch	4	0	0		
Magdalen Colledge	5	10	0		
New Colledge	1.	6	0	Dr Pinke. x s.	15
St Iohns Colledge	3	0	0		
Merton Colledge	1	10	0		
Brasennose Colledge	1	01	0	Dr Ratcliffe 5 s.	
Corpus Christi Colledge	1	12	(blank)		
Wadham Colledge	4	5	0		20
Exeter Colledge	1	18	0		
Queens Colledge	1	10	0		
Trinity Colledge	1	2	0		
Oriell Colledge	1	12	0		
Bailioll Colledge	1	10	0		25
Lyncoln Colledge	1	13	0		
Vniuersitie Colledge	1	0	0		
Iesus Colledge	0	10	0		
Pembroke Colledge	1	10	0	Dr Clayton 5 s.	
Magdalen hall	0	10	0		30
Hart hall	0	10	0	Dr Iles x s.	
Albon hall	1	10	0		
Edmund hall	1	0	0		
St Mary hall	0	13	0		
Gloster hall	2	0	0		35
Newe Inne	1	0	0			

To ye Right Worshipfull Master Doctor Smith Vicehancellor of ye
Vniuersitie of Oxonia & to ye Right Worshipfull ye Seuerall
Heades of Colledges & Halles in ye same Vniuersitie   40

24/ 12: 2 corrected over 0   38/ Vicehancellor: for Vicechancellor
29/ Pembroke: 2 minims in MS

The humble petition of Iohn Pollie, Edward Gollege ⌈°Iohn Garrett°⌉
& Thomas Hallwood priuiledged men musitians & teachers
of Musick to many Gentlemen in Colledges & Halles in
ye Vniuersitie of Oxonia

Whereas it hath pleased some of our worthy freinds in ye vniuersitie of Oxonia   5
to sollicite ye Right Worshipfull Master Vicechancellor & ye Right worshipfull
ye seuerall heades of Colledges & Halls in ye same vniuersitie for ye erectinge
& appropriatinge vnto ye sayde vniuersitye a companie of skillfull musitians for
ye due performance of such seruice as shalbe requyred of them by ye vniuersitie,
both for their loude musicke in ye Wynter morninges to ye seuerall Colledges   10
& halles & to particular priuiledged persons of qualitie within ye sayde
vniuersitie, and with with very commendable lowe musicke to be allwayes in
readinesse to wayte vppon all occasions of ye vniuersitie; And withall haue
recommended & nominated vnto your worships, vs your humble petitioners
vppon whose honestie, skill, & very deliberate care, it shall rest to prouide 4   15
others in their seuerall kindes skillfull musitians to make vp ye number of .7.
to ye good content of your worships & ye rest of ye honorable Corporation of
ye saide Vniuersitie. These are therefore humbly to entreate your worships, yat
as it hath pleased you out of your good affectiones & likinge to ye cause, to
giue your seuerall Consentes & agreementes to this our humble petition, so   20
wee are further imboldned to become humble suters vnto you, that out of
your goodnesse you would be pleased to grant vnto vs ye honor of wearinge
ye vniuersitie Recognisance ye Booke with .7. seales cutt either in plate or
wrought in rich gold needle worke; that when we shalbe knowen by your
honorable recognisance to be seruantes to ye vniuersitie, we may with more   25
credit & lesse delaye of time, furnish our selues with ye aforesaide number of
seauen a befittinge number for a right broken consort. And further we craue
of your worships, yat when vppon our due & diligent seruice made vnto ye
vniuersitie & vppon our well deseruinge in this behalfe, you would be pleased
to grant vnto vs, that once in ye yere we maye repayre to your seuerall Colledges   30
& halles to tender our seruice and musicke vnto your seuerall companies, &
then receiue such voluntary benevolences as ech particular person shall thinke
fitt in his owne goodnesse & discretion to gratifie our seruice therein./
[Taken] ∧⌈Transcribed out of⌉ ye originall of this, which I had of Master
Doctor Smith Warden of Wadham Colledge 1632   35

I am told that this was ye first petition exhibited about this businesse for a
seuerall Companye of Musitians for ye vniuersitie

°Prouided allwayes that ye boyes and newe pretences to ye Musitians aforesaide,   40
be included in this businesse and in euery other Act or Actes that shall concerne

12/ with with: *dittography*

ye saide musitians of ye vniuersitie, or any companie societee or corporation
that maye perhaps hereafter be procured.

The mens names	The Boyes names
Iohn Iarrett	Francys Taylor
Iohn Pollie	Thomas Curteis
Thomas Holwode	William Rogers
Iohn Stacy	Iohn Moore
Thomas Iones°	

5

The Towne Musitians   10

The first originall of them here, I finde not; though in ye passage concerninge
ye conflict [betw] that was sometime ∧⌈here⌉ betwixt ye Scolleres and ye

® 1297

Townesmen in ye .26. of king Edward ye first, amonge ye articles of ye saide
schollers against them, it is recorded, that, in festo Sancti Mathiæ Apostoli,
citatione communitatis villæ præhabita et collecta multitudine innumerabili   15
tam Indigenarum quam forensium, campana communi pulsata, cum sonitu
cornuum, præfati Burgenses in manu armata insultum schol⟨..⟩ibus Vniuersitatis
prædictæ ex præcogitata malitia hostiliter dederunt &c. (blank) which, whether
it should be taken for a noise of cornets, and so implied that ye Towne had
such Musitians ∧⌈of their owne⌉ at that time, [I kno], or also from any other   20
place, I knowe not. But I thinke, that they had but a small gatheringe of ye
vniuersitie that yere for such their musicke, if they were ye Townes musitians,
and for puttinge ye Schollers thus vnto ye horne.

f 108   25

Againe, that ye Vniuersitie maye lawfully haue a company of Musitians to
themselues without any wronge done to ye Towne, it is thus proued.

First because, indeede, and de iure ye Towne cannot sett vp any such companie   30
by their owne authoritie; because ye profession of ye liberall sciences belongeth
wholly to ye vniuersitie; but Musicke is one of ye liberall sciences &c. Ergo
&c: and they cannot practice it, but they must teach it. And by ye same reason,
they maye as well take vppon them to licence Grammarians & Schoolemasters,
which belongeth wholly & only to ye vniuersitie, in this place: and so we haue   35
ordered in our newe statutes. &c:

Secondly [by] ⌈in⌉ ye composition made in .37°. of .Henry .6. betwixt ye
vniuersitie & ye Towne. there are .3. thinges to be obserued.
first, that all feed men of ye vniuersitie (that is to saye all such as take any   40

p 502, l.40–p 503, l.8/ °Prouided … Thomas Iones°: *in Langbaines hand*
3/ The mens names: *underlined*

manner of fees or wages for seruice done to ye vniuersitie in any kinde
whatsoeuer) shalbe priuiledged men, with all their menyall men &c.
belonginge to them.

But those whom they formerly called ye Towne musitians, did take fees and
wages of ye vniuersitie. *(blank)* Ergo they were in ye true right and state of   5
priuiledged men, and should haue byn accounted & reputed for priuiledged
men: and if so, then it followeth, that ye vniuersitees intent, to haue a
companie of Musitians to themselues, is not against ye Townes liberties, or
preiudicious to them: naye it is very consonant therevnto; seinge that they
are bounde to allowe and mainetayne their composition with vs. &c: 10

Secondly, by ye same composition, All seruants takinge clothinge or hire by
ye yere, and so proportionably by ye halfe yere, or quarter of ye yere &c. are
to be allowed for priuiledged persons. Therefore ye Towne Musitians takinge
heretofore (before ye Vniuersitie had a companye of their owne) such wages   15
of ye vniuersitie and schollers, [were to be] as seruants vnto them, were to
be accounted priuiledged persons: Therefore in the vniuersities takinge to
themselues such a companie of their owne, & appropriated to their owne vse,
there is no wronge done vnto ye Towne therein. And ye Towne is to allowe it.

      20

Thirdly, ye same composition supposeth, that there maye be priuiledged men
per obsequium, and by retainement; as takinge wages and hire of schollers,
and yet not beinge of their necessarye familie or attendance: And then againe,
it is supposed by ye same composition that priuiledged men maye sett vp
what trade or profession they will, within ye vniuersities precincts: therefore,   25
why maye they not sett vp ye profession of Musicke, and be Musitians,
applienge themselues to ye vniuersities seruice, and to all others allso, when
they shalbe lawefully required therevnto.

which thinges, if they be so, then why should ye Towne haue any companie
of Musitians at all, when as this Authoritie is originally ye vniuersities and   30
none else. Would they haue a companie ∧⌈of their owne⌉ for ye vniuersitie to
mainetaine them, and yet not to be of ye priuiledge of ye vniuersitie? sure, if
ye vniuersitie vnderstande thereof, they will neuer yeelde therevnto.

The Towne refused to paye part of their fee farme (as they are bounde) to ye   35
maintenance of ye poore Almes men of St Barthelmewes, vnlesse they might
haue ye choice of them, themselues (and not ye Colledge) and vnlesse they
were free men of ye Towne. Then why should ye vniuersitie mainetayne ye
Towne musicians, vnlesse they would be priuiledged mens?

23/ familie: *second i altered from* a
36/ St Barthelmewes: *St Bartholomew's Hospital, in Cowley*
37/ ye Colledge: *Oriel College, which owned the hospital*

Wilson, *History of Great Britain (1653)*   TC Library: N.7.5
flyleaf*

The authour of this history Mr Arthur Wilson was a fellow-[⟨.....⟩] com*m*oner
of Trinity Coll*edge* in Oxon*ia*, when Dr Kettell was President, for the space of   5
one whole yeare, ⌈1632⌉ being then in his full ripeness of age; during which
time he was very punctuall in frequenting the Chappel and Hall, and in
observing all orders of ye Colledge & Vniversity. He had little skill in the
Latin tongue, less in the Greek, a good reading in the French, & some
smattering in the Dutch. He had travailed in Germany, [and] France, and   10
[⟨......⟩] Spain. He was well seen in the Mathematicks & was a commendable
Poet. He made some Comedies, which were acted at Black Friers in London,
by the Kings players, & in the Act-time at Oxon*ia* with good applause,
himself being present.
Part of this book he composed in Trinity Colledge, some yeares before the   15
civill warrs. He attended on Robert Devereux Earle of Essex from his youth,
from whom he afterwards recieved an yearly pension. So that the reader may
the less wonder if he finde him somwhat fals-byassed, favouring y*a*t Earle &
his allyes, and vnderprizing such as were more in the Kings favour. His carriage
was very courteous and obliging, and such ‸⌈as⌉ might become a well-bred   20
Gentleman. Having had good knowledge of him, & some acquaintance
with ‸⌈him⌉ I thought good to give the Reader this advertisement.
                                                        Ed*ward* B°athurst°

...

                                                                              25

Hannisters' Registers   OCA: L.5.2
f 213v*

...

xix° Octobris 1631

William/
Garrett./

®Iohn Baldwin

Memorandum that then William Garrett sonne of William Garrett of   30
Begbrooke in the Countie of Oxon. Laborer hath putt himself App*re*ntice
to Iohn Baldwin of the Citty of Oxon. Musici*o*n to learne his art & him after
the mann*er* of an Apprentice to serue from the feast day of St Bartholomew
Thappostle now last past vnto the full end and terme of Eight yeares from
thence next following & fully to be Compleate & ended And in thend of the   35
said terme the said Master shall giue vnto his sayd app*re*ntice double app*a*rrell
fitting for such an Apprentice and one Cloake & one good Instruem*en*t

...

9/ reading: *altered from* readiness *or vice versa*
23/ B°athurst°: *expanded by later hand*

f 215v*

...

10° Nouembris 1631

Iohn Payne
® Roberte Duke
debet

Memorandum That then Iohn Payne Sonne of George Payne of the Cittie
of Oxon. Musition hath put himselfe Apprentice to Roberte duke of the   5
Cittie of Oxon. Musicion to learne his arte and him after the manner of
an Apprentice to serue from the ffeast day of St Michaell Tharchangell
now last past vnto the full ende and terme of Eight yeares from thence next
followinge and fullie to be compleate and ended And in thende of the said
Terme the said Master shall giue vnto this said Apprentice double apparrell   10
fittinge for such an Apprentice

...

f 216v

...   15

xxx° Nouembris 1631

Thomas Younge

Memorandum that then Thomas Young sonne of Richard Young of
Winchington in the Countie of Buckinghamshire yeoman hath putt himself

® Arthur Henton

apprentice to Arthur Henton of the Cittie of Oxon. Instruement maker to
learne his arte & him after the manner of an Apprentice to serue from the   20
date hereof vnto the full end & terme of [Seauen yeares] Nyne yeares from
thence next following & fully to be Compleate & ended And in thend
of the said Terme the said Master shall giue unto his Apprentice double
apparrell fitting for such an Apprentice.

...   25

St Martin Churchwardens' Accounts   ORO: PAR 207/4/F1/1, item 167
single mb col 1*   *(1 April 1632–21 April 1633) (Receipts)*

...

Item receaued more att Hocktide aboue   30
all chardges   iij li. vj s. vj d.

...

1632–3
All Souls College Bursars' Accounts   Bodl.: MS. D.D. All Souls c.295   35
mb 12*   *(2 November–2 November) (Rewards)*

...

De xx s: giuen to hjs Maiesties Trumpeters.

...

18/ Winchington ... Buckinghamshire: *Upper or*   30/ Hocktide: *9–10 April 1632*
  Lower Winchendon, Buckinghamshire

Balliol College Bursars' Accounts   BC Arch: Computi 1615–1662
f 103   *(7 July–18 October 1633)* *(Expenses noted)*

...

To his M*a*iesties trumpetters   00. 10. 0.

...   5

Jesus College Bursar's Book   JC Arch: BU:AC:GEN:1
p 30   *(30 November–30 November)* *(Collections)*

...

To the Kings Trumpeters   0   10   0   10

...

p 32   *(Various expenses)*

...

The Vniu*e*rsity Musitians   0   10   0   15

...

Magdalen College Liber Computi   MC Arch: LCE/18
f 3v   *(Internal and external payments)*

...   20

Musicis in festo Bursariorum   5 s.

...

Buccinatorib*us* regis   1 li.

...

                                                                                                              25

New College Bursars' Accounts   NC Arch: 7650
mb 9   *(25 December–25 March)* *(Internal expenses)*

...

...So*lutum* Musicis oppidanis 6 s. 8 d....

...   30

(24 June–29 September)
...So*lutum* to his M*a*iesties Trumpetters from Woodstock 10 s....

...

                                                                                                              35

Oriel College Treasurers' Accounts   OC Arch: S 1.C.1
f 297v   *(Internal expenses)*

...

Item Buccinatoribus Regijs   0 11 0

...   40

The Queen's College Long Rolls   QC Arch: LRC
f 11 col 2   *(7 July–7 July) (External expenses)*

...

Mauritio Fidicini Ian*uarij* 1.   0 1 6

...

Tibicinib*us* Oxon*iæ*   0 10 0

...

St John's College Computus Annuus   SJC Arch: Acc.I.A.17
f 22v   *(25 March–24 June) (Allowances)*

...

It*em* ead*em* for ye Musitians   xij li. xij s. vj d.

...

f 23   *(24 June–29 September) (Internal and external expenses)*

...

X   It*em* given to ye Kings Trumpetors   xx s.

...

Trinity College Bursars' Books   TC Arch: I/A/3
f 22   *(24 June–29 September) (Expenses)*

...

Regijs Tubicinib*us*   0 10 0

...

University College Bursar's Journal   UC Arch: BU3/F1/2
f [74v]*   *(Thomas Rockley's expenses)*

...

[For admissio*n* to ye dancing schoole   1 2 0]

...

f [77]

...

for his quarteridg to ye dancer   0 [2] 2 6

...

f [78v]

...

at the reuells   0 5 0
qu*ar*teridg at dancing schoole   0 2 6

...

12/ ead*em*: *ie, the ninth week, 20–7 May 1633*

quart*er*idg to ye dauncer　　　　　　　　　　　　　　　0 2 6

...

for fencer et dancer　　　　　　　　　　　　　　　　　0 9 6

...

City Council Minutes　OCA: C/FC/1/A1/003
f 43　*(26 September)*

...

The Musitions
to haue such
allowance for
playinge on the
king*es* hollidaies
& other tymes
to the Citty as
the mayor &
thirteene shall
thinck fitt

Item M*aste*r Mayor shewinge to this howse that the Musitions haue noe
allowance from this Citty for theire playinge to this Citty on the King*es*
Hollidayes and when the Mayor cometh from London and other publike
meeting*es* and that the Cittizens refuse to accompany m*aste*r Mayor to the
Sermon on the King*es* Hollidaies for that this Cittie hath taken away an old
Custome of Allowance of Wyne and Cakes at Pennilies Bench It is now agreed
that the said Musitions shall haue soe much money geuen them out of the
treasure of this City toward*es* the buyeinge of them Cloakes as M*aste*r Mayor

They are allso
to sett downe
what shalbe
spent at
Penniles benche

and the Thirteene shall thincke fitt And alsoe they are desired to sett downe a
c*er*ten som*m*e that shalbe spent at Penniles benche on the king*es* hollidaies
And that the Chamberlins not exceedinge that som*m*e soe sett downe shall
have allowance thereof./

Audited Corporation Accounts　OCA: P.5.2
f 222　*(Chamberlains' payments)*

...

Item ffor Bread and Beare at the hall on the
Coronac*i*on day　　　　　　　　　　　　　　　1　0　0
Item for Wine at the Bench and geven to
the waites　　　　　　　　　　　　　　　　　0　16　0

...

f 222v

...

Item p*ai*d to the kinges Trumpeters　　　　　　　　1　0　0

...

St Martin Churchwardens' Accounts　ORO: PAR 207/4/F1/1, item 169
single mb col 1　*(21 April 1633–6 April 1634)* *(Receipts)*

...

Inprimis Receaued att Hocktide aboue
all Chardges　　　　　　　　　　　　v li. iiij s. iiij d. ob.

9/ M*aste*r Mayor: *William Charles*　　　39/ Hocktide: *29–30 April 1633*
39/ Inprimis: *in display script*

Item receaued att Whitsontide and all
chardges paid   xvij li. viij s. iiij d.
...

c 1633   5
St Peter le Bailey Churchwardens' Accounts   ORO: PAR 214/4/F1/76–7
mb [1]*   *(Expenses)*

Item paid for mending my wals which were
broken at witsontide the halfe   3 d. 10
...

1633–4
All Souls College Bursars' Accounts   Bodl.: MS. D.D. All Souls c.295
mb 13   *(2 November–2 November) (Various expenses)*   15
...
De v s. To Trumpeters on Act Tuesday
...

Balliol College Bursars' Accounts   BC Arch: Computi 1615–1662   20
f 108v   *(7 July–18 October 1634) (Expenses noted)*
...
It*em* to the trumpetters   050
...

                                                                         25
Jesus College Bursar's Book   JC Arch: BU:AC:GEN:1
p 38   *(30 November–30 November) (Annuities)*
...
To ye Universitie Musitians   0 10 0.
...   30

Magdalen College Liber Computi   MC Arch: LCE/19
f 3v   *(Internal and external payments)*
...
Musicis in festo Bursar*iorum* & fundatoris obitu   10 s. 35
...

1/ Whitsontide: *9–15 June 1633*
17/ Act Tuesday: *15 July 1634*

Merton College Bursars' Accounts MCR: 3.2
f 2v *(26 July–22 November 1633)* *(External expenses)*
…

…Buccinatoribus Regijs 10 s.

New College Bursars' Accounts NC Arch: 7651
mb 8 *(25 December–25 March)* *(Internal expenses)*
…

…So*lutum* Musicis oppidanis 6 s. 8 d.…
…

The Queen's College Long Rolls QC Arch: LRC
f 12 col 2 *(7 July–7 July)* *(External expenses)*
…

Buccinatoribus Regis 1 0 0

…
Mauritio ffidicinj 0 1 6

…
Tibicinibus Oxon*iæ* 0 10 0
…

St John's College Computus Annuus SJC Arch: Acc.I.A.18
f 22v* *(25 March–24 June)* *(Internal and external expenses)*
…

It*em* To ye Carpenter for worcke donne by him
at ye ffounders Showe ij s. vj d.
…

(Allowances)
Item 6ª for ye Musitians xj li. iiij s

…

St John's College Short Book SJC Arch: Acc.III.D.4
f 27 *(25 December–25 March)* *(Allowances)*
…

It*em* to ye Musitions Imposit*i* for yeir Liveries
hebd*omada* 7ª. ⌈I*ohn* Stacie⌉ xxxiij s.
…

30/ 6ª: *ie, the sixth week, 5–11 May 1634*
37/ hebd*omada* 7ª: *10–16 February 1633/4*

Vice-Chancellors' Accounts   OUA: WP/β/21(4)
p 226   *(22 July 1633–26 July 1634)*

...

Item for Gloues giuen when ye King was at Woodstock   25 0 0
Item to ye Waytors & to ye Trumpetters   3 0 0   5

...

OUS   ***Chancellor Laud, Corpus Statutorum (1634)***   STC: 19005
sig Hh2v*   *(Of forbidden amusements)*

...   10

2) L.241.b.   Item quòd, intra Vniuersitatem Oxon*iensis* aut eius præcinctum, absque
L.262.a.   speciali venia Vice-cancellarij, nec² Funambuli nec Histriones (qui quæstus
causa in Scenam prodeunt) nec Gladiatorum certamina siue spectacula
permittantur; nec Academici aut Scholares eisdem intersint. Histriones
verò, Funambuli, & Gladiatores contrauenientes incarcerentur. Et Scholares   15
(si qui ad huiusmodi spectacula confluentes deprehensi fuerint) non Graduati,
arbitrio Vice-cancellarij vel Procuratorum puniantur vel castigentur: Graduati
autem, sex solidos & octo denarios Vniuersitatis fisco singuli pendant,
toties quoties.

...   20

Thomas Crosfield's Diary   QC Library: MS 390
f 65v*

...

1   All Saints day, being on ye Friday was deferred till Sunday, we haveing had an   25
election & Scrutiny ye wednesday before of w*h*ich see – M.S. 8./
The Kings maiesties declaration to his subiects concerning lawfull Sports to be
vsed, on ye Sunday after divine Service, first published by *K*ing Iames after his
returne from Scotland through Lancashire. May 24. 1618./ for these 2 reasons
cheifely, bec*ause* barring ye people fro*m* such lawfull recreations 1. May hinder   30
ye conversion of many from Popery, whom ye Priests would p*er*swade to p*er*sist
obstinate bec*ause* they would pretend there is no tolerable recreatio*n* allowed
in o*ur* religion. 2. it hinders the com*m*on people fro*m* such exercises as may
make their bodies more able for warre, – ɪ, such are ₐ⌈1⌉ dauncing. 2. Archery.
3. leaping. 4. vaulting. also May game, moris daunces, [May ganles] May poles,   35
Whitson-ales: This is conceived to be published
                                                to the opposition of some doctrine
                                                taught by some of our divines.
This declaration is ratifyed & published by *K*ing Charles vpon occasion that in
some Counties, Vnder p*re*tence of takeing away abuses, there hath bene a   40

25m/ 1: *1 November 1633*   40/ Vnder: V *written over another letter*

generall forbidding, not onely of ordinary meeteings, but of The Feasts of ye
dedication of the Churches, commonly called Wakes./
October 18. [&] Anno Regni sui 9º after his returne from Scotland./
...

f 67*

...

Ianuarij .1.   Consuetudines
                Tempore nativitatis   3. Musica per morrice

...

f 67v*

...

1634 February   A great maske or showe presented to ye King.
14
...

ff 68–8v*   (15 July)

...

            ⎧ 1. The Palsgraues family
Spectacula   ⎪ 2. His maiesties Hokus Pokus
Oxonij hoc   ⎨ 3. Dancing vpon the rope.
anno   ⎪ 4. Hierusalem in it's glory, destruction   The story deuided
            ⎩ into 5 or 6 parts invented by mr Gosling, some times schollar
to mr Camden, Enginer, who bestowed the Dodar (a blacke
Indian bird) vpon ye anatomy schoole. his wife dying left him
some meanes in a chest which a maid-servant cunningly
getting ye key of her master conveyed away & soe he now
glad to get his liuing by vseing his wits for such inventions. |

(18 July)
One Richard Kendall about ye age of 50. or vpwards, belonging to ye Company
of players of Salisbury Court that came to Oxford this yeare came to see me &
related vnto me diuerse particular stories vizt.
1.   of his particular state & education in his youth at Kirkby Lonsdall where
      he serued his Apprenteship to a Talor, & afterward went to Cambridge
      where he stayd but litle, & then went to London where he became
      seruant to Sir William Slingsby & nowe he is one of ye 2. Keepers of
      the wardrobe of the said Company.

...

1–2/ The Feasts ... Churches: in display script   37/ one: o altered from 1
21–2/ hoc anno: ie, at the Act, held on 14 July 1634

5. of the seuerall
    Companies of
    Players in London
    which are in
    number 5.

{

1. The Kings Company at ye priuate house of
   Blackfriars: The masters or cheife whereof | Mr Talor
   are | Mr Lowen
2. The Queen's servants at ye Phoenix in Drury lane.
   Their master Mr Beeston, Mr Boyer, Shirley
   Robinson, Clarke   5
3. The Princes Servants at ye Red bull in St Iohns
   street, ye cheife Mr Cane a gold smith, mr Worth
   mr Smith 2000 li.
4. The Fortune in Golden-Lane, ye cheife Mr William
   Cartwright, Edward Armestead, Iohn Buckle, Iohn   10
   Kirke
5. The Company of Salisbury Court at ye further

end of fleetstreet against ye Conduit: The cheife whereof are 1. Mr Gunnell
a Papist. 2. Mr ∧⌜Iohn⌝ Yongue. 3. Edward Gibbs a fencer. 4. Timothy
Reed. 5. Christofer Goad. 6. Samuel Thompson. 7. Mr Stuffeild. 8. Iohn   15
Robinson. 9. Courteous Greuill. These are ye cheife whereof .7. are
called sharers. ie. such as pay wages to ye servants & equally share in the
overplus: Other servants there are as 2 Close keepers | Richard Kendall
                                                      | Anthony Dover. &c.
   of all these companies ye first if they please may come to Oxon., but none
without speciall lettres from the Chancellor obtained by meanes of ye Secretary   20
[f⟨..⟩] ⌜to⌝ the vicechancelor./ Mr Gunnell akin to ye Nappers/ A ∧⌜Crosse⌝
[mischance] happened to this company because of a boy yat quarrelled with
a Scholar in ye Tauerne./ They came furnished with 14 playes. And lodged
at ye Kings Armes, where Franklin hath about 3 li. a day while they stay. ie.
for euery play 4 nobles besides ye benefit of Seats.   25
…

Audited Corporation Accounts   OCA: P.5.2
f 225v*   *(Keykeepers' accounts)*
…   30
Item paid the Musitions by acte of
Comon councell towardes the payement
for theire Cloakes   5 0 0
…

35

St Martin Churchwardens' Accounts   ORO: PAR 207/4/F1/1, item 171
single mb col 1   *(6 April 1634–29 March 1635) (Receipts)*
…
Inprimis Receaued att Hocktide aboue
all chardges   v li. x s. ix d.   40

39/ Inprimis: *in display script*   39/ Hocktide: *14–15 April 1634*

Item receaued att Whitsontide and all
chardges paid   xviij li. j s. ij d.
...

St Michael at the North Gate Churchwardens' Accounts   5
ORO: PAR 211/4/F1/3, item 195
single mb col 2   *(6 April 1634–29 March 1635)* *(Receipts of Edward*
  Warde, churchwarden)
...
Inprimis gained at Hocktide   lviij s.   10
Item gained at Whitsontide   x li. v s. vij d.
                                    Summa   xiij li. iij s. vij d.
...

St Peter le Bailey Churchwardens' Accounts   ORO: PAR 214/4/F1/78   15
single mb*   *(Rendered 31 March 1635)* *(Receipts)*
...
Item of Thomas Byshopp for money gotten
at Whitsuntide   xj s.
...   20
Item receaved for Hocking moneys at
Hocktide last   xxij s.
...

1634–5   25
Balliol College Bursars' Accounts   BC Arch: Computi 1615–1662
f 113v   *(7 July–18 October 1635)* *(Expenses noted)*
...
Item to his Maiesties Trumpeters   0 10 0
...   30

Brasenose College Bursars' Roll of Account   BNC Arch: U.B.21
f 35*   *(21 December–21 December)* *(Gifts and rewards)*
...
To a Piper uppon Christmas day   xij d.   35
...

1, 11, 19/ Whitsontide, Whitsuntide: *25–31 May 1634*
10/ Inprimis: *in display script*
10, 22/ Hocktide, Hocktide last: *14–15 April 1634*

Paid to a piper in the Hall on Easter Monday   xij d.

...

August. *(blank)* To ye Kings Ma*iesties*
Trumpetters   xx s.

...   5

Brasenose College Junior Bursars' Accounts   BNC Arch: A.8.7
f 24*   *(21 December–25 March)* *(Expenses noted)*

...

Item to Pigeon for singinge in the Hall   i s. 10

...

Jesus College Bursar's Book   JC Arch: BU:AC:GEN:1
p 47   *(30 November–30 November)* *(Annuities)*

...   15

To the Vniversity Musicians   0 10 0

...

Hocking woemen   0 2 0

...

                                                                                           20

p 49   *(Various expenses)*

...

Kings Trumpeters   0 10 0

...

                                                                                           25

Magdalen College Liber Computi   MC Arch: LCE/20
f 3v   *(Internal and external payments)*

...

Musicis pro festo Bursar*iorum* et
puerorum interludio   10 s. 30

...

Buccinatoribus Regis   13 s. 4 d.

...

New College Bursars' Accounts   NC Arch: 7653
mb 6   *(25 December–25 March)* *(Internal expenses)*   35

...

...So*lutum* Musicis oppidanis 6 s. 8 d....

...

1/ Easter Monday: *30 March 1635*

mb 7   *(24 June–29 September)   (External expenses)*

...

...So*lutum* to the King*es* Trumpeters 10 s. 0....

...

                                                                                    5

Oriel College Treasurers' Accounts   OC Arch: S 1.C.1
f 308   *(Internal expenses)*

...

Ite*m* Buccinatorib*us* regijs   0 10. 0

...   10

The Queen's College Long Rolls   QC Arch: LRC
f 14v col 1   *(7 July–7 July)   (External expenses)*

...

Mauritio Fidicini   1 s. 6 d. 15

...

St John's College Computus Annuus   SJC Arch: Acc.1.A.19
f 22   *(25 December–25 March)   (Internal and external expenses)*

...   20

Item allowed by the Colledge [for] ⌈towards⌉
the making of a stage & scaffolds & setting out
a Comedy & a Tragedy   xxiiij li. xv s.

...

                                                                                    25

(Allowances)
Item 10ᵃ for the Actors bill   xxxvj li. v s.

...

f 23   *(24 June–29 September)   (Internal and external expenses)*   30

...

Ite*m* To ye Kings Trumpeters   xx s.

...

Trinity College Bursars' Books   TC Arch: I/A/3   35
f 39v   *(24 June–29 September)   (Expenses)*

...

Tubicinib*us* Regis   10 s.

...

27/ 10ᵃ: *ie, the tenth week, 2–8 March 1634/5*

Thomas Crosfield's Diary   QC Library: MS 390
f 71v*

...

At our
Act besides
ye playes at
ye Kings armes
other things
were to be
seene for
money, as

> 1. Dansing on ye rope at ye racket Court, by ye blew bore
> 2. Hokus pok*us* below ye flower de luce.
> 3. The lion, besides all hallowes
> 4. The Camells at ye Crowne
> 5. The witches of Lancashire ouer ag*ains*t ye Kings Head,
> their 1 Meetings
> 2 Tricks
> 6. Hierusalems {destruction & Repa̅ration} at mute hall.
> 7. The Waterworkes besides the beare.
> 8. A person with a clouen foot ouer ag*ains*t mute hall.
> 9. The beginning of ye world besides Carfax.
> 10. A wolfe &/

...

St Martin Churchwardens' Accounts   ORO: PAR 207/4/F1/1, item 173
single mb col 1   *(29 March 1635–17 April 1636) (Receipts)*
...

Inprimis Receaved at Hocktide	iiij li.
It*em* receaued at Whitsuntide	vj li. xj s. ix d. ob.

...

St Mary Magdalen Churchwardens' Accounts   ORO: PAR 208/4/F1/62
mb [1]*   *(Rendered 19 April 1636) (Receipts)*
...

°Item gotten bye the towne sids men at Hocktide	0j li. 2 s. j0°

...

St Michael at the North Gate Churchwardens' Accounts
ORO: PAR 211/4/F1/3, item 197
single mb col 1   *(29 March 1635–17 April 1636) (Receipts)*
...

Item gained at Hocktyde	lvj s.
Item gained at Whitsontyde	xxij s. iij d.

...

5/ Act: *13 July 1635*
21/ Inprimis: *in display script*
21, 29, 36/ Hocktide, Hocktyde: *6–7 April 1635*

22, 37/ Whitsuntide, Whitsontyde: *17–23 May 1635*
29/ 0j li. 2 s. j0: *ie, £1 2s 10d*

St Peter in the East Churchwardens' Accounts   ORO: PAR 213/4/F1/3
f 41v*   *(3 April 1635–26 April 1636)* *(Receipts)*
...

Item in hocking money	3	6	6
Item for Whitsun ale all things discharged	5	0	0

...

f 42   *(Payments)*
...

Item for two plaites for the May pole	0	1	0

...

1635–6

All Souls College Bursars' Accounts   Bodl.: MS. D.D. All Souls c.295
mb 9*   *(2 November–2 November)* *(Rewards)*
...

De xx s. to the king*es* Trumpetters by the last Burs*ar*
...

De xxv li. given by consent to M*aste*r vicechanclor for the king*es* m*ai*esties
Entertaynem*ent*
...

De °xx s. To ye Kings Trumpet*er*s.°

Balliol College Bursars' Accounts   BC Arch: Computi 1615–1662
f 120   *(7 July–18 October 1636)* *(Expenses noted)*
...

It*em* to his M*a*iesty's Trumpetters	0	10	0

...

Christ Church Expense Account for Plays   ChCh Arch: D.P.iii.c.1, item 27
p [1]*

> Money Layd out for his Maiesties Entertaynment by Dr. ffell,
> Dr. Estcote, & Dr Saunders Delegates for the Vniu*e*rsity.
> August 29: An*n*o d*om*ini 1636.

	li.	s.	d.
To the Designers for the Sceenes, w*i*th all things thereunto belonging per Acquiet*antias*	260	0	0
To the property Menn for apparrell, ut pat*et* per Acquiet*antias*	318	0	0

4/ hocking: *Hocktide was 6–7 April 1635*   19/ M*aste*r vicechanclor: *Richard Baylie*
5/ Whitsun: *Whitsuntide was 17–23 May 1635*

To the Musitians (vizt:) To Mr. Lawes & his Brother 45 li.:
Mr: Day and his Boyes 20 li.: Mr: Homes 13 li. 6 s. 8 d.
˄⌜Mr.⌝ Mell 12 li. Mr: Iones 10 li. Their Diett per Billam
10 li. 12 s. 10 d. To Mr. Lowe 6 li. 13 s. 4 d. Mr Goodall
3 li. Mr. Coleman j li. A Booke for Mr. Iones Chanter of   5
Christchurch j li. In toto ut patet per Acquietantias   122   12   8
Apparrell for Mr: Lawes, Mr. Homes, & Mr. Dayes Boyes,
per Billas   12   12   8
To Mr. Stoakes the Dancing Master for Composing &
performing 3 Dances and for Pumpes and some apparrell,   10
ut patet per acquietantias   22   0   0
To Mrs: Morgan the Tyrewoman for Seuerall heades of haire
& Diuers other Tyres, and for hir Iourneyes & paynes, ut
patet per Billas et Acquietantias   29   15   0
For 23 Dozen & 3 pound of waxe Candles at j s. 6 d. the   15
pound 20 li. 18 s. 6 d. And for 3 Boxes to packe them in
4 s. 6 d. In toto per Acquietantias   21   3   0
[For Tallow Candles for the Tireing roomes Musicke roomes
& for the Backe part of the Sceenes ut patet per Billam]   ⟨…⟩   0   ⟨…⟩]
For 2 Dozen & ten Torches per Billam   1   8   4 20
For Bootes, Shooes, and Spurrs, ut patet per Diuersas Billas   3   16   6
To the Brasiers for 12 Candlestickes, Loane of 6 flagons
per Billam   0   9   0
To the Apoulsterer[s] for Buckram, & 2 Curtaines for ye
Sedan for one Curtaine for the Musicke roome & for   25
workmanship per Billam   1   4   6
To the Ioyner for boardes to make the Sedan, & for
wormanship per billam   0   11   6
To Diuers workmen for attending and watching 6 Nights
and 6 Dayes and for takeing Downe the Sceenes, & frames,   30
and for Laying them up per Billam   5   0   0
For Loane of Linnen for the Musitians, ut patet per Billam   0   5   0
For wood and Coale for the Tireing roomes, Musicke roomes
and used about Soudering the Branches ut patet per Billam   1   0   0
To the Tayler for Mr. Caryes Suite per Billam   2   14   8 35
To the Tayler for altring of players Cloathes, & for Brushing
foulding, and Layinge them up in the Trunkes per Billam   1   0   0
To Mr. Stutvill for Binding of Bookes for ye King & Queene
and for other thinges ut patet per Billam   1   12   6

2/ Homes: *corrected from* Iones   28/ wormanship: *for* workmanship
17/ 21: *corrected over* 22

To the Barbers per Billas	1	10	0	
To Mr. Taylor for his Iourney, & for Loane of Cloathes	15	6	8	
For the use of Branches ⌈per Billam⌉	19	19	0	
Fancies Picture	1	10	0	
Vniuersity Musicke	2	0	0	5

Summa totalis 843 li. 15 s. 6 d.

Corpus Christi College Bursars' Accounts CCCA: C/1/1/9
mb 9 col 1* *(External expenses)*

… 10

To the Kings Trumpeters at the Kings Coming
to Oxford. 1 0 0

…

Jesus College Bursar's Book JC Arch: BU:AC:GEN:1 15
p 54 *(30 November–30 November) (Annuities)*

…

The Vniuersity Musicke. 1 10 0

…

To the hocking women. 0 2 6 20

…

p 58 *(Various expenses)*

…

To the Kings Trumpetters. 0 10 0 25
For the wholle Societye towards their Majesties
Entertainement 5 0 0

…

Magdalen College Liber Computi MC Arch: LCE/21 30
f 3v *(Internal and external payments)*

…

Musicis pro festo Bursariorum 0: 5 s. 0:

…

Buccinatoribus Domini Regis 1 li. 0: 0 35

…

Merton College Bursars' Accounts MCR: 3.2
f 15v *(31 July–20 November) (External expenses)*

… 40

…pro Regijs Buccinatoribus vj s.…

f 18   *(18 March–29 July)*

...

...Pro Collegio ad Excipiendam Regiam Maiestatem 20 li....

...

New College Bursars' Accounts   NC Arch: 7655
mb 7   *(25 December–25 March)* *(Internal expenses)*

...

...So*lutum* Musicis Oppidanis 6 s. 8 d....

...

(24 June–29 September) *(External expenses)*
...So*lutum* to Doc*t*or Baylie vicechancelor for the entertainement of the King
50 li. 0.... So*lutum* to the King*es* Trumpetters, when his Ma*ies*tie came to
Oxford 10 s. 0...

...

Oriel College Treasurers' Accounts   OC Arch: S I.C.1
f 312v   *(External expenses)*

...

Item solut*um* Dom*i*no Vicecancellario in adventum
Serenissi*mi* Regis, in vsum Dom*i*ni præpositi et
sociorum [vt patet] *per* Acquit*antiam*   10 0 0

...

f 313   *(Internal expenses)*

...

Item Regijs Buccinatorib*us*   0 10 0

...

The Queen's College Long Rolls   QC Arch: LRC
f 15v col 2   *(7 July–7 July)* *(External expenses)*

...

Buccinatoribus Dom*i*ni Regis   1   0   0
Mauritio Fidicinj   0   1   6

...

f 16 col 1

...

Fidicinibus Vniversitatis pro *pr*esentj et elapso anno   1   0   0

...

f 17 col 2   *(7 July 1636–7 July 1637)*

...

Aug*usti* 24. Buccinatorib*us* D*omi*ni Regis   01 00 00

...

                                                                                                                             5

St John's College Computus Annuus   sjc Arch: Acc.i.A.20
f 20v   *(29 September–25 December) (Internal and external expenses)*

...

It*em* allow'd by the Coll*ege* towards a show acted
Dec*ember* 7th   x s. x 10

...

f 21*   *(25 December–25 March) (Allowances)*

...

Item eâd*em* for the Actors   vj li. xviij s. 15

...

Item 14tâ for the Musitians   xij li. x s.

...

f 22   *(24 June–29 September) (Internal and external expenses)*   20

...

Item to his Ma*ie*sties Trumpeters August 23   xx s.

...

Trinity College Bursars' Books   tc Arch: I/A/3   25
f 51   *(Expenses)*

...

Solut*um* pro Rege et Reginâ excipiendo   10 0 0
Solut*um* Buccinatoribus Regijs   0 10 0

...   30

University College General Accounts   uc Arch: BU2/F1/1
p 59*   *(18 March 1635/6–10 March 1636/7)*

...

Imp*rimis* to Malin for whiteing the Hall & buttery   35
against the K*ings* comeing to Oxf*ord*   0 10 0

...

10/ x s. x: xˢx. *in ms; for* x s. x d. *or* xx s. (?)
15/ eâdem: *ie, the seventh week, 8–14 February 1635/6*
17/ 14tâ: *ie, the fourteenth week, 21–7 March 1636* (?)

p 61*

…

To Pattin for 3 dayes levelling the quadrangle
& cleansing the backside against ye K*ings*
comeing   0 2 9   5

…

Register of Congregation and Convocation   OUA: NEP/Supra/R
ff 132–2v*

…   10

Whereas the businesses of the Vniu*e*rsity at this time were many and Matters
of diuers Natures & Consequence would interuene each other if the time were
strictly Computed, I thought fitt therefore to place those Actes & decrees
wh*ich* Concerne his Ma*i*estyes Entertainment one after another.
        Orders sett Downe & agreed vpon the 25th Day of Iuly 1636 by the   15
                heads of Colledges and Halls Assembled together to pr*e*pare &
                        pr*o*uide for his Ma*i*estyes Entertainment by the Vniuersity of
                                Oxon. in August next following.
Inprimis, that the Vniuersity shall pay towards all guifts, Charges & Burthens
whatsoeuer ariseing by this Entertainment 200 li. and no more.   20
In the second place the seuerall Heads of Colledges there did acknowledge and
Consent vnto the ancient Valewations and Assesments of their seuerall Colledges
then pr*e*sented by Dr. Baylie Vicechancellor.
In the third place Iesus Colledge Wadham Colledge & Pembroke Colledge were
valewed & rated in the pr*e*sence of their seuerall Gouernours for this purpose 25
& Entertainment onely Vizt. Wadham Coll*edge* 200 li., Iesus Coll*edge* 200,
Pembroke Coll*edge* 200.
In the fourth place it was ordered that the Corporation & Body of euery
Colledge should bee rated and Assessed by it selfe, and besides euery Com*m*oner
in or of that Body should bee rated and assessed by the Pole.   30
In the fift place that euery perticular Colledge should bee rated after 5 li.
for euery hundred they were Assessed and valewed at 34º Elizabeth*æ*
vizt.

Christs Church	2000 li.	Brasenose Coll*edge*	300 li.	Vniu*e*rsity Coll*edge*	100
Magdalen Colledge	1200	Queens Coll*edge*	260	Baylioll Coll*edge*	100 35
New Colledge	1000	Exeter Coll*edge*	200	Christs Church & St
All Souls Coll*edge*	0500	Oriel Coll*edge*	200	Iohns at this time were
Corp*us* Chri*s*ti Colledge	500	Trinity Coll*edge*	200	exempted from all
Merton Coll*edge*	400	Lincoln Coll*edge*	130	payment in regard
St Iohns Colledge	400			of other perticular 40
				Charge.	

Euery perticular Com*m*oner is to bee rated and Assessed as followeth Vizt.

	li.	s.	d.
Euery Earls Sonne	1	13	4
Euery Barons Sonne	1	0	0
Euery ffellow Commoner			
or Vpper Commoner	0	10	0
Euery Master of Arts			
which is but an Ordinary			
Commoner	0	5	0
Euery Ordinary Commoner	0	5	0
The lowest sort Vsually			
called Battellers	0	3	4

It was then Ordered that a Scedule or Bill conteying the seuerall names, Degrees
and Qualities of euery Commoner and Batteller should bee transcribed out
of their seuerall Buttery books and brought to Master Vicechancellor on
Wednesday Morning next at farthest: wherein according to their ranke in the   15
house they shall bee Assessed and the Bill Cast vp into one generall summe.
It was there allsoe ordered that if the summe which should bee gathered by
these meanes should exceed and proue more then should bee Vsefull and
necessary, the Ouerplus should bee refunded in Proportion: and if it proue
Defectiue & too little to Discharge this Entertainment, it is to bee made vp   20
by the Rate and Taxes vt supra.

Dr Iackson President of Corpus Christi Colledge
was not at this Meeting, who afterward did
protest against this Taxe and Assessement because
they were rated more then Merton Colledge and   25
so great a summe as 500 li. might bee preiudiciall
to the Colledge in regard of their Mortmayne,
but towards the Entertainment the Colledge sent
in to the Vicechancellor Twenty ffiue pounds.

In the Morning between 8 & 9 of the Clocke vpon Thursday beeing the   30
Eleuenth Day of August 1636 the delegats appoynted by Convocation to
Ouer-see the High-wayes and the Streets in the Vniuersity, and likewise
to Order and sett downe what shall be fitt for the Vniuersity to performe in
publike against the Kings Maiestyes comeing and dureing the time of his
presence and abode here did meet in the Tower of the Schooles vizt. Dr ffell,   35
Dr Pincke, Mr Estcott Collegii Wadhami, Mr Turner Collegii Mertonensis,
Mr Stringer Collegii Noui; Mr Langton, Mr Law Collegii Magdalensis and
they did decree as followeth

...

12/ conteying: for conteyning
15/ Wednesday ... next: 27 July 1636

ff 133-3v*

...

5. ffor the greater Expedition and more suddain dispatch of this busines, the Bellman in Master Vicechancellors name is to require all manner of persons to remoue their Blocks and Dirt from before their dores, & pitch all such places   5 as are any way faulty and that presently they goe about it. If any shall neglect his duety herein & bee of the priuiledge, he shall lose the benefitt thereof and bee dispriuiledged; if he bee a Townsman and refuse to performe & submit to these Orders he shall be discommoned and Interdicted all Trade & Commerce with the Priuiledge after the 20th of August next immediately following or   10 otherwise seuerely punished.

6 That the Scauenger forthwith sett himselfe on worke in Ridding the streets of dirt ffilth & Rubbidge & all manner of vncleannes that may make Nuisances in the streets: and that this bee done euery wheare within his walke vpon perill of the seuerest punishment to bee inflicted on him by Master Vicechancellor. | 15

> In the Tower of the Schooles vpon the 12th Day of August after Dinner
> Dr Pincke, Dr Clayton Dr Bainbridge, Mr Estcott Mr Goode
> Procurator Iunior, Mr Turner, Mr Stringer, Mr Langton
> Delegats appoynted by Conuocation for his Maiesties
> Entertainment did Order & Conclude as followeth.   20

1   That at the Ringing of a Bell (at a time appoynted by Master Vicechancellor), those Men whose names are here vnderwritten vizt Master Vicechancellor, Sir Nathaniel Brente, Dr Prideaux, Dr Wilkinson Dr Radcliffe, Dr ffell, Dr Pincke, Dr Iackson, Dr King Iunior, Dr ffrewen, Dr Potter of Queens Colledge, Dr Walker, Dr Shelden, Dr Morris, Dr Clayton, Dr Bainbridge, Dr Zouche, Mr   25 Estcott, Mr Wheare, Mr Ayrie Mr Rouse, Mr Twine, Mr Turner, Mr Stringer, and as many Doctors and heads of houses besides as will bee at the Charge of Gownes & ffootcloths, shall repayre to St Iohns Colledge gate, and from thence together with Master Vicechancellor shall ride two & two to meet the Kinge (according to their seniority in the Vniuersity) euery Doctor rideing   30 vpon a ffootcloth and wearing a scarlett gowne and hood, and euery Master of Arts vpon a ffootcloth and wearing a wide sleeud Gowne & silke hood. The three Esquire Bedells shall allsoe ride before Master Vicechancellor in their formalities vpon ffootcloths bearing their staues; and all this Company shall meet the King at the farthest precincts of the Vniuersity, where they shall all   35 alight from their horses and Master Vicechancellor shall make an Oration to the Kinge the Bedells haueing first deliuered vp their staues to the Chancellor,

Collation with Bodl.: MS. Twyne 17 (T) pp 187–90:   16 August] August 1636 T
26 Mr Stringer] T omits   35 farthest] farther T

37l deliuered: 2 minims in MS

& the Chancellor to the Kinge. And it shall not bee lawfull for any schollar of any degree to goe out to meet the Kinge, or to bee att or vpon the way where the Kinge is to come vpon payne of a Moneths Imprisonment. They that ride to meet the Kinge are in their retourne to alight in Christs-churche there to wayt vpon his Maiesty and to Kneele vpon their Knees while the Vniuersity   5
Orator doth deliuer an Oration.

2.   At the Ringing of the Bell by Master Vicechancellors appoyntment, all the rest of the Doctors, Bachelors in all ffaculties Masters & Bachelors of Arts and Vndergraduats shall stande in Ranke one by one on both sides of the street from Christchurch toward North-gate as his Maiesty passeth by in   10
this Order. ffirst Doctors, then Bachelors in Diuinity, after them Masters of Arts and Bachelors in Law in Physicke, next Bachelors in Arts, then Schollars of Howses in their schollars gownes & Capps, and after them Commoners, all in the Habits belonging to their degrees. and shall stand there quietly till the King and his Trayne are past, and then Depart euery   15
man to his Colledge or Hall. The Noble men of the Vniuersity shall stand in the Church aboue the students &c of Christs-church, next to the Entrance into the Quire.

f 134*   20
...

4. There shall bee presented to the Kinge immediately after the Vicechancellors speech A Bible in ffolio with a Veluett Couer, richly Embroydered with the Kings Armes in the middest and allsoe a payre of Gloues, [and] to the Queen a payre of Gloues; to the Count Palatine a Booke and a payre of Gloues and   25
to his brother Rupertus a paire of Gloues and to some other great personages as shall bee thought fitt by our Chancellor.

...

7 It was likewise Ordered that the Count Palatine & his Brother and the rest of the Nobility that will bee Created or Incorporated, shall be presented by   30
Sir Nathaniel Brente Knight, Doctor of Law and Warden of Merton Colledge, (with some short speech to the Count Palatine,) vnles some Noble man desire to doe it. Whosoeuere of the Vniuersity are to be Created doctors in any ffaculty shall bee presented by the Professor of that faculty. They vnder the degree of Noble-men that shall bee made Masters of Arts shall bee presented   35
by some one to bee appoynted by the Vicechancellor.

Collation continued: 10 street] streetes *T*   12 in Physicke] & physicke *T*
34 shall bee] he shalbe *T*

23/ richly: c *written over* s

f 134v*

...

10.   At the Kings departure from the Vniuersity the iunior Proctor is to make an
Oration to him in Christs church Quadrangle or in such place as our Lord
chancellor or his Vicechancellor shall appoynt.   5

11.   If the King depart from the Vniuersity solemnly as he came in, then at the
Ringing of a Bell, as before all the Doctors, Masters & Schollars of the
Vniuersity shall stande in Rankes after the manner aforesaid, from Christs
church gate that way as the King is to goe

An Aduertisement for Heads of Howses to deliuer   10
with great charge vnto their Companies.

That they admonish all such as are vnder their Charge that they appeare no
wheare abroad dureing the Kings beeing heere without their Capps, and such
Colour and fashion in their Apparell as the statute prescribeth. And perticulary
that they beware that they weare not any long-hayre, nor any Bootes, nor   15
Double stockins Rolled downe, or hanging loose about their Legges as the
manner of some Slouens is to doe. Nor weare their Gownes hanging loosely
with the Capes belowe their shoulders. And whatsoeuer Graduats or
Vndergraduats shall offend against this Order shall forfeit to the Vniuersity
toties quoties 10 s., or else bee Imprisoned or otherwise corrected according   20
to the Discretion of such of the ouerseers of manners & behauiour by these
Delegats appoynted as shall find him faulty.

By the same Delegates assembled on the 16th day of August
it was farther enacted as followeth.

...   25

f 135*

4   The Doctors that haue Scarlett Gownes shall weare them whensoeuer they
appeare in Publike dureing the Kings beeing here.   30

5.   That no man of any Degree shall presse in to see any of the Playes saue onely
such as shall bee allowed by Tickets giuen them by the Lord Chamberlain:

...

7   That Master Vicechancellor would bee pleased to giue out a strict Inhibition
to keep Schollers from goeing to Woodstock or troubling the King any where   35
else in his sports. Which was accordingly Done.

8.   If any Man shall offend against any of these Orders he shall (besides the

Collation continued: 18 the] their *T*   29 The] Those *T*   36 Which ... Done.]
T omits

3/ iunior Proctor: *Thomas Good*   35/ troubling: r *corrected from* l

Ordinary Punishments of the Statutes presently to bee Inflicted on him) bee
entered allsoe into the Black-booke and so kept from his Degree.

…

f 138* 5

…

°Here is wanting ye letter of thanks of ye Vniuersity to ye chancellor for his
deliuery of their letters to ye Queen about their play called ye Royall slaue.
dat. December 12, 1636. principio Qui in commodum nostrum, quasi &c.
in Gestis cancellariatus Laud, p. 128.° 10

°19 December   Auspicatum opus quo Mater nostra Academia gratias & indulgentiam obtinuit
1636.°   à Serenissimâ Reginæ Maiestate
Die Lunæ 19o Decembris, Anno Domini 1636 Causa Conuocationis erat vt
Literæ quas Serenissima Reginæ Maiestatas ad Academiam misit publicarentur
tenoris subsequentis. 15

…

The Great Charter   OUA: Long Box XIX
mb 14   *(5 March)*

… 20

°Certamina et   …Insuper, tum Dominus Edwardus quondam Rex Anglie primus, per
spectacula°   quoddam Breve suum gerens datum apud Chertsey duodecimo die Novembris
Anno Regni sui tricesimo tercio Vicecomiti Comitatus Oxonie directum
Iustas et Burdeicias sive aliquod aliud factum Armorum, vnde Scholarium
Vniversitatis Oxoniensis quies contra libertates eiusdem Vniversitatis quoquomodo 25
impediri seu turbari valeat, prope Villam Oxonie teneri aut haberi prohibuisset
provt per idem Breve plenius constat: Nos de vberiori gracia nostra ac ex certa
sciencia et mero motu nostris per presentes pro nobis heredibus et Successoribus
nostris predictis Cancellario Magistris et Scholaribus et Successoribus suis damus
et concedimus per presentes, quod ipsi Cancellarius vel viccecancellarius aut 30
eius locumtenens pro tempore existens, ne qua huiusmodi Iuste Burdeicie
hastiludia facta Armorum Torneamenta Adventure vel cuiuscunque generis
spectacula ociosa et vana aut contentiosa, lucrandi, iocandi vel spectandi causa
populo presentari vel exhiberi solita vnde scholares a studijs suis avocari
poterint, infra Vniversitatem Oxoniensis eiusve precinctum vel infra Civitatem 35
Oxonie cuiusque Subvrb, seu per quinque Milliara circumquaque, absque

7–10/ Here is … Laud, p. 128.: *in Anthony Wood's*   21/ tum: *for* cum
hand   22–3/ duodecimo … tercio: *12 November 1305*
21–2m/ Certamina et spectacula: *in Brian Twyne's*   36/ Subvrb: *for* Subvrbia; *abbreviation mark missing*
hand   36/ Milliara: *for* Milliaria (?)

speciali dict*i* ipsius Cancellarij eiusve Vicecancellar*ij* aut locumtenen*tis*, et
vtriusq*ue* vel alterius Procurator*um* ipsius Vniversitat*is* pro temporis existen*tis*
assensu et consensu prius obtento, habeantur aut fiant; Et tam pro nobis
qu*am* hered*ibus* et Successorib*us* nostris imperpetuum, plenam potestatem et
authoritatem dict*is* Cancellar*io*, Magistris et Scholarib*us* et Successorib*us* suis   5
per presentes damus et concedim*us* omn*es* et singul*os* qui imposterum aliqua
vel aliquod premissor*um* infra limit*es* predict*os* absq*ue* ipsius Cancellarij
vicecancellar*ij* eiusve locumtenen*tis* et Procurator*um* Vniversitat*is* vel alterius
eor*un*dem assensu et consensu prius obtento (vt premittitur) offere aut exhibere
conabuntur, per se vel Officiarios seu Ministros suos inhibend*i* vel repellend*i*   10
et statim extra precinct*um* sive Iurisdicc*i*onem huiusmodi exterminand*i* et
ablegand*i* eciam Refractarios et Immorigeros, ad bene placitum suum
incarcerand*os*…

…

15

Chancellor's Court Inventories   OUA: Hyp/B/13
f [1]*   *(12 October)* *(Inventory of John Gerrard, University musician)*
…

It*em* his musicke books	0	15	0

…
20

In the shop

…

It*em* foure treble violins, three tenor violins two			
base viols, two Bandora's, two Lutes two Cittarnes,			
a sackbut, a duble Curtall, two single Curtals,			
A mute Cornet, two Recorders, two Tenor			
Cornets, a Church Cornet, foure treble Cornets,			
a Church Curtall	6	13	4

…

30

OUM   ### Archbishop Laud's Expenses for the Royal Visit   PRO: SP/16/348
f [2]*   *(30 August)*

Chardges for the Kings entertaynment at Oxford Aug*ust* 30. 1636.
…
35

Item to the Vniu*er*sity Wayt*es*	1	0	0
Item to the Towne Wayt*es*	1	0	0

…

Item to the knight Marshalls Men. ⌈4 li.⌉ &			
⌈3 li. 10 s.⌉ Kings Tru*m*petters	7	10	0

…

Item giuen Mr Dayes & Children   0   10   0

…

f [4]*.

…   5

Item payd for the stage & Comedy &c vt patet   394   13   0

…

The whole Chardge of the
Entertaynment commeth to
Vt patet   2666 li. 1 s. 7 d.   *Adam Torless*   10
Besyd the prouisions which wear sent me in./

Robert Gill's Petition   PRO: SP/16/304
single sheet*

                                                                          15

To the right Honorable the Lords and others of his Maiesties
most Honorable priuie Councell../.

® *Received* 18th
December 1635.

The humble peticion of Robert Gill Keeper of his Maiesties
Lyons and Leoperds in the Tower of London./.

Humbly sheweth   20
That whereas your peticioner hath served his sacred Maiestie that nowe is
by the space of diuerse years last past And his ffather, and his Grandfather,
his Maiesties father and Queene Elizabeth of blessed memory for many yers
before in that antient office of the custody of the Lions and Leoperds in ye
Tower of London, as appeareth by seuerall Pattents graunted vnto them   25
vnder ye greate Seale of England with all care & diligence to the vttermost of
their power. And whereas alsoe his late Maiestie for the better encouraginge
of them in ye said office was graciously pleased by his Lettres pattents dated
the one & Twentith daye of Iuly in the Tenth yeare of his said Maiesties
Raigne, to graunte vnto them that from thence forth noe person or persons, 30
whatsoeuer should att any tyme or tymes hereafter carry or convey nor cause
to be carried or conveyed any Lyon Lyonesse or Leoperd into any parte of
this Realme of England or Dominion of Wales to shew them or carry them
about to any place or places for gaine or profitt vpon payne of his Maiesties
displesure & such forfeiture punishment & ymprisonment as by any lawes   35
or statuts of this Realme can or may be inflicted vpon yem for yeir contempt
& disobedience in that behalfe, as by the said Lettres pattents more plainly
maye appeare./.

Yet notwithstanding may it please your good Lordships soe it is yat one   40
Thomas Warde in Contempt of his Maiesties Lettres pattents & in

disobedience to his Maiesties lawes notwithstanding he hath byn warned
to ye contrary and hath byn prohibited by publique authoritie both by the
Vice Chauncellor of Oxford & Cambridge yet he hath very contemptuously
gon about ye Country with a Lyon both att the act of Oxford and att
Sturbrige faier in Cambridge & diuerse other places to shew it for mony,   5
And since hath parted with it to one Martin Baccas & Iohn Watson who
in ye like contemptuos manner doth carry ye said lyon about ye Country
to make profitt by shewing of him notwithstanding he is growen soe feirce
& savage yat he had almost killed a Childe, byting him by ye heade &
tearing him so yat he laye a long tyme and cost xx^{ty} nobles ye cure, And   10
likewise bitt his Keeper soe yat he lay viij weeks of ye soore as it wilbe
proved by affidavit of ye Keeper of the said lyon. All which is to ye great
contempt of his Maiestie the daunger of his subiects & to ye great hindrance
of your petitioner his Maiesties servant./.

                                                                                  15
In Consideracion whereof may it please your good Lordships to call theis
parties before you, yat for their contempt to his Maiestie they may receave
suche a Condigne punishment as shall seeme best to your Lordships wisedomes
& discretions/.

                                                                                  20
                      And your peticioner shall ever be bound &c/

Letter of George Garrard to Viscount Conway   PRO: SP/16/331
ff [1v–2]*   (4 September)

                                                                                  25
…Munday Morning all repard' to St Iohns to attend the Archbishop;
Earles, My Lord Newcastle, Barons, Bishops, heads of houses, Doctors, I
among the rest, who had Six Buckes to present him, at least to tell him
of, from my Lord of Salisbury. He was vnder the Barbers hands when I
Came; But at lenghth he came forth, Courteous he was to all, but walked   30
most and entertain'd longest my Lord Cottington; Shewing him his new
building, the Roomes where he ment to Entertayne the King, and the Hall
where the Play was to bee… At One of the Clocke the Vniuersitye bell
rung out to call all the Students of Qualitye in theyre degrees to wayte on
his Grace theyre Chancellor to meete hys Maiestye nere two miles out of   35
towne, on horsebacke all riding on footeclothes, | This sight or entry I
wente to see, Afterwards I liued as I vse to doe att London, when Feasts,
Masques, and Playes are there, heare of them, but neuer see them. Since
the King was to come to a Citye, as well, as to an Vniversitye; The Maior

39/ The Maior: *Martin Wright*

and townesmen had some part in the Shewe at the Entry, Three score
townesmen rode first in blacke satten dobletts and Cloth hose, with blacke
Coates garded with Veluett, and theyre towne Clercke in a Veluett Coate
with a chaine of Gold about his Necke, then about 20 Aldermen in scarlett,
by the Eldest of them rode, there Recorder, Mr Whistler ... Then came   5
many Senior Masters, Peter Turner vpon a veluet footecloth, which he
borrowed of *Sir* Abraham Dawes, next Batchilors of Deuinitye, then
*Docto*rs in all Sciences, Three Bishops, Winchester, Oxford, and Norwich
The *Lo*rd Treasurer single, the Kings two mace bearers goeing before him,
a trovpe of his owne Gentlemen walking by his horse side; Then the Maior   10
of Oxford carying the Mace; Last of all the Sixe beadles of the Vniversitye
carying theyre staues before the Vicechancellor, His Grace next to the
Kings Coach, brauely mounted on his horse and footecloth, attended with
store of his Gentlemen who walked by him on foote; The King once enterd
Bocardoe, the Streetes were lind with masters and Batchelors and other   15
students, Commoners and Schollers of houses, vntill he enterd Christchurch
Gates, where he lodgd; When the Vniversitye first mett him, the
Vicechancellor made the Speech, here at Christchurch the Vniuersitye
Orator. Mr Stroade, who is of that house... That Night a Play was in
Christchurche hall presented to his Ma*ies*tye, fitter for schollers then a   20
Court, My *Lo*rd Canarvan flewe out against yt, Sayd it was the worst, that
euer he sawe, but One that he sawe at Cambridge; Tuesday the cheife
day of Entertainment is Come...

f [2v]*   25

...Then [made] the Vicechancellor made a speech, and dissolud the
Convocation. His Grace, this done, repayres to the King to wayte on his
Ma*ies*tye to the library, where at his Entry Will Herbert made a fine
Oration in latine to ye King and deliuerd yt as finely, which did not a   30
litle please my lord Chamberlayne; There the King spent more then an houre,
and was loth to leaue the Place, But dinner call him away to St Iohns; where
also his Ma*ies*tye stayd long before the Queene came; but the new building
and other entertainments gaue his Ma*ies*tye much Content...

                                                                               35

ff [3–3v]*

...Dinner done, and all ye meate consumed; They went to the Play,

6/ footecloth: l *corrected over another letter*   32/ call: *for* called
16/ Commoners: *5 minims in* MS

which was ^⌈not⌉ done vntill after sixe; how it was liked, Ile tell you
God willing when I meete you at Sion; The Dialogue is too long,
which hapned that night at my Lord Cottingtons at Supper, to relate
in this letter vpon the Censure of this Play, be you sure to call for yt,
Ile there tell it your Lordship. The Play done theyre Maiestyes retornd   5
to Christchurch to Supper, then had another Play, the Persian Slaue,
excellently written by a yong Master of Art one Cartwright, sumptuously
sett out, and acted to admiration, Generally liked by all ye Court, and
Vniuersitye, but my Lord Chamberlayne soe transported with yt, that
he swore mainely, he neuer saw ^⌈such a Play⌉ with all his Propertyes   10
before; Nay the next morning when theyre Iudgments had cooled vpon
yt, They were of the same Opinion. Both courts went away about 9 in
ye morning, The Archbishop feasts the Heads of houses and Doctors
at St Iohns on Wensday, a hope then was, that St Iohns Play shold
haue bin playd againe, to the Vniversitye, but the Vnrulines of the   15
Multitude of Schollers prevented yt, Then all repayred to Christchurch,
assuring themselues to haue theyre last Play acted againe, but there
was no Candles to be gott, The Cannons wold not be at that charge,
though the Actors were willinge, This Sir William Beecher told mee
at Hatfield who came thence two dayes after mee. His Grace went   20
thence on Thursday after dinner; and is retorned to Croyden. Having
left behind | of all his honorable Actions and deportments, a very
worthy fame....

Letter of Thomas Read to Sir Francis Windebank   PRO: SP/16/331   25
f [1]*   (8 September)

Honoratissime Avuncule.
    Extremas Easce Comædiæ partes, proram (vt ita dicam) et puppim
acquisiui; quæ fortassis sine scenâ placere possunt. Curiales elegantias   30
nobis licet attingere non fas sit, imitari tamen quis vitabit? Apollinem
non in arenam provocamus, sed Deum veneramur Tutelarem. Cæteri
Musarum nostrarum partus adhuc delitescunt. Quod si olim in
publicum prodierint, vestræ, non censuræ committam, sed tutelæ;
cum sciam, Te non Aristarchum studiorum Academicorum fore, sed   35
Mæcenatem.
                    Honoris vestri observantissimus
                            Consanguineus
                    Thomas Reade.
E Collegio Novo Septembris 8.   40
        1636

Thomas Crosfield's Diary   QC Library: MS 390
f 75v

...

2.   Seene a bull baiting in St Clem*ent*s
where the manner is thus

NB   1. 1 d. a piece for euery person
that goes in & 2 d. in a chamber.
2. The Bull master may strike the
doggs if two set on at a time.

{   1. The Doggs .10. or 12. are brought
chained into ye yard, where tyed their   5
anger or courage such as to bite or
breake ye chaines they are tyed with.
2. The Bull brought in w*i*th hornes
buttened, & tied to ye stake, walkes
about, ye dogs one at once set on: if   10
he catch him aboue coller, cheifely by
ye nose accounted victor./ after all
haue playd ouer round they com*m*only
haue a second boute –.

3. In the throwing or tossing of the doggs often they are kill'd or maimed,   15
but y*a*t to saue them men run & catch them in the fall. & keep them
backe from ye fiercenes & eager onset, whereby otherwise they would be
quite quash't, maimed or slaine by the Bull y*a*t watcheth their onset.
4. If the bull be cun*n*ing he will neuer run away, but warily watch ye very
first onset of the dog, & he receiues encouragem*ent* fro*m* his masters   20
strokeing of him. [⟨..⟩]

...

f 76

...   25

17   The Musicke kept in o*ur* Coll*edge* vpon the day in the afternoone: most fit./
...

ff 77–8*

...   30

25   Orders set downe & agreed vpon Iuly .25º. 1636. by the Heads of
Colledges & Halls, assembled together to prepare & prouide for his
ma*ie*sties entertainment by the vniuersity in August next following
1   Inprimis that ye vniuersity shall pay towards all gifts, charges & burdens
w*hat*soeuer arising by this entertainem*ent* 200 li. & no more.   35
2.   In ye 2^d place the seuerall heads of Colledges did acknowledge & consent
vnto the ancient valuations & assessm*ents* of their seuerall Colledges there
presented by Dr Baily Vicechancelor. This valuation was made in Queene
Elizabeths time when she was entertained by ye vniuersitie vizt

7m/ 2.: *2 February 1635/6*
26m/ 17: *17 February 1635/6*
31m/ 25: *25 July 1636*

31–3/ Orders ... following: *preceded by a drawing
of a hand with a pointing index finger*

Christ Church 2000 li.   valued all according
Magdalen Colledge 1200 li.   to ye old rent, aboue which
New Colledge 1000 li.   all now improued
Queens Colledge 260 li. &c.

3.   In the 3ᵈ place, Iesus Colledge, Waddam Colledge, & Pembrok Colledge were   5
     valued & rated in ye presence of their seuerall gouernors for this purpose &
     entertainement for [ancient] they were not anciently valued.

4.   In ye 4th place it was ordered yat ye corporation & body of euery Colledge
     should be rated & assessed by it selfe. And besides euery commoner in or of
     yat body should be assessed & rated by the pole   10

5.   In ye fifth place, that euery particular Colledge should be rated 5 li. for euery
     hundred they were assessed, as heretofore.

Euery Earles son   1. 13. 4.
Euery Barons son   1. 0. 0.
Euery fellow Comoner & vpper Commoner   0. 10. 0.   15
Euery ⌃⌐ordinary⌐ Master of Arts [or]   0. 5. 0.
Euery ordinary Commoner   0. 5. 0.
Euery one of ye lower sort called Battellors
  ⌃⌐or Soiounors⌐   0. 3. 4.
Poore schollars nothing./   20

6.   6. Also it was agreed yat a Schedall should be made for euery Colledge wherein
     ye names of all according to ye said rate should be taxed & summed vp &
     giuen to ye Vicechancelor,

and if ye   ⎧   Overplus to what shalbe expended, then
summe be   ⎨   ye same to be refunded in proportion.   25
                   ⎩   Defectiue, then the same must be made vp
                           according to ye same rate

Summa pro Collegio   13 li.
     pro Scholaribus   12 li. 10 s./ |
                                                                        30

August. 1636.

28.   The presents giuen to ye ⎧ Kinge: a bible of Edin[g]burgh print
                              ⎪ worth 80 li.
                              ⎨
                              ⎪ Queene Camdens Elizabeth
                              ⎩ Palsgraues, Hookers Ecclesiasticall policy.   35
     The maior, a Syluer bowle, richly adorned.

---

p 535, l.38–p 536, l.4/ This valuation … &c.: these   28–9/ Summa … 10 s./: these lines are set in a box
    lines are written in a box occupying part of the right-   at the bottom right side of the page
    hand side of the page   31/ 1636.: underlined
19/ Soiounors: underlined; for soiournors   32m/ 28.: for 29; the king arrived in Oxford on
21–7/ 6. Also it … same rate: these lines are set in a   29 August 1636
    box on the right side of the page

These were presented to them after that first about 2 of ye Clocke, the
Doctors & Citizens had rid towards woodstocke to meet him, there 2.
speeches one by ye vicechancelor/ th'other by ye Recorder & they came in
before ye King in this manner. First a trumpeter before ye townesmen which

were all either apparrelled in $\left\{\begin{array}{l}\text{Satin dublets \& cloth breeches, as ordinary}\\ \quad\text{townesmen of any degree.}\\ \text{Skarlet gownes, so ye maior \& thAldermen:}\\ \quad\text{\& 2 bayles}\end{array}\right.$ 5

29   Next to them were .1. such as rid in wide sleeu'd gownes & footclothes, vizt
mr Stringer Greeke professor, mr Rous library keeper, mr Principall Airay, mr   10
Turner, mr Twine ye 2: proctors.7.
2. The Doctors in Skarlet to ye number of about 20.

3. After ye Doctors   1. The Bishop of $\left\{\begin{array}{l}\text{Winchester, Dr Curle.}\\ \text{Oxford, Dr Bancroft.}\\ \text{Norwich, Dr Wren.}\end{array}\right.$ 15
    rid the
    Bishops thus.

          2. The Bishop of London,
             Dr Iuxon, Lord Treasurer
             with 2 mases before him.
          3. The Archbishop with ye
             Bedles before him, next   20
             before ye King

4. Then ye King & Queene, with ye Palsgraue & his brother in a Coach/.
5. After them followed ye Lord Chamberlane, Lord Cottington & ye guard/
These were passengers/; The spectators also were ranked in their orders vizt.

Without Bocardo all ye 4 Companyes of ye towne $\left\{\begin{array}{l}\text{Shoemakers}\\ \text{Tailors}\\ \text{Fullers \&c}\end{array}\right.$ 25

Within Bocardo from thence to Christ Church. 1. vndergraduates.
      2. Bachlors of Art. 3. Masters of Art & Bachlers of Law. 4. Bachlors of
      Diuinity all in their formalities.   30
6. when ye king & Queene & Palsgraue were lighted out of their Coach within
Christ Church the orator made a speech & ye Vice Chancelor deliuered ye
bookes vt supra./
7. After Supper ye Play, Prudentius, with intellectus agens & ye rellious
passions was acted from 7. a clocke till .9. or .10. at night: all this vpon   35
Munday.

30   The day following being Tuesday his maiesties entertainment was thus ordered
     ...

2–3/ there 2. speeches ... Recorder: *written in left*
   margin and marked with a + for insertion here
9m/ 29: *29 August 1636*
33/ vt supra: *underlined*

34/ Prudentius: *ie,* The Floating Island
34/ rellious: *for* rebellious
37/ The ... Tuesday: *30 August 1636*

10 & 11. vsque ad 1am The King accompanied with th'archbishop came on
foote from Christ church through Cat street into ye Diuinity Schoole, & then
went vp into ye Schooles where the Earle of Pembrokes son of Exon' Colledge
made a speech vpon his Knees, which was well accepted by his Maiestie...
2a post meridiem. Then comeing out of ye Library, [the] Queene met him at   5
ye gate & so they went to dinner at St Iohns, a Comedy after dinner till 7. a
clocke, then returned to Christ Church to Supper, & after supper a Comedy
vizt ye Royall Slaue was acted with good applause of King & Queene./ |

September 1. 1636.   10

1.   The day following being Wednesday ye King & Queene departed about 9
a clocke & went to Winchester & thence to Henley that night; having first
saluted all ye Doctors in Christ church Quadrangle...

...

2.   The Comedyes were acted before ye Schollars at Christchurch for yeir money...   15

...

Laud, *Diary of His Own Life (1695)*   Wing: L586
p 53   *(29–31 August)*

...   20

August 29. Munday, King Charles and Queen Mary entred Oxford, being to
be there entertain'd by me as Chancellor of the University.
August 30. On Tuesday, I entertained them at St. John's Colledge. It was St.
Fœlix his Day; and all passed happily. Charles Prince Elector Palatine, and his
Brother Prince Rupertus, was there. These two were present in Convocation;   25
and with other Nobles, were made Masters of Arts.
August 31. Wednesday, They left Oxford, And I returned homewards, the Day
after: Having first entertained all the Heads of Houses together.

A   ### Laud, *Historical Account (1700)*   Wing: L596   30
pp 100–1*   *(15 July)*

Sir,

My Letters to
the Vice-
Chancellour
about the
settlement of
the Plays in
Oxford against
his Majesties
coming.

Since I writ last to you, the Dean of Christ-Church came to me, and
acquainted me with two things, which are very necessary you should both   35
know and remedy.
    The one is, that the University seems to be unwilling to contribute to the
Charge of the Plays, which are to be at Christ-Church. Now this charge, as
by reason of their Building, they are not able to bear alone; So I must needs

10/ 1636.: *underlined*
11/ Wednesday: *31 August 1636*
39/ Building: *the extension of the buildings in Peckwater and Canterbury Quadrangles*

acknowledge, there is no reason, that they should, whatever their ability be: For the King is to be entertained by Oxford, not by Christ-Church. And that he lyes there, is but for the Conveniency of the place, where there are so many fair Lodgings for the great Men to be about him. Indeed if Christ-Church men will say, they will have no Actors, but of their own House, let them bear 5 the charge of their own Plays on God's name: But if they will take any good Actors from any other College or Hall, upon trial of their sufficiency to be as good, or better than their own; then I see no reason in the World, but that the whole University should contribute to the Charge. And I pray see it ordered, and let your Successour follow you accordingly. 10

The University to contribute to the Plays at Christ-Church

The other is, that since the University must contribute to this Charge, (for so it was done when King James came, and at the last coming of Queen Elizabeth, both within my own memory) I hold it very fit, that all the Materials of that Stage, which are now to be made new, and the Proscenium and such Apparel whatever it be, as is wholly made new, shall be laid up in 15

The materials of the Plays to be safely laid up and kept.

some place fit for it; to which the Vice-Chancellour for the time being shall have one Key, and the Dean of Christ-Church the other, that it may not be lost, as things of like nature and use have formerly been. And if any College or Hall shall at any time for any Play or Show that they are willing to set forth, need the use of any, or all of these things, it shall be as lawful, and free 20 for them to have and to use them, as for Christ-Church; Provided that after the use, they do carefully restore them to the place whence they were taken. And to the end these things may be kept with the more safety and indifferency to the University, I think it very fit that an Inventory be made of them, and that one Copy thereof remain with them, at Christ-Church, and the other in 25 such fit and convenient place, as the Vice Chancellour and the Heads shall agree on. For my part I think it fittest, that an Inventory should be kept in the |

® My Letters concerning the business of the Plays to be registred.

University Registry, that so you may not only have access to it, so often as you shall have cause, but also leave it ready for direction in future times in like Cases of expence. And I think it not amiss, that these my Letters which 30 concern the ordering of these Businesses, should be Registred also.

And further, that the University may see, how the Money, which they allow towards these Charges is expended, I think it very requisite, that your self and the Heads should name three or four Men of good experience in those things,

® Four experienced men to be appointed to look to the rates of the Materials for the Plays.

that may see at what Rates all things are bought and paid for: And an Accompt 35 delivered in to the Vice-Chancellour and the Heads, at such time, as the Vice-Chancellour, shall call for them. And also that, their Hands be set to both Copies of the above named Inventories. I have thought upon Dr. Fell, Dr. Sanders, and the Warden of Wadham, as very fit Men for this purpose; And if you and the Heads shall think it requisite to joyn any more to them, you 40 may name whom you please.

For the Play, which I intend shall be at St. John's, I will neither put the University nor the College to any Charge, but take it wholly upon my self.

And in regard of the great trouble and Inconvenience, I shall thereby put upon that House, as also in regard it shall set out one of the Plays by it self, I think there is great reason in it, and do therefore expect it, that no Contribution should be required from St. John's towards the Plays at Christ-Church. And I pray let me have an Accompt from you of the settlement of these things. So I   5
leave you to the Grace of God, and rest,
Croydon, Iuly
15. 1636.   Your loving Friend
                                        Willelmus Cantuariensis

...   10

p 102   *(29 August)*

Concerning my
Entertainment
of the King at
Oxford.

I came into
Oxford to
make things
ready for this
entertainment
upon Thursday
August 25.
I came in
privately at
Dinner hour,
having sent
most of my
Servants thither
the night
before, and my
self lay that
night at my
Lord of
Oxford's.

This year his Majesty and the Queen invited themselves to me to Oxford, and brought with them Charles, Prince Elector Palatine, and his Brother   15
Prince Rupert, being both then in England. They came into Oxford at the end of this Summer's Progress on Munday August 29. The Vice-Chancellour made a very good Speech unto them, where my self and the University met them, which was a mile, before they entred the Town. That Speech ended, they passed along by St. John's, where Mr. Tho*mas* Atkinson made another   20
Speech unto them very brief, and very much approved of by his Majesty afterwards to me. Within Christ-Church Gate, Mr. William Strode the University Orator entertained them with another Speech, which was well approved. Thence the King accompanied his Queen to her Lodging, and instantly returned, and went with all the Lords to the Cathedral. There   25
after his Private Devotions ended, at the West Door Dr. Morris, one of the Prebendaries entertained him with another short Speech, which was well liked. And thence his Majesty proceeded into the Quire, and heard Service. After Supper they were entertained with a Play at Christ-Church, which was very well penn'd, but yet did not take the Court so well.   30
...

pp 103–5*   *(30–1 August)*
...
...the King with the Princes and the Nobles, my self also waiting upon him,   35
went to the Library, where the King viewed the New Building and the Books, and was entertained with a very neat Speech made by the Son of the Earl of Pembrook and Montgomery, then Lord Chamberlain.
      Then the word was brought up, that the Queen was come. So the King went into the Coach to her, and they went away to St. John's to dinner, the   40
Princes and Nobles attending them.

36/ the New Building: *the north range of Canterbury Quadrangle*

When they were come to St. John's, they first viewed the New-Building, and that done, I attended them up the Library Stairs; where so soon as they began to ascend, the Musick began, and they had a | fine short Song fitted for them, as they ascended the Stairs. In the Library they were Welcomed to the College with a short Speech made by *(blank)* one of the Fellows.   5

...

When Dinner was ended, I attended the King and the Queen together with the Nobles into several withdrawing Chambers, where they entertained themselves for the space of an hour. And in the mean time I caused the Windows of the Hall to be shut, the Candles lighted, and all things made   10
ready for the Play to begin. When these things were fitted, I gave notice to the King, and the Queen, and attended them into the Hall, whither I had the happiness to bring them by a Way prepared from the President's Lodging to the Hall without any the least disturbance; And had the Hall kept as fresh and cool, that there was not any one person when the King and Queen came into   15
it. The Princes, Nobles, and Ladies entred the same way with the King, and then presently another Door was opened below to fill the Hall with the better sort of Company, which being done, the Play was begun and Acted. The Plot was very good, and the Action. It was merry, and without offence, and so gave a great deal of content. In the middle of the Play, I ordered a short Banquet   20
for the King, the Queen, and the Lords. And the College was at that time so well furnisht, as that they did not borrow any one Actor from any College in Town. The Play ended, the King and the Queen went to Christ-Church, retired and supped privately, and about 8 a Clock, went into the Hall to see

The latter Play at Christ Church acted over again by the Queen's Players at Hampton Court.

another Play, which was upon a piece of a Persian Story. It was very well penn'd   25
and acted, and the strangeness of the Persian Habits gave great Content; so that all Men came forth from it very well satisfied. And the Queen liked it so well, that she afterwards sent to me to have the Apparel sent to Hampton Court, that she might see her own Players act it over again, and see whether they could do it as well, as t'was done in the University. I caused the University   30
to send both the Clothes, and the Perspectives of the Stage; and the Play was acted at Hampton Court in November following. And by all Men's confession the Players came short of the University Actors. Then I humbly desired of the King and the Queen, that neither the Play nor Cloathes, nor Stage might come into the Hands and use of the Common Players abroad, which was   35
graciously granted. |

But to return to Oxford. This Play being ended, all Men betook themselves to their rest, and upon Wednesday Morning August 31. about Eight of the Clock, my self with the Vice-Chancellor and the Doctors attended the coming forth of the King and Queen; and when they came, did our Duties to them.   40

5/ *(blank): name apparently not entered in MS; indicated by 2 dashes by printer*

They were graciously pleased to give the University a great deal of thanks; and I for my self, and in the Name of the University, gave their Majesties all possible thanks for their great and gracious Patience and Acceptance of our Poor and mean Entertainment: So the King and the Queen went away very well pleased together.   5

...

   My retinue (being all of my own, when I went to this Entertainment) were between 40 and 50 Horse; though I came privately into Oxford, in regard of the nearness of the King and Queen, then at Woodstock. There was great store of Provision in all kinds sent me in towards this   10 Entertainment; and yet (for I bare all the Charge of that Play, which was at St. John's, and suffered not that poor College to be at a penny Loss or Charge in any thing) besides all these sendings in, the Entertainment cost me *(blank)*

                                                                              15

Entertainment of King Charles I   Bodl.: MS. Twyne 17
pp 191–2*   *(29–30 August)*

This summer for Keepinge of ye Towne cleene from ye sickenesse against ye kinges cominge there was neither Assises nor act kept in Oxford †®   20
Acta primae diei
29 .August. beinge mundaye .1636. [about te] at ye ringinge of ye great bell at St Maries we gott on horsebake, and rod vp to St. Iohns college where ye
®ye .3. Squire beadles ridinge before on their footcloathes in chaines of gold, & their staues — Chancellor & ye [ot] vicechancellor was: And [then to] from thence togither with ye Vicechancellor & our whole companie of Riders in our footclothes,   25 wide sleaued gownes & hooddes, we rod [towarde W] vp Woodstocke Waye as farre as abut Aristottles well, & there in ᴧ⸢ye⸣ broad greene ᴧ⸢high⸣ waye, we stood still. My Lords grace our chancellor, accompanied with my Lord Treasurer, ye Bishop of Wynchester, & Bishop of Norwich, & ye Bishope of Oxford all in one coach (as I thinke) [followed after] who followed vs, came   30 vp thither allso: [& at ye kinges commin] A while after came ye kinge & queene, and Ye Palsgraue & his brother, all in one coach. Ye kinge & Queene sittinge on ye [west] ⸢east⸣ side of ye coach. Then presently alightinge from our horses, [we] & ye Bishops from their coach, we all flocked to ye kinges coach, where kneelinge downe on ye greene high   35 waye, ye vicechancellor made a oration to ye kinge, of about a quarter of an houre longe: & ye chancellor deliuered vp ye .3. staues to [his] ye kinge, who gaue them backe to ye chancellor againe & hee to ye Beadles and here I thinke ye presents were giuen allso which beinge done, our Chancellor, & ye ᴧ⸢other⸣

14*l (blank): amount apparently not entered in MS; indicated by 8 dots by printer*
37–9*l & ye chancellor ... allso: entered between the lines and extended into the right margin*

Bishops mounted on horsebacke, as all we did allso & forward we came by
two & two (ye Iuniors [in ye] foremost) towarde ye Towne.
The Mayor & his Brethren stood about a bowe shoot from vs, towarde ye
Towne, & while their speech was makinge, we of ye vniuersitie ranked
ourselues on ye west side of ye high waye standinge still there vntyll ye   5
Townesmen, some in their blacke coates, & others in their skarlett gownes,
came by; & then we put on againe as before, & had senioritie of them, and
so we entred ye Towne. |

When we came to Christchurch gate, ye Aldermen and thirteene with ye other
Townesmen, rode on[wards] towarde Grantpont where they stood still. But   10
we of ye vniuersitie, rode all into Christchurch quadrangle, where an oration
was made by ye orator of ye vniuersitie, a little within ye ∧⌈great⌉ gate.
Then ye *king* rode in his coach towarde ye hall, where ye Canons (as I thinke)
receiued him, & had him to ye church .&c.
That night he ∧⌈and ye queene and palsgraue⌉ supped at Christchurch, and   15
after supper, they heard a playe acted in Christchurch hall, penned by Mr
Strode ye orator of ye vniuersitie called, passions calmed, or ye settlinge of ye
flotinge Ilande. My *Lord* Archbishops grace and my Lord Treasurer, lay at
St Iohns

20

But ye Mayor
bearinge his
mace on his
shoulder came
[into ye colled]
waited vppon
ye Kinge into
Christchurch
quadrangle &
after ye oration
was made he
deliuered ye
kinge ye boll,
as I thinke.

Acta 2ᵃᵉ diei 30ᵐᵒ Augusti
…abut ten of ye clocke, his ma*ie*stie & ye two palsgraues, [wen] accom*p*anied
with my Lords Grace our Chancellor ∧⌈and⌉ ye other Bishops & many other
of ye nobilitie, [we] with ye Bedles goeinge before them [ye] [with ye] ⌈hauinge
ye⌉ vppe end of their staues beinge carried vpwards, went on foote ∧⌈to⌉ ye   25
schooles to see ye Library, where they were entertayned with a Speech made
by one of my *Lord* Chamb*er*lanes suns then [studie] beinge a scholler of
Exceter Coll*ege*. And at dinner time they went all to St Iohns, where they
were royally feasted by my *Lord* Archbishope [Et] and sawe a playe acted there
in ye coll*ege* hall called, ye hospitall of louers   30
The vicechanc*ellor* & *p*roctors sate in their vsuall places but for ye chancellor
himselfe, there was erected a Chayre behinde ye vicechanc*ellor*, where he sate,
& ye Doctors behinde him close vnder ye windows…

p 193*   *(30–1 August)*   35

Towarde night they returned to Christchurch where they supped, & after
supper, they heard another playe acted in Christchurch, called ye Royall Slaue
made by one Mr Cartwright w*hich* playe beinge full of shewes & p*ar*takinge
of ye nature of a maske, was [better] farre better liked then Mr Strodes playe &c   40

10/ Grantpont: *Grandpont, the street leading from Christ Church Meadow Gate south to Folly Bridge*
30/ ye hospitall of louers: *added in different ink by the same hand*

Act*a* 3o diei

Vppon Wednesday morninge ye Doctors in their skarlett gownes & those that
fett in ye kinge att ye first, were warned to wayte vppon ye his ma*i*estie at
Christchurch at ye kinges lodginge; where ye kinge & queen & ye two
palsgraues tooke coach (beinge alltogether in one coach) [about] betwixt   5
eight & nine of ye cloke in ye morninge, & dep*ar*ted ouer south bridge...
But neither did ye mayor appeare waytinge vppon yat kinge at his dep*ar*ture,
nor ye vniu*er*sitie goe any further wi*t*h him
An obseruation after ye k*i*nge was come in, that all ye waye as he came in
neither schollers nor Townesmen did crie viuat.   10

...

p 194*   *(1–2 September)*

...

Vppon Thurseday after dinner my L*ord* Archbishops Grace & my L*ord*   15
Treasurer dep*ar*ted from St Iohns. And then ye playe w*hi*ch was acted before
ye kinge on ye tuesdaye in ye afternoone should haue byn rep*re*sented [to ye]
againe to ye vniu*er*sitie & to ye strangers, Courtiers & others then beinge
ˌ⌐as yet⌐ in ye Towne: but such was ye vnrulinesse of ye yonger schollers
to come in, that [they] vppon their breakinge in [⟨.⟩] ye strangers & others   20
could not be placed, doe what ye vicechancellor could; and so there was no
playe at all. [Neu*er*thelesse, vppon ye mundaye after, it was acted.]

°Mr Cartwright   Vppon fridaye in ye afternoone Cartwrights playe was acted at Christchurch
& Mr Maynes   before ye vniu*er*sitie; and Mr Strodes playe in ye afternoone vppon likewise
playes sent for   vppon saturdaye. And so ended all ye solemnities of ye kinges co*m*minge   25
vp to London   .&c.
vi*de* postea
p. 199. et 201°   ...

p 199*

...   30

In November 1636. ye Queens Ma*i*estie sent to Christchurch to desire ye
coll*ege* that she might borrowe ye plaie of ye Royall Slaue, together wi*t*h
all ye Persian attire & apparrell wherein it was acted at Christchurch, and
allso wi*t*h all ye curious contriuinges of ye stage, and ye strange shutts, &
conueyances of ye scenes that were in that playe; and they were all bestowed   35
vppon her Grace by ye vniu*er*sitie & ye coll*ege* & Edgarly ye Carrier had
them vp to Hampton Court in his waggon. Mr Maines playe allso [though n]
of Christchurch, though not acted at Oxford before ye kinge & Queene at
Oxford, yet it was sent for vp: and in Christmas weeke both Mr Cartwright

3/ ye his ma*i*estie: *for* his maiestie
23–6m/ Mr Cartwright ... et 201: *in Anthony Wood's hand*
24–5/ vppon likewise vppon: *dittography*

& Mr Mayne, ye poets, were sent for vp to Hampton Court, to see ye
settinge forth of their playes before ye Kinge & Queene.

p 201*

A goodly stage made at Christchurch from ye vpper-ende of ye hall allmost
to ye hearth, after ye newe fashion with [open] 3 or 4 openinges at ech side
thereof, and partitions much resemblinge ye deskes in a library, out of which
ye Actors issued forth on ech side, and these partitions they could drawe in at
their pleasure vppon a sudden, and thrust out newe in their places accordinge
to ye nature of ye scene, like ∧⌜churches⌝ dwellinge houses, pallaces or ye like,
which bred great varietie & admiration: [At ye vpper ende of ye stage was] and
ouer all, delicate payntinge resemblinge ye Cloudes & Sky cullur &c
At ye vpper ende, a great fayre shutt of two leaues ∧⌜painted curiously on ye
outside⌝ that opened and shutt together againe without any visible helpe;
within which was set forth ye emblem of ye ∧⌜whol⌝ playe in sumptuous
manner to behold: therein was ye perfect resemblance of ye billowes of ye sea
rollinge vp & downe, and an artificial Iland with churches & houses, wauinge
vp & downe really & flotinge in ye same in one whole peice, ye rockes & trees
∧⌜& hilles,⌝ in & about ye shores thereof, in ye playe of ye passions calmed:
and, after that, many other fine peices of worke and landscips at sundry
openinges thereof, did appeare; & there was a chayre came glidinge in vppon
ye stage without any visible helpe &c. but in ye other playe called ye Royall
Slaue ∧⌜where within those shutts as a curious temple and ye sun shininge on
it⌝ there was much more varietie of ye scene, and curious prospects of forests
& ye like, within those great shutts spoken of before, with villages, & men
visibly appearinge in them goinge vp & downe here & there, about their
businesse &c.

Heylyn, Cyprianus Anglicus (1668)   Wing: H1699
p 318*   *(29 August)*
…

  Such were the benefits which the University received from him in this
present year. And that he might both do himself and the University some
honour in the eye of the Kingdom, he invites the King, the Queen, the Prince
Elector, and his Brother, to an Academical entertainment, on the twenty ninth
day of August then next following, being the Anniversary day, on which the
Presidentship of St. John's Colledge was adjudged to him by King James. The
time being come, and the University put into a posture for the Royal visit,

5

10

15

20

25

30

35

8/ and: *written over other letters*   33/ him: *William Laud, archbishop of Canterbury*
13/ Cloudes: C *corrected from* S

their Majesties were first received with an eloquent Speech as he passed by the
house, being directly in his way betwixt Woodstock and Christ-Church, not
without great honour to the Colledge, that the Lord Archbishop, the Lord
Treasurer, the Chancellor, the Vice-Chancellor, and one of the Proctors,
should be at that time of the same foundation. At Christ-Church his Majesty   5
was entertained with another Oration by Strode, the University Oratour; the
University presenting his Majesty with a fair and costly pair of Gloves (as their
custome was) the Queen with a fair English Bible, the Prince Elector with
Hookers Books of Ecclesiastical Politie, his brother Rupert with Cæsars
Commentaries in English, illustrated by the learned Explanations and   10
Discourses of Sir Clement Edmonds. His Majesty was lodged in Christ-Church,
in the great Hall whereof (one of the goodliest in the World) he was entertained,
together with the Queen, the two Princes, and the rest of the Court, with an
English Comedy, (but such as had more of the Philosopher than the Poet in it)
called, Passions Calmed, or the settling of the Floating Islands....   15

p 319*   (30–1 August)

...After dinner he entertains his principal Guests with a pleasant Comedy,
presented in the publick Hall; and that being done, attends them back again   20
to Christ-Church, where they were feasted after Supper with another Comedy,
called, The Royal Slave; the Enterludes represented with as much variety of
Scenes and motions as the great wit of Inigo Jones (Surveyor General of his
Majesties Works, and excellently well skilled in setting out a Court-Masque to
the best advantage) could extend unto. It was the day of St. Felix (as himself 25
observeth) and all things went happily. On Wednesday the next morning the
Court removed, his Majesty going the same night to Winchester, and the
Archbishop the same day, entertaining all the Heads of Houses at a solemn
Feast; order being given at his departure, that the three Comedies should be
acted again, for the content and satisfaction of the University in the same   30
manner as before, but only with the Alteration of the Prologues and Epilogues.
...

Langbaine, English Dramatick Poets (1691)   Wing: L373
pp 53–4*   (30 August)   35
...

   Royal Slave, a Tragi-Comedy; presented to the King and Queen by the
Students of Christ Church in Oxford, August 30. 1636. Presented | since to
both Their Majesties at Hampton-Court by the King's Servants. This Play
gave such Content to Their Majesties, and the whole Court, as well for the   40
stately Scenes, the Richness of the Persian Habits, the excellency of the Songs,
(which were set by that admirable Composer, Mr. Henry Lawes, Servant to

his Majesty King Charles the First, in his publick and private Musick:) as for
the noble Stile of the Play it self, and the ready Address and graceful Carriage
of the Actors (amongst which Dr. Busby, the famous Master of Westminster
School approv'd himself a second Roscius); that they unanimously acknowledged
that it did exceed all things of that Nature which they had ever seen. The Queen   5
in particular so much admired it, that in November following, she sent for
the Habits and Scenes to Hampton-Court: she being desirous to see her own
Servants represent the same Play, (whose profession it was) that she might the
better judge of the several Performances, and to whom the Preference was due.
The Sentence was universally given by all the Spectators in favour of the Gown: 10
tho' nothing was wanting on Mr. Carthwright's side, to inform the Players as
well as the Scholars, in what belong'd to the Action and Delivery of each Part.
...

Verses Spoken in St John's Library   Bodl.: MS. Malone 21   15
ff 52v–3   *(30 August)*
...

      Verses spoken in St Iohns Library at ye Entertainment
           [at ye] of ye King and Queene anno 1636
As ye King and Queene ascended the Library staires a deepe base ran division   20
in Carolo Maria and was answerd on ye other side of the staires by a treble
running division Maria Carolo the Musicke ended appeares a young Scholler
as in a rapture saying |

Were they not Angells sung? did not mine eares   25
Drinke in a sacred Anthem from the spheares
Was I not blest with Charles & Maries name
Names wherein dwells all Musicke? tis the same
Hearke, I myselfe but spake Charles & Mary
And 'tis a Poem, nay tis a Library   30
                     he kneeles downe

All haile to your dread Majesty, whose power
Will deigne to feast in our Apollo's bower
And what place fitter for a royall payre
Then this where ev'ry booke presents a choice fare   35
Here Virgills well drest Venison, here the wine
Made Horace sing so sweet, here you may dine
With your rich Cleopatra's warlike love
Nay you feast and frolicke here with Iove
                points to the Gallory of Ivy 40

Next view the bower which is as yet all grene
Nor are there yett the rose and Lilly seene

A bower w*hich* had, 'tis true, beene beautify'd
With Catechiseing Arras on each side
But we ye Baptists sonnes did much desire
To make it like the dwelling of our sire
A groave or desart, wee (dread Leige) you'le guesse   5
Even our whole Colledge in a wildernesse
Your eyes and eares being fed tast of the feast
Which hath its pompe and glory from [the] ⌈its⌉ guest./

City Council Minutes   OCA: C/FC/1/A2/3   10
ff 12–12v*   *(12 August)*

…

It*em* [that pe] it is agreed that Pennilesse benche & Northgate [&] shalbe
whited & painted [at] & such other ∧⌈publyke⌉ places [amended] amendable
by this Cittie shalbe repaired by m*aste*r Chamberlain*es* as in their discrec*io*n*es* | 15
shalbe thought meet & needfull And they to be allowed for the same vppon
their Accompt/

It*em* [that] it is agreed [that eu*er*] at this Councell That any sume of money
not exceedinge one hundred Pownd*es* that shalbe thought fitt by m*aste*r Mayor   20
the Aldermen Thirteene & Bayliff*es* to be [vsed towardes] taken vppe for the
Citties vse ag*ains*t his Ma*ies*ties Cominge shalbe borrowed for this Cittie &
the seale of the Cittie geuen for the repayment thereof

…

                                                                        25

f 13*

…

Item it is agreed that these Citizens next vndernamed…

…

                                                                        30

ff 13v–14*

…

Shall on Munday the xxix^th of this instant August beinge the day on w*hich*
his Ma*ies*ties intendeth to com*m*e to this Cittie repaire to the Guihall of this
Cittie and from thence togeather w*ith* m*aste*r Mayor shall ride two and two   35
to meet the kinge accordinge to their places, eu*er*y Alderman and Assistant
ridinge vppon their foot clothes in their Skarlett gownes with Tippett*es* and
eu*er*y off them haueinge a footeman handsomlie suted all alike by his side and
both the[s] Bailliff*es* vppon ffooteclothes hauenge skarlett gownes and White
staues in their handes and rideinge next behind the assistant*es* and their   40

34/ Guihall: *for* Guildhall   39/ White: *corrected from* Whate
39/ hauenge: *corrected from* hauienge

Sargeants and some others behind them and all the rest of the Citizens aboue
named haueinge a satten doublett and other suteable apparell with Blacke
Coates and a handsome horse [g] & furniture and as many more Citizens as
shall please soe to fitt themselues shall alsoe ride before master Maior And all
this Companie before named shall meete the kinge at the farthest place of our   5
liberties or in some Convenient place[s] near thend of our ffranchises towards
wooluercutt when all that are in skarlet Master Recorder with the Towne clarke
and Mace bearer shall alight from their horses and Master Recorder | to make
an oration to his Maiestie And then Master Maior to present to his Maiestie at
the chardge of this Cittie a peece of plate or gloues and gloues to the Queenes   10
Maiestie and the Palsgraue as Master Maior and his bretheren and Master
Bailiffs shall thinke fitt
But it is agreed by this house that if any of these [house] Citizens shall ∧⌈not⌉
come [to] soe prepared as aforesaid Then he or they cominge soe vnprepared is
[not] to be put backe by order of this house And if any aboue named shall faile   15
herein haueinge noe iust cause to bee allowed by Master Maior Then euery
person soe failinge to forfeit .5 li. to the vse of this City to be levied by distresse
…

f 14v*   (5 September)   20
…

Item master Mayor shewed this house That his maiestes officers demaunded
35 li. for their ffees ouer & aboue 5 li. geuen by master Mayor [& x⟨.⟩] with the
consent of his brethren to ∧⌈the⌉ heraldes & [⟨..⟩] xx s. to the Coachman [& x s.
to the Trumpeters] & x s. to the kinges footemen & xx s. to the Queenes   25
footemen [And withall shewing That the same 35 li. so⟨.⟩] [wherevppon this
howse think] which ∧⌈35 li.⌉ [⟨…⟩] master Mayor hath not yet paid [as] it beinge
a farre greater some then euer was paid by this Cittie. But praieth the advize of
this howse who are [⟨….⟩] all vnwillinge to paie soe great a some if otherwise it
may be avoyded [But wherein] ⌈And therefore⌉ they desire master Mayor his   30
brethren & master Bayliffes to consider thereof & to [take ⟨..⟩] inquire whether
the [⟨…⟩] ∧⌈payment thereof⌉ may be avoyded & if not that then they would
doe therein as shall seeme best to them for the good of this Cittie And in the
meane ∧⌈tyme⌉ this howse doth allowe of the other ∧⌈particuler⌉ paymentes
[allreadie ⟨..⟩] aboue mencioned And if master Mayer shalbe questioned for   35
more payment thereof It is [fullie] ⌈vnanimouslie⌉ agreed by this howse That
he shalbe defended at the charge of this Cittie.
…

f 15*   (20 September)   40
…

Item [That] it is agreed that the dauncinge Schoole [so des⟨..⟩ed] latelie [⟨..⟩]
leased by this Cittie to Iohn Buseley and a lane held by Corpus Christi Colledge

shalbe viewed & [Co] the termes to ronne therein ⌈& the yearelie rent therof⌉ pervsed [And to that] in which [part] master mayor & [this] ⌈th⟨...⟩⌉ shall Accompany him at the viewing of the repaires are desired to doe/

City Council Minutes   OCA: C/FC/1/A1/003

f 68v*   *(23 September)*

...

A new Lease of the dauncinge Schoole graunted to Stoakes and Bossely

Item it is agreed that Iohn Bossely executor of his late father Iohn Bossely and William Stoakes who bredd vpp the said Iohn Bossely thexecutor and other the Children of the said Iohn Bossely Deceased shall haue a new Lease of the dauncinge Schoole vnder the old rent and Covenants with Capons for one and Twentie yeares for five poundes fyne

...

City Council Minutes   OCA: E.4.5

f 6v   *(23 August)*

...

It is agreed that the kinge shalbe presented with a [paire of gloues] Peece of plate about 4 or 5 and Twentie Pounde price and one paire of gloues And [for] that the Queene shalbe presented with another paire of gloues/ And likewise yat the Pallesgraue & his brother shalbe [lik] presented eache of them with a paire of gloues

...

f 7   *(30 August)*

...

It is agreed That in respect the heraldes haue dealt verie curteouslie with master Mayor & his brethren at his maiesties entrance into the Cittie in state five Poundes shalbe geuen them

...

f 7v*

Thomas davis
         &   } Master Bailiffes †
William Stephenes

Martin Wright esquire maior

The order of master Mayor and his Brethrens rideinge to meete kinge Charles the nyne and Twentith daie of August Anno domini 1636 togeither with the presentes which were presented vnto him & where togeather allso with the manner of their Rideinge in their Returne

ffirst Master Mayor his brethren & cittizenes herevnder named mett in the

guildhall of the said Cittie on the daie aforesaid about one of the Clocke
in the afternoon vppon Ringinge of the [⟨...⟩] Common Bell at Carfax
Churche viz.

master Mayor   5
master Recorder
master Alderman Potter
master Alderman Smith
master Alderman Sare
master Alderman Goode   All these ˰⌜Ride⌝ in Skarlett 10
mr Southam   & footeclothes (except the
mr Cooper   Recorder) who rode in a
mr Charles   blacke gowne & a footeclothe
°mr Harris°   [⟨.⟩] (most of them haueinge
mr Nixon   a footeman ˰⌜in [wh⟨...⟩]⌝ suite
                               of greene⌝ by their side & the 15
mr Chillingworth⎫   Alderman Boswell mayor & Aldermen & one
mr Cockram   ⎬ As deputies to mr dewe &   more [rideinge] haueinge
mr Thomas Smith⎭   mr willmott   Tippettes

⟨...... ..⟩vis ⎱ Bailiffes rideinge in Scarlett & footeclothes with white   20
⟨........⟩tephens ⎰ staves in their handes

⟨.⟩Towneclarke with his footecloth & a chaine of gold with a footeman
⟨.... .⟩ainten Macebearer with his footeman/

                                                                                   25
          mr Chambers   ⎫ mr hilliard   ⎫
          mr Reston   ⎪ mr Boweman   ⎪
          mr Griffin   ⎪ mr Shurley   ⎬ All these haueinge been
          mr Browne   ⎪ mr dennis   ⎪ Bailiffes or haueinge
⟨...⟩rowne mr Sympson   ⎪ mr hawkes   ⎭ Bailiffes places rode in
          mr Nicholas daniell⎬   satten doublettes   30
⟨....⟩ ⟨...⟩ mr Iones   ⎪
          mr whistler   ⎪
          mr Iohn Smith ⎪
          mr Thomas weekes⎭
                                                                                   35

Audited Corporation Accounts   OCA: P.5.2
f 230   *(Chamberlains' payments)*
...

Item paid for keepinge the Leades at the   40
kinges cominge   0 02 0
Item paid for eight Staves for the eight Constables   0 04 0

Item for two Sugarloues given to Mrs Smith
for the Steward*es* entertainment   1 11 8

...

f 232*   *(Keykeepers' receipts)*   5

...

Item paid to mr Painton the some of twenty five pound*es*
seaventeene shillinges and eight pence by him disbursed for
a paire of gloues presented to our hono*ra*ble Steward and for
ent*er*taininge his L*or*dshippe at his Com*m*inge to this Citty   10
in his Ma*ie*sties progresse hither   25 17 8

...

Item paid to mr Painton for foure paire of gloues for the
Kinges Ma*ie*stie the queenes Ma*ie*stie the Palsgroue and
duke Robert & for one silver & guilt bolle w*i*th a Cover   15
and for the Herald*es* and other of his Ma*ie*sties servant*es*   46 13 0

Indentures and Leases Book   OCA: D.5.6
f 5v*   *(26 September)*

                                                                              20

William ⎤   ⎤
Stoakes ⎥ and   ⎬ their Lease †
Iohn Bosseley ⎦   ⎦

This Indenture made the six and Twentith day of September in the
[Thirteenth] [Thirteenth] Twelfeth yeare of the raigne of our sou*er*aigne   25
Lord Charles by the grace of god kinge of England Scotland ffraunce and
Ireland defendor of the faith etc Betweene the Maior Bailiffes and Com*m*in*a*ltie
of the Cittie of Oxon. in the County of Oxon. of thone p*ar*te And William
Stokes of the said Cittie dauncinge Master and Iohn Bosseley of the said
Cittie dauncinge Master of the other p*ar*te witnesseth that the said Maior   30
Bailiffes and Com*m*in*a*ltie of their one assent & Consent for Diu*er*se good
causes and considerac*i*ons them therevnto especially movinge haue deuised
graunted and to ffarme letten And by these present*tes* for them and their
Successors doe deuise graunt and to ffarme lett vnto the said William Stokes
and Iohn Bosseley All that their vpper roome Soller or Chamber called or   35
knowne by the name of the dauncinge Schoole now in the Tenure of the
said William Stokes and Iohn Bossely togeather w*i*th the Stayres & passage
therevnto accustomed w*hi*ch said room sollar or Chamber is scituate lieinge &

24/ This Indenture: *in display script*
30/ witnesseth: *in display script*
32/ haue: *in display script*

beeinge neare vnto the Northgate of the said Cittie of Oxon. in the Countie
of Oxon. and reacheth over parcells of a Tenement and houses there now in
thoccupacion of william Hedges Butcher and extendeth throughout the whole
length thereof vnder a Certaine Cocklofte now in thoccupacion of the said
William Hedges And abbuteth Sowthward vppon certaine Roomes heretofore   5
Leased by the said Maior Bailiffes and Comminaltie vnto one Iohn Stacy
...

f 6v
...   10
...provided furthermore and it is Covenaunted by & betwixt the said parties
to these presentes That if the said William Stoakes and Iohn Bosselie their
executors administrators or assignes or any of them shall at any tyme or tymes
hereafter duringe the said tearme wittingly or willingly permitt or suffer his
or their Schollar or Schollars or any other person or persons whatsoeuer to   15
daunce in and vppon the said demised roome Sollar or Chamber or any parte
or parcell thereof betweene the houres of tenne of the Clocke in the night and
five of the Clocke in the morninge That then this present Indenture demise
and graunt and euery Article Clause and sentence herein conteyned shall cease
and be vtterly void Any thinge herein conteyned to the contrarie thereof in   20
any wise notwithstandinge...
...

St Martin Churchwardens' Accounts   ORO: PAR 207/4/F1/1, item 175
single mb col 1*   *(Rendered 25 May 1637)* *(Receipts)*   25
...

Inprimis Receaued att both the Hocktides   06   14   05
...

St Michael at the North Gate Churchwardens' Accounts   30
ORO: PAR 211/4/F1/3, item 199
single mb col 1   *(17 April 1636–9 April 1637)* *(Receipts)*
...
Item receiued at Hocktide   4   3   0
...   35

11/ provided: *in display script*
27/ Inprimis: *in display script*
27/ both the Hocktides: *25–6 April 1636 and 17–18 April 1637*
34/ Hocktide: *25–6 April 1636*

St Peter in the East Churchwardens' Accounts   ORO: PAR 213/4/F1/3
f 45*   *(26 April 1636–21 April 1637) (Receipts)*
...
Inprimis receiued for hocking money   3   14   0
...   5

f 45v   *(Expenses)*
...
To Goodman Mountague for cutting the weeds
from the Church wall and for carrying them away   10
against the Kings comming   0   0   6
...

Inventory of the Goods of George Payne   ORO: I 144/3/13
single mb*   *(28 January)*   15
...
It*em* 1 basevyoll 1 bandore 1 Cytherne 1 Cornet
w*i*th other instrum*en*ts   1 li. 0 0
...
                                                                                              20

1636–7
All Souls College Bursars' Accounts   Bodl.: MS. D.D. All Souls c.295
mb 11*   *(2 November–2 November) (Rewards)*
...
De vj li. v s. to M*aste*r vicechanceler for his Magistyes intertainement p*ate*t   25
per quitam
...

Balliol College Bursars' Accounts   BC Arch: Computi 1615–1662
f 128v   *(7 July–18 October 1637) (Expenses noted)*   30
...
It*em* to his M*a*iesties trumpeters   0. 10. 0.
...

Jesus College Bursar's Book   JC Arch: BU:AC:GEN:1   35
p 66   *(30 November–30 November) (Annuities)*
...
Vniversitie Musitians   00: 10: 0
...

4/ hocking: *Hocktide was 25–6 April 1636*   25/ M*aste*r vicechanceler: *Richard Baylie*

p 68 *(Various expenses)*

...

To Master Vicechancelor towards his Maiesties
entertainment, a 2d payment 02 10 0

... 5

Merton College Bursars' Accounts MCR: 3.2
f 21 *(29 July–18 November 1636) (External expenses)*

...

...Buccinatoribus Regijs 10 s.... 10

New College Bursars' Accounts NC Arch: 7656
mb 9 *(25 December–25 March) (Internal expenses)*

...

...Solutum Musicis Academicis 6 s. 8 d.... 15

...

(External expenses)
...Solutum to Doctor Baylie Vicechancelor for ye Kings intertaynment
12 li. 10 s. 0.... 20

...

The Queen's College Long Rolls QC Arch: LRC
f 17 col 2* *(7 July–7 July) (External expenses)*

... 25

Mauritio Fidicini 00 01 6

...

f 17v col 1

... 30

Aprili 7. Tibicinibus Vniuersitatis
Oxoniensis 00 10 00

...

St John's College Computus Annuus SJC Arch: Acc.I.A.21 35
f 22 *(25 December–25 March) (Internal and external expenses)*

...

Item allowed for 3 playes xl s./.

...

(Allowances)
Item ead*em* p*ro* Ludis   iij li. xviij d.
...
Item 13ᵃ [s] p*ro* Musicis   xiij li. vj s. viij d.
...   5

f 23   *(24 June–29 September) (Internal and external expenses)*
...
Item to ye Kings Trumpeters   x s.
...   10

SJC   ***Letter of the Vice-Chancellor to the Chancellor***   PRO: SP/16/344
f [2]*   *(16 January)*
...
Young Charles May p*re*sented us with a mock-shew on Saturday last, ye   15
subiect was slovenrie it selfe, ye marriage of Grobian's daughter, to Tantoblin;
but ye cariadg and acting soe hansom and cleane, that I was not better pleased
with a merriment these many yeares.
...
                                                                                                        20

Vice-Chancellors' Accounts   OUA: WP/β/21(4)
p 234   *(22 July 1636–7 August 1637) (Debits)*
...
It*em* de pecunijs receptis primâ et 2ᵈâ vice a Collegijs
et Aulis in excipiendo regiam Maiestatem.   718   9   4   25
...

(Extraordinary expenses)
Inprimis layd out in ye two Comedies att Christchurch
(ye third Comedie for his M*aie*sty being acted at St Iohns   30
Colledge at ye p*ro*per charge of his Grace) for ye Kings
entertainement vt patet p*er* billas   843 15 6

Letter of Edward Rossingham to Sir Thomas Puckering
BL: MS Harleian 7000   35
f [2v]   *(11 January)*

...Vpon 12.th night, The Royall Slaue, which had bene acted at Oxford before
their M*aie*sties the last sommer, was acted by the kings Players at Hampton

---

2/ eadem: *ie, the tenth week, 27 February–5 March*   4/ 13ᵃ: *ie, the thirteenth week, 20–6 March 1637*
   1636/7   15/ Saturday last: *14 January 1636/7*

Court. These Players had procurd from the vniversity, all there apparell and the Schenes w*h*ich the vniversity did not altogether approue of, but yet they sent them, but with a letter to my lord chamberlaine, that because they had provided that intertaynment for there ma*ie*sties only, ag*ain*st their coming to Oxford, they umbly besoght that what they had done for the intertaynment 5 of their ma*ie*sties might not bee made common vpon a stage, and this was the request of the vniversity in generall....

...

Thomas Crosfield's Diary   QC Library: MS 390   10
f 176v*   *(6 January)*

...

An abusiue booke reprehending the Archb*isho*p & B*isho*p of London – for goeing to playes at Oxford when ye King was there: some Copyes sent to Dr Fell, Dr Wilkinsen, Mr Rogers, Mr Hobbs – as tho they were approuers 15 of that Doctrine
Custome about this time in our Country .1. of Seeking ye flower in the well .2. of borrowing the frying pan – agmine in vno.

...

20

f 79v*

...

9. Musick [nigh] ⌈kept⌉ ⎰ 1. after chapter read Musica flatilis at ye
    vpo*n* ye day when ⎱   Hall window
                       2. in ye hall 3 lessons & a song by a boy 25
                       3. after dinner play'd first to m*aste*r Prouost
                       4. Returned into ye Hall & there, ye Conny
                          songs & some of Rob*er*t Luggs setting./

Burton, For God and the King (1636)   STC: 4141   30
pp 49–50*   *(5 November)*

Esay 22.12   ...Nor are they content, to abuse our pious Princes eares in the Pulpit, but
13. 14.   also on the Stage. O pyous, holy, reverend, grave, gracious Prelates, whose
        Academicall Entertainment of pious and religious Kings and Princes (in stead 35
        of learned and Scholasticall disputations, or exercises intable to the condition
        of a learned Academy) is a scurrilous Enterlude, and this in disgrace of that,
        which is the greatest beauty of our religion, to wit, true piety and vertue!...
        Nay, as if this had not been sufficient, this is done in the very heat and
        height of Gods Tragedy, still in Acting in the Imperiall City, when we were 40

23m/ 9.: 9 February 1636/7   36/ intable: *for* suitable

all mourning, yea, and every moment as | dying men. Was this a time then
of Entertaining the Court, and poysoning their eares with Enterludes, and
thereby provoking the Lord further to plague the Kings good people, when
you should rather have mooved his Majesty (whom you & wee al know to be
forward enough to hearken to such a motion) to have called a true Fast, with   5
Prayer and Preaching over the Land? And was that a time of Enterludes? Why
did you not feare some Plague to grow in such a mighty assembly? When
notwithstanding Preaching is made dangerous by you, for feare of the plague;
which should be a meanes (as it hath beene formerly) to drive away the plague,
by bringing the people to true humiliation and reformation. Whereas your   10
guelded Fast-book (contrary to the Proclamation) I am sure brought us for a
hansell, a double increase of the Plague that weeke, to any weeke since the
Plague began: and most terrible weather withall, to the Kings great losse, and
the Mercheants, the angry countenance of heaven ever since pouring Gods
wrath upon this your hypocritical Mockfast. But by the way take this with   15
you: As, when the Lord calls to Fasting, you fall a Feasting: So there is a hand
writing over you on the wall, the prophet Esay will tell you from the Lord,
Surely this iniquity shall never be purged away from you, till ye dye sayeth
the Lord. But now do not exclame, as if I spake against such intertainment
of our Gracious Soveraigne, & his noble Court, as is indeed honorable, grave,   20
and sutable to such a Majesty & Traine, for whom I am ready to Sacrifice my
deerest blood, if need were....

Burton, *A Divine Tragedie* (1636)   STC: 4140.7
p 12*   25
...

Example. 32.

Also at Oxford a carpenter undertaking to mend a Stage in S. Iohns
Colleidge on the Satturday night, for the finishing wherof he must of
necessity spent some part of the Lords day morning, that the Stage might   30
be ready against the Munday following, he that night fell backward from
the Stage, being not farre from the ground, and brake his neck, and so
ended his life in a fearfull Tragedy.

...
    35

p 46*

Bishops saith Augustine Contra Bril. l.3 c.6.) were all wont vaine dances to

---

30/ spent: *for* spend
38/ Augustine Contra Bril. l.3 c.6: *for* Augustine Contra parm. l.3 c.6; *reference is to Augustine's* Contra
    epistulam Parmeniani *3.6(29)*
38/ Contra ... c.6.): *opening parenthesis omitted*

reprove, But now they are so farre from it, that they to dance doe love. Thomas
Lovel his Dialogue. Witnes their late Oxford prophane plaies and dances. †
Neh.13.17.18.   …ye that in these dolefull daies of Plague and pestilence suppresse, neglect
all publike fasting, preaching and praying, which now if ever should be cried
up & practised, and in stead thereof give your selves, over to dancing, feasting,   5
playing, Sabbath breaking, so draw downe more wrath and plagues upon us…
…

Heylyn, A Briefe and Moderate Answer (1637)   STC: 13269
pp 75–6   10
…

  Hitherto for the generalls. And there are some particulars, on which you
spend your malice more than all the rest; you descant trimmely, as you thinke,
in the Newes from Ipswich, on my Lord of Canterbury, with your Arch-pietie,
Arch-charitie, if Belzebub himselfe had beene Arch-bishop, | Arch-agent for   15
the devill, and such like to those. A most triumphant Arch indeed to adorne
your victories. His costly and magnificent enterteinment of the king at Oxford,
you cry out against in your sayd Pulpit libell, for a scurrilous enterlude, made in
disgrace of that which is the greatest beauty of our religion, to wit true pietie,
and learning: and will him in his shrift to confesse, how unseemely it was for   20
him, that pretendeth to succeede the Apostles, p. 49.…

pp 78–9

…First for the enterteinment, of his Majestie at the universitie, tell me I pray   25
you of all loves, how would you have contrived it better, had you beene master
of the Ceremonies for that place and time? Would you have had a sermon?
Why the king had one. Would you have fitted him with Academicall exercises?
there was as little want of that: Orations in the fields, the Church, the Colledges,
the Convocation, and the Library. Would you have left out playes? When did   30
you ever know an Academicall enterteinment of the king without them. Would
you have had the playes in Latine? Consider that the Queene | was a principall
guest, and they were commanded to be in English. But sir conceale your griefe
no longer. I know what tis that troubles you, and makes you call it scurrillous
enterlude, and say that it was made in disgrace of pietie. All that offends you   35
is, that Melancholico, a Puritan passion in one of the commedies, was in
conclusion marryed to Concupiscentia; In case you doe not like the wedding,
why did you not come thither to forbid the banes. The Spartans used to shew
their drunken slaves unto their children, the better to deterre them from so
base a vice. And how know you but that the representing of that humour on   40

3m/ Neh.13.17.18.: *Neh 13.17–18*

the open stage, may let men see the follies of it, and so weane them from it.
But however the person you so grossely abuse, could not possibly have leisure,
farther than in the generall to command all things should be without offence,
which he most carefully did....

5

Mr Moore's Revels   Bodl.: MS. Ashmole 47
ff 122v–6*

...

Mr Moores revells nere
Eastgate in Oxon. 1636 |

10

The Prologue
ffaine would wee say youre welcome but we knowe
Till you please, wee can't truely tell you soe
Tis not the table richly spread with meate   15
That can enforce ye Peevish guest to eate
Well may the entertainer doe his best,
But tis th'acceptance maks his cheere a feast
I'le ffetch what w'have prepar'd but know not till
y'approove of't whether w'have done well or ill   20
your censure maks it eyther thus you see
T'is you must make ye welcome and not we
Now since your welcome lyes in your owne powers
If y'are not wellcome t'is your fault not ours
1   25
     Then came in ye Anti-masque being
     six moores (mr moore himselfe being
     one) having six blacke buckram
     coats laced with yellow straw
     each of them bearing a javlin in   30
     his hand
See what I have brought you here I thinke ther's none
Will doubt whether these negroes are our owne
Where should ye sutty visag'd Indian nest
But here? or where ye moare but here i the east   35
Where some of these are natives but ye rest
Are strangers meerely come at their request |
To doe them service: and theyle not dispayre
Though theyre blacke you'le bee candid as y'are ffayre

24/ ours: *a horizontal line extending across the page*   35/ i: *for* in
   separates the prologue from the anti-masque

If with your countenance they may bee grac't
They're sure to well ffavour'd though ill fac't
If by your smiles their sports may be advanct
Though th'are ill visag'd y'are well countenanc't
If you'le proclaime them candid who'le deny   5
Th'are whit who dare say blacke vnto their eye
When with such ffavour t'have your censure past
None will bee soe vnnaturall as't cast
Their blacknesse in their teeth which nature set
Like studs of Ivory in a fframe of jet   10
Let none suspect their innocence or ffeare
Their harmelesse hands though armed with a speare
These inoffensive javelins were design'd
ffor noe intent but this to be resign'd
vnto your feete, I'me sure they cold not grace   15
their vallour, yats best embleam'd by their fface
ere theyle looke Pale or white or blush they'le dye
Their nere fforsake their colours though they ffly
But yet they came not hither to expresse
Their active armes but their feet and nimblenesse   20
Afford them but a circle ere they'le part
They'le erayse theire nimble spirits by their blacke art, |
Could they but cast their figures here you'd ffind
six spirits raysed without a conjuring wind
such as is wont to spoyle a churches paint   25
And curse vs with ye downe fall of a saint
soe harmelesse are these sports yat women may
veiw as securely as a puppy play
Ile leave them to your censure you yat know
Better then they can beg how to bestow   30
ffreely your suffrage, may you please to deign
your prosperous smyles vnto them may th'obtaine
your wonted ffavour which theyle strive to doe
Their grand and Mr Moore shall thanke you too
And count this title cheif'st of his renoune   35
To pay such annuall tributes to his crowne
    The six moores danc't, after which
    being ended they left ye stage and went
    downe to lay aside their blacke-coats

2/ to: *for* to be   18/ Their: *for* They'le
8/ as't: *for* as t'

And to come vp againe and dance a
country dance made purposely ffor
them in ye meane while ffoure litle
boyes drest ffor apes stole a way
ffoure of their coates who soe soone   5
As ye moores left ye stage each of
the Apes had an inkehorne in his
hand to blacke themselves |
To resemble ye moores and yat they might
see to doe it exactly one of them   10
had a lookinglasse; ye speech
The ioyffull moore hath chang'd his native hew
And pensive sable being made ffayre by you
H'as left his mourning weeds chusing to bee
Invested with your glorious livery;   15
Since hees your candidate after this night
Since y'have smild of's blackenesse heele be white
          But yats not all my message
I've brought a second course here by their shaps
Each courteous eye may reade them to be Apes   20
But if here any curious critticks bee
Soe well verst in Apes Physiognomy
As mistrust them heres a glasse will show
If theyle looke in't whether th're apes or no
But should wee dresse them by each censures glasse   25
That which we mean't an ape might proove an asse
But to returne to our owne apes this messe
Of mimicks have seene th' moores expresse
Themselves soe nimbly here are come to trye
If they could counterfeit activitye   30
If you'le but clap them on I know theyle skip
ffreelye without ye menace of a whippe
ffayne would they imitate them in their looke |
And smutty visage else they nere had tooke
Such paines as these vnlesse they'd an intent   35
To try ye ladyes new experiment
Who spot and blacke their ffaces to repayre
Theire white who vse to foule their ffaces ffayre
Had you nere seene these coats before you'd guesse
Th'were ne[a]re made ffor them by their tediousnesse   40
Taylo[u]rs you know good honest souls wont wrong
Their customers to make their cloths too long

They stole this ffrom ye AEthiops which shows
Their fingers are ffarre nimbler then their toes
since they're soe nimble ffinger'd it were meete
They'd [stann⟨.⟩] ⌐dance¬ vppon their hands steale with their ffeete
But ffeare them not Ile warrant you theyle proove   5
Theeves onely in this to steale a way your love
  After these had danced ffollowed ye
  grand masque ffor eight and after
  yat ye masques single, and ffrench dances
  And a country dance made purposely [ffor them]   10
  ffor yem at the end of which one of [th] which one
  of them concluded ye revells with this Epilogue
your pardon and our thanks ye last wee vow
In ffull obsequiousnesse as due to you
The former wee could begg with fawning knee   15
And ffainted grudge without Idolatrye; |
But twere too superstitious wee but aske
That every modest dance night were a masque
That with your charity as you thinke meete
you'd cover ye transgressions of your ffeete   20
Had not some daring spirit prest within
The confines of our circle here had beene
more order and lesse error but wee ffinde
our starrs are good since your aspects are kind
The harmelesse shades are layd againe but you   25
must give an Item to our spirits too
our leggs being weakened goodnesse commands
you'd lead vs off by your asisting hands
  The second night being ye last
  Publique night had ye same   30
  speeches onely a new Epilogue
Our sports have here their Period and wee [see]
must circumcise our halting orchestrye
The Genius of the times forbids this art
ffor who can rightly rayse an heavy hart?   35
If any crime hath here committed beene
Count it your fault to encourage vs to sinne
ffor whilst your goodnesse blest vs with a smile
Our ffrisking soules danc't Anticke all ye while

11/ of which one of [th] which one: *dittography*
16/ ffainted: *for* ffained (?)

within ye duller earth our brests and wee
did ffeare ye stones would practise dancery
If envy wrong vs still with ffalse report
wee claime ye ffreedome of a schollers Court |
If this grand Iury say w" have err'd [this while] tis true   5
Our guilty or not guilty comes ffrom you
yet loath would every soule yat sins by night
Have all his workes of darkenesse brought to light
ffor severall ffaults wee here arraigned stand
expecting our last sentence ffrom your hand   10
  The third night being private ffor
  Gentlewomen, had onely a new
  Prologue ye epilogue was ye same
  with the ffirst Publique night
ffayre ones why fflocke you hither? what have wee   15
you can expect besids deformitye?
Perhaps was this you came ffor to expresse
your Beautyes lustre by our vglinesse
The sparkling Diamond's then most clearely set
When t[h]is incircled in a Pale of Iet   20
The radiant Lustre of ye Pearle appeares
Best when it dangles in an AEthiops eares
The glorious day would not seeme halfe so bright
were it nere muffled with its foyle ye night
And may our blacklings which Ile ffetch bee made   25
your beautyes ff[l]oyle may they become your shade
youle worke a miracle beyond our hope
you'le wash a black ˄⌐a⌐ more without a trope

City Council Minutes   OCA: C/FC/1/A1/003   30
f 74   *(22 May)*
 ...

Stokes &
Boseley their
Lease graunted
to bee sealed/.

Item it is agreed that the Lease of the dauncinge Schoole graunted to William
Stokes and Iohn Bosley and now reade shalbee sealed soe that there bee
inserted a Clause for a couple of Capons yearely or foure shillinges in lieu   35
thereof at theleccion of *Master* Maior for the tyme beeinge/ Togeather with
a lycence if they shall desire the same/.
 ...

5/ w" have: *for* wee have *or* w'have *(?)*
19/ then: n *corrected from* re

f 75v*   *(18 September)*

...

A Lease of the dauncinge Scoole graunted to William Stoakes & Iohn Boseley with a lycence of 10 yeares

Item at this Councell it is agreed that the Lease of the dauncinge Scoole now reade and graunted to William Stokes and Iohn Bosely shalbee sealed with the Seale of this Cittie And that they shall haue a lycence for lettinge the   5
same for tenne yeares or under to such persons as Master Maior for the tyme beeinge and the rest of the Thirteene with the Bailiffes for the yeare or the maior parte of them shall vnder their hands giue consent vnto/.

...

10

1637–8
All Souls College Bursars' Accounts   Bodl.: MS. D.D. All Souls c.295
mb 10   *(2 November–2 November)* *(Various expenses)*

De xx s. to the Kings Trumpetters   15
...

Balliol College Bursars' Accounts   BC Arch: Computi 1615–1662
f 134v   *(7 July–18 October 1638)* *(Expenses noted)*
...   20
Item Buccinatoribus Regijs   0 10 0
...

Brasenose College Bursars' Roll of Account   BNC Arch: U.B.21
f 60v   *(21 December–21 December)* *(Gifts and rewards)*   25
...
December 25. Paid to ye Piper in ye Hall   xij d.
December 26. Paid to ye Whitney Singers   xij d.
...
March .27 Giuen to Piper in the Hall   vj d. 30
...
August: 4. Giuen by Master Principal to ye
Kings Trumpetters   xx s.
...

35

Jesus College Bursar's Book   JC Arch: BU:AC:GEN:1
p 77   *(30 November–30 November)* *(Annuities)*
...
Vniversity Musitians   01 10 00
...   40

p 80   *(Various expenses)*

...

To His Maiestys Trumpeters   00 10 00

...

Magdalen College Liber Computi   MC Arch: LCE/23

f 3v   *(Internal and external payments)*

...

Buccinatoribus regis   1 li. 0 s. 0 d.

...

New College Bursars' Accounts   NC Arch: 7657

mb 7   *(25 December–25 March)* *(Internal expenses)*

...

...So*lutum* Musicis Academicis 6 s. 8 d....

...

(24 June–29 September)

...So*lutum* to ye Kings Trumpetters 10 s. 0...

...

Oriel College Treasurers' Accounts   OC Arch: S I.C.1

f 323   *(Internal expenses)*

...

Ite*m* Buccinatoribus Regijs   00 10 00

...

The Queen's College Long Rolls   QC Arch: LRC

f 18v col 2   *(7 July–7 July)* *(External expenses)*

...

Ian 2. Tibicinibus Oxon*iæ* eo die quo
hospites invitavimus   0   5   0

...

Tibicinib*us* Oxon*iæ* pro Antelucana Musica
tempore brumalj   0   10   0

...

Mauritio Tibicinj Ian 1.º   0   1   6

...

f 20 col 2   *(7 July 1638–7 July 1639)*

...

Imprimis Aug*usti* 21. Buccinatoribus D*omi*nj Regis   1   0   0

...

St John's College Computus Annuus   SJC Arch: Acc.I.A.22
p 43   *(25 December–25 March)* *(Internal and external expenses)*
...

Item allowed for ye Founders Shew   xxx s./.
...   5

p 44   *(25 March–24 June)* *(Allowances)*
...
Item *pro* Musicis   xvij li. ix s. iiij d.
...   10

p 45   *(24 June–29 September)*
...
Item to his Maiesties Trumpeters   xx s.
...   15

Trinity College Bursars' Books   TC Arch: I/A/3
f 72   *(25 March–24 June)* *(Expenses)*
...
Buccinatoribus regijs   10 s.   20
...

University College General Accounts   UC Arch: BU2/F1/1
p 90   *(17 March 1637/8–22 March 1638/9)* *(Minor expenses)*
...   25
To the Kings Trumpetters   0 16 0
...

H.L., Jests from the Universitie (1638)   STC: 15105
pp 15–16   30

On a Welchman in Oxford.
At a stageplay in Oxford, a Cornish man was brought forth to wrestle with
foure Welchmen, one after the other, and when he had put them all to the
worst, hee called out a loud have you any more Welchmen? which words a   35
scholler of Iesus Colledge, being himselfe of the Brittish Nation I tooke in
great endagine, insomuch that he leapt upon the stage and threw the Player
in earnest, and saide have you any more, &c.
...
                                                                                      40
pp 22–3*
...

On a Player coughing.

A Player being slain upon the stage, was troubled with a suddain cough, which hee endeavouring to suppresse was mani-|festly seene to shake and move, and at last did cough indeed. At which the Spectators laughing, one of his owne Company standing by, said that hee was wont to drinke in his pottage.

...   5

City Council Minutes   OCA: C/FC/1/A1/003
f 85*   *(3 September)*

...

Sampsons
sonne &
William
Hilliard & his
eldest sonne
made free

nonne but
Apprentices to
Musitions
shalbe admitted
ffree

Item at this Counsell it is agreed that Sampsons sonne and William Hilliard   10
and his eldest sonne beeinge the Cittie waytes shalbee admitted free of this
Cittie for the officers ffees, and a leather buckett, But it is agreed that hereafter
none but the[ir] Apprentices of such Musitions as shalbee free of this Cittie
shalbee admitted to bee of the Cittie Waytes And it is further agreed that
euery one of these three Musitions shalbee bound to prepare Scutchens with   15
silver Chaines at their own Chardges and to Leaue the same to this Cittie at
their death or other leauing of their places And this bond to bee taken before
they are made or els some sufficient man to vndertake that they shall seale
such bondes

                                                                                              20

Audited Corporation Accounts   OCA: P.5.2
f 238   *(Chamberlains' payments)*

...

Item paid to the kinges Trumpetters   00   10   00

...   25

Cordwainers' Minutes   Bodl.: MS. Morrell 20
f 86   *(Rendered 9 November)* *(Payments at the dinner)*

...

Item to the Musicke   0 6 0   30

...

St Martin Churchwardens' Accounts   ORO: PAR 207/4/F1/1, item 179
single mb col 1   *(Rendered 12 May 1639)* *(Receipts)*

...   35

Inprimis receaved att Hocktide   04   04   04
Item receaved at Whitsontide & midsomer
for money then gained   16   00   00
Item receaved for the Maypole   00   15   00

...   40

36/ Inprimis: *in display script*   37/ Whitsontide: *16–22 May 1638*
36/ Hocktide: *5–6 April 1638*

Archdeacon's Court Book   ORO: MS.Oxf.Arch. papers Oxon.c.13
f 306*   *(16 December)*

contra Edwardum Brookes parochie sancti Michaelis for working vpon St
Andrewes day last past   5
Citatus personaliter die Martis vltimo per Tomlinson iuratum &c. facta 3ª.
preconizacione &c. Comparuit: iuratus &c. et obiecto provt supra negat
that hee [onlie] did worke on St Andrewes day last nor his servantes to his
knowledge but if they did it was contrary to his will for hee did forbid
in proximum: them to doe it. Unde Dominus decrevit ffamulos citandos &c: 10
contra Iacobum Dudley eiusdem parochie Similiter
Citatus similiter &c. facta 3ª. preconizacione &c Comparuit: et fatetur that
hee did worke on St. Andrewes day about the Stage at Baliol Colledge which
was to bee suddenly finished Unde Dominus monuit eum to doe soe noe more.
Et ad interessendum in proximo ad videndum vlteriorem processum &c: 15
contra Iohannem Watson parochie sancti Thome Similiter:
Citatus similiter &c facta 3ª. preconizacione &c: Comparuit et Respondet
similiter per omnia: Et monitus similiter &c
contra Iohannem Symmonds et Thomam Coxe eiusdem parochie
Quesiti Die predicto &c per Tomlinson iurati &c: Comparuerunt et fatentur   20
similiter & dominus monuit similiter vt supra:

…

1638–9
Jesus College Bursar's Book   JC Arch: BU:AC:GEN:1   25
p 88   *(30 November–30 November)* *(Annuities)*

…

Vniversity Musitions   00 10 0

…
                                                                              30

Magdalen College Liber Computi   MC Arch: LCE/24
f 3v   *(Internal and external payments)*

…

Musicis pro festo Bursariorum   0 5 0

…
                                                                              35

Merton College Bursars' Accounts   MCR: 3.2
f 32v   *(27 July–23 November 1638)* *(External expenses)*

…regijs buccinatoribus 10 s.…   40

…

8/ St Andrewes day last: *30 November 1637*

New College Bursars' Accounts   NC Arch: 7660
mb 8   *(25 December–25 March)* *(Internal expenses)*

...

...*Solutum* Musicis Academicis 6 s. 8 d....

...   5

The Queen's College Long Rolls   QC Arch: LRC
f 20 col 2   *(7 July–7 July)* *(External expenses)*

...

Ian*uarij* 1. Mauritio Tibicinj   0   1   6   10
Tibicinibus Oxon*iæ* pro Antelucana Musicâ
tempore brumalj   0 10   0

...

St John's College Computus Annuus   SJC Arch: Acc.I.A.23   15
f 71v*   *(25 December–25 March)* *(Internal and external expenses)*

...

It*em* allowed towards ye founders shew   L s.
...

                                                                         20
(Allowances)
Item 11ᵃ *pro* Musicis   xx li. ij s. iiij d.
...
Item 12ᵃ *pro* Ludis Scenicis   v li. v s.
...   25

St John's College Short Book   SJC Arch: Acc.III.D.4
f 72*   *(Loans)*

...

x   Item lent to ye Musitians. 10bris. 10º   4 10   0   30
...
x   Item Lent to ye Musitions   3   0   0
...
x   Item lent ye Musitians Mar*ch* 11
    ⌐*(signed)* Thomas *Curtise*⌐   2   0   0   35
...
x   Impr*imis* to Mr Atkinson for ye Playes
    ut p*atet* *per* billas Computi   v li. xix s. vij d.
                (signed) Thomas Atkinson.

...   40

22/ 11ᵃ: *ie, the eleventh week, 4–10 March 1638/9*   24/ 12ᵃ: *ie, the twelfth week, 11–17 March 1638/9*

x Item paid to Thomas Halwood Musician
(signed) ⌜Thomas Halwod⌝ iiij s.

…

f 72v 5

[Payd to Mr Atkinson for ye Playes as appeares
by his hande verso folio v li. xix s. vij d.]

…

10

Vice-Chancellors' Accounts OUA: WP/β/21(4)
p 239 *(16 July–13 July) (Extraordinary expenses)*

…

Item for Gloves given att Woodstock when
ye King was there 26 10 0 15

…

Item to ye Kings Trumpetters 1 0 0

…

Robert Woodforde's Diary NC Arch: 9502 20
f [297]

9o. Iulij 1639
I prayed and went to Oxford … the act ended this day.

… 25

10o Iulij
This place here is prodigiously profane I perceave for drunkennesse swearinge
& other debauched Courses, stage playes &c Lord reforme these seminaryes if
it be thy will for the Lordes sake.

… 30

Hannisters' Registers OCA: L.5.2
f 340

…

Willelmus Hilliard Iohannes Hilliard and William Stronge Musitions 35
gratis admissi fuerunt in Libertates huius Ciuitatis soluendo tantum feoda
officiariorum et quilibet eorum sitelle Corporate Et prestiterunt sacramenta
sua corporalia [v] &c/.

…

35/ Willelmus … Stronge: *in display script*

Audited Corporation Accounts   OCA: P.5.2
f 241v   *(Chamberlains' payments)*

...

Item for tenne dozen of Bread when M*aste*r Maior			
went the ffranchises	00	10	00
Item paid for six dozen of Cakes two cheeses &			
one Barrell of Beare att the same tyme	00	19	08
Item to Mr Penn for the vse of his potts & for			
such as were broken & lost att the ffranches	00	03	04
Item to Mr Rayman for thofficers and botemens			
dinner at the ffranchises	01	11	00
Item to the drummers att the same tyme	00	05	00
Item to the ffreemen that went the ffranchises to			
drinke when they come home	00	10	00
Item to six boatemen for rowinge M*aste*r Maior			
at ye ffranches	00	04	00

...

Item to George Tredwell for laieinge two plancke*s*			
at the ffranchises in Ch*ris*tchurch meade	00	01	00

...

St Mary Magdalen Churchwardens' Accounts   ORO: PAR 208/4/F1/64
single mb   *(Rendered 7 April 1640) (Receipts)*

...

⟨.⟩tem Receyued att hocktide   iiij li. iij s.

...

1639–40

Brasenose College Junior Bursars' Accounts   BNC Arch: A.8.10
f 17v*   *(21 December–25 March) (Expenses noted)*

...

giuen the Whitney men	0	01	0

...

Jesus College Bursar's Book   JC Arch: BU:AC:GEN:1
p 99   *(30 November–30 November) (Annuities)*

...

Vniuersity Musitians	1	0	00

...

4/ M*aste*r Maior: *Thomas Smith*
25/ hocktide: *22–3 April 1639*

Magdalen College Liber Computi   MC Arch: LCE/25
f 3v   *(Internal and external payments)*

...

Musicis pro festo Bursariorum   0 5 s. 0

...   5

New College Bursars' Accounts   NC Arch: 7661
mb 9   *(25 December–25 March)* *(Internal expenses)*

...

...Solutum Musicis Academicis 6 s. 8 d.   10

...

The Queen's College Long Rolls   QC Arch: LRC
f 21v col 1   *(7 July–7 July)* *(External expenses)*

...   15

Ianuarij 1 Mauritio tibicini   0   1   6

...

Tibicinibus Oxoniæ pro antelucanâ Musicâ
tempore brumali   0   10   0

...   20

St John's College Computus Annuus   SJC Arch: Acc.I.A.24
f 23   *(25 December–25 March)* *(Allowances)*

...

Item Impositi for a play ⌈°Hebdomada. 5ta.°⌉   v li. viij s. v d. 25

...

Item set on for the Musitians bill ⌈°Hebdomada. 13.°⌉   xvj li. ij s. iiij d.

...

f 24   *(24 June–29 September)* *(Internal and external expenses)*   30

...

Item towarde ye Founders Show att Christmas   xx s.

...

Thomas Crosfield's Diary   QC Library: MS 390   35
f 87*

...

1.   1. Morrice ye gardiner goeing to euery fellowes chamber with Musike 6 d.
     or 12 d. of each

     ...   40

25/ Hebdomada. 5ta.: *20–6 January 1639/40*   38m/ 1.: *1 January 1639/40*
27/ Hebdomada. 13.: *16–22 March 1639/40*

City Council Minutes   OCA: C/FC/1/A1/003
f 103*   (17 February)

...

Item William Stronge sonne of Sampson Stronge is elected to bee one of the
Musitions of this Cittie in the roome of George Paine deceased soe that he   5
first become bound for redeliuerie of the as other the Musitions are/

...

Audited Corporation Accounts   OCA: P.5.2
f 244v   (Chamberlains' payments)   10

...

Item paid to William Laude for beare for the freemen
when they Came from the ffranchises   00   10   00
Item paid George Tredwell for Laieing twoe plancks
for Master Maior when he went the ffranchises   00   01   00 15
Item paid then to Richard Cooke for twoe Drummes   00   05   00
Item paid then to boatemen that rowed Master Maior
for their Dinners   00   15   00
Item for a barrell of beare at the ffranchises and the
Carriage thereof   00   10   00 20
Item for bread Cheese and Cakes at the same tyme   00   19   00

...

Item paid Mr Rayman for the officers Dinners when
Master Maior went the ffranchises   01   00   00
...   25

Cordwainers' Minutes   Bodl.: MS. Morrell 20
f 89v   (Rendered 6 November) (Payments at the dinner)

...

Item to the Musitions at the Dinner   0 6 0 30
...

St Martin Churchwardens' Accounts   ORO: PAR 207/4/F1/1, item 181
single mb col 1   (Rendered 25 May 1641) (Receipts)

...   35
Item Receaved for the Hocking money   03   00   00

...

6/ of the: word omitted; probably scutchen as in OCA: C/FC/1/A2/3, f 71
15/ Master Maior: John Smith
36/ Hocking: Hocktide was 13–14 April 1640

St Mary Magdalen Churchwardens' Accounts   ORO: PAR 208/4/F1/65
mb [1]   *(Rendered 27 April 1641) (Receipts)*

...

Rece*yve*d att Hocktide   iiij li. iiij s.

...   5

St Peter in the East Churchwardens' Accounts   ORO: PAR 213/4/F1/3
f 51v   *(7 April 1640–28 April 1641) (Receipts)*

...

Item of the Hockers   3   16   0   10

...

1640–1
Brasenose College Junior Bursars' Accounts   BNC Arch: A.8.11
f 21   *(25 March–24 June) (Expenses noted)*   15

...

giuen to the Whitney singers at Chr*is*tmasse   0   01   06
giuen to the Pyper of Hincsey   0   01   06.

...   20

f 59v   *(29 September–21 December)*

...

giuen ye piper of Whitney   0   01   6

...   25

Jesus College Bursar's Book   JC Arch: BU:AC:GEN:1
p 111   *(30 November–30 November) (Annuities)*

...

Vniversity Musicians   01   00   00

...   30

New College Bursars' Accounts   NC Arch: 7663
mb 9   *(25 December–25 March) (Internal expenses)*

...

...So*lu*tum Musicis Academicis 6 s. 8 d.   35

...

The Queen's College Long Rolls   QC Arch: LRC
f 23 col 1   *(7 July–7 July) (External expenses)*

...   40

Mauritio Tibicini Ian*u*ar*ij* 1   0   1   6

4/ Hocktide: *13–14 April 1640*   10/ Hockers: *Hocktide was 13–14 April 1640*

Tibicinib*us* Oxoni*æ* *pro* Musicâ Antelucanâ
tempore brumali   0   10   0

...

St John's College Computus Annuus   sJc Arch: Acc.i.A.25   5
f 24*   *(25 December–25 March) (Allowances)*

...

Item 12ª *pro* Musicis   vj li. xv s. viij d.

...
                                                                              10

Audited Corporation Accounts   oca: P.5.2
f 247v   *(Chamberlains' payments)*

...

Item for Cakes Bred & Chese at the ffranchizes   1   1   4
Item for a Barrell of Beare and Caridge of the same   15
at the same time   0   10   0
Item for a Kinderkin of Beare for the ffreemen when
they came from the ffranchizes   0   5   0
Item to George Tredwell for laieinge the plancks at
the ffranchizes in *Christ* Church meade   0   1   0 20
Item to Richard Cooke for Two drom*m*es at the
same time   0   5   0
Item for the Boatemen at the same time   0   16   0

...
                                                                              25

1641–2
Jesus College Bursar's Book   Jc Arch: BU:AC:GEN:1
p 122   *(30 November–30 November) (Annuities)*

...

The Univirsitie Musitians   01   00   00 30

...

p 125*   *(Various expenses)*

...

The Hocking women for two yeares   00   05   00 35

...

The Trumpeters of ye Earle of Pembroke and
other Lords for Ireland   00   05   00

...

8/ 12ª: *ie, the twelfth week, 15–21 March 1640/1*

Lincoln College Calculus 1641–2   LC Arch
f 15   *(5 June–3 December 1642)*   *(Internal expenses)*
...

To ye Kings Trumpeters Iuly 9   x s.
...

To ye Kings trumpeters 10 s.
...

Magdalen College Liber Computi   MC Arch: LCE/27
f 3v   *(Internal and external expenses)*
...

Buccina*toribus* Regijs   1 li.
...

Merton College Bursars' Accounts   MCR: 3.2
f 56   *(18 March–29 July)*   *(External expenses)*
...

...Buccinatoribus per Vicecustodem 6 s. 8 d....
...

New College Bursars' Accounts   NC Arch: 7665
mb 10   *(25 December–25 March)*   *(Internal expenses)*
...

...So*lutum* Musicis Academicis 6 s. 8 d.
...

Oriel College Treasurers' Accounts   OC Arch: S I.C.1
f 341   *(Internal expenses)*
...

Ite*m* Buccinatoribus quorundam Nobilium   00 05 00
...

The Queen's College Long Rolls   QC Arch: LRC
f 24v col 2   *(7 July–7 July)*   *(External expenses)*
...

Tibicinibus Oxoni*æ*   0   10   0
...

Mauritio tibicini Ian*uarij* 1   0   1   6.
...

St John's College Computus Annuus   SJC Arch: Acc.I.A.25
f 25v*   *(29 September–20 November) (Expenses)*

...

Item left to pay for the playes   iij li. x s.

...   5

St John's College Computus Annuus   SJC Arch: Acc.I.A.26
f 24*   *(25 December–25 March) (Allowances)*

...

Item 11o *pro* Musicis   v li. ix s. viij d.   10

...

St John's College Short Book   SJC Arch: Acc.III.D.4
f 29*   *(Loans)*

...   15

[Musitions bill. 6 li. 15 s. 8 d.
Item Lent Stacy & Curtis in part of their bill
thirty shillings   xxx s.
                    (signed) Iohn Stacie
                    (signed) Thomas Curtise]   20

...

University College General Accounts   UC Arch: BU2/F1/1
p 155   *(25 March 1642–24 March 1642/3) (Minor expenses)*

...   25
Item to the Princes Trumpetters   0 10 0
Item to the Princes Footmen   0 6 0
Item to the Kings Footmen   0 15 0
Item to Prince Ruperts Trumpetters   0 7 0
Item to ye Drummers of Ye Lifeguard   0 2 6   30
Item to ye Kings, Princes, & Dukes Coachmen   0 7 0
Item to ye Kings Trumpiters   0 5 0

...

Wallington, 'God's Judgement on Sabbath Breakers'   BL: Sloane MS 1457   35
f 67*

A memoriall of Gods Iudgment on them yat set vpon yat cvsed Maypole
    & A memoriall of Gods Iudgments on mockers especially that new

10/ 11o: *ie, the eleventh week, 26 February–6 March 1641/2*
38/ cvsed: *for cvrsed*

reproachful Name that now they giue to those y*at* striue to walke
in the ways of God in Calling them Round Head

®II Petrus iii.⌈3⌉

This first vnderstand that there shall come in the
Last days mockers, which will walke after their Lvst

I   5

1642   May the first in the parish of Hollowell in the Citie of Oxford there was a
Maypole to be set vp And he y*at* was the Chife setter vp of it being desierous
to make some addition to the Pole sporte Sets vpon the pole the picter of a
man in a Tub. And said that was the picter of a Round Head, which picter
is reported to be made in derision of a Godly man a Manciple of one of the 10
Colledg*es* in Oxford & the reason why it was to represent him was because
he was a godly honest man haueing repetion of sarmans in his house: This
picter being vp this man would haue them shoot at the picter of the Round
Head (the end of the sport was to deride those who were of that goodnesse) In
the Conclusion some brought Muskets & other pieces to shout at ye picter 15
And one a saruant of the man whose delight this game was shot and did hit
the picter at which the Master fell a laughing and one a sudden sunke down
falling into a conultion fit and hath bene sick euer since and now at this
present ∧⌈writing hereof⌉ for any thing reported to the Contrary Whether he
will liue or die that must be left to him to iudge who hath the issues of life 20
and death in his owne hand.

If you turne backe to page the *(blank)* you may see amonge the Sabbath
brekers many the like fereful examples of the like sort at the Maypole sport.

City Council Minutes   OCA: E.4.5   25
f 31*   *(23 May)*

…

Richard Pickeringe Barber sworne saith that on ffrydaie last beinge the
xx^th of this May he this d*e*pon*en*t & Edwin Golledge goinge toward*es*
merton College mett w*ith* daniell woolmaster who told [this] the said   30
Edwi*n* that his brother was Preachinge in a tubbe on the May polle in
Holliwell and said allso that if it had not been for such puritane[s] [as]
Rog*ues* as he there had not been such a tumult in the kingdome or word*es*
to that effect.

35

Edwi*n* Golledge saith the like.

…

3m/ II Petrus iii.⌈3⌉: *2 Pt 3.3*
12/ repetion: *for* repetition
18/ conultion: *for* conuultion
19/ writing hereof: *written in left margin and marked for insertion here*

Cordwainers' Minutes   Bodl.: MS. Morrell 20
f 95   *(Rendered 18 November)* *(Payments at the dinner)*

...

Item gaue the musick   0 5 0

...   5

St Michael at the North Gate Churchwardens' Accounts
ORO: PAR 211/4/F1/3, item 204
single mb col 2*   *(Receipts)*

...   10

Item gotten by hockeinge in the said parishe in the
yeare 1642 which is towardes the buyeinge of a palle   4   17   6

...

(29 May 1643)   15
°Richard Swetnam & John Hamblin are to be cald to account for the mony
gotten by the whitson ale for which they will make the parish no account°

...

1642–3   20
Merton College Bursars' Accounts   MCR: 3.2
f 61v   *(18 November–24 March)* *(External expenses)*

...

...Maiestatis regiæ Buccinatoribus ex consensu 10 s.... Tympanistis regijs
ex consensu 5 s. Buccinatoribus Principis Ruperti ex consensu 10 s....   25

...

St John's College Short Book   SJC Arch: Acc.III.D.4
f 64*   *(Loans)*

...   30

[Item ⌜november .28.⌝ Lent vnto Iohn Stacye the sume
of Thirty Shillings   30 s.
               (signed) Iohn Stacie]

...

11–12/ hockeinge ... 1642: *Hocktide was 18–19 April 1642*